Pharmacy Law
Desk Reference

THE HAWORTH PRESS
Titles of Related Interest

Pharmacy Law
Desk Reference

Delbert D. Konnor, PharmMS, PharmBS, RPh
Editor

Routledge
Taylor & Francis Group

NEW YORK AND LONDON

Transferred to Digital Printing 2009 by Routledge
270 Madison Ave, New York NY 10016
2 Park Square, Milton Park, Abingdon, Oxon, OX14 4RN

For more information on this book or to order, visit
http://www.haworthpress.com/store/product.asp?sku=5790

or call 1-800-HAWORTH (800-429-6784) in the United States and Canada
or (607) 722-5857 outside the United States and Canada

or contact orders@HaworthPress.com

PUBLISHER'S NOTE
The development, preparation, and publication of this work has been undertaken with great care. However, the Publisher, employees, editors, and agents of The Haworth Press are not responsible for any errors contained herein or for consequences that may ensue from use of materials or information contained in this work. The Haworth Press is committed to the dissemination of ideas and information according to the highest standards of intellectual freedom and the free exchange of ideas. Statements made and opinions expressed in this publication do not necessarily reflect the views of the Publisher, Directors, management, or staff of The Haworth Press, Inc., or an endorsement by them.

Cover design by Marylouise E. Doyle.

Library of Congress Cataloging-in-Publication Data

Pharmacy law desk reference / Del Konnor, editor.
    p. ; cm.
  Includes bibliographical references and index.
  ISBN-13: 978-0-7890-1821-2 (hard : alk. paper)
  ISBN-10: 0-7890-1821-7 (hard : alk. paper)
  ISBN-13: 978-0-7890-1822-9 (soft : alk. paper)
  ISBN-10: 0-7890-1822-5 (soft : alk. paper)
    1. Pharmacy—Law and legislation—United States. [DNLM: 1. Legislation, Pharmacy—United States. 2. Pharmaceutical Services—legislation & jurisprudence—United States. QV 733 AA1 P536 2006] I. Konnor, Delbert D.

KF2915.P4.P533 2006
344.7304'16—dc22

                                                                2006006572

CONTENTS

Chapter 17. Medicare and Medicaid   339
Susan C. Winckler

Chapter 18. Certification in Pharmacy: Advanced-Level Credentials, Including Specialty Certification   353
Richard J. Bertin

ABOUT THE EDITOR

Delbert D. Konnor, PharmMS, PharmBS, RPh, is President of The Del Konnor Group, LLC, and DEA Solutions Group, LLC, which he established in 2001 after sixteen years as President and Chief Executive Officer of the Pharmaceutical Care Management Association. He served as official spokesperson for the PCMA on matters of legislation, healthcare benefits, and managed care pharmacy.

Mr. Konnor has served as Vice President of Professional Services at the American Association of Retired Persons (AARP) Pharmacy Service, head of the Drug Enforcement Administration's Voluntary Compliance Program, and Director of the White House Conference on Prescription Drug Misuse, Abuse, and Diversion. He has been Assistant to Executive Vice President and Director of Association Affairs at the National Association of Retail Druggists (now the National Community Pharmacists Association or NCPA), and is the author of "The Evolution of PBMs–An Overview: From Mail Order Pharmacy to Pharmacy Benefits Manager," which appeared in *Drug Injury: Liability, Analysis and Prevention, Second Edition.*

Pharmacy Law Desk Reference
© 2007 by The Haworth Press, Inc. All rights reserved.
doi:10.1300/5790_a

CONTRIBUTORS

Jacqueline E. Artinger, JD, Associate General Counsel, Prescription Solutions/Ovations, A UnitedHealth Group Company, Irvine, California (Jacqueline.Artinger@rxsol.com)

Kenneth R. Baker, JD, PharmBS, Executive Director, Pharmacy Compounding Accreditation Board; formerly, Senior Vice President and General Counsel, Pharmacists Mutual Insurance Company, Washington, DC (Ken.Baker@phmic.com)

Richard J. Bertin, PhD, RPh, Executive Director, Board of Pharmaceutical Specialties, Washington, DC (rbertin@aphanet.org)

Marla J. Campbell, BScPharm, PharmD, Associate Clinical Professor, Department of Pharmacy Practice, University of Connecticut, Clinical Faculty–Ambulatory Care, Storrs, Connecticut (mcampbell pharmd@hotmail.com)

Norman A. Campbell, MBA, JD, PhD, Professor Emeritus, Social and Administrative Sciences, College of Pharmacy, University of Rhode Island, Kingston, Rhode Island (nca4902u@postoffice.uri.edu)

Garry Carneal, JD, MA, President, InforMed Medical Management Services, Annapolis, Maryland (garrycarneal@informed-llc.com)

Carmen A. Catizone, MS, RPh, DPh, Executive Director/Secretary, National Association of Boards of Pharmacy, Mount Prospect, Illinois (catizone@nabp.net)

Sandra J. Creta, BS, JD, Associate, Quarles & Brady Streich Lang, LLP, Phoenix, Arizona (screta@quarles.com)

Jennifer Devine, JD, LLM, Senior Staff Attorney, United States Pharmacopeia, Rockville, Maryland (jad@usp.org)

Margaret L. Eaton, PharmD, JD, Senior Research Scholar, Center for Biomedical Ethics, Stanford University, Palo Alto, California (Maggie@ronandmaggie.com)

Richard A. Feinstein, JD, Partner, Boies, Schiller & Flexner LLP, Washington, DC (rfeinstein@bsfllp.com)

Pharmacy Law Desk Reference
© 2007 by The Haworth Press, Inc. All rights reserved.
doi:10.1300/5790_b

Brian A. Gallagher, RPh, JD, Vice President Regulatory Compliance, Rite Aid Corporation, Harrisburg, Pennsylvania (bgallagher@riteaid .com)

Thomas George, RPh, JD, Pharmacy Manager, Coram Healthcare, Inc.; and President, Drugkey LLC, Las Vegas, Nevada (tgeorge@ drugkey.com)

Moira Gibbons, RPh, PharmD, JD, Accreditation Program Manager, National Association of Boards of Pharmacy, Mount Prospect, Illinois (mgibbons@nabp.net)

Jacqueline A. Henson, BA, JD, MBA, Partner, McKenna Long & Aldridge LLP, Washington, DC (jhenson@McKennaLong.com)

Daniel A. Kotchen, JD, Associate, Boies, Schiller & Flexner LLP, Washington, DC (dkotchen@bsfllp.com)

Melissa A. Madigan, PharmD, JD, Associate, Smith, Rickert & Smith, Downers Grove, Illinois (mmadigan@smithrickert.com)

Roger N. Morris, RPh, JD, Partner, Quarles & Brady Streich Lang, LLP, Phoenix, Arizona (rmorris@quarles.com)

Francis B. Palumbo, PhD, JD, Director, University of Maryland Center on Drugs & Public Policy, Baltimore, Maryland (fpalumbo@rx .umaryland.edu)

Larry R. Pilot, RPh, Esq, Partner, McKenna Long & Aldridge LLP, Washington, DC (lpilot@mckennalong.com)

Edward D. Rickert, RPh, JD, Partner, Smith, Rickert & Smith, Downers Grove, Illinois (edr@smithrickert.com)

George E. Rippel Jr., JD, Law Offices of George E. Rippel, Jr., Baltimore, Maryland

Sharon Horn Roddan, PharmD, JD, Adjunct Assistant Professor, University of Southern California, Los Angeles, California (sroddan@ix .netcom.com)

Martha M. Rumore, PharmD, JD, FAPhA, Attorney at Law, Katten Muchin Rosenman LLP, New York, New York (Martha.rumore@kattenlaw .com)

F. Nicholas Willard, MA, President, The Willard Consultancy, Alexandria, Virginia (nwillard@comcast.net)

Susan C. Winckler, RPh, JD, Vice President of Policy and Communications and Staff Counsel, American Pharmacists Association, Washington, DC (swinckler@aphanet.org)

Foreword

Those of us who graduated from pharmacy school in the 1960s or 1970s have witnessed tremendous and exciting changes in the practice of our profession. As an attorney as well as a pharmacist, I know that the regulatory framework governing pharmacy has also changed dramatically over the past thirty-five years. Understanding those changes in pharmacy law, and how they affect the practice of pharmacy, will be critical to our profession's success in the coming years.

That's where this book comes in. It is designed to help pharmacists, leaders of the profession, healthcare decision makers, regulators, and lawmakers gain insight into what is expected of the profession by government and the courts.

Because the subject matter of this work is so comprehensive, it could not have been written by any one person. It is, rather, the product of the efforts of numerous respected authorities in various aspects of pharmacy law. While key chapters in the book address contemporary topics in pharmacy law, the focus of this work is on providing the reader with a framework for understanding how and why the profession is regulated.

I expect that this book will serve as required reading in pharmacy schools throughout the country. This book is more than a textbook. It is a foundation work that will serve widely as a desk reference for law offices, pharmacy boards, professional societies, and healthcare facilities across the country. As a past president of the American Society for Pharmacy Law, I understand the value and importance of this book and its inherent contribution to pharmacy literature.

This is a book that will influence our understanding of pharmacy law for a generation to come.

Joseph G. Valentino, JD, RPh
Senior Vice President and General Counsel (Retired)
The United States Pharmacopeial Convention, Inc.

Pharmacy Law Desk Reference
© 2007 by The Haworth Press, Inc. All rights reserved.
doi:10.1300/5790_c

Preface

No profession in America is more closely regulated than pharmacy—and for good reason. The decisions that pharmacists make every day, the medicines they select, and the counsel they provide to patients have the potential to heal the sick, alleviate pain, and extend our lives. But they also have the potential to do great harm.

As one who has served both as a practicing pharmacist and as a regulator of the profession, I know firsthand how important it is for people on both sides of the regulatory fence to understand each other's role. In that regard, I've always believed that our country's small but dedicated community of pharmacist-attorneys is in a unique position to serve as a critically important liaison between government and the profession.

This book is a collaboration involving many leading members of that community. A nationally recognized authority in one or more aspects of pharmacy law authors each chapter. Many of these authors are active in the American Society for Pharmacy Law—an organization in which I have held membership for many years.

This book, though, is also a product of the support and guidance I received from others, including my friend and colleague Dr. Peter A. Previte, Professor of Social and Administrative Sciences, Ohio Northern University, College of Pharmacy, who critiqued my original outline and book proposal. and my son, D. Daniel Konnor II, who was always willing to provide input, advice, and support. Most important, though, this book owes its existence to my friend and colleague Dr. Albert I. Wertheimer, Director, Center for Pharmaceutical Health Services Research, Temple University, School of Pharmacy, whose constant encouragement and assistance helped me carry this project through to completion.

I must confess, however, that the seed for this endeavor was planted many years before the first chapter was written. Indeed, it is the book I wish was available to my students when I taught pharmacy law years ago at Wayne State University, College of Pharmacy. I hope it will offer our next generation of pharmacy students a solid grounding in the legal and regula-

Pharmacy Law Desk Reference
© 2007 by The Haworth Press, Inc. All rights reserved.
doi:10.1300/5790_d

tory issues that impact our profession. I am also hopeful that this work will serve as a valuable reference for the organizations representing America's pharmacists, for the state pharmacy boards and federal agencies that regulate the profession, and for others with a stake in improving the laws and regulations governing pharmacy to protect the public.

The more government administrators and lawmakers know about pharmacy practice, the more likely they will be to design and implement effective regulations that serve the public interest. And the better pharmacists understand the regulatory and legislative framework that shapes their practice, the better they will be able to carry out their responsibilities to patients.

It is this belief that has served as the inspiration for this book.

Delbert D. Konnor

Chapter 1

The Function, Evolution, and Historical Development of the Law

Martha M. Rumore

GOVERNMENT ORGANIZATION AND FUNCTION

There are three branches of government: executive, legislative, and judicial. Legislatures create statutory law by enacting bills which become laws. The judiciary makes common law, which is found in court decisions. However, it is impossible for the legislature to make all the necessary rules or for the judicial branch to handle all of the cases. Certain fields require nonlegal expertise. Therefore, Congress created the administrative agencies, often referred to as the fourth branch of government, which create administrative law. Agencies act like courts or legislatures by making rules or deciding cases. Administrative agencies may be called commissions, boards, bureaus, divisions, or agencies.

AGENCY ORGANIZATION AND FUNCTION

Agencies protect us against false advertising, unfair trade practices, unwholesome food, mislabeled drugs, air and water pollution, fraud in the sale of securities or land, unsanitary restaurants and hospitals, unsafe products, and sale of narcotics. Agencies dispose of many times the number of court-handled cases. Agencies also promulgate regulations via a process known as "notice and comment" rulemaking.

The *United States Government Manual* provides detailed descriptions and organization charts for each federal administrative agency.[1] The Food and Drug Administration (FDA), for example, is composed of various "centers" such as the Center for Drug Evaluation and Research (CDER) and the

Pharmacy Law Desk Reference
© 2007 by The Haworth Press, Inc. All rights reserved.
doi:10.1300/5790_01

Center for Biologics Evaluation and Research (CBER). Located within each center are various offices. For example, within CDER is the Office of Pharmaceutical Science, the Office of Generic Drugs, the Office of New Drugs, the Office of Compliance, and the Office of Drug Safety. The centers play an important role in both administrative and judicial enforcement activities. The FDA has enforcement power over manufacturing procedures for (and the finished) food, drug, cosmetic, medical device, and biologic products that are moved in interstate commerce, and it is responsible for enforcement of the Federal Food Drug and Cosmetic Act. The FDA shares or coordinates enforcement responsibility for certain products through established relationships often formalized in Memorandums of Understanding (MOUs) and other interagency agreements with other federal agencies such as the Drug Enforcement Administration and U.S. Customs Service. The FDA enforces the following acts, among others: the Federal Food, Drug, and Cosmetic Act; the Orphan Drug Act; the Drug Price Competition and Patent Term Restoration Act (Hatch-Waxman Amendments); the Federal Anti-Tampering Act; the Fair Packaging and Labeling Act; and the Prescription Drug User Fee Act. The addition, the FDA regulates the advertising of prescription drugs.[2]

Food and drug laws are located in Title 21 of the Code of Federal Regulations, as described in Table 1.1. The entire Title 21 may be keyword searched at the FDA's Web site. Examples of the wealth of information available at www.fda.gov include guidance documents and manuals, the *Regulatory Procedures Manual, Federal Register,* the *Orange Book* searchable by generic name, warning letters, and *The Handbook for Requesting Information and Records from FDA.* In addition to formal rulemaking, the FDA issues guidelines to help with compliance with the requirements of the regulations.[3] These guidelines are not a legal requirement; however, the

TABLE 1.1. Code of federal regulations.

Code number range	Description of subjects
1 to 99	FDA, General
100 to 169	Food for Human Consumption
170 to 199	Food fo Human Consumption
200 to 299	Drugs, General
300 to 499	Drugs for Human Use
500 to 599	Animal Drugs, Feeds, and Related Products
600 to 799	Biologics
800 to 1299	Medical Devices and Radiological Health
1300 to 1404	Drug Enforcement Administration, Department of Justice

FDA has stated that it will not recommend legal action against a person or product if the procedures in a current FDA guideline are followed. FDA interpretation of its own regulations or another statute are not regulations. FDA sources include more than twenty manuals that contain technical and compliance information. Some examples of manuals are the FDA Compliance Policy Guides Manual, which is used by field officers in interpreting regulatory policies, and the FDA Compliance Program Guidance Manual, which provides inspection details. A company can also seek an "advisory opinion" concerning the FDA's compliance posture on a certain matter.[4] Knowledge of these tools is invaluable in establishing voluntary compliance programs.

Other agency functions are also of interest to health professionals. The Consumer Product Safety Commission (CPSC) enforces the Consumer Product Safety Act of 1972, the Federal Hazardous Substances Labeling Act, and the Poison Prevention Packaging Act.[5] Although most FDA-regulated products are exempt from these statutes, medical devices are subject to the Federal Hazardous Substances Act, and all FDA-related products are subject to the Poison Prevention Packaging Act. The Drug Enforcement Administration (DEA) is responsible for placing controlled substances on the federal "schedule" and enforces the Federal Controlled Substances Act of 1970. The Federal Trade Commission (FTC) regulates the advertising of foods, over-the-counter (OTC) drugs, medical devices, and cosmetics. In addition, the FTC may take action to prevent unfair methods of competition and other unfair or deceptive acts or practices involving advertising, labeling, and other promotional practices. Within the FTC, the Bureau of Competition is responsible for enforcing antitrust laws such as the Sherman Antitrust Act and the Clayton Act.

Other agencies include the Environmental Protection Agency (EPA), aimed at protecting the environment, and the Occupational Safety and Health Administration (OSHA), which implements the Federal Occupation Safety and Health Act of 1970 that requires employers to provide safe working conditions for their employees.

THE COURT SYSTEM

Court decisions are collected chronologically in volumes called case reporters and are summarized by subject matter in reference works called case digests. Federal courts have three levels: a trial level, an appellate level, and a final appellate level. At the federal level, the trial courts are called the U.S. District Courts. Trial courts are courts of original jurisdiction that make determinations of law and of fact, with juries often making the determinations of fact.

Discovery enables one party to examine the evidence of the other party. A subpoena is a written document issued by the court, by the legislature, or by an agency if empowered to do so. A violation of a subpoena is considered "contempt." There are two types of subpoenas: *testificatum,* in which the individual is asked to testify at a particular time and place, and *duces tecum,* in which the individual is asked to produce records.

Documents prepared by the parties called pleadings (complaint, answer, interrogatories) and motions are filed before and during a trial; exhibits are submitted into evidence during the trial and a record (or transcript) is made. Pleadings, motions, exhibits, and transcripts are usually available only directly from the court in which the litigation was conducted.[6]

Federal intermediate appellate courts are known as the United States Court of Appeals. There are thirteen Federal Courts of Appeals, each of which covers a particular geographic area known as a circuit. Appellate courts are not trial courts, but rather review whether the trial judge correctly applied the relevant points of law to the facts. Appellate courts accept written briefs (statements prepared by the counsel arguing the case) and frequently hear oral arguments. Many appellate courts sit in panels smaller than the full court. When the full court meets, it is referred to as an *en banc* proceeding.[7]

The final appellate court in the United States is the Supreme Court. The Supreme Court is the highest authority in the United States on questions of federal law and constitutional law. State courts of last resort are the highest authorities on questions of state law. There are some matters over which a state or federal court has exclusive jurisdiction and some matters over which a state court has concurrent jurisdiction with the federal courts. Most libraries collect copies of the briefs and records filed in the Supreme Court and of the court of last resort of the state in which they are located.

The number and type of state courts vary with the individual state. In New York, the highest court is the New York Court of Appeals. It has jurisdiction in both criminal and civil matters, but appellate only. The court reviews only questions of law, except in two instances in which it reviews the facts: on appeal from a criminal judgment imposing the death penalty and from an appellate division decision reversing or modifying a judgment, finding new facts, and directing that a final judgment be entered on new facts.[8]

The intermediate appellate court in New York is called the Appellate Division of the Supreme Court. There is one in each of four judicial departments. The court reviews both the law and the facts and has some original jurisdiction in certain areas, i.e., admission and supervision of attorneys.[9]

Two rungs below New York State's highest court is the supreme court, a misnomer since it is not supreme. The supreme court is a single court of statewide jurisdiction, with a branch in each county. There is also a county court in each county outside New York City, a surrogate's court, family court, court of claims (reserved for claims against the state or by the state), New York City criminal court, New York City civil court, district courts, city courts, and town and village courts.[10]

Each level of the federal courts has at least one case reporter for its decisions.[11] Cases from the U.S. Supreme Court are found in the *United States Reports* ("U.S."), which is the official reporter. Supreme Court decisions are also found in unofficial reporters where helpful editorial features are added by the publishers: *Supreme Court Reporter* ("S. Ct.") and the *United States Supreme Court Reports Lawyers' Edition* ("L.Ed.").

U.S. Court of Appeals decisions from all circuits are found in the *Federal Reporter* ("F."-1880-1924; "F.2d"- 1924-present). From 1880 to 1932, U.S. District Court opinions were reported along with U.S. Court of Appeals decisions in the *Federal Reporter.* Since 1932, they have been published in the *Federal Supplement* ("F.Supp.").

Decisions of state courts are published in state cases reporters as well as regional reporters. For example, New York State cases appear in the *North Eastern Reporter* as well as reporters all the way down to its trial level courts. The *North Eastern Reporter* ("N.E. or N.E.2d") includes appellate opinions from Illinois, Indiana, Massachusetts, New York, and Ohio.

Case reporters are organized either by jurisdiction, by geography, or by subject. An example of cases reported chronologically by subject is the *United States Patent Quarterly.* The topical arrangements of court decisions are published in case digests. These digests, in effect, serve as indexes to the case reporters. A digest is a set of books that takes brief summaries (digests) of the legal principles in a case and lists each under the appropriate topic or heading. A single case may appear under several different subjects. Examples include the *Federal Practice Digests, Education Law Digest,* and the *U.S. Supreme Court Digest.* Digests are particularly useful in locating cases interpreting constitutions.[12]

A court case typically includes the following: name or title of the case (also called the "caption"); citation to the case; docket number (numerical designation assigned by a court); date of decision; prefatory statement (explains the nature of the case, its disposition in the lower court, and disposition in the appellate court), e.g., affirmed or reversed; syllabus or headnote (brief summaries of the rules of law or significant facts in a case); names of counsel; statement of facts; opinions of the court; and the decision, with judgment or decree.

The opinion of a court is the explanation of the court's decision. The "majority opinion" is written by one member of the court and represents the principles of law the majority on the court deem operative in a given decision. A member of the majority may also write a "concurring opinion" elaborating on individual reasoning. When more judges join a concurring opinion, but not yet a majority of the court, it is known as a "plurality opinion." The views of a minority are expressed as a "dissenting opinion." A *per curiam* opinion is an opinion of the entire majority, as distinguished from an opinion written by a specific judge. A "memorandum opinion" is a brief holding of the whole court in which the opinion is limited or omitted.

ORDER OF PRECEDENCE OF AUTHORITY

Although people are equal before the law, not all laws are equal. Some laws are more important than others. In general, the order of precedence of authority is the U.S. Constitution, federal statutes, federal regulations, state constitutions, state laws, and local laws and ordinances. The Constitution is the supreme law of the land; the first ten amendments place limits on government power and are known as the Bill of Rights.

Legal authority is any published source of law setting forth legal rules, legal doctrine, or legal reasoning that can be used as a basis for legal decisions.[13] Legal authority can be categorized as primary or secondary. Primary authority includes case law, legislation, constitutions, and regulations and opinions of administrative agencies. Secondary authority includes treatises, law reviews and other scholarly journals, *American Law Reports Annotations* ("A.L.R."), and loose-leaf services. Only primary authority can be "binding" (also called mandatory), meaning that a court or other decision maker believes the authority applies to the case before it and must be followed. Secondary authority can be only persuasive, meaning that a decision maker can, if so persuaded, follow it.[14]

Under what has come to be called the doctrine of precedent, the decision of a common law court not only settles a dispute between the parties involved but also sets a precedent to be followed in future cases among other litigants.[15] The doctrine of precedent encompasses *stare decisis,* which is the principle that the decision of a court is binding authority on the court that issued the decision and on lower courts in the same jurisdiction for the disposition of factually similar controversies.[16] In contrast, *dictum* (or *obiter dictum*) is language in an opinion that is arguably not necessary to the opinion. Dictim refers to what is said "by the way." Although dictum is not binding on future courts, it might be persuasive.[17] It is important to be aware of the fact that commonly yesterday's dictum develops into today's doctrine. Further, courts have much leeway in interpreting cases. No two cases are exactly the same, and at some point every case can be distinguished from all others.

ENACTMENT OF LEGISLATION

How a Bill Becomes a Law

Congress is responsible for federal criminal law, all laws governing the operation of federal departments and agencies, treaty approval, power to declare war, investigative power (when aimed at the executive branch this is called "oversight"), confirming or rejecting the president's nominees, and impeachment for "high crimes and misdemeanors. Via "congressional oversight" Congress oversees the activities of particular agencies. Congress also allocates money for the operation of federal departments and agencies via the appropriations process.

The Senate and House of Representatives make up the Congress. A "bill" is proposed legislation, not yet passed and, therefore, not law. A bill must be introduced in either the Senate or House of Representatives by a member of those legislative bodies. House seats are apportioned on the basis of population, whereas each state, regardless of population, elects two members to the Senate. Much of the work of Congress is conducted by committees with jurisdiction over a particular area of public policy. Almost every bill is sent to a committee or several committees, which normally pass them on to subcommittees. Committees schedule public hearings on bills where testimony is taken from bill sponsors, administration officials, outside experts, and any special interest groups. Next the bill undergoes "markup" where committee members go over it section by section, voting on proposed changes and redrafting the bill in view of what they have learned about the subject.

The full committee may at this point adopt the bill as written, amend it, or kill it. If adopted, the bill is sent to "the floor," meaning for vote by the House and Senate. House bills go to the House Rules Committee. Time for debate is limited, and floor action is often completed in a timely fashion. In the Senate, however, debate is often extensive, with elaborate rules of decorum. Once a bill is passed in either the full Senate or House, it is sent to the other chamber for consideration. Frequently, the House and Senate pass different versions of a bill. The differences are resolved via a "conference agreement," i.e., a compromise version which must then be repassed by both houses before being sent to the president for signing. If the president signs, it becomes law. Alternatively, the president can veto the bill, where it is then sent back to the Senate and House for another vote. If both chambers vote for it by at least a two-thirds majority, it becomes law despite the president's veto, thereby overriding the veto.

The *Congressional Record* is a verbatim transcript of the proceedings of the Senate and House. It includes the "Daily Digest" summarizing floor action, committee activities, committee meetings, and hearings scheduled. The Government Printing Office (GPO) was established to act as the "public printer" for the entire federal government, including Congress. Most federal publications are available at the GPO Web site.

Legislative History

Unfortunately, not all laws are clearly written. The entire process of enacting a law creates a legislative history which often serves as an important guide in determining the legislative intent and clarifying vagarities. In interpreting the meaning of a law, one can review the changes resulting from the committee process via the committee report. Other important items of legislative history are statements made during debates and changes made to a bill while it worked its way through Congress. Almost every printing of a bill represents a distinct step in its progress toward enactment and may ultimately be a significant document in its legislative history. The full text of congressional bills can be reached over the Internet by taping into the bulletin board of the House of Representatives or via Thomas, an Internet site that provides access to a wide variety of congressional documents, including bills.

Hearings do not have to be held on every bill, but when they exist, they aid in interpreting the provisions of the bill. Hearings may be published in the *Monthly Catalog of U.S. Government Publications* and in *CIS/Index*. Since 1970, *CIS/Index* has provided abstracts of testimony and indexing under the name of each witness.

Committee reports reflect the committee's proposal after the bill has been studied, hearings held, and amendments made.[18] They frequently contain the revised text of a bill and analysis of its content and intent. There will be a report only for bills that make it out of committee. Committee reports are indexed in the *Monthly Catalog of U.S. Government Publications,* the *CIS/Index,* and, occasionally, the *Congressional Record.* Congressional debates are found more or less verbatim in the *Congressional Record.*

Other Congressional documents, such as special studies and reports, are indexed and listed in the *Monthly Catalog of U.S. Government Publications. CIS* stands for Congressional Information Service. This reference separates the House and Senate into committees and subcommittees and divides publications for each into hearings, reports, and prints.

Finding Statutes

Like regulations, laws are published immediately upon enactment. When a bill is enacted, it is assigned a Public Law Number, e.g., 105-2. The first three numbers indicate the session of Congress, and the number following this is the number of the bill passed during that session of Congress. A permanent collection of the laws of each session of Congress is published by the Government Printing Office and called the *United States Statutes at Large* (abbreviated as "Stat."). The statutes are a chronological arrangement of the laws published as they become law, in no logical subject order. The codified version published by the U.S. government is found in the *United States Code* ("U.S.C.") and in two commercially published editions, *United States Code Annotated* ("U.S.C.A.") and *United States Code Service* ("U.S.C.S."). Published every six years, the United States Code is a consolidation of statutes arranged according to subject matter. Between editions, a supplementary volume is issued annually as an update for that year. To find a statute in the U.S.C., you can use the index, the Table of Titles and Chapters, the Tables of Acts cited by popular name, and the conversion tables. The FDCA begins at 21 USC 321; to locate it you would look for United States Code, Title 21, section 321. These are available in the government documents sections of most libraries.

U.S.C.A. and U.S.C.S. are annotated versions of the U.S.C. Both have detailed indexes, references to regulations promulgated and published in the C.F.R., popular name tables, and other tables. Both are updated with annual pocket parts, freestanding supplements, and periodic pamphlets (called advance sheets). The biggest difference is that each set organizes the case annotations according to different subject headings and may not include the same cases as the competing set. For legal research, the easiest way to locate a law is via its U.S. Code number.

Individual states also routinely publish session laws and statutory codes but vary widely in organizing and publishing these laws.

CODE OF FEDERAL REGULATIONS

Regulations are often the details to put statutes into effect. Regulations are also arranged chronologically in the *Federal Register* ("Fed. Reg.") and according to specific regulatory topics in *The Code of Federal Regulations* ("C.F.R."). FDA and DEA regulations are located in Title 21. The CFR is divided into 50 titles from "Accounts" to "Wildlife." There are over 150 CFR volumes. Each title is further divided into chapters, subchapters, parts, subparts, and sections. Federal administrative agency decisions are available from the agencies themselves.

Ordinarily research into the regulations of a federal agency begins with the C.F.R., since the C.F.R. pulls all the regulations together into one place. However, since the C.F.R. is updated on an annual basis, it is necessary to check the *LSA: List of CFR Sections Affected.* The LSA indicates *Federal Register* pages of any proposed or new rules affecting the C.F.R. In addition, as the LSA does not bring C.F.R. completely up to date, it is necessary to consult the last *Federal Register* issue of each month not covered by the LSA to be assured that no changes in the regulation have been promulgated.

What Is a Regulation?

Congress has delegated to agencies the power to promulgate "regulations" (also known as "rules") which are binding and can be legally enforced.[19] Regulations interpret and enforce statutes and must be consistent with the statute or risk being declared invalid by the federal courts.

In addition, regulations must be developed and issued in accordance with the Administrative Procedures Act or they are not enforceable.[20] In 1935, Congress enacted the Federal Register Act which provided for

1. filing of documents with the Office of the Federal Register,
2. placement of documents on public inspection, and
3. publication of documents in the Federal Register.

In 1946, the Administrative Procedures Act

1. introduced the right of the public to participate in the rulemaking process by commenting on proposed rules,
2. required that the effective date of a regulation not be less than thirty days from the date of publication unless in an emergency, and
3. provided for publication of agency statements.

Development of a Regulation

Regulations begin with an "Advance Notice of Proposed Rulemaking" or "Intent to Publish" in the *Federal Register.* Then they appear as a "Proposed Rule," whereby comments are invited within a time limit of sixty days to possibly one year. A hearing may also be scheduled to obtain public viewpoints. The agency analyzes all comments and arrives at an equitable decision. It is published in final form as a "Final Rule." Figure 1.1 provides an overview of this process. After a regulation is issued, it may be struck down by the courts.

Administrative law can be very complex to research. Not only must the regulations and decisions created by the administrative agency be found, but researchers must also find, interpret, and update the legislation the agency is administering and the judicial opinions interpreting the regulations, adjudications, and legislation.

What Is Not a Regulation

Petitions are not regulations. An interested party can petition an agency to establish, amend, or revoke a rule or any part thereof. If the agency head finds the petition has reasonable merit, notice of its filing and availability is published in the *Federal Register,* with a request for comment within a time limit. Any agency may also publish its own version of such a proposal.

Interim or temporary rules are also not regulations. They are effective as of the day of enactment but for a short or definite period of time. They have

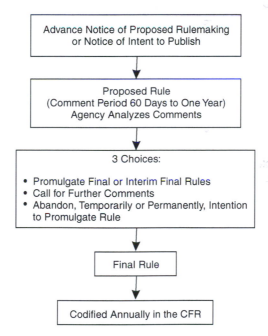

FIGURE 1.1. Regulation development process.

the same effect as a final rule in that they amend the CFR and give an effective date.

Adjudications

Many agencies have the power to receive evidence and decide controversies via "administrative adjudications" presided over by administrative law judges (ALJ). Final adjudications are often published and available to review as agency interpretations. These adjudications can be appealed to the courts.

The Freedom of Information Request

The Freedom of Information Act (FOIA) established the rights of private citizens to obtain information from federal government agencies. First passed in 1966 and strengthened in 1974, Congress enacted the FOIA which has opened thousands of government file cabinets to public scrutiny. The FOIA states that any person has the right to see and copy documents produced by any federal agency. The FOIA does not apply to the federal judiciary or elected officials of the federal government, private companies, persons who receive federal contracts or grants, tax-exempt organizations, or state and local governments. State and local governments have adopted their own versions of the FOIA, even though not federally mandated to do so.

Before enactment of the FOIA, the burden was on the individual to establish his or her right to examine government records. For those denied access there were no judicial remedies. Originally, the act was designed to establish more uniform procedures among the agencies in both rule making and adjudication, thus putting a new system of accountability into effect. In addition, the agency must reply within ten days of receipt of a FOIA inquiry. Delay is, nevertheless, common. Although the law states that an agency may receive a time extension only in exceptional or "unusual circumstances," agencies extend these deadlines regularly. Although the agency is mandated to reply within ten days of inquiry receipt, the actual information requested may take up to several months to be distributed. "Freedom of Information" must be stated on the request. Each request appears in a public log, which itself is available on request. There may be a fee for photocopying time or per page copied.[21]

Exhibit 1.1 lists the information that must be published in the *Federal Register* by each federal agency.[22] For example, under FOIA the FDA will

EXHIBIT 1.1. Types of available general information.

1. Central and field office locations, staff organizations
2. Methods by which the public can secure information
3. General methods by which its functions are channeled and determined
4. Rules of procedure, availability and description of necessary forms
5. Policy statements and substantive rulings of general applicability
6. Each agency must make the following available for public inspection and copying:
   - All final opinions whether concurring or dissenting, as well as orders given in the adjudication of cases
   - Those statements of policy and opinions which are informally adopted by the agency and not published in the *Federal Register*
   - Administrative staff manuals
   - All other records except those expressly exempted by law, upon request, within published rules for time, place, and fees
   - Agency proceedings

release information on test protocols, information relating adverse drug events, product experience and consumer complaints, approved New Drug Applications (NDAs) and Abbreviated New Drug Applications (ANDAs), administrative enforcement records such as recall letters, and manufacturing facility inspection reports.[23,24] Nondisclosable portions will be deleted prior to release. However, the FDA will uphold the confidential status of an IND. This information is considered nondisclosable under the trade secret exemption of the FOIA. Release of information may follow a sponsor's termination or withdrawal of the IND. In addition, under Executive Order 12958 which became effective October 15, 1995, there is automatic declassification of most U.S. government files more than twenty-five years old. Categories of information which are exempted from disclosure are found in Exhibit 1.2. The stamping of documents as "confidential" or "trade secret" by the person or company submitting said document does not obligate an agency to regard them as such.[25] Whenever an FOIA request is denied, the agency must inform the requestor of the reason for the denial and the right to appeal. Many agencies require that appeals be filed within thirty days. Whenever an administrative appeal is denied, the requestor may then file for judicial appeal in court.

EXHIBIT 1.2. Exempted categories of information.

- Classified national defense and foreign policy secrets
- Internal agency rules—agency personnel and medical records
- Trade secret and confidential business information
- Investigatory files for law enforcement purposes
- Information exempt under other laws
- Internal management matters
- Bank examination records
- Inter and intra agency memoranda
- Certain mineral, geological, and geophysical information

SECONDARY SOURCES OF THE LAW

There are a number of legal encyclopedias on a wide variety of topics arranged alphabetically. Examples are *Corpus Juris Secundum* ("C.S.J.") and *American Jurisprudence, Second* ("Am. Jur. 2d"). Other secondary sources are treatises, book-length analyses of legal topics, and legal periodicals, which consist of law journals and law reviews. The *Index to Legal Periodicals and Books* is a primary finding aid for legal periodicals. Since 1993, it has indexed books. The *Current Law Index* is another primary finding aid for legal periodicals.

Of course, many of the aforementioned legal resources can be accessed with a computer and are searchable using key words and phrases. Examples include LEXIS and WESTLAW, which offer access to cases, statutes, secondary sources, law reviews, mass media, and other information and services that are constantly being expanded and updated. Moreover, many Internet sources are available for government information. See the Appendix for a compilation of these sources.

It is hoped that this overview of the function, evolution, and historical development of the law will assist pharmacists in developing a fundamental ability to use legal materials.

APPENDIX: ELECTRONIC RESOURCES

Supreme Court Calendar
www.supremecourtus.gov/oral_arguments/argument_calendars.html

Senate Calendar
www.gpoaccess.gov/calendars/senate/index.html

U.S. Senate
www.senate.gov

U.S. House of Representatives
www.house.gov

Congressional Record via GPO Access
www.gpoaccess.gov/crecord/index.html

Congressional Record via Thomas
thomas.loc.gov

Federal Register
www.gpoaccess.gov/fr/index.html

Food and Drug Administration
www.fda.gov

U.S. Code
www.gpoaccess.gov/uscode/index.html

Library of Congress
www.loc.gov/index.html

NOTES

1. *The United States Government Manual,* Washington, DC: U.S. Government Printing Office.

2. 21 U.S.C. §§ 352(n), 378.

3. 21 C.F.R. § 10.90(b).

4. 21 C.F.R. § 10.85.

5. *Compilation of Statutes Administered by the Consumer Product Safety Commission* (CPSC), Washington, DC, April 1992.

6. Jacobstein JM, Mersky RM, and Dunn DJ. *Legal Research Illustrated,* 6th Edition. New York: Foundation Press; 1994, 4-6.

7. McFeeley ND. *En Banc* Proceedings in the United States Court of Appeals. *Idaho L. Rev.* 24:255 (1987-88).

8. Const. Art. VI, § 3(a).

9. Jud. L. § 90, CPLR 9401.

10. Siegel DD. *New York Practice,* 3rd Edition. St. Paul, MN: West Group; 1999, 13-22.

11. Wren CG, and Wren JR. *The Legal Research Manual.* 2nd Edition. Madison, WI: Adams & Ambrose Pub.; 1986, 10-11.

12. Schultz NL, and Sirico LJ. *Legal Research Law Outlines.* Santa Monica, CA: Casenote Pub. Co.; 1996, CO-6-7.

13. Marvell TB. *Appellate Courts and Lawyers* 129 (1978).

14. Merryman JH. The Authority of Authority, *Stan. L. Rev.* 6:613 (1954).

15. Powell LF. *Stare Decisis* and Judicial Restraint. *Wash & Lee L. Rev.* 47:281 (1990).

16. Aldisert RJ. Precedent: What It Is and What It Isn't, When Do We Kiss It and When Do We Kill It? *Pepperdine L. Rev.* 17:605 (1990).

17. Greenwalt K. Reflections on Holding and Dictim. *J. Legal Ed.* 39:431 (1989).

18. Berring RC. *Finding the Law.* 10th Edition. St. Paul, MN: West Pub. Co.; 1989, 168-186.

19. 5 U.S.C. §551(4).

20. 5 U.S.C. §553.

21. Nader R. *The Freedom of Information Act: A Users Guide.* Washington, DC: Freedom of Information Clearing House; 1992.

22. Freedom of Information Act, U.S.C. § 552, 309-312.

23. Pendergast WR. Problems and Opportunities Under the Public Information Regulation of the FDA. *Food, Drug Cosm L. J.* 30:326-337 (1975).

24. Marlene SB. Acquiring Food and Drug Administration Information Under the Freedom of Information Act. *Med. Ref. Serv. Quarterly* 7(4):19-29 (1988).

25. The Struggle Against Secrecy. *The New York Times.* 1996 Jan. 3: v145 PA 14(L) col. 1.

Chapter 2

Forms of Business Organization

Francis B. Palumbo
George E. Rippel Jr.

INTRODUCTION

When entering any type of business venture, many considerations must be taken into account. The type of business is quite important, in that it could be a small business, perhaps a community pharmacy, or it could be a large business, such as a major pharmaceutical manufacturer. In between are many other possible scenarios, including small group practices or consulting businesses. Each type of business has its own method of operation, its own financial needs, its own needs for governance such as a board of directors or shareholders, and its own expected profitability. In deciding what form of organization to use in conducting business, it is important to look at issues such as these and decide what is best for the short run, the medium run, and the long run. That is to say, when a small business is being put together the individuals might not have need for a regular corporate structure but may opt to enter into a partnership or some other form of organization. As the business grows and prospers, their organizational needs would be different and they may in fact need to take on the structure of a larger corporation. Many of our large corporations grew out of one individual's hard work and foresight.

There are, of course, tax considerations to be taken into account. As the organization becomes complex the tax situation would change considerably. For example, taxing a large corporation with thousands of shareholders is quite different from taxing a sole proprietor. One of the most important considerations in choosing a form of organization is liability. As this chapter develops, it will become clear that the personal financial exposure of a member of a business will vary, depending on the type of business organization under which that person operates. Limited liability is a very attractive

Pharmacy Law Desk Reference
doi:10.1300/5790_02

motivator for entering into a corporate or similar structure. In a nutshell, when a member of a business relies on the concept of limited liability, he or she would not be liable personally for any more than has been invested in that particular business. Thus, personal assets, such as homes, automobiles, furnishings, jewelry, and so forth, are protected from business creditors.

FORMS OF ORGANIZATION

The Sole Proprietorship

The sole proprietorship is probably the simplest and least costly of all the forms of organization.[1] The sole proprietorship essentially costs nothing to establish, since an individual merely starts doing business, hopefully collecting revenues and keeping track of expenditures. There is a substantial tax advantage to operating as a sole proprietorship. The owner of a sole proprietorship pays taxes only once on the profits of the business. The profits are calculated differently depending on whether the business has inventory. For example, consider a pharmacy with annual sales of $2 million. The cost of goods sold, i.e., the amount of money paid for the inventory that was sold, is $1.54 million. This leaves a gross profit of $460,000. Out of this $460,000, all of the expenses of the pharmacy are paid, including rent, heat, other utilities, supplies, equipment, and salaries of the owner and employees. For this example that total amount is $372,000, leaving a net profit of $88,000 ($460,000 minus $372,000). The owner of the sole proprietorship would pay taxes on the $88,000 plus any salary that he or she took out of the business during the year. Both of these figures, however, would be lumped together and taxed only once. So if the owner had been paid $100,000 and the business generated a profit of $88,000, the total taxes would be calculated based on $188,000 and would be filed with the owner's 1040 form. One major disadvantage of the sole proprietorship is the fact that the owner of a sole proprietorship cannot enjoy the limited liability offered by corporate status. Thus, the owner of a sole proprietorship could be personally liable for all the losses of the business. This begs the question as to why anyone would wish to conduct business as a sole proprietorship. It may be much less expensive from an accounting and legal services standpoint. The owner may also have confidence that he or she is adequately insured to take care of any liability losses. And the business may be sufficiently healthy so that the owner does not feel that he or she needs any more than a sole proprietorship.

Partnerships

The partnership is a more complex form of organization than the sole proprietorship, primarily because more than one party is involved. A partnership is defined as an association of two or more persons to carry on, as co-owners, a business for profit.[2] Thus, decision making is now spread across multiple individuals, and so are profits and losses. Like a sole proprietorship, the partnership does not enjoy limited liability. Thus, the partners can be personally liable for the obligations of the partnership itself. Under the law, each partner is presumed to be liable for the tort and contractual obligations of the other partners. Having said that, when entering into a partnership agreement, the partners may often specify the proportion of profits or losses to be enjoyed or borne by each individual of the partnership depending on each person's investment. Partners should be encouraged to have a written agreement when entering into a partnership, even though this is not absolutely required under the law. The agreement can serve to establish the expectations of the parties regarding many aspects of the business, not only the distribution of profits or losses. With regard to the issue of unlimited liability and partnerships, despite the fact that a partnership agreement might be in place, each partner may be jointly and severally liable if the partnership is on the losing end of a lawsuit. For example, if a court awards a large judgment to a plaintiff against a partnership, the partners are all jointly or severally (individually) liable to be sure that judgment is paid. So if one partner has very little in the way of income or assets and another partner has a great deal, the partner with the better ability to pay may end up paying all or most of the judgment despite what may be written in the partnership agreement. Generally speaking, the actions of any one partner will bind the entire partnership, in that that particular partner would be perceived as an agent of the partnership. Thus, except for extraordinary actions such as divestiture of partnership assets, any partner can bind the partnership.

The discussion thus far in this section has been about the concept of a general partnership. Another type of partnership, a limited partnership, also exists under the law and is something entirely different from a general partnership. A limited partnership is a partnership formed by two or more persons under a specific state statute, the Revised Uniform Limited Partnership Act.[3] Limited partners are basically mere investors. That is, someone can invest money in a limited partnership and enjoy the fruits of profits generated by that partnership, but their liability would be limited only to the extent of their investment in that partnership. Usually a limited partnership would have a managing partner who would be responsible for the day-to-day activities of the partnership and who could be liable for losses incurred by the partnership. The limited partners would be investors only. However, if a limited partner were to engage in management or decision making in the partnership, his or her limited partnership status would no longer exist and the individual could be liable for obligations of the partnership beyond his or her particular investment in that partnership.

Taxes for a general partnership are somewhat different from those of a sole proprietorship with regard to the actual filing. Partnerships generally file a form 1065 partnership return, but it is information only. It is otherwise known as a pass-through return in that the partnership itself does not pay income taxes. All the profits or losses are passed on to the partners and are reported to those partners on an IRS form K-1. Each partner then takes the information from that K-1 form and incorporates it into his or her personal income tax return. Thus, the partnership profits are treated similarly to sole proprietorship profits from a tax standpoint.

Corporations

The decision to incorporate can be based on a number of factors, which may include timing, the size of the business, the number of principals in the business, and the need for a limited liability.[4] Often corporations are formed at the inception of the business, but at other times the forming of the corporation represents a change of entity from another form of organization such as a sole proprietorship or a partnership.

A number of mechanics are involved in forming a corporation.[5] First, one must file articles of incorporation in his or her particular state. These articles would include the following:

1. *The name of the corporation.* The name should always end with a corporate designation such as Corp. or Inc. or some similar designation. This puts the public on notice that you are incorporated and entitled to limited liability.
2. *Specific purpose clause.* This basically details the reason for the existence of your corporation. For example, if your purpose is to conduct business as a pharmacy, then this should be listed in the specific purpose clause.
3. *General "catch-all" clause.* This more general clause would allow you to expand into other areas of business without having to refile your articles of incorporation with the state. It may say, for example, that this corporation can engage in any other business that is related to the specific purpose clause in any manner.
4. *The principal place of business of the corporation.*

5. *The name and address of the resident agent of the corporation.* This would be an individual within the state of incorporation who is authorized by the corporation to accept service of process and other legal notices on behalf of the corporation. So if a corporation is a defendant in a lawsuit, service on the resident agent would be considered service on the corporation. It should also be noted that anyone over the age of eighteen can generally serve as an incorporator. Often this may be the corporation's attorney or accountant, but it can also be a principal of the corporation.

6. *Authorization of capital stock.* This generally appears in the articles of incorporation and details the number of shares of stock that the corporation will be authorizing. This is a total number of shares and is not necessarily the number of shares that will actually be issued in the beginning years of the corporation.

7. *Board of directors.* In this section the initial board of directors will be listed by name. Otherwise the articles of incorporation may contain a provision waiving initial creation of a board of directors.

8. *Duration of the corporation.* A corporation can be perpetual, in which case there is no need to renew the charter. However, it may also have a limited duration, under which circumstance the charter would need to be renewed at the close of that period. If the corporation is to end at a certain time, it would be advisable to specify a limited duration in the articles of incorporation, thereby saving the members of the corporation money by not having to go through the corporation dissolution process.

After the articles of incorporation are filed with a particular state's version of the office of corporations or assessments, and after that office has accepted the articles of incorporation, the members (soon to be shareholders) of the corporation would hold an organizational meeting where the bylaws are adopted. At this meeting they would elect directors of the corporation and appoint the officers of the corporation, such as president, vice president, secretary, and treasurer. The duties of each of these would be generally spelled out in the bylaws at this meeting. Basically, the board of directors makes long-term decisions, and the officers of the corporation carry out the decisions of the board of directors. Ideally the board would not be involved in day-to-day management unless a board member is also an officer of the corporation.

At the organizational meeting, the board will also issue the stock in an amount and denomination necessary and appropriate for the initial capitalization of the corporation. Recall that in the articles of incorporation the total number of shares was authorized or enumerated. At this organizational meeting, and at subsequent meetings of the board, shares may actually be issued. There are generally two prohibitions on issuance of stock. First, stock may not be issued in return for promises to do future services for the corporation. Second, stock may not be issued to an individual who signs a promissory note to acquire that stock.

There are different types of corporations. The first is a regular corporation, or C-corporation. This is generally reserved for larger companies where the entity may anticipate going public at some point in time. The major advantage of this type of corporation is that it provides for the potential infusion of capital for expansion at a later time. Of course, there are always disadvantages. In this case the disadvantage, depending on one's point of view, is that the corporation is now owned by the shareholders and there is less autonomy on the part of the individuals who established the corporation. A regular corporation is also subject to double taxation. Basically, when the corporation itself generates net profit, the corporation must first pay tax on the profit before any profits are distributed to the shareholders. Upon distribution of those profits (or dividends) to shareholders, the shareholders must also pay tax on those when filing their personal income tax. So, basically the net profit is taxed twice, once on the corporation and once to the shareholders.

Many states recognize an entity called a close corporation.[6] This is usually utilized by families who want to keep all the corporate assets and decisions inside the family or another small group of people. Generally a close corporation requires that all extraordinary transactions have unanimous consent of the members of the corporation. These would include merger with another corporation, consolidation, dissolution, or sale of substantially all the assets. Often there are restrictions on the transfer of stock. For example, a shareholder who wishes to sell must first offer the stock to the corporation and then to the other shareholders.[7] If a corporation is going to be formed as a close corporation this should be noted in the articles of corporation that are filed with the state. Often a close corporation is the next step for a sole proprietorship where the business is growing and where liability concerns become an issue. With a close corporation, there is also the necessity of a buy-sell agreement among the members in the event of the death or disability of one of them or in the event of some type of shareholder deadlock on a particular issue. With a close corporation, formalities of notice are dispensed with.

The next type of corporate entity is an S-corporation. These election to become an S-corporation is filed on an IRS form 2553. The election to become an S-corporation takes places at the time of the organizational meeting within seventy-five days of the creation of the corporation in order to be valid for that particular tax year. An S-corporation cannot have more than seventy-five shareholders, and it requires IRS approval. As with a regular corporation (and a close corporation), S-corporation members enjoy limited liability. In addition, income in an S-corporation is treated the same as it is for a sole proprietorship or a partnership, that is, there is no double taxation.

A "professional corporation" is used widely by individuals who are members of certain recognized professions such as medicine, law, accounting, and other recognized service professions.[8] Individuals would need to refer to the statute on professional corporations for their particular state to determine whether they belong to a profession that is recognized by the legislature as one that would qualify for professional corporation status. A professional corporation's members enjoy limited liability for things such as contracts, leases, and other business types of obligations. However, membership in a professional corporation cannot insulate the professional from malpractice or professional liability claims. So, for example, merely because a physician is a member of a professional corporation, that physician is not insulated from personal liability for medical negligence.

Limited Liability Company

The newest business entity in existence is the limited liability company (LLC). These are set up by specific statutes in various states and are different from regular corporations at the point of inception or creation. Individuals file articles of organization instead of articles of incorporation for a limited liability company. In addition, in lieu of officers, directors, and shareholders, this type of corporate entity has members. The business is governed by an "Operating Agreement" signed by all of the members. In addition to the limited liability feature of a corporate entity, the LLC offers further protection of the members from things such as shareholders' derivative suits, since there are no shareholders to bring suit. This type of entity is often desirable when a venture has a limited duration; however, it is not necessarily limited only to ventures with a limited duration. It has some of the trappings of both a corporation and a partnership. As in a corporation, there is the limited liability feature. However, the members of an LLC are taxed as if they were in a partnership,[9] that is, each member receives a K-1 and files it with his or her income taxes.

PIERCING THE CORPORATE VEIL

It is very important for a corporation or an LLC to follow the laws and rules of its state very closely with regard to formation, meetings, notices, and other matters required by law. Plaintiffs or creditors are often anxious to try to get to a shareholder's or member's personal assets by "piercing the corporate veil." If they can show that your business entity is defective in some essential manner, your limited liability protection may dissipate and they may be able to reach your personal assets.

CONCLUSION

Decisions as to the form of organization when conducting any business venture are often quite complex. In addition to legal issues, personality and relationship issues often play a major role. It is important for the professional or businessperson to secure appropriate and competent legal and accounting representation or advice in attempting to establish and maintain their particular form of organization under which they operate. It is also important to realize that forms of organization can be changed as the needs of the business venture dictate. For example, what may have started out as a sole proprietorship might blossom into a full-blown C-corporation with hundreds or thousands of employees. It is difficult, if not impossible, to delineate all of the situations in which a particular corporate entity would be ideal. Suffice it to say that this chapter has provided some general guidance to the reader to be able to sit down with the appropriate business and legal professionals and engage in an informed discussion on the issues.

NOTES

1. Henn, Harry G. *Law of Corporations.* St. Paul, MN: West Publishing Company; 1970, 43-46.

2. Ibid., Uniform Partnership Act, Section 6.

3. Henn, *Law of Corporations,* p. 65.

4. Ibid., pp. 92-103.

5. Macey, Jonathan R. 1997. Corporation Practice Guide. In Richard H. Kravitz (ed.), *Corporation.* New York: Aspen Law and Business; 1997: 715-716, 1301-1404,

6. Ibid., pp. 1151-1181.

7. Clark, Charles C. 1986. *Corporate Law.* Boston: Little, Brown and Company; 1986.

8. Henn, *Law of Corporations,* pp. 103-106.

9. Bishop, Carter C., *Limited Liability Companies: Tax and Business Law.* Valhalla, NY: Warren Gorham and Lamont; 2001.

Chapter 3

Federal Food, Drug, and Cosmetic Act

Larry R. Pilot

INTRODUCTION

In 1906, the Pure Food and Drugs Act (the Act) was enacted into law.[1] The simple objective of this congressional initiative was to assure the purity of food and drugs distributed in the United States and provide existing federal government departments with the authority to assure compliance with this Act.* Since that time there have been many changes to the Act and considerable growth of the government agency responsible for the enforcement of applicable laws. This agency is the Food and Drug Administration (FDA), and its activities are followed so closely by the press that hardly a day passes when there is not some story which mentions the FDA.

Why is it important for pharmacists to know about the history, responsibility, and performance of the FDA? The state is responsible for the licensure of pharmacists and, to a limited extent, the articles that are made available to the consumer through pharmacists and pharmacies. However, it is the FDA that regulates these articles and evaluates whether those who manufacture, compound, distribute, clinically investigate, or dispense these articles are in compliance with federal law. The responsibilities of the FDA, as these may affect pharmacists, range from proper storage of drugs and devices through record keeping as part of the management of drugs or

---

*This Act described in five pages unlawful activities related to adulteration or misbranding of foods and drugs. The definition of "drug" and the identification of adulteration made explicit reference to the United States Pharmacopoeia and the National Formulary, a distinction that continues to the present.

devices used during clinical investigations. Any failure by the pharmacist to comply with a range of laws and regulations* administered by the FDA can subject the pharmacist to significant civil and/or criminal penalties, even though the pharmacist has no knowledge of or intent to commit a prohibited act.

The scope of federal government responsibility and authority expanded greatly during the twentieth century, in particular with reference to drugs, devices, biologics, certain food and dietary supplements, and radiological products. The contents of this chapter cannot condense the volumes of law and regulations that relate to the lawful commercial or investigational availability of articles subject to regulation by the FDA.† Within a typical chain pharmacy, the FDA has responsibility for the regulation of all prescription and over-the-counter (OTC) drugs, all cosmetics, packaged foods, infant formula, vitamins and minerals, dietary supplements, medical devices, and radiological products such as microwave ovens, cell phones, and televisions.

The history of what is generally known as "food and drug law" and the expansion of FDA responsibility reflects a century of public policy initiatives and decisions. Consequently, on a daily basis, consumers use or experience the use of a wide variety of goods and services that are directly subject to the authority of the FDA. From use of a toothbrush and toothpaste in the morning and prior to bedtime, the normal activities of the day are filled with examples of the benefits provided by a complex and diversified consumer and health industry. The pharmacist who practices in community or hospital pharmacy is a major player in the process of delivering many of these benefits to consumers. The pharmacist is also subject to various compliance responsibilities and the possibility of enforcement sanctions as these relate to the dispensing/discovery of drugs and devices.

Knowledge of the basics of food and drug law are important assets to every pharmacist who functions in the vast arena of activities that are subject to the pervasive regulatory authority of the FDA.

---

*Congress has authorized the federal government (i.e., the FDA) to promulgate specific regulations that will have the force and effect of law. Development of these regulations requires publication of a proposal in the Federal Register (Fed. Reg.) inviting public comment. The comments are reviewed and analyzed by the FDA and could result in changes to, withdrawal of, or publication of a new proposed regulation. If the process is completed, a final regulation along with an explanatory preamble will be published in the Fed. Reg. identifying an effective date. The final regulation then appears in Title 21 of the Code of Federal Regulations (C.F.R.). For example, regulations relating to Investigational New Drugs (IND) appear in 21 C.F.R. Part 312.

†The FDA estimates that 25 cents of every dollar spent by consumers for goods is for articles subject to regulation by the FDA.

HISTORY

From 1906 to 1938, there were no major developments in laws affecting the purity of foods and drugs. There was no authority to review the safety or effectiveness of drugs prior to commercial distribution. If the federal government believed that drugs or foods were adulterated or misbranded, the burden to prove such allegations in federal court was the responsibility of the federal government. Early efforts to amend the law were unsuccessful, until reports of severe injury and death associated with the consumption of a liquid sulfanilamide preparation were publicized. This preparation, as manufactured by the manufacturer, utilized diethylene glycol to form the solution. The toxicity of this medication and the reports of death or adverse incidents were sufficient to prompt Congress to agree on passage of the federal Food, Drug, and Cosmetic Act of 1938 (FFDCA). This major legislative accomplishment formed the basis for the present law. Numerous major amendments to this law have occurred because of deficiencies in existing provisions of the FFDCA and changes brought about by advances in technology or alterations in public policy.

Beginning with the 1938 FFDCA and moving to the present, some of these major changes are described as follows.

FFDCA—1938

This comprehensive legislative initiative[2] identified and/or defined various articles subject to explicit requirements, prohibited acts, government inspectional authority, and various penalties for violations.

The terms *drugs, new drug, cosmetic, food,* and *device* were defined, and specific sections of the FDA applied to each of these articles. For example, any "new drug" was to be subject to prior approval for safety before it could be manufactured for distribution into interstate commerce. Medical devices and cosmetics were made subject to the provisions of FFDCA for the first time. Prohibited acts applicable to the various articles were identified, as well as the penalties to be applied to the articles and those responsible for committing the prohibited act.

Most of the prohibited acts revolved around the concept of expanded descriptions of adulteration and misbranding, and these concepts continue to represent the centerpiece for FDA allegations of violations. Penalties for violations included seizure of the article, injunctive relief to prevent continuation of a violation, and criminal prosecution as either a misdemeanor or felony. The government was authorized to make inspections of various types of facilities and collect samples for analysis. However, enforcement of the FFDCA through application of penalties was the responsibility of the Department of Justice (DOJ). The government could refuse to approve a new drug that it considered to be unsafe; however, for drugs and devices that were in commercial distribution at the time of passage of the 1938 FFDCA, the DOJ had the burden to prove in federal court that there was interstate commerce, that a violation had occurred, and that appropriate penalties should be directed by the federal court.

Drug Amendments of 1962

Between 1938 and 1962, the most notable amendments to the FFDCA related to food[3] and color additives.[4] Congressional efforts to amend the FFDCA relative to drugs were unsuccessful until publicity about the teratogenic effects of Thalidomide, a sedative drug used in Europe.

These major drug amendments of 1962[5] required FDA approval of any new drug for effectiveness, as well as safety. These amendments also required that the FDA review those new drugs approved since 1938 for effectiveness, a process which ultimately took more than a decade. In addition, the FDA undertook to evaluate the safety and effectiveness of various categories of over-the-counter drugs. This continuing process has resulted in the publication of specific monograph regulations identifying acceptable ingredients for use in OTC drugs.

Medical Device Amendments of 1976

Because of the phenomenal growth of the medical device industry and a U.S. Supreme Court decision that confirmed FDA discretion to regulate some devices as new drugs, a major initiative began in 1969 to develop a legislative modification to the FFDCA that would apply to devices.* Representatives of industry, consumer, and healthcare groups, the federal government, and Congress agreed on an approach that would be enacted into law on May 28, 1976. This approach recognized the difference between drug and device premarket evaluation and established requirements applicable to investigational and commercially available devices that were significantly broader and more comprehensive than those applicable to drugs and new drugs.

---

*The Supreme Court in 1969 considered *United States v. Bacto-Unidisk,* 89 S. Ct. 1410 (1969) and decided that the FDA had the authority to regulate antibiotic sensitivity discs used on agar petri dishes as drugs and new drugs. This decision reversed an earlier court decision that these discs, which were used for neither treatment nor diagnosis, were devices. Consequently, the FDA had discretionary authority to regulate devices as drugs in order to implement the broad "remedial" function of the FFDCA as determined by the FDA.

Infant Formula Act of 1980

Except for certain specific types of infant products subject to regulation as drugs, infant formula products were subject to regulation as foods. However, in 1979 publicized incidents of death and injury that related to consumption of a defective infant formula manufactured by a pharmaceutical company prompted passage of amendments. These amendments[6] identified required nutrients for formulas, provided recall authority, and authorized the FDA to promulgate quality-control regulations.

Dietary Supplement Health and Education Act of 1994

These amendments[7] were propelled by growing public interest about dietary supplements for claims that exceeded those normally associated with vitamins and minerals also subject to regulation under the FFDCA. As a result, manufacturers/distributors of such products were authorized to market these products with limited health claims after acceptable notification from the FDA for use as a dietary supplement or new dietary ingredient. Limited labeling claims were required to avoid regulation as new drugs.

Various other minor and major amendments to the FFDCA have been enacted since 1938, and new congressional initiatives are expressed with each session of Congress. The legislative process is necessarily dynamic because of national and international issues, some of which are prompted by new discoveries and needs for regulatory reform.

FOOD AND DRUG ADMINISTRATION

The FDA is responsible for the premarket review or required notifications/submissions and enforcement of requirements that apply to various articles identified in the FFDCA.* The activities of those who manufacture, distribute, clinically investigate, and/or promote such articles are also subject to compliance with laws and regulations relating to these articles. The FDA is a component of the Department of Health and Human Services (HHS), and the Commissioner of Foods and Drugs reports to the HHS Secretary.

---

*The terms *drug, new drug, device,* and *dietary supplement* are a few of the terms defined in the FFDCA in Section 201 of Title 21 in the United States Code ("U.S.C."). For example, the term *drug* is identified at 21 U.S.C. § 201(g).

The resources of the FDA are applied through headquarters in the Washington, DC, area and approximately twenty District Offices throughout the United States. The structure of the Office of the Commissioner is described in Figure 3.1.

The principal organizations within the FDA that report to the commissioner are the Office of Regulatory Affairs (ORA) and six different Centers. The ORA is responsible for management of field resources located in approximately twenty District Offices and scores of resident posts. These resources consist primarily of inspectors or laboratory personnel whose responsibilities are to assure compliance with laws and regulations administered by the FDA.* For example, inspectors will inspect facilities and, where objectionable conditions are observed, these will be communicated to management of the inspected facility. Inspectional observations conveyed on an official FORM FDA 483 are reviewed by District Office personnel to determine whether enforcement action is indicated. Generally if enforcement is indicated, a recommendation is forwarded to the responsible Center for review and concurrence.

Each of the six Centers is responsible for scientific review of data and establishment of policy relating to approval, clearance, market experience, and specific requirements of law applicable to the type of article subject to the jurisdiction of the Center. These are as follows.

Center for Drug Evaluation and Research (CDER)

The CDER permits use of an Investigational New Drug (IND) upon acceptable review of submission by a sponsor. It approves new drugs through review of a New Drug Application (NDA) and generic drugs through review of an Abbreviated New Drug Approval Application (ANDA). They CDER also maintains establishment registration and drug-listing information, reviews adverse experience reports, provides surveillance over safety and effectiveness of drugs and labeling/advertising claims, and makes and/or confirms field recommendations for enforcement actions.

Center for Diseases and Radiological Health (CDRH)

The CDRH permits use of device clinical investigations through acceptable review of an Investigational Device Exemption (IDE) by a sponsor. It

---

*The inspectional authority of the FDA inspectors and limitations are described in the FFDCA at 21 U.S.C. § 704.

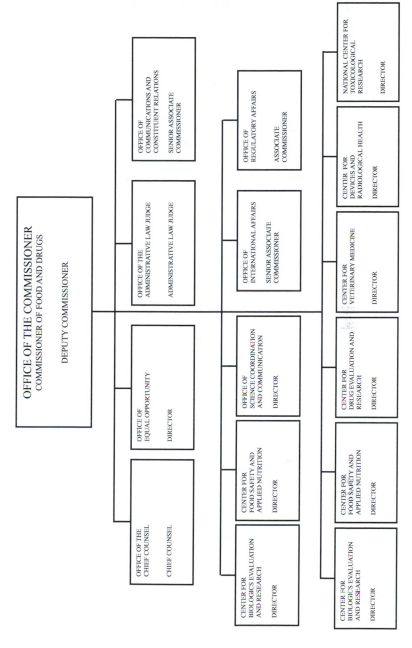

FIGURE 3.1. Department of Health and Human Services, Food and Drug Administration.

clears substantially equivalent devices for commercial distribution through acceptance of a premarket 510(k) notification and approves new devices through review and approval of a premarket approval (PMA) application. The CDRH assures safety of radiological products (e.g., TVs, microwave ovens, x-rays, laser establishment programs), and compliance with standards. The center also maintains registration and device listing information, provides surveillance over safety and effectiveness of devices and labeling/advertising claims, and makes and/or confirms field recommendations for enforcement actions.

Center for Biological Evaluation and Research (CBER)

The CBER administers provisions of the Public Health Service Act (PHSA)[8] relating to blood products, vaccines, and related products as well as some provisions of the FFDCA. It permits the use of new biological products through product and establishment licensure, maintains surveillance over safety of the nation's blood supply and related products, and makes and/or confirms field recommendations for enforcement action.

Center for Food Safety and Nutrition (CFSAN)

The CFSAN is responsible for safety and labeling of the packaged food supply; clearance of color additives for foods, drugs, and devices, and clearance of direct and indirect (e.g., packaging) food additives; recognition of lawful dietary supplements and new dietary ingredients; and safety of cosmetics. It makes and/or confirms field recommendations for enforcement action.

Center for Veterinary Medicine (CVM)

The CVM permits use of animal drugs through approval of New Animal Drug Applications (NADA) and is responsible for safety and effectiveness of animal drugs and devices as well as accuracy of labeling claims. It makes and/or confirms field recommendations for enforcement actions.

National Center for Toxicological Research (NCTR)

The CTR manages research activities relating to toxic substances and risk assessment related to the various articles subject to jurisdiction of the FDA. This Center is located in Arkansas, and unlike the other five Centers has no specific product jurisdiction relating to clearance, surveillance, or compliance.

General Responsibilities of Centers and Districts

Each of these Centers is responsible for a variety of activities that are to assure lawful commercial distribution of the various articles for which the FDA has jurisdiction. Premarket review of various types of required submissions will determine whether new articles or new claims for existing articles are lawful. Both the Center and the Office of Regulatory Affairs through its twenty District Offices cooperate in surveillance activities to assure continuous compliance of new and existing articles with a broad array of regulatory requirements.

District Office personnel are responsible for investigating complaints relating to performance and claims. This is accomplished through the use of inspectors and compliance officers who have authority to inspect facilities and gather information. A major function of the inspector is to inspect facilities to determine compliance with various regulations. For example, manufacturers of pharmaceuticals are expected to comply with regulations that define current Good Manufacturing Practice (cGMP). These regulations appear in Title 21 of the Code of Federal Regulations (CFR) at Parts 210 and 211 (i.e., 21 CFR Parts 210, 211). If the District Office believes that any person* has violated provisions of a law or regulation, it generally will present its recommendation as supported by evidence to the appropriate Center. Compliance personnel within the Center will review the recommendation and either accept or reject it. The recommendation could be limited to issuance of a Warning Letter† or could result in proceedings to apply civil and/or criminal penalties. Because these possibilities generally begin with the collection of evidence during an inspection and proceed through organizational components of the FDA and ultimately through the Department of Justice or local U.S. Attorney for resolution in a federal court, a brief description of this process as applied to drugs in interstate commerce is provided.

---

*The term "person" as defined at 21 U.S.C. § 201(e) "includes individual, partnership, corporation, and association."

†The FDA exercises flexibility in its application of laws and regulations. Through publication of various procedures, policies, and guidance documents available to the public, the FDA expresses its intention. For example, the Warning Letter policy of the FDA is described to prompt voluntary compliance when the FDA believes that a violation of the FFDCA or other law has occurred and is continuing.

SURVEILLANCE, ENFORCEMENT, AND RESOLUTION

The FDA Inspection

The FFDCA authorizes FDA inspectors to inspect facilities where articles, in particular drugs and devices, are manufactured or held for sale in interstate commerce. These inspections begin with the appearance of the inspector and presentation of credentials along with a printed notice of inspection on a FORM FDA 482. The inspection is to occur at reasonable times, in a reasonable manner, and within reasonable limits as authorized by specific provisions of the FFDCA. During the inspection, those subject to the inspection have rights as well as responsibilities. Upon completion of the inspection, if the inspector has made observations of objectionable conditions these will be conveyed on a FORM FDA 483 and management of the facility will have the opportunity to discuss these with the inspector. The inspected facility can provide a written response to the observations in addition to discussing these during a conference with management. Generally, a report of the inspection and any management conference is prepared. This report is identified as the Establishment Inspection Report (EIR), and the content of the EIR often will determine whether the District Office will recommend an enforcement action to the appropriate Center.

The Center Review and Office of Commission Review

When the District Office makes a recommendation to a Center, the recommendation is supported by the FORM FDA 483, any response from facility management, the EIR, and any other items of evidence gathered during the inspection. The compliance office in the Center will review the recommendation and either reject, accept, or request more information relating to the recommendation. If the recommendation for a Warning Letter is appropriate, then this is issued by the District Office or the Center for foreign inspections or other reasons.

A recommendation for seizure, injunction, or prosecution is referred to the Office of the Commissioner for acceptance or rejection. If accepted, the recommendation is forwarded to the FDA Office of Chief Counsel.

The FDA Office of Chief Counsel Review

The Office of Chief Counsel is an organization within the Department of Health and Human Services Office of the General Counsel, and it exists to provide counsel to the FDA. Because the FDA has no authority to engage in litigation on its own initiative, it must convey its recommendation to the Civil Division of the department or the local U.S. Attorney in the event of article seizure.

DEPARTMENT OF JUSTICE, CIVIL DIVISION

This division will determine whether to accept or reject a recommendation or request more evidence. In the event that a recommendation for injunctive relief is accepted, attorneys for the Civil Division and the FDA Office of Chief Counsel will generally work together. If counsel for the defendant is known, there will be a contact to initiate a possible settlement, including execution of a consent decree. If a settlement cannot be accomplished, the matter must be resolved through a trial. It is the DOJ which must sustain the burden of proof during trial.

A recommendation for criminal prosecution may involve a notice to those who could be prosecuted for an informal hearing, but this is not required. However, the recommendation for prosecution is preceded by the review of a grand jury. Unlike the procedure for seizure or injunction, where discovery can occur prior to trial, there is no similar discovery opportunity prior to indictment. However, the DOJ is obligated to provide certain information and does have the responsibility to prove to the trial jury beyond a reasonable doubt the guilt of the defendant (i.e., individual and/or entity such as a corporation).

Once a verdict is rendered, either party has the opportunity to file an appeal with the Court of Appeals for the Federal District Court. The decision of the Court of Appeals can be appealed to the U.S. Supreme Court, which can either accept or reject the opportunity to render a final judgment. Numerous disputes involving the activities of pharmacists or pharmacies have been pursued on appeal, and a recent Supreme Court decision involved the right of pharmacists to compound medications.[9]

PROVISIONS OF FFDCA DIRECTLY APPLICABLE TO PHARMACISTS AND PHARMACIES

General

Pharmacists have the legal responsibility to dispense drugs on the order of a practitioner licensed by the state. Consequently, physicians, dentists, podiatrists, and other licensed practitioners can direct that a prescription drug, as identified by the FDA, an OTC drug, or one to be compounded by the pharmacist be dispensed to a patient. Generally, the regulatory interest of the state and the FDA is to assure that patients are served and protected through the lawful activities of the pharmacist and the licensed practitioner. However, some provisions of the FFDCA or policies* established by the FDA have a direct impact on the practice of pharmacy. These include the Prescription Drug Marketing Act of 1987[10] and the Pharmacy Compounding provisions of the Food and Drug Administration Modernization Act of 1997.[11]

Prescription Drug Marketing Act of 1987 (PDMA)

A by-product of the growth of the pharmaceutical industry was the opportunity to provide samples of prescription drugs to licensed practitioners. The objective of this practice was to provide samples of prescription drugs through pharmaceutical sales representatives in order to encourage licensed practitioners to prescribe a particular manufacturer's prescription drug for patients. This practice existed for decades without major incident. However, a committee of the U.S. Congress[12] undertook an investigation of these practices during the mid-1980s. This investigation identified a significant number of examples of questionable practices. These practices ranged from the adulteration of samples through repackaging and subsequent resale to questionable diversion, reimportation of previously exported drugs, and counterfeiting.

As a result, changes to the FFDCA were made through new subsections 502(c) and 503(d), and prohibited acts and penalties were also identified.[13] A primary objective of these changes was to apply controls to the distribution of samples in order to prevent varieties of abuse that could have a harmful effect on patients. Consequently, the distribution of samples became subject to extensive record-keeping requirements to reduce the possibility of diversions that were considered unlawful. Manufacturers, wholesalers/distributors, and pharmacists became subject to the additional burden of limiting distribution of samples and maintaining accurate records of such distribution. Recipients of lawful distribution of samples, such as pharmacists, must execute a written receipt to the manufacturer or distributor of record. The PDMA also imposed restrictions on the resale of prescription drugs by hospitals, charitable institutions, and other healthcare facilities.

---

*The FDA maintains a number of documents, manuals, etc., which provide reference to FDA policy, procedures, etc. Many of these are also available to the public through the FDA Web site or through request under the Freedom of Information Act (FOIA). In addition, various "guidance" documents are prepared and available to give guidance to the FDA and those responsible for compliance with various provisions of the FFDCA.

Because these institutions often receive prescription drugs at reduced costs, the subsequent resale by these institutions raised issues about the integrity of the chain of control and unfair competition with wholesale distributors. Although these are exceptions, the restrictions applicable to these institutions greatly reduced the purchase for resale of prescription drugs.

The PDMA also required the FDA to promulgate regulations to establish minimum standards, terms, and conditions for the state licensing of wholesalers. On September 14, 1990, the FDA finalized "Guidelines for State Licensing of Wholesale Prescription Drug Distributors," which are located in 21 CFR Part 205. It is the responsibility of each state to apply these guidelines to their licensing of wholesalers.

Pharmacy Compounding—Food and Drug Administration Modernization Act of 1997

Although the actual compounding of drugs to the order of a licensed practitioner diminished considerably soon after passage of the 1938 amendments, pharmacists continue to have the responsibility to compound when presented with a prescription order. Under some circumstances, community or hospital pharmacists may be in a position to compound a volume of a drug in anticipation of the prescription order that is likely to be issued for a patient. This practice has prompted the FDA to express the concern that such activities constitute manufacturing, for which the pharmacist is obligated to comply with FDA regulations describing current Good Manufacturing Practice.

For many years there has been tension between the FDA and the pharmacy profession over the distinction between compounding and manufacturing. The FDA did issue various statements of policy on this subject, including Compliance Policy Guides, but these statements do not have the force and effect of law.

The 1997 amendments created a new section 503A to the FFDCA which is applicable to pharmacy compounding. The objective of this section is to enable the pharmacist to engage in compounding activities that would not subject pharmacists to accusations that such compounding constituted manufacturing because of compounding in bulk for future dispensing in anticipation of the receipt of a prescription order. The FFDCA does provide explicit requirements as to permissible conduct and the FDA has documented a policy (Compliance Policy Guide 7132.16), but confusion and disagreement remain.

In 1999, a group of pharmacists that specialized in drug compounding filed a complaint against the FDA (i.e., HHS secretary) to prevent prosecution for their activities to promote their capability to compound drugs. These pharmacists were fearful of prosecution because of possible disagreement with the FDA over whether their advertising and promotional activities were contrary to the provisions of the 1997 amendments. They prevailed at the district court level but were reversed in part by the Court of Appeals. The Supreme Court decided the dispute in a lengthy opinion which declared that the "free speech" restrictions in 503A of the FFDCA were unconstitutional. Consequently, pharmacists could advertise and promote their capacity to compound drugs.[14] Although the Supreme Court declared a victory for free speech surrounding the provisions of section 503A of the FFDCA, the controversy over distinction between pharmacy compounding and manufacturing continues. At least one pharmacy has received a warning letter from the FDA expressing the FDA belief that their activities relating to compounding constitute manufacturing. However, there has been no federal court litigation to resolve any dispute. If such disputes continue and there is litigation, the ultimate resolution could be through a decision by the Supreme Court or legislative action by the U.S. Congress.

SUMMARY

The United States is a country of laws intended to assure order in our society. Debate about the necessity for, quality of, or appropriate application of these laws is not likely to cease. Pharmacists recognize their obligations to comply with provisions of law that are part of their responsibility to maintain their license to practice pharmacy. Knowledge of the function and authority of the FDA is becoming increasingly important to the practice of pharmacy, because of the broad mandate that the FDA has to serve the public interest.

Most pharmacists during the course of their practice in retail, hospital, institutional, or academic environments are not likely to be affected directly by the responsibility of the FDA, yet it is essential to be reminded that the drugs dispensed by pharmacists exist because the FDA has the authority to determine if a new drug can be approved for distribution as well as what can remain available. The FFDCA provides the FDA with considerable authority to apply and enforce the act. When disagreements cannot be resolved through application of the administrative process, the federal court system is the forum for ultimate resolution of any dispute.

The content of this chapter is intended to provide a very basic understanding of the FDA, its statutory mandate, and the scope of its authority as it impacts on the practice of pharmacy. The FDA as a named organization existed for most of the twentieth century, and current Internet technology will enable the reader to locate the FDA and learn about new initiatives and responsibilities. For more information about the FDA, log on at www.fda.gov.

NOTES

1. June 30, 1906, ch. 3915, 34 Stat. 768.
2. June 25, 1938, Pub. L. No. 75-717, 52 Stat. 1040.
3. September 6, 1958, Pub. L. No. 85-929, 72 Stat. 1784.
4. July 12, 1960, Pub. L. No. 86-618, 74 Stat. 396.
5. October 10, 1962, Pub. L. No. 87-781, 76 Stat. 780.
6. September 26, 1980, Pub. L. No. 96-359, 94 Stat. 1190.
7. October 25, 1994, Pub. L. No. 103-417, 108 Stat. 4325.
8. July 1, 1944, ch. 373, 58 Stat. 682. The FFDCA is the major law which the FDA is authorized to administer. However, there are other laws or portions of laws which the FDA is authorized to administer as directed by the Secretary of the Department of Health and Human Services.
9. *Thompson v. Western States Medical Center,* 122 S. Ct. 1497, April 29, 2002.
10. Apr. 22, 1988, Pub. L. No. 100-293, 102 Stat. 95.
11. Nov. 21, 1997, Pub. L. No. 105-115, 111 Stat. 2296.
12. 133 Cong. Rec. S1054-02 (1987); 133 Cong. Rec. H3021-01 (daily ed. May 4, 1987) (Statement of Rep. Waxman) (1987). (Resulted in Prescription Drug Marketing Act of 1987.)
13. Pub. L. No. 100-293.
14. *Thompson v. Western States Medical Center.*

Chapter 4

The Pharmacist's Responsibility Under the Controlled Substances Act and Related Matters

Delbert D. Konnor

Practicing pharmacists are charged with many responsibilities under federal and state laws and regulations. The federal law that regulates controlled substances is the Controlled Substances Act (CSA) of 1970. The CSA became effective May 1, 1971, and consolidates into one piece of legislation a number of laws passed by Congress since the Harrison Narcotic Tax Act of 1914, the first comprehensive federal legislation to control addicting drugs.

This chapter brings together those regulations considered a minimum in any discussion of the pharmacist's responsibility under the law. Covered in this chapter are the schedules of controlled substances, prescription requirements, prescription records, purpose of issuance of prescription orders, record-keeping requirements, dispensing requirements, how to deal with forged, altered, and stolen prescription blanks, registration, inventories, disposal, and long term care facilities, among other important areas that affect a pharmacist's ability to order, stock, and dispense controlled substances. See Chapter 22, "Electronic Prescribing," for a discussion on electronic prescription orders for controlled substances.

The information in this chapter is taken liberally from the Drug Enforcement Administration Pharmacist's Manual (April 2004). The Pharmacist's Manual is a publication of the DEA's Office of Diversion Control to assist pharmacists in their understanding of the Federal Controlled Substances Act of 1970 and its implementing regulations as they pertain to pharmacy practice. The CFR is a codification of the general and permanent rules published in the Federal Register.

The DEA has long been recognized for reaching out to its registrants to seek their support in enforcing the law and controlling diversion of legiti-

Pharmacy Law Desk Reference
© 2007 by The Haworth Press, Inc. All rights reserved.
doi:10.1300/5790_04

mate controlled substances by relying on voluntary cooperation (compliance). Furthermore, the agency recognizes the value of controlled substances in healthcare and its key role established by Congress to safeguard the American public against drug abuse and diversion. A list of DEA Field Offices with Diversion Program Managers is included in the appendix to this chapter.

BACKGROUND

The Drug Enforcement Administration within the U.S. Department of Justice is the responsible federal agency for enforcing the Controlled Substances Act of 1970 (Title 21, United States Code, Section 800 et. Seq.) and its implementing regulations (Title 21, Code of Federal Regulations, Part 1300 to End) regarding the handling of controlled substances and regulated chemicals.

The DEA does not routinely inspect pharmacies for controlled substances violations. This function is usually conducted by appropriate state agencies. The DEA does concern itself with complaints of diversion from pharmacies and investigates "doctor shoppers" and prescription forgers when such activities are confirmed through review of pharmacy records.

Since its creation, the DEA has focused on the diversion and abuse of controlled substances and, more recently, drug products containing listed chemicals—ephedrine- and pseudoephedrine-containing over-the-counter (OTC) products are examples. The DEA continues to state that most drug diversion occurs at the retail level. Thus, the practicing pharmacist plays an important role in supervising the proper control of prescription medicine and OTC drug products. This further emphasizes the pharmacist's key role to safeguard the healthcare of the patient and prevent diversion. The pharmacist and the prescribing practitioner share responsibility for ensuring proper therapeutic drug usage of patients, whose healthcare is critical to their decisions.

The CSA authorizes pharmacists to dispense controlled substances when bona fide prescription orders are issued by practitioners authorized to prescribe controlled substances. Under the CSA, a valid prescription order must be issued for a legitimate medical purpose by a practitioner acting in the usual course of professional practice. While this responsibility rests on the prescriber, a corresponding responsibility rests upon the pharmacist who dispenses the prescription medicine. A prescription order that is not written for a legitimate medical purpose is not considered to be a valid prescription order within the meaning of the law. The individual who knowingly dispenses such a purported prescription order, as well as the individual issuing it, can be subject to criminal and/or civil penalties.

Regular monitoring of DEA information to keep current in changes can be done through the DEA's Web site (www.dea.gov). You can access the DEA's diversion control program by using the hyperlink for the Office of Diversion in the DEA Web site or go to www.deadiversion.usdoj.gov. This site includes newsletters, listings of DEA Diversion and Registration Field Offices, online forms and applications, DEA manuals and other publications, and items on the DEA's diversion control program.

SCHEDULES OF CONTROLLED SUBSTANCES

The controlled substances and their derivatives listed under the CSA can be found in the Code of Federal Regulations, Title 21 under Part 1308—Schedules of Controlled Substances.

The drugs and drug products under the jurisdiction of the CSA are divided into five schedules. Controlled substances in Schedules II through V have an accepted medical use in the United States, and Schedule I substances do not. The characteristics and some examples of the drugs in each schedule are presented next.

Schedule I Substances

The substances in Schedule I have a high abuse potential and no accepted medical use in the United States. This is the only schedule that includes drugs that are not available for prescribing, dispensing, or administering. The DEA does allow for research involving Schedule I substances. This requires a separate registration as a researcher. Some examples of substances classified as Schedule I narcotics include heroin and propiram. Some hallucinogenic substances found in Schedule I include LSD, marijuana, and MDMA (Ecstasy).

Other examples of Schedule I substances are the depressant methaqualone, gamma hydroxybutyric acid (GHB), and the stimulant methcathinone.

Schedule II Substances

Substances in Schedule II have a high abuse potential with severe psychological or physical dependence liability, have an accepted medical use in the United States, and are available for practitioners to prescribe, dispense, and administer.

Some examples of single entity Schedule II narcotics include morphine, codeine, hydrocodone, and opium. Other Schedule II narcotic substances and their common name-brand products include hydromorphone (Dilaudid®), methadone (Dolophine®), meperidine (Demerol®), oxycodone (Percodan®, OxyContin®), and fentanyl (Sublimaze®).

Some examples of Schedule II stimulants include amphetamine (Dexedrine®, Adderall®), methamphetamine (Desoxyn®), and methylphenidate (Ritalin®). Other Schedule II substances include cocaine, amobarbital, glutethimide, pentobarbital, and secobarbital.

Schedule III Substances

The substances in Schedule III have an abuse potential less than those in Schedule II, but more than Schedule IV substances.

Some examples of Schedule III narcotics include products containing less than 15 milligrams of hydrocodone per dosage unit (Vicodin®, Lorcet®, Tussionex®), and products containing not more than 90 milligrams of codeine per dosage unit (codeine with acetaminophen, aspirin, or ibuprofen).

Other Schedule III substances include anabolic steroids, benzphetamine (Didrex®), phendimetrazine, and any compound, mixture, preparation, or suppository dosage form containing amobarbital, secobarbital, pentobarbital, dronabinol (Marinol®), or ketamine.

Schedule IV Substances

The substances in Schedule IV have an abuse potential less than those listed in Schedule III and more than substances in Schedule V.

Some examples of Schedule IV narcotics include propoxyphene (Darvon®), butorphanol (Stadol®), and pentazocine (Talwin-NX®).

The following benzodiazepine substances are also found in Schedule IV: alprazolam (Xanax®), clonazepam (Klonopin®), clorazepate (Tranxene®), diazepam (Valium®), flurazepam (Dalmane®), halazepam (Paxipam®), lorazepam (Ativan®), midazolam (Versed®), orazepam (Serax®), prazepam (Verstran®), temazepam (Restoril®), triazolam (Halcion®), and quazepam (Doral®).

Other Schedule IV substances include barbital, phenobarbital, chloral hydrate, ethchlorvynol (Placidyl®), chlordiazepoxide (Librium®), ethinamate, meprobamate, paraldehyde, methohexital, phentermine, diethylpropion, pemoline (Cylert®), mazindol (Sanorex®), and sibutramine (Meridia®).

Schedule V Substances

The substances in Schedule V have an abuse potential less than those listed in Schedule IV and consist primarily of preparations containing limited quantities of certain narcotic and stimulant drugs generally for antitussive, antidiarrheal, and analgesic purposes. Some examples are cough preparations containing not more than 200 milligrams of codeine per 100 milliliters or per 100 grams (Robitussin AC®, Phenergan with Codeine®), and buprenorphine (Buprenex®).

REGISTRATION REQUIREMENTS

Every pharmacy that dispenses any controlled substance must be registered with the DEA. The DEA does not register pharmacists; pharmacists must obtain their license to practice pharmacy from their state regulatory authority. To obtain a DEA registration, a pharmacy can request a DEA Form-224 (Application for New Registration) from any DEA Registration Field Office or from the DEA Headquarters Registration Unit in Washington, DC, at 1-800-882-9539 (Registration Contact Center). DEA Form 224 is also available online and in PDF format at www.deadiversion.usdoj.gov. DEA Form 224 is fully interactive, including the acceptance of electronic credit card payments.

The completed DEA Form-224 must be submitted to the following address:

Drug Enforcement Administration
Registration Unit
Central Station
P.O. Box 28083
Washington, DC 20038-8083

Pharmacy registrations must be renewed every three years. The cost of the registration is noted on the application form. The certificate of registration must be maintained at the registered location and kept available for official inspection. If a person owns and operates more than one pharmacy, each place of business must be registered.

Every pharmacy currently registered with DEA will receive a renewal application approximately forty-five days before the registration expiration date. The renewal application will be sent to the address listed on the current registration certificate. If the renewal form is not received within thirty days before the expiration date of the current registration, the pharmacy should contact the DEA registration unit for their state and request a renewal registration form.

New Pharmacy Registration

Pharmacies seeking to become registered for the first time must request a DEA Form-224 (Application for New Registration) from any DEA Registration Field Office or the DEA Registration Unit in Washington, DC, at the address listed under Registration Requirements.

Any pharmacy engaged in co-op buying of controlled substances must also register as a distributor with the DEA. To obtain this registration, a pharmacy must meet distributor (wholesaler) security and record-keeping requirements.

An affidavit system for expediting pharmacy applications may be used to obtain a DEA registration number for a new pharmacy or for transferring ownership of an existing pharmacy. If the pharmacy has been registered by the state licensing agency, the applicant may include an affidavit to verify the existence of the state license with its application (21 CFR 1301.17).

Chemical Registration Requirements

Under DEA chemical control regulations there is an exemption from the registration requirement for a retail distributor. A retail distributor is defined as a grocery store, general merchandise store, drugstore, or other entity or person whose activities as a distributor of legal drug products containing listed chemicals pseudoephedrine, phenylpropanolamine (PPA), combination ephedrine, and single-entity ephedrine are limited almost exclusively to sales for personal use, both in number and volume of sales, either directly to walk-in customers or in face-to-face transactions. Personal use means the distribution of below "threshold quantities" in a single transaction to an individual for legitimate medical use.

Federal law requires any person who is engaged in the wholesale distribution of drug products containing List I chemicals to obtain a registration as a chemical distributor. A distributor who does not meet all the requirements for a retail distributor is a wholesale distributor.

Community (retail) pharmacies that are registered to handle controlled substances need not obtain a separate DEA chemical registration for retail distribution of drug products containing pseudoephedrine, phenylpropanolamine, combination ephedrine, and single-entity ephedrine which are regulated as List I chemicals. If a pharmacy desires to engage in the wholesale distribution of bulk quantities of these drug products, the pharmacy will have to register with the DEA as a chemical distributor, because these activities fall outside of the definition of retail distributor. Therefore, the pharmacy would be subject to the registration requirements that apply to wholesale distributors. To obtain a DEA Chemical Distributor registration, a pharmacy can request DEA Form-510 (Application for Registration) from any DEA Registration Field Office.

For additional information see Chemical Requirements: Comprehensive Methamphetamine Control Act of 1996 later on in this chapter.

Denial, Revocation, or Suspension of Registration

Diversion of legitimately manufactured controlled substances is a serious problem in the United States. Registrants serve as the nation's primary guardians for preventing diversion and controlling legitimate access to these drugs. The CSA provides the federal government with additional legal resources for taking action against those registrants who contribute to the diversion problem. The U.S. Attorney General has the authority to suspend or revoke a DEA registration upon a finding that the registrant has

1. materially falsified any application filed;
2. been convicted of a felony relating to a controlled substance or a List I Chemical;
3. had his or her state license or registration suspended, revoked, or denied;
4. committed an act which would render his or her registration inconsistent with the public interest; or
5. been excluded from participation in a Medicaid or Medicare program.

Denial of Registration in the Public Interest

The CSA gives the U.S. Attorney General authority to deny any application for DEA registration or renewal if it is determined that issuing a controlled substance registration would be inconsistent with the public interest. In determining the public interest, the CSA states the following factors will be considered:

1. The recommendation of the appropriate state licensing board or professional disciplinary authority
2. The applicant's experience in dispensing or conducting research with respect to controlled substances

3. The applicant's conviction record under federal or state laws relating to the manufacture, distribution, or dispensing of controlled substances
4. Compliance with applicable state, federal, or local laws relating to controlled substances
5. Such other conduct which may threaten the public health and safety

Termination of Registration

Any registrant who discontinues his or her business or transfers it to another person must notify the nearest DEA Registration Field Office in writing before terminating the pharmacy's registration. Along with the notification of termination of registration, the pharmacist should send the DEA Certificate of Registration and any unused Official DEA Order Forms (DEA Form-222). The pharmacist should write or stamp the word VOID across the face of each Official DEA Order Form before returning them to the DEA. The notification to the DEA should also indicate where the controlled substance inventories and records will be kept and how the controlled substances were transferred or destroyed.

Records involving controlled substances must be kept available for two years for inspection and copying by the DEA. This requirement applies even though the business has been discontinued.

Transfer of Business

A registrant transferring a pharmacy business to another registrant shall notify the nearest DEA Registration Field Office at least fourteen days before the date of the proposed transfer and provide the following information:

1. the name, address, and registration number of the registrant discontinuing business;
2. the name, address, and registration number of the registrant acquiring the pharmacy;
3. whether the business activities will be continued at the location registered by the current business owner or moved to another location (If the latter, give the address of the new location.); and
4. the date on which the controlled substances will be transferred to the person acquiring the pharmacy.

On the day the controlled substances are transferred, a complete controlled substances inventory must be taken and a copy of the inventory must be included in the records of both the person transferring the business and the person acquiring the business. Exhibit 4.1 is a model format for an affidavit to expedite the process for transferring the ownership of a pharmacy.

If the registrant acquiring the pharmacy owns at least one other pharmacy licensed in the same state as the pharmacy being transferred, the registrant may apply for a new DEA registration prior to the date of transfer. The DEA will issue a registration which will authorize the registrant to obtain controlled substances at the time of transfer. But the registrant may not dispense controlled substances until the pharmacy has been issued a valid state pharmacy license.

A DEA registration application for transferring ownership of an existing pharmacy can be expedited if the applicant includes an affidavit verifying that the pharmacy has been registered by the state licensing agency. The affidavit verifying the existence of the state license should be attached to the initial application for registration.

DISPOSAL OF CONTROLLED SUBSTANCES

The pharmacy may hire an outside firm to inventory, package, and arrange for the transfer of its controlled substances to another pharmacy, supplier, or manufacturer. The pharmacy is responsible for the actual transfer of the controlled substances and for the accuracy of the inventory and records. The pharmacy may also transfer the drugs to a distributor registered with the DEA to destroy drugs (reverse distributor). The pharmacy may not turn over any controlled substances to a distributor unless it is registered to destroy controlled substances. The pharmacy is responsible for verifying that the reverse distributor is registered with the DEA.

The records involving the transfer or destruction of controlled substances must be kept readily available for two years for inspection and copying by the DEA. The two primary methods for disposing of controlled substances are transfer to another registrant or destruction as explained later on in this chapter.

Transfer of Controlled Substances

If a pharmacy goes out of business or is acquired by a new pharmacy, it may transfer the controlled substances to another pharmacy, supplier, manufacturer, or distributor registered to dispose of controlled substances.

EXHIBIT 4.1. AFFIDAVIT FOR TRANSFER OF A PHARMACY (21 CFR, SECTION 1301.17(b))

I, _____,
the _____ (Title of offi-
cer, partner, or other position) of _____
(Corporation, partnership, or sole proprietor), doing business as
_____ (Store name) hereby
certify: (1) That said company was issues a pharmacy permit No.
_____ by the _____
(Board of Pharmacy of Licensing Agency) of the State of _____
_____ and a DEA Registration Number ____
_____ for a pharmacy located at _____
_____ (Number and Street), __
_____ (City) _____
(State) _____ (Zip Code); and (2) That said company
is acquiring the pharmacy business of _____
_____ (Name of Seller) doing business as
_____ with DEA Registra-
tion Number _____ on or
about _____ (Date of Transfer) and
that said company has applied (or will apply on _____
_____ (Date) for a pharmacy permit from the
Board of Pharmacy (or Licensing Agency) of the State of _____
_____ to do business as _____
_____
(Name of Pharmacy) at _____
(Number and Street) _____
(City) _____ (State) _____ (Zip Code).

This statement is submitted in order to obtain a Drug Enforcement Administration registration number.

I understand that if a DEA registration number is issued, the pharmacy may acquire controlled substances but may not dispense them until a pharmacy permit or license is issued by the State board of pharmacy or licensing agency.

I understand that if any information is false, the Administration may immediately suspend the registration for this pharmacy and commence proceedings to revoke under 21 U.S.C. 824(a) because of the danger to public health and safety. I further understand that

(continued)

(continued)

any false information contained in this affidavit may subject me personally and the above-named corporation/partnership/business to prosecution under 21 U.S.C. 843, the penalties for conviction of which include imprisonment for up to four (4) years, a fine of not more than $30,000.00 or both.

_____

Signature (Person who signs Application for Registration)

State of _____

County _____

Subscribed to and sworn before me this _____ day of

_____ 20_____.

_____

Notary Public

To transfer Schedule II controlled substances, the receiving registrant must issue an Official DEA Order Form (DEA Form-222, U.S. Official Order Form—Schedules I & II) to the registrant transferring the drugs. The transfer of Schedule III-V controlled substances must be documented in writing to show the drug name, dosage form, strength, quantity, and date transferred. The document must include the names, addresses, and DEA registration numbers of the parties involved in the transfer of the controlled substances.

To Another Pharmacy

On the day the controlled substances are transferred, a complete inventory must be taken, documenting the drug name, dosage form, strength, quantity, and date transferred.

In addition, DEA Form-222 (Official DEA Order Form) must be prepared to document the transfer of Schedule II controlled substances. This inventory will serve as the final inventory for the registrant going out of business and transferring the controlled substances. It will also serve as the initial inventory for the registrant acquiring the controlled substances. A copy of the inventory must be included in the records of each person. It is not necessary to send a copy of the inventory to the DEA. The person acquiring the controlled substances must maintain all records involved in the transfer of the controlled substances for two years.

To Another Supplier or Manufacturer

Any pharmacy may transfer controlled substances to a supplier or a manufacturer. The pharmacist must maintain a written record showing the following:

1. The date of the transaction
2. The name, strength, form, and quantity of the controlled substance
3. The supplier's or manufacturer's name, address, and, if known, registration number
4. DEA Form-222—The official record for the transfer of Schedule II substances

To a Reverse Distributor Registered to Dispose
of Controlled Substances

Any pharmacy may forward controlled substances to DEA-registered reverse distributors who handle the disposal of drugs. (Also see Disposal of Controlled Substances.)

Destruction of Controlled Substances

The DEA recommends that any pharmacy seeking to dispose of controlled substances first contact the nearest DEA Diversion Field Office for disposal instructions. In no case should drugs be forwarded to the DEA unless the registrant has received prior approval from the DEA. The DEA procedures established for the destruction of controlled substances shall not be construed as altering in any way the state laws or regulations for the disposal of controlled substances. Requests from registrants seeking authorization to destroy controlled substances without DEA presence or requests from nonregistrants desiring to dispose of controlled substances will be handled as follows.

Once-a-Year DEA Authorization for Destruction

Once each calendar year community (retail) pharmacies may request DEA authorization to destroy damaged, outdated, or otherwise unwanted controlled substances. The pharmacy must complete DEA Form-41 (Registrants Inventory of Drugs Surrendered), listing all drugs to be destroyed. In addition, the pharmacy must prepare a letter requesting permission to destroy the controlled substances, proposing a date and method of destruction, and listing the names of at least two people who will witness the destruction. The witnesses should be a licensed physician, pharmacist, midlevel practitioner, nurse, or state or local law enforcement officer.

Both documents must be received by the nearest DEA Diversion Field Office at least two weeks prior to the proposed destruction date. After reviewing all available information, the DEA office will then notify the registrant in writing of its decision. Once the controlled substances have been destroyed, signed copies of the DEA Form-41 must be forwarded to the DEA. The pharmacist should contact local environmental authorities prior to implementing the proposed method of destruction to ascertain that hazards are not associated with the destruction.

Exception to DEA Authorization for Destruction

Prior DEA authorization to destroy controlled substances is not necessary when an authorized member of a state law enforcement authority or regulatory agency witnesses the destruction. Copies of a DEA Form-41 or state controlled substance destruction form must be forwarded to the local DEA Diversion Office after the destruction.

Reverse Distributors Authorized to Destroy Controlled Substances

A pharmacy may at any time forward controlled substances to DEA-registered reverse distributors who handle the disposal of drugs. The pharmacist may contact the local DEA Diversion Field Office for an updated list of those reverse distributors in their area. When a pharmacy transfers Schedule II substances to a reverse distributor for destruction, the reverse distributor must issue an Official DEA Order Form (DEA Form-222) to the pharmacy. When Schedule III-V controlled substances are transferred to a reverse distributor for destruction, the pharmacy should document in writing the drug name, dosage form, strength, quantity, and date transferred. The DEA-registered reverse distributor who will destroy the controlled substances is responsible for submitting a DEA Form-41 to the DEA when the drugs have been destroyed. A DEA Form-41 should not be used to record the transfer of controlled substances between the pharmacy and the registered reverse distributor disposing of the drugs.

"Blanket Authorization" for Destruction
of Controlled Substances

The DEA will issue a "blanket authorization" for destruction of controlled substances on a very limited basis to those registrants who are associated with hospitals and clinics or other registrants having to dispose of used needles, syringes, or other injectable objects only. This limited exception is granted because of the probability that those objects have been contaminated by hazardous bodily fluids. The pharmacist should contact the local DEA Diversion Field Office for information about how to request such an authorization. The DEA will evaluate requests for a blanket authorization based on the following guidelines:

1. Frequency of destruction (i.e., daily, weekly) and volume of drugs involved that warrant such authorization
2. Method of destruction (Drugs must be destroyed in such a manner that they are beyond reclamation.)
3. Registrant's past history
4. Security at the pharmacy or registered location
5. Name and position of the individual responsible for the destruction

Those registrants granted blanket authorization to destroy controlled substances must complete DEA Form-41.

SECURITY REQUIREMENTS

The DEA requires pharmacies to keep Schedule II, III, IV, and V controlled substances in a locked cabinet or dispersed through the noncontrolled stock to deter theft. An electronic alarm system is recommended.

Request for Employment Waiver for Certain Pharmacy Employees

A pharmacy registrant (i.e., the registrant or corporation which owns the pharmacy) must not employ in a position which allows access to controlled substances anyone who has been convicted of a felony relating to controlled substances or who, at any time, has had an application for DEA registration denied, revoked, or surrendered for cause. "For cause" means surrendering a registration in lieu of, or as a consequence of, any federal or state administrative, civil, or criminal action resulting from an investigation of the individual's handling of controlled substances.

However, pharmacies desiring to employ an individual who meets this definition may request an exception to this requirement (see 21 CFR 1307.03) from the DEA. The employer must have a waiver approved before hiring the applicant. A waiver request should be sent to DEA Headquarters, Office of Diversion Control, Washington, DC 20537.

A pharmacy registrant who applies for such a waiver should understand that the following factors will be considered:

1. A detailed description of the nature and extent of the applicant's past controlled substances violations
2. Activities of the applicant since the violation
3. Current status of the applicant's state licensure
4. Extent of applicant's proposed access to controlled substances
5. Registrant's proposed physical and professional safeguards to prevent diversion by the applicant if employed
6. Status of employing registrant regarding handling of controlled substances
7. Other pertinent information uncovered by DEA in its investigation of the applicant's or registrant's handling of controlled substances
8. Such a waiver should not be considered unless there are valid reasons to believe that diversion is unlikely to occur

Controlled Substance Theft or Loss

Notify DEA and Local Police

Immediately upon discovery of a theft or significant loss of controlled substances, a pharmacy, as required by regulation, must contact the nearest DEA Diversion Field Office by telephone, facsimile, or a brief written message explaining the circumstances. A pharmacy should also notify the local police as may be required by state law. If there is a question as to whether a theft has occurred or a loss is significant, a registrant should err on the side of caution and report it to the DEA. The DEA must be notified directly. This requirement is not satisfied by reporting the theft or significant loss in any other manner. For example, a corporation which owns/operates multiple registered sites and wishes to channel all notifications through corporate management or any other internal department responsible for security must still provide notice directly to the DEA "upon discovery" and keep a copy for its records.

Complete DEA Form-106

A pharmacy shall also complete DEA Form-106 (Report of Theft or Loss of Controlled Substances). To obtain a DEA Form-106, contact the nearest DEA Diversion Field Office. The DEA Form-106 will formally document the actual circumstances of the theft or significant loss and the quantities of controlled substances involved, once this information has been determined conclusively. The pharmacy should send the original DEA Form-106 and a copy to the appropriate DEA Diversion Field Office and keep a copy for its records.

The DEA Form-106 must include the following information:

1. Name and address of firm (pharmacy)
2. DEA registration number
3. Date of theft
4. Name and telephone number of local police department notified
5. Type of theft (night break in, armed robbery, etc.)
6. Listing of symbols or cost code used by pharmacy in marking containers (if any)
7. Listing of controlled substances missing from theft or significant loss

If Investigation Finds No Theft or Loss

If after an investigation of the circumstances surrounding the theft or significant loss it is determined that no such theft or significant loss occurred, no DEA Form-106 need be filed. However, the registrant should notify the DEA in writing of this fact in order to resolve the initial report and explain why no DEA Form-106 was filed regarding the incident.

Registrant's Responsibility for Identifying "Significant Loss"

Although the CSA regulations do not define the term "significant loss," it is the responsibility of the registrant to use his or her best judgment to take appropriate action. A significant loss depends, in large part, on the business of the pharmacy and the likelihood of a rational explanation for a particular occurrence. What would constitute a significant loss for a pharmacy may be viewed as comparatively insignificant for a hospital or distributor.

Further, the loss of a small quantity of controlled substances, repeated over a period of time, may indicate a significant problem for a registrant, a problem which must be reported to the DEA, even though the individual amounts of missing controlled substances are not, in and of themselves, significant. Registrants must report a loss upon discovery.

In particular, a pharmacist should be alert for suspicious or unexplained losses. Any signs of a break in, physical entry, or armed robbery should be reported. The burden of responsibility is on the registrant to identify what is a significant loss and make the required report to the DEA.

Some factors to consider for determining significant loss include the following:

1. The schedule of the missing items
2. The abuse potential of the missing items
3. The abuse potential in your area of the missing substance
4. The quantity missing (one tablet versus one bottle or container)
5. Is this the first time this loss has occurred? Has a similar loss occurred before?
6. Was this loss reported to local law enforcement authorities?
7. If there is a question as to whether a loss is significant, a registrant should err on the side of caution and report it to the DEA

If it is determined that the loss is not significant, place a record of the occurrence in your theft and loss file for future reference.

In-Transit Loss

When all or part of a shipment disappears, or never reaches its intended destination, the supplier is responsible for reporting the in-transit loss of controlled substances to the DEA. A pharmacy is responsible for reporting any loss of controlled substances after a pharmacist has signed for or taken custody of a shipment. If it is discovered after that point that an in-transit loss or theft has occurred, the pharmacist must submit a DEA Form-106.

Breakage/Spillage

DEA policy on breakage of controlled substances does not constitute a "loss" of controlled substances. When there is breakage, damage, or spillage or some other form of destruction, any recoverable controlled substances must be disposed of according to DEA requirements. Damaged goods may be disposed of through shipment to a reverse distributor or by a DEA-approved process for the destruction of controlled substances. When this disposal occurs, it must be reported to the DEA on a DEA Form-41 (Registrants Inventory of Drugs Surrendered).

Controlled Substance Registrant Protection Act of 1984

Robberies, burglaries, and assaults on pharmacists and other registrants by those seeking controlled substances are a serious problem in the United States. These crimes result in property loss, serious injury to professionals and bystanders, and trafficking which serves to fuel the drug abuse problem.

Federal Investigation

The Controlled Substances Registrant Protection Act of 1984 (CSRPA) provides for the federal investigation of drug thefts and robberies if any of the following conditions are met:

1. Replacement cost of the controlled substances taken is $500 or more.
2. A registrant or other person is killed or suffers "significant" bodily injury during the commission of the robbery or theft of a controlled substance.
3. Interstate or foreign commerce is involved in planning or executing the crime.

Penalties Upon Conviction

The perpetrator convicted of violating the CSRPA's provisions is subject to the following penalties:

1. Conviction for commission of burglary or robbery can result in a maximum $25,000 fine and/or 20 years imprisonment.
2. Conviction for use of a dangerous weapon in the commission of the crime can result in a maximum $35,000 fine and/or 25 years imprisonment.
3. If death results from the crime, the convicted person can receive a maximum $50,000 fine and/or life imprisonment.

RECORD-KEEPING REQUIREMENTS

Every pharmacy must maintain complete and accurate records on a current basis for each controlled substance purchased, received, distributed, dispensed, or otherwise disposed of. All records of controlled substances must be maintained for two years. This record-keeping system allows a controlled substance to be tracked from the time it is manufactured to the time it is dispensed to the ultimate user. (Record-keeping requirements for List I Chemicals are contained in the Chemical Requirements section.)

All records concerning controlled substances must be maintained for at least two years for inspection and copying by duly authorized DEA officials. Records and inventories of Schedule II controlled substances must be maintained separately from all other records of the registrant. All records and inventories of Schedule III, IV, and V controlled substances must be maintained either separately from all other records or in such a form that the information required is readily retrievable from the ordinary business records. (Record-keeping requirements for prescription orders are detailed in the Prescription Records section.)

Readily retrievable means that

1. certain records are kept by automatic data processing systems or other electronic or mechanized record-keeping systems in such a manner that they can be separated out from all other records in a reasonable time, and/or
2. records are kept on which certain items are asterisked, redlined, or in some other manner visually identifiable apart from other items appearing on the records.

Records That Must Be Maintained

1. Official Order Forms (DEA Form-222).
2. Power of Attorney authorization to sign Order Forms
3. Receipts and invoices for Schedule III, IV, and V controlled substances as well as "threshold quantities" of List I chemicals
4. All inventory records of controlled substances, including the initial and biennial inventories
5. Records of controlled substances distributed or dispensed (i.e., prescriptions) and threshold amounts of List I chemicals distributed
6. Report of Theft or Loss (DEA Form-106)
7. Inventory of Drugs Surrendered for Disposal (DEA Form-41)
8. Records of transfers of controlled substances between pharmacies
9. DEA registration certificate

DEA Official Order Forms (DEA Form 222) are the required records of receipt and sale for Schedule II controlled substances.

Central Record Keeping

A registrant desiring to maintain shipping and financial records at a central location other than the registered location must notify the nearest DEA Diversion Field Office. Unless the registrant is informed by the DEA that the permission to keep central records is denied, the registrant may begin maintaining central records fourteen days after notifying the DEA. Central record-keeping requirements are described in 21 CFR, 1304.04. Central record-keeping permits are no longer issued by the DEA.

CHANGE OF BUSINESS ADDRESS

Any time a pharmacy moves to a new physical location or the postal address changes at the same location, a new DEA certificate reflecting the new address must be obtained. It is the pharmacy's responsibility to notify the DEA about a change of address before the effective date of the move.

A written request for modification of registration should be sent to the DEA Registration Field Office responsible for the state. If the modification is approved, the DEA will issue a new certificate of registration and, if requested, new Schedule II order forms (DEA Form-222, Official Order Form). A Renewal Application for Registration (DEA Form-224a) will be sent to only the registered address on file with the DEA. The renewal application cannot be forwarded.

AFFIDAVIT FOR RENEWAL
OF RETAIL CHAIN PHARMACY REGISTRATION

Corporations that own or operate a chain of pharmacies may submit a single DEA Form-224b (Retail Pharmacy Registration Affidavit for Chain Renewal) that covers all the chain's pharmacy registrants. This affidavit, along with a list of the corporation's registrations, is provided in lieu of a separate DEA application for each pharmacy registration. No registration may be issued unless the completed affidavit is received by the DEA. The corporation should retain a copy of this affidavit with its readily retrievable records for the duration of the registration covered by the affidavit. The corporation must answer the questions listed on the affidavit as they pertain to each registrant.

The original affidavit along with the registration fee and the list of registrations should be mailed to the following address:

Registration Chain Renewal
U.S. Department of Justice
Drug Enforcement Administration
Central Station
P.O. Box 28083
Washington, DC 20038-8083

PRESCRIPTION ORDER REQUIREMENTS

To dispense controlled substances, a pharmacist must know the requirements for a valid prescription order. A prescription order is a valid request for medication which is dispensed to or for an ultimate user. A prescription order is not a request for medication which is dispensed for immediate administration to the ultimate user (e.g., an order to dispense a drug to an inpatient for immediate administration in a hospital is a medication order).

A prescription order for a controlled substance must be dated and signed on the date when issued. The prescription order must include the patient's full name and address, and the practitioner's name, address, and registration number. The prescription order must also include the drug name, strength, dosage form, quantity prescribed, directions for use, and number of renewals. Where an oral prescription order is not permitted, a prescription order must be written in ink or indelible pencil or typewritten and must be manually signed by the practitioner. An individual (i.e., secretary or nurse) may be designated by the practitioner to prepare prescription orders for the practitioner's signature. The practitioner is responsible for making sure that the prescription order conforms in all essential respects to the law and regulations.

Who May Issue

A prescription order for a controlled substance may be issued only by a physician, dentist, podiatrist, veterinarian, midlevel practitioner, or other registered practitioner who is

1. authorized to prescribe controlled substances by the jurisdiction in which the practitioner is licensed to practice and
2. registered with DEA or exempted from registration (i.e., Public Health Service and Bureau of Prison physicians).

Purpose of Issue

To be valid, a prescription order for a controlled substance must be issued for a legitimate medical purpose by a practitioner acting in the usual course of sound professional practice. The practitioner is responsible for the proper prescribing and dispensing of controlled substances. However, a corresponding responsibility rests with the pharmacist who dispenses the prescription order. A request for controlled substances that purports to be a valid prescription order but is not issued in the usual course of professional treatment, or for legitimate and authorized research, is not a valid prescription order within the meaning and intent of the CSA. The individual who knowingly dispenses such a purported prescription order, as well as the individual issuing it, will be subject to criminal and/or civil penalties and administrative sanctions.

A prescription order may not be issued to allow an individual practitioner to obtain a supply of controlled substances for the purpose of general dispensing to the practitioner's patients. Therefore, a prescription order written for office stock or "medical bag" use is not a valid request.

Schedule II Substances

Schedule II controlled substances require a written prescription order, which must be signed by the practitioner. There is no time limit when a Schedule II prescription order must be dispensed after being signed by the practitioner. However, it is the pharmacist's responsibility to determine that the prescription medication is still needed by the patient (e.g., a narcotic prescription dispensed several weeks after being written). Federal regulations place no quantity limits on any prescription orders. For Schedule II controlled substances, an oral request is permitted only in an emergency situation. (See Emergency Dispensing).

Renewals

Renewing a Schedule II prescription order is prohibited.

Facsimile Prescription Orders for Schedule II Substances

To expedite dispensing prescription orders, a prescriber may fax the Schedule II prescription order to a pharmacy, as authorized in a final rule published in May 1994. This rule requires that the original Schedule II prescription order be presented to the pharmacist and verified against the facsimile at the time the controlled substance is actually dispensed. The pharmacist must make sure the original document is properly annotated and filed with the records that are required to be kept.

In an emergency, a practitioner may transmit a prescription order for a Schedule II controlled substance by facsimile or telephone to the pharmacy, and the pharmacist may dispense the prescription order. However, the prescribing practitioner must provide a written, signed prescription order to the pharmacist within seven days, and the pharmacist must notify the DEA if the written prescription order is not received from the prescribing practitioner within the seven-day period required by the CFR (see Emergency Dispensing).

Exceptions for Schedule II Facsimile Prescription Orders

The DEA also grants three exceptions to the facsimile prescription order requirements for Schedule II controlled substances. The facsimile of a Schedule II prescription order may serve as the original prescription order as follows:

1. A practitioner prescribing Schedule II narcotic controlled substances for a patient undergoing home infusion/intravenous (IV) pain therapy may transmit the prescription order by facsimile. The practitioner's agent may also transmit the prescription order to the pharmacy. The pharmacy will consider the facsimile prescription order a "written prescription order" and no further prescription order is required. All normal requirements of a legal prescription order must be followed.
2. Practitioners prescribing Schedule II controlled substances for patients in long term care facilities (LTCF), which are normally dispensed and delivered to the facility by the pharmacy, may transmit a prescription order by facsimile to the dispensing pharmacy. The practitioner's agent may also transmit a prescription order to the pharmacy. The facsimile prescription order serves as the original written prescription order for the pharmacy. No further original prescription order is required.
3. A practitioner prescribing a Schedule II narcotic substance for a patient in hospice care as certified by Medicare under Title XVIII may transmit a prescription order to the dispensing pharmacy by facsimile. The practitioner's agent may also transmit a prescription order to the pharmacy. The practitioner will note on the prescription order that it is for a hospice patient. The facsimile prescription order serves as the original written prescription order.

Schedule III-V Substances

A prescription order for controlled substances in Schedule III, IV, and V issued by a practitioner may be communicated either orally, in writing, or by facsimile to a pharmacist and may be renewed if so authorized on the prescription order.

Renewals

Schedule III and IV controlled substances may be renewed if authorized by the prescribing practitioner on the prescription order. However, the prescription order may only be renewed up to five times within six months after the date of issue. After five renewals or after six months, whichever occurs first, a new prescription order is required. A patient is permitted to request a renewal of an existing Schedule III-V controlled substance prescription order by sending an e-mail to the pharmacy or by telephone. Schedule V controlled substances may be renewed only as authorized on the prescription order by the prescribing practitioner.

When a prescription order for any controlled substance in Schedule III, IV, or V is renewed, the following information must be entered on the back of the prescription order: the dispensing pharmacist's initials, the date the prescription order was renewed, and the amount of drug dispensed on the renewal. If the pharmacist only initials and dates the back of the prescription order, the pharmacist will be deemed to have dispensed a renewal for the full face amount of the prescription order.

Computerization of Prescription Information

A pharmacy is permitted to use a data processing system as an alternative to the manual method for the storage and retrieval of prescription order renewal information for Schedule III, IV, and V controlled substances.

The computer system must provide online retrieval of original prescription information for those prescription orders which are currently authorized for renewal. The information must include, but is not limited to, the original prescription number, date of issuance, full name and address of the patient, the prescriber's name, address, and DEA registration number; the name, strength, dosage form, and quantity of the controlled substance prescribed; and the total number of renewals authorized by the prescriber.

In addition, the computer system must provide online retrieval of the current renewal history for Schedule III, IV, or V controlled substance prescription orders. This information must include, but is not limited to, the name of the controlled substance, the date of renewal, the quantity dispensed, the dispensing pharmacist's identification code, or name/initials for each renewal, and the total number of renewals dispensed to date for that prescription order. The pharmacist must verify and document that the renewal data entered into the system are correct. All computer-generated prescription order/renewal documentation must be stored in a separate file at the pharmacy and be maintained for a two-year period from the dispensing date. To meet the CFR record-keeping requirements, the pharmacy's computer must comply with the following guidelines:

1. If the system provides a hard copy printout of each day's controlled substance prescription order renewals, each pharmacist who renewed those prescription orders shall verify their accuracy by signing and dating the printout, as they would sign a check or legal document.
2. This printout must be provided to each pharmacy which uses the computer system within 72 hours of the date on which the renewal was dispensed. The printout must be verified and signed by each pharmacist who dispensed the renewals.
3. In lieu of such a printout, the pharmacy shall maintain a bound log book or separate file in which each pharmacist involved in the day's dispensing signs a statement verifying that the renewal information entered into the computer that day has been reviewed by the dispensing pharmacist and is correct.
4. A pharmacy computer system shall have the capability of printing out any renewal data which the pharmacy must maintain under the Controlled Substances Act. For example, this would include a renewal-by-renewal audit trail for any specified strength and dosage form of any controlled substance, by either brand or generic name or both, dispensed by the pharmacy. Such a printout must include the following:
   - Prescribing practitioner's name
   - Patient's name and address
   - Quantity dispensed on each renewal
   - Dispensing date for each renewal
   - Name or identification code of the dispensing pharmacist
   - Original prescription number
   In any computerized system employed by a user pharmacy, the central record-keeping location must be capable of providing a printout to a requesting pharmacy of the above information within 48 hours.
5. In case a pharmacy's computer system experiences downtime, the pharmacy must have a backup procedure to document in writing renewals of Schedule III, IV, and V controlled substances. This proce-

dure must ensure that renewals are authorized by the original prescription order, that the maximum number of renewals has not been exceeded, and that all required data are retained for online entry as soon as possible.

6. A pharmacy may use one only of the two systems described (i.e., manual or computer).

Facsimile Prescription Orders for Schedule III-V Substances

Prescription orders for Schedule III-V controlled substances may be transmitted by facsimile from the practitioner or an employee or agent of the individual practitioner. The facsimile prescription order is considered to be equivalent to an original written prescription order.

Telephone Authorization for Schedule III-V Prescription Orders

Only the practitioner can prescribe controlled substances, and this authority cannot be delegated to anyone else. A prescription order issued by a practitioner may be called in to a pharmacist by the practitioner or an employee or agent of the individual practitioner. It is the pharmacist's responsibility to ensure that these telephone prescription orders are valid and properly authorized by the practitioner (see Pharmacist's Guide to Dealing with Forged, Altered, and Stolen Prescription Orders).

Transfer of Prescription Information

The DEA will allow the transfer of original prescription information for Schedule III, IV, and V controlled substances for the purpose of renewal dispensing between pharmacies on a one-time basis, if permissible under state law (see Prescription Requirements section).

Pharmacies electronically sharing a real-time, online database may transfer up to the maximum renewals permitted by law and the prescriber's authorization. Such systems must contain the information required for a valid prescription order.

Midlevel Practitioners

Midlevel practitioners (MLPS) are registered and authorized by the DEA and the state in which they practice to dispense, administer, and prescribe controlled substances in the course of professional practice. Examples of MLPs include, but are not limited to, healthcare providers such as nurse practitioners, nurse midwives, nurse anesthetists, clinical nurse specialists, physician assistants, optometrists, ambulance services, animal shelters, veterinarian euthanasia technicians, nursing homes, and homeopathic physicians.

MLPs may receive individual DEA registration granting controlled substance privileges. However, such registration is contingent upon authority granted by the state in which they are licensed. The DEA registers MLPs whose states clearly authorize them to prescribe, dispense, and administer controlled substances in one or more schedules. The fact that an MLP has been issued a valid DEA registration number (beginning with the letter M) will be evidence that he or she is authorized to prescribe, dispense, and/or administer at least some controlled substances.

However, it will still be incumbent upon the pharmacist who dispenses the prescription order to ensure that the MLP is prescribing within the parameters established by the state in which he or she practices. MLP authority to prescribe controlled substances varies greatly by state. Check with your state licensing or controlled substances authority to determine which MLP disciplines are authorized to prescribe controlled substances in your state.

PRESCRIPTION MONITORING PROGRAMS

A prescription monitoring program is a state-administered data collection system used to gather prescription information. This information may be made available to state and federal investigators on a need-to-know basis.

Many states have adopted either a multiple-copy prescription program or an electronic data transmission system because these programs have proven to be an effective tool for detecting diversion, for developing pharmacist and physician medical education programs that heighten awareness about diversion, prescription drug abuse, drug trends, and for tracking effective use of prescription medication within a state. For the pharmacist, the data can be used to identify potential "doctor shoppers" and those who attempt to obtain controlled substances by fraud, forgery, or deceit.

In the states that have adopted these programs, a large part of their success has been attributed to the pharmacists' participation. The DEA strongly endorses prescription monitoring programs and works closely with the states on these programs.

PRESCRIPTION RECORDS

Pharmacies have three options for filing prescription records under the Code of Federal Regulations. If there is a conflict between federal and state requirements for filing prescription orders, the DEA recognizes that the pharmacy must choose a filing system that would comply with both federal and state law (Title 21 USC, Section 903).

All prescription records must be readily retrievable for DEA inspection. Controlled substance prescription orders must be filed in one of the following three ways:

1. Option 1 (Three separate files)
   - a file for Schedule II drugs dispensed,
   - a file for Schedule III, IV and V drugs dispensed, and
   - a file for prescription orders for all noncontrolled drugs dispensed
2. Option 2 (Two separate files)
   - a file for all Schedule II drugs dispensed and
   - a file for all other drugs dispensed (noncontrolled and those in Schedule III, IV, and V).

   If this method is used, a prescription order for a Schedule III, IV, and V drug must be made readily retrievable by use of a red "C" stamp not less than one inch high.
3. Option 3 (Two separate files)
   - A file for all Schedule II-V controlled substances. If this method is used, a prescription for a Schedule III, IV, or V drug must be made readily retrievable by use of a red "C" stamp not less than one inch high.
   - A file for prescription orders for all noncontrolled drugs dispensed.

If a pharmacy has an electronic record-keeping system for prescription orders which permits identification by prescription number and retrieval of original documents by prescriber's name, patient's name, drug dispensed, and date dispensed, then the requirement to mark the hard-copy prescription order with a red "C" is waived.

INVENTORY REQUIREMENTS

Inventory means a complete and accurate list of all stocks and forms of controlled substances in the possession of the registrant as determined by an actual physical count.

The CFR also requires that all inventories be maintained at the registered location in a readily retrievable manner for at least two years for copying and inspection. In addition, the inventory of Schedule II controlled substances must be kept separate from those for all other controlled substances.

Initial Inventory

When issued a DEA registration, a registrant must take an initial inventory, which is an actual physical count of all controlled substances in their possession. If no stocks of controlled substances are on hand, the registrant should make a record showing a zero inventory. There is no requirement to submit a copy of the inventory to the DEA.

The Code of Federal Regulations (CFR) requires that the inventory include the following:

1. the inventory date
2. the time the inventory is taken (i.e., opening or close of business)
3. the drug name
4. the drug strength
5. the drug form (e.g., tablet, capsule, etc.)
6. the number of units/volume
7. the total quantity

The DEA recommends that the inventory record include the following:

1. the name, address, and DEA registration number of the registrant
2. the signature of the person or persons responsible for taking the inventory

Biennial Inventory

Following the initial inventory, the registrant is required to take a biennial inventory (every two years), which requires the same information as the initial inventory of all controlled substances on hand. The biennial inventory may be taken on any date within two years of the previous inventory date. There is no requirement to submit a copy of the inventory to the DEA.

When taking the inventory of Schedule II controlled substances, an actual physical count must be made. For the inventory of Schedule III, IV, and V controlled substances, an estimated count may be made. An actual physical count must be made if the container holds more than 1,000 dosage units and has been opened.

Inventorying Newly Scheduled Controlled Substances

When a drug not previously controlled is scheduled, the drug must be inventoried as of the effective date of scheduling.

Inventory of Drugs for Destruction or No Longer Saleable

Each controlled substance that is (1) damaged, defective, or impure and is awaiting disposal, (2) held for quality control purposes, or (3) maintained for extemporaneous compoundings must be inventoried.

The Code of Federal Regulations requires that the inventory include the following:

1. the inventory date
2. the drug name
3. the drug strength
4. the drug form (e.g., tablet, capsule, etc.)
5. the total quantity or total number of units/volume
6. thw reason why the substance is being maintained
7. Whether the substance is capable of being used in the manufacture of any controlled substance in finished form

ORDERING CONTROLLED SUBSTANCES

Schedule II Substances

Only Schedule I and II controlled substances are ordered with a DEA Form-222. An Official Order Form is required for each distribution, purchase, or transfer of a Schedule II controlled substance.

When a controlled substance has been transferred by the DEA from Schedule II to another schedule at the federal level, in many states it remains in Schedule II pending any legislative or administrative actions that may result from the federal action. Many states require that transactions involving substances that they classify as Schedule II be made via DEA Form-222 Official Order Forms. Where federal and state laws or regulations conflict, the stricter one applies. When the use of DEA Form-222 Official Order Forms for the transfer of a controlled substance is not required under federal law, its use as mandated by these states does not violate federal law and is therefore permitted.

Requesting Official Order Forms

Official Order Forms can be initially requested by checking "block 3" on the application for new registration (DEA Form-224). There is no charge. Send the form to the following address:

Drug Enforcement Administration
Registration Unit
Central Station
P.O. Box 28083
Washington, DC 20038-8083

Once a registrant has received Official Order Forms (DEA Form-222), a separate requisition form (DEA Form222a) will be mailed to the registrant to request additional Official Order Forms. The registrant may also request Official Order Forms by calling either the DEA Headquarters Registration Unit (toll free: 1-800-882-9539) or the nearest DEA Registration Field Office.

Each book of DEA Official Order Forms consists of seven sets of forms. Each pharmacy is provided a maximum of six books at one time unless its needs exceed this limit. In such a case, the pharmacy should contact the DEA Registration Field Office serving their state.

Completing Official DEA Order Forms

When ordering Schedule II substances, the pharmacist is responsible for filling in the number of packages, the size of the package and the name of the item. Each Official DEA Order Form must be signed and dated by a person authorized to sign a registration application. (See Power of Attorney to Sign an Official DEA Order Form.) When the items are received, the pharmacist must document on the purchaser's copy (copy 3) the actual number of packages received and the date received.

Official DEA Order Forms must be maintained separately from the pharmacy's other business records. However, this does not preclude a registrant from attaching a copy of the supplier's invoice to the related DEA Order Form.

The Code of Federal Regulations requires that the Official DEA Order Form must be "complete, legible, and properly prepared, with no signs of alteration, erasure or change of any description." A supplier may refuse to accept an order for any of these reasons. However, the DEA has acknowledged a supplier may accept some minor changes or alterations. For example, suppliers may correct Official DEA Order Forms that have minor errors, which lack inconsequential information, or an incorrect date unintentionally annotated by the purchaser. If an order is refused, the supplier should return Official DEA Order Form copies 1 and 2 to the purchaser with a statement explaining the reason the order was refused.

DEA policy does not preclude the substitution of identical products differing in packaging size from those initially ordered, provided that the actual quantity received does not exceed the amount initially ordered and that the National Drug Code number reflected is that of the actual product shipped. For example, a distributor may substitute 5 bottles of 100 2 mg tablets for 1 bottle of 500 2 mg tablets or any variation thereof.

Power of Attorney to Sign an Official Order Form

Any registrant (pharmacy) may authorize one or more individuals, whether or not they are located at the registered location, to obtain and execute Official Order Forms by granting a power of attorney to each such individual. The same person who signed the most recent application for registration or renewal registration, as well as the individual being authorized to obtain and execute Official DEA Order Forms, must sign the power of attorney.

The person who signed the power of attorney may revoke the power of attorney at any time. It is necessary to grant a new power of attorney when the pharmacy completes a renewal registration only if a different person signs the renewal application. The power of attorney should be filed with executed Official Order Forms as a readily retrievable record. The power of attorney is not submitted to the DEA.

Suggested formats for granting and revoking power of attorney are shown in Exhibits 4.2 and 4.3.

Lost or Stolen DEA Order Forms

When the pharmacist has not received a shipment of controlled substances, he or she should first contact the supplier to determine whether the original DEA Form-222 was received. If the original order form has been lost or stolen, the pharmacist must complete a second order form so the supplier can fill the original order. The pharmacist must also prepare a statement which includes the first order form's serial number and date, and verify that the drugs ordered were never received. Attach a copy of the statement to the second order form that is sent to the supplier. The pharmacist must keep a copy of the statement with copy 3 from the first and second order forms.

EXHIBIT 4.2. POWER OF ATTORNEY FOR DEA ORDER FORMS

_____ (Name of registrant)
_____ (Address of registrant)
_____ (DEA registration number) I,
_____ (name of person granting power), the undersigned, who is authorized to sign the current application for registration of the above-named registrant under the Controlled Substances Act or Controlled Substances Import and Export Act, have made, constituted, and appointed, and by these present, do make, constitute, and appoint _____
(name of attorney-in-fact), my true and lawful attorney for me in my name, place, and stead, to execute applications for books of official order forms and to sign such order forms in requisition for Schedule I and II controlled substances, in accordance with Section 308 of the Controlled Substances Act (21 U.S.C. 828) and part 1305 of Title 21 of the Code of Federal Regulations. I hereby ratify and confirm all that said attorney shall lawfully do or cause to be done by virtue hereof.

(Signature of person granting power) I, _____
(name of attorney-in-fact), hereby affirm that I am the person named herein as attorney-in-fact and that the signature affixed hereto is my signature.

Witnesses:

1 _____
2 _____

Signed and dated on the _____ day of _____ in the year _____ at _____.

A pharmacy, upon discovery of the loss or theft of unused order forms, must immediately report the loss to the nearest DEA Diversion Field Office, and provide the serial numbers of each lost or stolen order form. If an entire book or multiple books of order forms are lost or stolen, and the serial numbers of the missing forms cannot be identified, the pharmacist must report the approximate date of issuance (in lieu of the serial numbers) to the DEA. If an unused order form reported stolen or lost is later recovered or found, the pharmacy must immediately notify the nearest DEA Diversion Field Office.

EXHIBIT 4.3. NOTICE OF REVOCATION OF POWER OF ATTORNEY

The foregoing power of attorney is hereby revoked by the undersigned, who is authorized to sign the current application for registration of the above-named registrant under the Controlled Substances Act or the Controlled Substances Import and Export Act. Written notice of this revocation has been given to the attorney-in-fact _____ this same day.

_____
(Signature of person revoking power)

Witnesses:

1 _____
2 _____

Signed and dated on the _____ day of _____ in the year _____ at _____.

Schedule III-V Substances

The registrant (pharmacy) must keep a receipt (i.e., invoice or packing slip) on which they record the date the drugs were received and confirm that the order is accurate. These receipts must be maintained in a readily retrievable manner for inspection by the DEA.

DISPENSING REQUIREMENTS

Required Information for Prescription Labels

The pharmacist dispensing a prescription order for a controlled substance must affix to the container a label showing the pharmacy name and address, the serial (prescription) number, date of initial dispensing, the name of the patient, the name of the prescribing practitioner, and directions for use and cautionary statements, if any, contained on the prescription order as required by law.

Federal Food and Drug Administration regulations require that the label of any drug listed as a "controlled substance" in Schedule II, III, or IV of the

Controlled Substances Act must, when dispensed to or for a patient, contain the following warning:

> Be aware that federal law prohibits the transfer of this drug to any person other than the patient for whom it was prescribed.

Schedule II Controlled Substances

A pharmacist may dispense a Schedule II controlled substance, which is a prescription drug as determined under the Federal Food, Drug, and Cosmetic Act, only pursuant to a written prescription order signed by the practitioner, except in an emergency situation as described in the following section.

Emergency Dispensing

"Emergency" means that the immediate administration of the drug is necessary for proper treatment of the intended ultimate user, that no alternative treatment is available (including a drug which is not a Schedule II controlled substance), and it is not possible for the prescribing practitioner to provide a written prescription order for the drug at that time.

In a bona fide emergency, a practitioner may telephone a Schedule II prescription order to the pharmacy or transmit the prescription order by facsimile to the pharmacy, and the pharmacist may dispense the prescription order provided that the following occurs:

1. The drug prescribed and dispensed must be limited to the amount needed to treat the patient during the emergency period. Prescribing or dispensing beyond the emergency period must be pursuant to a written prescription order.
2. The prescription order must be immediately reduced to writing by the pharmacist and must contain all information, except for the prescribing practitioner's signature.
3. If the prescriber is not known to the pharmacist, the pharmacist must make a reasonable effort to determine that the telephone authorization came from a valid practitioner, by verifying the practitioner's telephone number with that listed in the directory and by making other good faith efforts to ensure proper identity.
4. Within seven days after authorizing an emergency telephone prescription order, the prescribing practitioner must furnish the pharmacist a written, signed prescription order for the controlled substance prescribed. The prescription order must have written on its face "Authori-

zation for Emergency Dispensing." The written prescription order may be delivered in person or by mail, which must be postmarked within the seven-day period. Upon receipt, the dispensing pharmacist must attach this written prescription order to the oral prescription order reduced to writing by the pharmacist. By law the pharmacist must notify the nearest DEA Diversion Field Office if the prescriber fails to provide a written prescription order within seven days. If the pharmacist fails to do so, the pharmacist's authority to dispense without a written prescription order will be void.

Partial Dispensing

A pharmacist may partially dispense a prescription order for a Schedule II controlled substance if the pharmacist is unable to supply the full quantity in a written or emergency oral (telephone) prescription order, provided the pharmacist notes the quantity supplied on the front of the written prescription order (or on a written record of the emergency oral prescription order). The remaining portion may be dispensed within seventy-two hours of the first partial dispensing. However, if the remaining portion is not or cannot be dispensed within the seventy-two-hour period, the pharmacist must notify the prescribing practitioner. No further quantity may be supplied beyond the seventy-two hours, except on a new prescription order.

Exception for Schedule II Prescription Orders at Long Term Care Facilities

An exception has been made for patients in long term care facilities (LTCF) and patients who have been diagnosed with a terminal illness. If there is any question whether a patient may be classified as having a terminal illness, the pharmacist must contact the practitioner prior to partially dispensing the prescription medication. Both the pharmacist and the prescribing practitioner have a corresponding responsibility to assure that the controlled substance is for a terminally ill patient. The pharmacist must record on the prescription order whether the patient is "terminally ill" or an "LTCF patient."

A prescription order that is partially dispensed and does not contain the notation "terminally ill" or "LTCF patient" will be deemed to have been dispensed in violation of the CSA. In such cases, prescription orders may be dispensed in partial quantities, including single dosage units. For each partial dispensing, the pharmacist must note on the prescription order (or other uniformly maintained, retrievable record) the date the prescription order was partially dispensed, the quantity dispensed, the remaining quantity, and the identification of the dispensing pharmacist. Such prescription orders are valid for a maximum of sixty days from the date of issue, unless terminated earlier by discontinuance of the medication.

Internet Pharmacy

The actual physical location of the pharmacy that purchases, stores, and dispenses controlled substances pursuant to prescription orders processed by the Internet site must be registered with the DEA. The Web site itself would not require a separate registration unless it is the same physical location, since the Web site does not store or dispense controlled substances. For example, some Internet pharmacies maintain a central pharmacy warehouse site and offices where prescription orders are verified and substances shipped; this location must be registered with the DEA as a community (DEA uses the term *retail* in most of its documents) pharmacy. Other Internet sites allow patients to pick up their prescription orders for controlled substances from a local pharmacy; these pharmacies must be registered with the DEA. In this case, the Internet "pharmacy" has no obligations under DEA regulations because the responsibility for assuring compliance with DEA regulations rests with the actual pharmacy where controlled substances are dispensed.

The pharmacy must have a license from the state in which the controlled substances are stored and dispensed and, in instances, from any state in which the pharmacy plans to conduct business with patients. Pharmacists should also be aware that many states require licenses for the Web site itself, since these sites often provide services such as patient counseling. Being an Internet pharmacy does not change the pharmacy's responsibilities under DEA regulations. The pharmacy is still authorized to sell controlled substances only when there is a valid prescription order from a DEA-registered practitioner who issued the prescription order in the usual course of their professional practice.

A pharmacist may dispense a Schedule II controlled substance only after the patient or prescriber provides an original signed prescription order prior to dispensing. The label on the dispensed prescription medication container must indicate the location that dispensed the controlled substance.

Some Internet pharmacies have doctors who prescribe substances based on an online questionnaire. Federal law requires that "A prescription for a controlled substance to be effective must be issued for a legitimate medical purpose by an individual practitioner acting in the usual course of his professional practice" (21 CFR 1306.04(a). Every state separately imposes a similar acting requirement under its laws. Under federal and state law, for a doctor to be acting in the usual course of professional practice, there must be a bona fide doctor/patient relationship.

For purpose of state law, many state authorities, with the endorsement of medical societies, consider the existence of the following four elements as an indication that the legitimate doctor/patient relationship has been established:

1. a patient has a medical complaint;
2. a medical history has been taken;
3. a physical examination has been performed; and
4. some logical connection exists between the medical complaint, the medical history, the physical examination, and the drug prescribed.

Electronic Transmission of Prescription Orders

The DEA continues to review this issue, although the agency has not issued any definitive requirements for secure electronic transmission of controlled substances prescription orders between the prescriber and the pharmacy. Such requirements relate to security and would include authentication of the prescriber, content integrity, and nonrepudiation of involvement by parties to a transaction.

Schedule III-V Controlled Substance Prescription Orders

A pharmacist may dispense a Schedule III, IV, or V controlled substance having received either a written prescription order signed by a practitioner, a facsimile of that prescription order transmitted by the practitioner or the practitioner's agent to the pharmacy, or an oral prescription order made by an individual practitioner. The pharmacist must promptly reduce the oral prescription order to writing.

Partial Dispensing

The pharmacist may partially dispense a prescription order for a Schedule III-V controlled substance if the pharmacist notes the quantity dispensed and initials the back of the prescription order. The partial dispensing may not exceed the total amount authorized in the prescription order. The dispensing of all renewals must be within the six-month limit.

It is permissible to dispense a prescription for a quantity less than the face amount prescribed, resulting in the actual number of renewals dispensed being greater than the number of renewals authorized on the prescription order.

Dispensing Without a Prescription Order

In states where limited quantities of Schedule V preparations may be sold over-the-counter, the pharmacist is responsible for making sure that such sales comply with state law. Schedule V controlled substances or any controlled substance listed in Schedule II, III, or IV which is not a prescription item under the Federal Food, Drug, and Cosmetic Act may be dispensed without a prescription order at retail provided that the following circumstances exist:

1. Such distribution is made only by a pharmacist and not by a non-pharmacist employee, even if under the direct supervision of a pharmacist. However, after the pharmacist has fulfilled professional and legal responsibilities, the actual cash, credit transaction, or delivery may be completed by a nonpharmacist.
2. Because there is no physician determining the medical necessity for a Schedule V over-the-counter product, the pharmacist must ensure the medical necessity of the need for the product.
3. Not more than 240 mL (8 fluid ounces) or not more than forty-eight solid dosage units of any substance containing opium, and not more than 120 mL (4 fluid ounces) or not more than twenty-four solid dosage units of any other controlled substance, may be distributed at retail to the same purchaser in any given forty-eight-hour period without a valid prescription order.
4. The purchaser at a retail outlet is at least eighteen years of age.
5. For the retail purchase of a Schedule V controlled substance, every customer the pharmacist does not know should be required to provide suitable identification, including proof of age, where appropriate.
6. A Schedule V bound record book is maintained which contains the name and address of the purchaser, name and quantity of controlled substance purchased, date of each sale, and initials of the dispensing pharmacist. This record book must be maintained for a period of two years from the date of the last transaction entered in such record book, and it must be made available for inspection and copying by officers of the United States, as authorized by the U.S. Attorney General.
7. Other federal, state, or local law does not require a prescription order.

Central Dispensing Pharmacy

A central dispensing pharmacy (DEA uses "central fill" as the descriptive term) dispenses prescription orders for controlled substances on behalf of community pharmacies with which central dispensing pharmacies have a contractual agreement to provide such services or with which the pharmacies share a common owner. When one community pharmacy receives a prescription order and a second community pharmacy prepares and subsequently delivers the controlled substance medication to the first community pharmacy for dispensing to the patient, the second pharmacy is engaging in a central dispensing activity.

Records must be maintained by both the central dispensing pharmacy and the community pharmacy that completely reflect the disposition of all controlled substance prescription orders dispensed. Central dispensing pharmacies are required to comply with the same security requirements applicable to community pharmacies, including the general requirement to maintain effective controls and procedures to guard against theft and diversion of controlled substances. Community pharmacies that also perform central dispensing activities are allowed to do so without a separate DEA registration, separate inventories, or separate records.

Central dispensing pharmacies are permitted to prepare both initial and renewal prescription orders, subject to all applicable state and federal regulations. Only a licensed pharmacist may dispense the prescription order. Both the practicing pharmacist on the staff of the pharmacy and the practicing pharmacist who dispenses the prescription order to the patient have a corresponding responsibility to ensure that the prescription order was issued for a legitimate medical purpose by an individual practitioner acting in the usual course of professional practice and otherwise in the manner specified by DEA regulations.

A central dispensing pharmacy will not be permitted to prepare prescription orders provided directly by the patient or individual practitioner or to mail or otherwise deliver a dispensed prescription order directly to a patient or individual practitioner. Community pharmacies are permitted to transmit prescription information to a central dispensing pharmacy in two ways. First, a facsimile of a prescription order for a controlled substance in Schedule II-V may be provided by the community pharmacy to the central dispensing pharmacy. The community pharmacy must maintain the original hard copy of the prescription order, and the central dispensing pharmacy must maintain the facsimile of the prescription order. The DEA also allows for the prescription information to be transmitted electronically by the community pharmacy to the central dispensing pharmacy. Both pharmacies must maintain the prescription information in a readily retrievable manner and comply with all applicable federal and state record-keeping requirements.

LONG TERM CARE FACILITIES

A long term care facility is defined in the Code of Federal Regulations as a nursing home, retirement care, mental care, or other facility or institution which provides extended healthcare to resident patients. In most cases, these facilities are not registered with the DEA, yet these healthcare facilities routinely maintain controlled substances issued via prescription order to their residents. These controlled substances are already outside the CSA closed drug distribution system since they have been dispensed to the ultimate user (i.e., patient). LTCFs frequently need to dispose of unused medications due to a change in patient medication or the patient's demise. For drug disposal instructions, contact the nearest DEA Diversion Field Office. In most cases, these LTCFs are regulated by state agencies and other federal mandates (FDA, Federal Nursing Home Guidelines, etc.).

The DEA is aware of the issues facing most LTCFs concerning the dispensing and handling of controlled substances. These are affected by a variety of state laws and circumstances. Pharmacists should check with their state agency for guidelines concerning controlled substances at LTCFs. In this chapter, regulations concerning LTCFs are also found in the Prescription Requirements section under Exceptions for Schedule II Facsimile Prescription, and in the Dispensing section under Exception for Schedule II Prescriptions at Long Term Care Facilities.

Emergency Kits for Long Term Care Facilities

The DEA has issued a policy statement that provides individual state licensing and regulatory boards with general guidelines for establishing specific rules concerning controlled substances used in emergency kits at long term care facilities. Here are the guidelines.

Guidelines for Emergency Kits in Long Term Care Facilities

The placement of emergency kits containing controlled substances in long term care facilities not registered with the DEA will be deemed in compliance with the Comprehensive Drug Abuse Prevention and Control Act of 1970 if the appropriate state agency or regulatory authority specifically approves such placement and sets forth procedures that require the following:

1. *Source of supply:* The LTCF must obtain controlled substances for the emergency kits from a DEA-registered hospital/clinic, pharmacy, or practitioner.
2. *Security safeguards:* Access to each emergency kit in the LTCF must be restricted, and the type and quantity of controlled substances which may be placed in the emergency kit must be specifically limited.
3. *Proper control, accountability, and record keeping:* The LTCF and the providing DEA-registered hospital/clinic, pharmacy, or practitioner must maintain complete and accurate records of the controlled substances placed in the emergency kit, including the disposition of these controlled substances, and take periodic physical inventories of the drugs.
4. *Administration of controlled substances:* In emergency medical situations when medication is needed from the emergency kit, only LTCF personnel who are authorized by an individual practitioner can administer the controlled substances (21 CFR 1306.11 and 21 CFR 2306.21).
5. *Prohibited activities:* Prohibited activities can result in the state revocation, denial, or suspension of having emergency kits containing controlled substances in an LTCF.

CONTROLLED SUBSTANCE DISTRIBUTION BY A PHARMACY

A pharmacy registered to dispense controlled substances may distribute such substances (without being registered as a distributor) to another pharmacy or to a practitioner to dispense, provided that the following conditions are met:

1. The pharmacy or practitioner is registered under the CSA to dispense controlled substances.
2. The pharmacy records that it distributed the controlled substances, and the recipient pharmacy or practitioner records that they received the controlled substances.
3. If a Schedule II controlled substance is distributed, the transfer must be documented on an Official DEA Order Form (DEA Form-222). The distributing pharmacy must record the following information on an Official DEA Order Form:
   • The name of the substance, the dosage form, and the quantity.
   • The name, address, and DEA registration number of the pharmacy or practitioner to whom it is distributed.

4. Five percent rule: The total number of dosage units of controlled substances distributed by a pharmacy may not exceed 5 percent of all controlled substances dispensed by the pharmacy during a calendar year. If at any time the controlled substances distributed exceeds 5 percent, the pharmacy is also required to register as a distributor.

NARCOTICS FOR PATIENTS WITH TERMINAL ILLNESSES OF INTRACTABLE PAIN

Controlled substances, particularly narcotic analgesics, may be used in the treatment of pain experienced by a patient with a terminal illness or intractable pain. These drugs have legitimate uses, and a pharmacist should not hesitate to dispense them when a prescription indicates they are for a legitimate medical purpose. (The CSA requires that a controlled substance prescription order must be issued for a legitimate medical purpose by a practitioner acting in the course of professional practice [Title 21 CFR 1306.04]. The CSA does not define "legitimate medical practice," nor does it set forth "standards of medical practice.")

According to the DEA, a pharmacist who dispenses controlled substances in good faith pursuant to a prescription order issued for a legitimate medical purpose need not fear any DEA action. It is the position of the DEA that controlled substances should be prescribed and dispensed when there is a legitimate medical need.

Inappropriate prescribing and dispensing of controlled substances, including opioid analgesics, may lead to drug diversion and abuse by individuals who seek these drugs for purposes other than legitimate medical use. However, pharmacists should recognize that drug tolerance and physical dependence may develop as a consequence of the patient's sustained use of opioid analgesics for the legitimate treatment of chronic pain. It is also important to understand that the quantity of drugs prescribed and frequency of prescription orders dispensed alone are not indicators of fraud or improper prescribing.

A pharmacist's professional judgment is the first step in determining the appropriate course of action when the pharmacist is presented with a prescription order that appears questionable. The pharmacist's judgment, in consultation with the prescriber, is the best way to verify that the prescription order is for a legitimate medical need. The pharmacist, in cooperation with the prescribing practitioner, has a responsibility to continue to monitor the patient receiving the controlled substance in order to prevent abuse or diversion.

NARCOTIC TREATMENT PROGRAMS

The Narcotic Addict Treatment Act of 1974 is the law that governs the use of narcotics and the treatment of addiction in the United States. In addition, the law designates which government agencies have responsibility for narcotic treatment programs, defines the terms "maintenance" and "detoxification," and explains who has to register to treat patients for drug dependence.

There are separate record-keeping and security requirements for narcotic treatment programs. The CFR requirements for narcotic treatment programs include the following:

- Official Order Forms (DEA Form-222) are required for all Schedule II narcotic transactions between a narcotic treatment program and any registrant, including a manufacturer, distributor, practitioner, or another narcotic treatment program.
- A narcotic treatment program registered with the DEA can handle only the narcotic substances applied for on the DEA Form-363 (New Application Registration) and that are approved for use in maintenance or detoxification.
- Controlled substances for treatment of conditions other than narcotic addiction cannot be administered, dispensed, or stored on the premises of a narcotic treatment program unless a physician has a valid practitioner registration at the program location.

Use of Methadone Outside a Narcotic Treatment Program

1. A practitioner may prescribe methadone or any other narcotic to a narcotic addict for analgesic purposes. However, a practitioner may not prescribe methadone or any other narcotic medication solely for the treatment of a patient's narcotic addiction. The individual must receive the narcotics at a registered narcotic treatment program. In this case, the narcotics can be dispensed or administered but not prescribed. (The regulations do not prohibit the prescribing, administering, or dispensing of methadone for analgesic purposes for medical conditions other than addiction.)
2. A practitioner who is not part of a narcotic treatment program may administer narcotic substances to an addicted individual to relieve that individual's acute withdrawal symptoms while the practitioner makes arrangements to refer the individual to a narcotic program. Not more than one day's medication may be administered at one time. This

treatment cannot last more than three days and may not be renewed or extended.
3. A hospital that has no narcotic treatment program on the premises may administer narcotics to a drug-dependent individual for either detoxification or maintenance purposes, if the individual is being treated for a medical condition other than narcotic addiction. Questions regarding any part of the Narcotic Addict Treatment Act of 1974 or its regulations should be directed to the nearest DEA Diversion Field Office.

U.S. POSTAL SERVICE MAILING REQUIREMENTS FOR CONTROLLED SUBSTANCES

U.S. Postal Service regulations permit mailing any controlled substances, provided that they are not outwardly dangerous or of their own force could cause injury to a person's life or health, if the following preparation and packaging standards are met:

1. The inner container of any parcel containing controlled substances is marked and sealed under the provisions of the Controlled Substances Act and its implementing regulations, and placed in a plain outer container or securely wrapped in plain paper.
2. If the controlled substances consist of prescription medicines, the inner container is also labeled to show the name and address of the pharmacy, practitioner, or other person dispensing the prescription order.
3. The outside wrapper or container is free of markings that would indicate the nature of the contents.

CONTROLLED SUBSTANCES FOR MEDICAL MISSIONS AND HUMANITARIAN CHARITABLE SOLICITATIONS

The DEA assists organizations and practitioners who provide charitable medical, dental, and veterinary treatment in foreign countries. In order for practitioners to hand carry controlled substances overseas, they must obtain approval from the DEA and the appropriate authority in the foreign country. Practitioners interested in cooperating with such medical missions should contact their local DEA Diversion Field Office or the International Drug

Unit, DEA, Office of Diversion Control, Washington, DC 20537, for instructions. Allow at least thirty days to obtain the necessary approvals.

If a pharmacy is asked to donate controlled substances to charitable organizations, contact your state controlled substance agency to determine if you have state authority to do so, and your local DEA Diversion Field Office for further guidance. The shipment of controlled substances abroad is considered to be an export, which may be done only by a DEA-registered exporter.

CHEMICAL REQUIREMTENTS: COMPREHENSIVE METHAMPHETAMINE CONTROL ACT OF 1996

Community (referred to as "retail" by DEA) pharmacies that are registered to handle controlled substances need not obtain a separate DEA chemical registration for retail distribution of pseudoephedrine, phenylpropanolamine, combination ephedrine, and single-entity ephedrine drug products. However, if the pharmacy is going to handle these products containing List I chemicals, then the pharmacy must comply with the record-keeping and reporting requirements of the Comprehensive Methamphetamine Control Act of 1996 (MCA). Record-keeping includes documentation of both receipts and sales of threshold amounts of List I chemical drug products. The MCA requirements also include reporting mail-order transactions, such as drugs delivered by the U.S. Postal Service or any private or commercial carrier.

It is unlikely that pharmacies will engage in transactions involving List II Chemicals in quantities that meet or exceed thresholds for record-keeping and reporting requirements. Therefore, this chapter summarizes only the requirements for List I chemicals. If the pharmacy engages in List II chemical transactions which meet or exceed threshold limits, then the pharmacy should contact the local DEA Diversion Field Office for further information.

Summary of MCA's Major Provisions That Concern Pharmacists

1. The MCA defines a retail distributor as a grocery store, general merchandise store, drugstore, or other entity or person whose activities as a distributor of pseudoephedrine, phenylpropanolamine (PPA), and combination ephedrine drug products are limited almost exclusively to sales for personal use, both in number and volume of sales, either to walk-in customers or in face-to-face transactions by direct sales. Personal use is defined as subthreshold sales in a single transaction to an

individual for legitimate medical use. All distributions of single-entity ephedrine are subject to the registration requirement.

2. Threshold quantities have been set for sales of listed chemicals contained in drug products. If the pharmacy engages in any above-threshold retail transactions of pseudoephedrine, PPA, combination ephedrine (more than 24 grams), and single-entity ephedrine drug products (more than zero grams), the pharmacy must maintain a record of these transactions for two years. Furthermore, the pharmacy must also obtain proof of identity from customers and report suspicious above-threshold retail transactions immediately to the DEA.

3. The threshold of 24 grams on retail sales does not pertain to blister packs of pseudoephedrine and PPA. The pharmacy may sell more than 24 grams of pseudoephedrine or PPA drug products in blister packs in a single transaction without the transaction being considered a "regulated transaction" subject to the MCA record-keeping and reporting requirements. Sales of over-the-counter drug products (blister packs) by retail distributors are not subject to the 24-gram threshold.

4. All transactions of ephedrine, pseudoephedrine, and PPA to nonregulated parties by postal, private, or commercial carrier must be reported to the DEA on a monthly basis, regardless of the size of the transaction, with the following exceptions.

   • Distributions of drug products by retail distributors that may not include face-to-face transactions to the extent that such distributions are consistent with the activities authorized for a retail distributor
   • Distributions of drug products pursuant to valid prescription orders
   • Distributions of drug products to a long term care facility for dispensing to or for use by a resident of that facility
   • Distributions of sample packages of drug products when such packages contain not more than two solid dosage units of the equivalent of two dosage units in liquid form, not to exceed 10 liters of liquid per package, and not more than one package is distributed to an individual or residential address in any thirty-day period

   The data required for such reports must include the following:
   • Name of the purchaser
   • Quantity and form of the ephedrine, pseudoephedrine, or PPA purchased
   • The address to which such drug products were sent
   • Date of each transaction
   • Other items of information which may be required by regulation

5. Retail distributors of List I chemical drug products who do not have a DEA registration may make infrequent and small quantity sales of pseudoephedrine, PPA, or combination ephedrine to another store,

if that store is in short supply of these products. However, retail distributors should be extremely cautious with such transactions, since they are required to limit their sales of these products "almost exclusively, both in number of sales and volume of sales" to "walk-in customers or in face-to-face transactions by direct sales."

- Therefore, depending upon a retailer's volume of sales, a single large quantity sale to another store could mean the retailer no longer satisfies the definition of "retail distributor" and would be required to register as a distributor of List I chemicals.
- Even if a retailer is able to complete this transaction without affecting its status as a retail distributor, a record of the transaction must be maintained if it meets the 9 gram threshold for pseudoephedrine and PPA or the 24 gram threshold for combination ephedrine drug products.

6. A person is subject to criminal prosecution who distributes a listed chemical, any other chemical, chemical product, or chemical equipment knowing or having reasonable cause to believe that such chemical, product, or equipment will be used in the illegal manufacture of a controlled substance.

Regulated Chemicals

Most of the chemicals regulated under the CSA will not be encountered in a pharmacy setting or in quantities subject to record-keeping and reporting requirements. List I chemicals are mostly precursors used for the manufacture of controlled substances and actually become part of the final drug molecule. Examples include anthranilic acid, ephedrine, ergotamine, norpseudoephedrine, pheny-lacetic acid, PPA, and pseudoephedrine. List II chemicals are mostly solvents and reagents that can be used in the manufacture of controlled substances. Examples include ethyl ether, potassium permanganate, acetone, and toluene.

Records for List I Chemicals

Records of regulated transactions must be maintained separately or distinguished in some manner from records for controlled substances. All such records must be maintained for a period of two years. It is suggested that the required records be maintained in a bound logbook like that used to record the dispensing of Schedule V controlled substances. Some states have passed legislation or regulations requiring that certain List I chemicals be dispensed pursuant only to a prescription order. In those jurisdictions, the prescription order will suffice as the dispensing record. Inventories of List I chemicals are not required.

Proof of Identity Requirement for Purchasers of List I Chemicals

Before List I chemicals can be dispensed, pharmacists must obtain proof of identity from cash purchasers or individuals buying threshold quantities of List I chemicals. Proof of identity must be in the form of a driver's license, one other form of identification, and the purchaser's signature. If the product is dispensed pursuant to a prescription order, regular prescription medication records will suffice.

Excessive or Unusual Purchases of List I Chemicals (Suspicious Orders)

Drug products containing ephedrine, pseudoephedrine, or PPA are usually sold to individuals in quantities for personal use. Combination drug products packaged for the retail market are the precursor material found at nearly 95 percent of the methamphetamine laboratories seized by DEA. This fact shows that pharmacists have an important role in preventing diversion of legitimate products to methamphetamine production. Pharmacists should be alert for persons who want to buy a large quantity of over-the-counter drug products containing these chemicals, since they can be used in the clandestine manufacture of controlled substances. Pharmacists should also be aware that persons seeking large quantities of List I chemical products from pharmacies frequently claim they will export the products.

Any regulated transaction for a List I chemical involving an extraordinarily large quantity, an uncommon method of payment or delivery, or any other circumstance that may lead the pharmacist to believe that the listed chemical will be used in violation of the law must be reported to the local DEA Diversion Field Office. Each report shall be made orally at the earliest practicable opportunity after the pharmacist becomes aware of the circumstances involved and as much in advance of the transaction as possible. Within fifteen days a written report of the transaction should be forwarded to your local DEA Diversion Field Office and must include the following information:

1. The name, address, and, if required, DEA registration number of each party to the regulated transaction

2. The date of the regulated transaction
3. The name, quantity, and form of packaging of the listed chemical or a description of the tableting machine or encapsulating machine (including make, model, and serial number)
4. The method of transfer (company truck, picked up by customer, etc.)
5. The type of identification used by the purchaser and any unique number on that identification

List I Chemical Security

Single-entity ephedrine products must be stocked behind a counter where only employees have access. However, there is no such requirement for pseudoephedrine or PPA drug products.

PHARMACISTS' GUIDE TO FORGED, ALTERED, AND STOLEN PRESCRIPTION BLANKS

A prescription order for a controlled substance must be issued for a legitimate medical purpose by an individual practitioner, acting in the usual course of sound professional practice. The law holds the pharmacist responsible for knowingly dispensing a prescription order issued not in the usual course of professional treatment. The DEA also expects that the pharmacist will make a reasonable effort to determine the identity of a practitioner—if the dispensing pharmacist does not know the practitioner.

The Drug Enforcement Administration recognizes that attempts to obtain legitimately manufactured controlled substances by misrepresentation—i.e., forged and altered prescription orders and stolen prescription order blanks—are serious problems confronting pharmacists and local law enforcement agencies. The passage of the Comprehensive Drug Abuse Prevention and Control Act of 1970 established more stringent controls over the dispensing of controlled substances by pharmacists. Even though these more stringent controls and the vigilance of pharmacists and law enforcement officials have helped curtail the fraudulent prescription problem, the issue of dealing with fraudulent prescription orders must remain a top priority for pharmacists.

The only way a forged, altered, or stolen prescription order blank can enter the system is by presentation to a pharmacist. Attempts may be made either by presenting the prescription order at the pharmacy or by an oral order of a person that purports to be a physician.

A prescription order represents any request by an authorized prescriber (practitioner as defined by the Controlled Substances Act) for the dispensing, or the administration, to a particular patient, of a particular quantity, of a particular drug, in a particular dosage form and strength, for use according to particular directions, to treat a particular condition of health, at a particular time.

The Drug Enforcement Administration, in its attempt to curtail or stop the diversion of legitimately manufactured controlled substances, encourages pharmacy and medical groups to cooperate with each other in local programs that address forged and fraudulent prescription orders. The DEA recognizes the practicing pharmacist's expertise and ability to spot fraudulent prescription orders.

Accepting Responsibility

According to the DEA, the abuse of prescription drugs (especially controlled substances) is a serious social and health problem in the United States. As a healthcare professional, the pharmacist shares responsibility for helping solve the prescription drug abuse and diversion problem.

The DEA outlines three major areas of responsibility for pharmacists:

1. Pharmacists have a legal responsibility to acquaint themselves with the state and federal requirements for dispensing controlled substances. Furthermore, pharmacists also have a legal and ethical responsibility to uphold these laws and to help protect society from drug abuse.
2. Pharmacists have a personal responsibility to protect their practices from becoming an easy target for drug diversion. Also, pharmacists must become aware of the potential situations where drug diversion can occur and safeguards that can be enacted to prevent this diversion.
3. Dispensing pharmacists must maintain a constant vigilance against forged or altered prescription orders. The law holds the pharmacist responsible for knowingly dispensing a prescription order that was not issued in the usual course of professional treatment.

Characteristics of Forged Prescription Orders

1. The prescription order looks too good. The prescriber's handwriting is too legible.
2. Quantities, directions, or dosages differ from acceptable medical usage.

3. Prescription orders are written on hospital blanks. If you don't know the prescriber, check with the hospital to verify both prescriber and the patient.
4. Prescription orders do not comply with acceptable standard abbreviations or appear to be textbook presentation.
5. Prescription order (the form itself) appears to be photocopied.
6. Directions written in full with no abbreviations.
7. Use of different color inks or written in different handwriting.
8. Quantity looks like it has been altered.
9. Apparent erasure marks are present.

Prevention Techniques

1. Know the prescriber and his or her signature.
2. Know the prescriber's DEA registration number.
3. Know the patient.
4. Use good professional practice and dispensing procedures.
5. Check the date on the prescription order. Has it been presented to you in a reasonable length of time since the prescriber wrote it?
6. When there is a question about any aspect of the prescription order, telephone the prescriber for verification or clarification.
7. If there is a discrepancy, the patient must have a plausible reason before the prescription medicine is dispensed.

Forged Prescription Orders: What to Look For

In the course of everyday dispensing by the practicing pharmacist it is important that various kinds of forged prescription orders be identified. If you believe that you have a forged, altered, or bogus prescription order, do not dispense it. Call your local police. Similarly, if you believe that you have discovered a pattern of prescription medicine abuses, contact your state Board of Pharmacy or your local DEA office.

The Forged Physician's Prescription Order

1. Printers, at the request of forgers, print prescription blanks in the form of pads either knowingly or unknowingly.
2. Legitimate prescription pads are stolen from physicians' offices, and prescription orders are written for fictitious patients.
3. Some patients, in an effort to obtain additional amounts of legitimately prescribed medicines, alter the prescription order.

The Forged Hospital Prescription Order

Pharmacists should question prescription orders written on hospital prescription order blanks. It is always best to call the hospital pharmacy to verify the prescriber. Some forgers use names and addresses of fictitious patients on these stolen blanks.

APPENDIX
DEA FIELD OFFICES
WITH DIVERSION PROGRAM MANAGERS

Atlanta

NW Georgia
North Carolina
South Carolina
Tennessee

75 Spring Street SW, Room 800
Atlanta, GA 30303
Telephone 404-893-7186
Fax 404-893-7138 (Diversion Program Manager)
404-893-7096 (Diversion Group)

Boston

Connecticut
Maine
Massachusetts
New Hampshire
Rhode Island
Vermont

JFK Federal Building
15 New Sudbury Street, Room 400E
Boston, MA 02203-0402
Telephone 860-240-3700

Fax 617-557-2348 (Diversion Program Manager)
617-557-2126 (Diversion Group)

Caribbean

Barbados
Dominican Rep
Grenada
Guadeloupe
Haiti
Jamaica Netherlands Antilles
Puerto Rico
Saint Martin
Trinidad and Tobago
U.S. Virgin Islands

Mailing Address:
P.O. Box 2167
San Juan, PR 00922-2167

Physical Address:
Second Street Bldg 17
Suites 400 and 500
Guaynabo, PR 00968
Telephone 787-775-1865
Fax 787-775-1855

Chicago

Illinois (north and central)
Indiana
Wisconsin
Minnesota
North Dakota

Kluczynski Federal Building
230 S. Dearborn Street, Room 1200
Chicago, IL 60604
Telephone 312-353-1234 or 800-478-7914
312-353-9166 or 800-478-7914
Fax 312-353-1476 (Diversion Program Manager)
312-353-1235 (Diversion Group)
312-353-1236 or 800-478-7642 (Minnesota)

Dallas

Oklahoma
North Texas

10160 Technology Blvd., East
Dallas, TX 75235
Telephone 214-366-6936
Fax 214-366-6902

Denver

Colorado
Montana
Utah
Wyoming

115 Inverness Drive, East
Englewood, CO 80112
Telephone 303-705-7331
Fax 303-705-7423

Detroit

Kentucky
Michigan
Ohio

431 Howard Street
Detroit, MI 48226
Telephone 313-234-4005
Fax 313-234-4065 (Diversion Program Manager)
313-234-4149 (Diversion Group)

El Paso

New Mexico
West Texas

El Paso Federal Justice Center
660 South Mesa Hills Drive, Suite 2000
El Paso, TX 79912
Telephone 915-832-6000 (main) or 713-693-3630
Fax 915-832-6302 (Diversion Program Manager)

Houston

South Texas

1433 West Loop South, Suite 600
Houston, TX 77027-9506
Telephone 713-693-3630
Fax 713-693-3661

Los Angeles

Central California
Guam
Hawaii
Nevada

255 East Temple Street, 20th Floor
Los Angeles, CA 90012
Telephone 213-621-6711
Fax 213-894-5924 (Diversion Program Manager)
213-894-3946 (Diversion Group)

Miami

Bahamas
Florida

8400 N.W. 53rd Street
Miami, FL 33166
Telephone 305-994-4704
Fax 305-994-4293

New Orleans

Alabama
Arkansas
Louisiana
Mississippi

3838 N. Causeway Blvd., Room 1800
Lakeway III

Metairie, LA 70002
Telephone 504-840-1372
Fax 504-840-1076

New York

New York

99 Tenth Avenue
New York, NY 10011
Telephone 212-337-1190
Fax 212-337-2895 (Diversion Program Manager)
212-337-2872 (Diversion Group)

Newark

New Jersey

80 Mulberry Street, 2nd Floor
Newark, NJ 07102
Telephone 973-273-5097
Fax 973-645-6297 (Diversion Program Manager)
973-297-4842 (Diversion Group)

Philadelphia

Delaware
Pennsylvania

William J. Green Federal Building
600 Arch Street, Room 10224
Philadelphia, PA 19106
Telephone 215-597-9540
Fax 215-597-3030

Phoenix

Arizona

3010 N. 2nd Street, Suite 301
Phoenix, AZ 85012
Telephone 602-664-5810
Fax 602-664-5820

St. Louis

Iowa
Kansas
Missouri
Nebraska
South Dakota
South Illinois

317 South 16th Street
St. Louis, MO 63103
Telephone 314-538-4712
Fax 314-538-4622

San Francisco

North California

Address 450 Golden Gate Avenue, 14th Floor
P.O. Box 36035
San Francisco, CA 94102
Telephone 415-436-7463
Fax 415-436-7810

Seattle

Alaska
Idaho
Oregon
Washington

400 2nd Avenue West
Seattle, WA 98119
Telephone 206-553-1257
Fax 206-553-1576

Washington, DC

District of Columbia
Maryland
Virginia
West Virginia

Mailing Address:
Techworld
800 K Street, NW, Suite 500
Washington, DC 20001

Physical Address:
801 I Street, NW, Suite 500
Washington, DC 20001
Telephone 202-305-8207
Fax 202-307-5823 (Diversion Program Manager)
202-305-8355 (Diversion Group)

Chapter 5

Principles of Professional Liability Insurance for Pharmacists

Kenneth R. Baker

OVERVIEW

From the viewpoint of the insurance client, insurance is about a single individual risk—the client's. In the relatively unlikely event that the client suffers a loss insured by the insurance contract, the insurance company agrees, subject to terms, conditions, and exclusions contained in the contract, to pay the loss. Viewed from the insurance company's perspective, insurance is a collection of individual risks. This combination of individual risks makes up a pool of risks and clients.

Although it is likely that one or more of these risks may have a covered claim in any given year, it is unlikely that a large number of the risks will have a claim in the same year. Premiums are collected from each of the individual risks insured, and this cash is invested. Throughout the year the premium income is used to pay claims and the expenses related to these claims. In addition, the insurance company must set aside a portion of its income as reserves against future claims. The money that is left is called *underwriting profit*. Underwriting profit is analogous to what pharmacy owners think of as "gross margin."

From the underwriting profit the insurance company pays its operating expenses. Whatever is left is added to the investment income, and together these make up the company's profits. A part of these profits is added to the company's surplus and a portion is returned to the company's shareholders or, in the case of a mutual insurance company, to its policyholders in the form of dividends.

When the insurance company is notified of a claim, or a potential claim, a claims representative must evaluate the information and set a reserve. A

Pharmacy Law Desk Reference
© 2007 by The Haworth Press, Inc. All rights reserved.
doi:10.1300/5790_05

reserve is an amount of money that is set aside to eventually pay the claim and the expenses of the claim. Typically, a reserve is reviewed several times during the life of a claim. Reserving is at best an art—it is certainly not a science. Claims representatives use their experience to estimate (some say guess) how much will eventually be paid, both directly for the claim and for expenses associated with the claim. Chronically overreserving or underreserving claims can create serious problems for the company. But, just like the collection of risks becomes a pool, so the reserving of individual claims creates one large reserve. It is this reserve pool that becomes important to the insurance company. This concept of pooling of risks and losses is central to the business of insurance. In part at least, it is what gives insurance companies the ability to insure so many businesses in total amounts several times the company's capital and surplus.

The other factor that allows small and medium-sized companies to write relatively large amounts of insurance is the concept of *reinsurance*. Reinsurance is a method of spreading the risk, not just among several policies, but also among several insurance companies. An insurance company will typically "sell" a part of each policy or risk. For example, an insurance company may insure a business for $1 million but decide that the most it can risk on this one business having a claim is $100,000. The insurance company will approach reinsurance companies who, for a portion of the premium, agree to take the risk of any loss above the $100,000 retained by the primary company. Because the majority of losses will be under $100,000, the primary (or underlying) insurer still bears most of the risk but is spared the occasional, catastrophic large loss.

Insurance is normally divided into three broad categories: life, health, and property and casualty (P&C). These types of insurance and the rules that govern them are sufficiently different for state regulators to require different types of licenses and to apply different requirements. The contract of the life insurance company is usually thought of as the most simple. Life insurance policies are relatively straightforward contracts involving a promise by the insurance company, in exchange for premiums, to pay the face amount of the policy if the insured dies while the policy is in force. Absent fraud in answering one or more relevant questions on the application, if the insured person dies, the company pays. Relatively speaking, there are few conditions, terms, or exclusions.

Health insurance policies, on the other hand, are full of conditions, terms, and exclusions. Books have been written on the nature, pricing, and underwriting of health insurance. The rule of large numbers (averages are accurate only if a large number of individuals are combined to reach that average) and the need for statistical data is critical in the health insurance business, as it is in all areas of insurance.

When healthcare costs were relatively stable and predictable, small and medium-sized health insurance companies could compete and be reasonably profitable. That changed with the explosion of new and costly medical devices and procedures in the past few decades. Today there are only a few large health insurance companies writing this line of insurance. In some ways the void left by the exit of the small and medium-sized insurance companies has been filled by the advent of health maintenance organizations (HMOs), which not only collect the premiums but also provide the medical services, allowing them to directly control costs.

The health insurance industry has in recent years gone through cycles of relative calm and profitability followed by years of crisis. During the lean years some companies exit the health insurance business, creating almost panic among those insureds whose insurance plan has been eliminated. The reasons for and the problems suffered by health insurance companies are too broad, too varied, and too large to be discussed here.

No insurance policy covers every eventuality. Insurance companies could not charge enough premiums to be able to afford to offer such all-encompassing policies, and generally insureds know and accept that some things will be excluded from coverage. This concept, accepted with P&C policies, is rejected by consumers of medical services. Not being able to repair your residence following an earthquake which is excluded from your homeowners policy would be difficult, but this disaster is eclipsed when compared with the news that your child's needed operation is not covered by your health insurance. The first is survivable; the second may not be.

Pressure on the insurance company in such an instance to "make an exception" to the contract language would be, and perhaps should be, tremendous. If the health insurance company, or any insurance company, loses the ability to control costs and to limit claims to those set forth in the insuring agreement, it must either raise premiums or exit the business. The statistical prediction of risk is based upon the risks defined as covered in the policy.

Pharmacists view health insurance companies through the somewhat distorted lens of the pharmacy benefit managers (PBMs), who have been successful in taking advantage of the unequal bargaining positions of the insurance companies (including the HMO models) and the pharmacies. The PBM sells to the insurance company their ability to control prescription costs better than the competing PBM. They have managed to create in the minds of insurance company managers an almost complete separation between costs of medication and costs of auxiliary medical services, including physician and hospital costs. The PBM is then able to dictate to several separate pharmacy organizations using a "take it or leave it" style of negotiations. The result of this separate and myopic view of medical treatment has been increased medical costs, including prescription costs.*

Insurance plans sold on an individual basis are combined by the insurance company into a group. The insurance company can then use the actuarial rules of averaging probable health used of large numbers of people as outlined earlier in this chapter. The risks associated with these averages are accepted by the insurance company. If the payouts are higher than predicted by the statistics, the insurance company will lose money. In an employer group, however, the insurance company is not ultimately at risk—the employer is. If the insurance company loses money this year, it increases premiums to the employer next year. Because of the loss history of the employer's group, competition among health insurance companies for this group is limited, and the employer must accept the higher premiums. With individual plans those insureds who did not use benefits (those people on whom the insurance company depends for profits) can individually seek lower prices if the company raises the price of their individual plans.

The model of health insurance that has evolved over the past fifty years in the United States is broken and needs repair. However, as long as there is sufficient money within the system to keep paying higher premiums, the current system is likely to limp forward until overcome by a crisis. Among the problems is that the antitrust laws, meant to ensure competition, have stifled competition. Health insurance, as it currently exists in this country, is a complicated and interwoven subject, which this discussion can only touch upon.

Property and casualty insurance, commonly referred to as P & C, includes a broad range of policies and risks. Individually, most people are familiar (usually only vaguely, however) with personal P & C policies—their homeowners policy and their automobile policy. We can also buy insurance on boats, private airplanes, works of art, and collections of almost anything imaginable. This chapter will not deal with these personal policies but will concentrate on commercial insurance, including individual pharmacist professional liability policies. Further, because of the emphasis on the profession of pharmacy, this chapter will limit inquiry to liability provisions of those commercial policies, with an emphasis on pharmacy malpractice coverages.

---

*The current state of unequal negotiation positions between pharmacies and PBMs can be compared to the status of employees in the eighteenth, nineteenth, and early twentieth centuries. Prior to the modern laws allowing collective bargaining, employers could dictate terms and wages of employment, knowing that if one worker did not accept their unilateral offer, others would. Employees were also aware of their inability to individually influence wage and condition dictates and were forced to accept the "take it or leave it" offers of employers. The legal inability of workers to form unions through which they could bargain with employers on a somewhat equal basis freed those who set wages and conditions from the necessity to negotiate.

UNDERWRITING

Insurance companies can be profitable because they pool together a large number of businesses and individuals and collect premiums from each. Statistically, only a small amount of these individual risks will have a claim in any given year, allowing the company to pay these claims out of the premiums collected from the larger pool, most of whom had no claim this year. In addition, the insurance companies are able to spread the risk among several insurance companies through the concept of reinsurance.

Insurance companies can further expand the possibilities of having a profitable year by selling insurance policies only to those businesses and individuals that are least likely to have a claim. The insurance company can dramatically increase profits by eliminating the most risky of potential insureds. In this way, the risk of paying more in claims than the company charged in premiums decreases dramatically. As the gambler might say, "You improve the odds by betting only on the good hands."

In the business of insurance the process of selecting the best risks is called *underwriting*. Underwriting begins with the selection of the type of businesses the insurance company decides it will insure. The focus may be broad, such as automobiles or private family residences or all retail businesses, or the focus may be narrow, such as only medical malpractice or only pharmacists and pharmacy-related businesses. The smaller the company, the more likely it will select a niche for concentration. This niche allows a company to collect special knowledge of the type risks it assumes and enables it to better select those within the niche. A narrow focus also gives an advantage to the individuals and businesses insured, as it allows the insurer to tailor its policies to fit specific needs of those whom it insures.

Once the insurance company has selected a market, such as pharmacy, it must find a means of selecting those within the market, i.e., pharmacists and pharmacies, who are least likely to suffer a loss—that is to say, the best risks. That is the job of the underwriter. The underwriter must be careful, however. If the criteria are so strict that only a few qualify, the pool of pharmacies and pharmacists insured will not be large enough to spread the risk. Underwriters know they will accept most of those within the selected niche (pharmacy) while weeding out those who are outside the norm. In order to perform this task, the underwriters must have knowledge of the businesses and individuals applying for insurance.

In order to get this knowledge, information must be collected. One source of this information is the insurance application. The application for a pharmacy asks such questions as the number of prescription orders dispensed; the income from all sources, including prescription orders; and whether there have been previous claims. The answers must, of course, be truthful, since they form part of the information upon which the insurance company bases its decision to insure. Typically, the application contains a statement that false answers may invalidate the policy.

Other sources of the underwriter's information may include physical inspection of the property or location by a company employee, the insurance agent, or another person specially hired for the purpose. Insurance companies may also ask for a list of all insurance claims over the past several years. The prospective insured may then be required to ask its present insurance company for a claims history or "loss run" to be provided to the new insurance company.

Another job of the underwriter is the pricing of the risk. Insurance companies are heavily regulated by the states and must file the rates it will charge for particular types of risks. Within that published rating structure, however, there will be various factors that the underwriter may take into consideration. If, for example, the pharmacy application includes coverage for the building in which the pharmacy is located, the rating may be determined by whether the building is constructed of brick or wood.

If the rate setting is done correctly—that is, it properly reflects the risk—and if the selection of insured is correct—this insured is less likely to have a claim—and if the cash flow is invested well, the insurance company will be profitable. If the insurance company is profitable, and if the competitive market is working, the insured will be rewarded with lower, or at least reasonable, rates. An additional benefit of all of these factors—selection, pricing, rating, investing, and competition—working well is that the insurance company continues operating and the insurance industry remains stable.

Insurance companies are, by the nature of their business, conservative organizations. At the same time, the industry is built on risks. Insurance companies do not fear risk. What they fear is insufficient statistical information and unknown risks. Occasionally a business will become unstable, meaning that the litigation environment, the number of claims, and the amounts paid out have suddenly increased. This means that the actuarial risks upon which premiums were based are no longer accurate. An example is medical malpractice insurance. After a period of stability, the number and amounts of claims increased in the 1970s and 1980s, and again in the 2000s. When this occurred, prices charged to the insureds' physicians increased and insurance companies began leaving the market. Pharmacy experienced a smaller version of this in recent years, when duties changed, claims increased, and pharmacies became involved in more class action and mass tort litigation. As a result, some insurance companies that had insured drugstores and pharmacies for years became nervous and began exiting the market.

If people took the time to read the provisions of several automobile policies from several different insurance companies, most would be struck by their finding that most automobile policies are surprisingly uniform. Not only would these people find that each policy covers the same risk and insures the same acts, but to a large extent, each states what it insures against and the conditions under which it covers them and the acts it excludes in the same language—often word for word. The same is true of homeowners policies and even most commercial policies.

The reason for these similarities is simple. Most insurance policies used in the United States are written by, and copyrighted by, the same organization—the Insurance Services Organization, usually referred to as ISO. ISO is a not-for-profit trade organization owned by member insurance companies, each of whom are entitled, for a fee, to use the ISO forms. In addition to the fee however, the member companies must agree to share their claims information with ISO, who uses the combined data to create a larger pool of statistical probabilities which, when combined with the individual company's expense and cost data, can be used to generate rates to be charged.

The use of the larger statistical pool more accurately predicts the likelihood of a claim occurring. The information from this extremely large number of insurance companies can be meaningfully combined, of course, only if each of these companies follows the same rules as to what risks are covered, when and where they are covered, and the conditions under which they are covered. In that case, generally, each company will pay a claim or reject a claim under the same circumstances. Thus, the insurance industry required uniform policies, and ISO was directed to write a policy that each company could adopt.

In order to avoid possible legal problems associated with adoption of uniform policies, the insurance industry, along with other interested groups, requested an exemption from the federal antitrust laws. Beginning in the late nineteenth century a series of federal laws were passed forbidding companies from entering into agreements or taking joint actions considered to be anticompetitive. The first major antitrust legislation, known as the Sherman Act, was passed in 1890. This was followed in 1914 by the Clayton Act and the Federal Trade Commission Act and in 1936 by the Robinson-Patman Anti-Discrimination Act.[1]

One of the insurance company arguments was that without the ability to share in the collection of data and the resulting increased statistical accuracy of the loss ratios, small companies could not compete with those companies large enough to use their own information in statistically sound calculations and ratings. There are still some very large insurance companies today that do not share information with ISO and do not use ISO policies. Over the years, however, these companies have adopted ISO definitions, language, terms, conditions, and coverages, until today there are few actual differences in even these policies. Another of the insurance industry demands was that the states adequately regulate the business of insurance—to which the states agreed. The result of these arguments and requests was the McCarran-Ferguson Act.[2]

The antitrust exemptions provided to the insurance industry by the McCarran-Ferguson Act are limited. McCarran-Ferguson in essence provides that the business of insurance shall be regulated by the several states, rather than by the federal government. The exception was that the federal antitrust laws would "be applicable to the business of insurance to the extent that such business is not regulated by State Law."[3] While allowing uniform policies and data collection, calculation, and dissemination, the law does not permit the companies to fix prices or to collude in any other manner. McCarran-Ferguson specifically exempted from its protection other federal laws[4] and parts of the Sherman Act: "Nothing contained in this chapter shall render the said Sherman Act inapplicable to any agreement to boycott, coerce, or intimidate, or act of boycott, coercion, or intimidation."[5] In spite of McCarran-Ferguson's limited exceptions to antitrust, the insurance industry is one of the most highly competitive sectors of the U.S. conomy.

A few years ago, some insurance companies, becoming disillusioned with some aspects of ISO services, formed a competing nonprofit services organization, which provides many of the same data collecting functions, information services, and policies to its member companies. The American Association of Insurance Services, or AAIS, also produces uniform insurance policies, and although there are some important distinctions, the basics of these policies are similar to the ISO versions.

Most P & C companies feel that they cannot control the statistical risk probabilities, and thus use AAIS's or ISO's numbers in deciding how to factor risk into the price of their policies. Each company adds this pooled risk calculation to their costs, adds what profit they need, and arrives at a final rate. The competitive prices charged are usually a factor of desired profit, how well the company can control its costs, and how well it underwrites. Good underwriting can change the statistical probabilities by selecting out of the pool only the best risks.

PROFESSIONAL PHARMACY LIABILITY COVERAGE

A pharmacist's first interest in a commercial policy covering his or her profession should be professional coverage. When reading the professional liability provisions, they need to consider that no policy covers all acts of every pharmacist. An insurance policy is no more than a contract—it is a promise by the insurance company accompanied by payment by the insured. As with any contract, it is important to understand what the promises are and the limitations of those promises. The "promises" are stated in the totality of the policy, including terms, limitations, conditions, exclusions, and declarations. One method insurance companies use to maintain the certainty that the statistics are as meaningful and as correct as possible is to write the policy to clearly state who is covered, what risk is covered, and the conditions under which those insureds and the risks are covered. These terms, conditions, and exclusions are contained in the language of the policy.

As discussed later in this chapter, pharmacists' professional liability coverage is typically found in two types of policies, each designed to fulfill a specific purpose. The primary policy covering most pharmacists' professional liability is the pharmacy's commercial liability policy. This policy is primary because it should be the first to respond, not just for the pharmacy, but also for any employed pharmacist sued while acting "in the course of the business"—i.e., performing their job. The second level of protection (or third level in the case of umbrella coverage for the pharmacy) is the personal, individual professional liability policy for the pharmacist. Both policies (pharmacy and pharmacist) are considered commercial coverage.

READING A PROFESSIONAL LIABILITY AND COMMERCIAL POLICY

Many people, including pharmacists, are intimidated by insurance contracts—they typically are long (a commercial policy may be in excess of fifty pages) and written in an unfamiliar, legalistic form. Any pharmacist involved in a business should use the services of a good attorney versed in business and insurance law. For a basic understanding, however, a law degree is not required to read an insurance policy. An insurance policy is best read with two principles in mind. First, like any contract, no words are without contextual meaning—the insurance company placed them there for a purpose. When reading the policy, ask "Why is this here?" The second principle in reading a policy is that all insurance policies are made up of four general elements that can be understood by reading the policy with five questions in mind. The first four questions are: How?, What?, When?, and Where? The fifth question—the one asked above: "Why is this here?"—is always in the background. It accompanies the others and should be kept in mind while reading any insurance policy or contract.

There is one step to take before reading for content. As with any contract, some words have the exact meaning set forth in the contract. In an insurance policy these exact meanings are found in the definitions section. Before plunging into the policy language, review the definitions used in the policy. At first, just review the section to note what words are defined. Then, as you read through the policy to answer the five questions, when you reach one of the defined words, go back to the definition section and study what that word means. The policy format helps with this since whenever a defined word is used in the policy the word is highlighted in some fashion.

At the risk of making the exercise feel like a class assignment with a quiz following, I suggest it may be helpful when reading an insurance policy to write down the five questions, so you can make a note of the answers as you read and the page on which you found the answer. Although almost all policies are arranged in a similar fashion, for the reasons discussed above, there are some differences from company to company. The process below follows the most typical policies.

How

Historically, the profession of pharmacy evolved differently from that of medical practice. Today's medical clinics and hospitals began as individual physicians charging a fee for services. Medical malpractice insurance developed to meet this need by writing policies that covered this individual, service-style business. These individual medical professional policies were the primary protection the physician had in the event of legal allegations of malpractice.

Pharmacy developed along the lines of a business model—a retail establishment selling services and products. When all prescription orders were compounded, the services were the art and science of combining ingredients to compound a product that was sold to the patient. Pharmacy policies developed as a form of business insurance—the business was the insured and the pharmacists, including the business owner, were an extension of the business. This business policy was the first, or primary, level of protection. Note, however, that even though these pharmacy policies are clearly intended to be primary, many contain language that says the policy is secondary to any other policy covering the same risk. The disadvantages to this language in a commercial business policy will be discussed later.

Individual pharmacy professional liability polices did not exist until the last third of the twentieth century. These individual policies were designed for the employed pharmacist who wanted to have personal protection against the increasing number of lawsuits in pharmacy and medicine. The concerns of the employed pharmacist were "What if the pharmacy does not have good professional pharmacy liability coverage?"; "What if only the drugstore is covered by the policy?"; and "What if the drugstore didn't pay the premium?" The employed pharmacists did not want to pay for primary insurance—they expected the drugstore to pay for that—they wanted a "just in case policy." This form of "just in case" coverage developed into the secondary or excess* individual professional policy available today.

There are advantages for both the pharmacy and the individual pharmacist in this primary first, secondary next, arrangement. For the pharmacist it means the individual policy can be priced as an excess layer of protection that will be required to pay only after the primary (pharmacy's) coverage has paid out its limit—typically $1 million. Since the risk of a claim reaching into the second million-dollar level is more remote, the price charged is less—usually less than $200 annually for $1 million of coverage. Physicians and other professionals marvel at the low prices paid by pharmacists for professional liability coverage. What they do not understand is that the price they are comparing with is excess coverage, whereas their policies are designed as primary.

There is also an advantage for the pharmacy in being certain that one policy is very specifically primary and the other is specifically secondary or excess.† The pharmacy's policy should cover all professionals working for the business.‡ This is important for several reasons, but among them is to ensure a coordination of defenses. Absent a conflict of interest between the parties, by covering all those against whom a professional claim is or can be asserted, the defense can be effectively united.

Commercial pharmacy policies who use language to claim they are secondary, for the purpose of dividing the costs of any claim, face the risk of the pharmacist's policy not sharing in the risk but defending the claim independently. There is then a tendency to shift blame for an error from the individual pharmacist to the employer's prescription process. Such a strategy is necessitated by the pharmacy's insurance company's position and is most likely to be advantageous to the individual, employed pharmacist and the plaintiff, but potentially disastrous for the pharmacy.

---

*Although there are definite policy language differences between a secondary policy and an excess individual professional liability policy, for the purposes of this discussion both will be treated as the second layer of protection (secondary) and the term *secondary* will be used to mean both.

†For the purposes of this discussion, both secondary and excess policies are treated as identical. Indeed, the secondary language is used for the same purpose as the excess language—to establish a clear distinction with the primary pharmacy policy and to set an order of use. Currently, to the best of the author's knowledge, only Pharmacists Mutual Insurance Company uses the excess language in its individual policies. It was felt that excess language more clearly established policy order, particularly when some "primary" policies say they are "secondary."

‡But, see, "Who?" section of this discussion later in the chapter.

The mutual advantage of a clear order of primary/excess policies is easiest seen through use of an example. A technician mistypes a label causing the patient to take twice the dosage prescribed. The technician is negligent and may be sued by the patient. The pharmacist checked the label, as was the pharmacist's duty, but missed the mistake made by the technician. The pharmacist was also negligent and could be sued by the patient. Since each is employed by the pharmacy to dispense prescription orders, the pharmacy can also be sued under the legal theory of respondeate superior, or "let the master respond." All three potential defendants have professional liability insurance policies.

The pharmacy's policy states that all employees of the pharmacy are insureds under the policy and that it (the pharmacy's policy) is primary. The policy for the pharmacist and the technician insure only them and each contains excess (or secondary) language, as explained in the policy preamble:

> This policy is specifically designed to be excess coverage for *you.* This policy is intended to be *your* personal professional umbrella policy, as it is excess to other professional liability policies and is rated to be excess. This insurance does not apply until the limits of *your employer's* professional liability coverage, including self insurance or deductible have been exhausted. In addition to being excess protection, this policy does protect *you* when *you* are not employed or when *you* are not protected by any other policy. This policy is designed to protect you, not *your employer* or their insurance company.

Unless the damages are extraordinary (or unusual facts indicating a conflict of interest between the defendants, not disclosed above, are at play), the pharmacist, technician, and the pharmacy will unite in one theory of defense. They will all be represented by the same insurance claims representative hired by the pharmacy's commercial insurance company and, if necessary, by the same attorney. In the professional pharmacy malpractice case outlined above, the dispute between the defendants and the plaintiff (patient) will be on damages, and the defense will concentrate on the question of proximate cause.

If, however, the pharmacy's commercial insurance policy has secondary language and the insurance company takes the position that the individual policies of the pharmacist and/or the technician must agree to share in the claim expenses on a pro rata basis* the case may take on a different perspec-

---

*The courts that have ruled on these disputes between the respective insurance companies have been divided in their rulings.

tive. The companies who wrote the individual policies may disagree, insisting that their policy comes into play only after the limits of the pharmacy's policies are exhausted. In this event, the initial handling of the claim may be delayed and the defenses bifurcated.

A delay in initially handling a claim may prove to be expensive and potentially frustrating to the patient, pharmacist, technician, pharmacy, and the insurance companies. A delay may be hard to avoid. If either insurance company, while insisting that their policy is the second layer of protection, begins to process the claim by contacting the claimant (patient or plaintiff) before there is an agreement between the companies, that company may be held to have accepted the primary position, which may be determinative in a later adjudication of the question.

When purchasing a commercial pharmacy insurance policy, the pharmacy or its attorney should examine the policy to answer the question of "How is the pharmacy covered?" Look for the "Other Insurance" clause as it applies to liability coverages (usually toward the back of the policy). Look for the statement: "This insurance is primary" or "This insurance is secondary." There is less concern as to primary and secondary in property coverage. Virtually all commercial policies declare themselves secondary in the event of a fire. As to professional liability, however, the pharmacy representative should be certain the policy is primary. This may save time and frustration in the event of a professional claim. Conversely, the pharmacist should look for language in an individual professional policy indicating it is "excess" or "secondary." There may, of course, be times that the pharmacist has determined that he or she wants, and is willing to pay for, primary coverage. This may particularly be the case if the pharmacist is working as an independent contractor, not an employee of the pharmacy.

Who

The second question to ask when selecting a professional liability policy, whether individual or commercial, is "Who is covered by the policy?" Most policies will have a section titled "Who Is Insured." An individual policy will usually cover only the pharmacist and not cover employers, employees, or co-workers. The pharmacy commercial policy, however, should cover the business entity, partners or the sole proprietor, and employees for all acts within the scope of their duties for the pharmacy. If the employed pharmacists and technicians are not included as insured under the pharmacy's policy, the above discussion of a united defense is academic.

Almost all policies use similar language under the "Who Is Insured" section, with one exception, important to pharmacy. The following clause is found in a large number of commercial policies: Under the provision titled "Who Is Insured" the policy states: "Your employees are insureds . . . except . . . none of your employees are insureds . . . if they perform, or fail to perform professional health care."[6]

This provision results in the employed pharmacist being an insured under the policy except when she or he dispenses a prescription order or performs other professional acts. In the case of a lawsuit for professional negligence, the insurance company may refuse to defend or indemnify the employed pharmacist. The employer's insurance company may also take the position it has the right to collect from the employed pharmacist any money it spent paying a judgment or claim against the pharmacy since the pharmacy (and thus the pharmacy's insurance company) had to pay only because of the pharmacist's negligence. This is known as vicarious liability.

Since most commercial policies used in the United States are not designed specifically for pharmacies or any professional business, it is not surprising that such a clause would be unnoticed by most insureds and even most insurance agents who sell and service these commercial policies. This clause, highly important to a pharmacy, is of no consequence to the vast majority of businesses—shoe stores, bakeries, bookstores, etc., who have this policy. The "Who Is Insured" clause is usually, but not always, found in the definitional section under "Insured."

One other problem should be considered if the employed pharmacist is not an insured under the pharmacy's policy. Most commercial policies contain a subrogation clause. Such a clause will usually be found under a subtitle of Subrogation Rights or Transfer of Rights of Recovery Against Others to Us. The effect of such a clause is that if the employed pharmacist is not an insured under the pharmacy's policy, the pharmacy, through the subrogation clause, has given its insurance company the right to sue any employed pharmacist alleged to be involved in an error to recover the insurance company's money. The suit against the employed pharmacist would be in the name of the pharmacy.

What

For a pharmacy, "What?" is a two-part question. The answer to the first part is usually not found as part of the definitions contained within the body of the policy but in the exclusions and endorsements to the policy. This first part involves the professional coverage afforded to the practice of pharmacy. Here there is a divergence in policy language. In some policies there is no mention of the profession of pharmacy in the body of the agreement. Instead, there is a broad exclusion exempting from coverage all professional acts. In these policies the pharmacy owner or the agent for the pharmacy needs to look at the endorsements attached to the policy for professional liability coverage.

Neglecting the examination of the policy until after a claim occurs can be hazardous. One pharmacy owner, having submitted a claim made by a patient for a medication error, received a letter saying the policy covering the business did not have professional liability coverage. On examining the policy, the pharmacy's insurance agent (the same one who has recommended the policy to the pharmacy owner) discovered that this was true. The pharmacy faced a malpractice claim that was not insured and the insurance agent, a personal friend of the pharmacy owner, faced an insurance malpractice claim.

Some policies specifically mention pharmacy and what is covered is found in an exclusion. This exclusion grants coverage as an exception. The contract excludes all professional acts "including pharmaceutical services," then it says: "However, an insured whose business includes a retail drugstore is not excluded." Obviously, the person who wrote the policy language did not understand the changes that have taken place in the practice of pharmacy over the past thirty years.

A problem, or potential problem, with such language is, What does it mean? What is included and what is excluded? Does the policy mean to exclude pharmaceutical manufacturing? If so, does it cover compounding? What is a "retail drugstore"? The contract does not define the term, so the pharmacy is left to speculate. What if the pharmacy is a community pharmacy but also includes nursing home services—typically closed pharmacy activities? If the pharmacy does some IV compounding for home care, it will not look like any pharmacy the insurance claims department ever experienced. The problem with a policy using outdated terms and older concepts of the profession is the pharmacy may discover what is covered only after a claim is filed.

Another common policy covering pharmacies today uses an ISO, or modified ISO, endorsement titled "Druggist Liability" and is the closest the insurance industry comes to a standard for pharmacy professional liability coverage. The endorsement reads, in part: "Damages include bodily damages and property damage for the rendering or failure to render professional services as a pharmacist." "Professional services as a pharmacist" are not defined. The "Druggist Liability" endorsements may or may not extend the definition of an insured to cover employed pharmacists.

Other types of policies present other problems. Typically, prior to the expansion of pharmacists' duties beginning circa 1980, the insurance industry looked upon "druggist liability" as essentially a products liability, not a professional liability, coverage. The products pharmacists supplied to their clients were either correct, as the doctor prescribed, or they were not correct. If the product (prescription medication) was correct, the pharmacy and the pharmacist were not sued. Even if the doctor made a mistake and prescribed a drug that the patient was allergic to or that was contraindicated for use with another drug the patient was taking, the error was the physician's and the pharmacist was not liable. If the pharmacy's product (prescription) was incorrect, it was because the pharmacist made a mechanical error* and the claim was a products liability/work product claim. Pharmacy liability coverage was thus covered as a products liability claim. There are still several policies covering pharmacies today that treat pharmacy professional claims in the same manner. Look for language that indicates that a prescription order must be dispensed for the damages to be covered or that "the product must change hands."

The problem for the pharmacy and its employees is that unless a product changes hands there is no coverage. From the point of view of the insurance company who still treats pharmacy claims as products liability claims, there is no problem. From the standpoint of the pharmacist, however, a claim could arise for advice given when no product or prescription order was purchased.

The second part of the "What" question is, "What damages are covered by the policy?" This is a limitation with all policies, as no insurance policy could afford to cover every loss and no insured could afford the premium on a policy that covered everything. There are four standard coverages in commercial insurance policies marketed in the United States. They are bodily injury, property damage, personal injury, and advertising injury. Bodily injury and property damage may be found in some individual policies as part of the term "occurrence." The coverages are typically defined as follows:

> *Bodily injury* means bodily harm, sickness, disease, or mental or emotional distress to a person. This includes required care, loss of services, and resulting death.

---

*A pharmacy mechanical error has come to be defined as a prescription which mistakenly contained the wrong drug (not the drug prescribed); or the correct drug, but the wrong strength of the drug; or a prescription on which the label was typed incorrectly (wrong label). The term "mechanical error" to describe this type of pharmacy mistake was first used in 1990 as part of the publication for the first Pharmacists Mutual Study of Claims against pharmacists. The term *mechanical error* was used to distinguish between allegations against pharmacists involving such traditional claims and claims alleging a failure to counsel; failure to warn the physician or patient of a contraindication or allergy; failure to take appropriate action to address overuse of prescription drugs, including addiction cases; failure to use child-resistant caps; or similar claims, for which the term "intellectual error" was coined in the same publication. See, Baker, K., *Pharmacists Mutual Study: Professional Claims Against Pharmacists,* ASPL Law Journal, ASPL 1990.

Property damage means physical injury to or destruction of property. This includes the loss of its use.

Personal injury means injury (other than bodily injury) within the coverage territory and during the policy period. It must arise out of one or more of the following offenses:

A. Oral or written publication of other than advertising material
   1. that slanders or libels a person or organization;
   2. that disparages a person's or organization's goods, products, or services; or
   3. that violates a person's right of privacy
B. False arrest, detention, imprisonment, or malicious prosecution
C. Wrongful entry into, or eviction of a person from, a room, dwelling, or premises that the person occupies

Advertising injury means injury within the coverage territory and during the policy period (other than bodily injury) arising out of one or more of the following offenses:

A. Oral or written publication of advertising material
   1. that slanders or libels a person or organization;
   2. that disparages a person's or organization's goods, products or services; or
   3. that violates a person's right of privacy
B. Misappropriation of advertising ideas or style of doing business
C. Infringement of copyright, title, slogan

Understanding these covered damages is important because of what is not covered. Typically, in the standard pharmacy commercial policy, the four damages listed above are covered except for the pharmacy professional coverage. Of these two, personal injury is the most critical for pharmacy. From the definition it is clear that this is where allegations of unauthorized release of medical and pharmacy records would fall. Although this has been important for at least the past decade, when claims for breach of confidentiality began being made against pharmacists, it is more so now, after the enactment of the federal Health Insurance Portability and Accountability Act (HIPAA) regulation.

The question of what damages are covered arise because of the wording of the insuring clause of most policies. When reading a commercial pharmacy policy for the answer to "What is covered," begin with the insuring clauses. Standard policies will have four or five insuring clauses. One, often referred to as the general liability clause, will contain a statement similar to the following: "We pay for all damages for which you are legally liable caused by bodily injury or property damages to which this insurance applies. . . ."

A similar insuring paragraph or clause, often called personal injury coverage, will replace the bodily injury or property damage phrase with "personal injury and advertising injury." Other insurance clauses may include "products liability," "property of others liability," and "incidental medical malpractice."

The "incidental medical malpractice" coverage may sound like pharmacy professional coverage, but, by its language, it excludes all professionals, including pharmacists acting within their profession, from its terms. It is meant to cover those with no medical training who provide emergency first aid. One insurance agent tried to convince a pharmacy owner, who could find no professional liability coverage in his pharmacy's commercial policy, that "incidental medical malpractice" covered this, until the pharmacist read the agent the language of that coverage. The pharmacy owner changed his insurance company, his policy, and his agent.

Even if all of these coverages are in the commercial pharmacy policy, they may not be in the professional coverage endorsement. The policy endorsement cited above covering "professional services as a pharmacist" protects the pharmacy and its employees only against damages for bodily injury and property damage. Personal injury and advertising injury are not mentioned in this endorsement.

In some ways this oversight may not be surprising for an industry that still refers to pharmacy professional coverage as "Druggist Liability." Until recently, the lay public generally did not think of pharmacy records as confidential. One episode of the popular television program *Law & Order* contained a scene of the two primary detectives discussing their frustration at not being able to get the physician's records of drugs prescribed for the main suspect, deciding to obtain the records from the suspect's pharmacy. One detective said to the other: "Who ever heard of a pharmacist-patient privilege."

Where

The answer to the question "Where is coverage afforded under the policy?" is usually found in the definitional section under "coverage territory." A common coverage territory is " . . . the United States, its possessions and Canada." Even though an insurance company may not be licensed in a particular state or market its products there, the policy will usually still be operative in that state. The "Where" question becomes important with mobile pharmacists who are licensed and may occasionally work in a number of jurisdictions and for pharmacies who do even only occasional mail order of prescription medications, including patients on vacation. The answer to the question of "Where" is actually somewhat broader than indicated here, but the extra depth of the definition of coverage territory is beyond the needs of this discussion.

A second "Where" limitation is that commercial business policies provide coverage only while the insured is "in the course of the conduct of the business." When the pharmacist is at home or working elsewhere, there will be no coverage under the pharmacy's business policy. The pharmacist needs coverage for the second business. Many beginning consultant pharmacists supplement their practice by working as consultants to hospitals or long term care facilities. As a consultant the pharmacist may work as an employee of the institution, as an employee of their regular employer, or as an independent contractor.

If the pharmacist is an independent contractor, he or she has only that protection he or she purchases for himself or herself. Independent contractors are not employees and are not usually under the protection of the business policy of the entity contracting for their services. An individual professional liability policy, however, may not be sufficient. The independent contractor has additional insurance needs. The individual professional liability policy protects the pharmacist only against claims involving professional acts. The independent contractor also needs general liability protection.

When

Claims Made versus Occurrence Coverage

All insurance policies contain limitations. Policies often have limitations that affect the business. There are generally two types of policies: occurrence and claims-made policies. If a claims-made policy is discontinued prior to a claim being made against the pharmacist, it may no longer provide protection.

Business policies will be written on either a claims-made or an occurrence basis. A claims-made basis means the accident (i.e., misdispensed prescription order) must occur during the policy period (or extended policy periods during which the insurance is renewed) and the claim must be made, or reported, during the same period. If either the accident (occurrence) that leads to the claim or the report of the claim does not fall within the time the policy is in effect, there is no coverage. An occurrence policy, on the other hand, requires only that the injury occur within the policy period. So long as this requirement is met, it does not matter when the claim is reported so long as it is within a reasonable time after the pharmacist becomes aware of the claim or potential claim. The policy may specify, however, a set amount of time for "reasonable." Generally speaking, pharmacists should look for an occurrence policy.

The following claim was reported to Pharmacists Mutual Insurance Company in 1990 and illustrates the problem associated with a claims made policy. The claim also gives an example of a time when a pharmacist may want an individual professional liability policy even though the presumption is the employer's policy will usually protect the employed pharmacist. The names and other identifying information have been changed.

John had worked at the hospital for over five years when he became involved in a law suit. John was employed as the chief outpatient pharmacist in a medium-sized pharmacy in a large city. Although he did not realize it until the lawsuit was filed, when he reviewed the records John could not deny he had made a mistake when filling the prescription for a child. The prescription called for Dilantin Suspension® 30 mg per 5 cc. John had filled the prescription with Dilantin Suspension® 100 mg per 5 cc.

The hospital was sued as well as John. One year *after* the prescription was misfilled, and almost one year *before* the suit was filed, the hospital administration decided to save money by discontinuing its insurance coverage and "self-insuring." The hospital did not purchase "tail coverage" to extend the time within which a claim could be filed. Since the policy was a claims-made policy and since no claim had been made by the time the policy was nonrenewed, and no "tail coverage" was purchased, the policy no longer covered the claim. The hospital and John were "on their own."

It took almost a year from the time the suit was filed to reach serious negotiations. By that time the hospital had declared bankruptcy, which meant John was on his own. John's individual policy became primary when it was recognized that the hospital's self-insurance was unable to respond. The suit was settled entirely by John's individual professional policy.[7]

As claims against pharmacies and pharmacists increase, claims-made policies will become more commonplace. Eventually, occurrence policies for pharmacy professional liability may become as hard to find as they are now for physicians and attorneys. Currently, however, pharmacists and pharmacies have a choice. In most cases, the choice is simple—occurrence policies have the advantage.

CONCLUSION

Pharmacy is a profession, but it is also a business. This chapter has concentrated on the unique part of the business of pharmacy and, from the insurance perspective, the unique part of the risk—professional practice of pharmacy. Throughout most of modern history, the risk of providing insurance to pharmacies has been relatively low. As a result, most insurance companies writing commercial insurance policies have been willing to write policies on pharmacies and have actively solicited the business. Over the past few years the risks and the insurance companies' perception of the risks have increased. Many insurance companies who previously sought out this business now shy away from it.

There are many factors influencing the perception of pharmacy as a business moving from low to medium or even high risk. One factor is that there have been increased claims against pharmacists and pharmacies. It is true that the entire country has become more litigious, but this explains only a part of the increase in claims and lawsuits. Another factor is that pharmacy is changing dramatically from a business performing mechanical functions to a profession in which pharmacists are making decisions based upon their knowledge, experience, and training.

In 1985, the Indiana Appellate Court in the case of *Ingram v. Hooks Drug Stores*[8] dismissed a lawsuit that had been filed against a pharmacy for the employed pharmacist's failure to warn of side effects associated with a prescription drug dispensed by the pharmacy. The court concluded that pharmacists' only legal duty was to properly dispense a prescription order as written by the physician. After reviewing many cases from across the United States up to that time, the court concluded the following:

> The decision of weighing the benefits of a medication against potential dangers that are associated with it requires an individualized medical judgment. This individualized treatment is available in the context of a physician-patient relationship which has the benefits of medical history and extensive medical examinations. It is not present, however, in the context of a pharmacist filling a prescription for a retail customer. The injection of a third-party in the form of a pharmacist into the physician-patient relationship could undercut the effectiveness of the ongoing medical treatment. We perceive the better rule to be one which places the duty to warn of the hazards of the drug on the prescribing physician and requires of the pharmacist only that he include those warnings found in the prescription.

In the year the Indiana court made its decision in *Ingram v. Hooks*, it was in step with the majority of the jurisdictions in the country. Within one year, however, the liability picture for pharmacists had begun to change. In 1986, a Pennsylvania court[9] found pharmacists had a duty to detect a physician's error in dosage on the face of the prescription order and to warn the patient and/or physician of the potential error. In 1990, the Tennessee Appellate Court[10] overruled earlier precedent that a pharmacist could not be held liable for failure to warn a patient of hazards associated with a drug. The court said that pharmacists have a duty to conform to the standards of practice of their profession and that it was for a jury to decide in this case if this pharmacist had lived up to that standard. Specifically, in this case the jury could decide if the pharmacist had a legal duty to recognize the drug interaction and warn the patient and physician of the foreseeable potential harm.

Many other cases followed, expanding the legal duty of the pharmacist. By 1993 most states had enacted statutes or pharmacy regulations based upon the federal OBRA 90 law mandating that pharmacists had a duty to counsel patients and perform a perspective drug review on all prescription orders before they are dispensed. In 1994, the Indiana Supreme Court[11] revisited the appellate court's 1985 view of the duties of a pharmacist and, without overruling the *Ingram* case, held that a pharmacist's duty went beyond dispensing the prescription order correctly and could include a duty to monitor a patient's drug use and to warn the physician of abuse and the patient of potential harm.

Although the courts have not been uniform in their opinions,[12] the clear tendency has been to recognize that pharmacists can be sued for professional duties above those involving dispensing prescription orders exactly as written by what one court referred to as "the omnipotent physician."[13]

Pharmacies have at the same time begun providing new professional services to their patients, including diabetes and asthma management. Although many of these services, such as bone scanning, involve little actual risk, to the layman they appear to be "medical-like" and thus risky. Add to this expansion of services and legally recognized duties the press' sensationalized reports of pharmacy errors and the state laws requiring pharmacies to institute systems to reduce prescription errors, and insurance companies rising fears appear understandable. The profession of pharmacy, once viewed as a simple mechanical service, is beginning to seem as complicated to insurance professionals as the insurance policy seems to pharmacists.

To some extent, of course, the insurance companies' view of pharmacy, as a profession taking on increased risk of liability, is correct. For each new duty there is increased risk. But the increased liability currently being taken on by the profession is not unduly great. The risk of insuring a pharmacy is no longer comparable to the risk of insuring a grocery store, but neither is it the risk associated with medical malpractice.

Still, in terms of both numbers and dollars, claims against pharmacists are increasing. Pharmacists Mutual Insurance Company has noted this trend over the past few years. In addition, the Pharmacists Mutual Claims Study continues to show an increase in the relative number of drug review (allergies, interactions, overuse, etc.) claims since 1989. Still, according to the same Pharmacists Mutual Claims Study, mechanical errors account for over 80 percent of the claims against pharmacists and pharmacies.

Legally and professionally, pharmacy has changed dramatically in the past few years and it continues to change. It is not surprising that insurance companies have been unable to change their policies as quickly as pharmacists think they should. Relatively speaking, pharmacy is a small market for most large insurance companies. Recognizing this, it is up to pharmacists, pharmacy owners, and managers to review their insurance policies and to ask questions to assure they have adequate coverage. The first step in doing so is to read and study their policies. It is hoped that this review of the principles of insurance will help in that study.

NOTES

1. See 15 U.S.C. 41 *et seq.*

2. 15 U.S.C. §§ 1011 *et. seq.*

3. 15 U.S.C. § 1012 (b).

4. 15 U.S.C. § 1014: "Nothing contained in this chapter shall be construed to affect in any manner the application to the business of insurance of the Act of July 5, 1935, as amended, known as the National Labor Relations Act (29 U.S.C. 151 *et seq.*), or the Act of June 25, 1938, as amended, known as the Fair Labor Standards Act of 1938 (29 U.S.C. 201 *et seq.*), or the Act of June 5, 1920, known as the Merchant Marine Act, 1920 (46 App. U.S.C. 861 *et seq.*)."

5. 15 U.S.C. § 1013 (b).

6. ISO Insurance Policy, #GA 000,009 © 1988, p. 9.

7. Pharmacist Mutual claim code DMPHL-DD045-A.

8. *Ingram v. Hooks,* 476 NE2d 881 (Ind. App. 1985).

9. *Riff v. Morgan Pharmacy,* 508 A.2d 1247 (1986).

10. *Dooley v. Everett,* 805 Sw2d 380 (Tenn. App 1990).

11. *Hooks Superx v. McLaughlin,* 642 N.E.2d 514 (Ind. 1994).

12. Compare generally the differences in the decisions of *Horner v. Spalitto,* 1 S.W.3d 519 (Mo. Ct App. Western Dist. 1999); *Happel v. Wal-Mart Stores, Inc.,* 766 N.E.2d 1118 (Ill 2002); and *Cottam v. CVS Pharmacy,* 436 Mass. 316 (Mass. 2002).

13. *Riff v. Morgan Pharmacy,* 508 A.2d 1247 (1986).

Chapter 6

Patent Law, Trademarks, and Copyrights

Martha M. Rumore

Patents, copyrights, trademarks, and related interests are known as intellectual property. Trademarks, patents, and copyrights are independent rights, and one does not preclude the other. All these rights may apply to a single product.

Innovation cannot occur unless companies that succeed in the marketplace can recoup their research, development, and marketing costs. That is the major function of intellectual property (hereinafter IP). IP is increasingly seen as playing a key global role in developing technologies for the next century.

TRADE DRESS

Traditionally "trade dress" referred to the manner in which a product was "dressed up" to go to market. The meaning of trade dress has broadened to include a product's basic shape and design, as well as its packaging, i.e., the total image of a product or service. Thus, for example, the interior decor of a pharmacy as well as the container of a pharmaceutical product may be protected as trade dress. To show trade dress infringement, a demonstration of likelihood of confusion is required. The assessment of likelihood of confusion is heavily fact based. Thus, the determination of likelihood of confusion is termed a finding of fact, and the burden of proof rests with the asserting party.[1]

Special attention has been provided for pharmaceutical product trade dress, where confusion may lead to damage or loss of human life. Courts have generally accepted a lesser threshold of confusing similarity when dealing with pharmaceuticals.[2] However, recent case law points to a significant reduction in the scope of protection for trade dress. Particularly, color

Pharmacy Law Desk Reference
doi:10.1300/5790_06

and shape have recently been afforded a more relaxed standard of protectability with regard to pharmaceutical products. In *Bristol-Myers Squibb Co. v. McNeil-P.P.C. Inc.,* the Second Circuit considered an appeal from a district court order granting a preliminary injunction against McNeil's use of the packaging for Tylenol PM®, finding that the trade dress infringed the plaintiff's rights in its Excedrin PM® packaging.[3] The court reversed the lower court ruling and held that there was no likelihood of confusion, due to the prominence of the brand names on the packages.

Subsequent courts have broadly interpreted this case as providing a general "brand name" defense to a trade dress infringement action. For example, in *Pfizer Inc. v. Astra Pharmaceutical Products Inc.,* the presence of brand names was found to distinguish plaintiff's Procardia XL® from defendant's Toprol XL®.[4]

The scope of trade dress protection was narrowed even further in *Conopco, Inc. v. May Dept. Stores,* where the Federal Circuit held that there was no likelihood of confusion between plaintiff's Vaseline Intensive Care® lotion and the defendant's "private label" version of the lotion.[5] The Conopco opinion virtually entitles private labelers to mimic the trade dress of well-known brand name products.[6]

Similarly, in *American Home Products v. Barr Laboratories,*[7] the court found no likelihood of confusion between Advil® and a generic ibuprofen product where the generic intentionally copied Advil's brown color. However, in *Par Pharm. Inc. v. Searle Pharms., Inc.,*[8] the blue color of Searle Pharmaceutical's Flagyl® tablets was found protectable.

PATENTS

By statute, a patent confers upon the owner the right to exclude others from making, using, or selling the patented invention throughout the United States for a specific period of time. Patent law is codified under 35 U.S.C. § 1-280[9] and regulated by the Patent and Trademark Office (PTO) pursuant to Title 37, Code of Federal Regulations.

Patents offer the strongest possible protection; they are valid for twenty years from when an application is first filed and only in the country where issued. There are three broad types of patents: utility, process, and design. A new drug pioneer, under the broad class of utility patents, can patent the drug itself, the process by which it is made, and its use.

Patents became more valuable to U.S. pharmaceutical manufacturers within the past five years as a result of increased foreign competition and U.S. trade deficits. Pharmaceutical companies are litigating their patents more aggressively. Some hope to force competitors to pay royalties, while others hope to eliminate competitors from the market.

Further, one of the considerations in choosing a target drug for marketing is the patent landscape surrounding that drug. Patent protection for pharmaceuticals does not differ significantly from that of other nonpharmaceutical inventions, the exception being the granting of patent term extensions and other nonpatent, de facto monopolies relating to pharmaceuticals.[10]

Patents are granted for new, useful, and nonobvious inventions. To receive a patent the invention must meet at least those criteria. Conditions for patentability are found in Exhibit 6.1. It is important to note that the applicants' own publication and commercial activities can be a statutory bar under 35 U.S.C. § 102(b) if too much time is taken in preparing the patent application.

The patent owner is entitled to exclude others from practicing the invention for a term of twenty years from the date the patent is filed.[11] Unlike

EXHIBIT 6.1. PATENT LAW

Patent laws state that a person shall be entitled to a patent unless

- the invention was known or used by others in this country, or patented or described in a printed publication in this or a foreign country, before the invention thereof by the applicant for patent,[a] or
- the invention was patented or described in a printed publication in this or a foreign country or in public use or on sale in this country, more than one year prior to the date of the application for patent in the United States,[b] or
- he had abandoned the invention,[c] or
- the invention was first patented or caused to be patented, or was the subject of an inventor's certificate, by the applicant or his legal representatives or assigns in a foreign country,[d] or
- the invention was described in (1) an application for patent by another filed in the U.S. before the invention by the applicant for patent or (2) a patent granted on an application for another filed in the U.S. before the invention by the applicant for patent.[e]

[a]35 U.S.C. § 102(a).
[b]35 U.S.C. § 102(b).
[c]35 U.S.C. § 102(c).
[d]35 U.S.C. § 102(d).
[e]35 U.S.C. § 102(e).

other countries, the U.S. system is a first-to-invent system whereas most of the world uses a first-to-file system. Patent rights are federal. There is no state patent protection.

Requirements for Patenting

The patent itself must include a written description of the invention. The term "specification" technically includes all of the parts of the patent application that satisfy the requirements of 35 U.S.C. § 112, including the description of the invention and the claims.[12] The specification must be in such clear, concise, and exact terms as to enable any person skilled in the art to which it pertains to make and use the invention and shall set forth the best mode contemplated by the inventor of carrying out the invention.

In addition, a patent may not be obtained if the differences between the subject matter sought to be patented and the prior art are such that the subject matter as a whole would have been obvious at the time the invention was made to a person having ordinary skill in the art to which said subject matter pertains.[13]

Once a patent has been issued, periodic maintenance fees must be paid to the PTO in order to maintain the patent in force. Maintenance fees are due at each of three-, seven-, and eleven-year anniversary dates from the date of issue of the patent.

Pharmaceutical patents may be obtained for the compound itself, intermediates, pharmacological effect (e.g., analgesic), dosage form, process of manufacture, and method of using. For example, dosage forms (e.g., sustained release) are patentable provided they contain an unobvious concentration of the "old" active ingredient and/or are combined with an unobvious ingredient or ingredients.[14]

An example of a dosage form patent claim appears in U.S. Patent No. 6,485,745, assigned to Novartis. Claim 1 of this patent reads as follows:

> A compressed solid dosage form comprising: (a) an active agent comprising an effective amount of valsartan or a pharmaceutically acceptable salt thereof; and, (b) at least one pharmaceutically acceptable additive; wherein the active agent is present in an amount of more than 35% by weight bases on the total weight of the compressed solid dosage form and wherein said dosage form exhibits accelerated release of the active agent.

An example of a method of making or process claim appears in U.S. Patent No. 5,776,495, assigned to Effik Laboratories. Claim 1 of this patent reads as follows:

A process for the production of a solid dispersion of 1 to 20% by weight of a surface active agent, 10 to 60% by weight of at least one therapeutic agent selected form the group consisting of progesterone and a mixture of progesterone and estradiol or an ester or ether thereof in a hydrophilic carrier having enhanced solubility in an aqueous media comprising dissolving the therapeutic agent in a volatile organic solvent containing a very hydrophilic polymer and without strong heat or vacuum evaporating the solvent to dryness to form a co-precipitate of therapeutic agent and hydrophilic binder.

Patents and Hatch-Waxman Amendments

The Drug Price Competition and Patent Term Restoration Act of 1984, known as the Hatch-Waxman Act, provides patent term extensions to compensate for the drug approval lag. Title I specifically authorizes Abbreviated New Drug Applications (ANDAs) under section 505(j) and section 505(b)(2) applications.[15] This section also provides for exclusivity. A generic drug receives 180 days of exclusivity if it is the first to file a complete ANDA containing a Paragraph IV certification, during which time no other generic companies may enter the market.[16]

Title II, the patent term restoration part of Hatch-Waxman, is extremely important to brand manufacturers because the patent usually issues long before clinical trials begin on the compound, and in the United States the twenty-year patent term runs from the time of filing the patent. A pioneer receives a patent extension term equal to half of the time of the IND period (time from IND approval through NDA submission) plus the time for NDA review.[17]

Patent term extension under Hatch-Waxman may not be based on a combination of active ingredients where the individual active ingredients have already been separately approved for marketing.[18] In *Arnold Partnership v. Rogan,* the court upheld the PTO refusal to extend a drug patent for the combination of the cough suppressant hydrocodone and the pain reliever ibuprofen.[19] Therefore, whereas the focus of the FDA approval process is the drug claimed by the patent as whole, the *Arnold* court explained that the focus of the patent extension statute is the active ingredient of that drug, whether as a single entity or in combination with another active ingredient.

A pharmaceutical manufacturer may, however, apply for a new patent on the unique combination claiming a novel pharmaceutical composition or method of making dosage forms with the unique combination. In general, the patent term for combination drug patents is extended only if one of the active ingredients has not been previously approved by the FDA.

New uses for old drugs may be patentable where the new use is not obvious. This is referred to commonly as "evergreening," i.e., the practice of using patents to block competition by discovering new uses for old drugs. A classic example of "evergreening" occurred with Epogen®, where the drug was actually approved as an orphan product with a very limited indication, and now enjoys many indications and is considered a blockbuster drug. A more limited type of evergreening is where a pharmaceutical manufacturer looks for new indications in different patient populations, e.g., pediatric patients. However, under Hatch-Waxman, patent term extensions are not granted for new uses or dosage forms of previously approved drugs.

The FDA allows innovator companies to list patents in the Orange Book without oversight. Consequently, a strategy pioneer pharmaceutical companies use to delay generic drug approval is to bootstrap some claims that do not involve the drugs themselves in the Orange Book. The NDA holder may list multiple patents that claim the approved drug or an approved method of using the drug product. Each may have a different expiration date and offer its own unique protection to the NDA product.[20] Subsequantly, all a patent holder needs to do is to tinker with a drug product formulation just enough to obtain a new patent, which is then listed in the Orange Book.[21]

Also pursuant to the Hatch-Waxman Amendments, the first company to file an Abbreviated New Drug Application with the FDA has the exclusive right to market the generic drug for 180 days. No other generic can gain FDA approval until this 180-day period expires. The purpose of the exclusivity period is to encourage generic entry.

Patents for drugs approved under 21 U.S.C. § 355 (c) must be listed in the FDA's Approved Drug Products with Therapeutic Equivalence Evaluations (commonly known as the "Orange Book").[22] The Orange Book is meant to provide generic manufacturers with a convenient tool to monitor drug patents covering brand-name drug products while, simultaneously, giving "NDA holders" the opportunity to obtain an automatic suspension of FDA approval for any ANDA that the NDA holder believes infringes on one of the Orange Book–listed patents. The FDA conducts only a brief review of the patents submitted. The Orange Book is meant to list patents only for active ingredients in the brand-name drug product and subject matter concerning the same (e.g., physical/chemical form), as well as the drug delivery system (e.g., formulation), but is not meant to encompass patents directed to the process of preparation of the brand-name product.

Typically the generic manufacturer files what is known as a Paragraph IV certification, alleging that the patent is invalid, is not infringed, or both. Once the innovator timely (i.e., forty-five days from notice of filing of Paragraph IV certification) files a patent infringement suit with respect to an Orange Book–listed patent which is the subject of a Paragraph IV certification, the act does not allow FDA to approve any generic equivalents for thirty months, or earlier upon a ruling in favor of the ANDA applicant from a U.S. federal district court.[23]

A firm understanding of the ramifications of patents listed in the Orange Book is particularly important to the generic manufacturer. The Orange Book–listed patent must be carefully reviewed first with respect to its claims to ensure that the proposed ANDA product active ingredient and/or formulation under consideration for development does not fall within the scope of its claims. A careful review of the patent claims, and an understanding of the limitations in those claims, including a thorough analysis of claim interpretation (e.g., a consideration of the meaning of terms in the claims in view of the specification and file history and prior art estoppels to the extent they exist) may be crucial to the determination of whether a proposed ANDA product could be considered to fall within the claims of an Orange Book–listed patent, or whether the NDA holder/patent owner can construe one or more patent claims in an Orange Book–listed patent to encompass the proposed drug product.

In any event, an early consideration of these issues by patent counsel and a thorough evaluation of such issues via a combined effort of different departments of the generic company (formulation, clinical, regulatory, marketing, and legal), prior to arriving at a final dosage form, may lead to the development of a product that stands a better chance of avoiding a colorable claim of infringement of a listed patent. This process, known as patent clearance, includes a consideration of patents in addition to those listed in the Orange Book, such as synthesis patents or patents for the process for manufacture of the formulation. Such patents should not be properly listed in the Orange Book, yet they may still be pertinent to a proposed ANDA product.

Patent clearance with respect to all existing U.S. patents is an important undertaking with respect to developing an ANDA product and should be an early consideration of the generic manufacturer, preferably prior to final selection of a drug delivery system and optimization of a proposed dosage form.

The U.S. PTO offers free online searching of patents (full text since 1976, full-page images since 1790). Other patent offices of the world offer patent searching capabilities online, including the United Kingdom (www.patent.gov.uk), Germany (www.dpma.de/suche/suche.html), Japan (www.ipdl.jpo-miti.go.jp/homepge.idpl), Australia (ipaustralia.gov.au), and Canada (patentsl.ic.gc.ca/intro-e.html). Commercial databases, which include Questal, (www.qpat.com), Derwent (www.dialog.com), Micropatent (www.micropatent.com), and Nerac (www.nerac.com), are also useful for full-text worldwide searching.

Once a search is completed, "designing around existing patents" would include addressing any patent issues that may arise based on the results of the patent searches for the active ingredient, the physical/chemical factors of the active ingredient, the formulation of the product, process for making the active ingredient, and, possibly, methods of treatment.

As a consequence of the provisions of the Hatch-Waxman Amendments, many low-cost generics have been marketed upon expiration of the patent on brand name drugs.[24] In addition, as provided in the reversal of *Roche v. Bolar*,[25] generic manufacturers obtained the right to test patented drugs prior to expiration of the patent. However, according to the Federal Trade Commission (hereinafter FTC), two specific provisions of Hatch-Waxman have been subject to abuse by companies attempting to delay generic competition: the automatic 30-month stay of generic drug approval pending patent challenges, and the 180-day market exclusivity for the first generic drug applicant. For example, one brand company delayed generic competition on a cancer drug by filing a patent on the brown bottle that it came in. In other cases brand companies are settling lawsuits by paying generic companies millions in return for keeping the generic equivalent off the market.[26] These "reverse licensing" payments from the brand to the generic not to market the generic version delays the initiation of the 180-day period. If the 180-day exclusivity period never begins, other generic companies cannot enter the market, thereby giving an indefinite patent term to the pioneer drug. There is also a trend toward "authorized generics" just prior to the 180-day exclusivity period, essentially trumping the 180-day exclusivity. Brand companies via licensing or patent settlement agreements are specifically authorizing generic versions of their drugs to come to market.

The current method of choice for extending exclusivity is adding new patents to the Orange Book shortly before the other listed patents are about to expire. Some common types of patents which may be issued after FDA approval are those for revised formulations, new uses, new crystalline forms, metabolites, or intermediates of the active ingredient. Obviously, the greater the number of Orange Book patents listed, the greater the hurdle for the ANDA applicant. The ANDA applicant must provide certifications to all listed patents that claim rights to the drug. The ANDA applicant who then files a Paragraph IV certification to this new patent will, in all likelihood, be sued for patent infringement. The pioneer company will be entitled to another thirty-month stay. By adding new patents to the Orange Book at the "right" time, pioneer companies were enjoying multiple thirty-month stays. The result was a de facto extension on the length of the patent term.

This frivolous listing of patents with multiple thirty-month stays was becoming a major barrier to generic drug entry. Since 1998 infringement suits have involved more patents per ANDA, resulting in multiple thirty-month stays. In 2002, the Federal Trade Commission issued a report citing some concerns it had about the brand industry attempting to extend patents on products.[27] According to the FTC study, there were cases involving several brand-name drugs between 1994 and 2000 in which repeated thirty-month stays delayed access to generic drugs.[28]

The pharmaceutical patent endgame has dramatically changed because of two legislative/regulatory changes. The first is FDA's Final Rule which went into effect on August 18, 2003, and curtailed the ability of brand names to extend patent life and has quickened the pace of entry of generic pharmaceuticals into the marketplace.[29] The second legislative change is the Medicare Prescription Drug Improvement and Modernization Act (MPDIMA) of 2003[30] in which provisions were also enacted closely mirroring the FDA's Final Rule and providing greater access to generic drugs.[31] The effect is strict limits on the thirty-month stay and clarification on the types of drug patents that can be listed in the Orange Book.

Under the new rule, brand manufacturers will no longer be able to receive multiple thirty-month stays on the consideration of ANDAs while possible patent infringements are investigated. Only one thirty-month stay is permitted for each ANDA or 505(b)(2) application. Before this, an NDA holder could obtain multiple thirty-month stays by listing additional patents after the first stay had been triggered. The new rule eliminates the potential for "stacked" thirty-month stays delaying generic entry.

MPDIMA modifies the notice provision requirement for ANDA applicants. Under the changes an ANDA applicant who is amending an ANDA to include a new Paragraph IV certification must only notify the patent holder and NDA holder only if the original ANDA did not previously include a Paragraph IV certification. If no notice is given, no additional stays on the ANDA can be asserted. Further, subsequent Paragraph IV certifications no longer trigger a new forty-five-day period within which the NDA holder may file suit.

The new rule eliminates a portion of the notice requirement required by the ANDA applicant and sets time limits for other portions.[32] Notice must be provided by generic applicants to NDA holders (1) if the Paragraph IV certification is in an ANDA, within 20 days of receiving notice from the FDA that the ANDA has been filed, or (2) if the Paragraph IV certification is in an amendment or supplement to the ANDA, at such time the amendment or supplement is filed.[33] However, to resolve infringement disputes prior to marketing, the ANDA applicant may voluntarily notify the NDA holder.*

---

*This would be prudent because a generic firm would be unwilling to enter the market while the patent situation is in flux because of the large damage exposure.

The NDA holder can then file a patent infringement suit at any time, but such suits will not result in a thirty-month stay of FDA approval.[34] For example, Aventis recently filed suit against five generic companies for infringing Orange Book method-of-use patents on the antihistamine Allegra® (fexofenadine). Five additional lawsuits were filed against the same five generic companies for infringement of non–Orange Book patents claiming fexofenadine intermediates and processes of making fexofenadine.[35]

The thirty-month stay is available only for patents listed by the innovator before the filing date of the ANDA. When a patent is listed after the filing of an ANDA but before approval of the ANDA, the thirty-month stay provisions will be triggered if the ANDA applicant has amended the ANDA to include the certification, before the date that the application is determined to be substantially complete.

The Final Rule and Medicare Amendments clarify FDA's new vision of the types of patents that should—and should not—be submitted for listing in the Orange Book. With the amendments the only patents that are currently permitted in the Orange Book are patents claiming either the "drug substance" (active ingredient) of the drug that is the subject of the NDA; patents claiming the "drug product" (formulation and composition) that is the subject of the NDA; product-by-process patents where claim is made to a drug that is made by a particular process; and method-of-use patents. Product-by-process patents are required to be listed only if the product can be identified as novel.*

Previously, an NDA applicant would merely file a declaration statement that the patent covers either the formulation, composition, or method of use.[36] This has now been replaced with a multipage "checklist"-type declaration form which requires identification of the relevant patent claims.†

The NDA holder must now submit information on each patent that claims the drug product (active ingredient) (including polymorphs), drug substance (formulation/composition), or a method of using the drug that is the subject of the NDA, amendment, or supplement and with respect to which a claim of patent infringement could be asserted. That is, patents having claims to methods of using that are not in the labeling must not be listed. To safeguard against listing inappropriately, the specific method-of-use claims and the labeling language related to that claim must be identified in the declaration forms. In addition, the Medicare Prescription Drug Im-

---

*Product-by-process patents claim a product by describing or listing process steps to wholly or partially define the claimed product. The patented, novel invention is the product and not the process that is used to make the product.

†False statements regarding the patents submitted to FDA could lead to criminal charges.

provement and Modernization Act of 2003 permits the applicant to counter-claim for an order requiring the patent holder to "correct or delete" the patent information submitted by the holder. The ANDA applicant may seek a delisting order "on the ground that the patent does not claim either: the drug for which the application was approved, or an approved method of using the drug."

A major change is that polymorph patents must now be listed. Specifically, if a patent claims a polymorph of the active ingredient in the drug product that is the subject of an NDA, and that polymorph is demonstrated to be the "same" as that active ingredient, the patent should be listed. However, the FDA final rule requires that the polymorph form claimed by the patent submitted for listing satisfy specific testing that demonstrates "sameness," particularly with respect to dissolution, solubility, and bioavailability. What effect does Orange Book listing of polymorph patents have? Possibly it makes it more difficult for generic companies to design around existing patents.

Process patents, i.e., those that claim the process used in manufacture of the drug product, packaging patents, metabolite patents, and patents claiming intermediates are not listable in the Orange Book.* According to the FDA rule, "Because metabolites exist only after the approved drug has been broken down inside the body, a patent claiming a metabolite does not claim the approved drug." The only circumstances where a metabolite-related patent may be listed is when it is in a method-of-use patent.[†]

Another change is that the Medicare Rx Drug Improvement Act permits the ANDA applicant to file suit for declaratory judgement if (1) the forty-five-day period has expired without the patent owner suing for infringement of the patent for which it has received notice of a Paragraph IV certification; and (2) if the Paragraph IV certification asserts noninfringement, the notice must include an offer of confidential access to the ANDA for the purpose of determining whether an action for infringement should be filed. A declaratory judgment sought is that the patent is invalid or will not be infringed. The purpose of the new language regarding declaratory judgments is to permit a generic company to get an early ruling on the validity of the branded company's patent. A second purpose was to allay concerns about the constitutionality of those provisions.[37]

---

*The rationale for not listing intermediates is that intermediates are in-process materials and, therefore, are not present in the finished drug product. In addition, for packaging, the exception is that patents claiming a container that is an integral part of the dosage form (e.g., prefilled drug delivery systems) should be listed.

[†]A metabolite patent would be listable if it meets all the requirements and claims an approved method of using an approved drug to administer a metabolite.

The new legislation also makes refinements to the provisions relating to the 180-day exclusivity period. Specifically, multiple companies are now eligible to qualify for the 180-day exclusivity if they all file their application on the first day of eligibility. "Shared exclusivity" refers to FDA awarding marketing approval, and the accompanying 180 days of exclusive generic marketing rights, to more than one manufacturer of a generic drug. Shared exclusivity encourages more manufacturers to develop generic drugs earlier, thus encouraging competition and providing earlier patent access. Previously, when different generic applicants had valid exclusivity claims on different patents for the same product, these competing claims for exclusivity would block one another so that no application could be approved.[38]

FDA's Final Rule and the Medicare Amendments to the Hatch-Waxman Act will have far-reaching effects on patenting of pharmaceuticals. It remains to be seen whether these changes will accelerate generic drug entry while preserving innovation in the U.S. pharmaceutical industry.

Pediatric and Orphan Drug Exclusivity

Section 111 of the Food and Drug Administration Modernization Act, "Pediatric Studies of Drugs," amended the FDCA to add section 505A. This section provides an additional six months of patent and nonpatent market exclusivity to pharmaceutical manufacturers that conduct acceptable studies in pediatric patients.*

In addition, the Orphan Drug Act of 1983, as amended, created a mechanism that awards seven years of exclusivity to pharmaceutical companies that obtain approval for drugs for rare diseases or conditions.

Anticompetitive Practices

On a global scale certain practices are allowed in an effort to prevent patent owners from abusing IP rights, "unreasonably" restraining trade, or hampering the international transfer of technology. Compulsory licensing is when a government allows someone else to produce a patented product or process without the consent of the patent owner. This is usually associated with pharmaceuticals.

Under the TRIPS Agreement, the phrase "other use without authorization of the right holder" appears and is tantamount to allowing compulsory

---

*These incentives were recently renewed in the 2002 Best Pharmaceuticals for Children Act.

licensing.[39] However, the agreement specifically lists the circumstances under which compulsory licensing in violation of patent rights might be justified.

Another anticompetitive practice occurs with parallel imports. Parallel or gray-market imports are not imports of counterfeit products or illegal copies. These are products made and marketed by the patent owner in one country and imported into another country without the approval of the patent holder. For example, suppose a company has patented a drug, which it makes in the United States and Argentina, but sells at a lower price in Argentina. If a second company buys the drug in Argentina at a price that is lower than the first company's price and imports it into the United States at a price that is lower than the first company's price, that would be a parallel or gray import.

Patent Validity

During the patent examination process, it may become apparent that one or more other patent applications currently being considered make similar or identical claims. An interference proceeding will then be commenced by the PTO with the objective of determining which applicant first conceived and reduced the patent to practice.

A U.S. patent is presumed to be valid.[40] Each claim stands alone as its own definition of the invention, and a presumption of validity attaches to each claim independent of the validity or invalidity of other claims.[41] The presumption of validity "places the burden of proof of facts, and the ultimate burden of persuasion to establish invalidity" on the challenger.[42] Patent invalidity may be asserted when prior art surfaces that challenges the validity of a patent on the grounds of novelty or obviousness. In general, a party challenging the validity of a patent must establish its invalidity by clear and convincing evidence.[43] Patent invalidity may be predicated on §102, §103, fraud, or inequitable conduct.

Under 35 U.S.C. §102, a claim is anticipated, and therefore invalid, when a single prior art reference discloses each and every element of the claimed invention.[44] If the reference fails to suggest even one limitation of the claimed invention, then the claim is not anticipated.[45]

Invalidity may also be predicated on a public use bar. In addition to prior art references as a basis of anticipation, nondocumentary activity may anticipate an asserted patent if that activity occurred more than one year before the patent was filed in the United States.[46] Under the public use bar, the Federal Circuit has defined "public use" as including "any commercial use of the claimed invention by a person other than the inventor who is under no limitation, restriction or obligation of secrecy to the inventor."[47] The question of public use requires an examination of whether any public use has ever occurred, no matter the frequency, and whether the public use can be corroborated.

Patent invalidity may also be predicated on the on-sale bar. As with the public use bar, the on-sale bar will invalidate an asserted issued patent if anticipatory activity occurred more than one year prior to the asserted patent's filing date.[48] Section 102(b) on-sale validity challenges are based on sale of the invention by the inventor or anyone else in the United States more than one year before the effective filing date of the inventor's U.S. patent application. An invention is on-sale when two conditions occur before the critical date: (1) the product must be subject to a commercial sale or offer for sale and (2) the invention must be ready for patenting.[49] Just as with a pubic use bar, on-sale activity must be corroborated. However, public use/on-sale art is difficult to find outside of litigation context.

Patent invalidity may be predicated on §103, i.e., obviousness. Obviousness under 35 U.S.C. §103 requires a determination of (a) the scope and content of the prior art; (b) the differences between the prior art and the claimed invention; (c) the level of ordinary skill in the art; and (d) the objective secondary indicia of obviousness.[50]

Under 35 U.S.C. §103, the subject matter of a claim is considered obvious, and therefore invalid, when the claimed "subject matter as a whole would have been obvious at the time the invention was made to a person having ordinary skill in the art to which said subject matter pertains." The teachings of more than one reference may be considered in combination, but only when there is some teaching or suggestion to support their use in combination.[51]

In order to invalidate a patent under 35U.S.C. §103 using a combination of prior art, there must be some reason, suggestion, or motivation found in the prior art whereby a person of ordinary skill would make the combination.[52] However, it is not necessary that the prior art specifically suggest making the combination. Such suggestion or motivation to combine prior art teachings can derive solely from the existence of a teaching, which one of ordinary skill in the art would be presumed to know, and the use of that teaching to solve the same or similar problem that it addresses.[53]

Patent invalidity can be predicated on fraud or inequitable conduct. Section 156(a) of the C.F.R. provides in pertinent part that "[e]ach individual associated with the filing and prosecution of a patent application has a duty of candor and good faith" when dealing with the Patent and Trademark Office. This duty is violated when any such individual affirmatively misrepresents a material fact, fails to disclose material information, or submits false information with an intent to deceive the Patent and Trademark Office.[54]

Fraud and inequitable conduct must be proved by clear, unequivocal, and convincing evidence with a heavy burden of persuasion on the accuser. In *Glaxo, Inc. v. Novopharm Ltd.,*[55] the Federal Circuit held that a defense of inequitable conduct may be established by clear and convincing evidence that (1) the patentee misrepresented facts to the Patent and Trademark Office; (2) the misrepresentation was material; and (3) the patentee acted with intent to deceive the Patent and Trademark Office. Where the level of materiality is high, intent may be inferred.[56]

Under 37 C.F.R. §1.56(b), information is "material" when it is not cumulative to information already of record or being made of record in the application, and (1) [I]t establishes, by itself or in combination with other information a prima facie case of unpatentability of a claim; or (2) [i]t refutes, or is inconsistent with, a position the applicant takes in: (i) [o]pposing an argument of unpatentability relied on by the [Patent] Office, or (ii) [a]sserting an argument of unpatentability." Depending on the nature, relevance, and materiality of the prior art found, the patent may be found unenforceable due to "inequitable conduct" for failing to disclose this art to the Patent and Trademark Office.

TRADEMARKS

The key statute concerning trademarks is the Lanham Act.[57] The term *trademark* includes any word, name, symbol, or device or any combination thereof

1. used by a person or
2. which a person has a bona fide intention to use in commerce and applies to register on the principal established by this Act, to identify and distinguish his or her goods, including a unique product, from those manufactured or sold by others and to indicate the source of the goods, even if that source is unknown.[58]

A trademark must be distinctive to serve its identification function. Marks are typically classified as (1) arbitrary or fanciful, (2) suggestive, (3) descriptive, or (4) generic.

A common synonym for "trademark" is a brand name. Trademarks identify the product as coming from a particular company. The distinction between trademarks and trade names is that the former identifies products whereas the later identifies businesses.

A dosage form shape or color can be a trademark. Color alone may be protected as a trademark or trade dress as described previously, even if the color is not part of an otherwise separable symbol or logo. The Lanham Act prevents others from replicating that color on the product or packaging if such use is likely to cause confusion. If the color is functional, that is, if it serves as a necessary element in the use of the product (utilitarian functionality) or is aesthetically pleasing (aesthetic functionality), then it may not be trademarked. The rationale behind the functionality doctrine is to prevent a color from being monopolized by a single company.

In *Norwich Pharmacal Co. v. Sterling Drug, Inc.*, the court referred to the pink color of Pepto-Bismol.[59] Colors for pharmaceutical capsules have been found to be nonfunctional.[60]

Trademarks As Property

Rights in a trademark generally arise automatically upon its first commercial use and have potentially unlimited duration. Although federal registration confers advantages, marks need not be registered. Common law rights may prevent others from using similar marks when consumers may be deceived as to source or sponsorship of goods or services. As a property right, a trademark exists only in connection with its associated product. A trademark cannot validly be transferred apart from the goodwill it symbolizes.[61]

Trademark Infringement

Trademark infringement is a type of unfair competition.[62] Litigation is prevented when the PTO finds that the goods are related and refuses registration. For pharmaceuticals, a doctrine generally referred to as "the doctrine of greater care" has been applied. This doctrine states that because drugs are potentially harmful to the prospective purchaser, a higher standard should be applied to medicinal products, thus lowering the threshold of finding a likelihood of confusion.[63]

For OTCs, private-label or store-brand, courts have interpreted the purposeful use of features borrowed from the national brands as a form of intentional copying under the trademark and unfair competition laws. This is true when the private-label company copies more than one important element of the national-brand packaging.[64]

In *Pfizer v. Perrigo Co.*,[65] the patentee brought a patent infringement and unfair trade practice action against Perrigo, parent company of several wholly owned subsidiaries. These subsidiaries manufacture and distribute

OTC pharmaceuticals to retail chains who in turn sell the products under the stores' brand names. Perrigo claimed it was simply a holding company and did not transact business anywhere, and as such the exercise of personal jurisdiction over it offended the Due Process Clause of the Fourteenth Amendment. The court found minimum contacts with the forum state and that the company had purposely availed itself to same.[66]

In *Hoffman-La-Roche, Inc. v. Medisca, Inc.*,[67] Roche filed a trademark infringement suit against Medisca for selling bulk ceftriaxone for use in compounding, claiming source confusion under the false designation section of the Lanham Act.[68] The defendants asserted that ceftriaxone is a generic mark because it is the common name that describes the chemical substance at issue. Roche's position was that even a generic mark is entitled to Lanham Act protection if a competitor uses it in a manner that engenders source confusion. The court held for Medisca, referring to the compounding exception under the FDC Act and sales of the product limited to compounding.

Trademark Dilution

In 1996, the United States enacted the Federal Trademark Dilution Act.[69] Unlike infringement actions, a dilution action does not focus on consumer confusion but is premised on conduct that weakens the distinctiveness or the good will associated with a mark.* Dilution pertains to highly distinctive, well-known trademarks.

There are three branches of dilution relief: (1) diminution in the uniqueness of the plaintiff's mark; (2) tarnishing of the mark; and (3) use of the mark in a manner that causes a likelihood of consumer confusion about the source, sponsorship, or affiliation of goods, services, or business.

Diminution of the uniqueness of the plaintiff's mark occurs when the plaintiff has a very strong mark, which the public closely associates with the plaintiff as a business or as a source of a particular type of good or service. The defendant uses the same or a similar mark on dissimilar goods or services. Here, the defendant's use whittles away or dilutes the strong association consumers have between the mark or trade name and the plaintiff.

Tarnishment occurs when the defendant's use of a similar mark casts the plaintiff's distinctive, well-known mark or trade name in a bad light and thus "tarnishes" the plaintiff's commercial image or reputation.

---

*In view of the lack of uniform definition of dilution and the fact that not all states have dilution statutes, the Federal Trademark Dilution Act provides uniform nationwide protection for famous marks.

NONPATENT PROTECTION

Trade Secrets

Some inventions can be commercially exploited while being kept secret. For example, a product may not reveal a chemical process that is used to make the product. A trade secret may consist of any formula, pattern, device, or compilation of information which is used in one's business, and which gives one an opportunity to obtain an advantage over competitors who do not know or use it.[70]

Trade Secret Protection

Trade secret protection protects works that can be and are kept secret. Trade secrets are governed by the Uniform Trade Secrets Act.[71] Trade secrets are difficult to keep, and anyone who learns a trade secret without wrongdoing (as by independent reverse engineering, discovery, or analysis) is legally free to use the knowledge.[72] Maintaining secrecy is often expensive; for some works it is impossible. Yet secrecy is an important option. In the case of, e.g., manufacturing processes, patent infringement may be impossible to detect and secrecy is not only possible but also may be preferred.

The PTO will accept and preserve for a limited time an informal description on an invention known as a "Disclosure Document." However, this document does not provide any form of legal representation.

In *Glaxo v. Novopharm,*[73] the brand manufacturer alleged that exhibits introduced at a previous patent infringement trial concerning the choice of solvent system, pH, temperature, and seeding were trade secrets. The court maintained if the manner of practicing the invention is a trade secret, then a disclosure sufficient to obtain a patent has not been made. Conversely, the owner of a valid patent will have disclosed the best method of practicing the invention, and thus no longer possess a valuable trade secret relating to the practice of the invention unless he or she later develops some unanticipated alternative practice.

In *Merck & Co. v. SmithKline Beecham Pharms. Co.,*[74] the court ruled a combination of known matters can be protectable so long as it is combined in a unique process not known to the industry. In *Merck v. SmithKline,* trade secret protection was given where it was established that the defendant had derived at least two steps of its fourteen-step process from the process that the plaintiff, as an exclusive licensee, sued upon.[75]

COPYRIGHT

A copyright is a property right in an original work of authorship that is fixed in tangible form.* Works of authorship under copyright are found in Exhibit 6.2. The current copyright law is codified at 17 U.S.C.A. § 101 et seq. The U.S. Copyright Act of 1976 (the "Copyright Act") provides protection to "original works of authorship," including "pictorial, graphic and sculptural works," such as fine, graphic, and applied art, photographs, prints and art reproductions, maps, globes, charts, diagrams, and models.[76]

A work of authorship must be "original" in order to qualify for copyright protection. This requirement has two facets: first, the author must have engaged in some intellectual endeavor of his or her own, and not just have copied from a preexisting source, Second, the work must exhibit a minimal amount of creativity.

Ownership of copyright usually rests with the author at the time the work is created. The exception is a "work made for hire," i.e., "a work prepared by an employee within the scope of the employment relationship, or is a work specially ordered or commissioned for use as a contribution to a collective work, as part of a motion picture or other audiovisual work, as a

---

*The actual definition under 17 U.S.C. § 102 states: (a) copyright protection subsists in original works of authorship fixed in any tangible medium of expression, now known or later developed, from which they can be perceived, reproduced, or otherwise communicated, either directly or with the aid of a machine or device. (b) In no case does copyright protection for an original work of authorship extend to any idea, procedure, process, system, method of operation, concept, principle, or discovery, regardless of the form in which it is described, explained, illustrated, or embodied in such work.

EXHIBIT 6.2. WORKS OF AUTHORSHIP

Under 17 U.S.C. § 102 works of authorship include the following categories:

- Literary works
- Musical works, including any accompanying words
- Dramatic works, including any accompanying music
- Pantomimes and choreographic works
- Pictorial, graphic, and sculptural works
- Motion pictures and other audiovisual works
- Sound recordings
- Architectural works

translation, as a supplementary work, as a compilation, as an instructional text, as a test, as an answer material for a test, or as an atlas, if the parties expressly agree in a written instrument signed by them that the work shall be a work made for hire."[77]

The owner of a copyright has the exclusive right to reproduce the copyrighted work, to prepare derivative works from it, to distribute it, and to perform or display the copyrighted work publicly.[78] Copyrights, like patents, are exclusively governed by federal statute. There is no state copyright protection. Copyrights may last to seventy years beyond an author's lifetime and are much more easily and inexpensively obtained.

Certain things are not entitled to copyright protection. These include "any idea, procedure, process, system, method of operation, concept, principle, or discovery, regardless of the form in which it is described, explained, illustrated, or embodied." This means that an idea may not be protected by copyright, although the author's particular expression of that idea may be protected.[79]

Current copyright law denies protection to compilations of facts unless such facts are arranged or organized with some minimal element of originality. Even then, it is the creative aspect of such arrangements or organization that may be protected and not the underlying facts themselves.[80] Legislation has been repeatedly introduced, advocated primarily by large database companies, aimed at codifying into law a new sui generis form of intellectual property protection for databases.

Copyright Infringement

Copyright infringement requires a showing of copying, which can be proven circumstantially by demonstrating that the defendant had access to the copyrighted work and that the defendant's work is substantially similar to that work.[81]

The copyright owner is entitled to a variety of remedies if there is an infringement, which include damages, attorney fees and costs, injunctions, and impounding and disposition of infringing articles. Criminal penalties are also available. Registration is unnecessary for copyright protection, but infringement actions cannot be brought by owners of works originating in the United States until registration is at least attempted. Failure to register unpublished works forfeits statutory damages and attorney fees for infringement commenced before registration. For published works registered within three months of publication, those remedies are available even for infringement commenced earlier.

Under certain circumstances, actions that would otherwise be considered copyright infringement are permitted as "fair use" of a copyrighted work. Copyright law provides that "the fair use" of a copyrighted work, including such use by reproduction in copies or by any other means…for purposes of criticism, comment, news reporting, teaching, scholarship, or research, is not an infringement of copyright.

Intellectual property provides important incentives for biomedical innovation. A large proportion of the patents annually granted in the world relate to pharmaceutical products and processes. However, the intellectual property landscape has become more complex, with more patents per innovation and more patenting for upstream inventions (e.g., targets for drug intervention). Intellectual property protection provides social and technological benefits in encouraging investors and creators, thereby encouraging new drug development and bringing social benefits.

NOTES

1. Robert C. Dorr and Christopher H. Munch, *Trade Dress Law,* Second Edition (New York: Aspen Law & Business, 1999) §2.03[C].

2. See generally *Ciba-Geigy Corp. v. Bolar Pharm. Co.,* 747 F.2d 844 (3d Cir. 1984).

3. 973 F.2d 1033, 24 U.S.P.Q.2d 1161 (2nd Cir. 1992).

4. 858 F. Supp. 1305, 33 U.S.P.Q.2d 1545 (1994).

5. 46 F.3d 1556, 32 U.S.P.Q.2d 1225 (Fed. Cir. 1994), *cert. denied,* 514 U.S. 1078, 1155 S. Ct. 1724 (1995).

6. Glenn Mitchell, Steven Wadyka, Hara Jacobs, and Melissa Lee, *U.S. Trade Dress Law* (International Trademark Association, 2002), pp. 143, 150-151.

7. 656 F. Supp. 1058 (1987), *aff'd* 834 F.2d 368 (3d Cir. 1987).

8. 227 U.S.P.Q. (BNA) 1024, 1028 (N.D. Ill. 1985).

9. 35 U.S.C. §1-280 (1982). Under §101, "Whoever invents or discovers any new and useful process, machine, manufacture, or composition of matter, or any new and useful improvement thereof, may obtain a patent therefore, subject to the conditions and requirements of this title." Case law and legal commentaries have dissected and defined the aforementioned section so that it may properly be used as a guide by which litigants may sue.

10. Jerome Rosenstock, *The Law of Chemical and Pharmaceutical Invention* (Frederick, MD: Aspen Law & Business, 2003), pp. 2-8.

11. 35 U.S.C. §173.

12. 37 C.F.R. §§1.71-1.75.

13. 35 U.S.C. §103

14. *Id.*

15. Abbreviated New Drug Application Regulations: Patent and Exclusivity Provisions, 59 Fed. Reg. 50,338-50,358, Oct. 3, 1984. A 505(b)(2) application seeks

approval of a new drug but at least some of the safety and efficacy date relied upon comes from studies conducted by third parties, not by, or on behalf of the applicant.

16. 21 U.S.C. §355(j)(2)(A)(vii)(I)(IV). A Paragraph IV certification states that the patent is not infringed or is invalid.

17. Pub. L. No. 98-417, 98 Stat. 1585 (1984) (codified as amended at 21 U.S.C. § 321) limiting the patent extension to no more than five years, for any patent, and the total effective patent life of the product, after the patent term is extended, cannot exceed fourteen years. Only one patent can be extended for each regulatory review period for any product. Further extensions are not available for different dosages or drugs containing salts of the same active ingredient.

18. E.D. Va. No. 1:02 v. 858 2/20/03 reported in 65 BNA's *Patents, Trademarks & Copyright J.* 406 (2003).

19. *Id.* The court found that the applicant had failed to satisfy the "first commercial marketing" requirement of the statute.

20. 21 C.F.R. §314.53(b), pertaining to patent listing requirements for NDAs.

21. See "Glaxo Bupropion Patents Are an Example of 'Orange Book' Abuse," 60 *FDC Reports, The Pink Sheet,* October 26, 1998.

22. The Orange Book is available at www.fda.gov/cder/ob/default.htm.

23. A Paragraph IV certification, required for 505(b)(2) and 505(j) ANDA filing, begins the process by which the question of whether the listed patent is valid or will be infringed by the proposed generic product will be answered by the courts prior to the expiration of the patent.

24. The Hatch-Waxman Amendments, 98 Stat. 1585 (1984); see generally H. REP. No. 98-857, pt. 1, at 14 (1984).

25. 733 F.2d 858 (Fed. Cir. 1984), *cert. denied,* 469 U.S. 856 (1984). See Krulwich, Statutory Reversal of Roche v. Bolar: What You See Is Only the Beginning of What You Get, 40 *Food Drug Cosm. L.J.* 519 (1985); Peter Safir, Hatch-Waxman Developments in 1988, 44 *Food Drug Cosm. L.J.* 359 (1989); Kevin McGough, Preserving the Compromise: The Plain Meaning of Waxman Hatch Exclusivity, 45 *Food Drug Cosm L.J.* 487 (1990); Terry Coleman, Waxman-Hatch Exclusivity Provisions Not Related to Patent Status, 46 *Food Drug Cosm L.J.* 345 (1991).

26. Schumer, Collins Reintroduce Measure to Close Loopholes Blocking Generic Drugs, 65 *BNA Patent, Trademark & Copyright,* 232-234, January 17, 2003.

27. Vonronica Kolidakis, Generic Industry Waiting to See Effect of FDA Final Rule, Possible Legislation, 1 *BNA pharm. law & indust.,* 921, August 22, 2003.

28. *Generic Drug Entry Prior to Patent Expiration,* Federal Trade Commission, July 2002. (reporting eight instances where late-listed patents resulted in multiple thirty-month stays on ANDA approval); see generally A Review of the FTC Report: Before the Subcommittee on Health, Oct. 9, 2002 (statement of Honorable L. Crawford, Acting Commissioner, U.S. FDA).

29. 68 Fed. Reg. 36675, June 18, 2003 (implementing regulations which were initially issued in 1994. FDA decided to implement the rule rather than wait to see what Congress would do with pending Medicare legislation. The Medicare legislation includes many of the FDA rule provisions). See generally Michelle Meadows, Greater Access to Generic Drugs, *FDA Consumer,* Sept-Oct 2003 (quoting the

Health and Human Services Secretary Tommy G. Thompson that the new FDA rule is expected to save consumers $35 billion over 10 years, as well as lower costs for state Medicaid programs and employer-provided coverage. To supplement the regulation, the FDA also launched an initiative called "Improving Access to Generic Drugs." The initiative involves revamping the FDA's review process to put generics into consumers' hands more quickly. President Bush's fiscal year 2004 budget request increases funding for the FDA's generic drug program by $13 million, the largest ever for that program, with the goal of speeding up generic drug reviews.

30. P.L. No. 108-173. December 8, 2003. Sections 1101-1104 of the act amends the Hatch-Waxman Act, 21 U.S.C. §355.

31. *See* 69 Fed. Reg. 9982, March 3, 2004 (where FDA sought comments on how to best implement the Hatch-Waxman reforms contained in the new Medicare law).

32. 21 C.F.R. §§ 314.52(a)(3) and 314.95(a)(3).

33. 21 U.S.C. § 355(j)(2)(B)(ii).

34. Deborah Shelton, *FDA's Final Hatch-Waxman Regulations,* at www .arentfox.com/publications/alerts/alerts/2003.html, visited December 24, 2003.

35. Aventis Pharmaceuticals Inc. v. Dr. Reddy's Laboratories, Ltd., D.N.J., No. 2:04-CV-01075-JAG-GDH, filed 3/5/04.

36. 21 C.F.R. § 314.53(c)(2)(i) (pertaining to the declaration that must be submitted).

37. *GOP Medicare Bill Reforms Law for Generic Drugs,* 67 PATENT, TRADEMARK & COPYRIGHT 49, 50, Nov. 21, 2003; see generally Donna A. Elfin, Hatch-Waxman Fix May Delay Market Entry of Generics, FTC Commissioner Leary Says, 2 Pharm Law & Indust, 260, March 5, 2004 (quoting the FTC Commissioner Thomas B. Leary as predicting that the declaratory judgement may deter generic entry as entry companies would be unwilling to enter the market while the patent situation is in flux).

38. FDA Talk Paper, *Department of Justice Appeals Court Decision Regarding FDA's Shared Exclusivity Determination for Generic Paroxetine Hydrochloride Tablets,* T04-04, Feb. 5, 2004; see FDA Web site at www.fda.gov/bbs/topics/ NEWS/2004/new01030.html. The date on which the first complete ANDA application is submitted to challenge a brand-name drug product is now disclosed on the FDA Web site. However, the name of the generic company will not be disclosed.

39. Article 31, The TRIPS Agreement.

40. 35 U.S.C. §282.

41. *Bausch & Lomb, Inc. v. Barnes-Hind/Hydrocurve, Inc.,* 796 F.2d 443, 446, 230 U.S.P.Q.2d 416, 418 (Fed. Cir. 1986), *cert. denied,* 484 U.S. 823 (1987).

42. *SmithKline Diagnostics, Inc. v. Helena Lab. Corp.,* 859 F.2d 878, 885, 8 U.S.P.Q.2d 1468, 1474 (Fed. Cir. 1988).

43. *Lindemann Machinenfabrik GmbH v. American Hoist & Derrick Co.,* 730 F.2d 1452, 1459, 221 U.S.P.Q. 481, 486 (Fed. Cir. 1984).

44. *Applied Medical Resources Corp. v. United States Surgical Corp.,* 147 F.3d 1374, 47 U.S.P.Q.2d 1289 (Fed. Cir. 1998), *cert.* denied, 119 S. Ct. 870 (1999).

45. *Atlas Powder Co. v. E. I. du Pont De Nemours & Co.,* 750 F.2d 1569, 1574, 224 U.S.P.Q. 409, 411 (Fed. Cir. 1984).

46. 35 U.S.C. §102(b).

47. *In re Smith,* 714 F.2d 1127, 1134, 218 U.S.P.Q. 976, 983 (Fed. Cir. 1983).

48. 35 U.S.C. §102(b).

49. *Pfaff v. Wells Electronics,* 525 U.S. 55, 48 U.S.P.Q.2d 1641 (1998).

50. *Monarch Knitting Mach. Corp. v. Sulzer Morat GmbH,* 139 F.3d 877, 881, 45 U.S.P.Q.2d 1977, 1981 (Fed. Cir. 1998).

51. *Id.*

52. *In re Sernaker,* 702 F.3d 989, 994, 217 U.S.P.Q. 1, 5 (Fed. Cir. 1983).

53. *In re Wood,* 599 F.2d 1032, 1036-37, 202 U.S.P.Q. 171, 174 (C.C.P.A. 1979).

54. *Molins PLC v. Textron, Inc.,* 48 F.3d 1172, 1178, 33 U.S.P.Q.2d 1823, 1826 (Fed. Cir. 1995).

55. 52 F.3d 1043, 34 U.S.P.Q.2d 1565 (Fed. Cir.), *cert. denied,* 516 U.S. 988 (1995)

56. *Paragon Podiatry Lab., Inc. v. KLM Lab., Inc.,* 984 F.2d 1182, 1189, 25 U.S.P.Q.2d 1561, 1567 (Fed. Cir. 1993).

57. 35 U.S.C. §§1051-1127.

58. 15 U.S.C. §1127.

59. Schumer, Collins Reintroduce Measure to Close Loopholes Blocking Generic Drugs, 65 *BNA Patent, Trademark & Copyright,* 232-234, January 17, 2003.

60. *Ciba-Geigy v. Bolar Pharm. Corp.,* 747 F.2d 844, 851 (3d Cir. 1984), *cert. denied,* 471 U.S. 1137 (1985).

61. *What Is a Trademark?* (Washington, DC: American Bar Association, 1995).

62. Siegrun D. Kane, *Trademark Law,* Third Edition (New York: Practicing Law Institute, 2001), pp. 1-7.

63. See, e.g., *Glenwood Laboratories v. American Home Products Corp.,* 173 U.S.P.Q. 19 (1971) (applying the doctrine of greater care to find a likelihood of confusion between "Myocholine" for dysphagia, abdominal distension, and urinary retention, and "Mysoline," an anticonvulsant); but see, e.g., *Schering Corp. v. Thompson Medical Co., Inc.,* 209 U.S.P.Q. 72 (S.D.N.Y. 979) (refusing to apply the doctrine and holding that "Polaramine," an antihistamine, was similar to "Prolamine," an appetite suppressant, but that the channels of trade were distinct as one product was OTC and the other prescription).

64. See generally Joseph Diamante and Darren Saunders, Four Federal Court Decisions Have Limited the Extent to Which Private-Label Manufacturers Can Copy the Packaging of the National-Brand Counterparts, *The Nat'l L. J.,* July 18, 1994, at B5.

65. 903 F. Supp. 14 (1995).

66. See generally *International Shoe Co. v. Washington,* 326 U.S. 310 (1945); *Hanson v. Denckla,* 357 U.S. 235 (1958).

67. No. 99 CV 163, 1999 WL 123578 (N.D.N.Y., March 3, 1999).

68. Section 43(a).

69. Pub. L. No. 104-98. The act adds a new section to Section 43 of the Trademark Act of 1946.

70. Roger M. Milgrim, *Milgram on Trade Secrets* (Matthew Bender & Co., 2003), April 2003 suppl., pp. 1-132.

71. 18 U.S.C.A. §1905. See Economic Espionage Act 18 U.S.C. §§ 1831-1839.

72. *What Is a Patent? A Guide for the IP Lawyer* (Washington, DC: American Bar Association, 2001), p. 23.

73. 931 F. Supp. 1280 (1996). *See also Glaxo v. Novopharm,* 110 F.3d 1562 (Fed. Cir. 1997).

74. 1999 Del. Ch. LEXIS 242, *judgment aff'd per curiam,* 746, A.2d 277, 2000 Del. LEXIS 45 (Del.), *decision aff'd,* 766 A.2d 442 (Del. 2000).

75. *Iid.*

76. 7 U.S.C. §§101, 102.

77. Frank H. Andorka, *What Is a Copyright?* (Washington, DC: American Bar Association, 2001), p. 10.

78. 17 U.S.C. §106.

79. Andorka, *What Is a Copyright?,* Section on Intellectual Property Law.

80. John W. Hazard, *Copyright Law in Business and Practice* (West Pub., 2002) suppl., pp. 1-2.

81. Mitchell et al., *U.S. Trade Dress Law,* p. 221.

Chapter 7

Pharmacy Trade Regulation

Richard A. Feinstein
Daniel A. Kotchen

Community pharmacies, wholesalers, pharmaceutical manufacturers, professional associations, and other pharmaceutical organizations are all subject to federal laws and regulations (as well as state counterparts) that govern business practices. These laws, which are primarily intended to operate for the benefit of consumers, generally fall into two broad categories: (1) laws that ensure vigorous competition among competitors, known as antitrust laws, and (2) laws that ensure consumers are not misled by marketing practices, known as consumer protection laws. These laws can be enforced through a federal enforcement agency specifically charged with regulating trade (primarily the Federal Trade Commission), state attorneys general offices, and private rights of action. This chapter generally summarizes antitrust laws applicable to the pharmaceutical industry, describes enforcement of these laws, discusses enforcement actions in the pharmaceutical industry, and sets forth practical suggestions as to how to minimize legal risks attendant to antitrust laws. In addition, this chapter briefly summarizes the scope of consumer protection laws applicable to the pharmaceutical industry.

ANTITRUST LAWS

Antitrust laws have two overriding purposes: (1) to ensure that competitors act independently in making business decisions, particularly decisions involving buying or selling products or services, and (2) to ensure that one or several firms are not able to capture a market through anticompetitive means (e.g., foreclosing competition through exclusionary conduct) as opposed to prevailing in competition on the merits due to superior business acumen.

Pharmacy Law Desk Reference
© 2007 by The Haworth Press, Inc. All rights reserved.
doi:10.1300/5790_07

Principally, four federal antitrust statutes apply to pharmaceutical firms: the Sherman Act, Clayton Act, Robinson Patman Act, and Federal Trade Commission Act.* Set forth is a general description of these laws and the activities they proscribe.

Sherman Act

The Sherman Act has two principal sections: Section 1, which governs concerted action between two or more firms or individuals, and Section 2, which principally governs unilateral activity by an entity that either has market power or a dangerous probability of achieving market power.

Section 1 of the Sherman Act, 15 U.S.C. § 1 (2002)

Section 1 of the Sherman Act prohibits "every contract, combination in the form of trust or otherwise, or conspiracy, in restraint of trade or commerce among the several States, or with foreign nations."

There are three elements to a Section 1 violation: (1) the existence of a contract or agreement, which can be express or implied, among two or more separate entities that (2) unreasonably restrains trade and (3) affects interstate or foreign commerce.[1] Almost all contracts in the pharmaceutical field have some effect on interstate or foreign commerce (i.e., contracts that involve interstate or international sales of products or services), but few of these contracts are likely to give rise to antitrust concerns. To understand the scope of the prohibitions under Section 1 of the Sherman Act, then, it is essential to understand the second element of the statute, which requires that a contract "unreasonably restrain trade" to constitute a violation.

Courts have established two broad categories of Section 1 offenses that constitute "unreasonable restraints of trade": (1) per se offenses and (2) contracts or agreements deemed illegal under the rule of reason. For categories of agreements that constitute per se offenses (see below), all that is generally needed to establish an antitrust violation is to prove the existence of the agreement itself.

The rule of reason, on the other hand, is a fact-intensive analysis that weighs an agreement's anticompetitive effects against any procompetitive justifications. To the extent that an agreement, on balance, harms competi-

---

*In addition, most states have enacted antitrust laws that parallel the federal antitrust laws and provide their own separate remedies in the event of a violation. This chapter focuses on the application of the federal antitrust laws to firms in the pharmaceutical industry. Parallel state antitrust laws generally incorporate the principles and theories underlying their federal law counterparts.

tion, it is unlawful under the rule of reason. In analyzing an agreement under the rule of reason, a court will typically require that (1) litigants define the relevant market in which to analyze the agreement's effects, (2) the plaintiff demonstrates how the agreement has harmed competition in the relevant market (e.g., limiting competitive choices), and (3) to the extent that the plaintiff meets its burden of establishing competitive harm, the defendant demonstrates how procompetitive aspects of the agreement (e.g., integrative efficiencies that lower prices) outweigh any anticompetitive effects.

Certain types of contracts and agreements have been frequently challenged under Section 1 and therefore are the subject of numerous court decisions, including the following:

1. *Agreements to Fix Prices*—Agreements between competitors regarding the prices they will charge customers are per se illegal, regardless of how reasonable or unreasonable the prices or whether the parties to the agreement agree to charge different prices, as explained by the Supreme Court:

> The aim and result of every price-fixing agreement, if effective, is the elimination of one form of competition. The power to fix prices, whether reasonably exercised or not, involves power to control the market and to fix arbitrary and unreasonable prices. The reasonable price fixed today may through economic and business changes become the unreasonable price of tomorrow. Once established, it may be maintained unchanged because of the absence of competition secured by the agreement for a price reasonable when fixed. Agreements which create such potential power may well be held to be in themselves unreasonable or unlawful restraints, without the necessity of minute inquiry whether a particular price is reasonable or unreasonable as fixed.[2]

Not just agreements to set prices themselves are per se illegal. Agreements that affect prices have also been held to be per se unlawful restraints of trade, such as agreements to set maximum or minimum prices, a pricing formula, discounts extended to customers, credit terms, bids cast prior to the awarding of a contract (called "bid rigging"), or any element of a price.

2. *Vertical Resale Price Maintenance Agreements*—Agreements in which suppliers of a product agree with resellers as to the minimum, maximum, or actual resale price at which a product will be sold are per se illegal.

3. *Agreements to Allocate Customers, Territories, or Products*—Agreements between competitors to decide which competitors will compete for certain customers or in certain geographic territories as well as which com-

petitors will market certain products are also per se illegal. This constitutes dividing markets and has been found to minimize competition on its face:

> One of the classic examples of a per se violation of a § 1 [of the Sherman Act] is an agreement between competitors at the same level of the market structure to allocate territories in order to minimize competition. Such concerted action is usually termed a "horizontal" restraint, in contradistinction to combinations of persons at different levels of the market structure, e.g., manufacturers and distributors, which are termed "vertical" restraints. This Court has reiterated time and time again that "(h)orizontal territorial limitations . . . are naked restraints of trade with no purpose except stifling of competition."[3]

This prohibition is not limited to agreements between firms that are currently competing; it extends to agreements between potential competitors—companies that could compete in the future, but agree not to compete: "[Territorial allocation] agreements are anticompetitive regardless of whether the parties split a market within which both do business or whether they merely reserve one market for one and another for the other."[4]

4. *Group Boycotts or Concerted Refusals to Deal*—Agreements between competitors to not deal with certain suppliers, customers, or other related companies are almost always found to be per se illegal:

> Group boycotts, or concerted refusals by traders to deal with other traders, have long been held to be in the forbidden category. They have not been saved by allegations that they were reasonable in the specific circumstances, nor by a failure to show that they "fixed or regulated prices, parceled out or limited production, or brought about a deterioration in quality." Even when they operated to lower prices or temporarily stimulate competition they were banned.[5]

Following the Supreme Court's decision in *Northwest Wholesale Stationers v. Pacific Stationery & Printing Co.,*[6] where the Court found that membership exclusion in a trade association did not amount to a per se illegal boycott (without a showing of market power), group boycotts cannot always be considered per se illegal. In some instances (i.e., where the design of the boycott or effect on competition is not clear on its face), it may be necessary to show that parties to a boycott have market power in order for the boycott to be deemed illegal.

5. *Tying Agreements*—Agreements in which the buyer of a product is required, as a condition of buying one product or service, to purchase a sec-

ond, distinct product or service can be per se illegal. An agreement will be considered an unlawful tying agreement if it meets the following elements:

> (a) two separate products or services are involved, (b) the sale or agreement to sell one product or service is conditioned on the purchase of another, (c) the seller has sufficient economic power in the market for the tying product to enable it to restrain trade in the market for the tied product, and (d) a not insubstantial amount of interstate commerce in the tied product is affected.[7]

As with the group boycott theory, following a Supreme Court decision,[8] not all tying agreements can be considered per se illegal without first considering an agreement's competitive effects. In *Jefferson Parish,* the Court noted that "as a threshold matter there must be a substantial potential for impact on competition in order to justify per se condemnation [of a tying agreement]."[9] As a result, a court may analyze a tying claim using an analysis that resembles the rule of reason.

6. *Exclusive Dealing Contracts*—Contracts in which a supplier of a product or service agrees to supply a purchaser of the product or service on an exclusive basis for a period of time are analyzed under the rule of reason. As explained by the Supreme Court, such contracts will generally be found unlawful if they have the effect of foreclosing competitors from the market:

> In determining whether an exclusive-dealing contract is unreasonable, the proper focus is on the structure of the market for the products or services in question—the number of sellers and buyers in the market, the volume of their business, and the ease with which buyers and sellers can redirect their purchases or sales to others. Exclusive dealing is an unreasonable restraint on trade only when a significant fraction of buyers or sellers are frozen out of a market by the exclusive deal.[10]

Section 2 of the Sherman Act, 15 U.S.C. § 2 (2002)

Section 2 of the Sherman Act prohibits any firm from monopolizing, attempting to monopolize, or conspiring to monopolize a market. Each of these offenses is described in the following.

A monopolization offense has two elements: (1) the possession of monopoly power in the relevant market and (2) the willful acquisition or maintenance of that power as distinguished from growth or development as a consequence of a superior product, business acumen, or historic accident.[11]

To satisfy the first prong of a monopolization claim, one must define a relevant market and show that a firm has a significant share of that market and/or has the ability to raise prices (or reduce output) within the market free from reasonable competitive constraints. In establishing that a monopolist has willfully acquired or maintained its market power (the second prong of a monopolization claim), it is not sufficient to merely show that a firm has acquired or maintained market power over time. Rather, a monopolist must have engaged in exclusionary acts that enabled it to establish or maintain its position in the market. Such exclusionary acts can include the following:

1. *Predatory Pricing*—A monopolization offense can arise when a firm prices a product or service below an appropriate measure of its production costs in an effort to drive rivals (who would presumably match the price) out of the market, and has a dangerous probability of recouping its losses (from the below-cost pricing) by raising prices after competition has been reduced. This theory requires that a firm have market power following its predatory pricing and during its "recoupment phase."
2. *Refusals to Deal*—When cooperation between competitors is necessary to effectively compete, a monopolist's decision not to deal with certain competitors could meet the second prong of the monopolization test.
3. *Leveraging*—When a monopolist uses its market power in one market to secure a competitive advantage in another market, it could constitute a monopolization offense.
4. *Sham Litigation*—If a monopolist knowingly files a suit (e.g., against a potential entrant) that is objectively baseless, it could constitute a monopolization offense (this theory is somewhat prevalent in cases involving patents).
5. *Foreclosure*—If a monopolist enters into contracts that foreclose the opportunity of other competitors to compete effectively (e.g., by limiting competitors' access to an essential raw material) it can be liable for monopolization.

Attempted monopolization is similar to monopolization inasmuch as it applies to a firm's predatory or anticompetitive conduct, but differs from monopolization to the extent that it applies to firms that do not have market power and therefore do not meet the first prong of a monopolization offense. The elements of attempted monopolization include "(1) that the defendant has engaged in predatory or anticompetitive conduct with (2) a specific intent to monopolize and (3) a dangerous probability of achieving monopoly power."[12] The third element of this test—the dangerous probability of achieving monopoly power—requires that a firm have a significant presence in the market (typically at least a 30 percent share of the market), but not necessarily sufficient market power to be considered a monopolist.

A conspiracy to monopolize exists when there is (1) a combination or conspiracy among two or more independent firms, (2) an overt act in furtherance of the conspiracy, and (3) a specific intent to monopolize.[13] Unlike monopolization and attempted monopolization offenses, a conspiracy to monopolize offense does not focus on a firm's market power. Rather, if two firms conspire to intentionally engage in conduct that would otherwise be unlawful under the second element of a monopolization offense (i.e., willful acquisition or maintenance of monopoly power), they would have committed a conspiracy to monopolize in violation of Section 2 of the Sherman Act.

Clayton Act

Two sections of the Clayton Act are pertinent here. Section 3 prohibits tying arrangements (discussed above), but only when the tied product and tying product are "goods, wares, merchandise, machinery, supplies, or other commodities"[14]—not services.*

Section 7 of the Clayton Act prohibits mergers or acquisitions the effect of which "may be substantially to lessen competition, or to tend to create a monopoly."[15] A merger or acquisition may be found to substantially lessen competition when the market at issue is highly concentrated and/or the merged entity will have a relatively significant share of the market. Also relevant to an analysis under Section 7 is the ease with which competitors can enter the market at issue. If entry is easy (i.e., if it takes less than a year and does not involve significant capital outlays), then it is less likely a merger could substantially lessen competition because the threat of potential entry will limit the ability of the merged entity to exercise market power by raising prices.

Robinson-Patman Act

The Robinson-Patman Act[16] prohibits price discrimination. That is, it prohibits sellers from discriminating in the prices, terms of sale, or advertising and other promotional allowances paid to competing purchasers of goods where competitive injury may result to disfavored purchasers or to

---

*Note that a tying offense under Section 1 of the Sherman Act can involve services.

the seller's competitors. The act applies only to sales of commodities (not services) of like grade and quality, and, in order for there to be a violation, there must be at least two sales of a commodity by the same seller at differing prices. The act was passed primarily to protect small businesses by preventing large businesses from exercising their superior buying power to demand non-cost-related price discounts that may result in an unfair competitive advantage. When a seller incurs different costs in selling its product or prices a product differently simply to meet a competitor's price, the Robinson-Patman Act will not likely condemn the pricing differentials.

Federal Trade Commission Act

Section 5(a) of the Federal Trade Commission Act[17] authorizes the FTC to enforce the antitrust laws. This section prohibits all "unfair methods of competition," which the FTC considers to include any conduct that would violate the Sherman Act, Section 7 of the Clayton Act, or the Robinson-Patman Act.[18] In short, the FTC has the authority to prosecute each of the established antitrust violations previously described, but only through Section 5(a) of the FTC Act.

ANTITRUST LAW ENFORCEMENT MECHANISMS AND PENALTIES

Enforcement Mechanisms

The antitrust laws can be enforced in three ways. First, a private party—such as a firm's supplier, competitor, or purchaser—can initiate a lawsuit alleging that it was or will be harmed by the firm's anticompetitive practice.

Second, a state's attorneys general office can initiate a lawsuit challenging the practices of a firm, alleging that a firm has violated state and/or federal antitrust laws. Such a suit is typically preceded by an investigation into the challenged practice. State attorneys general offices generally have subpoena power even during investigations, meaning that they can subpoena firms for documents and testimony to determine whether a claim can be made that a certain practice violates antitrust laws.

Third, and most important, antitrust laws are enforced by the federal government. Two federal antitrust enforcement agencies enforce the antitrust laws: the Department of Justice (DOJ) and the Federal Trade Commission (FTC). The DOJ has exclusive federal enforcement jurisdiction to prosecute criminal antitrust claims, which typically arise in the most egregious of circumstances, such as when competitors specifically agree on the prices each will charge for competing products. Criminal antitrust enforcement, though, is much less common than civil enforcement. Historically, the FTC is the federal enforcement agency that generally investigates and prosecutes civil antitrust claims in the pharmaceutical industry. Over the past ten years, the FTC has actively scrutinized business practices and proposed acquisitions in the industry and, as described in the next section, brought a number of enforcement actions.

In enforcing the antitrust laws, the FTC first investigates potential violations. FTC investigations can be initiated by a complaint to the government by a competitor, customer, or supplier regarding a firm's business practices, or by public reports about a firm's business practices. During investigations, which are not public, the agency has the authority to subpoena documents and testimony from parties (including both corporate entities and individuals) that may have information relevant to the investigation. Investigations will often span months and sometimes even more than a year, during which time staff attorneys at the FTC gather facts relevant to the potential violation. If the staff attorneys believe that the matter under investigation should give rise to an enforcement action, they submit an enforcement recommendation to the FTC's commissioners seeking approval to commence an enforcement action. The FTC has five commissioners appointed by the president, and a majority of these commissioners must approve each enforcement action by the FTC.

An enforcement action can include (1) filing a lawsuit in either federal or administrative court (the forum depends on the remedy sought) or (2) entering into a consent decree. Consent decrees are agreements between the targets of an investigation (called "respondents") and the FTC, where respondents agree to terms that presumably assuage the FTC's antitrust concerns. In the merger context, this may mean that two firms that plan to merge agree to divest assets to another competitor (or potential competitor). In the nonmerger context, this may mean that a firm will agree to not engage in certain conduct—conduct that is presumably the focus of the FTC investigation—for some period of time (typically five to ten years). Firms that enter consent decrees do not admit any violation of the antitrust laws; all that is admitted is that the firms are subject to the FTC's jurisdiction.

It is not uncommon for FTC investigations to be terminated without any enforcement action, but even investigations that do not lead to cases can be burdensome, time-consuming, and disconcerting in that they involve uncertain outcomes. As discussed later in this chapter, given the burdens and uncertainties of an FTC investigation, firms should be mindful of the antitrust laws in conducting activities and should avoid even the appearance of impropriety. Legal counsel should be consulted regarding planned practices that may raise antitrust concerns. Moreover, the FTC has an "Advisory Opinion" process in which staff attorneys review planned business practices and comment on their antitrust implications.* This process typically involves supplying FTC attorneys with documents regarding a planned practice and making business persons available for interviews to discuss the planned practice. Although this review procedure requires some time and resources (as well as the risk that the FTC attorneys will advise that a planned practice not be initiated), it can be a useful tool to minimize future antitrust scrutiny of a practice. To learn more about the Advisory Opinion process, visit the FTC's Web site (www.ftc.gov).

Penalties

Penalties for violating the antitrust laws are severe. The Department of Justice may prosecute Sherman Act violators as criminal felons. Employees, officers, directors, or agents who authorize or participate in a per se offense can be imprisoned for up to three years and can be fined up to the greatest of (1) $350,000 (per count); (2) twice the gross pecuniary loss caused to victims of the crime; or (3) twice the gross pecuniary gain the individual derived from the crime. Further, in most circumstances, the U.S. Federal Sentencing Guidelines mandate incarceration for individuals who have engaged in a criminal antitrust offense. Where in the past, judges often placed such individuals on probation given their status in the community, now such individuals (including high-level corporate officers) must routinely serve time in prison.

Moreover, for criminal offenses, a corporation can be fined up to the greatest of (1) $10 million (per offense), (2) twice the pecuniary loss caused to the victims of the crime, or (3) twice the gross pecuniary gain a firm derived from the crime.

Separate from criminal penalties, a violation of an antitrust law can subject a firm to civil penalties. Private parties (such as customers, suppliers, or competitors) and state attorneys general offices can bring civil suits to recover three times their actual damages caused by an antitrust violation, plus attorneys' fees and court costs. Treble damage judgments in civil suits can amount to tens or even hundreds of millions of dollars. In addition, the FTC

---

*For examples of FTC advisory opinions concerning the pharmaceutical industry, see Northeast Pharmacy Service Corporation, letter issued July 27, 2000, FTC Advisory Opinion, available at www.ftc.gov; Orange Pharmacy Equitable Network, letter issued May 19, 1999, FTC Advisory Opinion, available at www.ftc.gov. Both of these opinions analyze antitrust implications of establishing networks of competing retail pharmacies and pharmacists to contract with health plans in delivering pharmaceutical-related services.

can seek disgorgement from a firm, requiring that the firm disgorge its ill-gotten gains from an illegal business practice.

Civil penalties can also include injunctive relief, which can preclude a firm from engaging in a challenged business practice.

ANTITRUST ENFORCEMENT IN THE PHARMACEUTICAL INDUSTRY

The following are brief summaries of recent, noteworthy antitrust enforcement actions in the pharmaceutical industry. The actions include suits by the federal government, states' attorneys general offices, and private parties. They also include consent decrees entered by the FTC.

Actions Involving Price Fixing

1. *Vitamins Price-Fixing Case:* The DOJ, states attorneys general, and private plaintiffs sued pharmaceutical manufacturers for an alleged conspiracy spanning nine years (1990-1999) to fix prices of vitamin blenders involving vitamins A, C, E, and a variety of the B-complex vitamins. The parties also alleged that the conspiracy involved agreeing to allocate sales volumes as well as agreeing to divide contracts to supply vitamin premixes to customers in the United States and rigging the bids for those contracts. The cases settled for record fines. The states attorneys general and private plaintiffs settled with seven firms for $1.1 billion. The DOJ obtained—through plea agreements—criminal fines of eight conspirators amounting to almost $900 million as well as convictions of top executives of two conspirators who agreed to prison sentences and personal fines.

2. *Institutional Pharmacy Network 126 F.T.C. 138 (1998) (consent order):* In this matter, which resulted in an FTC consent order, the FTC alleged that five institutional pharmacies formed the "Institutional Pharmacy Network" (IPN) to enable the firms to fix prices and restrain competition among institutional pharmacies in Oregon, leading to higher reimbursement levels for serving Medicaid patients in Oregon long-term institutions. According to the FTC, the pharmacies that formed IPN provided 80 percent of the institutional pharmacy services to patients in Oregon and therefore had sufficient market power to increase reimbursement levels. The consent order prohibits IPN and the individual pharmacy respondents from entering into similar such arrangements.

Actions Involving Market Allocations
and Agreements Not to Compete

1. *Biovail Corporation/Elan Corporation*—No. C-4057 (FTC consent order issued August 15, 2002) (FTC Commission Actions: August 20, 2002, available at www.ftc.gov): In this matter, which resulted in an FTC consent order, the FTC alleged that an agreement between Biovail Corporation ("Biovail") and Elan Corporation ("Elan") constituted an illegal agreement not to compete.

Biovail and Elan filed Abbreviated New Drug Applications (ANDAs) with the FDA to market competing 30 mg and 60 mg generic versions of a brand product named Adalat. The parties did not compete with these products, but instead entered into a distribution agreement. Pursuant to the agreement, in exchange for specified payments and profit sharing, Elan appointed Biovail as the exclusive distributor of Elan's 30 mg and 60 mg generic versions of Adalat. Biovail, through a distributor, marketed Elan's 30 mg product and marketed its own 60 mg product. At the time of the FTC consent decree, Biovail did not market its own 30 mg product, nor was Elan's 60 mg product marketed.

The FTC alleged that the Biovail/Elan distribution agreement provided an incentive for Biovail and Elan not compete against each other and therefore could be construed as an agreement not to compete. Biovail and Elan entered a consent decree with the FTC in which they agreed to terminate the agreement and not enter a similar such agreement in the future.

2. *Agreements Not to Compete Involving Payments from Brand Name Pharmaceutical Firms to Potential Generic Competitors:* Between 1999 and 2003, one of the most active areas of antitrust enforcement has involved agreements between brand-name pharmaceutical firms and potential generic competitors that filed ANDAs to market generic versions of the brand-name manufacturers' products. These agreements share the following characteristics: (a) they purport to resolve some aspect of patent litigation between the parties, (b) the brand name manufacturers make significant payments to their potential generic entrants, and (c) the potential generic entrants agree to not market their products for some period of time. The FTC, states' attorneys general offices, and private plaintiffs have challenged a number of these agreements, alleging that they constitute unlawful market allocations. These challenges have resulted in three court decisions, all of which are on appeal (as of this writing). Two of the decisions found that the agreements at issue constituted market allocations and, thus, were per se unlawful.[19] The other decision found the agreement lawful under the rule of reason, reasoning that the agreement ensured generic market entry before patent

expiration and that the payments from the brand-name manufacturer to the potential generic entrant were not in return for the generic agreeing not to compete.[20]

Group Boycotts

1. *Baltimore Metropolitan Pharmaceutical Association, Inc. and Maryland Pharmacists Association,* 117 F.T.C. 95 (1994) (consent order). In this matter, which resulted in an FTC consent order, the FTC alleged that the Maryland Pharmacists Association and the Baltimore Metropolitan Pharmaceutical Association conspired to boycott the Baltimore city government employees' prescription-drug plan in order to force higher reimbursement rates for prescription medicines. Under the consent order, the respondents are prohibited from entering into, organizing, or encouraging any agreement between or among pharmacies to refuse to enter into, or to withdraw from, any participation agreement offered by a third-party payer.

2. *Chain Pharmacy Association of New York State, Inc.,* 114 F.T.C. 327 (1991) (consent order). In this matter, which resulted in an FTC consent order, the FTC alleged that the Chain Pharmacy Association (Chain) and its members conspired to boycott the New York State Employees Prescription Plan, in order to increase reimbursement rates. The order prohibits Chain from organizing or entering into any agreement among pharmacies to withdraw from or refuse to enter into third-party payor prescription drug plans. The FTC also entered consent orders with the individual members of Chain.

Tying Agreements

1. *Sandoz Pharmaceuticals Corporation,* 115 F.T.C. 625 (1992) (consent order). In this matter, which resulted in an FTC consent order, the FTC alleged that Sandoz unlawfully required purchasers of its schizophrenia drug, clozapine, to also purchase distribution and patient-monitoring services from Sandoz. The order prohibits Sandoz from requiring any purchaser of clozapine, or a patient taking clozapine, to buy other goods or services from Sandoz.

Exclusive Dealing Agreements/Exclusionary Conduct

1. *Biovail Corporation,* C-4060 (consent order issued October 2, 2002) (FTC Commission Actions: October 4, 2002, available at www.ftc.gov). In this matter, which resulted in an FTC consent order, the FTC alleged

Biovail illegally acquired the exclusive license to a drug patent in order to prevent generic competition to its antihypertension drug Tiazac. According to the FTC, Biovail then wrongfully listed the acquired patent in the FDA's Orange Book, which—pursuant to the FDA regulatory scheme—enabled Biovail to secure a second thirty-month stay of generic entry through patent litigation. The order precludes Biovail from taking any action that would trigger the thirty-month stay and requires Biovail to divest at least a portion of the exclusive license to its original owner.

2. *FTC v. Mylan Laboratories et al.,* 62 F. Supp. 2d 25 (D.D.C. 1999) (FTC Commission Actions: November 29, 2000, available at www.ftc .gov). In this matter, the FTC sued Mylan Laboratories and three Mylan raw material suppliers (Profarmaco S.R.L., Cambrex Corporation, and Gyma Laboratories), alleging that the defendants violated Sections 1 and 2 of the Sherman Act by entering into exclusive licensing contracts for the supply of raw material necessary to produce Mylan's generic versions of lorazepam and clorazepate. These contracts, the FTC alleged, foreclosed the ability of other pharmaceutical competitors to produce competing generic versions of lorazepam and clorazepate, which enabled Mylan to increase prices. Thirty-four states' attorneys general offices as well as private plaintiffs also sued, challenging the same agreements. Mylan settled the litigation with the FTC, states, and several private plaintiffs, agreeing to pay $100 million to purchasers of lorazepam and clorazepate during the period in which its exclusive contracts were in place. The defendants also agreed to an injunction barring them from entering into similar agreements in the future.

3. *RxCare of Tennessee, Inc. et al.,* 121 F.T.C. 762 (1996). In this matter, which resulted in an FTC consent order, the FTC alleged that RxCare of Tennessee used a "most favored nation" clause (MFN) to discourage pharmacies from discounting, and to limit price competition among pharmacies in their dealings with pharmacy benefits managers and third-party payors. The MFN clause at issue required that if a pharmacy in the RxCare network accepted a reimbursement rate from any other third-party payor that is lower than the RxCare rate, the pharmacy must accept that lower rate for all RxCare business in which it participates. Combined with RxCare's market power (the network included 95 percent of all chain and independent pharmacies in Tennessee), the complaint alleged that the MFN clause forced some pharmacies in the network to reject lower reimbursement rates for prescription orders they dispense for patients covered by other health plans. The order bars RxCare from including the MFN clause in its pharmacy agreements.

Mergers and Acquisitions

In recent years, the FTC has reviewed a number of mergers and acquisitions in the pharmaceutical industry and issued a number of consent decrees in which the parties to a proposed acquisition agreed to divest assets. In addition, the FTC authorized court challenges to three proposed transactions, two of which were withdrawn; the third proposed transaction was litigated and won by the FTC. Since 1994, the FTC's announced enforcement actions regarding mergers and acquisitions in the pharmaceutical industry include the following:

Involving Court Challenges

- *FTC v. Cardinal Health, Inc.* and *FTC v. McKesson Corp.,* 12 F. Supp. 2d 34 (D.D.C. 1998) (FTC successfully challenged a proposed merger between McKesson and AmeriSource as well as a proposed merger between Cardinal Health and Bergen-Brunswig).
- Rite Aid Corporation and Revco D.S., Inc., FTC File No. 961-0020 (preliminary injunction authorized April 17, 1996) (FTC Commission Actions: April 17, 24, 1996, available at www.ftc.gov) (Rite Aid withdrew its proposed acquisition of Revco after the FTC authorized a court challenge to block the transaction).
- Cytyc Corp. and Digene Corp., FTC File No. 0210098 (preliminary injunction authorized June 24, 2002) (FTC Commission Actions: June 24, 2002, available at www.ftc.gov) (Cyctc and Digene withdrew a proposed merger after the FTC authorized a court challenge to block the transaction).

Involving Consent Orders

- Baxter International Inc. and Wyeth, C-4068 (consent order issued December 20, 2002) (FTC Commission Actions: December 20, 2002, available at www.ftc.gov).
- Amgen Inc. and Immunex Corporation, C-4946 (consent order issued September 3, 2002) (FTC Commission Actions: September 6, 2002, available at www.ftc.gov).
- Glaxo Wellcome plc and Smith Kline Beecham plc, C-3990 (consent order issued January 26, 2001) (FTC Commission Actions: January 23, 30 2001, available at www.ftc.gov).

- Pfizer Inc. and Warner-Lambert Company, C-3957 (consent order issued July 27, 2000) (FTC Commission Actions: July 28, 2000, available at www.ftc.gov).
- Hoechst AG and Rhone-Poulenc, C-3919 (consent order issued January 18, 2000) (FTC Commission Actions: January 28, 2000, available at www.ftc.gov).
- Zeneca Group plc, C-3880 (consent order issued June 7, 1999) (FTC Commission Actions: June 10, 1999, available at www.ftc.gov) (concerning Zeneca's acquisition of Astra).
- Merck and Medco (consent order issued February 18, 1999) (FTC Commission Actions: February 24, 1999, available at www.ftc.gov).
- Roche Holding Ltd., 125 F.T.C. 919 (1998) (consent order) (concerning Roche's acquisition of Corange Ltd.).
- American Home Products Corp., 123 F.T.C. 1279 (1997) (consent order) (concerning American Home Product's acquisition of Solvay's animal health business).
- Baxter International, Inc., 123 F.T.C. 904 (1997) (consent order) (concerning Baxter's acquisition of Immuno International).
- Ciba-Geigy, Ltd., 123 F.T.C. 842 (1997) (consent order) (concerning the merger of Ciba-Geigy and Sandoz).
- J.C. Penney Company and Eckerd Corporation and Rite Aid, 123 F.T.C. 778, 795 (1997) (consent orders).
- CVS Corporation and Revco, 124 F.T.C. 161 (1997) (consent order).

MINIMIZING ANTITRUST RISK

In light of the antitrust issues noted above, the severe consequences that can result from antitrust violations, and the burdens and uncertainties of government investigations, firms in the pharmaceutical industry should avoid the following agreements and business practices:

- Do not agree with competitors on the prices or terms to sell or buy products or services. This could be considered price fixing and a violation of Section 1 of the Sherman Act.
- Do not have understandings with competitors to stay out of each others' markets or to stay away from each others' customers. In addition, do not have understandings as to which services or products will be offered by which competitors. This could be considered market allocation and a violation of Section 1 of the Sherman Act.

- Do not agree with competitors not to deal with certain suppliers, customers, or other competitors. This could be considered a group boycott or concerted refusal to deal and a violation of Section 1 of the Sherman Act.
- Do not condition the purchase of one product (or service) upon the purchase of a second product (or service) so that a customer who wants one has to buy both. This could be considered a tying arrangement in violation of Section 1 of the Sherman Act or Section 3 of the Clayton Act.
- Do not agree with a customer on a price or a price level at which the customer will resell a product. This could be considered vertical price maintenance and a violation of Section 1 of the Sherman Act.
- Do not charge different prices for the same product to similarly situated customers. This could constitute a violation of the Robinson-Patman Act. Two exceptions to this rule include cost savings passed along to a customer that costs less to serve and lower prices charged to a customer if necessary to match a competitor's price.
- Do not set prices below costs in order to drive out or punish competitors or discourage new entry into the market. This could be considered predatory pricing and a violation of Section 2 of the Sherman Act.
- Do not take advantage of control over a source of supply or of a facility to drive out of the market other competitors who rely on that source of supply or facility. This could be considered a form of monopolization and a violation of Section 2 of the Sherman Act.
- Do not initiate a lawsuit against a competitor without a legal basis and simply to impose costs on the competitor. This could be considered sham litigation and a violation of Section 2 of the Sherman Act.

In addition to existing business practices, appearances of impropriety can also subject a firm or individual to antitrust risk. In this regard, the greatest potential for antitrust problems arises from relations with and communications among competitors. As discussed above, certain agreements among competitors are per se illegal. All that is needed to establish a violation of the antitrust laws is to prove the existence of any of these condemned agreements. An "agreement" condemned by the antitrust laws is not limited to a written, signed contract. It can include a simple understanding between competitors, established during a dinner conversation or over a glass of wine. For example, a discussion between employees of two competitors about avoiding price wars or discounts, followed by price stabilization between the two firms, could expose the firms and individuals to criminal and civil antitrust liability.

In light of the potential for antitrust liability stemming from communications with competitors, it is advisable to strictly limit the substance of conversations with competitors. The following topics should be avoided:

- Prices, discounts, bids, or any other terms or conditions of sale
- Sales territories, marketing plans and practices, distribution plans and practices
- Refusals to deal with a customer or any supplier
- Selection, retention, or quality of either customers or suppliers
- Profits, profit margins, or market shares
- New products or product innovations as well as the type or quality of production of products

CONSUMER PROTECTION LAWS

The primary federal consumer protection law, enforced by the FTC, is Section 5(a) of the FTC Act[21] which condemns marketing practices that are either deceptive or unfair.*

Deceptive Practices

In a 1983 Policy Statement on Deception (available at www.ftc.gov), the FTC set forth the elements of a deceptive marketing practice that violates the FTC Act. This statement defines these elements as follows:

First, there must be a representation, omission, or practice that is likely to mislead the consumer. Practices that have been found misleading or deceptive in specific cases include false oral or written representations, misleading price claims, sales of hazardous or systematically defective products or services without adequate disclosures, failure to disclose information regarding pyramid sales, use of bait-and-switch techniques, failure to perform promised services, and failure to meet warranty obligations.

Second, the FTC examines the practice from the perspective of a consumer acting reasonably in the circumstances. If the representation or practice affects or is directed primarily to a particular group, the FTC examines reasonableness from the perspective of that group.

Third, the representation, omission, or practice must be a "material" one. The basic question is whether the act or practice is likely to affect the consumer's conduct or decision with regard to a product or service. If so, the

---

*Similar to the federal antitrust laws, states typically have counterparts to this federal consumer protection law, which is enforced by state attorneys general offices.

practice is material, and consumer injury is likely, because consumers are likely to have chosen differently but for the deception. In many instances, materiality, and hence injury, can be presumed from the nature of the practice. In other instances, evidence of materiality may be necessary.

Thus, the FTC will find deception if there is a representation, omission, or practice that is likely to mislead the consumer acting reasonably in the circumstances, to the consumer's detriment.

Unfair Practices

In the FTC Act Amendments of 1994,[22] Congress codified the phrase "unfair acts and practices" to mean a practice that "causes or is likely to cause substantial injury to consumers which is not reasonably avoidable by consumers themselves and not outweighed by countervailing benefits to consumers or to competition."[23] Examples of unfair practices include (1) making a promotional claim regarding a product with a reasonable basis; (2) marketing products—or using promotions—that may be physically injurious; and (3) engaging in sales practices that are inconsistent with other statutes or public policies (i.e., billing credit cards without permission).

Examples of FTC Enforcement of Consumer Protection Laws in the Pharmaceutical Industry

FTC enforcement of consumer protection in the pharmaceutical industry has focused on false, misleading, or unsubstantiated statements made in consumer advertising. For instance, on July 19, 2000, the FTC sued Rexall Sundown, Inc., alleging that Rexall made false and unsubstantiated claims while marketing its dietary supplement, Cellasene. The FTC claimed that Rexall made unsubstantiated advertising statements regarding Cellasene's ability to reduce cellulite, such as the following: "Unlike massages and creams, Cellasene works from within, nutritionally, to help *eliminate* cellulite." The FTC also alleged that Rexall falsely represented that it had clinical evidence establishing Cellasene's efficacy. As of this writing, the FTC's suit is pending in the United States District Court for the Southern District of Florida. A copy of the FTC's complaint is available at www.ftc.gov.

Similarly, on August 31, 2000, the FTC sued several participants involved in the allegedly deceptive advertising of weight-loss products referred to as the "Enforma System." According to the FTC, the Enforma System was promoted chiefly via televised thirty-minute infomercials, which claimed that consumers who used it could lose weight without dieting or exercising, regardless of what they ate. The FTC alleged that this claim, and other supporting statements, were false and unsubstantiated. As of this writing, the FTC's suit is pending in the United States District Court for the Central District of California. The FTC seeks a permanent injunction prohibiting the defendants from engaging in deceptive practices and would require the payment of consumer redress. One defendant has settled with the FTC, agreeing not to make additional unsubstantiated claims and to pay consumer redress of $10 million. A copy of the FTC complaint is available at www.ftc.gov.

The FTC also entered into consent decrees with Del Pharmaceuticals, Pfizer Inc., and Care Technologies, Inc., regarding the FTC's allegations that the companies made false and unsubstantiated claims regarding their over-the-counter head lice treatments. Examples of the allegedly false and unsubstantiated claims include statements that a product "erases head lice completely" and is "100 percent effective in laboratory testing in killing lice and eggs." The consent orders prohibit the respondents from making similar such unsubstantiated claims in the future and, for a two-year period, requires the respondents to make a disclosure in promotional materials that their lice products require reapplication for complete effectiveness. For copies of the consent orders, see Care Technologies Inc., C-3840 (consent order issued December 14, 1998) (FTC Commission Actions: December 23, 1998, available at www.ftc.gov); Del Pharmaceuticals, Inc. and Del Laboratories, Inc., C-3837 (consent order issued December 8, 1998) (FTC Commission Actions: December 23, 1998, available at www.ftc.gov); Pfizer Inc., C-3841 (consent order issued December 14, 1998) (FTC Commission Actions: December 23, 1998, available at www.ftc.gov).

NOTES

1. ABA Section of Antitrust Law, Antitrust Law Developments, at 10 (4th ed. 1997).

2. *United States v. Trenton Potteries,* 273 U.S. 392, 397-98 (1927).

3. *United States v. Topco Assoc.,* 405 U.S. 596, 608 (1972) (citing cases).

4. *Palmer v. BRG of Georgia, Inc.,* 498 U.S. 46, 49-50 (1990).

5. *Klor's, Inc. v. Broadway-Hale Stores,* 359 U.S. 207, 212 (1959) (citations omitted) (quoting *Fashion Originators' Guild v. FTC,* 312 U.S. 457, 466 (1941).

6. 472 U.S. 284 (1985).

7. ABA Section of Antitrust Law, Antitrust Law Developments, at 178 (4th ed. 1997).

8. *Jefferson Parish Hosp. Dist. No. 2 v. Hyde,* 466 U.S. 2 (1984).

9. *Id.* at 16.

10. *Jefferson Parish Hospital District No. 2 v. Hyde,* 466 U.S. 2, 45 (1984).

11. *United States v. Grinnel Corp.,* 384 U.S. 563, 570-71 (1966).

12. *Spectrum Sports, Inc. v. McQuillan,* 506 U.S. 447, 456 (1993) (citing cases).

13. ABA Section of Antitrust Law, Antitrust Law Developments, at 302 (4th ed. 1997).

14. 15 U.S.C. § 14 (2002).

15. 15 U.S.C. § 18 (2002).

16. 15 U.S.C. §§ 13-13b, 21a (2002).

17. 15 U.S.C. § 45(a) (2002).

18. See "A Brief Overview of the Federal Trade Commission's Investigative and Law Enforcement Authority" available at www.ftc.gov/ogc/brfovrvw.htm.

19. *In re: Cardizem CD Antitrust Litigation,* 105 F. Supp. 2d 682 (E.D. Mich. 2000) (on appeal to the Sixth Circuit Court of Appeals); *In re: Terazosin Hydrochloride Antitrust Litigation,* 164 F. Supp. 2d 1340 (S.D. Fla. 2000) (on appeal to the Eleventh Circuit Court of Appeals). The firms party to the agreements in both of these cases entered consent decrees with the FTC in which they agreed not to enter similar such agreements. See *FTC v. Hoechst Marion Roussel, Inc., Carderm Capital L.P., and Andrx Corp.,* D. 9293 (consent order issued May 8, 2001) (FTC Commission Actions: May 11, 2001, available at www.ftc.gov); *Abbott Laboratories and Geneva Pharmaceuticals, Inc.,* No. C-3945, C-3946 (consent orders issued May 22, 2000) (FTC Commission Actions: May 26, 2000, available at www .ftc.gov).

20. *In the Matter of Schering Plough Corp. et al.,* No. 9297, 2002 WL 1488085 (F.T.C. June 27, 2002) (on appeal to the Federal Trade Commission).

21. 15 U.S.C. § 45(a)(1) (2002).

22. Pub. L. No. 103-312, 108 Stat. 1691, 1695 [codified at 15 U.S.C. §§ 41-57c (1994)].

23. § 9, 108 Stat. At 1695 [codified at 15 U.S.C. § 45(n) (1994)].

Chapter 8

Administrative Law

Sharon Horn Roddan

INTRODUCTION

The subject of pharmacy administrative law is the procedural foundation for many of the matters addressed in the other chapters of this book. Regardless of your specific area of practice in pharmacy or the pharmaceutical profession, you will, without question, be regulated by many administrative agencies. Administrative agencies are units of government created to carry out specific tasks. Either the legislative or the executive branch may form these administrative agencies, but, quite interestingly, the agencies are charged with legislative, executive, and judicial power. For example, some of the agencies with whom you will likely interact will be the state Board of Pharmacy, the state and federal Food and Drug Administrations, the Drug Enforcement Administration, the National Labor Relations Board, perhaps even the Internal Revenue Service, the United States Patent and Trademark Office, or many other national, state, and local agencies which oversee a particular body of substantive law.

Today, administrative law is so fundamental to American jurisprudence that state, national, and model administrative procedure acts set forth generalized procedures for the quasi-judicial or administrative adjudication of topic-specific laws, rules, statutes, codes, and regulations.

THE NEED FOR ADMINISTRATIVE TRIBUNALS

Right now, you might be wondering why and how these very powerful agencies, which largely regulate your practice, were formed. These agencies are neither legislative bodies nor courts of law, yet how did they get their both their quasi-judicial (adjudicative) and quasi-legislative (rule making) powers?

Pharmacy Law Desk Reference
© 2007 by The Haworth Press, Inc. All rights reserved.
doi:10.1300/5790_08

As our civilized society grew, it became apparent that a system was needed to create order for regulating diverse bodies of laws, rules, and statutes. The judicial burden could be made more efficient by establishing specific agencies to regulate, enforce, and adjudicate specialized issues thereto without resorting to the court system for each issue.

On the other hand, however, the delegation of both the creation of regulatory standards and the enforcement of those standards might subject an individual controlled by a particular agency to unfair or arbitrary adjudication. The 1927 words of Justice Felix Frankfurter recognizing this fact are as true today as they were when they were penned:

> Because of the danger of arbitrary conduct in the administrative application of legal standards . . ., our administrative law is inextricably bound up with constitutional law. But after all, the Constitution is a Constitution, and not merely a detailed code of prophetic restrictions against the ineptitude and inadequacies of legislatures and administrators. Ultimate protection is to be found in the people themselves, their zeal for liberty, their respect for one another and for the common good—a truth so obviously accepted that its demands in practice are usually overlooked. But safeguards must also be institutionalized through machinery and processes. These safeguards largely depend on a highly professionalized civil service, and adequate technique of administrative application of legal standards, a flexible, appropriate and economical procedure (always remembering that "in the development of our liberty insistence upon procedural regularity has been a large factor"[3]), easy access to public scrutiny, and a constant play of criticism by an informed and spirited bar.

So, to protect against damaging the constitutional rights of those who must comport with the actions of agencies, various administrative procedure acts (state, national, and model) have been created.

SEPARATION OF POWERS

How does this concept of administrative law seem fair? If our constitutional checks and balances system is based upon the separation of powers of the three branches of government—the legislative branch, the judicial branch, and the executive branch—how is it possible that an administrative agency has such comprehensive powers as those listed previously? Our courts protect this checks and balances system. Judicial review has been established to protect a regulated party from an agency acting illegally, unconstitutionally, mistakenly, or outside its scope of practice.

The practice of pharmacy or pharmaceutics is increasingly more technical. To defer regulatory issues and matters to specialists in the field is often highly desirable. Courts frequently defer to the recommendation of the agency. Table 8.1 is a comparison of forums in enforcement cases in the majority of jurisdictions.

DELEGATION OF LEGISLATIVE POWER

In some ways it may seem strange to you that we vote for legislators to draft and enact our laws, and then those very legislators turn around and delegate their legislative power (i.e., rule making) to an administrative agency. How can this be? Strictly speaking, the legislature cannot delegate its legislative power. But in realty, the various legislative bodies frequently allow administrative bodies to make rules. This doctrine known as the delegation of legislative power has two important prongs. In order to delegate its power to a particular agency, (1) the legislature must establish the fundamental policy choices, which leaves the agency with the duty to implement the details, and (2) the power which the legislature has vested to the agency must be within that particular agency's scope or the delegation will be held to be invalid. However, over the years the Supreme Court has uniformly upheld the broad delegation of rule making to agencies even to the point in 1963 of upholding *no* standards at all (*Arizona v. California,* 373 US 546). Generally an agency will limit its scope by adopting its own standards for rule making on a case-by-case basis.

DUE PROCESS HEARING REQUIREMENT

Since it is clear that agencies are now vested with broad powers, how can an individual be protected when an agency plans to take action against him or her? The United States Constitution states:

> All persons born or naturalized in the United States, and subject to the jurisdiction thereof, are citizens of the United States and of the State wherein they reside. No State shall make or enforce any law which shall abridge the privileges or immunities of citizens of the United States; nor shall any State deprive any person of life, liberty, or property, without due process of law; nor deny to any person within its jurisdiction the equal protection of the laws. (Fourteenth Amendment, Section 1)

TABLE 8.1. Comparison of forums.

Agency	Court
Initial adjudication	
Senior agency official decides.	Until case is filed, identity of decision maker is uncertain.
Political attitude of decision maker is consistent in most cases.	Political attitudes and personal opinions vary for each judge.
Standardized regulation; it is uniformly controlled.	Different trial judges may rule inconsistently in similar cases.
It is an expert forum for technical issues.	There is a relative ignorance of technical issues.
Administrative prosecutions usually proceed in adversary mode from beginning.	
Procedures	
Rules of evidence are usually modified.	Rules of evidence apply.
Discovery may be limited or unavailable in administrative forum; usually unavailable on subsequent judicial review.	Discovery is usually available (except on applications for preliminary or emergency relief).
Presiding officer (administrative law judge [ALJ]) usually makes recommendation, but not decision.	Presiding officer (trial judge) makes decision.
Adjudicatory proceeding is usually public in theory, but private in fact.	Proceeding is public; a big case may be a media circus.
Remedies	
Senior agency official determines remedy and can usually retain primary authority to monitor and assess compliance.	Judge determines remedy and may retain primary authority to monitor and assess compliance.
Agency is more likely to make examples of egregious or recidivist violators.	Trial judges often lack sufficient experience with program to identify and heavily penalize egregious or recidivist violators.
Emergency relief is often unavailable except by drastic remedy of summary abatement.	Temporary restraining orders and preliminary injunctions are more commonly available.
Enforcement of administrative orders requires judicial support.	Violation of judicial orders triggers contempt liability.
Judicial deference to agency	
Courts are usually very deferential to adjudicating agency's interpretation of technical data, statutes, and policy.	Courts may give prosecuting agency's interpretation of technical data, statutes, policy great weight, or may treat prosecuting agency as just another litigant.
Agency's factual findings on nontechnical issues receive same deference on judicial review as trial findings receive on appellate review.	Appellate courts generally defer to trial court's findings of fact.

THE RIGHT TO AND ADEQUACY OF NOTICE

The landmark oase concerning the issue of when must an administrative agency hold a hearing before taking action against a party is found in *Goldberg v. Kelly,* 397 US 254 (1970).

In 1968, in New York City, John Kelly was disabled and unemployed, and Angela Velez was a single parent with four children. Both Kelly and Velez were on welfare. Suddenly, with no notice of pending termination, the state of New York ceased paying their welfare benefits. John Kelly was penniless. Angela Velez was unable to pay her rent and she and her children were evicted.

Kelly and Velez joined on public assistance and filed a lawsuit stating that they have a right to a hearing before losing their benefits. Nearly four years later, the U.S. Supreme Court agreed with the plaintiffs, holding that

> the Nation's basic commitment has been to foster the dignity and well-being of all persons within its borders. We have come to recognize that forces not within the control of the poor contribute to their poverty. . . . Welfare, by meeting the basic demands of subsistence, can help bring within the reach of the poor the same opportunities that are available to others to participate meaningfully in the life of the community. . . . Public assistance, then, is not mere charity, but a means to "promote the general Welfare and secure the Blessings of Liberty to ourselves and our Posterity." The same governmental interests that counsel the provision of welfare, counsel as well its uninterrupted provision to those eligible to receive it; pre-termination evidentiary hearings are indispensable to the end.

The Court continued that it would be "unconscionable" to discontinue welfare benefits without a hearing in the face of such "brutal need." That termination of benefits deprives eligible recipients of the means to live while they await their hearing decision.

What Type of Hearing Is Required?

The *Goldberg* court identified the components of "rudimentary due process" for us. As such,

1. the hearing must be held at a meaningful time and in a meaningful manner;
2. timely and adequate notice detailing for the proposed termination must be given;

3. there must be an effective opportunity to confront and cross-examine adverse witnesses and to present arguments and evidence orally;
4. informal procedures and suspension of the rules of evidence would be permitted;
5. there is a right to counsel, but not appointed counsel;
6. when the decision is rendered it must rest solely on legal rules and evidence adduced at the hearing, and the decision must state the reason for the decision and the evidence relied on; and
7. there must be an impartial decision maker who has not participated in making the determination under review.

Although not mentioned in *Goldberg,* another component of basic due process is the right to judicial review in the event the individual disagrees with the administrative decision.

So, the general rule is that a hearing must occur before the deprivation of liberty or property occurs. Hearing timing is often of the utmost importance, particularly if the agency should act first and later hold a hearing. As seen in the Goldberg case, the damage to the plaintiff could be irreparable.

Your professional pharmacist license is a form of "property" protected by due process. The state board of pharmacy will grant licenses to individuals upon completion of certain statutory requirements. (Usually this is a specific number of internship hours, the successful graduation from a recognized college of pharmacy, and a passing score on the state licensing examination.) [For further reading, see *Milligan v. Pharmacy Board* 204 NE 2d 504 (Mass. 1965) regarding the right to a hearing on disputed facts for an applicant seeking a pharmacy license.]

If a state board of pharmacy moves to revoke or suspend a pharmacist's license, the agency generally will provide notice and an opportunity for the pharmacist to be heard. However, when it is necessary for the protection of the public interest the state is entitled to suspend a license prior to a hearing [*Barry v. Barchi,* 443 US 559 (1979)]. Likewise, there is always an emergency exception when the protection of public health or safety is an issue [*North American Cold Storage Co. v. Chicago,* 211 US 300 (1908); *Fahey v. Mallonee,* 332 US 245 (1947)].

So, just about the time the fundamental fairness of administrative due process becomes clear, along comes the 1976 Supreme Court case *Mathews v. Eldridge,* 424 US 319 (1976), which established a "balancing test" to determine when a state is able to act first and hold a hearing later. Under the holding in this case the court considers (1) the private interest that would be affected by the official action; (2) the risk of erroneous deprivation of such interest with the current procedures; and (3) the government's interest.

The facts in the Eldridge case are rather similar to *Goldberg*. However, here the Court tackles the issue as to whether the due process clause of the Fifth Amendment requires prior to the termination of Social Security disability benefit payments that the recipient be afforded an opportunity for an evidentiary hearing.

Eldridge was first awarded Social Security disability benefits in June 1968. In March 1972 he received a questionnaire from the state agency charged with monitoring his medical condition. He completed the questionnaire. The state received reports from the Eldridge physicians and determined that Eldridge's disability benefits ceased in May 1972. Rather than exhausting his administrative remedies, as set forth in his denial letter, Eldridge contended that due process required a predetermination hearing, relying exclusively upon the Court's decision in *Goldberg* (which established a right to an "evidentiary hearing" prior to termination of welfare benefits). The district court held for Eldridge, as did the Court of Appeals for the Fourth Circuit. But the U.S. Supreme Court *reversed.* The Court held that

> Eligibility for disability benefits, in contrast [to Goldberg and welfare benefits], is not based upon financial need. Indeed, it is wholly unrelated to the worker's income or support from many other sources, such as earnings of other family members, workmen's compensation awards, tort claims awards, savings, private insurance, public or private pensions, veterans' benefits, food stamps, public assistance, or the many other important programs, both public and private, which contain provisions for disability payments affecting a substantial portion of the work force.

Second, the Court looked at the fairness and reliability of the existing pretermination procedures and the probable value, if any, of additional procedural safeguards and found that the current procedures were adequate in disability proceedings.

Finally, the Supreme Court balanced the government's interest, including the fiscal and administrative burdens of additional procedures. In reaching this third prong of the balancing test, the Court states, "At some point the benefit of an additional safeguard to the individual affected by the administrative action and to society in terms of increased assurance that the action is just, may be outweighed by the cost."

Just in case you were wondering how the Court viewed administrative agencies, this case further states, "Substantial weight must be given to the good-faith judgments of the individuals charged by Congress with the administration of social welfare programs that the procedures they have provided to assure fair consideration of the entitlement claims of individuals."

The same balancing test that is used for the timing of the hearing is used to determine what elements the hearing must contain. Due process requires (1) notice, (2) the opportunity to confront adverse witnesses, (3) the right to have an attorney present, although the state is not required to pay for same, (4) the reasons for the determination are stated and based solely on legal rules and evidence presented at the hearing, and (5) an impartial decision maker is present at the hearing.

THE PROCESS OF ADMINISTRATIVE ADJUDICATION

The preceding discussion begs the question, "How does administrative law impact me in the practice of pharmacy?"

All state boards of pharmacy authorize board of pharmacy inspectors to conduct inspections of pharmacies. These inspections may be routine (generally once every three years) or they may be more frequent, for example, upon receiving a complaint.

Routine Inspections

Routine inspections are in most states unannounced. Upon arrival at the pharmacy, the inspector will, as unobtrusively as possible, typically review the pharmacy's operations, which may include the following (depending upon the state):

1. completed self-assessment form and compliance with the form;
2. quality assurance program;
3. patient consultation compliance;
4. CURES compliance/controlled substance record keeping;
5. compounding equipment;
6. acquisition and disposition records; prescription documents and inventory; and
7. security and sanitation practices.

Although these procedures may vary slightly from state to state according to the particular law of that state, suffice it to say that a procedure similar to the one to be described below will be followed.

If the inspector believes an infraction or violation of pharmacy law has taken place, an order of correction will be noted on the inspection report.

This order simply notifies the licensee of the violations of law that the inspector believes occurred and directs the licensee to comply within thirty days by submitting a corrective action plan to the inspector. Alternatively, the licensee can contest the order by requesting an informal office conference with the executive officer. However, if no office conference is requested, compliance with the order is not an admission of the noted violation. The order of correction is not a citation, nor is it a disciplinary action. A copy of the order of correction and the corrective action plan must be maintained on the pharmacy premises for at least three years from the date of issuance. An investigation may be opened by the inspector if the violations are of a more serious nature.

Issuance of Citations and Fines

The executive officer issues citations and fines and considers the following factors:

1. gravity of the violation;
2. good or bad faith of the cited person or entity;
3. history of previous violations;
4. evidence that the violations were or were not willful;
5. extent to which the cited person or entity has cooperated with the board's investigation;
6. extent to which the cited person or entity has mitigated or attempted to mitigate any damage or injury caused by the violation;
7. other matters as may be appropriate; and
8. the number of violations found in the investigation.

Fine Amount

In the state of California, the board's regulation provides that a fine can be up to a maximum of $5,000 per licensee for each citation. If an investigation involves multiple licensees (e.g., a staff pharmacist, the pharmacist-in-charge, a pharmacy technician, and the pharmacy), each licensee may be cited and fined. The amount of each fine will depend on which of the previously named factors are present and applicable to each licensee. The amount of the fine is determined on a case-by-case basis.

Request for an Office Conference

A licensee has fourteen calendar days after service of a letter of admonishment or a citation and fine to request an office conference, pursuant to Title 16 of the California Code of Regulations (16 CCR) section 1775.4(b).

Appeal Process for Citation and Fines

If a hearing is not requested, payment of a fine does not constitute an admission of the violation charged. A licensee has thirty days after service of the citation and fine to file a written appeal (request for a hearing). Appeals are referred to the attorney general's office and proceed in accordance with the Administrative Procedure Act (a copy is provided at the end of this chapter).

Complaint Investigation

When the board of pharmacy receives a complaint or uncovers potential violations of the law through its own efforts, the matter may be assigned for investigation either to an enforcement analyst or to an inspector. During the course of the investigation, evidence is obtained to determine if the alleged violation of law occurred. As part of the investigation, the licensee may be asked for documents (e.g., business records, patient records, and/or policies and procedures) and/or for statements regarding the events that allegedly transpired.

Licensees are encouraged to respond in a timely and accurate manner, as the information is used as part of the investigative record. A licensee's responsiveness or nonresponsiveness may be considered as mitigation or aggravation. The licensee may want to contact an attorney in his or her state experienced with pharmacy board matters to discuss the matter and if necessary seek legal representation before proceeding.

If it is believed that a violation of pharmacy law took place, the licensee may be advised of the alleged violation through an Order of Correction (Business & Professions Code [B&PC] section 4083) on the inspection report. This order simply notifies the licensee of the violations of law that the inspector believes occurred and directs the licensee to comply within thirty days by submitting a corrective action plan to the inspector.

After the investigation is completed and there is a determination by the inspector or enforcement analyst that the law was violated, the case is referred to a supervising inspector for review. If the supervising inspector determines that there was no violation or that the violation was so minor that it does not merit any action, the case may be closed with the Order of Correction only, and the matter goes no further.

Recommended Actions

If after review by a supervising inspector, it is determined that action may be warranted, the case is referred to the board's executive officer. The executive officer, with the assistance of the supervising inspectors, reviews the matter and determines the appropriate course of action. The types of potential action include the following:

1. *Case Closure—No Further Action.* The executive officer may decide that no action is warranted. This may occur when the executive officer finds that there has been no violation, that the violation is so minor that it does not merit an action, or that the mitigating circumstances are such that it would be best not to pursue an action. The matter then ends.
2. *Order of Correction.* If an Order of Correction has been issued, the licensee can contest the order by requesting an office conference with the executive officer. However, if no office conference is requested, compliance with the order is not an admission of the noted violation. The order of correction is not the board's final or formal determination regarding the matter, nor is it a citation or a disciplinary action. A copy of the order of correction and the corrective action plan must be maintained on the pharmacy premises for at least three years from the letter's date of issuance. The order of correction will not be considered a public record for purposes of disclosure.
3. *Further Investigation.* The executive officer may decide that there is insufficient evidence to determine whether a violation occurred or whether any action is warranted. The executive officer may then send the matter back for further investigation.
4. *Letter of Admonishment.* After review, the executive officer may issue a Letter of Admonishment to the licensee for failure to comply with pharmacy law. The letter will include a reference to the statute or regulation violated, a description of the nature and facts of the violation, and a notice to the licensee of available appeal rights.
5. *Citation and Fine.* May be as set earlier.
6. *Refer to the Attorney General's Office.*

Issuance of Orders of Abatement

The board is authorized to issue an order of abatement, requiring a person or entity to whom a citation has been issued to demonstrate how future compliance with pharmacy law will be accomplished. In such cases a licensee may be required to do such things as submit a corrective action plan and complete up to six hours of continuing education courses in subject matter specified in the order of abatement (CA B&PC Section 4314).

California Code and Administrative Procedure Act

This section will focus upon the Government Code and the Administrative Procedure Act of California. This is included for teaching purposes. As you read through these selected sections, you will note the safeguards against arbitrary actions which have been put in place. Your state or specific practice modality may be controlled by other similar acts. Regardless of the geographic specifics, this section, which focuses on portions of the California Code and Administrative Procedure Act, is illustrative of the codification of the administrative procedural function of agencies.

CALIFORNIA CODES
GOVERNMENT CODE
SECTIONS 11150-11162

11150. It is the policy of this State to vest in the Governor the civil administration of the laws of the State and for the purpose of aiding the Governor in the execution and administration of the laws to divide the executive and administrative work into departments as provided by law.

11151. Each department shall maintain an office and the director of each department who is a member of the Governor's council shall reside at Sacramento. Each department shall adopt and keep an official seal.

11152. Subject to the approval of the Governor, the head of each department may arrange and classify the work of the department and consolidate, abolish, or create divisions thereof. So far as consistent with law the head of each department may adopt such rules and regulations as are necessary to govern the activities of the department and may assign to its officers and employees such duties as he sees fit. For the betterment of the public service, he may reassign to any employees under the chief of any division, such duties as he sees fit.

11152.5. Wherever, pursuant to this code, any state department, officer, board, agency, committee, or commission is authorized to adopt rules and regulations, such rules and regulations which are building standards, as defined in Section 18909 of the Health and Safety Code, shall be adopted pursuant to the provisions of Part 2.5 (commencing with Section 18901) of Division 13 of the Health and Safety Code unless the provisions of Sections 18930, 18933, 18938, 18940, 18943, 18944, and 18945 of the Health and Safety Code are expressly excepted in the provision of this code under which the authority to adopt the specific building standard is delegated. Any building standard adopted in violation of this section shall have no force or effect. Any building standard adopted prior to January 1, 1980, pursuant to this code and not expressly excepted by statute from such provisions of the State Building Standards Law shall remain in effect only until January 1, 1985, or until adopted, amended, or superseded by provisions published in the State Building Standards Code, whichever occurs sooner.

11153. Except as otherwise provided by law, each division of a department shall be in charge of a chief who shall be appointed by the head of the department and receive such compensation as is fixed according to law. When a new division is created and a new chief appointed the salary of the chief shall be fixed by the Governor until fixed by the Legislature and shall not exceed the compensation paid for like services.

11154. Except as otherwise provided by law, the head of each department may, with the approval of the Governor, appoint such officers and employees as are necessary; and prescribe their duties, and fix their salaries in accordance with classifications made by the State Personnel Board.

11155. The head of a department has no authority to obligate the State for salaries in excess of money available by law for that purpose.

11156. In addition to any bonds required by the Director of General Services the head of each department may require any officer or employee in his department to execute an official bond in such amount as he determines.

11157. The Attorney General is the legal adviser of each department in all matters relating to the department and to the powers and duties of its officers. Upon request of the head of a department, the Attorney General, or under his direction, the district attorney of any county in which the proceeding is brought, shall aid in any investigation, hearing, prosecution or trial had under the laws which the department is required to administer, and shall institute and prosecute all necessary actions or proceedings for the enforcement of such law and for the punishment of all violations thereof.

11158. The sheriffs in the several counties shall execute all lawful orders of a department in their counties.

11159. Whenever a department succeeds to and is vested with the duties, powers, purposes, responsibilities and jurisdiction of a State agency, deputy, employee, or employment, the name or designation of the State agency, deputy, employee, or employment and of its several members, officers, deputies and employees, when used in any law then in force or thereafter enacted, shall be construed to mean the department, as though the title of the department had been specifically set forth in the law.

11160. Whenever a department is invested with the power and is charged with the duty of administering and enforcing any law which imposes a duty or jurisdiction or confers an authority upon any State agency, deputy or employee, to administer its provisions, the duty, jurisdiction, and authority are hereby imposed upon and transferred to the department and its officers, deputies and employees with the same effect as if the name of the department occurred in the law in each instance in lieu of the name of the State agency, the member, officer, deputy or employee, as the case may be.

11161. Every person is subject to the same obligations and duties, and has the same rights as if the rights, powers and duties imposed upon and transferred to a department were exercised by the State agency, deputy or employee designated in the laws administered by departments created in conformity with this chapter. Every person is subject to the same penalties, civil or criminal, for failure to perform any obligation, or duty, or for doing a prohibited act as if the obligation or duty arose from or was prohibited by the State agency, deputy or employee, designated in the laws administered by the department.

11162. Every State officer, deputy and employee is subject to the same penalties, civil or criminal, for any offense as are prescribed by existing law for the same offense by any officer, deputy or employee whose powers or duties are devolved upon him under any law creating a new department. No law creating a new department affects any act done, ratified, or confirmed, or any right accrued or established, or any offense committed, or any action or proceeding had or commenced in a civil or criminal cause before such law takes effect; but such right may be enforced, offense punished and action or proceeding prosecuted and continued by the department having or acquiring jurisdiction of the subject matter to which such litigation or proceeding pertains, with the same effect as if the transfer of such rights powers, duties, responsibilities and jurisdiction had not been made to the department.

CALIFORNIA GOVERNMENT CODE
SECTIONS 11500-11529

11500. In this chapter unless the context or subject matter otherwise requires:

(a) "Agency" includes the state boards, commissions, and officers to which this chapter is made applicable by law, except that wherever the word "agency" alone is used the power to act may be delegated by the agency, and wherever the words "agency itself" are used the power to act shall not be delegated unless the statutes relating to the particular agency authorize the delegation of the agency's power to hear and decide.

(b) "Party" includes the agency, the respondent, and any person, other than an officer or an employee of the agency in his or her official capacity, who has been allowed to appear or participate in the proceeding.

(c) "Respondent" means any person against whom an accusation is filed pursuant to Section 11503 or against whom a statement of issues is filed pursuant to Section 11504.

(d) "Administrative law judge" means an individual qualified under Section 11502.

(e) "Agency member" means any person who is a member of any agency to which this chapter is applicable and includes any person who himself or herself constitutes an agency.

11501. (a) This chapter applies to any agency as determined by the statutes relating to that agency.

(b) This chapter applies to an adjudicative proceeding of an agency created on or after July 1, 1997, unless the statutes relating to the proceeding provide otherwise.

(c) Chapter 4.5 (commencing with Section 11400) applies to an adjudicative proceeding required to be conducted under this chapter, unless the statutes relating to the proceeding provide otherwise.

11502. (a) All hearings of state agencies required to be conducted under this chapter shall be conducted by administrative law judges on the staff of the Office of Administrative Hearings. This subdivision applies to a hearing required to be conducted under this chapter that is conducted under the informal hearing or emergency decision procedure provided in Chapter 4.5 (commencing with Section 11400).

(b) The Director of the Office of Administrative Hearings has power to appoint a staff of administrative law judges for the office as provided in Section 11370.3. Each administrative law judge shall have been admitted to practice law in this state for at least five years immediately preceding his or her appointment and shall possess any additional qualifications established by the State Personnel Board for the particular class of position involved.

11503. A hearing to determine whether a right, authority, license or privilege should be revoked, suspended, limited or conditioned shall be initiated by filing an accusation. The accusation shall be a written statement of charges which shall set forth in ordinary and concise language the acts or omissions with which the respondent is charged, to the end that the respondent will be able to prepare his defense. It shall specify the statutes and rules which the respondent is alleged to have violated, but shall not consist merely of charges phrased in the language of such statutes and rules. The accusation shall be verified unless made by a public officer acting in his official capacity or by an employee of the agency before which the proceeding is to be held. The verification may be on information and belief.

11504. A hearing to determine whether a right, authority, license, or privilege should be granted, issued, or renewed shall be initiated by filing a statement of issues. The statement of issues shall be a written statement specifying the statutes and rules with which the respondent must show compliance by producing proof at the hearing and, in addition, any particular matters that have come to the attention of the initiating party and that would authorize a denial of the agency action sought. The statement of issues shall be verified unless made by a public officer acting in his or her official capacity or by an employee of the agency before which the proceeding is to be held. The verification may be on information and belief. The statement of issues shall be served in the same manner as an accusation, except that, if the hearing is held at the request of the respondent, Sections 11505 and 11506 shall not apply and the statement of issues together with the notice of hearing shall be delivered or mailed to the parties as provided in Section 11509.

Unless a statement to respondent is served pursuant to Section 11505, a copy of Sections 11507.5, 11507.6, and 11507.7, and the name and address of the person to whom requests permitted by Section 11505 may be made, shall be served with the statement of issues.

11504.5. In the following sections of this chapter, all references to accusations shall be deemed to be applicable to statements of issues except in those cases mentioned in subdivision (a) of Section 11505 and Section 11506 where compliance is not required.

11505. (a) Upon the filing of the accusation the agency shall serve a copy thereof on the respondent as provided in subdivision (c).

The agency may include with the accusation any information which it deems appropriate, but it shall include a post card or other form entitled Notice of Defense which, when signed by or on behalf of the respondent and returned to the agency, will acknowledge service of the accusation and constitute a notice of defense under Section 11506. The copy of the accusation shall include or be accompanied by

(1) a statement that respondent may request a hearing by filing a notice of defense as provided in Section 11506 within 15 days after service upon the respondent of the accusation, and that failure to do so will constitute a waiver of the respondent's right to a hearing, and

(2) copies of Sections 11507.5, 11507.6, and 11507.7.

(b) The statement to respondent shall be substantially in the following form:

Unless a written request for a hearing signed by or on behalf of the person named as respondent in the accompanying accusation is delivered or mailed to the agency within 15 days after the accusation was personally served on you or mailed to you, (here insert name of agency) may proceed upon the accusation without a hearing. The request for a hearing may be made by delivering or mailing the enclosed form entitled Notice of Defense, or by delivering or mailing a notice of defense as provided by Section 11506 of the Government Code to: (here insert name and address of agency). You may, but need not, be represented by counsel at any or all stages of these proceedings.

If you desire the names and addresses of witnesses or an opportunity to inspect and copy the items mentioned in Section 11507.6 of the Government Code in the possession, custody or control of the agency, you may contact: (here insert name and address of appropriate person).

The hearing may be postponed for good cause. If you have good cause, you are obliged to notify the agency or, if an administrative law judge has been assigned to the hearing, the Office of Administrative Hearings, within 10 working days after you discover the good cause. Failure to give notice within 10 days will deprive you of a postponement.

(c) The accusation and all accompanying information may be sent to the respondent by any means selected by the agency. But no order adversely affecting the rights of the respondent shall be made by the agency in any case unless the respondent shall have been served personally or by registered mail as provided herein, or shall have filed a notice of defense or otherwise appeared. Service may be proved in the manner authorized in civil actions. Service by registered mail shall be effective if a statute or agency rule requires the respondent to file the respondent's address with the agency and to notify the agency of any change, and if a registered letter containing the accusation and accompanying material is mailed, addressed to the respondent at the latest address on file with the agency.

11506. (a) Within 15 days after service of the accusation the respondent may file with the agency a notice of defense in which the respondent may:

(1) Request a hearing.

(2) Object to the accusation upon the ground that it does not state acts or omissions upon which the agency may proceed.

(3) Object to the form of the accusation on the ground that it is so indefinite or uncertain that the respondent cannot identify the transaction or prepare a defense.

(4) Admit the accusation in whole or in part.

(5) Present new matter by way of defense.

(6) Object to the accusation upon the ground that, under the circumstances, compliance with the requirements of a regulation would result in a material violation of another regulation enacted by another department affecting substantive rights.

(b) Within the time specified respondent may file one or more notices of defense upon any or all of these grounds but all of these notices shall be filed within that period unless the agency in its discretion authorizes the filing of a later notice.

(c) The respondent shall be entitled to a hearing on the merits if the respondent files a notice of defense, and the notice shall be deemed a specific denial of all parts of the accusation not expressly admitted. Failure to file a notice of defense shall constitute a waiver of respondent's right to a hearing, but the agency in its discretion may nevertheless grant a hearing. Unless objection is taken as provided in paragraph (3) of subdivision (a), all objections to the form of the accusation shall be deemed waived.

(d) The notice of defense shall be in writing signed by or on behalf of the respondent and shall state the respondent's mailing address. It need not be verified or follow any particular form.

(e) As used in this section, "file," "files," "filed," or "filing" means "delivered or mailed" to the agency as provided in Section 11505.

11507. At any time before the matter is submitted for decision the agency may file or permit the filing of an amended or supplemental accusation. All parties shall be notified thereof. If the amended or supplemental accusation presents new charges the agency shall afford respondent a reasonable opportunity to prepare his defense thereto, but he shall not be entitled to file a further pleading unless the agency in its discretion so orders. Any new charges shall be deemed controverted, and any objections to the amended or supplemental accusation may be made orally and shall be noted in the record.

11507.3. (a) When proceedings that involve a common question of law or fact are pending, the administrative law judge on the judge's own motion or on motion of a party may order a joint hearing of any or all the matters at issue in the proceedings. The administrative law judge may order all the proceedings consolidated and may make orders concerning the procedure that may tend to avoid unnecessary costs or delay.

(b) The administrative law judge on the judge's own motion or on motion of a party, in furtherance of convenience or to avoid prejudice or when separate hearings will be conducive to expedition and economy, may order a separate hearing of any issue, including an issue raised in the notice of defense, or of any number of issues.

11507.5. The provisions of Section 11507.6 provide the exclusive right to and method of discovery as to any proceeding governed by this chapter.

11507.6. After initiation of a proceeding in which a respondent or other party is entitled to a hearing on the merits, a party, upon written request made to another party, prior to the hearing and within 30 days after service by the agency of the initial pleading or within 15 days after the service of an additional pleading, is entitled to

(1) obtain the names and addresses of witnesses to the extent known to the other party, including, but not limited to, those intended to be called to testify at the hearing, and

(2) inspect and make a copy of any of the following in the possession or custody or under the control of the other party:

(a) A statement of a person, other than the respondent, named in the initial administrative pleading, or in any additional pleading, when it is claimed that the act or omission of the respondent as to this person is the basis for the administrative proceeding;

(b) A statement pertaining to the subject matter of the proceeding made by any party to another party or person;

(c) Statements of witnesses then proposed to be called by the party and of other persons having personal knowledge of the acts, omissions or events which are the basis for the proceeding, not included in (a) or (b) above;

(d) All writings, including, but not limited to, reports of mental, physical and blood examinations and things which the party then proposes to offer in evidence;

(e) Any other writing or thing which is relevant and which would be admissible in evidence;

(f) Investigative reports made by or on behalf of the agency or other party pertaining to the subject matter of the proceeding, to the extent that these reports (1) contain the names and addresses of witnesses or of persons having personal knowledge of the acts, omissions or events which are the basis for the proceeding, or (2) reflect matters perceived by the investigator in the course of his or her investigation, or (3) contain or include by attachment any statement or writing described in (a) to (e), inclusive, or summary thereof.

For the purpose of this section, "statements" include written statements by the person signed or otherwise authenticated by him or her, stenographic, mechanical, electrical or other recordings, or transcripts thereof, of oral statements by the person, and written reports or summaries of these oral statements.

Nothing in this section shall authorize the inspection or copying of any writing or thing which is privileged from disclosure by law or otherwise made confidential or protected as the attorney's work product.

11507.7. (a) Any party claiming the party's request for discovery pursuant to Section 11507.6 has not been complied with may serve and file with the administrative law judge a motion to compel discovery, naming as respondent the party refusing or failing to comply with Section 11507.6. The motion shall state facts showing the respondent party failed or refused to comply with Section 11507.6, a description of the matters sought to be discovered, the reason or reasons why the matter is discoverable under that section, that a reasonable and good faith attempt to contact the respondent for an informal resolution of the issue has been made, and the ground or grounds of respondent's refusal so far as known to the moving party.

(b) The motion shall be served upon respondent party and filed within 15 days after the respondent party first evidenced failure or refusal to comply with Section 11507.6 or within 30 days after request was made and the party has failed to reply to the request, or within another time provided by stipulation, whichever period is longer.

(c) The hearing on the motion to compel discovery shall be held within 15 days after the motion is made, or a later time that the administrative law judge may on the judge's own motion for good cause determine. The respondent party shall have the right to serve and file a written answer or other response to the motion before or at the time of the hearing.

(d) Where the matter sought to be discovered is under the custody or control of the respondent party and the respondent party asserts that the matter is not a discoverable matter under the provisions of Section 11507.6, or is privileged against disclosure under those provisions, the administrative law judge may order lodged with it matters provided in subdivision (b) of Section 915 of the Evidence Code and examine the matters in accordance with its provisions.

(e) The administrative law judge shall decide the case on the matters examined in camera, the papers filed by the parties, and such oral argument and additional evidence as the administrative law judge may allow.

(f) Unless otherwise stipulated by the parties, the administrative law judge shall no later than 15 days after the hearing make its order denying or granting the motion. The order shall be in writing setting forth the matters the moving party is entitled to discover under Section 11507.6. A copy of the order shall forthwith be served by mail by the administrative law judge upon the parties. Where the order grants the motion in whole or in part, the order shall not become effective until 10 days after the date the order is served.

Where the order denies relief to the moving party, the order shall be effective on the date it is served.

11508. (a) The agency shall consult the office, and subject to the availability of its staff, shall determine the time and place of hearing. The hearing shall be held in Oakland if the transaction occurred or the respondent resides within the First or Sixth Appellate District, in the County of Los Angeles if the transaction occurred or the respondent resides within the Second or Fourth Appellate District other than the County of Imperial or San Diego, in the County of Sacramento if the transaction occurred or the respondent resides within the Third or Fifth Appellate District, and in the County of San Diego if the transaction occurred or the respondent resides within the Fourth Appellate District in the County of Imperial or San Diego.

(b) Notwithstanding subdivision (a):

(1) If the transaction occurred in a district other than that of respondent's residence, the agency may select the county appropriate for either district.

(2) The agency may select a different place nearer the place where the transaction occurred or the respondent resides.

(3) The parties by agreement may select any place within the state.

(c) The respondent may move for, and the administrative law judge has discretion to grant or deny, a change in the place of the hearing. A motion for a change in the place of the hearing shall be made within 10 days after service of the notice of hearing on the respondent.

11509. The agency shall deliver or mail a notice of hearing to all parties at least 10 days prior to the hearing. The hearing shall not be prior to the expiration of the time within which the respondent is entitled to file a notice of defense.

The notice to respondent shall be substantially in the following form but may include other information:

You are hereby notified that a hearing will be held before (here insert name of agency) at (here insert place of hearing) on the _____ day of _____, 20__, at the hour of _____, upon the charges made in the accusation served upon you. If you object to the place of hearing, you must notify the presiding officer within 10 days after this notice is served on you. Failure to notify the presiding officer within 10 days will deprive you of a change in the place of the hearing. You may be present at the hearing. You have the right to be represented by an attorney at your own expense. You are not entitled to the appointment of an attorney to represent you at public expense. You are entitled to represent yourself without legal counsel. You may present any relevant evidence, and will be given full opportunity to cross-examine all witnesses testifying against you. You are entitled to the issuance of subpoenas to compel the attendance of witnesses and the production of books, documents or other things by applying to (here insert appropriate office of agency).

11511. On verified petition of any party, an administrative law judge or, if an administrative law judge has not been appointed, an agency may order that the testimony of any material witness residing within or without the state be taken by deposition in the manner prescribed by law for depositions in civil actions under Article 3(commencing with Section 2016) of Chapter 3 of Title 4 of Part 4 of the Code of Civil Procedure. The petition shall set forth the nature of the pending proceeding; the name and address of the witness whose testimony is desired; a showing of the materiality of the testimony; a showing that the witness will be unable or cannot be compelled to attend; and shall request an order requiring the witness to appear and testify before an officer named in the petition for that purpose.

The petitioner shall serve notice of hearing and a copy of the petition on the other parties at least 10 days before the hearing.

Where the witness resides outside the state and where the administrative law judge or agency has ordered the taking of the testimony by deposition, the agency shall obtain an order of court to that effect by filing a petition therefor in the superior court in Sacramento County. The proceedings thereon shall be in accordance with the provisions of Section 11189.

11511.5. (a) On motion of a party or by order of an administrative law judge, the administrative law judge may conduct a prehearing conference. The administrative law judge shall set the time and place for the prehearing conference, and shall give reasonable written notice to all parties.

(b) The prehearing conference may deal with one or more of the following matters:

(1) Exploration of settlement possibilities.

(2) Preparation of stipulations.

(3) Clarification of issues.

(4) Rulings on identity and limitation of the number of witnesses.

(5) Objections to proffers of evidence.

(6) Order of presentation of evidence and cross-examination.

(7) Rulings regarding issuance of subpoenas and protective orders.

(8) Schedules for the submission of written briefs and schedules for the commencement and conduct of the hearing.

(9) Exchange of witness lists and of exhibits or documents to be offered in evidence at the hearing.

(10) Motions for intervention.

(11) Exploration of the possibility of using alternative dispute resolution provided in Article 5 (commencing with Section 11420.10) of, or the informal hearing procedure provided in Article 10 (commencing with Section 11445.10) of, Chapter 4.5, and objections to use of the informal hearing procedure. Use of alternative dispute resolution or of the informal hearing procedure is subject to subdivision (d).

(12) Any other matters as shall promote the orderly and prompt conduct of the hearing.

(c) The administrative law judge may conduct all or part of the prehearing conference by telephone, television, or other electronic means if each participant in the conference has an opportunity to participate in and to hear the entire proceeding while it is taking place.

(d) With the consent of the parties, the prehearing conference may be converted immediately into alternative dispute resolution or an informal hearing. With the consent of the parties, the proceeding may be converted into alternative dispute resolution to be conducted at another time. With the consent of the agency, the proceeding may be converted into an informal hearing to be conducted at another time subject to the right of a party to object to use of the informal hearing procedure as provided in Section 11445.30.

(e) The administrative law judge shall issue a prehearing order incorporating the matters determined at the prehearing conference.

The administrative law judge may direct one or more of the parties to prepare a prehearing order.

11511.7. (a) The administrative law judge may order the parties to attend and participate in a settlement conference. The administrative law judge shall set the time and place for the settlement conference, and shall give reasonable written notice to all parties.

(b) The administrative law judge at the settlement conference shall not preside as administrative law judge at the hearing unless otherwise stipulated by the parties. The administrative law judge may conduct all or part of the settlement conference by telephone, television, or other electronic means if each participant in the conference has an opportunity to participate in and to hear the entire proceeding while it is taking place.

11512. (a) Every hearing in a contested case shall be presided over by an administrative law judge. The agency itself shall determine whether the administrative law judge is to hear the case alone or whether the agency itself is to hear the case with the administrative law judge.

(b) When the agency itself hears the case, the administrative law judge shall preside at the hearing, rule on the admission and exclusion of evidence, and advise the agency on matters of law; the agency itself shall exercise all other powers relating to the conduct of the hearing but may delegate any or all of them to the administrative law judge. When the administrative law judge alone hears a case, he or she shall exercise all powers relating to the conduct of the hearing. A ruling of the administrative law judge admitting or excluding evidence is subject to review in the same manner and to the same extent as the administrative law judge's proposed decision in the proceeding.

(c) An administrative law judge or agency member shall voluntarily disqualify himself or herself and withdraw from any case in which there are grounds for disqualification, including disqualification under Section 11425.40. The parties may waive the disqualification by a writing that recites the grounds for disqualification. A waiver is effective only when signed by all parties, accepted by the administrative law judge or agency member, and included in the record. Any party may request the disqualification of any administrative law judge or agency member by filing an affidavit, prior to the taking of evidence at a hearing, stating with particularity the grounds upon which it is claimed that the administrative law judge or agency member is disqualified. Where the request concerns an agency member, the issue shall be determined by the other members of the agency. Where the request concerns the administrative law judge, the issue shall be determined by the agency itself if the agency itself hears the case with the administrative law judge, otherwise the issue shall be determined by the administrative law judge. No agency member shall withdraw voluntarily or be subject to disqualification if his or her disqualification would prevent the existence of a quorum qualified to act in the particular case, except that a substitute qualified to act may be appointed by the appointing authority.

(d) The proceedings at the hearing shall be reported by a stenographic reporter. However, upon the consent of all the parties, the proceedings may be reported electronically.

(e) Whenever, after the agency itself has commenced to hear the case with an administrative law judge presiding, a quorum no longer exists, the administrative law judge who is presiding shall complete the hearing as if sitting alone and shall render a proposed decision in accordance with subdivision (b) of Section 11517.

11513. (a) Oral evidence shall be taken only on oath or affirmation.

(b) Each party shall have these rights: to call and examine witnesses, to introduce exhibits; to cross-examine opposing witnesses on any matter relevant to the issues even though that matter was not covered in the direct examination; to impeach any witness regardless of which party first called him or her to testify; and to rebut the evidence against him or her. If respondent does not testify in his or her own behalf he or she may be called and examined as if under cross-examination.

(c) The hearing need not be conducted according to technical rules relating to evidence and witnesses, except as hereinafter provided.

Any relevant evidence shall be admitted if it is the sort of evidence on which responsible persons are accustomed to rely in the conduct of serious affairs, regardless of the existence of any common law or statutory rule which might make improper the admission of the evidence over objection in civil actions.

(d) Hearsay evidence may be used for the purpose of supplementing or explaining other evidence but over timely objection shall not be sufficient in itself to support a finding unless it would be admissible over objection in civil actions. An objection is timely if made before submission of the case or on reconsideration.

(e) The rules of privilege shall be effective to the extent that they are otherwise required by statute to be recognized at the hearing.

(f) The presiding officer has discretion to exclude evidence if its probative value is substantially outweighed by the probability that its admission will necessitate undue consumption of time.

11514. (a) At any time 10 or more days prior to a hearing or a continued hearing, any party may mail or deliver to the opposing party a copy of any affidavit which he proposes to introduce in evidence, together with a notice as provided in subdivision (b).

Unless the opposing party, within seven days after such mailing or delivery, mails or delivers to the proponent a request to cross-examine an affiant, his right to cross-examine such affiant is waived and the affidavit, if introduced in evidence, shall be given the same effect as if the affiant had testified orally. If an opportunity to cross-examine an affiant is not afforded after request therefor is made as herein provided, the affidavit may be introduced in evidence, but shall be given only the same effect as other hearsay evidence.

(b) The notice referred to in subdivision (a) shall be substantially in the following form:

The accompanying affidavit of (here insert name of affiant) will be introduced as evidence at the hearing in (here insert title of proceeding). (Here insert name of affiant) will not be called to testify orally and you will not be entitled to question him unless you notify (here insert name of proponent or his attorney) at (here insert address) that you wish to cross-examine him. To be effective your request must be mailed or delivered to (here insert name of proponent or his attorney) on or before (here insert a date seven days after the date of mailing or delivering the affidavit to the opposing party).

11515. In reaching a decision official notice may be taken, either before or after submission of the case for decision, of any generally accepted technical or scientific matter within the agency's special field, and of any fact which may be judicially noticed by the courts of this State. Parties present at the hearing shall be informed of the matters to be noticed, and those matters shall be noted in the record, referred to therein, or appended thereto. Any such party shall be given a reasonable opportunity on request to refute the officially noticed matters by evidence or by written or oral presentation of authority, the matter of such refutation to be determined by the agency.

11516. The agency may order amendment of the accusation after submission of the case for decision. Each party shall be given notice of the intended amendment and opportunity to show that he will be prejudiced thereby unless the case is reopened to permit the introduction of additional evidence in his behalf. If such prejudice is shown the agency shall reopen the case to permit the introduction of additional evidence.

11517. (a) A contested case may be originally heard by the agency itself and subdivision (b) shall apply. Alternatively, at the discretion of the agency, an administrative law judge may originally hear the case alone and subdivision (c) shall apply.

(b) If a contested case is originally heard before an agency itself, all of the following provisions apply:

(1) An administrative law judge shall be present during the consideration of the case and, if requested, shall assist and advise the agency in the conduct of the hearing.

(2) No member of the agency who did not hear the evidence shall vote on the decision.

(3) The agency shall issue its decision within 100 days of submission of the case.

(c) (1) If a contested case is originally heard by an administrative law judge alone, he or she shall prepare within 30 days after the case is submitted to him or her a proposed decision in a form that may be adopted by the agency as the final decision in the case. Failure of the administrative law judge to deliver a proposed decision within the time required does not prejudice the rights of the agency in the case. Thirty days after the receipt by the agency of the proposed decision, a copy of the proposed decision shall be filed by the agency as a public record and a copy shall be served by the agency on each party and his or her attorney. The filing and service is not an adoption of a proposed decision by the agency.

(2) Within 100 days of receipt by the agency of the administrative law judge's proposed decision, the agency may act as prescribed in subparagraphs (A) to (E), inclusive. If the agency fails to act as prescribed in subparagraphs (A) to (E), inclusive, within 100 days of receipt of the proposed decision, the proposed decision shall be deemed adopted by the agency. The agency may do any of the following:

(A) Adopt the proposed decision in its entirety.

(B) Reduce or otherwise mitigate the proposed penalty and adopt the balance of the proposed decision.

(C) Make technical or other minor changes in the proposed decision and adopt it as the decision. Action by the agency under this paragraph is limited to a clarifying change or a change of a similar nature that does not affect the factual or legal basis of the proposed decision.

(D) Reject the proposed decision and refer the case to the same administrative law judge if reasonably available, otherwise to another administrative law judge, to take additional evidence. If the case is referred to an administrative law judge pursuant to this subparagraph, he or she shall prepare a revised proposed decision, as provided in paragraph (1), based upon the additional evidence and the transcript and other papers that are part of the record of the prior hearing. A copy of the revised proposed decision shall be furnished to each party and his or her attorney as prescribed in this subdivision.

(E) Reject the proposed decision, and decide the case upon the record, including the transcript, or upon an agreed statement of the parties, with or without taking additional evidence. By stipulation of the parties, the agency may decide the case upon the record without including the transcript. If the agency acts pursuant to this subparagraph, all of the following provisions apply:

(i) A copy of the record shall be made available to the parties. The agency may require payment of fees covering direct costs of making the copy.

(ii) The agency itself shall not decide any case provided for in this subdivision without affording the parties the opportunity to present either oral or written argument before the agency itself. If additional oral evidence is introduced before the agency itself, no agency member may vote unless the member heard the additional oral evidence.

(iii) The authority of the agency itself to decide the case under this subdivision includes authority to decide some but not all issues in the case.

(iv) If the agency elects to proceed under this subparagraph, the agency shall issue its final decision not later than 100 days after rejection of the proposed decision. If the agency elects to proceed under this subparagraph, and has ordered a transcript of the proceedings before the administrative law judge, the agency shall issue its final decision not later than 100 days after receipt of the transcript. If the agency finds that a further delay is required by special circumstance, it shall issue an order delaying the decision for no more than 30 days and specifying the reasons therefor. The order shall be subject to judicial review pursuant to Section 11523.

(d) The decision of the agency shall be filed immediately by the agency as a public record and a copy shall be served by the agency on each party and his or her attorney.

11518. Copies of the decision shall be delivered to the parties personally or sent to them by registered mail.

11518.5. (a) Within 15 days after service of a copy of the decision on a party, but not later than the effective date of the decision, the party may apply to the agency for correction of a mistake or clerical error in the decision, stating the specific ground on which the application is made. Notice of the application shall be given to the other parties to the proceeding. The application is not a prerequisite for seeking judicial review.

(b) The agency may refer the application to the administrative law judge who formulated the proposed decision or may delegate its authority under this section to one or more persons.

(c) The agency may deny the application, grant the application and modify the decision, or grant the application and set the matter for further proceedings. The application is considered denied if the agency does not dispose of it within 15 days after it is made or a longer time that the agency provides by regulation.

(d) Nothing in this section precludes the agency, on its own motion or on motion of the administrative law judge, from modifying the decision to correct a mistake or clerical error. A modification under this subdivision shall be made within 15 days after issuance of the decision.

(e) The agency shall, within 15 days after correction of a mistake or clerical error in the decision, serve a copy of the correction on each party on which a copy of the decision was previously served.

11519. (a) The decision shall become effective 30 days after it is delivered or mailed to respondent unless: a reconsideration is ordered within that time, or the agency itself orders that the decision shall become effective sooner, or a stay of execution is granted.

(b) A stay of execution may be included in the decision or if not included therein may be granted by the agency at any time before the decision becomes effective. The stay of execution provided herein may be accompanied by an express condition that respondent comply with specified terms of probation; provided, however, that the terms of probation shall be just and reasonable in the light of the findings and decision.

(c) If respondent was required to register with any public officer, a notification of any suspension or revocation shall be sent to the officer after the decision has become effective.

(d) As used in subdivision (b), specified terms of probation may include an order of restitution. Where restitution is ordered and paid pursuant to the provisions of this subdivision, the amount paid shall be credited to any subsequent judgment in a civil action.

(e) The person to which the agency action is directed may not be required to comply with a decision unless the person has been served with the decision in the manner provided in Section 11505 or has actual knowledge of the decision.

(f) A nonparty may not be required to comply with a decision unless the agency has made the decision available for public inspection and copying or the nonparty has actual knowledge of the decision.

(g) This section does not preclude an agency from taking immediate action to protect the public interest in accordance with Article 13 (commencing with Section 11460.10) of Chapter 4.5.

11520. (a) If the respondent either fails to file a notice of defense or to appear at the hearing, the agency may take action based upon the respondent's express admissions or upon other evidence and affidavits may be used as evidence without any notice to respondent; and where the burden of proof is on the respondent to establish that the respondent is entitled to the agency action sought, the agency may act without taking evidence.

(b) Notwithstanding the default of the respondent, the agency or the administrative law judge, before a proposed decision is issued, has discretion to grant a hearing on reasonable notice to the parties. If the agency and administrative law judge make conflicting orders under this subdivision, the agency's order takes precedence.

The administrative law judge may order the respondent, or the respondent's attorney or other authorized representative, or both, to pay reasonable expenses, including attorney's fees, incurred by another party as a result of the respondent's failure to appear at the hearing.

(c) Within seven days after service on the respondent of a decision based on the respondent's default, the respondent may serve a written motion requesting that the decision be vacated and stating the grounds relied on. The agency in its discretion may vacate the decision and grant a hearing on a showing of good cause. As used in this subdivision, good cause includes, but is not limited to, any of the following:

(1) Failure of the person to receive notice served pursuant to Section 11505.

(2) Mistake, inadvertence, surprise, or excusable neglect.

11521. (a) The agency itself may order a reconsideration of all or part of the case on its own motion or on petition of any party. The power to order a reconsideration shall expire 30 days after the delivery or mailing of a decision to respondent, or on the date set by the agency itself as the effective date of the decision if that date occurs prior to the expiration of the 30-day period or at the termination of a stay of not to exceed 30 days which the agency may grant for the purpose of filing an application for reconsideration.

If additional time is needed to evaluate a petition for reconsideration filed prior to the expiration of any of the applicable periods, an agency may grant a stay of that expiration for no more than 10 days, solely for the purpose of considering the petition. If no action is taken on a petition within the time allowed for ordering reconsideration, the petition shall be deemed denied.

(b) The case may be reconsidered by the agency itself on all the pertinent parts of the record and such additional evidence and argument as may be permitted, or may be assigned to an administrative law judge. A reconsideration assigned to an administrative law judge shall be subject to the procedure provided in Section 11517.

If oral evidence is introduced before the agency itself, no agency member may vote unless he or she heard the evidence.

11522. A person whose license has been revoked or suspended may petition the agency for reinstatement or reduction of penalty after a period of not less than one year has elapsed from the effective date of the decision or from the date of the denial of a similar petition. The agency shall give notice to the Attorney General of the filing of the petition and the Attorney General and the petitioner shall be afforded an opportunity to present either oral or written argument before the agency itself. The agency itself shall decide the petition, and the decision shall include the reasons therefor, and any terms and conditions that the agency reasonably deems appropriate to impose as a condition of reinstatement. This section shall not apply if the statutes dealing with the particular agency contain different provisions for reinstatement or reduction of penalty.

11523. Judicial review may be had by filing a petition for a writ of mandate in accordance with the provisions of the Code of Civil Procedure, subject, however, to the statutes relating to the particular agency. Except as otherwise provided in this section, the petition shall be filed within 30 days after the last day on which reconsideration can be ordered. The right to petition shall not be affected by the failure to seek reconsideration before the agency.

On request of the petitioner for a record of the proceedings, the complete record of the proceedings, or the parts thereof as are designated by the petitioner in the request, shall be prepared by the Office of Administrative Hearings or the agency and shall be delivered to petitioner, within 30 days after the request, which time shall be extended for good cause shown, upon the payment of the fee specified in Section 69950 for the transcript, the cost of preparation of other portions of the record and for certification thereof. Thereafter, the remaining balance of any costs or charges for the preparation of the record shall be assessed against the petitioner whenever the agency prevails on judicial review following trial of the cause. These costs or charges constitute a debt of the petitioner which is collectible by the agency in the same manner as in the case of an obligation under a contract, and no license shall be renewed or reinstated where the petitioner has failed to pay all of these costs or charges. The complete record includes the pleadings, all notices and orders issued by the agency, any proposed decision by an administrative law judge, the final decision, a transcript of all proceedings, the exhibits admitted or rejected, the written evidence and any other papers in the case. Where petitioner, within 10 days after the last day on which reconsideration can be ordered, requests the agency to prepare all or any part of the record the time within which a petition may be filed shall be extended until 30 days after its delivery to him or her.

The agency may file with the court the original of any document in the record in lieu of a copy thereof. In the event that the petitioner prevails in overturning the administrative decision following judicial review, the agency shall reimburse the petitioner for all costs of transcript preparation, compilation of the record, and certification.

11524. (a) The agency may grant continuances. When an administrative law judge of the Office of Administrative Hearings has been assigned to the hearing, no continuance may be granted except by him or her or by the presiding judge of the appropriate regional office of the Office of Administrative Hearings, for good cause shown.

(b) When seeking a continuance, a party shall apply for the continuance within 10 working days following the time the party discovered or reasonably should have discovered the event or occurrence which establishes the good cause for the continuance. A continuance may be granted for good cause after the 10 working days have lapsed if the party seeking the continuance is not responsible for and has made a good faith effort to prevent the condition or event establishing the good cause.

(c) In the event that an application for a continuance by a party is denied by an administrative law judge of the Office of Administrative Hearings, and the party seeks judicial review thereof, the party shall, within 10 working days of the denial, make application for appropriate judicial relief in the superior court or be barred from judicial review thereof as a matter of jurisdiction.

A party applying for judicial relief from the denial shall give notice to the agency and other parties. Notwithstanding Section 1010 of the Code of Civil Procedure, the notice may be either oral at the time of the denial of application for a continuance or written at the same time application is made in court for judicial relief. This subdivision does not apply to the Department of Alcoholic Beverage Control.

11526. The members of an agency qualified to vote on any question may vote by mail or another appropriate method.

11527. Any sums authorized to be expended under this chapter by any agency shall be a legal charge against the funds of the agency.

11528. In any proceedings under this chapter any agency, agency member, secretary of an agency, hearing reporter, or administrative law judge has power to administer oaths and affirmations and to certify to official acts.

11529. (a) The administrative law judge of the Medical Quality Hearing Panel established pursuant to Section 11371 may issue an interim order suspending a license, or imposing drug testing, continuing education, supervision of procedures, or other license restrictions. Interim orders may be issued only if the affidavits in support of the petition show that the licensee has engaged in, or is about to engage in, acts or omissions constituting a violation of the Medical Practice Act or the appropriate practice act governing each allied health profession, or is unable to practice safely due to a mental or physical condition, and that permitting the licensee to continue to engage in the profession for which the license was issued will endanger the public health, safety, or welfare.

(b) All orders authorized by this section shall be issued only after a hearing conducted pursuant to subdivision (d), unless it appears from the facts shown by affidavit that serious injury would result to the public before the matter can be heard on notice.

Except as provided in subdivision (c), the licensee shall receive at least 15 days' prior notice of the hearing, which notice shall include affidavits and all other information in support of the order.

(c) If an interim order is issued without notice, the administrative law judge who issued the order without notice shall cause the licensee to be notified of the order, including affidavits and all other information in support of the order by a 24-hour delivery service. That notice shall also include the date of the hearing on the order, which shall be conducted in accordance with the requirement of subdivision (d), not later than 20 days from the date of issuance. The order shall be dissolved unless the requirements of subdivision (a) are satisfied.

(d) For the purposes of the hearing conducted pursuant to this section, the licentiate shall, at a minimum, have the following rights:

(1) To be represented by counsel.

(2) To have a record made of the proceedings, copies of which may be obtained by the licentiate upon payment of any reasonable charges associated with the record.

(3) To present written evidence in the form of relevant declarations, affidavits, and documents.

The discretion of the administrative law judge to permit testimony at the hearing conducted pursuant to this section shall be identical to the discretion of a superior court judge to permit testimony at a hearing conducted pursuant to Section 527 of the Code of Civil Procedure.

(4) To present oral argument.

(e) Consistent with the burden and standards of proof applicable to a preliminary injunction entered under Section 527 of the Code of Civil Procedure, the administrative law judge shall grant the interim order where, in the exercise of discretion, the administrative law judge concludes that:

(1) There is a reasonable probability that the petitioner will prevail in the underlying action.

(2) The likelihood of injury to the public in not issuing the order outweighs the likelihood of injury to the licensee in issuing the order.

(f) In all cases where an interim order is issued, and an accusation is not filed and served pursuant to Sections 11503 and 11505 within 15 days of the date in which the parties to the hearing on the interim order have submitted the matter, the order shall be dissolved.

Upon service of the accusation the licensee shall have, in addition to the rights granted by this section, all of the rights and privileges available as specified in this chapter. If the licensee requests a hearing on the accusation, the board shall provide the licensee with a hearing within 30 days of the request, unless the licensee stipulates to a later hearing, and a decision within 15 days of the date the decision is received from the administrative law judge, or the board shall nullify the interim order previously issued, unless good cause can be shown by the Division of Medical Quality for a delay.

(g) Where an interim order is issued, a written decision shall be prepared within 15 days of the hearing, by the administrative law judge, including findings of fact and a conclusion articulating the connection between the evidence produced at the hearing and the decision reached.

(h) Notwithstanding the fact that interim orders issued pursuant to this section are not issued after a hearing as otherwise required by this chapter, interim orders so issued shall be subject to judicial review pursuant to Section 1094.5 of the Code of Civil Procedure. The relief which may be ordered shall be limited to a stay of the interim order. Interim orders issued pursuant to this section are final interim orders and, if not dissolved pursuant to subdivision (c) or (f), may only be challenged administratively at the hearing on the accusation.

(i) The interim order provided for by this section shall be:

(1) In addition to, and not a limitation on, the authority to seek injunctive relief provided for in the Business and Professions Code.

(2) A limitation on the emergency decision procedure provided in Article 13 (commencing with Section 11460.10) of Chapter 4.5.

Chapter 9

Professional Practice Acts

Norman A. Campbell

Irrespective of the type and location of a pharmacy practice, the owners (individuals, entrepreneurial enterprises, not-for-profit organizations), pharmacists, and pharmacy students must be cognizant of the guiding principles that govern the practice of pharmacy and all that might come to entail.

ESTABLISHING THE PRACTICE PARAMETERS

It is important to point out the legal framework discussed in this chapter is centered upon the practice of pharmacy to be distinguished from what commonly might be considered "drug laws." The definition of pharmacy, how it is practiced, by whom, where, and under what conditions are central to the authority granted to states and related jurisdictions by the U.S. Constitution. As a general rule, the practice of any profession or the legal parameters established for many occupations are vested in state, district, territory, or commonwealth legislative and regulatory bodies. The U.S. Congress and federal agencies may influence professional practice indirectly, as will be addressed subsequently.

One should also be aware before going forward that in addition to the pharmacy practice act, on which this discussion is centered, states will have other prevailing statutes which are modeled after federal acts. Two examples are the Federal Food, Drug, and Cosmetic Act (FDCA) and the Federal Controlled Substances Act (CSA), discussed earlier in this text. The states usually have related names and content, establishing dual jurisdiction with the federal authorities.

While a given jurisdiction's pharmacy practice act will establish the basic structure as envisioned by its legislature, as with statutory law generally, it will be the responsibility of a state regulatory agency to address the

Pharmacy Law Desk Reference
© 2007 by The Haworth Press, Inc. All rights reserved.
doi:10.1300/5790_09

specifics. Names of this body vary from state to state. For this discussion the term *board of pharmacy* will be used for simplicity and uniformity.

GENERAL PROVISIONS OF A PHARMACY PRACTICE ACT

It is important to amplify the constitutional authority alluded to above with respect to the creation of a pharmacy practice act. Paramount in this regard is the state's responsibility and authority to protect the public health and safety of its citizens. By defining health professions such as pharmacy and establishing by statute and regulation who may engage in the practice of such a profession, the state may ensure that persons not qualified to perform the controlled activities will be prohibited from exposing citizens to dangerous behavior. Said behavior may range from misleading prospective consumers of pharmacy services to illegal practice of the profession to illicit distribution of otherwise legal drugs and related health products. The matter of specific qualifications will be discussed further.

Definitions of the "practice of pharmacy" are critical to developing operational professional parameters in the several jurisdictions. Over time, these definitions have undergone considerable modification and amendment due to the influence of professional leaders nationally as well as in the various states.

As the profession of pharmacy has evolved, the state definitions have been addressed across the country with varying results. The traditional activities of prescription interpretation, evaluation, dispensing, record keeping, drug regimen review, patient counseling, and so forth have been expanded in some state acts to include such activities as prescribing and drug administration, including immunization. Just as the practice of pharmacy has been modified over time, so too have there been changes in who may perform certain activities formerly considered in law to be the sole domain of a pharmacist. Primary among these activities are those more recently relegated to pharmacy technicians and, under certain conditions, pharmacy interns.

One is advised to check the statutes and regulations of a state of interest to determine the breadth of the definition of pharmacy practice in that jurisdiction. The National Association of Boards of Pharmacy (NABP), a membership organization of boards of pharmacy, has developed and published the "Model State Pharmacy Act and Model Rules of the National Association of Boards of Pharmacy" (Model Act), which serves as a guide to individual state boards in dealing with their respective legislatures. It is created by a collaborative process involving committees, consultant specialists in pharmacy law, hearings, and convention voting, thus representing a consensus document. Information on this document and other related topics to be addressed subsequently may be found at the NABP Web site www.nabp.net.

THE BOARD OF PHARMACY

Since legislative bodies are composed of elected officials from across a wide spectrum of occupational and educational backgrounds, they and legislative staff members cannot be expected to be experts in all the phases of pharmacy or any other profession. As a consequence, the act will call for the appointment of a hands-on regulatory body which has been identified as the board of pharmacy. Once again, the composition of the board varies from state to state. The number of members ranges, from as few as three persons to as many as sixteen. As with the definition of practice, boards also have undertaken structural change over time. Although it was long the tradition for the majority of board members to come from pharmacists practicing in independent community pharmacies, recognition of the changing professional roles and activities has led to expansion of numbers and diversity. Increasingly, health-system pharmacists have become integral to boards as the result of laws and/or policy decisions. The consumerism movement motivated the appointment of nonpharmacists to most pharmacy boards with the goal of open government, balance, and oversight. Only a handful of boards have no public member. On those boards that do include nonpharmacists, this group is in the minority on the panel, often becoming quite knowledgeable advocates for pharmacy. Actively practicing pharmacists continue to be in the majority, given the need to have intimate knowledge of the practice of pharmacy to carry out the body's statutory and regulatory mission.

Acts vary widely in terms of a minimum number of years of practice experience to qualify for selection and appointment. In several states, there is no time frame. Ten years of experience is the longest practice requirement. Although usually appointed by the governor, in a small number of jurisdictions board members are appointed by another public official granted this authority by statute; it may be a health director, for example. Many states do not address service limits, while many have adopted two or three terms of three to six years each.

Board Duties and Responsibilities

A pharmacy practice act generally will spell out in broad terms the powers and duties of the state board of pharmacy. These cover a range of activities. For example, the board shall be charged with the regulation of the practice of pharmacy and the enforcement of all laws relating to pharmacy in that jurisdiction. The examination of applicants for pharmacists' licenses will be a board duty, along with the establishment of qualifications for licensure of pharmacists, interns, technicians, and other classes of pharmacy personnel as may be recognized in that state.

Boards generally are authorized to conduct hearings relating to license suspension or revocation and related matters and may issue subpoenas. They are granted authority to promulgate regulations necessary to carry out the purposes of the statute. These may include establishing criteria for license renewal, such as continuing education requirements as a condition of relicensure, as well as assessing administrative penalties where warranted for failure to comply with statutory or regulatory provisions.

ADDITIONAL PROVISIONS OF THE ACT

Licensing requirements may be provided for all persons seeking to engage in the practice of pharmacy or an ancillary role, the operation of a pharmacy, a wholesale activity, a manufacturing facility, or other entity subject to the act, within or without the jurisdiction. For example, states may license out-of-state pharmacies or other distributors or entities which do business in that state as they define such activity.

A wide spectrum of activities may be set forth in a state act and concomitant regulations dealing with categorical controls and requirements. Some of these will be addressed in detail further in this chapter and include, but are not limited to, who may practice pharmacy in the jurisdiction; how they shall be screened; definition of a pharmacy generally and any special categories authorized; credentialing of support personnel such as pharmacy technicians; drug product selection; prescription price posting; drug regiment review; and patient counseling.

Often the act is amended to include such practice modifications when federal statutes or regulations establish a need for change. As an example, drug regimen review and patient counseling provisions were not codified in most jurisdictions until Congress established these activities as minimum services for Medicaid patients under provisions in the Omnibus Budget Reconciliation Act of 1990 (OBRA-90). These practice reforms were mandated generally for all patients, not only Medicaid beneficiaries.

Also noteworthy is that legislatures often respond to board recommendations and those of professional associations and societies of pharmacists advocating for adoption of practice reforms that have been instituted voluntarily and shown to be beneficial to patient care. This phenomenon may be characterized as an evolutionary question of whether the law drives practice or practice drives the law. It is clear that both are responsible at different times in raising the level of pharmacy practice and quality of care. Since all jurisdictions do not act in concert, often a time frame of years is required to bring about uniformity with respect to the state-to-state response to reform stimuli.

PHARMACIST LICENSING REQUIREMENTS

Provisions discussed in this and subsequent sections contain both statutory and regulatory references. As noted earlier, uniformity from one jurisdiction to another with respect to what topics appear in the act versus regulations makes it more efficient to commingle the information for discussion.

One of the initial considerations to be found is a detailing of the qualifications to be a pharmacist licensed by examination. These may include a minimum age statement as well as a general reference to moral and professional character. For many years, some states maintained a U.S. citizenship standard, granting provisional licenses to noncitizens for a specified time period in which citizenship was to be obtained. These have been repealed or judicially struck down in recent years.

Candidates presenting themselves for a license generally must provide evidence of graduation with a first professional degree in pharmacy from a school or college of pharmacy program accredited by the Accreditation Council for Pharmacy Education (ACPE), formerly known as the American Council on Pharmacy Education. It is possible that during the degree transition period all states may not have identified a single degree designation (i.e., BS, BPharm, PharmD) yet, but may list multiple entry-level degrees in the interim.

Alternatively, in most jurisdictions, a mechanism exists for a foreign pharmacy graduate to obtain certification of educational equivalency. This may be accomplished by passing the NABP's Foreign Pharmacy Graduate Equivalency Examination (FPGEE) and the following standardized language proficiency examinations: Test of English as a Foreign Language (TOEFL) and Test of Spoken English (TSE).

The candidate must also demonstrate having completed to the board's satisfaction that jurisdiction's prelicensure professional experience requirements, referred to generally as internship. It is important to document precisely that a candidate's internship meets the state's total hours requirement as well as the time frames, practice activities, and supervisory criteria set forth in the statute and/or regulations governing this activity. It would behoove the candidate to determine these requirements as early in the pharmacy education process as possible.

With respect to these variable internship laws, it should be noted that states may establish rules pertaining to such areas as who may serve as a preceptor; what is a suitable internship site; how an intern is defined, and so forth. Often, a state requires that a pharmacist will have practiced for a minimum of number of years in the jurisdiction before being authorized to serve as a preceptor for pharmacy interns. A further requirement may be that practice activities during this time shall include dispensing of prescription orders. As pharmaceutical education and pharmacy practice have evolved and changed over time, boards have demonstrated a willingness to accept innovative practitioners and their sites as suitable internship practitioners and venues.

Generally, practice sites that meet local regulatory criteria are deemed proper locations at which interns may receive qualified experiences. In addition to traditional community and institutional pharmacies, states may recognize nuclear pharmacies, nursing home consulting services, IV therapy pharmacies, and pharmacy benefits management organizations, to name just a few.

States usually establish a licensing or registration procedure which enumerates such items as when in the pharmaceutical education process a student may apply to commence earning internship credit; limits as to how much time may be logged during an academic year and/or per week during vacations; limits on the activities performed by the intern; ratio of pharmacists to interns in a given pharmacy as well as span of control issues (i.e., the number of interns who may be on duty under one pharmacist at a time, etc.).

All U.S. jurisdictions currently recognize the North American Pharmacist Licensure Examination (NAPLEX), developed and administered under the supervision of the NABP, as the qualifications standard for determining practice competence. Candidates may submit the score earned to a single state board or to several states under the NAPLEX Score Transfer Program. It should be noted that not all states participate in this program, and there are varying time frames within which this option may be exercised. All other requirements established by each state must be satisfied therein as well. These may include passing the Multistate Pharmacy Jurisprudence Examination (MJPE), the NABP pharmacy law examination, and/or a state board–developed law exam, as well as an additional requirement such as a practical examination, a personal interview, a calculations test, etc. It is important to note the mechanisms described above all result in a pharmacist being licensed by examination, whether in a single jurisdiction or in several via the score transfer route.

Procedures are enacted in most jurisdictions for a pharmacist licensed by examination in one state pursuant to practicing in that state to transfer that license to another state upon satisfying a variety of requirements. This process generally has been referred to as *reciprocity,* and the term may be found in state practice acts and regulations.

Historically, the underlying justification for reciprocity as articulated by the NABP membership was that a candidate for transfer of license would have satisfied the requirements in the state in which he or she is seeking licensure at the time the license by examination was granted. Length and quality of practice since that license was awarded and other character-related tests would need to be satisfied as well (i.e., in good standing where licensed by examination). MJPE and/or the state's law exam or other additional requirements may need to be satisfied as well.

LICENSE RENEWAL

Each state determines its specific criteria for granting renewal of licenses of pharmacists in that jurisdiction. In general terms, these requirements embody having maintained the license in good standing during the time period for which it was granted.

Since the 1970s, state boards have adopted and legislatures have mandated continuing education as a relicensing criterion. The details vary somewhat from state to state but usually include the number of hours or credits as determined by the statutory or regulatory definition. The most widely accepted standard is the Continuing Education Unit (CEU), whereby one hour of instruction equates to .1 CEU. Most states may require fifteen hours or 1.5 CEU per year since the most recent renewal, be that an annual or biennial time frame.

The fifteen hours may be dictated in terms of topics, live programs versus print or electronic material, balance of presentation media, and the certification of providers of continuing education. As an example, a specific number of hours of continuing education might be required in the subject area of pharmacy law or HIV instruction. A state may limit the number of hours of instruction which may be obtained through written or electronic media programs, requiring a minimum quantity of the total credits to be earned at live programs.

Boards require pharmacists' continuing education credits to be provided by recognized providers who meet the criteria established by statute or regulation in their jurisdiction. The American Council for Pharmacy Education, the agency noted earlier as the body which accredits pharmacy professional degree programs, is the most widely accepted approval body for continuing education providers. Many states also recognize programs approved by the Accreditation Council for Continuing Medical Education (ACCME), the principal body which oversees medical education programs.

In addition, some boards provide a mechanism for preapproval of programs internally, so participants may receive credit for completion of these activities.

The accrediting bodies' recognition of a program is widely considered a quality control mechanism upon which contributors to the content, participants, and licensing boards may rely. Accreditation criteria require timely and detailed advanced clearance of each specific program. ACPE, for example, requires documentation several weeks before presentation of the presenters' credentials, goals and objectives, CEUs to be awarded, etc. Pretest and posttest requirements and individual program evaluations also are among the items of interest to the accrediting agency.

These data are included in the reaccreditation review process for the provider institutions or organizations that regularly present continuing professional education programs.

PHARMACY TECHNICIANS

As the profession of pharmacy has undergone substantial change over time, the role of the pharmacist has been evolving from predominantly compounding to counting and measuring prefabricated dose forms prepared by pharmaceutical manufacturers to an increasingly cognitive and consultative service-oriented practice. Concomitant with this evolutionary phenomenon, boards of pharmacy responded to the need to address the roles of nonpharmacist personnel who are involved in the provision of pharmaceutical care and drug distribution in their respective states' pharmacies. Over time, a variety of terms have emerged to refer to that person, such as drug clerk, ancillary, supportive, assistant, and a variety of related titles. By and large, "pharmacy technician" is the most widely accepted term in both general use and state laws.

Attention has focused in large measure on who may perform the manipulative and administrative activities surrounding the delivery of the drug product involved to the patient for whom it was prescribed, as well as the limits of those actions. Further, boards are concerned about the supervising pharmacist's roles and responsibilities in the safe and efficient performance of these services.

Individual jurisdictions deal with the menu of technician activities in a number of ways, but often they permit the supervised technician to perform some electronic functions such as entering a prescription order or health-system drug order into the computer system employed in that pharmacy while generating a label as well as other relevant accompanying printed materials. The technician may then remove the bulk drug container from the shelf and count or pour the prescribed quantity into a dispensing container, all subject to verification by a pharmacist. Compounding, including weighing ingredients, and fabricating the final IV or other dose form may be permitted. Telephoned prescription renewal authorizations may be taken by pharmacy technicians in some states as well. Some states expressly provide for technicians to check other technicians' work in what have been referred to over time as "tech check tech" programs. Most either prohibit the practice or do not address the issue. Often the statutes or regulations will include a list of prohibited activities, such as drug utilization review, patient counseling, prescription clarification, and new orders.

Most states provide for licensing or registering technicians. The qualifications are not as uniform among the jurisdictions as they are for pharmacists, due largely to the variability in educational and training mechanisms in place to be recognized as such. When requirements are established, they run the gamut from on-the-job training in a pharmacy, to a formalized, in-house training program in a community or institutional or other pharmacy, to educational institution training, one provided by a branch of the U.S. Armed Services of the U.S. Public Health Service, or completion of a program accredited by the American Society of Health-System Pharmacists (ASHP).

Successfully completing the Pharmacy Technician Certification Board (PTCB) examination is another avenue of recognition. It always is important to check an individual state's requirements well in advance of applying for educational/training recognition.

Technicians in some jurisdictions are required to earn continuing education credits as a prerequisite for relicensure or recertification. Those hours may need to be earned in ACPE- or ACCME-accredited programs, though the process is not as formalized in most states as it is for pharmacists.

As with pharmacy intern supervision, boards address this issue with respect to pharmacy technicians as well. A flat number of technicians per pharmacist may be established to cover all practice venues, or differing requirements may exist for sites and practice modalities which a board deems could still be accommodated without endangering patient safety.

LICENSING ENTITIES

For purposes of the ensuing discussion, the term *entity* is selected to encompass a broad range of business-related activities in for-profit as well as not-for-profit environments. Not all pharmacy boards exercise enforcement authority over all such activities, and those set forth herein serve as examples. As in all areas of the law related to pharmacy practice, it is important to look to a respective state's statutes and regulations for detailed clarification.

The first entity that bears consideration is the pharmacy. One should look first to the definitions section of the pharmacy practice act to determine the parameters set forth there. Generally, a pharmacy may be designated as that portion of the premises where prescription compounding and dispensing and related activities are performed and drugs are stored. This is in contrast to the alternative of designating the entire retail establishment, or "drug-store," as the pharmacy.

There are numerous general and special provisions provided in the various states with respect to pharmacies and their operational requirements. As an example, specific dimensions may be mandated for the areas referred to above. The overall dimensions of the pharmacy area and such items as the types and size of practice areas for pharmacists and supportive personnel may be established. Equipment such as refrigeration units, balances, glassware, mortars and pestles, and related profession tools often are included in the checklist used in the inspection process. Likewise, certain reference materials may be enumerated, both print and electronic media.

A pharmacist is designated as the registrant or pharmacist-in-charge for purposes of providing a responsible person with whom the board may communicate in the event of the need to do so. In recent years, states have begun moving toward the establishment of corporate responsibility, concomitant with that of the identified pharmacist.

Adequate staffing by professional and supportive personnel is another criterion appearing in many state laws. The underlying philosophy is the pharmacy personnel must be able to provide pharmaceutical services in an efficient and safe manner. Generally, the registrant or pharmacist-in-charge is expected to have responsibility for the performance of pharmacy staff members, whether the supervisor is on the premises or not.

Many of the above rules also may be applicable in an institutional or health-system pharmacy, usually located in a hospital or related site. There are, of course, some differences due to the variability in drug distribution and pharmacy practice in these facilities. The Joint Commission on the Accreditation of Healthcare Organizations (JCAHO) standards, though they do not have the force of statutes or regulations, provide added controls over institutional pharmacies.

It would be useful to examine a given state board's authority with respect to an institutional pharmacy. It is possible another state agency, perhaps a public health office, etc., might exercise enforcement jurisdiction over the pharmacy as a component of a hospital which the agency regulates. In such a case, the board would retain its powers over the pharmacists and other licensed or registered pharmacy personnel employed in that institution.

Some states recognize specialized pharmacy practice and sites in which these activities are performed. For example, a pharmacy that provides pharmaceutical services to a nursing home or hospice care facility, etc., may be responsible for additional supervisory and/or record-keeping activities, above and beyond those expected in servicing more traditional ambulatory care patients in the community pharmacy.

A board may have in place additional special physical, equipment, and handling requirements for the compounding of sterile pharmaceuticals prepared in response to a validly executed prescription order or institutional order. Examples of these provisions might be the use of laminar or vertical flow hoods under appropriate conditions and the sterile technique procedures required.

Another specialized area where policies vary from state to state is the nuclear or radiological pharmacy. Generally, these facilities are involved in distributing or redistributing radioactive material. In addition to requirements of space and equipment which might be imposed by the board, these facilities also need to meet the standards of state and federal agencies which have jurisdiction over their activities. Special pharmacist licensing might also be necessary to practice in such an entity, perhaps including relicensure requirements for specialized continuing professional education credits in the area of nuclear pharmacy or medicine.

A category of license in place in most, but not all, states is what has been characterized as a "nonresident pharmacy." Although specific provisions may vary across jurisdictions, the generally regarded purpose of such a license is to provide a board with enforcement authority over a pharmacy not licensed in its state which intends to ship, mail, or deliver prescription drugs and/or devices into the state under conditions and circumstances recognized under applicable federal and state laws.

The general rule is pharmacists licensed and practicing in a nonresident pharmacy are not required to become licensed in the state into which that nonresident pharmacy is sending the prescription drug or device. In a small number of states, a pharmacist license is required for the pharmacist-in-charge or any pharmacist entering the licensing state to provide services.

As with the generally accepted business law provision relative to foreign corporations (foreign being interpreted to mean out-of-state), a board may require the nonresident pharmacy to designate a resident agent in the state for service of process. This means that a pharmacy board needing to contact the pharmacy enterprise legally for an enforcement procedure or a party seeking a legal remedy against the pharmacy enterprise need not go to the nonresident party's home state to gain recourse. The agent may be served with the appropriate legal documents and it would have the full force and effect of having done so at the out-of-state business address. In the absence of identifying such an agent, the usual procedure is that as a condition of receiving the license the nonresident pharmacy owner agrees service on the secretary of state in the licensing jurisdiction shall be sufficient.

Among other conditions of licensure might be that the nonresident pharmacy shall maintain a valid and unexpired license or registration to operate a pharmacy in compliance with the granting state's law. In addition, they may be required to comply with prescription processing and dispensing regulations of the state into which they are making shipments.

In addition to those more traditional pharmacy and pharmacy-related entities regulated by state boards, some jurisdictions provide for licensure of manufacturers, wholesalers, distributors, and similar activities. Provisions may include a licensing requirement which applies to these enterprises, wherever located, that engage in distribution of prescription drugs into, out of, or within the state.

Information required may include such items as the name(s) of the business, address(es), and phone number(s) of all sites where permitted activities are carried out; the FDA manufacturing license number if appropriate; and related data relative to the corporate leadership and membership if applicable. Further, the entity would need to document its current license or registration in the home jurisdiction(s). This shall include the qualifications and professional experience and record of compliance with legal requirements in all states in which the firms are conducting business. Broadly, the areas of interest generally relate to personnel, facilities, security, storage, and record keeping, as well as compliance with federal and state laws as mentioned.

It is once again noteworthy that all states may not provide for the licensing of out-of-state business entities of these types. Consequently, it is important to check the statutes and regulations of any states in which such an enterprise is being proposed.

BOARD SANCTIONS AGAINST LICENSES

Failure to meet all the requirements set forth in any state's pharmacy laws is a valid reason for a board to deny any of the licenses provided by their statutes and regulations.

Once granted there are numerous bases upon which a license may be suspended or revoked. In addition, enabling legislation may grant the board authority to impose other forms of discipline. It is important to note the differences between a suspension and a revocation of a license. Generally, when a license is suspended, the licensee is temporarily prohibited from practicing pharmacy for a specified time (e.g., six months or two years) or until some specific disciplinary action or remediation has been satisfactorily completed. For example, a board may suspend the license of a pharmacist who is deemed to require additional continuing pharmacy education beyond the annual renewal requirements. The board could establish the duration of the suspension to coincide with the documentation of the satisfaction of that disciplinary action. Usually there is a provision for application to reinstate the suspended license to good standing.

When a license is revoked, essentially it places the former licensee in the same category of a person who never held a license. Rather than simply filing an application for reinstatement, if circumstances permit, it may be necessary for the candidate to follow the procedures set forth for the granting of an initial license in the jurisdiction. Of course, if the violation is deemed to be so egregious as to disqualify the former licensee from ever again being licensed in that state, that person may be barred permanently from practicing therein.

A broad range of violations appear in state statutes and regulations. Some representative types of proscribed activities include the following. A license holder may be sanctioned for having procured a license through fraud, misrepresentation, or deceit. The licensee may have violated state or federal law relating to pharmacy practice, drug distribution, or other activity which conflicts with board requirements. Drug or alcohol dependence or use while rendering professional services may be another basis for suspension or revocation of a license to practice pharmacy. Mental incapacity, when determined by a competent legal tribunal, may result in loss of license as well. Varying definitions of unprofessional conduct also may be considerations upon which boards may act.

As pharmacy practice continues to grow and evolve, administrative action by boards and judicial decisions provide additional bases upon boards may take action against the license of a pharmacist. Improper implementation and compliance with a state's drug product selection law may lead to sanctions. Drug regimen review and patient counseling provisions adopted by the states provide further measures of professional competence upon which a board may reach a decision concerning a licensee.

Federal and state confidentiality and patient records protection laws open yet another avenue for potential violations.

The important message to be learned concerning professional practice acts and their resulting regulations is that they should be read and referenced while recognizing they are subject to amendment over the practitioner's years of service. Further, board interpretations may vary over time as well.

RESOURCES

Richard R. Abood and David B. Brushwood, *Pharmacy Practice and the Law* (Gaithersburg, MD: Aspen, 1994).

FingLaw, Home Page (available at www.findlaw.com).

Joseph L. Fink III, Jesse C. Vivian, and Kim Keller Reid, *Pharmacy Law Digest,* 36th Edition (Germantown, PA: Facts and Comparisons, 2002).

National Association of Boards of Pharmacy, *2005 Survey of Pharmacy Law* (Mount Prospect, IL: NABP, 2005). [CD-Rom]

National Association of Boards of Pharmacy, Home Page (available at www .nabp.net).

Chapter 10

Labor and Employment Law

Roger N. Morris
Sandra J. Creta

INTRODUCTION

The relationship between employer and employee is shaped by several factors. A primary factor is the agreement between the individual employer and employee. They agree to the specific terms of their relationship—what the employer will pay, the employee's job duties, the code of conduct at the workplace, the hours the employee will be required to work, and what will occur upon the termination of the relationship. The employment relationship is also shaped by the labor market. If labor is scarce, employees can command better working conditions and higher wages. If labor is plentiful, employers pay lower wages and offer fewer benefits. Last, but not least, the law plays a very significant role in shaping an employment relationship throughout each person's working life, beginning with child-labor laws and ending with laws that prohibit age discrimination.

This chapter is designed to help pharmacist employers understand the employment relationship and the various federal and/or state laws that govern this relationship. Understanding these laws will help employers avoid costly and unintentional mistakes. Treating employees fairly and being aware of the laws against discrimination will also boost employee morale and help longevity. This chapter is intended to provide a general understanding only, and employers are encouraged to become familiar with their own state's laws and practices.

EMPLOYMENT CONTRACTS

The employment relationship is a contractual relationship, whereby the employee agrees to perform certain services and the employer agrees to pay

Pharmacy Law Desk Reference
© 2007 by The Haworth Press, Inc. All rights reserved.
doi:10.1300/5790_10

for these services. The parties, subject to state and federal laws, are free to negotiate the terms of employment as they see fit. An employer is not required to hire anyone, and an employee cannot be compelled to perform services for any employer—these decisions are left for the individuals to decide.

At Will Employment

In the United States, unless there is an express agreement to the contrary, the relationship between an employer and an employee is presumed to be "at will." In an at will employment relationship, either the employee or the employer can sever the relationship at any time for good cause or no cause without being guilty of a legal wrong. Cause is not required to end an employment relationship. An important caveat is that an employer may not terminate an employee for any reason that is forbidden by state and federal law, such as sex, race, age, religion, disability, or national origin. Despite this historical and long-standing presumption that employment is at will, the at will employment doctrine has begun to erode and can be altered by the parties, state or federal law, or the actions or statements of the employer, such as the publication of an employee handbook containing promises of continued employment. Following is a discussion of the ways that an at will employment relationship can be altered.

Express Contracts

Although employment contracts without express terms are presumptively at will, an employee can overcome the at will presumption by establishing a contract term that is either expressed or inferred from the words or conduct of the parties.[1] If an employer and employee enter into an employment contract for a fixed period of time, an employer that terminates an employee prior to the expiration of the agreement may be liable for breach of contract. Employees who terminate their employment prior to the expiration of the agreement cannot be compelled to work, but may be liable for money damages caused by their breach of contract. If an employer and an employee wish to have an employment contract for a specific period of time, this contract should be in writing and signed by both parties. Oral agreements that are for an indefinite period of time, such as "for life," or that exceed one year often do not withstand legal scrutiny and, in most states, will not be recognized by the courts.

Implied Contracts

In certain situations the at will rule may be modified by promises, practices, or policies that create a reasonable expectation of job security. These implied contracts are inferred from the conduct, policies, or statements of the parties. Promises of job security, whether written or spoken, may be construed as creating a contractual relationship that limits the employer's absolute right to discharge.[2] For example, in some states, an employee handbook that sets forth a progressive discipline policy or that includes seniority rights for employees may be deemed to create contractual rights that can be enforced by employees.

Wrongful Discharge

A wrongful discharge claim is a tort claim that can arise from an employment relationship. Wrongful discharge claims come in all shapes and sizes depending on the state of employment. Employees can allege a wrongful discharge in breach of an implied contract, in violation of public policy (the whistle-blower claim), in retaliation for their exercise of a recognized state or federal right, or in retaliation for refusing to engage in conduct that is protected by public policy.

Some states, in an effort to stem the tide of employment litigation, have attempted to limit the types of wrongful discharge actions that can be brought by employees. For example, Arizona has enacted legislation that bars employee tort claims for wrongful discharge if a state statute provides a remedy for the alleged conduct. Thus, an employee who alleges that she has been fired for complaining of sexual harassment cannot sue for wrongful termination—she must seek relief under the Arizona Civil Rights Act.[3] Other states, such as California, recognize a broad range of wrongful termination claims including claims for wrongful termination for refusing to sign an unenforceable contract.[4]

DUTIES OWED TO THE EMPLOYER

The law recognizes at least three general obligations that employees owe to their employers. Employees are required to be loyal to their employers, to maintain the confidentiality of employer trade secrets, and to honor agreements with their employers. Employers and employees are free to agree that additional obligations and duties will be owed, as in the case of restrictive covenants. A restrictive covenant generally takes the form of an agreement not to compete or a nonsolicitation agreement. The extent to which agreements between employers and employees will be enforced varies greatly from state to state. Following are general explanations of the duties owed by employees and of restrictive covenants.

The Duty of Loyalty

General agency principles impose duties of loyalty upon employees. Unless an agreement to the contrary exists, employees have a duty to act for the employer's benefit in all matters connected with the scope of employment.[5] The higher an employee is in an organization's structure, the more duties that employee will likely owe to the employer. For example, most states have laws that prohibit officers and directors of a corporation from usurping corporate opportunities, and most states recognize that officers and directors owe fiduciary obligations to the corporation. In addition, under most state laws, partners owe fiduciary obligations to one another.

Trade Secrets

Common law prohibits an employee from learning trade secrets and proprietary information in the course of a confidential relationship and then using that information to compete with his or her employer. Most states have codified this common law duty by enacting trade secret acts that provide for damages and injunctive relief for misappropriation of trade secrets. In addition, the wise employer that develops and creates confidential information will have employees execute confidentiality agreements that define confidential information and provide for specific remedies in the event of a breach by the employee. Such agreements provide an additional cause of action to an employer whose information has been wrongfully taken.

In general, for information to be deemed a trade secret or confidential, it must derive independent economic value, actual or potential, from not being generally known to and not being readily ascertainable by proper means by other persons who can obtain economic value from its disclosure or use. Employers must use reasonable efforts to maintain secrecy—if the information is common knowledge and is easily accessible within the public domain, a court will not be likely to protect the information as a trade secret.[6]

Restrictive Covenants

In most states, with some exceptions, courts will enforce legitimate agreements that limit the employee's right to compete against the employer after termination of employment; however, only reasonable restraints will be enforced. Covenants that are overly broad or that lack consideration are not enforceable. In assessing whether a restrictive covenant is reasonable, courts routinely scrutinize the time and territorial limitations in such covenants. Territorial limitations that are citywide or greater and that prohibit competition within a state's largest cities have been rejected.[7] However, a statewide restriction that precludes only the solicitation of customers of the former employer may not be deemed unreasonable and oppressive if it is not broader than necessary to protect the employer's interest. A covenant not to compete should not be longer than is required to permit an employer to find and train a replacement to effectively carry on the employer's interests.

Employers are also prohibited from enforcing a postemployment restrictive covenant simply to eliminate competition per se. Depending on the state, a covenant found to be overly broad or overreaching may be modified by a court to make it enforceable. Employers should strive to draft restrictive covenants that are as narrow and as tied to the employer's business interests as possible, as courts will generally not enforce restrictions that are not tied to an employer's business. Before implementing any restrictive covenant, employers should research their state laws to determine whether such covenants would be enforceable and what types of restrictions have been upheld in past cases.

CIVIL RIGHTS LAWS

The Americans with Disabilities Act

The Americans with Disabilities Act of 1990 (ADA) requires employers to provide "reasonable accommodations to the known physical or mental limitations of an otherwise qualified individual with a disability who is an applicant or employee," unless the employer can demonstrate that any accommodation would impose an undue hardship on it.[8] The ADA defines a qualified individual with a disability as "an individual with a disability who, with or without reasonable accommodation, can perform the essential functions of the employment position."[9] Disability is defined as (1) a physical or mental impairment that substantially limits one or more of the major life activities of such individual; (2) a record of having such an impairment; or (3) being regarded as having such an impairment. To qualify as disabled under subsection (1) above, a claimant must initially prove that he or she has a physical or mental impairment. A physical impairment, the type most often claimed by employees in ADA discrimination claims, is defined as "Any physiological disorder or condition, cosmetic disfigurement, or anatomical loss affecting one or more of the following body systems: neurological;

musculoskeletal; special sense organs; respiratory, including speech organs; cardiovascular; reproductive, digestive, genito-urinary; hemic and lymphatic; skin; and endocrine."[10]

Merely having an impairment does not make one disabled for purposes of the ADA. Claimants also need to demonstrate that the impairment limits a major life activity, which can include, but is not limited to, walking, seeing, hearing, and performing manual tasks.[11] A person claiming protection under the ADA must demonstrate that the limitation on the major life activity is "substantial," meaning that the person is unable to or is severely restricted in performing a major life activity that the average person in the general population can perform.[12] When determining whether a person is substantially limited in a major life activity, the following factors should be considered: (1) the nature and severity of the impairment; (2) the duration or expected duration of the impairment; and (3) the permanent or long-term impact, or the expected permanent or long-term impact of or resulting from the impairment.[13]

Once an employer learns that an employee has a disability, the ADA prohibits the employer from discriminating against that individual. Discrimination includes

> Not making reasonable accommodations to the known physical or mental limitations of an otherwise qualified individual with a disability who is an applicant or employee, unless such covered entity can demonstrate that the accommodation would impose an undue hardship on the operation of the business of such covered entity.[14]

Reasonable accommodations may include job restructuring, part-time or modified work schedules, reassignment to a vacant position, and acquisition or modification of equipment or devices, among other things.

In order for an employer to determine the appropriate accommodation, it may be necessary for the employer to initiate an informal, interactive process with the employee who needs an accommodation. The purpose of this process is to identify the precise limitations resulting from the disability and potential reasonable accommodations that could overcome those limitations. The interactive process usually is triggered by the employer's learning of an employee's possible disability and request for accommodation.[15] The information, including the request for an accommodation, does not need to come directly from the employee, and may be provided by a third party, such as a family member or a doctor.[16] The employee also does not need to use any specific terms to initiate the interactive process. If the employer knows of an employee's disability, that the employee is experiencing difficulty in the workplace due to the disability, or that the disability prevents the employee from requesting an accommodation, then the employer may have an obligation to initiate the interactive process and/or to provide reasonable accommodation.

The Age Discrimination in Employment Act

The Age Discrimination in Employment Act of 1967 (ADEA) was originally enacted in order to protect older workers from being arbitrarily dismissed or discriminated against based upon their age. The ADEA prohibits discrimination in hiring, promotion, assignment, compensation, discharge, and working environment against persons who are age forty or over.[17] This prohibition applies to employers that have twenty or more employees who work twenty or more calendar weeks a year, as well as to labor organizations, employment agencies, and to most state and political subdivisions.[18] The ADEA applies to employees who are younger than forty, and does not apply to independent contractors, individual supervisors, Indian tribes, or religious institutions.[19]

An employee who is forty or older does not have a cause of action simply because he or she is terminated or disciplined. The following are permissible actions under the ADEA:

1. acting based upon a bona fide occupational qualification (BFOQ) reasonably necessary to the normal operation of a particular business (e.g., a flight controller);
2. differentiating employees on reasonable factors other than age;
3. discharging or disciplining an individual for good cause (e.g., tardiness or intoxication);
4. taking action in an effort to comply with foreign laws when the workplace is in a foreign country; and
5. acting pursuant to a bona fide seniority system or employee benefit plan (such plans may not be enacted as the means for evading compliance with the ADEA).[20]

A BFOQ is an age-related job-related qualification. To determine whether a BFOQ exists, the job qualification necessitating an age requirement must be reasonably necessary to the essence of the particular business and the age requirement must be more than just a convenient way to sort employees. Reasonable factors other than age are items such as prior experience, skills, or education. These factors may appear to correlate with age, but are not age. This exception to the ADEA allows employers to take actions negatively impacting older workers when the motivating factor for the action is not the employee's age. For example, an employer can act out of concern for excessive costs, even if those costs are correlated with seniority, a factor related to age. An employer may also refuse to hire an overqualified applicant, even though being overqualified is correlated with age.

Under the ADEA, "good cause" for terminating an employee means a reason, whether it is decreasing revenues, poor performance, poor attitude, or harassment of a co-worker. This standard does not negate the "at will" employment concept, but if an employer terminates an individual who is forty or older and elects to retain an employee who is twenty-five, the employer needs to be able to articulate a good-faith basis for this decision. Accordingly, when making decisions regarding termination or discipline, it is essential to document the thought processes and reasons for each decision.

Title VII of the 1964 Civil Rights Act

Title VII of the 1964 Civil Rights Act (Title VII) provides that it is illegal to discriminate in hiring, promotion, assignment, compensation, discharge, and working environment on the basis of sex, religion, national origin, race, or color.[21] Everyone is protected by Title VII, including men, women, heterosexuals, and homosexuals. Harassment, including sexual harassment, is a form of discrimination and can occur against men as well as women and against heterosexuals as well as homosexuals.

Harassment

Harassment is defined as verbal or physical conduct that creates an intimidating, hostile, or offensive work environment or that unreasonably interferes with an employee's work performance. Examples of harassment include the following:

1. verbal conduct—epithets, negative stereotyping, derogatory jokes and comments, gender-based, racial, religious, or national origin slurs or unwanted sexual or sex-oriented invitations, statements, or comments; socially unacceptable words, taunts, or expressions in the workplace;
2. written materials or visual conduct—derogatory or sexually oriented posters, photography, cartoons, drawings or gestures, or written materials that show hostility because of sex, race, color, religion, national origin, age, or disability;
3. physical conduct—assault, unwanted touching, blocking normal movement, interfering with work, and "flashing";

4. threats or demands to submit to requests as a condition of continued employment or to avoid some other loss; and
5. retaliation for having reported or threatened to report harassment.

Sexual harassment is defined as unwelcome sexual advances, requests for sexual favors, and other verbal or physical conduct of a sexual nature when

1. submission to such conduct is made either explicitly or implicitly a term or condition of an individual's employment; or
2. submission to or rejection of such conduct by an individual is used as the basis for employment decisions affecting such individual; or
3. such conduct has the purpose or effect of unreasonably [*Faragher v. City of Boca Raton,* 524 U.S. 775, 788 (1998)] interfering with an individual's work performance or creating an intimidating, hostile, or offensive working environment.[22]

Employer Liability for Harassment

An employer will automatically be liable for sexual harassment if the supervisor is the harasser and if the harassment results in a tangible employment action, such as termination, discipline, discharge, or demotion.[23] An employer can also be liable for harassment if the employer does not have policies in place to prohibit harassment, if an employer fails to respond to a complaint of harassment, or if an employer knows or reasonably should know about harassment and fails to take any action.

A good antiharassment policy that is communicated to all employees is essential to protect employers. Policies should include establishing complaint and investigation procedures and making employees feel that the employer is sensitive to and will not tolerate harassment. A policy must also include a statement that an employee will not be retaliated against for making a complaint of harassment or discrimination.

Equal Employment Opportunity Commission

The EEOC was established by Title VII of the Civil Rights Act of 1964 and began operating on July 2, 1965. The EEOC is the agency responsible for the admistration and enforcement of Title VII of the Civil Rights Act of 1964.[24] The agency also has the authority to administer and enforce the following federal statutes: (1) the Age Discrimination in Employment Act of 1967; (2) the Equal Pay Act (EPA) of 1963; (3) Title I and Title V of the

Americans with Disabilities Act of 1990; (4) Section 501 and 505 of the Rehabilitation Act of 1973; and (5) the Civil Rights Act of 1991.

The EEOC coordinates all federal equal employment opportunity regulations, practices, and policies. The EEOC interprets employment discrimination laws, monitors the federal-sector employment discrimination program, provides funding and support to state and local fair employment practices agencies, and sponsors outreach and technical assistance programs. Any individual who believes he or she has been discriminated against in employment may file an administrative charge with the EEOC.

A charge must be filed before the EEOC has jurisdiction to investigate.[25] After investigating the charge, the EEOC determines if there is "reasonable cause" to believe discrimination has occurred.[26] If "reasonable cause" is found, the EEOC attempts to conciliate the charge by reaching a voluntary resolution between the charging party and the respondent. If conciliation is not successful, the EEOC may bring suit in federal court. As part of the administrative process, the EEOC may also issue a right-to-sue-notice to the charging party, allowing the charging party to file an individual action in court without the agency's involvement.

Many, if not all, states have a state agency that acts in a capacity similar to the EEOC. In some states, the EEOC contracts with the state agency to process discrimination charges. Charges with state agencies are filed under state and local laws prohibiting employment discrimination as well as federal laws enforced by the EEOC.

THE HIRING PROCESS

Interviews

During the hiring process, which includes any screening process or interviews, employers must be careful not to ask questions that might indicate that an employer is making decisions on the basis of any protected category. Questions that would involve a person's religion, family status, status as a veteran, marital status, age (unless the age is a bona fide occupational qualification—such as requiring employees who serve alcohol to be twenty-one years of age), religion, sexual orientation, or disability should be avoided at all costs. Employers may give and act upon the results of any professionally developed ability test provided that the test is not designed, intended, or used to discriminate because of race, color, religion, sex, age, disability, or national origin. Any ability test must bear a rational relationship to the job the applicant is seeking. For example, a math test would be reasonable for an applicant for a cashier position but not for an applicant for a janitor position. Information that cannot be requested on an employment application likewise cannot be asked of applicants during interviews or through other means.[27]

Medical Examinations

An employer may not require a medical examination or make inquiries of a job applicant as to whether the applicant is disabled. However, employers can make inquiries into the ability of an applicant to perform job-related functions. Any preemployment examinations need to be established as job related and consistent with business necessity. In addition, if an applicant has met all of the qualifications for the job and has been offered the job, the employer may require a postoffer physical, provided that all entering employees are subjected to such an examination regardless of disability. Moreover, employers may conduct voluntary medical examinations which are part of an employee health program available to employees at that work site. All information obtained regarding the medical condition or history of an applicant needs to be collected and maintained on separate forms, in separate medical files, and should be treated as a confidential medical record.[28]

Genetic Testing

In many states, it is against the law to fail or refuse to hire, to discharge, or to otherwise discriminate against any individual based on the results of a genetic test received by the employer. Furthermore, the EEOC Compliance Manual indicates that the EEOC believes that genetic predisposition to disease does in fact constitute a protected disability under the ADA. Thus, discrimination on the basis of genetic information may be unlawful under the ADA.[29] In addition, Congress is considering legislation that would ban genetic discrimination in employment and health insurance.[30]

Credit Checks

It is lawful for employers to conduct credit checks on applicants for employment. In order for an employer to gain access to these reports, the employer must adhere to the strict disclosure and consent requirements set forth in the Federal Credit Reporting Act (FCRA) and applicable state law.[31] First, the employer must notify the applicant or employee that the information is being sought. This notification must be in writing, and may not contain reference to any other subject. Next, the employer must obtain the proper written consent from the applicant or employee. In some states, it is unlawful for the employer to request or require any waiver of rights by any consumer. Finally, an employer who considers a credit report in making a determination to deny a consumer employment, promotion, or retention as an employee shall disclose to such consumer the name and address of any consumer reporting agency which has furnished such employer with a consumer report on such consumer.

Immigration

The Immigration Reform and Control Act (IRCA) requires that employers properly verify the employment eligibility of all their workers. An employer may face criminal and civil penalties for (1) failing to verify or incompletely verifying the work authorization on form I-9; (2) knowingly hiring an unauthorized worker; and (3) knowingly continuing to hire a person after their work authorization ends.[32] The Illegal Immigration Reform and Immigrant Responsibility Act (IIRAIRA) amendments to the IRCA remove some of the more difficult employer compliance issues. The IIRAIRA reduced the number of documents available for I-9 verification. The act also added a good-faith defense for procedural or technical violations of the paperwork provisions of IRCA. Under this new provision, an employer is said to have complied with the paperwork requirement if there was a good-faith effort to comply with the act.[33]

WAGE AND HOUR LAWS

Fair Labor Standards Act

The Fair Labor Standards Act (FLSA) establishes minimum wage, overtime pay, equal pay, record keeping, and child labor standards for employees who are within its coverage and who are not exempt from specific provisions. Specifically, the FLSA places a floor on wages and a ceiling over hours of employment. The FLSA regulates employment in industries that affect interstate commerce and provides coverage to employees in all fifty states, the District of Columbia, and all U.S. territories. However, the FLSA does not preempt any state laws that establish higher minimum wages or more stringent labor standards. It is administered and enforced by the Department of Labor, Wage-Hour Division, which is charged with the responsibility of promulgating regulations pertaining to matters specifically left by Congress to agency rule making.[34]

Minimum Wage

The FLSA mandates that every employer shall pay to each of its employees a minimum wage of not less than $5.15 an hour.[35] This law applies to all employees who are engaged in commerce or in the production of goods for commerce, or who are employed in an enterprise engaged in commerce or in the production of goods for commerce.

Child Labor

The FLSA regulates the employment hours and conditions of persons under eighteen years of age. In general, the minimum employment age for minors in nonagricultural work is fourteen. Employees who are fourteen and fifteen can work only during nonschool hours, three hours in a school day, eighteen hours in a school week, eight hours on a nonschool day, forty hours on a nonschool week, and only between the hours 7:00 a.m. and 7:00 p.m. during the school year (Labor Day through May 31). There is no limit on the number of hours an employee who is sixteen years of age or older can work.

Exceptions to the minimum age laws established by the FLSA exist. For example, at any age, minors may perform household chores in a private home, baby-sit, deliver newspapers, perform in radio, television, movie, or theatrical productions, and work in a family-owned business, unless the business is mining or manufacturing or is hazardous. Most states have enacted their own child labor laws, many of which are very similar to the provisions in the FLSA. To the extent that a state's law differs from the FLSA, the law that is the most protective of the minor will control.

Break Periods

Under the FLSA, rest periods are counted as compensable working time if they are for a period twenty minutes or less. Meal times are also compensable unless (1) they are generally thirty minutes or longer; (2) employees are relieved of all duties, including answering the telephone; and (3) employees are free to leave their duty post. It is not necessary that employees be free to leave the premises if they are otherwise completely free from duties during the meal period. All employees should be encouraged to leave the immediate area adjacent to their work stations and to perform no tasks during their meal period.[36]

Overtime

Employees who work in excess of forty hours in any seven-day work-week must receive compensation at a rate not less than one and one-half times the regular hourly rate at which the employee is paid. The workweek must be fixed, regular, and consist of seven consecutive twenty-four-hour periods. The workweek does not have to coincide with a calendar week. It may begin any day, at any hour.[37]

If an employer has established procedures for not working overtime and the employee violates the procedures, the employer is still responsible for payment if it has direct, or indirect, knowledge of the additional work; however, the employee may be subject to disciplinary action by the employer.[38] If the employee fails to notify the employer or deliberately prevents the employer from acquiring knowledge of the overtime work, the employer's failure to pay for the overtime hours is not a violation of the FLSA.[39]

Records Retention

The FLSA requires employers to keep certain payroll and personnel information and records. Some of the information required includes name, address, and social security number; date of birth; sex and occupation; rate and basis of pay; work schedule and total hours worked; and copies of all employment contracts and collective bargaining agreements. The records must be maintained for at least three years.[40] In addition, each employer is required to keep true and accurate work records for such periods of time and containing such information as each state's departments of labor or economic security require. Many states require that these records shall be open to inspection and may be copied by a state agency or its authorized representatives at any reasonable time and as often as necessary.

State Wage Statutes

In some states, most provisions governing employment practices and working conditions are superceded by, or are substantially identical to, the FLSA. Other states have implemented laws that require payment of a higher minimum wage or increased overtime pay. For example, California requires an employer to pay overtime for hours worked in excess of eight hours in a single workday.[41] In addition, many states have laws governing the frequency of pay, deductions from pay, payment upon termination or resignation, automatic deposits, and garnishments. Employers should become familiar with their states' laws.

EMPLOYEE RIGHTS

Union Relations

The National Labor Relations Act (NLRA), enacted in 1947, protects both union and nonunion employees. The NLRA gives employees the right to organize and to collectively bargain with their employers.[42] It also protects employees from retaliation for participating in collective bargaining or other protected activity and prohibits employers from threatening employees or from promising benefits to avoid unionization.[43] If a labor union approaches an employer, the employer has two choices. It can voluntarily acknowledge the union or it can require the National Labor Relations Board to conduct an election to determine whether the majority of employees support the union.[44]

Once a union has been recognized, the employer is required to bargain in good faith with the union regarding terms and conditions of employment. The terms and conditions of employment are subjects for mandatory bargaining between the employer and the labor union, and include items such as wages, hours, benefits, and working conditions. The failure of an employer or a union to bargain in good faith may constitute an unfair labor practice.[45] Employers are not required to agree to all union requests, and employees are permitted to strike to support their bargaining demands.[46]

Some states are "right-to-work" states, which means that no person can be denied the opportunity to obtain or retain employment because of nonmembership in a labor organization. Employers in "right-to-work" states are not allowed to enter into any agreement which excludes any person from employment or continuation of employment because of nonmembership in a labor organization. Employees are not obligated to pay union dues, and agreements which would require the payment of union dues, or equivalent fees, to a union as condition to obtaining or retaining employment are prohibited. In other states, union membership, which necessarily includes union dues, might be mandatory for certain jobs.

Health and Safety

Under the Occupational Safety and Health Act of 1970 (OSHA), employers are required to maintain a safe workplace and to comply with promulgated health and safety standards.[47] OSHA gives employees the right to receive information and training from their employers regarding workplace safety, hazards, testing, accidents, and standards and rules. OSHA also requires employers to train their employees regarding hazardous chemicals and working conditions, and protects employees from retaliatory discharge or discrimination based on their exercise of rights afforded by OSHA. Employees may (1) file complaints about occupational safety and health; (2) institute or cause to be instituted proceedings under OSHA; (3) testify in any proceeding under OSHA; and (4) cooperate with investigations.[48] OSHA does not give employees the right to refuse to work if they believe workplace conditions are unsafe or unhealthful.

OSHA works closely with state agencies to enforce OSHA standards and to investigate employee complaints of hazardous workplaces or of discrimination or retaliation. Approximately twenty-three states currently operate OSHA-approved state plans, and many states have local enforcement offices as well. Employers should be aware of hazards and potential safety concerns within their workplaces and should investigate any concerns to determine whether they are in compliance with state and federal law.

Leaves of Absence

Family and Medical Leave

The federal Family and Medical Leave Act (FMLA) requires employers with fifty or more employees to provide eligible employees with one or more years on the job up to twelve weeks of job protected leave (1) for the birth of a child and to care for the child; (2) for the placement of a child with the employee for adoption or foster care; (3) to care for the employee's spouse, son, daughter, or parent with a serious health condition; and (4) because a serious health condition makes the employee unable to perform the functions of his or her job.[49] FMLA applies to private-sector employers who employ fifty or more employees for each working day during each of twenty or more calendar workweeks in the current or preceding calendar year, all public agencies regardless of the number of employees employed, all public and private elementary and secondary schools regardless of the number of employees employed, and any person acting directly or indirectly in a covered employer's interest to any of its employees.[50]

Employees who are eligible for FMLA benefits must be employed by a covered employer and must have been employed by the employer for at least twelve months, which need not be consecutive months, have worked for at least 1,250 hours during the twelve-month period immediately preceding the beginning of the leave, and be employed at a worksite where fifty or more employees are employed by the employer within seventy-five miles of that worksite.[51]

Employers must maintain any preexisting group health coverage for employees during leave under the same terms and conditions as if the employee had continued to work, and must not deprive employees of accrued employment benefits as a result of FMLA leave.[52] When the employee's leave ends, an employer generally must reinstate the employee to the same or an equivalent position with equal employment benefits, pay, working conditions, and other terms and conditions of employment.[53] Some states have adopted their own family and medical leave laws, which may be more favorable to employees than the FMLA. Employers should check with their own state's laws and regulations to determine whether other family and medical leave laws may apply.

Military Leave

The Uniformed Services Employment and Reemployment Rights Act (USERRA) obligates employers to provide leave to employees who are serving in the uniformed services, reinstate employees who are returning from military leave, and train or otherwise qualify returning employees.[54] USERRA also prohibits employers from discriminating against employees because of their past, present, or future military obligations. Under USERRA, employees are entitled to leave for active duty, active duty for training, initial active duty for training, inactive duty training, full-time National Guard duty, and absence from work for fitness for duty examinations. If an employee was employed only briefly or for a nonrecurrent period of time prior to his or her leave and had no reasonable expectation of continued employment, then the employee will not be entitled to reinstatement. With certain exemptions, if an employee's cumulative military leave absences exceed five years, the employee will not be entitled to reinstatement rights.

State Leave Laws

Many states have adopted leave laws to enable employees to vote and to participate in jury duty. Most states allow employees between two and four hours of time off from work to vote, and most states have enacted laws prohibiting employers from taking actions to discourage employees from serving as jurors. A few states even require employers to compensate employees who are on jury duty. In addition, some states have adopted victim's rights laws to allow victims of crimes to attend the trials of the accused perpetrators and parental leave laws that allow parents to attend parent-teacher conferences or other school activities. Employers must investigate their own state's laws to determine any other leave requirements.

Workers' Compensation

Most states have laws requiring employers to participate in the state workers' compensation system, either by purchasing workers' compensation insurance or through self-insurance. In general, an employee's sole remedy for an injury arising out of the employment relationship is a claim under the workers' compensation law, unless the injury is the result of the employer's intentional conduct. Employees may elect to reject the terms of the workers' compensation law. If they provide written notice of such election to the employer prior to sustaining any injuries, employees may maintain an action at law for damages. In virtually all states, discharging an employee for filing a workers' compensation claim is prohibited.

TERMINATION OF EMPLOYMENT

Unemployment Compensation

Virtually all states maintain a fund from which unemployment benefits are paid. These funds are generally maintained by mandatory contributions from employers. The purpose of unemployment compensation is to provide benefits for a limited time to individuals who are available and willing to work but are unemployed through no fault of their own. Each state's standards for employers that are required to contribute and the standards for employee eligibility for unemployment compensation differ and must be examined on a case-by-case basis.

Plant Closing Laws

The Worker Adjustment and Retraining Notification Act (WARN) is potentially relevant whenever a company orders mass layoffs or plant closings.[55] Whether a business is subject to WARN depends upon the number of persons employed by that business and the number of those employees that are laid off due to cutbacks in the workforce or the closing of a place of business.[56] Essentially, WARN requires employers with 100 or more workers to notify workers and communities 60 days in advance of (1) closures that affect 50 or more workers and (2) layoffs that either (i) affect one-third of the workforce or (ii) involve 50 or more workers. In addition to WARN, many states have adopted their own plant closing laws. When employers are considering a plant closing or a mass layoff, they should investigate which state laws, if any, apply.

COBRA

The Comprehensive Omnibus Budget Reconciliation Act of 1974 (COBRA) requires that employee health plans covered by the Employee Retirement Income Security Act (ERISA) provide a continuation of health coverage to certain individuals. The coverage obligation exists for plan sponsors of each group health plan unless the small employer plan exception applies. The small employer exclusion applies to those employers with fewer than twenty employees on a typical business day in the preceding calendar year.[57]

The plan sponsor of a covered health plan must allow each qualified beneficiary to elect continuation coverage under the terms of the plan, subject to paying an appropriate premium. There are, at present, six qualifying events that can trigger the continuation coverage obligation: (1) the death of the covered employee; (2) the termination (other than by reason of such employee's gross misconduct) or reduction of hours of the covered employee's employment; (3) the divorce or legal separation of the covered employee from the employee's spouse; (4) a covered employee's entitlement to benefits under Title XVIII of the Social Security Act; (5) a dependent child's ceasing to be a dependent child under the generally applicable requirements of the plan; and (6) a bankruptcy proceeding initiated on or after July 1, 1986, by an employer providing retiree health benefits.[58]

Severance Pay

Ordinarily, employers are not required to pay severance pay to terminated employees. If an employer has a policy or practice of paying severance pay, it might create an express or implied contract to pay severance pay. Providing severance pay to some employees but not to others might give rise to a claim of discrimination from employees who were not offered severance pay. In the event an employer pays severance pay to only selected individuals, the employer should be able to demonstrate a legitimate business reason for this decision. In general, it is recommended that employers who pay severance pay require employees to sign a release of claims as a condition of receiving severance pay.

Releases

Employers who require their employees to sign a release of claims in exchange for severance pay or other benefits should be aware that the Age Discrimination in Employment Act provides that a waiver of claims under the ADEA will not be effective unless it (1) is written in a manner that is calculated to be understood by the employee (or the average eligible employee); (2) does not waive claims arising after the execution of the waiver; (3) represents that the employee was given consideration to which he or she was not otherwise entitled in exchange for the waiver; (4) advises the employee to consult with an attorney prior to signing; (5) gives the employee at least twenty-one days to consider the agreement (forty-five days are required if the release is being obtained as a result of an exit incentive or other program offered to a class of individuals); and (6) provides that employees may revoke or cancel the agreement within seven days of signing it.[59]

Employers who obtain waivers as a result of an exit incentive or other program must also provide information to employees regarding who was eligible for the plan and the criteria that the employer used to determine eligibility.[60] In addition, individual states may also require that specific language be included in a release to effectively waive claims. Employers should investigate the requirements of a release on a case-by-case and stateby-state basis.

NOTES

1. See, e.g., *Wagenseller v. Scottsdale Memorial Hospital,* 710 P.2d 1025 (Ariz. 1981).

2. *Leikvold v. Valley View Comm. Hosp,* 688 P.2d 170 (Ariz. 1984).

3. A.R.S. § 23-1501(3)(b).

4. See, e.g., *D'Sa v. Playhut, Inc.,* 102 Cal. Rptr.2d 495 (Ct. App. 201).

5. See, e.g., Restatement (Second) of Agency § 387; *Jet Courier Service v. Mulei,* 771 P.2d 486 (Colo. 1989).

6. See A.R.S. § 44-401(4), patterned after the Uniform Trade Secrets Act, which has served as a model for several states.

7. *Oliver/Pilcher Ins. v. Daniels,* 715 P.2d 1218 (Ariz. 1986); *Truly Nolen Exterminating v. Balckwell,* 610 P.2d 483 (Ariz. 1980); *Bryceland v. Northey,* 772 P.2d 36 (Ariz. 1989).

8. 42 U.S.C. § 12112(b)(5)(A).

9. 42 U.S.C. § 12111(8).

10. 45 C.F.R. § 84.3(j)(2)(i).

11. 45 C.F.R. § 84,3(j)(2)(ii).

12. 29 C.F.R. § 1630.2(j).

13. 29 C.F.R. § § 1630.2(J)(2)(i)-(iii).

14. 42 U.S.C. § 12112(b)(5)(A).

15. *Barrett v. U.S. Air, Inc.,* 228 F.3d 1105, 1111 (9th Cir. 2000).

16. *Taylor v. Phoenixville Sch. Dist.,* 184 F.3d 296, 312 (3d Cir. 1999).

17. 29 U.S.C. §§ 623 and 631.

18. 29 U.S.C. § 630(b).

19. 29 U.S.C. § 630(f).

20. 29 U.S.C. § 623(*l*).

21. 42 U.S.C. § 2000(e)-2(a).

22. *Harris v. Forklift Systems, Inc.,* 510 U.S. 17, 21 (1993).

23. *See Faragher v. City of Boca Raton,* 524 U.S. 775 (1998).

24. 42 U.S.C. § § 2000e-4 and 5.

25. *Graniteville Co. v. EEOC,* 456 F.2d 32, 35 (4th Cir. 1971).

26. 42 U.S.C. 2000e-6(b).

27. James K. Cowan Jr., *Interviewing Job Applicants: Can I Ask This Question,* 19 NO. 3 ACCA Docket 40 (2001) (available at Westlaw.com).

28. 42 U.S.C. § 12112.

29. EEOC Directive 915.002 (Mar. 15, 1995).

30. The Genetic Nondiscrimination in Health Insurance and Employment Act, H.R. 602, 107th Cong. (2002).

31. 15 U.S.C. § 168; *Credit Data of Ariz., Inc. v. State of Ariz.,* 602 F.2d 195 (9th Cir. 1979).

32. 8 U.S.C. §§ 1324a and 1324b.

33. 8 U.S.C. §§ 1324(b)(6).

34. 29 U.S.C. § 201, *et seq.*

35. 29 U.S.C. § 206.

36. 29 C.F.R. §§ 785.18, 785.19.

37. 29 U.S.C. § 207.

38. *Newton v. City of Henderson,* 47 F.3d 746 (5th Cir. 1995).

39. *Forrester v. Roth's I.G.A. Foodliner, Inc.,* 646 F.2d 413 (9th Cir. 1981).

40. 29 C.F.R. §§ 516.0 to 516.34.

41. Cal. Labor Code § 510.

42. 29 U.S.C. § 157.

43. 29 U.S.C. § 158(a).

44. See, e.g., 29 U.S.C. § 481, *et seq.*

45. 29 U.S.C. § 158(d).

46. 29 U.S.C. § 158(g).

47. 29 U.S.C. § 651, *et seq.*

48. 29 U.S.C. § 657.

49. 29 U.S.C. § 2612(a).

50. 29 U.S.C. § 2611(4)(A).

51. 29 U.S.C. § 2611(2)(A) & (B).

52. 29 U.S.C. § 2614(a)(2).

53. 29 U.S.C. § 2614(a)(1)(B).

54. 38 U.S.C. § 4301, *et seq.*

55. 29 U.S.C. § 2101, *et seq.*

56. 29 U.S.C. § 2101(a)(1).

57. 29 U.S.C. § 1161(b).

58. 29 U.S.C. § 1163.

59. 29 U.S.C. § 629(1)(A)-(G).

60. 29 U.S.C. § 629(1)(h).

Chapter 11

Taxation

Jacqueline A. Henson

INTRODUCTION

Whether you are a sole proprietor of a pharmacy operation, a member of a partnership or a limited liability company that operates a pharmacy, a shareholder of an incorporated pharmacy operation, or an employee of any of the foregoing, you will be subject to a variety of taxes as the result of your activities. This chapter begins with the general theories of taxation, including the constitutional underpinnings of taxation and the limitations on the taxing power. It then provides a general overview of the basic framework of federal income taxation and describes the federal income taxation applicable to individuals, partnerships, and corporations. The remaining sections discuss other federal taxes, including Social Security taxes, the Medicare tax, and excise taxes. Finally, the chapter concludes with a discussion of state and local taxation.

GENERAL THEORIES OF AND TYPES OF TAXATION

A "tax" is a compulsory contribution from a person or entity made to a government unit for a common interest. Two general theories used to describe taxation include the benefit theory and the ability to pay theory. Under the benefit theory, taxes are assessed in terms of the amount of benefits and services received by the taxpayer. The greater the benefit that the taxpayer receives, the greater the tax that taxpayer must pay. For example, the more cigarettes one smokes, the more cigarette tax one pays.

The ability to pay theory uses a proxy to determine a person's ability to pay a tax. Typical measures of ability to pay are income, property, and sales. The more income one earns, the more ability one should have to pay more

Pharmacy Law Desk Reference
© 2007 by The Haworth Press, Inc. All rights reserved.
doi:10.1300/5790_11

tax. Property wealth is determined by how much property one owns. A sales tax relates positively with the amount of sales that one generates.

Taxes are often levied as a percentage, called the tax rate, of a certain value, referred to as the tax base. The most common tax base is the income one generates. An ad valorem tax is one in which the tax base is the value of a good, a service, or a type of property. Sales taxes, tariffs, property taxes, inheritance taxes, and value-added taxes are examples of ad valorem taxes. These types of taxes are typically imposed at the time of a transaction but may be imposed on an annual basis or in connection with a significant event.

An important feature of tax systems is whether they are flat, progressive, or regressive. In a flat tax scheme, the percentage of tax does not depend on the base. Hence, the tax is proportional to how much you earn, how much you have, or how much you spend. A tax may be regressive (the more you have the lower the tax rate) or progressive (the more you have the higher the tax rate). Progressive taxes reduce the tax burden for people with smaller incomes, since they take a smaller percentage of their income. The federal income tax is an example of a progressive tax. A sales tax, on the other hand, is an example of a regressive tax.

CONSTITUTIONAL CONSIDERATIONS

Article I, Section 8 of the Constitution states that "Congress shall be empowered to lay and collect Taxes, Duties, Impose and Excises, to pay the Debts and provide for the common Defense and general Welfare of the United States; but all Duties, Impose and Excises shall be uniform throughout the United States." In *United States v. Butler,*[1] the Supreme Court interpreted Article I to provide that Congress has broad authority to tax and spend for the general welfare. The only limitation on Congress's broad power to tax and spend is that it may not violate other constitutional provisions. Subsequent cases have affirmed Congress's expansive authority under the taxing and spending clause. In *Steward Machine Company v. Davis,*[2] the Supreme Court upheld the constitutionality of the federal unemployment compensation system created by the Social Security Act. In *Helvering v. Davis,*[3] the Court upheld the constitutionality of the Social Security Act, which is supported exclusively by federal taxes.

Historically, the Supreme Court drew distinctions between "direct" and "indirect" taxes when considering the constitutionality of taxes. Article I, Section 2 of the Constitution states that "Direct Taxes shall be apportioned among the several States which may be included within this Union, according to their respective Numbers." Article I, Section 9 provides that "No capitation or other direct tax shall be laid unless in proportion to the census." Initially, the Supreme Court narrowly defined what is a direct tax and thus limited congressional authority to impose various kinds of taxes. Direct taxes were limited to poll taxes (taxes that levy a set amount per individual) and taxes on real property; indirect taxes were taxes imposed on rights, privileges, and activities. In *Pollack v. Farmer's Loan & Trust Co.,*[4] the Supreme Court, by a 5-4 vote, declared unconstitutional the federal income tax. The court reasoned that because the income tax collected revenue gained from property, among other sources, it was a direct tax that must be apportioned among the states. In 1913, the Sixteenth Amendment was added to the Constitution to overturn that decision and to permit a federal income tax. The Sixteenth Amendment provides that "Congress shall have power to lay and collect taxes on incomes, from whatever source derived, without apportionment among the several States and without regard to any census or enumeration." As a result, federal courts evidentially abandoned the distinction between direct and indirect taxes.

U.S. TAXATION OVERVIEW

Taxation in the United States may involve payments to at least three different levels of government: local government (possibly including municipal, township, district, and county governments), state government, and the federal government. Local government is financed largely by property taxes and fees and sometimes income tax. State government is financed mainly by a mix of sales and/or income taxes. The federal government is financed primarily by income taxes.

Most U.S. tax laws are not properly indexed to inflation. Either they ignore inflation completely or they are indexed to the consumer price index, which tends to understate real inflation. In a progressive tax system, not indexing the brackets to inflation has the effect that there is a tax increase every year, even if Congress passes no tax law. That is because an individual's income will naturally go up at the inflation rate, and the progressive taxation system causes the person to pay a greater percentage of his or her income in taxes.

FEDERAL INCOME TAX

The federal income tax forms the bulk of taxes collected by the U.S. government. Depending on income, it ranges from 0 to 35 percent of a taxpayer's income. The income tax is progressive because it takes a larger percentage of the income from higher-income individuals and entitites.

Individuals

U.S. citizens are subject to tax on their worldwide income. Generally, foreigners are treated as U.S. residents for U.S. income tax purposes if they (a) are lawful permanent residents (that is, they hold an immigrant visa ("green card") at any time during the calendar year) or (b) meet a "substantial presence" test.[5] This substantial presence test is met generally if the person is present in the United States for at least 31 days during the current calendar year and the total number of days present in the United States in the current and two immediately preceding years is at least 183.

An individual's taxable income is determined by aggregating items of gross income and then reducing such amount by the aggregate items of deduction and credit. In general, gross income is defined broadly to include all income from any source except where the Internal Revenue Code specifically provides otherwise. Gross income includes salaries, tips, and wages from employment, dividends, interest, gains from the sale of property, and other accretions of wealth realized by the individual taxpayer. However, a gain is not taxable until recognized. Moreover, with limited exceptions, the appreciation of an asset is not considered income until it is recognized by a sale, exchange, transfer, or conversion.

The U.S. income tax system includes both tax deductions and tax credits. The most common deduction for individuals is mortgage interest on a personal home and contributions to charitable organizations. Business expenses, such as dues paid by pharmacists to pharmacy-related associations and other pharmacist-employee expenses may, be treated as deductions, although subject to a 2 percent floor. For 2005, taxpayers who do not participate in an employer-sponsored pension plan may contribute up to $4,000 ($4,500 if age fifty or above) into an individual retirement account and may deduct that contribtion from their gross income.[6]

There are two ways for an individual to calculate income tax. The regular way, as noted above, is based on the gross income minus any applicable deductions and then a marginal tax percentage is applied according to the taxpayer's income bracket. From this result, any applicable tax credits are subtracted and the result is the income tax owed. If the result is a negative number due to refundable tax credits, the taxpayer is entitled to a tax refund even if no tax had been paid.

The second way, the alternative minimum tax (AMT), is based on the taxpayer's gross income plus any tax preference items such as paper gain on exercised stock options. Adding back tax preference items almost guarantees a much higher taxable income in this alternative calculation. This higher income base is multiplied by 26 or 28 percent depending on taxpayer income. Special tax rates apply to net longer term capital gain and qualified dividends. The taxpayer pays the higher of the regular tax liability or the AMT liability. The AMT was designed to prevent people from using loopholes in the tax law to avoid tax.

Corporations

Corporations that are incorporated under the laws of the United States or any of the states are subject to U.S. taxation on their worldwide income, just like individuals. This is true regardless of the status of their shareholders or the site of the corporation's management and control. The U.S. system of taxation treats a corporation as a separate and distinct entity taxable separate from its shareholders. Therefore, income is taxed at the corporate level when earned, and that income is taxable again at the shareholder level. Certain intercompany dividends may be excluded to some extent, and there is certain beneficial tax treatment on dividends received by individuals.

Like taxation of an individual, a corporation's taxable income is determined by aggregating items of gross income and reducing such amount by the aggregate items of deduction. Gross income for a corporation typically includes business income (net of the cost of goods sold), dividends, interest, gains from the sale of property, and other additions to wealth.

U.S. corporations are entitled to deduct all ordinary and necessary expenses paid or incurred during the taxable year in carrying on a trade or business. However, some expenses, although ordinary and necessary from a business standpoint, are never deductible. Prime examples are lobbying expenditures and political contributions. Even if otherwise ordinary and necessary, other business expenditures that are capital in nature will not be deductible currently. These capital expenditures are generally deductible only through depreciation, depletion, or amortization over the statutory recovery period for the property. In addition, other expenses are deductible, subject to limitation.

A corporation's tax liability is determined by multiplying an applicable corporate tax rate by the corporation's net income. There are eight brackets of corporate tax rates, as shown in Table 11.1.

Every U.S. corporation subject to income tax is required to file an annual income tax return. A return must be filed even if the corporation has no in-

TABLE 11.1. Taxable income brackets, 2005.

Over	But not over	Pay +	% on excess	of the amount over–
$0	$50,000	$0	15	$0
50,000	75,000	7,500	25	50,000
75,000	100,000	13.750	34	75,000
100,000	335,000	22,250	39	100,000
335,000	10,000,000	113,900	34	335,000
10,000,000	15,000,000	3,400,000	35	10,000,000
15,000,000	18,333,333	5,150,000	38	15,000,000
18,333,333	. . .	0	35	0

come or if no tax is due.[7] This return is due by the fifteenth day of the third month following the close of the taxable year. An extension of time to file a return may be granted. Nonetheless, the time for paying the tax due is unaffected by any extensions received.

In addition, payors of dividends, interest, or royalties of $10 or more to any person or entity during a calendar year must file an information return for each category. Payments in the ordinary course of a trade or business of $600 or more to another person likewise require the filing of an information return. Generally, information returns must be sent to the payee by January 31 following the calendar year in which the payments are made, and filed with the IRS by February 28 following the calendar year in which payments are made.

An S-Corporation is a "small business corporation" whose shareholders have all consented to the corporation's choice to be taxed in a manner similar to a partnership. That is, the S-Corporation does not pay any income tax. Instead, the corporation's income and deductions are passed through to the shareholders who report the income and deductions on their own income tax returns.

A small business corporation (1) must be a domestic corporation organized under the laws of any state or U.S. territory; (2) must have only individuals, estates, or certain trusts as shareholders; (3) must have only U.S. citizens or residents as shareholders; and (4) must have only one class of stock.[8] For 2005, an S-Corporation can have no more than 100 shareholders.

The corporation must elect S-Corporation status, with the unanimous consent of its shareholders, on or before the fifteenth day of the third month of its taxable year. If timely filed, the election is effective in the year in which it is made.

Limited Liability Companies and Partnerships

LLCs may be treated as either a partnership or a corporation for U.S. income tax purposes, depending upon various factors. Therefore, special care must be taken to ensure partnership status if desired. A business entity not required to be treated as a corporation for federal inxome tax purposes may choose whether to be taxed as a corporation or as a partnership.

U.S. partnerships are treated as conduits and therefore are not subject to U.S. taxation. Rather, their partners are subject to U.S. taxation on their distributive shares of the partnership's income, whether actually distributed to them or not. No additional tax is imposed upon the distribution of previously undistributive income. Therefore, the partnership form of doing business in the United States, unlike the corporate form, subjects the income of the business to only one layer of taxation imposed at the partner level. The determination of a partnership's taxable income as well as most elections affecting the computation of a partnership's taxable income, however, are made at the partnership level.

The taxable income of a partnership generally is computed in the same manner as that of an individual except that certain deductions (for example, charitable contributions, personal exemptions, foreign income taxes, and net operating losses) are not allowed. However, certain items of income and deduction which retain their character when passed through to the partners are excluded from the ordinary business income of the partnership and must be separately stated so that any individual limitation on the includibility or deductibility of such items can be applied at the individual partner's level. These items generally include capital gains and losses, gains and losses on the sale of business property, charitable contributions, dividends eligible for the dividends received deduction, and foreign income taxes.

Under the conduit approach, partners are required to report their distributive shares of the partnership's ordinary income and separately stated items on their individual income tax returns. Partners that are U.S. corporations report this amount as other income on their U.S. corporate income tax returns. A partner's distributive share generally is determined by the partnership agreement. Allocations under a partnership agreement generally are respected as long as they have substantial economic affect (that is, the allocations to the agreement follow the economics of the agreement).

Regulations issued in 1996 (the "check the box rules") allowed taxpayers to elect to treat domestic entities as either partnerships or corporations for federal income tax purposes. As a result, it is generally possible to create corporate-like entities such as LLCs that are treated as partnerships for tax purposes without regard to management characteristics, dissolution provisions, or restrictions on the transfer of non–publicly traded interest.

SOCIAL SECURITY TAX

The next largest tax at the federal level is the Social Security tax. Under the Federal Insurance Contributions Act (FICA), an employer is required to withhold Social Security taxes (including hospital insurance tax) from wages paid to an employee during the year and must also match the tax withheld from the employee's wages. For 2005, the combined tax rate is 7.65 percent, which consists of a 6.2 percent component for Old Age Survivors and Disability Insurance (OASDI) and 1.45 percent component for hospital insurance (Medicare). The OASDI rate applies only to wages up to $90,000 in 2005. This threshold increases every year and has been increasing faster than inflation. There is no cap on wages subject to the Medicare tax.[9]

If an employee works for more than one employer, each employer must withhold and pay FICA taxes on the wages paid.

Self-employed people are responsible for both parts of the social security tax. The Medicare tax is used to pay for medical care for qualifying persons, usually people over the age of sixty-five.

Dividend and interest income, however, is not subject to Social Security or Medicare taxes.

OTHER FEDERAL TAXES

The United States has an income tax to support unemployment insurance. This tax is based on the first $7,000 of wages paid during the calendar year to each employee. The full rate of tax is 6.2 percent, but the employee is allowed a partial credit against this tax based on state unemployment insurance tax liability.[10]

The United States also has a tax to pay for retraining of displaced workers; this tax is assessed only on employers.

Employers pay these taxes directly to federal banks, which use the money to retire short-term treasury debt. For this reason, most employers maintain an account at a federal bank.

The United States also maintains federal excise taxes on gasoline and other fuels used by vehicles. Higher profile excise taxes exist on distilled spirits, tobacco products, and some firearms.

STATE INCOME TAX

All states also have their own tax system. Typically there is a tax on real estate, and there may be additional income taxes, sales taxes, and excise taxes. Oil- and mineral-producing states often have a severance tax, which is similar to an excise tax in that tax is paid on products produced, rather than on sales. Taxes on hotel rooms are common and politically popular because the taxpayers usually do not vote in the jurisdiction levying the tax.

The following states do not levy an individual income tax: Alaska, Florida, Nevada, South Dakota, Texas, Washington, and Wyoming. New Hampshire and Tennessee tax only interest and dividend income. Delaware, Oregon, Montana, and New Hampshire have no state or local sales tax. Alaska has no state sales tax but allows localities to collect their own sales taxes up to a state-specified maximum. California has all the mentioned taxes, which can result in taxes that exceed 51 percent of income for many workers.

CITY AND COUNTY TAX

Cities and counties may levy additional taxes, for instance to improve parks or schools, or pay for police, fire departments, local roads, and other services. As in the case of the IRS, they generally require a tax payment account number. Other local governmental agencies may also have the power to tax, notably independent school districts.

Local government taxes are usually property taxes but may also include sales taxes and income taxes. Some cities collect income tax on not only residents but also nonresidents employed in the city.

NOTES

1. 297 U.S. 1(1936).
2. 301 U.S. 548 (1937)
3. 301 U.S. 619 (1937)
4. 157 U.S. 429 (1895)
5. I.R.C. § 7701(b)(1).
6. I.R.C. § 219(b)(5)(B).
7. I.R.C. § 6012(a)(2).
8. I.R.C. § 1361(b).
9. I.R.C. 3101, 3111, and 3121(a).
10. I.R.C. § 3301.

Chapter 12

Contracts

Jacqueline E. Artinger

This chapter will cover the area of contracts. It is meant as a general overview and is not to be used in place of competent legal counsel. Included will be an overview of the law of contracts, the anatomy of a typical contract with sample language, and the reasons behind the inclusion of these provisions.

Contracts, also known as "Agreements" or "K's," are made up of terms and conditions which put the parties on notice of their respective duties, obligations, and benefits. Quite often the shorter, less painful route is to avoid entering into the negotiating, drafting, and executing process of a contract. Frequently though, regret follows this decision.

Most states have what are known as the "Statute of Frauds" laws. These dictate when a contract, or agreement, must be in writing to be actionable. These typically include contracts for the sale of land, sale of goods over the amount of $500, marriage contracts (such as prenuptial agreements), contracts taking longer than one year to perform, and promises to pay the debt of another. Typically contracts related to pharmacy will fall under the Statute of Frauds because of either the dollar amount involved or because service agreements are typically for a period of time longer than one year.

A contract contains terms and conditions which must be specific enough to prevent ambiguity. The goal is to have a document that both parties can perform under with a sense of fairness and good faith. When one party takes a "hard nose" approach to negotiating an agreement, neither party ends up feeling good about the experience, and typically resentment prevents performance to the level that would have otherwise been achieved.

Attorneys these days are trained to write in "plain English." However, old habits die hard. There are certain "terms of art" that will take much longer to be replaced with plain English. There are traditional terms and conditions that are standard to most contracts, and these are still robust with

Pharmacy Law Desk Reference
© 2007 by The Haworth Press, Inc. All rights reserved.
doi:10.1300/5790_12

"legalese." It is always wise to retain an attorney to review all contracts before signing, especially when the stakes are high.

The Parol Evidence Rule prevents oral testimony from being submitted that would vary, add to, or contradict the written agreement. For this reason, it is important that the terms and conditions are clear enough so that the intents of both parties are clearly represented.

The Uniform Commercial Code (UCC) governs the sale of goods. It has "looser" standards than statutory contract law. The goal is to keep business moving along so the requirements are not as strict. Such examples are the parameters of what is considered an offer or acceptance. The UCC recognizes that businesses conduct "deals" everyday that call for looser standards. If contracts had to be strictly complied with on a day-to-day basis, businesses would have to shut down or continue at a snail's pace. States vary as to whether they have adopted the UCC "as is," or with some modification thereof. An attorney in your state can advise you as to the current status in your state.

REQUIREMENTS OF A CONTRACT

A contract must have an offer, acceptance, and consideration. A contract is not valid until the offer has been accepted. An offer can usually be withdrawn before it is officially "accepted." The acceptance must be clear to the person issuing the offer to put the "offeror" on notice that his or her offer has been accepted. Acceptance should be in writing, but especially under the UCC, acceptance may be oral. Your goal should simply be to make sure the offeror is aware that you want to consummate the deal.

Consideration is the area that has the most controversy and is most frequently contested. Consideration is the "bargained for exchange." There must always be a "give and take" in a contract. Typically it is a product or service supplied on the one side and money paid on the other side. If one side is not committed to a benefit or a detriment, then the contract can be considered "illusory." This results in neither party having to perform under the agreement. The government (such as the Department of Justice, Office of Inspector General, etc.) is always reviewing agreements to see if they are illusory. Typical instances are when pharmaceutical companies are paying money to a pharmacy. There must always be a benefit derived by the pharmaceutical company. If the agreement is used simply to funnel money to the recipient, then more likely than not, the contract will be deemed illusory (and likely will also violate several state or federal laws on kickbacks, etc.).

Once the offer, acceptance, and consideration are satisfied, then the final negotiations and drafting of the formal agreement may take place.

A typical contract has an introductory paragraph, which identifies the parties; the recitals, which explain the purpose for the agreement; the general terms and conditions, which lay out the obligations of each party; and the signature lines. The agreement must be signed, at a minimum, by the "party to be charged." This means that if you were going to sue the other side for breach, you must have their signature on the agreement. If not, you will not be able to hold the other party to the terms and conditions.

There are also what are called "implied in fact" contracts, but they are atypical. This is when the performance of each party never makes it into a written agreement. The court may find that it would simply not be fair to let the other (breaching) party off the hook, so the court will hold that an agreement existed, albeit not in writing. You still have the Statute of Frauds issues, etc., to contend with, so it is simply easier to put the agreement in writing.

ANATOMY OF A SAMPLE CONTRACT

The following contains the parts of a typical agreement and the reasons behind the inclusion of such provisions:

Introductory Paragraph

> This PURCHASING AGREEMENT, dated as of _____ 200____, (this "Agreement"), is made and entered into by and between (insert name of party), a (insert state) corporation, d.b.a. _____, as seller ("Seller" or "Company"), and (insert name of party), a (insert state) corporation, d.b.a. _____ as buyer ("Buyer"), with reference to the following facts:

This provision identifies the parties, gives a date to the inception of the agreement, and allows for the assigning of nicknames to the parties, which provides for ease in identification throughout the agreement. Quite often "Buyer" and "Seller" are used, and this is fine, so long as they are defined somewhere in the agreement. By doing this in the beginning, it is clear to the reader who is obliged to the agreement.

Recitals

RECITALS:

WHEREAS, Seller manufactures, sells, markets, and/or distributes widgets ("Company Products" or "Products") to companies which use Company Products and to other entities which distribute or resell such Products; and

WHEREAS, Buyer is in the business of distributing Company Products in the United States and in Europe; and

WHEREAS, Seller desires to provide Buyer with certain special Company Products and Buyer desires to purchase such special Company Products upon the terms and subject to the conditions set forth in this Agreement.

NOW THEREFORE, in consideration of the above recitals and their representations, warranties, conditions, covenants, and promises exchanged by the parties herein below, and for adequate consideration, the receipt and sufficiency of which is hereby acknowledged, Seller and Buyer hereby agree as follows:

The Recital section lays out the reasons for the agreement. It tells the role each party plays. Here, one party manufactures widgets and the other party needs to purchase widgets for its distribution business. Both parties agree that Buyer will buy widgets from Seller and each will abide by the terms and conditions that will follow. The part that follows the Recitals is where the rubber hits the road. The terms and conditions are actionable for any potential breach situation and both parties are put on notice as to what their respective obligations are.

Terms and Conditions

1. DEFINITIONS

Except as may be defined elsewhere herein, the capitalized terms used in this Agreement shall have the meanings ascribed to them in this Section 1.

1.01. The term "Affiliate" shall mean and refer to any entity, whether partnership, corporation, individual, firm, or otherwise, which either Company or Buyer, directly or through one or more intermediaries, owns or controls, or which owns or is common control with either Company or Buyer.

1.02. The term "Agreement" shall mean and refer to this Purchasing Agreement, dated as of (Insert Date), 200____, made and entered into by and between Company and Buyer, together with any and all exhibits attached hereto, as from time to time may be amended in accordance with the terms hereof or by operation of law.

1.03. The term "Bid Price" shall have the meaning ascribed to it in section 4.01 below.

1.04. The term "Buyer" shall mean and refer to (Insert Name), a (Insert State) corporation, with its principal place of business located at (Insert Address).

1.05. The term "Company" or "Seller" shall mean and refer to (Insert Name), a (Insert State) corporation, with its principal place of business located at (Insert Address).

1.06. The term "Company Product(s)" shall mean and refer to any widget, whether custom designed or of stock specifications which is, as applicable: (i) manufactured, sold, marketed, and/or distributed by Company for resale to the consuming public; (ii) approved, if necessary by applicable state or federal agency; and (iii) set forth on Exhibit "A" attached hereto, as from time to time may be amended, revised, or updated by the mutual written agreement of Company and Buyer.

The definitions may be placed in several locations in an agreement. The two most common places are directly after the Recitals or in a separate exhibit. If placed in an exhibit, it is wisest to make it the first exhibit. The definition section is where words or phrases are defined that are open to several or more possible meanings. By clearly defining them here, you clear up any ambiguities up front. There are two philosophies on drafting contracts—be as specific as possible or as vague as possible. Which route you choose will depend on whether you want a broad interpretation or a narrow interpretation. Vague will give you a broad interpretation, while very specific descriptors will allow for only narrow interpretations. Remember that the "specific" will control over the "general," and the Parol Evidence Rule will allow for oral testimony to define "trade of art" phrases if they are not defined clearly enough in the agreement.

Duties and Obligations of the Parties

2. OBLIGATIONS OF COMPANY

2.01. *Provide Company Products.* Company shall provide Buyer with the Company Products requested at their respective Bid Prices. Company shall deliver the Company Products requested within ten (10) calendar days of receipt of Buyer's purchase order. The Company Products shall be delivered CIF (Cost-of-Goods, Insurance, and Freight) to Buyer.

2.02. *Standards.* Company represents, warrants, covenants, and agrees that, at all times during the term of this Agreement, Company shall do, or cause to be done, and shall maintain each of the following:

2.02.01. Compliance with any and all federal and state rules, regulations, and statutes, and registration requirements governing the conduct and operations of Company's business and the testing, approval, manufacture, sale, and distribution of all Company Products;

2.02.02. Use of its best efforts to ensure that any and all Company Products sold to Buyer hereunder or distributed to a Designated Wholesaler are of the highest quality.

2.02.03. *Company,* at its sole cost and expense, shall maintain throughout the term of this Agreement and, if coverage is provided on a claims-made basis, for a period of four years following termination of this Agreement, comprehensive liability insurance including general liability, contractual liability, and products liability coverages (with a vendor's endorsement in favor of Buyer, in the minimum amount of one million dollars ($1,000,000) per occurrence and three million dollars ($3,000,000) annual aggregate.

All insurance required under this Agreement shall be provided by insurers who are agencies licensed to do business in the State of (Insert Buyer's State) and who have obtained an A.M. Bests' rating of A: VIII or better.

A certificate of insurance shall be issued to Buyer prior to the Commencement Date and upon the renewal of the insurance coverage specified in this Section. The certificate shall provide that Buyer shall receive thirty (30) days' prior written notice of cancellation or material reduction in the insurance coverage specified in this Section. Notwithstanding anything to the contrary, if Company has a claims-made based policy and anticipates that such policy (or policies) will be cancelled or not renewed, Company agrees to exercise any option contained in said policy (or policies) to extend the reporting period to the maximum period permitted; provided, however, that Company need not exercise such option if the superseding insurer will accept all prior claims. Notwithstanding any other provision of this Agreement, failure to provide the certificate of insurance shall be grounds for immediate termination of this Agreement.

2.04. *Maintain Records.* During the term of this Agreement and for a period of thirty-six (36) months following the expiration or other termination hereof, Company shall keep and maintain adequate records, books, and files, respecting the sale of Company Products under this Agreement.

3. OBLIGATIONS OF BUYER

3.01. *Maintain Licensure.* Throughout the term of this Agreement, Buyer shall remain duly licensed to operate a distributorship for widgets and other related or nonrelated products.

3.02. *Payment.* Buyer shall pay for the Company Products provided by Company in accordance with the provisions of Section 4 below.

3.03. *Maintain Records.* During the term of this Agreement and for a period of thirty-six (36) months following the expiration or other termination hereof, Buyer shall keep and maintain adequate records, books, and files respecting the purchase of Company Products under this Agreement.

The duties and obligations of the two parties follow the definitions section. Note that this sample agreement is from the perspective of the Buyer and certain terms and conditions are more favorable to the Buyer. An example of this is the insurance requirement. Logically, it makes sense for the seller (manufacturer) of the product to be contractually obligated to carry insurance, but it is not necessarily unreasonable for the buyer to also have to maintain insurance. In a completely reciprocal agreement, both parties would be obligated to perform all duties and obligations that are common to both parties. A determining factor is who has more control or more of a potential liability.

Payment Terms

4. PAYMENT AND PAYMENT TERMS

4.01. *Bid Price of the Company Products.* Buyer shall purchase the Company Products for the price (the "Bid Price") set forth on Exhibit "A" opposite each Company Product's name. The parties will renegotiate the Bid Price every two years.

4.02. *Payment Terms.* Buyer shall pay Company with terms of 2/90, net 120 upon receipt of the invoice for the Company Products purchased. The obligations of this Section 4.02 shall survive the expiration or other termination of this Agreement.

4.03. *Modifying the Bid Price.* If the Bid Price for any Company Product expires during the initial term or any renewal term of this Agreement, then Company and Buyer shall negotiate, in good faith, to arrive at a new Bid Price for such Company Product. Any Bid Price applicable under the terms of this Agreement may be modified by attaching a new, revised, or supplemental Exhibit "A" to the Agreement, which exhibit shall be dated and signed by both Company and Buyer.

Payment terms should reflect the agreed upon terms. This is a necessary provision in a purchase or service agreement. If there are any "special" provisions, such as paying by electronic fund transfer (EFT), then they should be added here. Penalties are not allowed in a contract in most states, but additional "fees" are. So, if the parties have agreed upon extra fees or interest for such things as late payments, they should also be added here.

Term and Termination

5. TERM AND TERMINATION

5.01. *Term.* The initial term of this Agreement shall commence on _____, 200____, (the "Commencement Date") and shall continue for a period of twenty-four (24) months thereafter. Upon the expiration of the initial term hereof, the term of this Agreement automatically shall be renewed for successive twenty-four (24) month periods on each anniversary of the Commencement Date.

5.02. *Termination.* The initial term or any renewal term of this Agreement may be terminated only as follows:

5.02.01. *Mutual Consent.* This Agreement may be terminated, with or without cause, at any time upon the mutual written consent of Company and Buyer.

5.02.02. *Good Cause.* Either party may terminate this Agreement for good cause upon thirty (30) calendar days prior written notice to the other party. Any notice given pursuant to this Section 5.02.03 shall describe the nature of the alleged misconduct or default and the precise action required to cure the default, if a cure is possible.

5.02.02.01. *Company Default.* Buyer shall have good cause to terminate this Agreement for, among other things, the repeated failure of Company to deliver the Company Products to Buyer when due or for Company's breach of any other material term, condition, or covenant of this Agreement.

5.02.02.02. *Buyer Default.* Company shall have good cause to terminate this Agreement for, among other things, Buyer's repeated failure to tender payment for the Company Products purchased hereunder when such payment is due or for Buyer's breach of any other material term, condition, or covenant of this Agreement.

5.02.02.03. *Cure Period.* Notwithstanding the foregoing, this Agreement shall not be deemed terminated if, within said thirty (30) day period, the breaching party cures the default or eliminates the good cause to the other party's reasonable satisfaction. In the event that a default or breach is incurable or not cured with the thirty (30) day period, then this Agreement shall be terminated upon the expiration of the thirty (30) day curative period.

5.02.03. *Insolvency.* Either Buyer or Company may terminate this Agreement if the other party files a petition in bankruptcy, makes a general assignment for the benefit of creditors, or has a petition in bankruptcy filed against it, a receiver or trustee appointed over its assets, or an attachment, seizure, lien, or levy made against a substantial portion of its assets which is not released or dismissed within thirty (30) calendar days. In such event, the termination of this Agreement shall be effective upon the insolvent party's receipt of written notice thereof.

The "Term and Termination" section tells how long the agreement will be in effect and under what circumstances it can or will be terminated. The term in this sample language is set up as an "evergreen" contract. This means that it keeps on going until one party breaches and does not cure or becomes insolvent. All agreements must have a termination point, whether it is included at the time of signing (". . . and shall commence for a period of two years.") or, as in this case, is left open to keep going until an event takes place to trigger a termination. Another option is to have an evergreen with an option to renew on the anniversaries or have a "without cause clause." A "without cause clause" allows either party to terminate at any time upon the giving of a certain number of days notice of termination to the other party. The issue with "without cause clauses" is that it allows either party to terminate at any time. This would not be beneficial if you have spent a long time negotiating the agreement and the terms are favorable to you. It all boils down to what can be negotiated.

Indemnification

6. INDEMNIFICATION OBLIGATION

Company shall indemnify, defend and hold harmless Buyer and its past, present, and future parents, shareholders, affiliates, subsidiaries, officers, directors, employees, agents, representatives, successors, transferees, and assigns (collectively, the "Buyer Group") from and against: (i) any and all losses, damages (of every kind and nature), liabilities, deficiencies, or obligations incurred or reasonably likely to be incurred by any member of the Buyer Group which results from or arises out of (a) the design, manufacture, storage, transportation, or any use of the Company's Products or (b) the Company's breach of or default under any representation, warranty, covenant, condition, or promise made by the Company under this Agreement; and (ii) any and all claims, actions, suits, proceedings, demands, judgments, settlement amounts, assessments, fines, interest, penalties, costs and expenses (including reasonable legal, accounting, experts' and other fees, costs and expenses) relating to or resulting from any of the foregoing (collectively "Losses and Expenses")

6.01. *Disposition of Claims.* After Buyer's receipt of notice of any claim by a third party which is the subject of indemnification pursuant to Section 6 above (collectively, "Action"), Buyer shall deliver to Company written notice (the "Notice of Claim") specifying the basis of the claim for indemnification hereunder. The failure of Buyer to give such Notice of Claim shall not relieve Company of its indemnification obligations hereunder unless such failure shall result in material prejudice to Company. Buyer shall be entitled, at the sole expense and liability of Company, to exercise full control of the defense, compromise, or settlement of any Action unless Company, within ten (10) business days after the delivery of the Notice of Claim, shall: (i) notify Buyer in writing of Company's intention to assume the defense thereof, and (ii) retain legal counsel reasonably satisfactory to Buyer to conduct the defense of such Action. Buyer and Company shall cooperate with the party assuming the defense of any such Action in accordance herewith in any manner that such party reasonably may request. No such Action may be settled by Company without the written consent of Buyer.

6.02. *Acknowledgments*. The parties to this Agreement hereby acknowledge that they are sophisticated business persons who were represented by legal counsel during the negotiations regarding this Agreement, including, without limitation, the provisions of this Section 6 regarding indemnification, and are fully informed regarding such provisions. They further acknowledge that the provisions of this Section 6 regarding indemnification fairly allocate the risks of the matters for which indemnification or reimbursement may be sought under this Agreement.

Indemnification is often the most contentious subject matter in an agreement. The lesser the risk of harm or of something "going wrong," the less important this section is. Let's face it: we are in a litigious environment. It doesn't take too much these days for one party to sue another, often over insignificant events. Indemnification protects the "innocent" party. For instance, if you are sued because of a defective product, but you did not manufacture it and you did not have any way to tell it was defective, then indemnification will reimburse you for monies you will spend in defending yourself and for any potential damages that you will have to pay. Indemnification provisions can vary in relation to what is covered, if there are any particular circumstances, or may be limited to a specific dollar amount.

Confidentiality

7. CONFIDENTIAL AND PROPRIETARY INFORMATION

7.01. *Inspection Rights.* Upon reasonable notice and at reasonable times, each party hereto shall have the right to examine and audit the books, records, and files of the other as they relate to the performance of this Agreement or the transactions contemplated hereunder. This right may be exercised by any employee, agent, representative, attorney, or accountant of the party requesting the audit or examination at any time during the term of this Agreement and for a period of up to six (6) months following the expiration or other termination of this Agreement for any reason whatsoever. The expense of the audit or examination shall be borne by the party requesting it. Both Company and Buyer shall provide any governmental agency exercising competent jurisdiction over Company, or Buyer with access to their respective facilities, equipment, books, and records relating to the performance of this Agreement.

7.02. *Confidential and Proprietary Information.*

7.02.01. *Confidentiality of this Agreement and Related Information.* This Agreement and all terms and conditions hereof are confidential. Any and all accounts, records, books, files, and lists respecting any transaction provided for or contemplated under this Agreement (the "Related Information") shall be confidential and proprietary to the party generating such information. Company shall not disclose this Agreement or any of Buyer's Related Information to any third party without the prior written consent of Buyer.

7.02.02. *Other Information Proprietary to Buyer.* Company acknowledges and agrees that Buyer (and/or its Affiliates) have developed or use certain symbols, logos, trademarks, trade names, service marks, patents, inventions, copyrights, copyrightable material, trade secrets, personnel information, operating manuals, memoranda, work papers, notes, reports, customer or client lists, business information, operational techniques, prospect information, marketing programs, plans and strategies, operating agreements, financial information and strategies, computer software and other computer-related materials in Buyer's business which are confidential or proprietary to Buyer (or its Affiliates) (collectively, "Buyer's Proprietary Information"). Company agrees to hold all of Buyer's Proprietary Information in strictest confidence and to not use, disclose, divulge, or exploit any such information for Company's own benefit (including use in Company's advertising or promotional materials except with Buyer's consent) or for the benefit of some third party without the prior written consent of Buyer, which consent may be refused for any or no reason.

7.02.03 *Proprietary Information Disclosed to Company.* Company and Buyer acknowledge that, during the course of this agreement, Company may have access to or make use of certain of Buyer's Proprietary Information, including this Agreement and Buyer's Related Information. However, Buyer shall remain the sole and exclusive owner of all of Buyer's Proprietary Information notwithstanding its disclosure to Company. Upon the expiration or other termination of this Agreement, for any reason whatsoever, Company shall immediately return to Buyer or destroy any and all of Buyer's Proprietary Information (including Buyer's Related Information) in Company's possession, including all copies, duplications, and replicas thereof.

7.03. *Confidential and Proprietary Information of Company.* Buyer acknowledges and agrees that Company (and/or its Affiliates) have developed or use certain symbols, logos, trademarks, trade names, service marks, patents, inventions, copyrights, copyrightable material, trade secrets, personnel information, operating manuals, memoranda, work papers, notes, reports, customer or client lists, business information, operational techniques, prospect information, marketing programs, plans and strategies, operating agreements, financial information and strategies, computer software and other computer-related materials in Company's business which are confidential or proprietary to Company (or its Affiliates) (collectively, "Company's Proprietary Information"). Buyer agrees to hold all of Company's Proprietary Information, including Company's Related Information, in strictest confidence and to not use, disclose, divulge, or exploit any such information for Buyer's own benefit (including use in Buyer's advertising or promotional materials except with Company's consent) or for the benefit of some third party. Upon the expiration or other termination of this Agreement, for any reason whatsoever, Buyer shall immediately return to Company or destroy any of Company's Proprietary Information in Buyer's possession, including all copies, duplications, and replicas thereof.

7.04. *Equitable Relief.* Company and Buyer acknowledge and agree that it would be difficult to measure the damages resulting from any breach of their respective obligations set forth in Section 7.02 and 7.03 above, that injury to such party (or its Affiliate) from any such breach would be impossible to calculate, and that money damages would therefore be an inadequate remedy for any such breach. Consequently, Company and Buyer agree that, in addition to any other rights or remedies which they may have, an injured party shall be entitled to injunctive and other equitable relief, without bond or other security, in the event of an actual or threatened breach by the other party of the covenants of Section 7.02 or 7.03, as the case may be. The obligations and the rights and remedies of the parties under this Section 7.04 are cumulative and in addition to, and not in lieu of, any obligations, rights, or remedies which they may have under applicable patent, copyright, and other laws, including the statutory and common laws governing unfair competition and misappropriation or theft of trade secrets, proprietary rights, or confidential information.

7.05. *Legal Disclosures.* Nothing contained in this Section 7 shall prevent or restrict either party from disclosing any confidential or proprietary information of the other party pursuant to a valid court order or as required under applicable statute, rule, or regulation or by any federal, state, county, municipal, local, or foreign government or governmental agency, bureau, commission, authority, or body, with competent jurisdiction over either party hereto or the requested information.

7.06. *Survival.* The Covenants and conditions of this Section 7 shall survive the expiration or other termination of this Agreement for any reason whatsoever.

It is always wise to have a section that covers information that is confidential and proprietary to each of the respective parties. Typically, not much confidential information will be exchanged in a simple, one-time purchase of a product, such as buying a scale. But if you are in a "relationship" or "partnership" with the other party and expect to have a long-term relationship, then it is highly likely that there will be a regular exchange of information that you would not want to have shared with the public at large, and especially with your competitor. This section provides the "instructions" as to what a party would consider confidential and what is expected when the relationship ends as it relates to shared or disclosed confidential information. At the same time, permission is granted to disclose if required by law. If required by law, you would be compelled to disclose anyway, but this will allow the disclosure to take place while not putting you in a breach of the agreement. A survival clause is added so that the other party does not have the right to share your confidential information with others just because the agreement containing the protections has terminated or expired. It adds additional duration of protection. The time may vary in each agreement because it will depend on the types of information that is expected to be shared and the type of industry involved. Some industries evolve at a snail's pace, which makes the information shared valuable for a long time, while other industries are changing at a fast pace, so the information is already stale the next day and is not noteworthy in a very short period of time. For the slower-evolving industries, the longer the protection the better.

Notices

8. NOTICES

Any and all notices, requests, consents, demands, or other communications required or permitted to be given hereunder shall be in writing and shall be deemed to have been duly given (i) when delivered, if sent by United States registered or certified mail (return receipt requested), (ii) when delivered, if delivered personally, or (iii) on the next business day, if sent by United States Express Mail or overnight courier, in each case to the parties at the following addresses (or at such other addresses as shall be specified by like notice) with postage or delivery charges prepaid:

If to Buyer:
(Insert name of Buyer)
(Insert address of Buyer)
Attn: President

If to Company:
(Insert name of Company)
(Insert address of Company)
Attn: President

A Notice provision spells out where official communications should be sent and to whom. This is to avoid the, "Well, I thought you wanted it sent to the Milwaukee office" scenario. This avoids miscommunication and works to ensure that amendments, price changes, purchase orders, etc., are sent to the correct address, so business can continue and performance will continue to be in compliance with the terms and conditions.

General Provisions, Broken Down One by One with Accompanying Explanations

9. GENERAL PROVISIONS

9.01. *Integrated Agreement.* This Agreement constitutes the final written integrated expression of all of the agreements between Company and Buyer with respect to the purchase and sale of Company Products and is a complete and exclusive statement of the terms relating thereto. This Agreement supersedes all prior or contemporaneous, written or oral, memoranda, arrangements, contracts, and understandings between the parties hereto with respect to the subject matter of this Agreement. Any representation, promises, or statements made by either party that differ in any way from the terms of this Agreement shall be given no force or effect. The parties specifically represent, each to the other, that there are no additional or supplemental agreements between them related in any way to the matters herein contained unless specifically included or referred to herein. No addition to or modification of any provision of this Agreement shall be binding upon either party unless embodied in a dated written instrument signed by Company and Buyer.

The "Integrated Agreement" provision is included in a contract to state that this is "it" as it relates to the subject matter of the agreement. This provision reinforces that any prior oral "promises" are not to be given consideration.

> 9.02. *Amendments.* This Agreement shall not be amended, modified, revised, supplemented, or terminated orally unless evidenced by a dated written instrument executed by Company and Buyer.

The "Amendment" provision is included in a contract to state that any modifications or amendments must be in writing and signed by both parties. This prevents a party from sending a letter or e-mail unilaterally changing the terms of the contract, such as a price increase. If both parties agree during the negotiations that price increases may occur at regular intervals, then that information can be clearly spelled out in the Exhibit or the body of the contract and would not require a separate amendment each and every time.

> 9.03. *Waivers.* The waiver by either party hereto of a breach of any provision hereunder shall not operate or be construed as a waiver of any prior or subsequent breach of the same or any other provision hereunder.

The "Waiver" provision is included in a contract to protect each party from inadvertently committing a "waiver." The law typically states that if a party starts to perform in a manner that is different from what is in the written agreement and the other party does not object, then the other party has committed a waiver and cannot thereafter force the "offending" party to perform in accordance with the written agreement. This provision allows for some leeway. There may be circumstances where you want to cut the other party "some slack" and not sue them for breach, but at the same time want to reserve your right to go back and demand that performance be in strict adherence to the written agreement.

> 9.04. *Severability.* In the event that any provision in this Agreement shall be found by a court or governmental authority of competent jurisdiction to be invalid, illegal, or unenforceable, such provision shall be construed and enforced as if it had been narrowly drawn so as not to be invalid, illegal, or unenforceable and the validity, legality, and enforceability of the remaining provisions of this Agreement shall not in any way be affected or impaired thereby.

The "Severability" provision is included in a contract to allow the "removal" of a term or condition that is subsequently determined to be illegal.

If this provision were not in the contract, the contract could be deemed invalid because you cannot have an agreement that is illegal. This also prevents having to have an immediate amendment to rectify the situation.

> 9.05. *Governing Law, Consent to Jurisdiction.* This Agreement shall be governed by and construed in accordance with the laws of the State of (Insert State name) and of the United States. Any legal action, suit, or proceeding arising out of or relating to this Agreement which is not subject to arbitration as provided in Section 9.07 below may be instituted in any state or federal court located within the County of (Insert name of County), State of (Insert name of State), and each party agrees not to assert, by way of motion, as a defense, or otherwise, in any such action, suit, or proceeding, any claim that it is not subject personally to the jurisdiction of such court in any inconvenient forum, that the venue of the action, suit, or proceeding is improper or that this Agreement or the subject matter hereof may not be enforced in or by such court. Each party further irrevocably submits to the jurisdiction of any such court in any such action, suit, or proceeding. Any and all service of process shall be effective against any party if given personally or by United States registered or certified mail, return receipt requested, or by any other means of United States mail that requires a signed receipt, postage prepaid, mailed to such party as herein provided. Nothing herein contained shall be deemed to affect the right of any party to serve process in any manner permitted by law or to commence legal proceedings or otherwise proceed against any other party in any other jurisdiction.

The "Governing Law, Consent to Jurisdiction" provision is included in a contract to make it more efficient if the parties end up in court over a disagreement as to performance or payment. It saves a lot of time if the parties, while not in the heat of a disagreement, can agree beforehand as to the place that a case will be tried and the determination of which state's laws will be applied. States' laws will differ in regard to contract law, privacy, etc., so it is wise to make the determination ahead of time and memorialize it in the agreement.

> 9.06. *Attorney's Fees.* In the event of any dispute involving the subject matter of this Agreement (including an arbitration), the prevailing party shall be entitled to its reasonable attorneys' fees and court or arbitration costs incurred in resolving or settling the dispute, in addition to any and all other damages or relief which a court or arbitrator may deem proper.

The "Attorney's Fees" provision is included in a contract to enable the prevailing party to recover their legal fees and costs if arbitration or a trial takes place. Attorney fees accumulate quickly and can be very costly. Parties are more inclined to hold the other party accountable if they know their attorney fees are recoverable.

> 9.07. *Arbitration.* Except that either party to this Agreement may seek injunctive relief or a prejudgment attachment in a court of competent jurisdiction, and except as otherwise specifically provided for herein, any and all controversies, disputes, or claims arising out of or relating to this agreement, or any part hereof, including, without limitation, the meaning, applicability, or scope of this section 9.07 and to the performance, breach, interpretation, meaning, construction, or enforceability of this Agreement, or any portion hereof, and all claims for rescission or fraud in the inducement of this Agreement, shall, at the request of either party, be settled or resolved by arbitration pursuant to the commercial rules and regulations of the American Arbitration Association (the "AAA") for the resolution of commercial disputes, except as modified herein below.
>
> Any party requesting arbitration under this Agreement shall make a demand on the other party by registered or certified mail with a copy to the AAA. The parties consent and agree to have such arbitration proceedings heard in (Insert name of City), (Insert name of State), or in the place closest thereto which the AAA may select for convenience of the arbitrator(s). The arbitration shall take place as noticed by the AAA regardless of whether one side to the dispute or controversy fails or refuses to participate.

The "Arbitration" provision is included in a contract to provide for arbitration first, then if desired, a subsequent trial. There are two types of arbitration. The first is "binding," and the second is "nonbinding." Binding arbitration is "binding" on the parties. The "loser" cannot appeal the verdict. In "nonbinding" arbitration, the nonprevailing party may, if desired, file a suit if it is unhappy with the arbitration award. Arbitration typically takes less time and costs less money. Depending on what the parties agree to, the level of formality will vary. The process can extend all the way to allowing full discovery with the taking of depositions to the awarding of all possible damages, including punitive damages. Any exceptions, such as injunctions, etc., to the arbitration requirement, need to be spelled out in the arbitration section. For arbitration to be binding, the agreement must state so in writing.

> 9.08. *Successors and Assigns.* This Agreement shall be binding upon the parties hereto and their respective successors, transferees,

and assigns. However, Company shall not assign its rights or delegate its duties hereunder without the prior written consent of Buyer, which consent shall not be unreasonably refused. For the purposes of this Section 9.08, an assignment of this Agreement shall be deemed to include any change by Company in its ownership or control in one or a series of related transactions which involve, among other things, a merger, reorganization, sale of all or substantially all of Company's assets, or sale of greater than fifty percent (50%) of Company's voting capital stock.

The "Successors and Assigns" provision is included in a contract to establish the parameters as to if and when an agreement may be "absorbed" by a new entity. It is not uncommon for one company to be purchased by another company. In this sample language, the Company must first obtain the permission of Buyer before an assignment may be completed. This would protect the Buyer in the case where a company that Buyer has had a past bad experience with, and would therefore choose not to have to be in a contractual relationship with, bought the other party. If the contract is favorable to one party, then that party will likely want to have a mandatory assignment provision to ensure that the deal continues even if a different party is now on the other side.

9.09. *Construction.* This Agreement has been drafted with the joint participation of each of the parties hereto and shall be construed to be neither against nor in favor of either party hereto, but rather in accordance with the fair meaning thereof.

The "Construction" provision is included in a contract to counteract the "Rules of Construction." The rules of construction apply when there is a controversy as to a meaning, etc., which results in the meaning being construed against the primary drafter of the agreement. The rules of construction are to protect the nondrafting party from the drafting party inserting language that is extremely one-sided and unilaterally in the favor of the drafter. This provision acknowledges that it was drafted with the joint participation of both parties and is not to be construed for or against either party.

9.10. *Articles, Sections, Exhibits, and Schedules.* References in this Agreement to articles, sections, exhibits, and schedules are to articles, sections, exhibits, and schedules of and to this Agreement. However, the article and section headings contained in this Agreement are for reference purposes only and shall not in any way affect the meaning or interpretation of this Agreement. All exhibits and schedules to this Agreement, either as originally existing or as the same from time to time may be supplemented, modified, or amended, are hereby incorporated in full herein by this reference.

The "Articles, Sections, Exhibits, and Schedules" provision is included in a contract to indicate that the headings, etc., are descriptive only and are not to be considered when determining definitions. Also, Exhibits must be stated as "incorporated by reference." If not, there is a real chance that they will not be considered to be a part of the contract. Quite often the "guts" of an agreement will be contained in the Exhibits. This allows for the formation of a "standard" agreement that can be used in various circumstances, with the specifics for each separate agreement to be contained in exhibits, which are then attached to the back of the "standard agreement."

9.11. *Counterparts.* This Agreement may be executed in one or more counterparts, each of which shall be deemed to be an original, but all of which shall be considered one and the same instrument.

The "Counterparts" provision is included in a contract to allow for different "copies" to be circulated at once, which is especially helpful when signatures are being obtained. This is where a reference to fax copies should be included if fax signatures are to be accepted.

Signature Block

IN WITNESS WHEREOF, Company and Buyer have executed this Agreement as of the date first written above.

Buyer: (Insert name of Buyer)
                                a (Insert State name) corporation

                                By: _____
                                (Insert name and title)

Company: (Insert name of Company/Seller)
                                a (Insert State name) corporation

                                By: _____
                                (Insert name and title)

Signature blocks are typically located at the end of an agreement and provide a place for both parties to sign. Only persons authorized and empowered by a party to contractually obligate the company or organization should sign a contract.

Exhibits

Exhibits are attached after the signature block and are typically used to lay out the specifics of the particular relationship of the parties. The center top of the page is labeled "Exhibit A." The numbering of the paragraph sections start over. The language should be in "plain English" and clear enough to explain exactly what each party is responsible for (although it is not atypical for the language to be very one-sided, especially in a purchase agreement). This is where description of the products should go, such as "Four (4) inch long Widgets. 1000 in the color blue, 1000 in the color red, and 5000 in the color orange. Price to be $5.00 each." You can be as simple as you want, or as detailed as you want, just remember that the specific controls over the general. If any warranties are to be included, this is the place to include them.

All agreements should have the description of the product(s) or service(s), the price, the time allowed for performance, and the quantity. If time is of the essence or you need specific details followed, these must also be included. For instance, you need the 5000 orange widgets by (insert date) and they MUST be orange, then you would need to state that the widgets *must* be in the color orange and delivery must be made on or before (insert date). The greater the extent the parties expectations are outlined in the agreement, the greater the odds that performance will match the parties' respective expectations.

SUMMARY

Contracts are necessary to put parties on notice of their duties and obligations. Hopefully the sample contract language and accompanying explanations of why the terms and conditions are typically included will help to clarify for you the world of contracts. It is always wise to seek legal counsel before you commit to a contract, versus having to seek legal counsel later to get you out of a bad contract or to protect your interests in a breach situation by the other party.

Chapter 13

Crimes and Torts

Norman A. Campbell

It is useful for pharmacists in all practice venues, as well as students preparing for the practice of pharmacy, to be informed of the potential legal pitfalls resulting from failure to meet their respective legal obligations. The purpose of this discussion is to provide a broad overview of the topic rather than a treatise on criminal and civil liability. The practitioner and student alike should consider it a guide to consider when faced with day-to-day decision making.

CRIMES

In general terms, a crime is a violation of penal law against the state. It may be committed by an act or failure to act which abridges societal norms. These statutory infractions usually carry with them penalties upon conviction which range from death to imprisonment or probation, to fines, to loss of privileges and/or ability to serve in public office or hold a professional license. The gravity of the crime determines the sentencing, based upon the act being categorized as a felony, the most serious offenses, or the less egregious misdemeanor which results in lower levels of penalties. These usually include fines and possible jail terms in a facility other than a penitentiary.

Prosecutors may bring a criminal action against a defendant when the facts warrant proceeding. A wide range of violations have been the bases for prosecutions of pharmacists through the years in various state courts as well as in the federal judicial system. Cases have arisen from such activities as diversion of controlled substances, fraud in insurance and/or federal or state government programs, dispensing violations, and homicide resulting from improper prescription dispensing, to name a few.

Whether the criminal conviction is the result of a business-related violation or one involving professional practice, it is important to be aware that a

Pharmacy Law Desk Reference
© 2007 by The Haworth Press, Inc. All rights reserved.
doi:10.1300/5790_13

state board likely will consider that disposition in making a determination with respect to the defendant's license to practice pharmacy or to register a pharmacy, or both. States may consider a felony conviction as a basis for revocation of a pharmacist's license as well as the disqualification of an applicant. Misdemeanors will be reviewed with respect to their impact on the professional competence and good moral and/or professional character.

As a consequence of conviction in a federal prescription program fraud case, usually the pharmacist will be barred from participation in any federally funded programs. This prohibition extends to the entity which employs the pharmacist. Consequently, even if the convicted pharmacist retains a license following a suspension or other sanction, it is unlikely the individual will be permitted to be employed in any pharmacy position given the extent to which the federal government provides payment for pharmaceutical services.

It should be noted that not only criminal acts arising from professional practice activities are of concern to the courts and, subsequently, a board. Examples of such acts are personal use of illegal substances or operating a motor vehicle while impaired, domestic violence, and so forth.

To summarize, criminal prosecutions are brought on behalf of the government (federal or state), reflecting the position of the people who represent society. The evidential standard in a criminal action holds the prosecution to prove the allegation(s) beyond a reasonable doubt in the view of a jury or judge.

TORTS

In contrast to the societal issues expressed above, a tort is a civil action between private parties for a breach of duty, fixed by law for which an action for damages may be commenced.

To understand this statement, it is useful to look at each provision in detail. The parties are individual persons who may be human beings or corporate or other business enterprises which are afforded most rights available to humans. The plaintiff alleges the defendant committed some act or failed to perform to an expected level, resulting in harm.

The basis for the lawsuit is generally to compensate the injured party for the harm inflicted by defendant. These payments are described as damages and will be discussed further.

In order to prevail in a tort action, the plaintiff must demonstrate that the defendant had a duty to the plaintiff and that the defendant breached that duty, resulting in harm, showing causation between the breach and harm to the plaintiff.

Duty may be established by a variety of means. When a licensed healthcare professional is the defendant, it is generally accepted that the healthcare professional owes a high duty of care to those who rely upon that licensed status. By virtue of holding oneself out as a pharmacist, for example, that person is saying, "You're in good hands when you rely upon me for professional services." One is expected to meet the standards of care generally accepted by members of the defendant's peer professional group. Means of determination of those standards will be addressed subsequently.

Breach of duty is determined by demonstrating the defendant failed to perform to the standard expected from an ordinary prudent pharmacist under similar circumstances. One may rely upon standards determined from multiple sources, including testimony from qualified "experts" in professional practice. Interpretation of the testimony from opposing expert witnesses provided by both parties poses a difficult task for a jury or court. Historically, the "locality rule" was a widely invoked defense. The underlying theory of this argument is "I acted as the ordinary prudent pharmacist in my geographic environs would have acted under these circumstances." For generations, courts accepted variability in levels of practice among pharmacists and other healthcare professionals in different community settings. In theory, practitioners in major urban medical centers were held to a higher, more sophisticated knowledge base than those in small, rural communities. In the early 1960s, courts began to consider a broader standard of practice. National norms became the measure of what a patient could expect from a party holding oneself out to be a competent practitioner of pharmacy or other healthcare profession. Early cases arose from medical practice cases, setting the new standard of care. The then availability of rapid dissemination of continuing education information and professional journal distribution were cited as creating a level informational playing field in all healthcare areas. Hence, the expert witnesses cited above usually are retained by plaintiff's counsel to demonstrate that national standard. How difficult it will be for the defense to acknowledge quality care when using the argument, "Well, that may be how they do things in other parts of the country, but we do it differently here in Anytown."

Harm or injury must have been suffered by the plaintiff. This may include physical injury, medical expenses, loss of income, and related issues. When translated into a financial measure, this total will be considered compensatory damages assessed against the defendant. The basis for this is to make the plaintiff "whole" for the harm suffered. When a jurisdiction permits and a court or jury so determines, punitive damages also may be assessed as "punishment" for the behavior of the defendant in the present case.

One of the most critical issues to be determined is the line of causation linking the harm inflicted upon the plaintiff to the breach of duty by the defendant. The alleged inappropriate activity from which the injury to the plaintiff arose must be shown to have been the proximate cause of that harm.

All four of the basic elements of duty, breach, causation, and harm must be demonstrated by the plaintiff to prevail in the case.

For example, a pharmacist may dispense the wrong medication on a prescription order. Although this is a breach of the very high duty of care owed to patients being served by that practitioner, if the patient or caregiver recognized the error without taking any of the drug product, no harm could be shown. Further, if the patient, while exiting the pharmacy with that incorrectly dispensed prescription order, were to fall and sustain bodily injuries, no causation would exist between the breach and the harm.

In contrast to the evidentiary standard required in a criminal case, in a civil action the plaintiff's threshold is a preponderance of evidence. This may be considered as tilting the balance on a scale in one direction.

NEGLIGENCE

Such activities as those outlined lead to a consideration of the concept of negligence, an act performed below the standard established by law for the protection of others. Misfeasance is carrying out a legal activity at a level which falls below that level which the plaintiff may reasonably have expected given the circumstances and what the ordinary, prudent pharmacist would have done under the same conditions. In the absence of the elements of causation and harm as described earlier, this sometimes is thought of as a "mistake."

If a professional act is performed in contravention of any state or federal law and results in harm, then it is considered malfeasance, or a "bad act." Examples will be described below. It is particularly important for the practitioner and future pharmacist to be aware this type of negligent behavior may be subjected to different judicial scrutiny to the benefit of the plaintiff's case. Depending upon the jurisdiction, such illegal acts may be deemed per se violations or be considered strict liability cases. Rather than meet the standard of the four elements outlined above, the documentation of the illegal behavior may suffice to meet the evidentiary standard. Using a sports metaphor, it would be closer to a forfeit than playing out an entire game to determine the score.

Nonfeasance is failure to attempt to carry out a professional responsibility to the plaintiff's detriment. The question here is not an error of commission (i.e., performing a task poorly), but rather an error of omission by not doing what an ordinary, prudent pharmacist would have done in these circumstances.

In some instances, it becomes problematic to differentiate from jurisdiction to jurisdiction whether certain acts fit into one of these categories. If a state does not address by statute or regulation a particular pharmacy practice, but peer activity supports it as a standard, a violation would be considered differently.

Of principal concern to the pharmacist are those violations that comprise what generally is considered malpractice, a term which has grown to mean professional negligence. The changing dynamics of healthcare and the profession of pharmacy make it difficult, if not impossible, to enumerate every expectation which a patient interacting with a pharmacist in any practice venue might reasonably expect. Several examples are set forth herein for illustrative purposes. One must recognize the expanding nature of this area almost daily as pharmacists create new roles and innovative practice models. As these roles evolve, it can be expected that courts will subsequently be dealing with cases arising from alleged negligence in performing them at expected levels.

At this juncture, it is important to advise pharmacists and students of the value and importance of purchasing a personal pharmacy malpractice insurance policy. Just as it would be imprudent to operate a motor vehicle upon the public highways without maintaining a valid liability insurance policy at minimum, it is even more unwise to fail to be covered by a professional liability policy. Some employee pharmacists rationalize their failure to have personal coverage by referring to coverage provided by the employer. It should be of concern that when/if the interests of the employer pharmacy or hospital are in conflict with that of the employee pharmacist, the insurance company's obligation is to its client (i.e., the entity which pays the premium). The lawyers representing the insurance company will likewise identify with the same client. For a relatively modest annual premium, the covered beneficiary has peace of mind and is assured of having a personal lawyer as well as funds to pay damages from other than the pharmacist's personal assets.

ISSUES FOR CONSIDERATION

Though somewhat disparate in their application and relationship, one to another, a variety of issues are set forth here to establish an awareness by pharmacists and students of their existence and potential tort liability implications.

As one considers the negligence discussion above, there usually is no concern that the act or failure to act which resulted in harm to the prospective plaintiff was consciously performed. In other words, it was an unintentional tort. However, it is important to keep in mind that on rare occasion an intentional act may be committed which can give rise to a civil and/or criminal action(s). As reprehensible as intentionally dispensing a prescription order improperly resulting in harm might be, it should be noted such cases exist. Such an act may be contemporaneously a tort and a crime. Since the criminal case is required to be tried with dispatch, when a conviction is rendered, this becomes a valuable tool for the plaintiff to demonstrate malfeasance.

Placing another person in fear of imminent bodily harm describes the act of assault, an intentional tort which also may result in criminal charges. The actual striking of another is considered battery. Although battery usually is considered upon a person, it could include property. Battery cases involving pharmacists are rare, but there have been situations that have brought employees in a pharmacy into conflict with patrons or other visitors to the pharmacy. Under the right conditions, these actions can involve the pharmacy as a defendant.

Long before the passage and implementation of the Health Insurance Portability and Accountability Act (HIPPA) by Congress, issues of confidentiality were important for pharmacists to consider. Electronically held protected health information (PHI) was not the sole concern. Anything said or implied by the pharmacist about a patient, prescriber, pharmaceutical manufacturer, professional colleague, or other individual would have been, and still is, fair game for a suit for defamation. In general terms, defamation implies that a statement made by the likely defendant about the plaintiff causes the third party to whom the information was transmitted to think less favorably of the party about whom the comment was offered. When that statement is uttered orally to a single party or small group of people, generally this act is considered slander and the resulting damages would be considered less onerous than if it were libel, the dissemination of the defamatory information were through a widely read publication such as a newspaper or via electronic media to a wide audience.

A defense which may be employed is truth. Although the defendant may argue this defense, it is not available if the motivation of defendant in circulating the information was malicious. For example, identifying a political candidate's diagnoses and drug regimens with the intent to create doubt about that person's capacity to serve, thus helping the competing candidate to whom the pharmacist is pledged, clearly would nullify the validity of the truth defense.

Offhand comments to patients about their physicians or other prescribing practitioners should be considered carefully, being offered only under very limited circumstances. "Wow, this drug product hasn't been used for your condition for years and years. I was surprised to find it still on the shelf. Your doctor must be an old-timer." Consider whether the patient would interpret such a statement favorably.

"You know that my professional colleagues at the pharmacy down the street are prone to frequent medication errors. You should take all your prescription orders dispensed there back to your doctor to assure accuracy." The reader should assess whether this statement rises to the level of slander.

HIPAA has helped to focus on the confidentiality of health information and should keep the issue in the forefront as implementation proceeds through the stages.

Another area of concern that is worthy of pharmacist and student consideration is the broad category of self-care and potential tort liability implications. OBRA-90 provisions concerning pharmacists maintaining patient profiles, conducting prospective drug use review, and patient counseling open another potential tort liability minefield. The statutory language lists among the background information to be included in a community pharmacy's profile is the patient's use of over-the-counter (OTC) drug products to the extent efforts to obtain such data are successful. With the growing trend of Rx-only to OTC status, pharmacists should be aware of potential drug-drug interactions, possible adverse drug events, or other problems related thereto. Health-system pharmacists should include OTC data in their drug use assessment process in their respective institutions. As manufacturers, citizen groups, insurers, or the FDA broaden their emphasis on such drug reclassification, pharmacists should be vigilant with respect to managing any potential risk arising from OTC use.

OBRA-90 does not address dietary supplements specifically. Since the Dietary Supplement Health and Education Act (DSHEA) was not enacted by Congress until 1994, this is understandable. Nonetheless, growing use of such products since implementation of this statute suggests pharmacists might be well served to consider treating them as outlined above with respect to OTCs irrespective of practice venue.

Texts and reference books have proliferated in recent years to assist pharmacists and other healthcare professionals in assessing OTC and dietary supplement products as to their risks. Many computer-assisted drug evaluation and interaction programs currently include these lines of products, serving practitioners well.

SOME DEFENSES

It is important to note that every case is unique in terms of its facts, evidence, and interpretation by the court or a jury. This is one caveat for relying too heavily on trial court cases in a variety of jurisdictions for more than trending. Cleary, appellate review and decisions from courts of last resort are another matter.

Consequently, the defenses discussed herein are provided for informational purposes to give students and pharmacists a frame of reference to guide their practice activities.

As indicated earlier in this chapter, plaintiffs need to demonstrate the duty, breach, causation, and harm required elements to sustain an action. Defendants would seek to defend first by attempting to show any one or all of these elements were not present. Many cases turn on showing proximate cause between the breach of a legal duty and the resultant harm or injury to the plaintiff. This means that said effect occurred without any intervening cause, leaving an unbroken line from the event to injury.

Defendants also, when circumstances permit, may attempt to invoke the defense of contributory negligence. This requires demonstrating that the plaintiff was negligent as well, thus contributing to the resulting harm. As with any other act, the party asserting negligence must demonstrate the other party knew or should have known the consequences of an act or failure to act. For example, if a patient who received another party's prescription medication, properly labeled, in error, took the drug and was injured, the defendant could assert plaintiff also was negligent. A court or jury would need to make the assessment whether contributory negligence existed and to what extent. In some jurisdictions any level of contributory negligence would be sufficient to provide a finding for the defendant. In yet other jurisdictions, a determination is made of the percentage of each party's contribution to the damages which arose in the case. For example, if $100,000 were determined to be the amount of damages and the plaintiff was determined to be 45 percent liable, then the defendant's liability would be $55,000 (55 percent of $100,000).

Another defense that might be asserted is assumption of the risk. The basis for this defense is that when fully informed of any potential risks associated with a particular activity, the party so advised agrees to proceed under the conditions described. Having done so, the expected harm was suffered. The defense in claiming plaintiff's assumption of the risk would describe the series of events as set forth here.

This is demonstrated in case law by persons being barred from successfully suing a baseball park's or hockey rink's management for injury arising from a ball or puck entering the stands and striking the plaintiff. One attending such an event is determined to have an awareness such events may occur. Entering the venue and sitting in "harm's way" would constitute assumption of the risk.

In terms of risk management, effective, documented patient counseling by a pharmacist may establish a basis for the assumption of the risk defense.

To summarize the contents above, it is important for the reader to recognize the differences between crimes and torts, while understanding the same act may fall into both categories. The difference is that the criminal act is deemed to have been committed against the state (society), while the tort is against another person.

The evidentiary standard in a criminal case is beyond a reasonable doubt, as opposed to the civil case preponderance of evidence, i.e., the balance of evidence in one direction or another.

To prevail in a civil action in tort, the plaintiff must show the defendant had a duty to the plaintiff and breached that duty, which can be shown to be the proximate cause of harm to the plaintiff. Negligence, performing below the standard established by law for the protection of others, is the lynchpin of tort litigation.

Pharmacists should consider the cautionary issues surrounding tort liability implications for practitioners. Understanding how one may avoid defamation and other intentional tort areas may be beneficial to current and future practitioners. Potential plaintiffs should be aware of the defenses of contributory negligence and assumption of the risk and how to practice effectively while considering these issues. A final caveat is that all facts situations are unique and must be dealt with as such. Recognizing some of these matters can be beneficial in the workplace.

BIBLIOGRAPHY

Richard R. Abood and David R. Brushwood, *Pharmacy Practice and the Law* (Gaithersburg, MD: Aspen, 1994).

Henry Campbell Black, *Black's Law Dictionary,* Revised Fourth Edition (St. Paul, MN: West, 1968).

FindLaw, Home page (available at www.findlaw.com).

Joseph L. Fink III, Jesse C. Vivian, and Kim Keller Reid, *Pharmacy Law Digest,* Thirty-Sixth Edition (Germantown, PA: Facts and Comparison, 2002).

Chapter 14

Agency

Norman A. Campbell

Irrespective of a pharmacist's practice site, specialty, or the organization's structure, it is useful to understand the basics of the law of agency and its applications. The relationships among the parties to an agency are best demonstrated in terms of contract law, but they have considerable application in tort as well. As this discussion develops, effort will be made to show both the similarities and differences.

PARTIES TO AN AGENCY RELATIONSHIP

To understand the principles of agency law, one must recognize the cast of characters involved. First, there is a principal, who generally appoints an agent to represent the principal in dealings with a third party. Critical to this understanding is the nature of what *represent* means in this context. Any face-to-face dealings occur between the agent and the third party in a manner which might be depicted as a broken line if it were being drawn graphically. A solid line would show the relationship between the principal and the third party, i.e., in a contract, this would depict the two contracting parties relative to the subject matter under consideration. A third line would be drawn between the principal and agent to indicate that contractual relationship as well.

It is important to note the third party shall be apprised of the fact the relationship with the agent is only as it relates to the contract the third party is contemplating with the principal.

An agent owes a fiduciary duty to represent the principal to the best of agent's ability. This implies getting the best deal possible or performing at one's best. Whatever the performance of the agent, provided this activity is within the scope of authority, the principal is liable for the agent under the doctrine of *respondiat superior,* which imputes the agent's acts to the principal.

Pharmacy Law Desk Reference
© 2007 by The Haworth Press, Inc. All rights reserved.
doi:10.1300/5790_14

Respondiat superior is of particular interest in a plaintiff's tort liability suit alleging pharmacist malpractice. Based on the "deep pockets" theory, it may be the goal of the plaintiff to seek damages from a reachable party with sufficient assets to satisfy a judgment. Typically, this would be a pharmacy chain or hospital corporation. The burden of the plaintiff would be to show that the pharmacist who is accused of malpractice performed the injurious act while acting in the capacity of an agent of the employing entity.

Mere employment is not sufficient itself to establish agency. In every organization there are employees working at a variety of levels. Thus, there may be a number of agency relationships within the organization, and each agent may serve in a different role. As a consequence, third parties should be on notice of the potential that an employee may not have the authority to represent the principal in a given situation. For example, who would expect a pharmacy student intern to have the authority to place an order for new equipment and fixtures for the pharmacy? In such a situation the third party would attempt to enter such a contract at his peril. On the other hand, it is possible for one to have broad, general authority on behalf of an employer as agent.

Simply noting a party working within the pharmacy may not be enough to reach a conclusion that this person is an agent of the enterprise. In fact, that person may not be an agent and may well not be an employee. For example, consider a scenario in which an outside computer technology consultant is working in the pharmacy. If that individual were to injure a patron or patient, a tort action against the enterprise under the doctrine of *respondiat superior* would likely fail for the inability to show an agency relationship. This person is an independent contractor. Consequently, the pharmacy is not liable for the injurious actions. One caveat, however, should be noted. In the event the pharmacy's management exercised specific control over the contractor to the extent the person's work was specifically performed according to these directions, a court could conclude the existence of an agency.

Who may be a principal? In general, anyone capable of contracting may be a principal. This would require meeting all the legal requirements established in a particular jurisdiction—age or mental capacity, among others. Whatever activity the principal is authorizing the agent to perform on his or her behalf must be one which the principal is capable of doing so himself or herself. The principal may be an individual or a business entity, for example a partnership or corporation. In the context of who would be a principal for an employed pharmacist, that enterprise could be a community pharmacy (independently owned or corporate chain), a hospital, pharmaceutical manufacturer, pharmacy benefits management company, or any other employing entity.

Who may be an agent? Unlike the criteria for being a principal, an agent may be anyone with sufficient legal capacity to understand the requirements of the role. Thus, minors may serve as agents for the sale of goods, for example, under the conditions they understand the nature of money, making change, and other related rules. Thus, even elementary-school-age children selling candy, cookies, or candles door to door for a school, church, or scout troop may be deemed agents of the organization which they represent. Virtually every employee in a community or institutional pharmacy or other entity may qualify as an agent from time to time, depending upon the specific role being undertaken when an issue arises.

APPOINTMENT PROCESS

A principal-agent relationship may be created expressly—"I hereby appoint you to be my agent in charge of prescription drug purchasing." Likewise, the authorization may be imbedded in an employment contract. The job description may spell out specific duties and authority.

At times, determining the existence of an agency is a more complicated process. For example, there may be created an *agency by ratification* when the conditions exist whereby the principal never appointed the apparent agent. However, the apparent agent holds himself out to be the agent of the principal. The third party, having no reason to believe otherwise, agrees to the contract with the principal. Not until after the contract was created did the principal learn what the agent had done on the principal's behalf. At that point, the principal ratified the contract entered into earlier on his behalf by the agent. Even if the third party were to attempt to repudiate at that juncture, it would not be possible. Upon ratification, the agency now exists *ab initio,* from the point in time when the contract was struck with the third party. It is important to note the creation of the agency after the fact legally existed at the time the contract was established, not necessarily when the contract was executed (i.e., transfer of the sale of personal property).

Another means of creating an agency without appointment is the *agency by operation of law (estoppel),* or *apparent authority.* In this situation, the principal does not appoint an agent, and may not intend that one exist. Nonetheless, a third party reasonably could conclude from the placement of an individual in a position whereby it appears that the party is an agent with authority to represent the principal. Pharmacy management policies which permit nonpharmacists to appear to third parties to be pharmacists may not argue no agency exists because such persons are not credentialed or licensed. Courts have repeatedly indicated principals are estopped (i.e., prevented) from taking this position when they "cloaked with the indicia of authority" those appearing to represent them.

DUTIES OF THE PARTIES

It is important to recognize several matters impacting on the agency relationships. Except for the unusual circumstances set forth in some states' real estate sales laws, an agent may represent only one party to a transaction. Consequently, the agent's fiduciary duty to the principal requires that the agent strive to represent the principal in the best possible manner as if the principal were carrying out the responsibilities alone.

Pharmacists, and organizations which employ them, frequently retain employment agencies or temporary employment firms. Where negotiations are necessary to determine pay rates, benefits, hours, working conditions, or the like, it would behoove the retaining party to determine whose position is being represented by the employment agency before proceeding with the relationship. Just as in the real estate broker situation, it defies the basic principles of agency to have the same party serve as agent for both parties to a contract.

A principal's responsibility is to honor any agreements entered into or activities performed on his behalf by the agent. The only exception would be if the agent had exceeded the authority granted by the creation of the agency. Generally, such a grant would be considered to be general authority, unless expressly limited. If it were limited, a mechanism needs to be in place to alert third parties such a limitation exists.

A common example arises in all pharmacies, which are authorized by the Drug Enforcement Administration (DEA) to purchase and sell Schedule II controlled substances. The order and receipt form supplied by the agency to create documentation of such purchases, DEA Form-222, is required to be executed when ordering by the pharmacy's registrant. In the absence of the registrant when an order is being generated, such as when that person is on vacation or off for the day, the DEA permits a person authorized by the registrant as demonstrated by a duly executed power of attorney for this limited purpose to execute the order. This is a form of limited agency, and documentation need only be on file in the pharmacy and available to inspectors upon request. Manufacturers or wholesalers to whom the order is sent are not required to receive such notification.

A business entity organized as a partnership of two or more persons also creates unique agency relationships and duties. In the absence of notice to third parties to the contrary, each partner is a general agent of the partnership and of every other partner. Therefore, each partner and the business entity are responsible for acts of any single partner. Hence, a very high degree of faith is required among the partners given this fiduciary responsibility. The use of a relatively new business entity, the limited liability partnership (LLP), was created to mitigate the classic liability issues just described. It is not uncommon for partners to divide management and other activities among the partners, giving each primary responsibility for one or more operational areas. But, as noted, such limitations are not binding upon third parties unless proper notice has been given in a manner that complies with the laws of a given jurisdiction. Usually, this would be legal notice in a newspaper recognized as the appropriate forum for the dissemination of such information.

AGENCY TERMINATION

It is important to recognize that an agency, be it for a single activity (i.e., purchase or sale of real property) or as part of an employment contract, does not continue in perpetuity. If the agency is created for a single activity such as sale of property, that agency is terminated with the expiration of the contract creating it. The former agent could not bind the former principal following such expiration. The addition, the agent could not bind the principal during the period of agency on a subject area not specified in the original appointment. For example, a pharmacist granted the power of attorney to execute C-II orders as described above could not now be considered an agent of the registrant for the purpose of hiring or firing personnel.

The least complicated mechanism for the termination of agency is agreement of the parties to terminate. Notwithstanding the simplicity of this method as it affects the principal and agent, a caveat must be considered with respect to third parties. In the absence of notice to others, a situation could develop whereby a third party reasonably could expect the former agency still was in place. As a consequence, the principal should issue appropriate legal public notice to the effect the parties have agreed to terminate the agency and the effective date.

At any given point in time, either party may exercise the option provided for in the appointment to terminate the agency. Once again, third parties with whom the agent may have been in contact need to be protected from what could be a misleading situation based upon past interactions with the agent.

Revocation by the principal is another specific method by which an agency may be terminated. Very simply, the principal, who created the agency by appointment, may decide to revoke or rescind that grant. An employer may decide a particular agency responsibility assigned to one employee may have been ill-advised. To rectify this matter, it would be necessary to revoke the agency with appropriate notice to third parties. The employer then would be free to assign that duty to another employee. Once again, there are limitations. Having appointed an agent for the purpose of hiring prospective employees, the principal is barred from revoking the agency after performance by the agent (i.e., identifying several qualified candidates for the principal). The principal may not avoid payment of commissions or fees by terminating the agency before retaining the new employee(s). Case law is replete with cases involving sellers of real property seeking to avoid broker commissions by agreeing with a ready and willing buyer introduced by a real estate broker to postpone signing a purchase-sale agreement until after the broker's agency agreement was revoked by the principal.

Yet another mechanism by which the agency may be terminated is renunciation by the agent. Essentially, this means the agent formally or voluntarily gives up or surrenders the authority granted by the principal in creating the agency. The rights of third parties again must be given due consideration and notice.

Rescission is the term used when a party rescinds either the appointment or acceptance of the responsibilities embodied in the agency agreement. Clearly, many of these termination mechanisms may overlap to some extent, but they are presented here to provide a broad range of possibilities to serve to raise awareness as pharmacists and students become engaged in such activities.

Several means of termination exist in the absence of activity attributable to either the principal or agent. Broadly, these are categorized as termination by operation of law. Briefly, these include death of a party to the agency. Clearly, the death of the principal creates impossibility of contract. Consequently, the agent would have no person to represent. Likewise, with the death of agent, no party exists to represent the principal.

Likewise, insanity of either party bars that person from eligibility to enter into a valid contract. Thus, the agency contract would be void upon determination of this status.

Given the special legal circumstances set forth in federal and state bankruptcy laws, any agency created by a principal who is, personally or as a business enterprise, subject to the bankruptcy court's jurisdiction is unable to effect any contractual relationships. The court-appointed trustee in bankruptcy assumes that role. Public notice will be handled by that individual for the protection of all creditors and others doing business with the principal.

Impossibility to perform, war, or other unusual events or changes also are possible means of terminating an agency by operation of law.

To recap, the law of agency involves a condition whereby a principal contracts with a third party via an appointed representative called an agent who deals directly with the third party. The principal is responsible for the activities of the agent under the doctrine of *respondiat superior.*

An agent should be distinguished from an employee or an independent contractor. Although an employee generally may be an agent, the extent of that agency will vary upon the determination of a job description and/or specific appointment. Unless specifically ordered to work in a certain manner, an independent contractor is not an agent.

Any party capable of contracting may be a principal, and any person with sufficient intellectual capacity to understand the consequences of the activities related to the agency may be an agent. Under certain conditions, an agency also may be created by ratification or by operation of law. A number of termination mechanisms are available, including some imposed by operation of law. Pharmacists and pharmacy students should remain cognizant of the rights, duties, and responsibilities created by the agency relationship.

BIBLIOGRAPHY

Richard R. Abood and David R. Brushwood, *Pharmacy Practice and the Law* (Gaithersburg, MD: Aspen, 1994).

Henry Campbell Black, *Black's Law Dictionary,* Revised Fourth Edition (St. Paul, MN: West, 1968).

FindLaw, Home page (available at www.findlaw.com).

Joseph L. Fink III, Jesse C. Vivian, and Kim Keller Reid, *Pharmacy Law Digest,* Thirty-Sixth Edition (Germantown, PA: Facts and Comparisons, 2002).

Chapter 15

The Interface Between Law and Ethics in Pharmacy Practice

Margaret L. Eaton

INTRODUCTION

There are times when adhering to laws and regulations does not sufficiently satisfy a pharmacist's obligation to act responsibly. In such cases, a
pharmacist who wants to maintain professional and personal integrity can
seek ethical guidance to help achieve this result. This chapter will describe
some major similarities and differences between the two systems of law and
ethics, will provide resources for ethical guidance in professional practice,
and give some advice for circumstances where there are no such resources.
Several references will be provided for further study since the subject matter is too dense and broad for adequate coverage in one small chapter.

THE LIMITATIONS OF LAW AS AN ETHICAL GUIDE

There are important similarities and differences between legal and ethical systems. Their connections stem from the fact that laws are based on
commonly shared notions of what constitutes acceptable conduct, and these
notions are usually derived from moral principles, such as rights, duties,
and justice. For instance, laws are often promulgated when certain practices
infringe on people's rights or are considered irresponsible or unfair. Laws
impose responsibilities on people to tell the truth or fully disclose information or prevent harm to others. The intertwined relationship between law
and ethics was described eloquently by Chief Justice Earl Warren in a
speech[1] he gave at the Jewish Theological Seminary: "In civilized life, law
floats in a sea of ethics. Each is indispensable to civilization. Without law,
we should be at the mercy of the least scrupulous; without ethics, law could
not exist."

Pharmacy Law Desk Reference
© 2007 by The Haworth Press, Inc. All rights reserved.
doi:10.1300/5790_15

On the other hand, legal and ethical systems are different in many ways. Laws are derived in political systems, are enforced, have predetermined punishments for action that deviates from what is prescribed, and use judges and a judicial system to interpret and say what the law is. Ethics operates in a broader sphere and is self-determined, voluntary, unenforced, and unenforceable. These similarities and differences produce interesting and sometimes problematical dilemmas for pharmacists who wish to both comply with the law and "do the right thing."

The law does not and cannot deal with all conduct, but much conduct has an ethical dimension that should not be ignored. When it is, new laws and regulations are passed to curb the censured conduct. There are even those who ascribe to the view that, since laws usually prescribe only minimum standards of behavior, it is frequently insufficient to simply do what is legally required or to refrain from illegal conduct. Studying a history of the drug laws in this country can make one an adherent to this view.

Drug laws in the United States have their roots in English law and arose in the nineteenth century to prevent the widespread adulteration of food and drugs and to prevent fraud. A seminal event in 1862 occurred after a druggist's assistant in England poisoned 400 people by accidentally putting arsenic in some peppermint lozenges. The public outcry over this disaster led the British Parliament to pass the Bill for Preventing Adulteration of Articles of Food and Drink. From this time on, the history of drug regulation both in Great Britain and the United States has been an oft-repeated pattern of incremental regulatory restrictions or litigation following drug-related tragedies caused by careless, irresponsible, or fraudulent conduct.[2] As further abusive practices come to the attention of legislators and regulators, new laws are enacted to restrict the conduct of or impose new responsibilities on healthcare practitioners, researchers, and industry professionals. (see Chapter 3, "Federal Food, Drug, and Cosmetic Act," for some of this history).

Because unethical behavior invites both legislation and litigation, a pharmacist who relies exclusively on what is currently legal can get into trouble by failing in a professional duty or engaging in questionable activity that is just outside the clear boundaries of the law. One example is a practice of some large pharmaceutical companies that pay chain pharmacies to mail or call patients about company drugs or competing products. The materials and messages urge patients to do such things as continue taking a currently prescribed drug, switch to a new form of the drug, or switch from a competitor's drug. Theses programs are not illegal. Although viewed by many as promotional material directed to patients on selected drugs, companies call the material "patient education," "patient compliance," or "disease management" programs. However, these programs raised several troubling ethical questions. Was this activity an improper invasion of the privacy of patients' prescription records? Was there a conflict of interest when pharmacists were being paid to urge patients to take a particular brand of drug? Was this interfering with the patient-physician relationship when the pharmacist advised a patient to take a drug other than one prescribed by the physician?[3] The programs continued and the questions mounted. Eventually, these programs were challenged in lawsuits brought by pharmacy customers against major chain pharmacies for invasion of privacy and in investigations by states' attorneys general and the Federal Trade Commission for possible violations of unfair and deceptive trade-practices laws. Congress and the Department of Health and Human Services considered new privacy laws and regulations to stop the practice.[4] Leaving aside the merits of the claims against the companies and pharmacists, which have not been resolved, this is a classic example of how ethically questionable but legal activity can lead to censure, litigation, regulation, and loss of trust in the profession. Although there may be nothing illegal at the time about an act or a failure to act, many situations deserve consideration of whether they are ethical, especially where the health, safety, or welfare of patients is at stake.

Laws can also violate moral principles. As an example, there are pharmacists who believe that laws that allow the dispensing of abortifacients are immoral. Such pharmacists believe that the use of these drugs causes the death of a human being who has an innate right to life and that anyone who participates in this process, therefore, acts immorally by violating this right. Once having arrived at this conclusion, the pharmacist must determine what his or her duty is to either protect this right or prevent the encroachment of the right. The pharmacist must also then grapple with the conflict between the right of fetus (which the law does not protect) and that of the mother or parents to control their procreation (which the law does protect). Where does duty lie when laws and morality conflict?

The availability of the abortifacient RU-486 also highlights another feature of the law; it often lags behind advances in biomedical science. This drug product can be used as a contraceptive, emergency contraceptive, and for early abortion, all of which are controlled by different legal protections and restrictions. The development of the product and growing medical knowledge about its uses has led to uncertainty about not only the legal status of contraception and abortion but also the laws governing women's access to these products and services, which are likewise treated differently in the law.[5] The fact that this product is also politically sensitive means that many legislators may be reluctant to address the legal uncertainties since they may be unwilling to risk alienating groups of constituents. While courts and legislatures may eventually resolve and clarify these laws, prescribing and dispensing pharmacists will have to guess about the legal status of the product and possibly wonder whether their professional actions conform to the law. Because courts and legislatures are often slow to address the consequences of biomedical advances, pharmacists and other health professionals often find themselves in this position.

Another reason that laws do not always give direct guidance is that they can be imprecise and ambiguous or different depending on the jurisdiction. Furthermore, legislators and judges can be uninformed about the practice of pharmacy and therefore fail to anticipate how a new law or ruling impacts a closely related area of professional practice. Modifying the law to improve clarity often takes extensive amounts of time since busy legislators need to be persuaded to sponsor legislation or amendments. Courts need a "case or controversy" before they can adjudicate a matter; therefore, judges must wait until a lawsuit is brought. Contentious court cases can take years to be resolved at the highest level before legal precedent can be set. And when it is set, court-made legal precedent is limited to the facts at hand and is therefore often too limited in nature to be broadly useful.

Laws can also be contested, leaving practitioners uncertain about whether the law as written is legitimate. This type of situation occurred when Oregon passed its controversial physician-assisted suicide law.* Almost immediately, multiple legal challenges made it unclear whether the law could be implemented. Among such challenges were the U.S. congressional efforts such as the Pain Relief Promotion Act, a bill that would have amended the 1970 Controlled Substances Act to make clear that narcotics cannot be used in physician-assisted suicide. Other congressional challenges have surfaced from time to time but have failed so far to block the Oregon law. In the meantime, similar and persistent efforts were made by the Drug Enforcement Agency (DEA) and the U.S. Attorney General. Initially, the DEA took the position that it was within their authority under the Controlled Substances Act to revoke the licenses of physicians who prescribed lethal doses of controlled drugs to aid the suicide of a terminally ill patient. This position also presumably applied to pharmacists who dispensed these medications for the same purpose. The attorney general at the time, Janet Reno, who was appointed in the Clinton administration, overruled this decision on the grounds that the federal Controlled Substances Act did not give the DEA the authority to interfere with the traditional state role of defining legitimate medical practices. With the subsequent Bush administration, however, the new attorney general, John Ashcroft, reversed the decision of former Attorney General Reno with a directive that instructed the DEA to enforce the position that assisting suicide is not a "legitimate medical purpose" within

---

*The Oregon Death with Dignity Act, passed by referendum in 1994, specifies that a physician may prescribe and pharmacists may dispense lethal medication that is to be used to hasten death for competent, terminally ill persons who voluntarily request it.

the meaning of the federal Controlled Substances Act and that prescribing and dispensing controlled substances to assist suicide violates the act and could lead to the suspension or revocation of professional licenses. In addition, Ashcroft filed a lawsuit in federal court that attempted to implement this interpretation of the CSA.[6] This lawsuit traveled through the appellate courts, and it was not until January 2006 (twelve years after the initial state law had passed) that the U.S. Supreme Court ruled in *Gonzales v. Oregon* that the attorney general had overstepped his authority and that he could not use the Controlled Substances Act to prohibit physicians from prescribing controlled substances for physician-assisted suicide in terminally ill patients. In a climate of such diverse and changing legal opinions, it is easy to see how a pharmacist can be uncertain about what his or her obligations are when involved in physician-assisted suicide or other legally challenged laws that impact the profession. As with the law in Oregon, it can take years for legal certainty to exist, making it unwise or impractical to wait to decide how to act.

Laws and regulations can change. Legislative bodies and courts have been known to alter what was once considered legally settled. This is the case currently with the legal status of the "learned intermediary" doctrine which protects pharmaceutical companies from liability to patients for failure to warn them directly of prescription drug risks so long as there are adequate warnings given to physicians and pharmacists. For years, courts were asked to reject this legal doctrine before the first court did so in 1999.[7] Often, the need for legal change is apparent long before law changes, which can lead to the question of whether it is ever appropriate to ignore the law. This situation existed in the 1965 Supreme Court case of *Griswald v. Connecticut,* 381 U.S. 479 (1965), a case that began when Griswald, the executive director of the Planned Parenthood League of Connecticut, and Dr. Buxton, the medical director of a Planned Parenthood clinic, were arrested. Both had been found to have violated the law by giving contraception information, instruction, medical advice, and prescription orders to married persons. The law in question, on the books since 1879, forbids the use of contraceptives by anyone. For decades, however, the law had been ignored and was only rarely enforced. Indeed, as a practical matter, the law was unenforceable, except indirectly in aiding-and-abetting situations such as the *Griswald* case. In addition, the law had lost much of its legitimacy since many believed that the use of marital contraceptives should be left to personal and private choice and was not a matter for state interference. Medical social policy also favored having birth control counseling and medical care widely available. Just as Griswald and Buxton had been, any pharmacist who dispensed contraceptives could have been prosecuted for aiding and abetting in a violation of the law. Although the Connecticut law was found to be unconstitutional, it took two subsequent Supreme Court cases to settle the question of whether the same constitutional right of access to contraceptives also applied to unmarried adults and to minors [see *Eisenstadt v. Baird,* 405 U.S. 438 (1972) and *Carey v. Population Services International,* 431 U.S. 684 (1977)]. Prior to and during the litigation that led to these Supreme Court decisions, some (perhaps many) pharmacists had been dispensing contraceptives and giving contraceptive advice contrary to the laws in their states. It is probably reasonable to assume that most of these professionals were doing so not because they believed the law would not be enforced but because of their perceived professional and ethical obligations to their patients.

Finally, the laws do not always clarify the boundaries of responsibility. The pharmaceutical industry, the FDA, and healthcare providers (physicians, pharmacists, nurses, etc.) each have a role in the medical product approval, prescribing, dispensing, and counseling process, but there are sometimes differences of opinion about where the responsibility of one entity ends and the other begins. For instance, the erosion of the "learned intermediary" doctrine described above has led to differences of opinion about who has the duty to warn the patient and how much the company or professional can legitimately rely on the other to fulfill this duty. The same questions exist with respect to "off label" prescribing and dispensing. "Off label" prescribing per se is not regulated by federal or state laws; it is considered the practice of medicine. But do physicians have the sole responsibility for determining what "off label" uses are appropriate? Even if dispensing pharmacists are arguably free from a legal duty to act, do they have an ethical obligation if they think that this prescribing is irresponsible? This issue came up with Genentech's recombinant human growth hormone (rhGH), approved and labeled for use in children with a rare form of dwarfism caused by lack of natural growth hormone. After the product was launched, physicians began prescribing rhGH to short healthy children to help them grow taller, to adults to improve athletic performance, to obese patients for weight loss, and for other "off label" uses. Little was known about the efficacy or safety of the product for these other uses, and concerns existed about the potential for harm, especially in children, from "off label" rhGH prescribing and dispensing. The fact that the drug came to be used to "treat" short stature was a combination of physician prescribing and pharmacist dispensing. Overt criticism was directed to Genentech and to physicians, questioning whether they were profiting from purposefully ignoring (or even condoning) irresponsible prescribing that could harm children.[8] The same question could have been directed to pharmacists who dispensed this product. Whether they had an obligation to monitor for irresponsible prescribing is more of an ethical rather than a legal question.

Given the above characteristics and vagaries of the law, a pharmacist familiar with ethical principles and reasoning can do the following: anticipate legal changes when legally acceptable conduct raises ethical questions and determine appropriate action in times of legal uncertainty such as when laws are silent, conflict, are ambiguous, or direct the pharmacist to act in ways considered unethical. The next sections of this chapter provide information about sources of ethical guidance and methods of analysis.

SOURCES OF ETHICS CODES AND GUIDELINES

Dispensing

Current pharmacy practice is quite diverse and, therefore, the pharmacist looking for guides to ethical professional conduct must consult several sources. For dispensing pharmacists, the American Pharmacists Association (APhA) wrote a general Code of Ethics, which has also been endorsed by the American Society of Health-System Pharmacists (ASHP) (see www.aphanet.org/pharmcare/ethics.html). This Code contains general provisions describing a pharmacist's obligations to patients, to maintain competence and professionalism, and to be responsive to the needs of the profession, the community, and society. The APhA Code contrasts with the one promulgated by the Royal Pharmaceutical Society of Great Britain,[9] which is both more specific and detailed about required ethical conduct and also, contrary to most codes of ethics, is enforced. When the Royal Society finds that a pharmacist has violated the Code of Ethics, he or she loses membership in the Society and the license to practice. Debates exist about how detailed codes of ethics should be and whether they should be voluntary or enforced. The American and British codes are examples of codes on either end of each spectrum. In between these two are specific statements of ethical positions promulgated by the ASHP Council on Legal and Public Affairs.[10] These statements include positions on a patient's right to choose, assisted suicide, conscientious objection of a pharmacist, nondiscriminatory pharmaceutical care, and the use of drugs in capital punishment.

Human Research

For pharmacists engaged in human research, several codes and guides of ethical conduct exist, and the body of literature on this subject is extensive. Current ethical standards for clinical research have their roots in the research atrocities that took place during World War II, carried out by physicians under orders from the Third Reich. The postwar Nuremberg Trials, which disclosed these research practices, resulted in the issuance of the Nuremberg Code,[11] the first major set of research ethics guidelines, which continues to inform current research standards. The principles of the Nuremberg Code were used to generate a more extensive moral code of conduct for medical researchers when the Declaration of Helsinki was adopted by the Eighteenth World Medical Association General Assembly at Helsinki, Finland, in 1964.[12] The Declaration of Helsinki was promulgated following a growing recognition that research abuses had occurred before Nazi Germany and were still continuing to occur in many countries, including the United States.*

The Declaration of Helsinki contains the same basic requirements as the Nuremberg Code—that the rights to autonomy and free choice of human subjects be respected and that the benefits of research should not outweigh the risk to subjects. However, the Declaration of Helsinki contains more specific provisions about how these rights should be preserved, and many of these have been topics for continuing debate in the medical research community. One important problem that the Declaration of Helsinki addresses is when the need to obtain scientific information is given priority over the interests of human subjects. To prevent this from happening, the Declaration provides that it is the duty of the researcher to remain the protector of the life and health of human subjects, and not to allow scientific or societal interests to take precedence over the well-being of the subject. Although most medical researchers do not dispute that the interest of human subjects should remain paramount, there are several disagreements about how the provisions of the Declaration of Helsinki should be interpreted. These disagreements concern what amount of human subject risk is reasonable to impose in the interests of science, whether it is necessary that human subjects stand to benefit from participation in or the results from clinical research,

---

*In 1966, Henry K. Beecher, an anesthesiologist at Harvard Medical School who had closely studied the Nuremberg Trials documents, published an article in the *New England Journal of Medicine* listing eighteen cases of nonconsensual and otherwise unethical research conduct. For instance, in 1963, researchers had injected live cancer cells into twenty-two patients in the Jewish Chronic Disease Hospital in Brooklyn, New York. This research was done without the knowledge of the patients involved and was intended to study the role of the immune system in fighting cancer. About the same time, mentally impaired children in the Willowbrook State School in New York were infected with live hepatitis A virus in an attempt to reduce the spread of fecalborne infections. The parents were not fully informed about the nature of this research. Beecher deplored the abuses even when the data collected were highly useful. He concluded, "An experiment is ethical or not at its inception; it does not become ethical post hoc—ends do not justify means. there is not ethical destriction between eds and means" (Beecher, 1966). These revelations and other abuses highlighted the need for more specific research standards and a heightened awareness of the ethical obligations of researchers (Lock, 1995).

whether it is legitimate to conduct research in humans only if the investigator is substantially uncertain about which of the comparative interventions (e.g, the drug or placebo) is better,* whether it is ever proper to combine medical treatment with medical research, and whether the use of a placebo control is justified in human research if treatment is available for the condition in question. These and other challenging questions require that any pharmacist who is responsible for human research be familiar with the codes and literature dealing with ethical conduct in research.

In the United States, public disclosure of human research abuses in the 1960s and 1970s (including the infamous Tuskegee study) led to the appointment of a U.S. national commission to clarify ethical guidelines for protecting human subjects.[13] The National Commission for the Protection of Human Subjects of Biomedical and Behavioral Research was created by the National Research Act of 1974[14] and operated until 1978. The commission was directed to consider the following:

1. the boundaries between biomedical and behavioral research and the accepted and routine practice of medicine,
2. the role of assessment of risk-benefit criteria in the determination of the appropriateness of research involving human subjects,
3. appropriate guidelines for the selection of human subjects for participation in such research, and
4. the nature and definition of informed consent in various research settings.

Because the commission met at the Belmont Conference Center of the Smithsonian Institution, the report that contained the outcome of its deliberations was called The Belmont Report.[15] The Belmont Report identifies three basic ethical principles related to human medical research: (1) respect for persons; (2) beneficence; and (3) justice. Respect for persons requires that individuals should be treated as autonomous agents and also that persons with diminished ability to exercise their autonomy are entitled to protection. Beneficence is defined as an obligation to "do no harm" to subjects and to maximize possible benefits and minimize the possible harms of research. The justice aspect addresses the question of who ought to receive the benefits of research and bear its burdens. The Belmont Report gave recognition to the notion that human medical research can be unethical if its

---

*Called the uncertainty principle, proponents often adhere to the notion that the proper degree of uncertainty exists when the investigator is in a state of equipoise—equally uncertain about which investigational intervention is better.

benefits and burdens are unfairly distributed, especially if the burdens fell disproportionately on vulnerable or disadvantaged people. Applying these ethical principles meant that to respect persons, investigators must obtain informed and voluntary consent from all human subjects. Beneficence requires a careful assessment of the risks and benefits of a clinical trial, a proper trial design to maximize the benefits and minimize and justify the risks. Application of justice principles requires that subjects be selected in a fair manner (individual justice) and also that vulnerable subjects such as children, prisoners, and the mentally incapacitated are protected (social justice).

Since the publication of the Belmont Report, multiple medical professional organizations have developed codes of research ethics, and the medical literature is replete with articles commenting on what constitutes ethical practice in this area of endeavor. For pharmacists, the American College of Clinical Pharmacy (ACCP) has a White Paper on research ethics topics that is a good place to start exploring this subject.[16]

Clinical Practice

Not so long ago (1967) the APhA Code of Ethics prohibited pharmacists from discussing the therapeutic effects or composition of a prescription with a patient. Although this prohibition no longer exists, there are still no codes of ethics in the United States that specifically apply to pharmacists engaged in advanced clinical practice with direct patient care responsibilities. Although it is interesting to reflect on why this is so, it does not mean that pharmacists lack resources for the ethical codes that apply to this vital aspect of practice. Because of the similarity in medical and clinical pharmacy practice, the Code of Medical Ethics for physicians is a valuable resource. This code, developed over 155 years ago and frequently updated by the American Medical Association (AMA), is a comprehensive ethics guide that covers issues such as the relationships with patients, patient consent, confidentiality, end-of-life care, and social policy issues. The AMA considers this Code of Medical Ethics to be the embodiment of professional self-regulation necessary for the practice of good medicine. In addition, the AMA's Council on Ethical and Judicial Affairs has developed extensive ethics resource material that is continually updated, including a set of Principles of Medical Ethics and a statement of the Fundamental Elements of the Patient-Physician Relationship, a collection of the codes of ethics within various medical associations, and much educational material applicable to clinical practice.[17]

For hospital-based pharmacists, the American Hospital Association has produced a Patient's Bill of Rights (see www.aha.org/aha/ptcommunication/partnership/index.html), which has been adopted in whole or in part by many other healthcare associations and in some state regulations that govern acute care hospitals and nursing homes. The rights enumerated serve as a delineation of the duty of a clinical pharmacist to promote these rights or to protect them from infringement.

BASICS OF ETHICAL REASONING

All of the above material is relevant to pharmacy practice and well worth the time to study closely. However, many codes of ethics suffer from some of the same problems as do the laws and regulations, i.e., they are too absolute, general, or ambiguous to be helpful in specific cases. Recently graduated pharmacists have some skills to deal with this gap since ethics instruction has become part of the professional practice courses in many schools of pharmacy, a curriculum inclusion endorsed by the APhA since 1988. There are also helpful textbooks available on the subject of biomedical ethics.[18] These resources can provide an understanding of ethical theories and the founding principles of healthcare ethics and how they are applied. This understanding can enhance the ability to reason through ethical dilemmas when the laws and codes of ethics are not sufficiently instructive.

In situations based on relationships between healthcare professionals and patients or research subjects, four principles are usually invoked to guide ethical reflection. These four principles are used as the starting place for reasoning through a moral problem in medicine and are autonomy, beneficence, nonmaleficence, and justice.* These four principles are in the forefront of medical ethics because they are rooted in the traditions of principled medical practice or have risen to prominence as importance has been placed on personal liberties and the rights of individuals and as concern has grown that the relevant consequences of medical treatment should extend beyond the patient to encompass the whole of society.[19] In addition, starting with the Belmont Report, the four principles have become the basis on which much medical law, regulations, codes, and guidelines have been developed. Below is a brief description of these four principles and how they can apply to a healthcare practice.

---

*These principles were derived from various types of ethical theory including utilitarianism, deontology, virtue-based theory, the ethics of care, and casuistry. For a description of how these theories evolved and relate to the ethical principles espoused in biomedicine, see TL Beauchamp and JF Childress, Types of Ethical Theory. In *Principles of Biomedical Ethics,* Fourth Edition. Oxford University Press, New York: 1994, pp. 44-119.

Autonomy

Autonomy developed as an important aspect of medical ethics since it mirrors the societal importance placed on individual freedom. Respect for autonomy of patients comes from the view that individuals in this society should be able to make medical choices for themselves free from controlling interference by others, such as by coercion, deceit, duress, or constraint. Autonomy in a healthcare setting has also come to mean that patients with diminished autonomy are entitled to protection. The principle of respect for persons thus divides into two separate moral requirements: the requirement to acknowledge autonomy and the requirement to protect those with diminished autonomy.[20]

Respect for autonomy is the ethical principle (although not the only one) that gives rise to the rules and duties associated with informed consent. Healthcare professionals who seek informed consent for treatment act in such a way as to promote the patient's ability to make healthcare choices that serve his or her interest; these actions include telling the truth, fully disclosing information, obtaining consent, and preserving confidentiality and privacy. Further, consent cannot be informed unless patients have a full understanding of the medical options available and their risks and benefits. Patients are also entitled to have a recommendation from the healthcare professional about what is believed to be the best course of action.

A feature of autonomy that is frequently an issue in clinical medicine is that of agency. Free agents make their own medical decisions, either to accept or reject recommended treatment. But there are many classes of patients who cannot act as free agents. These include young children, some patients with mental illness, those who have lost their ability to reason because of illness or injury, or those who cannot make rational choices because they are overwhelmed either physically, pharmaceutically, or psychically by their disease. Those who feel under duress can also fall into the category of questionable free agency, such as prisoners who, despite assurances to the contrary, feel that refusing to volunteer for a research study will negatively impact their chances for parole. Other patients can be under duress from family members to accept or reject recommended treatment. Healthcare providers have a responsibility to seek consent for treatment when patients can fully participate in the consent process, such as when the effects of axiolytics or anesthesia have dissipated or when patients are free from the controlling influences of others. When this cannot be accomplished, patients with permanently or temporarily diminished decision-making capacity are entitled to have others make medical decisions on their behalf and in their best interest. These healthcare agents (also called surrogates) can be appointed by courts (guardians or conservators), exist by virtue of family relationship (e.g., spouses or parents of a minor), or can be appointed in advance by the patient. Regardless of how they come to serve in the role, healthcare agents should be persons with a close personal relationship to the patient and should show care and concern for the patient's welfare. Healthcare agents who know the patient's treatment preferences should disclose and abide by them, even if contrary to their own preferences and values. When the treatment preferences of the patient are not known, decisions about what treatment is in the patient's best interest should come from those who are familiar with the patient's activities, health, religious beliefs, and values.

It is easy to see how these rules and duties of informed consent have flowed from the ethical principle of respect for patient autonomy. As much as can be, this autonomy is to be promoted. However, one of the primary areas of conflict in healthcare ethics exists when a healthcare professional believes that a patient or surrogate, exercising or serving personal autonomy, has made a medical choice that is detrimental to the health or well-being of the patient. In these cases, the principle of respect for autonomy clashes with the duty to benefit the patient.

Beneficence and Nonmaleficence

In a common translation of the Hippocratic Oath, it states: "I will use treatment to help the sick according to my ability and judgment, but I will never use it to injure or wrong them." As in the oath, it is difficult to separate the duty to do good for patients from the duty to not harm them. Implicit in the concept of beneficence is that doing good is what is intended and that active steps will be taken to prevent or remove harm. Beneficence also includes the utilitarian principle that good should be maximized and harm minimized. Nonmaleficence requires that the healthcare professional refrain from causing harm to a patient. Although often considered to be two sides of the same coin, these two principles are often distinguished by viewing nonmaleficence as a more passive obligation (beneficence requires more active involvement) and by the notion that healthcare professionals have a duty to all patients not to harm them but a duty to benefit only some. The duties to benefit and refrain from harming patients are seen as part of a healthcare provider's obligation that flows from the fact that professionals have superior training and knowledge and are in a position to know better what will best promote the patient's health. Patients, on the other hand, are typically dependent, anxious, vulnerable, and exploitable and need to trust that the healthcare professional will do what is best for them.

The principles of beneficence and nonmaleficence can encompass the professional values of keeping patient medical information confidential, telling patients the truth about their medical condition, having empathy for patients, maintaining professional skills, or advocating for patients. However, promoting each of these values does not always lead to one particular conclusion of what should be done in any particular case. In a healthcare context, deciding how to benefit and not to harm patients can be easy (a child has pneumonia and will die without treatment, so the patient's allergy history is checked as is the sensitivity of the bacteria and the appropriate antibiotic is prescribed) or problematical (in a state that allows it, a dying patient presents a prescription order for a controlled substance to aid in his suicide and the pharmacist, on the basis of a moral belief, refuses to dispense the drug). Even truth-telling can raise problems when, e.g., close family members say that informing a patient that he has an incurable cancer will make him lose hope and ruin the little time he has left to live. It is also sometimes difficult to determine how far the obligations of beneficence and nonmaleficence go. Some pharmacists believe that they have an obligation to benefit patients financially by advocating diligently (and sometimes crossing swords with physicians) to dispense generics. Others believe that their duty to patients extends only to the health aspects of pharmaceutical practice. In another example, a wife may demand, under threat of litigation, that all life-saving medical intervention be provided for her permanently unconscious husband and the healthcare providers, intending to relieve the suffering caused by mechanical and pharmacologic support, want to remove what they believe to be futile medical treatment and switch the patient to palliative care. How far do the professionals go to work for what they believe is right for the patient, especially when they risk getting sued for their efforts? Pharmacists who participate in the care of such a patient by advising on a narcotic regimen that can alleviate pain and distress need to also deal with the fact that the narcotic may easily depress respiration and cause the patient's death. The so-called "double effect" principle* that applies to the use of narcotics in palliative care parallels this ethical conflict in medicine. Normally, one primary way that healthcare professionals provide benefit is when they preserve life. However, in this situation, does it benefit or harm to preserve a life without awareness? It may be similarly difficult to decide who can best make this determination. This example also raises the question of whether the financial costs of intensive medical interventions at the end of life are justifiable. Such a question raises the ethical principle of justice.

---

*The principle of double effect exists and is ethically (and sometimes explicitly legally) defensible when the practitioner intends a beneficial effect (relief of pain and suffering) but does not intend and yet can foresee a harmful effect (the patient's death).

Justice

Justice has to do with fairness in the distribution of the benefits and burdens of society. Justice issues come into play in healthcare in several ways. Justice can require that patients should be treated fairly so that, for instance, similarly situated patients with the same disease are entitled to the same quality of healthcare. Another example is that we do not place the burdens of human research on a racial minority group of patients for the primary benefit of the majority. These examples invoke the formal principle of justice that equals must be treated equally and that unequals can be treated unequally so long as the differences between them are relevant to the healthcare at issue.

Difficulties in applying this notion of justice as fairness occur when attempting to decide in what respects people should be treated equally and what is relevant to a determination of whether people are equal. To address especially this last question, the material principles of justice come into play. Need is a powerful material principle of justice in medicine, and it is common to hear that patients should be treated equally if their need for medical care is equal. Not all patients have equal need, however, which can justify treating them unequally. When public health officials decide who is entitled to the first flu vaccines of the season, those with the greatest need get first access and, e.g., everyone who is immunocompromised is treated equally in this respect. Need can also be used to justify having some patients who presented their prescription orders first wait longer for their medication than someone who came to the pharmacy later. Basing medical treatment allocation on need alone can, however, cause problems when, for instance, one very sick patient consumes enormous amounts of healthcare resources and finances, resulting in fewer resources for others.

Other material principles that can be applied when distributing the benefits of society include merit (used in determining salaries and promotions), contribution to society (used in retirement programs and awards), and effort (used in unemployment benefit programs). These are much more difficult to justify in medicine. For instance, transplanting an organ into a revered sports hero who does not meet typical medical transplant criteria can lead to accusations that it is unfair to distribute such a precious medical resource based on the contributions this person made to society when another potential recipient who could have lived longer with the organ was denied. Giving each person an equal share (another material principle used, for instance, to determine access to elementary and secondary education) is often difficult or impossible in healthcare because of constrained resources. Justice issues are further imbedded in healthcare since the ability to pay is another factor in determining who gets access to treatment. Great debates exist on how to remedy situations when medically insured and wealthy patients have access to healthcare when, arguably, their need is not as great as others who cannot pay. Triage is another formulation of distributive justice employed in medicine. In acute care settings such as emergency departments and battlefield medicine, triage invokes several of the material principles of justice which results in offering treatment first to those most salvageable, needy, and, if relevant, to those most important to return to the battle or the local disaster at hand.

As healthcare budgets (including those for prescription drugs and dispensing and service fees) become more constrained and contested, justice issues will proliferate. Questions will include whether access to prescription drugs is an entitlement. Who should pay for or subsidize the cost of drugs? Where patients' lives depend on access to certain drugs, what principles of distributive justice should govern? Because they have a unique perspective on how prescription drugs impact the lives and health of patients, pharmacists should be fully engaged in these important debates. Being well versed in the ethical principles of distributive and social justice will be important to the ability to contribute to this discourse.

Applying the Four Principles of Medical Ethics

Ethical problems in medical care usually involve either conflicts between ethical principles or differences in how the principles are interpreted. In the simplest formulations of ethical conflict resolution, the four major ethical principles described above are considered equally binding unless one conflicts with another, such as when a healthcare professional decides that he should contradict a patient's wishes in order to protect the patient from harm. When deciding that one principle should dominate in a conflict, a professional should take care to ensure that the dominance is necessary and then act in such a way as to minimize infringing the other principles.

Applying the principles in a situation where there are no consensus rules of conduct, a pharmacist may decide, for example, that he or she cannot honor a patient's request to renew a long-term, vitally necessary but potentially toxic prescription order because it appears that the patient has been noncompliant with necessary monitoring.* Normally, this kind of situation

---

*Such a situation existed when physicians failed, despite the labeling instructions, to order tests for liver toxicity for more than half of patients taking the antidiabetic drug Rezulin®. The drug was eventually withdrawn after reports of more than sixty deaths caused by liver failure among patients taking the drug (Hilts, PJ. Drug's Problems Raise Questions on Warnings. *The New York Times*, 2001, August 21;Sect. F:1).

can be easily remedied by a call to the physician. However, the pharmacist knows that this physician does not insist on monitoring, especially when, as in this case, the patient views monitoring as excessively burdensome and expensive. A pharmacist faced with this situation must be sure of the facts and then must balance the duties of protecting the patient from harm, doing the good that can be done, and allowing the patient to make medical decisions for himself (in this case, that his need for the drug outweighs the burdens, risks, and costs of submitting to monitoring). In doing this, the pharmacist can decide to ask the patient to supply medical information so that the pharmacist can determine the medical risks and benefits of dispensing or not dispensing and then dispense an appropriately limited supply of the drug—enough for the patient to have time to either visit the lab or see his physician. As with most cases, knowledge promotes autonomy and the pharmacist should fully explain the reasons that monitoring is necessary to the patient's health and the consequences of further noncompliance. It is also wise to consider who else is affected by the actions taken, e.g., if the pharmacist suspects that the physician is similarly lax and possibly negligent in having other patients opt to forgo drug toxicity monitoring, should the pharmacist have a discussion with the physician to advocate for safe practices for other patients? Deciding how far the scope of concern should extend (e.g., to the patient's finances? to the prescribing physician? to the physician-patient relationship? to other patients?) is another factor to consider in addressing such an ethical problem.

Notice the gap between the identification of ethical principles that apply to the situation and the determination of what should be done. In the process of arriving at a conclusion of what constitutes right action, the pharmacist had to reason through the ethical dilemma of how to preserve a patient's right to control the circumstances of his healthcare (respecting autonomy) while preventing harm to the patient and doing the good that can be done (nonmaleficence and beneficence), while at the same time deciding how far to extend the scope of obligation. Becoming facile with such ethical reasoning processes can best be accomplished with ethics education and training. The textbooks cited above are a good place to start such an endeavor. In addition, hospital-based pharmacists, especially those at academic medical centers, often have ready access to this type of training. Hospital ethics committees are another avenue for training and service in this field. For other pharmacists, the APhA, AMA, and other healthcare associations provide ethics education and resources that can assist in becoming adept at incorporating an ethical aspect into professional practice decision making.

CONCLUSION

Adherence to the law is required but does not set the limits of responsible pharmacy practice conduct. Decisions about which action is right can be guided by consulting the codes of professional and ethical conduct. For situations where neither the law nor the codes supply adequate guidance, having a basic understanding of medical ethical principles and how they are applied will assist in developing an enlightened and responsible professional practice.

NOTES

1. Available from www.conservativeforum.org/authquot.asp?ID=639.

2. Food and Drug Administration. Milestones in U.S. food and drug law history. 1999 May 3. Report #BG99-4. Available from vm.cfsan.fda.gov/mileston.html.

3. O'Harrow R. Plan's access to pharmacy data raises privacy issue. *The Washington Post,* 1998 Sept 27;Sect. A:1.

4. Zimmerman A and Armstrong D. Use of pharmacies by drug makers to push pills raises privacy issues. *Wall Street Journal,* 2002 May 1;Sect. A:1.

5. Wyser-Pratte RC. Protection of RU-486 as contraception, emergency contraception and as an abortifacient under the law of contraception. *Oregon Law Review* 2000; 79:1121-1156.

6. News Release, Attorney General reinstates DEA position on the dispensing of controlled substances to assist suicide. November 6, 2001. Available from www.usdoj.gov/dea/pubs/pressrel/pr110601.html.

7. *Perez v. Wyeth Laboratories, Inc.* 734 A.2d 1245 (August 9, 1999).

8. Kolata G. Selling growth hormone for children: The legal and ethical questions. *The New York Times* 1994 August 15;Sect. A:2.

9. Available from www.rpsgb.org.uk/.

10. Available from www.ashp.org/bestpractices/Ethics.html.

11. The Nuremberg Code, from Trials of war criminals before the Nuremberg Military Tribunals under Control Council Law No. 10. U.S. Government Printing Office. 1946-1949. Available from www.ushmm.org/research/doctros/Nuremberg_Code.htm.

12. World Medical Association. Declaration of Helsinki. *JAMA* 1997;277:909-914.

13. Department of Health, Education, and Welfare. Belmont Report: Ethical Principles and Guidelines for the Protection of Human Subjects of Research. Report of the National Commission for the Protection of Human Subjects of Biomedical and Behavioral Research. 44 *Fed. Reg.* 23, 192, April 18, 1979.

14. National Research Act of 1974, Public Law No. 93-348.

15. Department of Health, Education, & Welfare, Belmont Report, April 18, 1979.

16. American College of Clinical Pharmacy. Ethical Issues Related to Clinical Pharmacy Research. *Pharmacotherapy* 1993;13:523-530. Available from www.accp.com/position.html.

17. Available from www.ama-assn.org.

18. Smith M, Strauss S, Baldwin J, et al., eds. *Pharmacy Ethics,* The Haworth Press, Binghamton, NY, 1991; Beauchamp TL and Childress JF. *Principles of Biomedical Ethics,* Fourth Edition. Oxford University Press, New York, 1994; Gillon R and Lloyd A. *Principles of Healthcare Ethics.* John Wiley & Sons Ltd., Hoboken, NJ, 1994; Weinstein BD. *Ethical Issues in Pharmacy.* Applied Therapeutics, Inc., Vancouver, WA, 1996; Buerki RA and Vottero LD. *Ethical Responsibility in Pharmacy Practice.* American Institute of the History of Pharmacy. Madison, WI, 1996; Buerki RA and Vottero LD. *Ethical Practices in Pharmacy: A Guidebook for Pharmacy Technicians.* American Institute of the History of Pharmacy, Madison, WI, 1997; Jonsen AR, Siegler M, and Winslade WJ. *Clinical Ethics,* Fourth Edition, McGraw-Hill, New York, 1998; Veatch RM and Haddad AM. *Case Studies in Pharmacy Ethics.* Oxford University Press, New York, 1999.

19. Gillon R. The four principles revisited—Reappraisal. In *Principles of Healthcare Ethics.* Gillon R, ed. John Wiley & Sons Ltd., Hoboken, NY, 1994, pp. 319-333.

20. National Commission for the Protection of Human Subjects of Biomedical and Behavioral Research. The Belmont Report: Ethical principles and guidelines for the protection of human subjects of research. Report No. GPO 887-809. Department of Health, Education and Welfare, Washington, DC, 1979. Available from www.nih.gov:80/grants/oprr/humansubjects/guidance/belmont.htm.

BIBLIOGRAPHY

Beecher HK. Ethics and clinical research. *New Engl J Med* 1966;274:1354-1360.

Lock S. Research ethics—A brief historical review to 1965. *J Int Med* 1995; 238:513-520.

Chapter 16

HIPAA Privacy in the Pharmacy

Brian A. Gallagher

WHAT IS HIPAA?

HIPAA stands for the Health Insurance Portability and Accountability Act of 1996. Although the act itself is quite lengthy, a small provision contains the legislative authority for protecting the privacy and security of a patient's personally identifiable health information.

One of the primary goals of the act was to standardize many aspects of electronic insurance claims processing and achieve "administrative simplification," theoretically resulting in tremendous cost savings. Through HIPAA, Congress empowered the Department of Health and Human Services (DHHS) to enact rules to make the various aspects of the law a reality. For pharmacies' purposes, the three most relevant rules are transaction sets, privacy, and security.

Although HIPAA applies to all health providers, this chapter will focus only on the aspects of the law most applicable to privacy implications for the pharmacy. Thus, this discussion will focus in large part on the final privacy rule and briefly explain transaction sets and security to place them in context.

Transaction Sets

Part of the theory behind HIPAA involves generating cost savings through administrative simplification accomplished by the standardization of electronically transmitted insurance claims. These claims are sent via "transaction sets," which are essentially electronic claims forms. Currently, there is no uniformity in these transactions sets. Instead, each payor has its own forms and codes. HIPAA intended to standardize these into a uniform claims processing methodology.

Pharmacy Law Desk Reference
doi:10.1300/5790_16

Instead of imposing a governmentally mandated group of transaction sets, the federal government opted to allow the National Council for Prescription Drug Programs (NCPDP) to set the standard transaction sets for pharmacy and then the government would "adopt" these standards and mandate that they be used across the pharmacy industry by incorporating them into rules under DHHS. NCPDP was chosen to define the transaction sets for pharmacy because it is the standards-setting organization for pharmacy claims processing. Membership is voluntary and is open to any person or entity that has any part in processing prescription claims. Therefore, key members of NCPDP include pharmacies, insurers, pharmacy benefits managers (PBMs), and software vendors. Although these standards are nominally voluntary, DHHS's adoption of the standard in rule effectively empowers NCPDP to make "law" within the contents of their standard. The standards-setting organizations for other healthcare groups (e.g., physicians, hospitals, etc.) created their own transaction sets for their own type of claims.

The standard created by NCPDP and adopted by rule by DHHS is commonly referred to as NCPDP Version 5.1 or simply "Five One." Originally, these new standardized transaction sets were to be fully implemented by October 15, 2002, and all providers were to send claims and all payors were to pay claims using only the new NCPDP 5.1 transaction sets. However, Congress enacted the Administrative Simplification Compliance Act (ASCA) extending the time for compliance until October 15, 2003, for those pharmacies and insurance companies that applied for the extension. Because a number of covered entities have not met the deadline, DHHS is giving extra time to meet the requirements under "compliance plans" on a case-by-case basis for those entities that have made and continue to make good-faith efforts toward compliance.

The federal government originally surmised that after the transaction sets became standardized and administrative simplification became a reality, healthcare information would be readily transferable and easily distributed. Therefore, the impetus to create a legal framework to protect health information became more urgent. In response to these concerns, Congress created two additional sets of rules to protect patient privacy and mandate security measures to safeguard patient data.

Security

The security rule became final in 2003 and was scheduled to take effect on April 20, 2005. Full explanation of the provisions of this rule is outside the scope of this chapter. However, because of the impossibility of keeping information private without securing it, privacy and security are inextricably linked. Thus, the privacy rule that is already in effect has what has been commonly termed a "minisecurity" provision that mandates taking steps to secure patient identifiable data.

The final security rule gives some guidance as to what is required by creating five security categories: "Administrative Safeguards," "Physical Safeguards," "Technical Safeguards," "Organizational Requirements," and "Policies, Procedures, and Documentation Requirements." These categories are further subdivided into twenty-two "standards" that must be instituted, coupled with forty-five "implementation specifications" outlining how to comply with the standards. Each standard or implementation specification is either "required" or "addressable." While the term "required" is self-explanatory, pharmacies should note that "addressable" does not mean optional. In other words, pharmacies must address all requirements in some form or fashion. The addressable standards simply give the pharmacy much more flexibility in the method of compliance.

Administrative requirements include establishing policies and procedures within the pharmacy to secure patient information, training employees on security procedures, and enforcing penalties for violations.

Technical security requirements mandate the use of security systems and methodologies such as biometrics and encryption of data.

Physical security consists of activities such as ensuring that computers are locked and other physical methods of providing security are followed.

The security rule provides few concrete requirements. Instead, the rule requires pharmacies to use "reasonable" methods to secure data. Obviously, the definition of "reasonable" is fluid, thus security requirements evolve as technology evolves.

Additional reference to a source specific to HIPAA security is advisable for more detailed information regarding the rule's mandates.

Privacy in General

HIPAA designates pharmacies and other healthcare providers as well as insurers and clearinghouses as "covered entities." Covered entities are directly regulated by HIPAA and are required to abide by all of the provisions of HIPAA. The definition does not clearly state whether the covered entity is the pharmacy and/or the pharmacist. Because of this ambiguity, prudence dictates that both the pharmacy and the pharmacist abide by the mandates of the law.

Covered entities can have either a direct or indirect treatment relationship with a patient. Caregivers with a direct treatment relationship, such as physicians and pharmacists, administer care to the patient themselves. Caregivers with an indirect treatment relationship, such as clinical laboratory personnel or radiology technicians, render care at the behest of a practitioner with a direct treatment relationship (e.g., performing a lab test that was ordered by a physician). Both direct and indirect treatment providers must maintain patient privacy.

WHAT INFORMATION DOES HIPAA PROTECT?

The "designated record set" constitutes the records that must be protected according to the mandates of the privacy rule. It consists of a group of records maintained by the pharmacy that comprise the medical and billing records about individuals maintained by the pharmacy or records used in whole or in part by the pharmacy to make decisions about individuals.

HIPAA titles the information subject to the privacy rule as "personally identifiable health information," commonly known as protected health information (PHI). For HIPAA protections to apply to a document in the pharmacy, the document must be PHI. Thus, the threshold inquiry requires application of a two-part test to determine if a document is PHI. First, the record must be personally identifiable (e.g., contain the patient's name, social security number, or other data identifying and linked to an individual patient). Second, it must contain health information about the patient. Health information is defined as any information, whether oral, written, or in any other format, that "relates to the past, present or future physical or mental health or condition of an individual or the past, present, or future payment for the provision of health care to an individual." Importantly, if the record is either not personally identifiable or does not contain "health information," then the record is not PHI and not covered by HIPAA.

OTHER PRIVACY LAWS

HIPAA creates a minimum level of privacy protection and does not eliminate or "preempt" state laws that grant greater privacy protections than HIPAA. Because HIPAA privacy constitutes only a guarantee of minimal privacy protections, states are free to impose more stringent restrictions on the uses and disclosures of information or other matters related to protecting a patient's privacy. Furthermore, because HIPAA does not repeal, supercede, or preempt existing state privacy laws, privacy protections often differ from state to state depending on the level of protection afforded by state law. Therefore, complying with the mandates of HIPAA will not, in all cases, assure full compliance with the law.

When conflicts between HIPAA and state law arise, covered entitles must comply with whichever law, state or federal, is more stringent. Determining whether HIPAA or a state law is more stringent requires covered entities to ascertain which law gives greater rights to the patient, provides for retaining more detailed records on the patient, or requires the covered entity to maintain these records for a longer duration. Essentially, whichever law, state or federal, gives more rights or protections to the patient is the more stringent law.

However, in certain instances pharmacies must comply with a few state laws that take away rights granted by HIPAA. Even though HIPAA is more stringent (i.e., giving patients greater protections), pharmacies are allowed to comply with these state laws because the states have a compelling need for PHI in limited circumstances. HIPAA specifically allows compliance with state laws mandating reports using PHI to prevent fraud and abuse, to assist the state with regulation of insurance and health plans, to report on healthcare delivery or costs, or "for purposes of serving a compelling need related to public health, safety or welfare," to comply with state regulations on controlled substances, or to meet reporting requirements of state law such on child abuse, disease, or injury, or "public health surveillance, investigation or intervention" (See the State Privacy Laws versus HIPAA section)

NOTICE OF PRIVACY PRACTICES

By April 14, 2003, pharmacies must have created and provided to patients a "Notice of Privacy Practices," including a number of requirements specified in the privacy rule. These notices are an essential component of HIPAA compliance. The entire notice should be written in plain language so that is understandable to the average reader.

The notice must contain a header stating, "This notice describes how medical information about you may be used and disclosed and how you can get access to this information. Please review it carefully." It also must include a number of required elements, including a description with at least one example of the types of uses and disclosures the pharmacy may make for payment, treatment, and healthcare operations, descriptions of other purposes for which the pharmacy is permitted or required to disclose PHI without the patient's permission, a statement that the pharmacy will comply with the most stringent law, that other uses will be made only if the patient has signed an authorization, and that this authorization can be revoked.

The notice must state what payment, treatment, and healthcare operations mean to the pharmacy and give examples of each. Obviously, these definitions and examples cannot exceed the bounds imposed by the definitions of these terms contained in the HIPAA privacy rule. Pharmacies are legally bound to comply with the privacy practices delineated in their notice.

The notice must specify the patient's rights under both state and federal law. Thus, because the state's privacy laws vary, notices differ not only from pharmacy to pharmacy but may also differ from state to state, even for pharmacies within the same chain.

Notices must be updated to accurately reflect both current law and the pharmacy's current privacy practices. Thus, if state or federal laws governing the privacy of healthcare records change or the pharmacy modifies their privacy practices, then the pharmacy must make corresponding changes to the notice to reflect the new law or policy. Pharmacies need not redistribute copies of a revised notice to patients who previously received an older version of the notice unless the patient asks for a copy of the new notice.

In addition to attempting to give the patient a copy of the notice, it must be posted in the pharmacy and copies of the notice must be available when the notice is revised.

If the patient receives services electronically, such as through an Internet pharmacy, the notice must be available electronically and the pharmacy may provide the notice via e-mail. Mail-order pharmacies may mail the notice to patients.

Acknowledgment

Under HIPAA, the notice of privacy practices and another document, called an "acknowledgment," are linked. At the patient interface, the initial action taken by a pharmacist is to make a good-faith effort to obtain the patient's written acknowledgment that the patient received the pharmacy's notice of privacy practices. So, in practice, the pharmacist is required to present the notice and then either secure a written acknowledgment or document why no written acknowledgment was received. Obtaining a written acknowledgment from the patient is not an absolute requirement. Thus, at the end of this interaction with the patient, the pharmacist is expected to have documented one of two things. Either the patient provided the written acknowledgment and the pharmacist has retained that acknowledgment, or the pharmacist should document his or her "good faith efforts" to obtain the patient's acknowledgment.

DHHS permits wide latitude in how the written acknowledgment is to be obtained. However, the acknowledgment must be in writing (although a signature is not required). Despite this flexibility, the rule does not allow the pharmacy to obtain a single signature from a patient for all purposes. DHHS said that "a pharmacist is permitted to have the individual sign or initial an acknowledgment within the log book that patents already sign when they pick up prescriptions, so long as the individual is clearly informed on the log book of what they are acknowledging and the acknowledgment is not also used as a waiver or permission for something else (such as a waiver to consult with the pharmacist)." Thus, the patient cannot sign to waive counseling or that they received the prescription combined with the signature for the acknowledgment of receipt of the notice of privacy practices. That writing must stand alone, so in many instances the pharmacist will have to get the patient to sign twice or perhaps three times during one transaction for a single prescription.

Once the patient has provided written acknowledgment, there is neither an expiration date for the written acknowledgment nor any requirement to provide a new acknowledgment even if the notice of privacy practices changes. However, if the patient requests a copy of any new notice, the pharmacy must have the new notice available and provide it to the patient.

Patients who frequent the same chain of pharmacies need only be provided that chain's notice of privacy practices once at the first date of service. Attempting to provide a second notice is not required if the patient subsequently goes to another pharmacy in that same chain.

Failure to obtain written acknowledgment of receipt of the notice of privacy practices does not automatically prohibit the pharmacy from using or disclosing PHI for payment, treatment, or healthcare operations provided that the pharmacy documents its good-faith effort to attempt to obtain the written acknowledgment. Failure to obtain the acknowledgment can occur for any reason, including a patient simply refusing to sign, provided that a good-faith effort is made and that effort is documented.

Electronic signatures or other writing complies with the written acknowledgment. Pharmacies must keep written acknowledgments or the good-faith efforts to obtain them on file for six years.

Payment, Treatment, and Healthcare Operations

Securing either the written acknowledgment or documenting the good-faith efforts to obtain it unlocks the door for the pharmacy to use or disclose PHI for payment, treatment, or healthcare operations as specified in the law and as stated in the pharmacy's notice of privacy practices.

For pharmacy, "payment" means activities undertaken by the pharmacy to obtain reimbursement for the provision of healthcare, including but not limited to eligibility determinations, coordination of benefits, billing, claims management, collection activities, and utilization review including pre-authorization of services, concurrent, and retrospective review.

Treatment is defined as "the provision, coordination, or management of health care and related services by one or more health care providers, including the coordination or management of health care by a health care provider with a third party; consultation between health care providers relating to a patient; or the referral of a patient for health care from one health care provider to another." Guidance issued by DHHS makes it clear that refill reminder programs are defined as treatment even if the reminder comes from a company hired by the pharmacy to perform the mailing and/or if a pharmaceutical manufacturer pays the pharmacy to provide the reminders. Preventive care and wellness programs are also included in the definition of treatment.

Under HIPAA, "health care operations" is a catchall category designed to allow covered entities to continue to use PHI without undue restrictions for necessary or valuable operations that do not fit easily into the other two definitions. This definition includes such pharmacy activities as selling a pharmacy's records to a successor pharmacy, conducting quality assessment and improvement activities, contacting other healthcare providers and patients about treatment alternatives, and "related functions that do not include treatment." Operations also include reviewing the competency of healthcare professionals, conducting medical reviews, legal services, auditing, including fraud and abuse prevention, and assessing compliance with the law, including HIPAA privacy.

These three definitions combined constitute what is essentially the day-to-day practice of pharmacy. Thus, fulfilling the acknowledgment requirement allows the pharmacy to use or disclose PHI for the vast majority of transactions in the course of the pharmacy practice.

TREATMENT VERSUS MARKETING

Critical to the thinking underlying privacy protections provided by HIPAA is attempting to distinguish between and to separate treatment from marketing. The goal is to not unduly curtail treatment activities but to limit marketing contact with patients to those communications that the patient chooses to receive. Often this distinction is difficult to draw and causes a potential for significant overlap, as many pharmacy activities contain elements of both treatment and marketing. For example, a pharmacist who recommends that the patient purchase a supplement to replenish some nutrients being depleted by drug therapy is, in essence, both treating the patient and marketing a product.

Under HIPAA, marketing is defined as "a communication about a product or service that encourages recipients of the communication to purchase or use the product or service." In pharmacy, a host of communications to the patient, from recommending an over-the-counter (OTC) drug to advising the patient to see a physician, contain at least an element of encouragement to buy a product (e.g., the OTC drug) or service (e.g., be examined by the physician). Thus, this broad definition of marketing seems as first blush to largely subsume treatment. Fortunately, communications for treatment, case management, or care coordination, recommending alternative treatments, therapies, to other healthcare providers or settings of care, or regarding a health-related product or service that is provided by or included in the patient's health benefits are specifically carved out of the definition of marketing. These communications are not marketing even if a third party, such as a drug company, pays the pharmacy to make the communication. Moreover, regardless of the purpose of the communication, face-to-face interactions between the pharmacist and the patient never constitute marketing under HIPAA.

When a program falls within the definition of marketing, however, all participating patients must affirmatively agree to participate in the program by completing a document called an "authorization" before a pharmacy can engage in marketing activities. HIPAA mandates that patients agree to participate in a marketing program by signing an "authorization" expressing their desire to be part of the program. A patient actively agreeing to participate in a marketing program is commonly referred to as "opting in" to the marketing program, as opposed to sending marketing materials to a patient and then allowing or requiring the patient to "opt out" of the program by requesting that they be removed from the marketing plan or from receiving additional unsolicited marketing materials.

Authorizations can be used for more than one marketing program provided that each program is adequately explained in the authorization.

Even if patients have completed an authorization and agreed to participate in a marketing program, they can still drop out of the program at any time simply by notifying the pharmacy of their decision.

HIPAA prevents coercing patients into a marketing program. Pharmacies cannot insist that patients sign the authorization opting into the marketing program or refuse to dispense a prescription order or treat the patient because the patient chooses not to participate in any marketing program.

Authorizations must contain specific elements and they must be complete. They must describe the PHI to be used or disclosed, include the person who will disclose the information and the person who will receive it, contain an expiration date, state that the patient can revoke it at any time including how to revoke, and that the information my be redisclosed by the person receiving the PHI. It must be written in plain language and contain the signature of the patient or the patient's personal representative. The pharmacy must provide the patient with a copy of the authorization.

Some of the ambiguity between treatment and marketing has been resolved, but overlap remains. Because of the vastly different legal requirements between treatment activities and marketing programs coupled with the significant potential penalties involved, legal counsel should be consulted whenever any doubt exists about whether an activity constitutes treatment or marketing.

MINIMUM NECESSARY

Using or disclosing PHI only on a "need to know" basis lies at the center of the conceptual underpinning of HIPAA privacy. In essence, the rule directs that only the minimum PHI be released to accomplish the purpose for which it is being used or disclosed and that this minimum amount of information be disclosed to only the minimum number of people needed to accomplish the goal. The rule states:

> When using or disclosing protected health information or when requesting protected health information from another covered entity, a covered entity must make reasonable efforts to limit protected health information to the minimum necessary to accomplish the intended purpose of the use, disclosure or request.

Pharmacies may develop and follow policies and procedures for complying with releasing only the minimum necessary information for routine disclosures. However, nonroutine disclosures must be handled on a case-by-case basis.

Disclosures for treatment purposes are exempted from the minimum necessary restrictions. Recognizing that the potential for unduly limiting information might interfere with patient care, HIPAA creates an exception for information used or disclosed for treatment purposes. Thus, a pharmacist may err on the side of disclosing all information to another health professional or pharmacist he or she believes may be necessary for patient care. However, the pharmacist may need to limit access by job classification or function. For example, a pharmacy intake clerk may need less access to certain PHI than a technician, and a technician may need less PHI than another pharmacist. These determinations will often turn on the staffing, prescription volume, and work flow in each particular pharmacy.

Although the minimum necessary restriction does not apply to uses or disclosures for treatment, HIPAA mandates that only the minimum necessary information be used or disclosed for payment or healthcare operations. Various payors request differing fields to pay claims. Transmitting any field that is designated as a "mandatory" field in the standard transaction sets included in NCPDP 5.1 does not violate HIPAA privacy. The ultimate determination of what fields exceed the minimum necessary restrictions does not turn on those fields requested by the payor. Despite the fact that a payor may not pay a claim unless certain fields are transmitted, in the final analysis, the pharmacist, and not the payor, is required to make this determination. The preamble to the rule explaining this section states:

> The pharmacist may infer that the information requested by the payor does not exceed the minimum necessary *if reasonable to do so* [emphasis added], and then does not need to engage in a separate minimum necessary assessment. If a pharmacist does not agree that the amount of information requested is reasonably necessary for the PBM to fulfill its obligations, it is up to the pharmacist and PBM to negotiate a resolution of the dispute as to the amount of information needed by the PBM to carry out its obligations and that the pharmacist is willing to provide, recognizing that the PBM is not required to pay claims if it has not received the information it believes is necessary to process the claim in accordance with its procedures, including fraud prevention procedures.

Unless either NCPDP or DHHS determines which fields exceed the minimum necessary, there will be no certainty in this area, with the pharmacist facing sanctions for making an inappropriate determination.

Uses or disclosures made pursuant to an authorization given by the patient, including marketing activities, are not subject to the minimum necessary requirements.

ADDITIONAL PATIENT RIGHTS

Besides the right to receive and acknowledge receipt of the pharmacy's notice of privacy practices, HIPAA affords patients with a number of additional rights. Some of these have more applicability in healthcare contexts such as hospitals or physician offices, but all apply to pharmacy and compliance may pose some significant logistical hurdles. The most important of these from a pharmacy perspective are the right to receive an accounting of disclosures, the right to inspect and copy their records, the right to request additional privacy rights or restrictions, the right to amend or append records, and the right to receive information at an alternative address.

Accounting of Disclosures

Patients have the right, upon request, to receive an accounting of nearly all disclosures made by the pharmacy for purposes other than payment, treatment, or healthcare operations. Other exceptions include disclosures to patients themselves or disclosures made pursuant to an authorization that the patient has signed for activities such as marketing. Pharmacies do not have to keep an accounting of uses or disclosures for marketing because the patient was already informed about them when he or she signed the authorization to opt into the marketing program.

Most significant in the practice of pharmacy, it appears that pharmacies must keep an accounting of disclosures to law enforcement authorities, Board of Pharmacy inspectors, the DEA and other regulators.

Although the pharmacy must create and maintain the record of what governmentally mandated disclosures were made and who received what PHI and when, in limited circumstances the authorities may request that this audit trail information be suspended for a time and not disclosed to the patient. This suspension is limited to thirty days if the request is made orally. The pharmacist must document oral requests, including the name of the requesting agency and official. Written requests must state that disclosing the information to the individual would "be reasonably likely to impede the agency's investigation" and specify the time limit of the suspension. Presumably, this suspension cannot be indefinite.

Inspecting and Copying Records

Except in very limited circumstances, patients have the right to inspect and copy their own records. The timeline for compliance depends on whether the records are stored on site at the pharmacy or off site. Pharmacies must retrieve and allow copies to be made within thirty days for records stored on site and sixty days if the records are housed off site. In addition, pharmacies may obtain an additional thirty-day extension if they inform the patient in writing of the extension.

Under HIPAA, pharmacies can charge a reasonable cost-based fee for retrieval and copying the records. However, because some states prohibit charging for the first copy of records and HIPAA requires that the pharmacy comply with the "most stringent" law, pharmacies may not be allowed to charge for copies in some states.

There are a few exceptions to a patient's right to inspect and copy their own records, and fewer still apply in the pharmacy context. The exceptions generally deal with psychiatric records or situations in which someone who is mentioned in the record might be endangered by disclosing their name to the patient. Obviously, this would rarely if ever occur in a pharmacy.

A pharmacist can legally deny access to a patient only pursuant to one of these limited exceptions. Such denial must be in writing and state the reasons for the denial. The patient has the right to appeal the denial. The pharmacist must designate another healthcare provider not involved in the original denial decision to rule on the appeal. This ruling must also be in writing within thirty days and provided to the patient. All of this documentation must be retained for six years.

Right to Request Additional Privacy Rights or Restrictions

Patients can request that pharmacies voluntarily grant them additional privacy rights not specified under HIPAA or mandated by state law. The pharmacy is not required to give the patient any additional rights or protections not afforded by HIPAA or state law. However, if the pharmacy does agree to additional privacy rights, then these must be documented and the pharmacy personnel must adhere to all of these requirements as well as duties under HIPAA and state law. When the pharmacist agrees to these additional rights, any violation of these also subjects the pharmacist to sanctions under HIPAA. These rights continue to exist until the pharmacist notifies the patient that they will no longer agree to them.

With all of the complexities of HIPAA, at first blush, many pharmacies may initially conclude that they will never agree to additional privacy rights or responsibilities. However, patients will undoubtedly make a number of quite reasonable and prudent requests that pharmacies will want to grant in the interest of good patient care. For example, a terminally ill cancer patient who is taking a number of controlled substances and is not able to personally come to the pharmacy may request that only certain individuals be allowed to pick up the prescriptions on the patient's behalf.

If the pharmacy does agree to grant additional rights or to assume additional responsibilities then these should be clearly and carefully documented and involved staff fully informed to avoid inadvertent violations.

Right to Amend or Append Records

In certain circumstances, patients have the right to request that the pharmacy amend their records or attach (append) additional information to the patient's records. These requests should be granted if they improve patient care and do not violate the law. For example, if the patient moves and their address is no longer valid, then the record should be appropriately corrected to include the new address. Or, if the patient has an allergy to a medication and the record does not reflect this, it should be modified to incorporate the correct information.

If the pharmacist agrees to amend or append a patient's record, the pharmacist must communicate the amendment to any other entities that have copies of the inaccurate records.

Conversely, some patients may request improper amendments or ask to append to their records information that the pharmacist feels is inappropriate. For instance, a patient may ask that accurate but potentially embarrassing information be deleted from the record or ask that an old prescription be destroyed when the law requires that the pharmacy maintain it.

If the record is "reasonably accurate and complete" or if someone else created the record, then the pharmacist may legally deny the patient's request to amend or append. The refusal must be in writing and given to the patient within thirty days. The patient is then allowed thirty days to file a written response to the denial, and the pharmacy is given another thirty days to submit a written rebuttal to the patient's response. Like other records mandated by HIPAA, all of this information must be linked in the patient's record and kept on file for six years.

Unlike requests for copies of records, there is no legal requirement to have someone not involved in the pharmacy's initial decision to deny the amendment to review the patient's appeal of that decision.

Although the law allows oral requests to append or amend, the pharmacy has the option of requiring written requests by stating in the notice of privacy practices that requests to amend or append must be in writing and include the patient's rationale for the request.

Use of Alternative Address

The ability of a patient to require the pharmacy to use an alternative address for the patient is the last patient right with significance for pharmacy. Patients have the right to require the pharmacy to send prescriptions or any other communications to an address other than the patient's home or primary address (e.g., a post office box). This obviously impacts mail-order pharmacy to a greater extent than other areas of pharmacy practice, but all types of pharmacies must be prepared to comply with these requests.

Patients can also require pharmacies to call them at a phone other than the patient's home or send mailings in a sealed envelope as opposed to a postcard.

RESPONSIBILITIES OF COVERED ENTITIES

In addition to granting patients the rights discussed above, HIPAA imposes a number of responsibilities on pharmacies. As a covered entity, pharmacies and pharmacists are required to do a number of things in addition to complying with all of the patient's rights, providing the notice, and protecting PHI.

Training the Pharmacy's Workforce

HIPAA requires that the pharmacy's "workforce" be trained about patient privacy and the pharmacy's privacy policies "as necessary and appropriate for members of the workforce to carry out their function" for the business. The workforce includes everyone who works in the pharmacy, including all full-time staff and individuals who might not be paid by the pharmacy, such as students, volunteers, floating staff, or interns. Any staff having access to PHI must be trained. Thus, consideration must be given to anyone who has access to PHI that might not initially come to mind, such as clerks at the front of the store if they ever help in the pharmacy or otherwise handle prescriptions, or personnel in the home office who might ever need to access PHI.

The rules are unclear as to whether every pharmacy employee, such as the CEO of a chain, must be trained if they do not have access to PHI.

HIPAA required that training occur prior to April 14, 2003, and any new employees hired after April 14 must be trained within a "reasonable time." If the pharmacy's policies and procedures or the law "materially" changes then employees must be given follow-up training. All staff training must be documented and this documentation retained for six years.

Appointing a Privacy Officer

Pharmacies must appoint a "privacy officer." One individual may serve in this capacity for an entire chain. The privacy officer is "responsible for the development and implementation of the policies and procedures of the entity." No more specifics about the training or the exact duties and responsibilities of the privacy officer are detailed in HIPAA. However, reason dictates that this person should be the contact for questions, complaints, and other HIPAA-related privacy activities.

Developing and Implementing Privacy Policies and Procedures

All covered entities, including pharmacies, must develop privacy policies and procedures to detail how all of the HIPAA requirements are going to be met. The pharmacy workforce must be trained and abide by these policies. Failure to create or adhere to the policies could subject both the pharmacy and the person violating the directive to HIPAA sanctions.

Additional Responsibilities of Covered Entities

Pharmacies and pharmacists, as covered entities, have several additional responsibilities that are not clearly explained in the HIPAA privacy rule. In essence, they must cooperate with DHHS in their efforts to obtain HIPAA compliance. The rule requires that they provide records and compliance reports as may be requested by DHHS, cooperate with complaint investigations, permit DHHS to have access to information, including access at any time and without notice, certify efforts to obtain information from other agencies, and aid attempts by DHHS to resolve complaints informally.

EDUCATING THE PUBLIC ABOUT HIPAA

One of the primary reasons for requiring pharmacists to use good-faith efforts to get the patient to sign a separate acknowledgment of receipt is to generate a conversation about patient privacy rights between the pharmacist and the patient. Although this discussion is not legally mandated anywhere in the privacy rule, the preamble to the final rule makes it abundantly clear that this interaction coincides with the spirit of the law if not its actual language.

The preamble states in pertinent part that

> The notice acknowledgement process is intended to provide a formal opportunity for the individual to engage in a discussion *with a health care provider* about privacy. At the very least, the process is intended to draw the individual's attention to the importance of the notice. The Department believes these goals are better accomplished by requiring a written acknowledgement . . . (emphasis added)

The duty is not exclusively on the pharmacist or other covered entity. The preamble continues,

> the Department continues to believe strongly that promoting individuals' understanding of privacy practices is an essential component of providing notice to individuals. . . . The Department anticipates that many stakeholders, including the Department, covered entities, consumer organizations, health educators, the mass media and journalists, and a host of other organizations and individuals, will be involved in educating individuals about privacy notices and practices.

Thus, many individuals and entities are expected to be involved in educating the public. However, with information coming from wide and varied avenues, confusion may occur. For example, a patient who visits a prescriber will receive the prescriber's notice of privacy practices and may engage in a conversation with them about it. Then, shortly thereafter, the patient comes to the pharmacy and receives the pharmacy's notice and another conversation may ensue. With the current state of uneven knowledge about HIPAA, differing and sometimes erroneous explanations may be given to the patient. Thus, pharmacies and pharmacists would be well served by having a methodology to handle question and/or have a good working knowledge of the notice and of HIPAA.

RECOGNIZED ENTITIES UNDER HIPAA

Hybrid Entities

Some pharmacies may opt to designate themselves as "hybrid entities." This provision was originally crafted to address concerns of businesses such as supermarkets that contain pharmacies, because these companies perform the functions of both covered entities and businesses that are not regulated by HIPAA. In the final rule, this provision has been expanded to allow pharmacies to designate the portions of the business that use PHI as "healthcare components" to be bound to follow the HIPAA rules while the other portions of the business ("non-healthcare components") are not required to abide by the HIPAA requirements.

If a pharmacy decides to designate a portion of the business as a non-healthcare component, firewalls must be created prohibiting PHI from being shared with the portion of the hybrid entity not required to comply with HIPAA. In hybrid entities, the employees in the non-healthcare component need not be trained in HIPAA privacy. However, if a clerk works primarily in the nonpharmacy component but occasionally assists in the pharmacy, then this person must be trained.

Organized Healthcare Arrangement

Certain entities, such as hospitals, qualify as an "organized healthcare arrangement" under HIPAA. These operations typically have an array of healthcare providers rendering care to patients as a team. An organized healthcare arrangement is defined as "a clinically integrated care setting in which individuals typically receive health care from more than one health care provider." Often, the various caregivers are not all employees of the same business. For example, a hospital might have physicians who are in private practice, while the pharmacists and nurses are hospital employees. All are giving care to the same patients in an organized healthcare arrangement. These entities need only provide a single joint notice and attempt to obtain the acknowledgement only once from each patient on behalf of all providers giving care. Therefore, because these entities will likely attempt to obtain acknowledgment upon admission, pharmacists working in a hospital setting will probably never be required to participate in the acknowledgment process. Other aspects of HIPAA are still applicable but will likely be administered according to the policies and procedures of the organized healthcare arrangement.

STATE PRIVACY LAWS VERSUS HIPAA

Unfortunately, as stated previously, compliance with HIPAA alone does not assure full legal compliance because pharmacies also must comply with "more stringent" state privacy laws. State laws vary widely in this regard and are often difficult to find. They may be in the form of statutes, rules and regulations, court opinions, or even state constitutions. They may change at any time, so keeping up with a myriad of changes, large and small, will be tedious and difficult.

When state and federal laws conflict, determining which controls can be tricky and open to significant interpretation. The general rule is that if a state law is "contrary" to HIPAA, meaning that it is either impossible for the pharmacy to comply with both the state law and HIPAA or the "state law "stands as an obstacle" to HIPAA compliance, then the pharmacy must comply with HIPAA.

However, "more stringent" state laws constitute a major exception to the general rule. "More stringent" means that the state law provides increased privacy protections, prohibits a use or disclosure of PHI that is allowed by the HIPAA rules (except for disclosures to DHHS during investigations or providing patients with their own PHI), grants patients superior rights to amend or access their PHI, provides more information to patients about uses or disclosures of PHI or about the patients' privacy rights and avenues to resolve breaches, or requires that records be kept longer or that more detailed information be reported. State laws that protect the patient's privacy by requiring the patient's express permission to use or disclose PHI or narrows the scope or shortens the duration of the permission, enhances protections under the permission, or decreases the coercive effect of the circumstances surrounding the permission all supercede HIPAA.

Several other specific types of state law take precedence over HIPAA. These include any state law that regulates the manufacture, registration, distribution, dispensing, or other use of controlled substances; is intended to prevent fraud and abuse, or to regulate insurance or health plans; is needed by the state to report on healthcare delivery or costs; or to serve a "compelling need related to the public health, safety or welfare."

Finally, state laws requiring information for the licensure of pharmacists and pharmacies and public health reporting mandates are superior to HIPAA restrictions.

WHEN PHI MAY BE DISCLOSED

Minors

If state law allows someone to act on behalf of a person, such as a parent acting on behalf of a minor, the pharmacy must treat such person as a personal representative with respect to PHI. However, two separate special exceptions to this general rule concerning minors and their legal representatives are germane to the HIPAA privacy discussion.

First, the law in many states gives patients, and particularly minor patients, enhanced privacy rights in certain circumstances. Some states allow minors to consent to treatment themselves, without parental involvement, for sensitive disease states such as sexually transmitted diseases (STDs), family planning, substance abuse treatment, or psychiatric conditions. Legislatures justify giving these minors the right to exclude parents from the decision-making process, because otherwise many children would not seek care if their parents were notified. Thus, in these limited circumstances, minors are permitted under HIPAA to provide written acknowledgment of receipt of the notice of privacy practices. Often, pharmacists are in a particularly poor position to know if these state laws apply because they do not know the minor's diagnosis and many medications, such as antibiotics, can be used for a wide array of conditions, some protected (e.g., STDs) and others unprotected by state law. Pharmacists must use judgment in these situations in deciding who must complete the acknowledgment.

Emancipated minors constitute the second special situation involving minors. A child becomes emancipated according to each state's law. Many states categorize certain persons under the age of majority (typically eighteen or twenty-one) as "emancipated minors," giving them the full legal rights of adults. For example, some states may say that a person over the age of sixteen and married is an emancipated minor able to legally act for himself or herself. Emancipated minors have the full rights of adults under HIPAA.

State laws vary greatly regarding both the special rights of minors and how to become an emancipated minor, so each state must be referenced individually.

Disclosures Without Patient Knowledge or Permission

In certain defined circumstances, HIPAA allows pharmacies and other covered entities to disclose PHI without any type of permission, consent, or authorization from the patient. There are a limited number of these exceptions, but distinctions are vague and contain detailed and distinct but closely related requirements for the various types of disclosures. The pharmacy's privacy officer should be knowledgeable about them and make the determination about whether to comply with any particular request for disclosure without the patient's permission. A pharmacist or privacy officer who is uncertain about the correct course of action should consult counsel for a detailed analysis of the particular facts and the nuances of the law.

As one of the patient rights created by HIPAA, disclosures to patients themselves or their representatives does not require any additional documented permission.

Disclosures without permission include an array of disclosures that may be required by law or necessary for law enforcement. They include

1. disclosures that are pursuant to another law that mandates disclosure and
2. disclosures for public health activities such as collecting vital statistics, controlling or preventing disease, public health surveillance, investigations, or interventions.

Some other situations warrant special comment.

Pharmacies may release PHI in response to a law enforcement request about a patient who may be a *victim of a crime*. The patient must agree to the disclosure or if the patient is not able to agree then the law enforcement official must represent that the information is necessary and the patient is not the target of the investigation, and that the investigation would be "materially and adversely affected by waiting" for the patient's agreement prior to the pharmacy disclosing the requested PHI.

Pharmacies may divulge PHI to report victims of abuse, neglect, or domestic violence if law requires the disclosure, if the patient agrees to the disclosure, or if the law expressly permits the disclosure and the pharmacist believes that disclosure is necessary to protect the patient or others. In most instances the pharmacy or pharmacist must notify the patient and give the patient the right to object to the disclosure.

Pharmacies can legally disclose PHI without the patient's permission or knowledge when participating in certain FDA activities, including reporting adverse events or product defects, tracking products, facilitating product recalls, repairs, or replacement (including finding and informing patients who received the drug about the recall), or conducting postmarketing surveillance mandated by the FDA.

Pharmacies may disclose PHI to a "health oversight agency," such as the Board of Pharmacy, for oversight activities authorized by law, including audits, civil, administrative, or criminal investigations or proceedings, inspections, licensure or disciplinary actions, or "other activities necessary for appropriate oversight" of the healthcare system or government benefit programs such as Medicare or Medicaid when the PHI is relevant to determine eligibility.

An important exception exists to the health oversight disclosure segment of the rule. If the individual whose PHI is being requested is also the subject of the investigation or other law enforcement activity and the investigation does not relate directly to the receipt of healthcare, a claim for public benefits, or qualifications for benefits when a patient's health is integral to the claim, the pharmacy cannot release the information without the patient's knowledge and assent. Presumably, in these situations the patient must be informed and have the opportunity to object to the disclosure.

Pharmacies may disclosure PHI for judicial and administrative proceedings, including court orders, provided that only the material specified in the order or request is released.

In complying with subpoenas, discovery requests, or any other lawful request that is made without a court order, the pharmacy must receive satisfactory assurances that the requestor has made "reasonable efforts" to ensure that the person whose PHI is being requested has been informed of the request or that the requestor has received a protective order. Many of these requirements seem to be created to give the patient the right to formally object and to attempt to block release of their PHI.

Pharmacies may disclose PHI to law enforcement if the pharmacist believes that a crime has occurred in the pharmacy. Thus, it seems that a pharmacist can still report to the appropriate authorities what he or she believes to be forged prescriptions. Other law enforcement situations in which the pharmacy may be required to disclose PHI without permission of the patient include the following:

1. as required by other law or court order, warrant, subpoena, or administrative request. However, special note should be taken by pharmacies because some states have laws that may bar the release of PHI pursuant to a subpoena;
2. to identify or locate a suspect, fugitive, material witness, or missing person;
3. in response to a request about an individual who may be a victim of a crime;
4. about an individual who has died as a result of criminal conduct; or
5. where the pharmacy believes that the PHI is evidence of criminal conduct that occurred at or in the pharmacy. Presumably, this gives the pharmacist the authority to contact the authorities about forged prescriptions.

Because HIPAA regulates only covered entities such as pharmacies and not courts or law enforcement, pharmacies are required to meet the documentation requirements that more logically should be the responsibility of the requesting entity. Pharmacies should always confirm the identity of the requestor and the agency they represent, obtain and make copies of any documents justifying the request, note what PHI was disclosed, the purpose of the disclosure, and the date, and any requested suspension of the audit trail requirements that may be requested. Before releasing PHI without the patient's permission, pharmacies are required to verify both the identity of the requestor and both their authority to make the request and to access the PHI. If statements or documents are used in making the request, the pharmacy must also memorialize and retain any oral or written statements, representations, or documentation made by the requestor.

Pharmacies can disclose PHI for law enforcement purposes provided that de-identified information could not be used. Again, these disclosures are limited to the terms specified in the request, such as a subpoena, court order, or administrative request. Pharmacies may make disclosures of PHI that are mandated by law, but they can divulge only the minimum amount of PHI necessary to comply with the law.

Because of the confusing nature of these requests and the attendant requirements, pharmacist should seek the advice of counsel when attempting to comply.

Whistleblowers

Employees or business associates of covered entities are permitted to disclose PHI if they believe in good faith that the covered entity is engaged in conduct that is unlawful, violates professional or clinical standards, or that the care or conditions of the covered entity potentially endangers patients, workers, or the public. PHI can be disclosed by these "whistleblowers" to health oversight agencies such as the Board of Pharmacy, DHHS, or an attorney that they hire to help them decide what, if anything, to do about the inappropriate actions of the covered entity.

Covered entities are forbidden by HIPAA to discharge, punish, or take any retaliatory action against a whistleblower. Pharmacies should consider having policies to deal with whistleblowers to avoid charges of retaliatory actions.

LIMITED EXCEPTIONS TO THE HIPAA PRIVACY RULE

De-identification

There are two approved methods of de-identifying PHI so that it is no longer subject to the requirements of the HIPAA privacy rule. The first method is commonly known as the "Safe Harbor" and is accomplished by stripping the data of a list of specified identifiers.

The safe harbor section of the HIPAA privacy rule lists a wide range of identifiers, the last of which is a broad catchall. The enumerated list in the rule is as follows:

    (A) Names;

    (B) All geographic subdivisions smaller than a state, including street address, city, county, precinct, zip code, and their equivalent geocodes, except for the initial three digits of a zip code if, according to the current publicly available data from the Bureau of the Census:

    (1) The geographic unit formed by combining all zip codes with the same three initial digits contains more than 20,000 people; and

(2) The initial three digits of a zip code for all such geographic units containing 20,000 or fewer people is changed to 000.

(C) All elements of dates (except year) for dates directly related to an individual, including birth date, admission date, discharge date, date of death; and all ages over 89 and all elements of dates (including year) indicative of such age, except that such ages and elements may be aggregated into a single category of age 90 or older;

(D) Telephone numbers;

(E) Fax numbers;

(F) Electronic mail addresses;

(G) Social Security numbers;

(H) Medical record numbers;

(I) Health plan beneficiary numbers;

(J) Account numbers;

(K) Certificate/license numbers;

(L) Vehicle identifiers and serial numbers, including license plate numbers;

(M) Device identifiers and serial numbers;

(N) Web Universal Resource Locators (URLs);

(O) Internet Protocol (IP) address numbers;

(P) Biometric identifiers, including fingerprints and voiceprints;

(Q) Full-face photographic images and any comparable images; and

(R) Any other unique identifying number, characteristic, or code, except as permitted by paragraph (c) of this section.

In addition, the pharmacy cannot have actual knowledge that the information could be used alone or in combination with other information to identify an individual who is a subject of the information.

The second methodology, known as the statistical method, requires that the covered entity use a method to de-identify the PHI (such as encryption) and engage an appropriately qualified statistician to certify that use of this methodology results in a "very small" risk that the PHI can be re-identified. The methodology used by the statistician must be documented.

Disclosing any encryption code or other means to re-identify the PHI constitutes disclosure of PHI and subjects the disclosing party to sanctions.

Whoever does the de-identification may retain a method to re-identify the data provided the re-identification methodology is "not derived from or related to information about the individual and is not otherwise capable of being translated so as to identify the individual; and the method is not disclosed or used for any other purpose."

Use of either the safe harbor or the statistical method means that the information is no longer PHI and removes the data from HIPAA regulation.

Research

HIPAA allows valid research to continue and relaxes the rules in the research context. The full discussion of the privacy rules for research is outside the scope of this chapter.

Incidental Disclosures

DHHS recognizes that certain minimal disclosures of PHI are necessary to the efficient operation of any healthcare facility and to provide treatment. In the pharmacy, typical examples of "incidental disclosures" are being overheard counseling a patient or announcing over a loudspeaker that a patient's prescription is ready for pickup. These incidental disclosures of PHI are an exception to the general rule and do not violate HIPAA privacy. However, pharmacists should exercise care in making incidental disclosures because the exception is a narrow one. The pharmacist must employ "reasonable safeguards" to reduce the chance of an incidental disclosure. For example, while announcing that a patient's prescription is ready may be acceptable, announcing the name of the drug or other sensitive information probably is not. Waiting patients should be urged to stand back from the counter while the pharmacist talks with the patient, signs should be posted to remind workers about confidentiality, and the pharmacist should lower his or her voice if possible (e.g., when the patient does not have a hearing problem).

Discarding old vials or prescription records containing PHI are probably not incidental disclosures and the PHI they contain are likely to be entitled to HIPAA protections. Therefore, discarded items containing PHI should be handled appropriately to avoid violations. However, a Guidance issued by DHHS maintains that the accidental discovery of PHI by a cleaning service employee is an incidental disclosure that does not violate HIPAA.

Although not truly an incidental disclosure, the Guidance issued by DHHS says that it is permissible for the pharmacist to leave messages about the patient on the patient's answering machine, but the pharmacist should use professional judgment and limit the amount of information left on the machine. Similarly, the pharmacist may disclose PHI for "quick, effective and high quality healthcare" such as discussing a prescription with a patient over the pharmacy counter, or with a physician or the patient over the phone.

Although there are many possible "incidental disclosures," pharmacies would be well served to take serious steps to minimize the chance of incidental disclosures rather than relying on this narrow exception to avoid either compliance efforts or liability.

Business Associates

The definition of a covered entity in the HIPAA statute is not broad enough to include every entity in our complex healthcare system that has access to PHI. Pharmacies regularly provide PHI to businesses such as software vendors who are not covered entities under HIPAA. To close this loophole, DHHS created the concept of a "business associate" of the covered entity. A business associate is defined as an entity (other than an employee of the pharmacy) that performs a function on behalf of the pharmacy (other than pharmacies in an organized healthcare arrangement) involving the use or disclosure of PHI. The activities on behalf of the pharmacy include claims processing or administration, data analysis, processing or administration, utilization review, quality assurance, billing, benefit management, practice management, and repricing. Other healthcare providers involved with the treatment of the patient are not business associates of the pharmacy.

Because DHHS is empowered to regulate only covered entities, DHHS mandated that covered entities enter into business associate contracts with noncovered businesses with which they share PHI. These contracts must provide the covered entity with "satisfactory assurances" that the business associate will not use or disclose PHI in a manner that would be impermissible for the covered entity. The contract must also require the business associate to get the same assurances from any companies (e.g., subcontractors) that they share PHI with to perform functions on behalf of the pharmacy. Pharmacies need not have business associate agreements with businesses that might inadvertently come in contact with PHI, such as a janitorial service. The law required that these contracts be in place by April 14, 2004. The first contract with a new business associate requires a business associate contract.

Pharmacies, as covered entities, must enforce these agreements by requiring the business associate to comply with the terms of the contract. If the pharmacy learns that the contract has been violated, then the pharmacy is required to encourage compliance and may be required to terminate the contract.

Business associates must aid the pharmacy in complying with HIPAA. Therefore, the contract must require the business associate to make PHI available for amendments and incorporate amendments agreed to by the pharmacy, make PHI available to allow the pharmacy to create an audit trail of disclosures when the patient requests an accounting of disclosures, and make its policies and records relating to PHI available when requested to allow DHHS to determine compliance with privacy requirements.

When the contract between the covered entity and the business associate concludes, the business associate must either destroy or return PHI to the pharmacy and not keep copies. If neither returning nor destroying the PHI is viable, the terms of the contract protecting the information must be extended until return or destruction of the PHI is feasible.

The privacy rule contains a suggested business associate contract, but using its exact language is not required.

COMPLYING WITH HIPAA
IN PHARMACY TRANSACTIONS

Deceased Individuals and Personal Representatives

Pharmacies must continue to comply with HIPAA regarding the PHI of deceased individuals. Thus, such PHI should be released only to the legally designated personal representative of the deceased patient, usually the executor or administrator of the patient's estate.

Personal representatives may also be designated for minor children or incompetent patients. These representatives possess the exact same rights under HIPAA as the patient themselves, and the pharmacy is required to treat them in all respects as standing in the place of the patient.

A pharmacy may elect not to treat someone as the personal representative of the patient if the pharmacy has reason to believe the patient is being subjected to domestic violence, abuse, or neglect by the person or if the pharmacy believes that treating the person as the personal representative will endanger the patient or that it is not in the best interests of the patient to treat the person as the patient's personal representative.

Friends and Family Picking Up Prescriptions

HIPAA permits the pharmacist to release filled prescriptions to the patient's family members, other relatives, or close personal friends. Under the privacy rule, the pharmacist is required to use his or her professional judgment in deciding if someone other than the patient is authorized by the patient to pick up a prescription. The law requires that the pharmacist be able to reasonably infer that the patient would not object to the person obtaining the prescription. HIPAA does not require that the names be submitted to the pharmacy in advance.

Although not legally mandated under HIPAA, when releasing the prescription to anyone other than the patient, it may be advisable for the pharmacist to document why he or she decided to allow the prescription to be released to a friend or family member (e.g., stating in the profile "the patient's husband picked up the prescription").

The same general rule applies to the pharmacist leaving messages with family members. The pharmacist "should use professional judgment to assure that such disclosures are in the best interest of the individual and limit the information disclosed."

Sale of the Pharmacy

HIPAA permits a pharmacy owner to sell the pharmacy to another entity that will perform pharmacy services, and permits the prospective purchaser to perform due diligence prior to the sale. Without this clarification the sale of a pharmacy would be virtually impossible because arguably every patient would be required to agree to allow their records to be transferred to the purchaser. However, state law may make this a requirement. Again, it is critical that both HIPAA and state law be determined in situations related to PHI and patient privacy.

CONSEQUENCES OF NONCOMPLIANCE

Right to File a Complaint

Any individual, not only a patient, who believes that a pharmacy is not complying with the HIPAA privacy requirements is entitled to file a complaint with the secretary of DHHS. These complaints must be filed in writing (either paper or electronically) and must name the pharmacy or pharmacist and detail the things that the pharmacy is allegedly doing improperly. The complaint must be filed within 180 days of when the person filing the complaint knew or should have known of the improper activity, unless this time limit is waived by DHHS "for good cause shown." There is no time limit for when DHHS has to begin or conclude any investigation. Pharmacies must cooperate with complaint investigations.

The rule requires DHHS to notify the covered entity in writing and to attempt to resolve the issue informally when possible. DHHS must also inform the pharmacy when they investigate the complaint and find no violation. DHHS will designate a place to file the complaints and may investigate them but is not required to do so.

Pharmacies cannot retaliate, refuse treatment, or otherwise attempt to dissuade individuals from filing complaints.

In addition to investigating complaints that are filed, the rule empowers the Office of Civil Rights of DHHS to periodically and randomly perform compliance reviews to ascertain if the pharmacy is operating within the bounds of HIPAA. However, DHHS has indicated that, at least initially, investigations will be complaint driven. Even so, DHHS has stated that they must "maintain the flexibility to conduct whatever reviews are necessary to ensure compliance with the rules."

Penalties and Enforcement

Pharmacies must require that employees protect patient privacy, require employees to follow company privacy policies, and sanction employees who inappropriately use, disclose, or access PHI. Such sanctions should include the possibility of discharge. However, pharmacies cannot punish whistleblowers who disclose PHI for whistle-blowing purposes.

Pharmacies must document the sanctions leveled against employees who violate the privacy policies. In addition, when the pharmacy learns of a violation, steps must be taken to keep the damage as slight as possible.

As previously stated, pharmacies must also enforce their business associate agreements and sanction noncompliant entities that inappropriately use or disclose the pharmacy's PHI.

DHHS designated the Office of Civil Rights (OCR) to enforce HIPAA privacy violations. HIPAA's privacy rule contains a broad array of criminal, civil, and administrative penalties. Sanctions run the gamut from routine violations carrying a penalty of a fine up to $100 for each violation up to $25,000 per calendar year to the most severe being up to 10 years in jail and $250,000 fine levied for using or disclosing PHI for "personal gain, commercial advantage or malicious harm."

The Centers for Medicare and Medicaid Services (CMS) enforces the portions of HIPAA that relate to transactions and code sets, security, and identifier rules. The agency has promulgated a HIPAA enforcement rule to specify how these rules will be enforced.

DHHS has indicated that they are more interested in compliance with the law than in sanctioning violators. Therefore, indications are that pharmacies not yet in full compliance but attempting to comply will be allowed to create a compliance plan rather than face penalties. DHHS stated in a briefing paper that

CMS will assemble an enforcement staff, write an enforcement regulation that outlines the enforcement program, implement the enforcement system and begin to accept complaints. . . . CMS intends to provide education and technical assistance to covered entities to help them achieve compliance, rather than seeking out noncompliant entities and imposing fines on them. If a covered entity is found to be noncompliant, CMS will work with them to achieve compliance and will only impose civil monetary penalties if these efforts fail.

There is no private right of action specified in HIPAA, meaning that individuals are not specifically authorized to bring civil actions against pharmacies that violate privacy rights, nor is enforcement by the state authorities expected. However, individuals, groups, or state governmental authorities may nonetheless attempt legal actions in state or federal courts based on privacy rights granted under HIPAA and/or state law.

BIBLIOGRAPHY

HHS Web site: spe.hhs.gov/admnsimp/Index.htm.
NACDS Web site: www.nacds.org.
WEDI Web site: www.wedi.org.
WEDI/SNIP Web site: www.wedi.org/snip/snip_hipaa.htm.

Chapter 17

Medicare and Medicaid

Susan C. Winckler

Through the Medicare and Medicaid programs, state and federal governments pay for nearly 33 percent of the nation's health expenditures.[1] Established through the Social Security Act, Medicare and Medicaid programs have a substantial impact on healthcare, including pharmacy practice. Beyond the direct effect on their beneficiaries and participating providers, third-party payors often follow Medicare coverage guidelines.

Whether a service is paid by Medicare or Medicaid is important in determining what happens in pharmacy practice. If payment for a service is denied or limited, adoption and expansion of that service are often limited, as such expansion relies on an individual patient's willingness to pay for such services. In addition, violating Medicare or Medicaid policy can result in significant sanctions, as well as exclusion from program participation.[2] This chapter will discuss the Medicare and Medicaid programs.

MEDICARE

Medicare is a health insurance program for individuals aged sixty-five years and older, some individuals with disabilities under age sixty-five, and individuals with end-stage renal disease (those with permanent kidney failure requiring dialysis or a transplant).[3] Established in 1966 for the elderly, coverage was expanded to the disabled in 1973. In 1999, more than 39 million individuals were enrolled in Medicare, including nearly 34 million beneficiaries over sixty-five years old and 5 million disabled.[4] Expenditures for Medicare in the year 2000, including costs for administration, healthcare fraud and abuse control, and quality improvement organizations, exceeded $219 billion.[5]

The Medicare program consists of two parts: Part A—Hospital Insurance and Part B—Medical Insurance.[6] Medicare Part A pays partial costs of

Pharmacy Law Desk Reference
© 2007 by The Haworth Press, Inc. All rights reserved.
doi:10.1300/5790_17

inpatient hospital services, skilled nursing facility services, hospice care, and some home health services. Most Medicare-eligible beneficiaries do not have to pay direct premiums to participate in Part A coverage, because they or their spouse paid Medicare taxes while they were working and thus contributed to the program. Enrollment in Part A is automatic upon turning age sixty-five, and nearly all Medicare beneficiaries participate in Part A. Medicare Part B helps pay for medically necessary physician visits, outpatient hospital services, physical and occupational therapists, some home health services, and a limited number of medical devices and prescription medications. Participation in Medicare Part B requires paying a monthly premium. Beneficiaries are strongly encouraged to participate in Part B as soon as they become eligible for benefits and may pay higher premiums if they wait to participate.

Medicare Part C is a combination of traditional Medicare Part A and Part B, operated in a managed-care approach. In 2006, Medicare Part C plans (known as Medicare Advantage programs) began offering coverage for prescription drugs. Prescription drug coverage must meet certain parameters outlined in the Medicare Prescription Drug, Improvement, and Modernization Act of 2003, including the scope of products covered, beneficiary cost-sharing, and access to pharmacies.

Beginning in 2006, Medicare Part D will become available to help pay for certain prescription drug expenditures and medication therapy management services. Participation in Medicare Part D will require most beneficiaries to pay a monthly premium (estimated at $35 per month in 2006). Low-income beneficiaries will pay a lower premium, if any, and will have a lower deductible and cost-sharing. Similar to the incentives for Part B participation, beneficiaries will be strongly encouraged to participate in Part D as soon as they become eligible for benefits, and may pay higher premiums if they wait to participate. If the beneficiaries receive sufficient prescription drug coverage from an employer or former employer, however, they will not pay a penalty to join Medicare Part D if that employer-sponsored coverage is eliminated and they then choose to join Part D.

Medicare and Pharmacists' Services

Medicare's impact on pharmacy practice is more significant for the products and services it fails to cover than for those that it does. For example, a common lament of pharmacists is that they are not recognized as "providers" under the Social Security Act.[7] As such, the Centers for Medicare and Medicaid Services (CMS), the administrative agency for the Medicare program, is not required to pay for pharmacist services, including pharmaceutical care.

This prohibition is not universal, however, as individual Medicare contractors may have the authority to pay for certain services in the absence of statutory or regulatory mandate. CMS makes national coverage determinations outlining whether Medicare will cover, or not cover, specific services, procedures, or technologies on a national basis. If a specific service is not mentioned in a national coverage determination, the Medicare contractor may determine whether to pay for the service.[8]

Although the lack of Medicare coverage does not prohibit other payors (including patients themselves) from paying for this service, some use the excuse of a lack of Medicare payment as an excuse for refusing payment. Many perceive lack of payment for pharmacist services in Medicare as a substantial barrier to changing pharmacy practice.

Medicare and Paying for Pharmaceuticals

With few exceptions and until the implementation of the new Medicare Part D in 2006, the Medicare program does not pay for medications used in the outpatient setting.[9] In 1995, approximately 35 percent of community-dwelling Medicare beneficiaries lacked outpatient prescription coverage.[10] Of the 65 percent with some form of prescription drug coverage, concern exists about the adequacy of their coverage.

The primary exception is a limited outpatient prescription drug benefit under Medicare Part B, covering 80 percent of Medicare's authorized payment after the beneficiary has met the deductible, currently $100. (Medicare does not pay the usual and customary charges for these products, but establishes a national formula to determine such payment.) The only outpatient prescription drugs covered under this limited benefit are

1. immunosuppressive drugs following discharge for a Medicare-covered organ transplant;
2. erythropoetin for the treatment of anemia for persons with chronic renal failure who are on dialysis;
3. oral anticancer agents used in chemotherapy if they have the same ingredients and are used for the same indications as those covered as non-self-administered drugs;
4. hemophilia clotting factors for hemophilia patients who are able to use such factors to control bleeding without medical supervision;
5. injectable osteoporosis drugs approved for treatment of postmenopausal osteoporosis, when the beneficiary is homebound and unable

to self-administer the drug. In addition, the attending physician must have certified the individual suffers from a bone fracture related to postmenopausal osteoporosis;

6. supplies (which include drugs) necessary for the effective use of covered durable medical equipment;
7. Hepatitis B vaccine for those beneficiaries at high or intermediate risk of contracting hepatitis B; and
8. diabetes testing supplies.[11]

Medicare also fully covers (with no cost sharing) a pneumococcal pneumonia vaccine when ordered by a physician and an influenza vaccine upon request (with or without a physician order).[12]

Medicare also pays for a few medications as a component of broader services, such as those associated with hospice care.[13] In hospice care, medications are included in the costs that must be covered by the per diem fee. This fee, however, is often insufficient to cover the medication costs and the costs of other services. In one example, sufficient morphine to stabilize a patient's pain at the end of life would cost more than $300 per day, using substantial amounts—if not all—of a per diem payment.[14] This conflict creates substantial problems in determining and providing appropriate services under the hospice benefit.

In inpatient care, Medicare covers medication costs as a component of diagnosis-related payment for the patient's full hospital stay.[15] Medicare pays most hospitals for their inpatient services at a predetermined rate for each discharge under a prospective payment system (PPS). PPS is not calculated on the actual costs of treatment, but rather is an adjusted average payment rate. In this program, some cases will yield payment in excess of costs and other cases yield payment in a lower amount than costs. By paying an average rate, hospitals are incentivized to increase efficiency and to treat a mix of patients to balance cost and payments. In the medication arena, then, medication treatment costs are covered in the same payment cap with physician and nursing services, general hospital operations, and so forth. Because medication costs are carefully monitored and targeted within the hospital costs, many pharmacists in health-system facilities have significant responsibilities to manage costs and optimize medication use.

Medicare beneficiaries also obtain prescription drug coverage through some Medicare+Choice plans. (The Medicare Prescription Drug, Improvement, and Modernization Act of 2003 changed the names of the programs to "MedicareAdvantage.") Prescription drug coverage in many of these programs is limited, and often beneficiaries find that the availability of alternative sources for prescription drug coverage is declining. With federal payments to many Medicare+Choice plans decreasing and the increasing share of the healthcare dollar allocated to drug therapy, plans may react by cutting the prescription drug benefit. Even those who currently have prescription drug coverage through HMOs often lack coverage for extreme drug expenditures. Ninety percent of beneficiaries who have drug coverage through Medicare+Choice plans have benefit limits on their prescription drug benefit such as caps on the dollar benefit amount or limits on number of prescription orders.[16]

Another source of Medicare coverage for prescription drugs is through privately purchased Medigap coverage. (Medigap plans are insurance plans available to Medicare beneficiaries to supplement the Medicare program.) Only three of the standardized plans—Plans H, I, and J—offer prescription drug coverage. All three plans have limits on the benefit, leaving seniors at risk for extreme drug expenditures. Premiums for these three plans are generally higher than the other Medigap plans, often making them unaffordable for seniors. Comparing Plan I (which has drug coverage) with Plan C (does not include drug coverage) in several metropolitan areas, premiums for Plan I can be more than double the premiums of the plan without drug coverage. Some observers claim that this higher premium for plans with drug coverage is due to adverse selection into plans with prescription drug benefits. In other words, seniors with high drug spending are more likely to choose a Medigap plan with drug coverage than a senior without such expenses or risk of such expenses.

Adequate prescription drug coverage is an important issue to the elderly because the aged account for a large portion of drug expenditures. The situation is not new. In 1987, the elderly were 12 percent of the population, yet they accounted for 34 percent of total pharmaceutical expenditures.[17] The same study noted that those with chronic illnesses have higher drug expenditures. For persons over age sixty-five, 37 percent of the elderly with three or more chronic illnesses accounted for 57 percent of drug expenditures.[18] These dynamics contributed to an extended discussion of how and when to add coverage for outpatient prescription drugs to the Medicare program.

In 2003, the United States Congress took a major step in that debate with the passage of the Medicare Prescription Drug, Improvement, and Modernization Act (MMA). The act established a voluntary benefit for prescription drug expenditures, beginning in 2006. Intended to be administered through private plan sponsors and the managed-care plans involved in Medicare Part C (MedicareAdvantage), beneficiaries are expected to have the choice of at least two different drug coverage plans. Because of funding limitations, however, the new benefit includes limits—the most noticeable being an average gap in coverage for annual prescription drug expenditures between $2,250 and $5,100. (The benefit will be delivered through private plan sponsors, so actual coverage gaps and other plan parameters may vary if the variation yields a benefit actuarially equivalent to the congressionally mandated parameters.) Most low-income beneficiaries will not face this gap in coverage.

Beyond payment for drug products, pharmacists are eligible for payment from Medicare for a few discrete services if quality parameters are met. In the states where pharmacists are authorized to administer medications, Medicare pays pharmacists for administering immunizations in addition to supplying the product.[19] When operating a program that meets certain parameters, a pharmacy may secure payment for providing diabetes self-management education services. The pharmacy (and any other provider seeking payment for these services) must meet the accreditation requirements of the American Diabetes Association. In addition, pharmacists may secure payment for services provided "incident to" a physician's services, although this payment option is limited.

In 2006, pharmacists will be eligible for payment for medication therapy management services for targeted beneficiaries under the new Part D benefit or the expanded drug coverage provided under Part C. Under the MMA, targeted beneficiaries include those with multiple chronic conditions who are using multiple medications and expected to incur prescription drug expenses of a designated amount. Considered a quality improvement measure essential for the new drug coverage, pharmacists are the only healthcare professionals designated as potential medication therapy management providers in the statute and in the proposed regulation (released in August 2004), although other healthcare professionals are not precluded from providing such services. The exact parameters of medication therapy management services are not, however, defined in the statute or in the proposed regulation. Rather, that definition is largely delegated to the private plans expected to offer the prescription drug programs. To facilitate plans' understanding of medication therapy management services, the American Pharmacists Association convened a process that yielded a consensus definition from eleven national pharmacist and pharmacy organizations.

The detail of Medicare-compensated medication therapy management services programs is expected to evolve with publication of final regulations in 2005 and the implementation of the benefit in 2006.

MEDICAID

Created in 1965, the Medicaid program is a state-federal partnership established to provide healthcare services to the indigent and disabled.[20] Medicaid is intended to help provide adequate medical care and health-related services to individuals and families with low incomes. In fiscal year

1998, 41.4 million people were enrolled in the Medicaid program and 40.6 million beneficiaries accessed services, including nearly 19 million children and 3.9 million elderly.[21] Enrollment in Medicaid is expected to grow by less than 5 percent in the next ten years, and children are expected to continue to represent the largest eligibility group of beneficiaries. Expenditures for Medicaid in 2000, excluding administrative costs, were $194.7 billion ($111.1 billion in federal and $83.6 billion in state funds).[22]

In contrast to Medicare, much of the control and design of Medicaid programs is determined by the individual states, territories, and the District of Columbia. Who is eligible for the program, the services provided, and the reimbursement for those services can vary from state to state as well as from year to year.

Congress establishes broad national guidelines for Medicaid programs, and states must comply with these requirements to secure federal funding. The guidelines include, for example, certain eligibility requirements— describing individuals who must receive Medicaid coverage, such as children whose family income is at or below 133 percent of the federal poverty level.[23] In 2001, the federal poverty level was monthly income of $759 or less for an individual, or $1,015 or less for a couple, or annual income of less than $9,108 for individuals, and $12,180 for a couple.

CMS provides federal administrative oversight and guidance for state programs, and administers the federal matching funds (or federal financial participation). The federal match varies with each state, determined by a formula comparing the state average per capita income with national income. The rate must be at least 50 percent but less than 83 percent.[24] For example, the federal match for Medicaid expenditures in New York State is 50 percent, while Mississippi's match is 77 percent.[25]

When defining Medicaid benefits, the federal government requires state coverage of some basic services such as inpatient hospital services, vaccines for children, and physician services. Of importance to pharmacists, coverage of outpatient medications is an *optional* service, although Medicaid programs in the fifty states and the District of Columbia include some coverage of these products.[26] The majority of these programs pay for medications in a traditional fee-for-service model, with compensation based on an estimate of product cost and a dispensing fee,[27] intended to pay for the dispensed medication, prospective drug utilization review, and an offer to counsel the beneficiary about their medication use.[28]

Even though payment for prescription drugs is an optional service, prescription drug coverage is one of the most popular Medicaid benefits: in fiscal year 1998, more than 19.3 million beneficiaries accessed this benefit, exceeding physician services as the most utilized Medicaid benefit. Although frequently used, expenditures for prescription drugs are not the highest component of Medicaid budgets. Prescription drug spending in 1998 in these programs was $11.7 billion, with expenditures for nursing homes and intermediate care facilities much higher, at more than $44 billion.

Although the federal government contributes substantially to program operations, Medicaid spending is a substantial portion of state budgets, often comprising more than 14 percent of total state general funds.[29] As states grapple with decreasing incomes and increasing Medicaid requirements, legislators face increasing pressure to limit Medicaid expenditures. As one of the highest components of Medicaid budgets, prescription drug expenditures become a target, and payments to pharmacies part of that target. In some situations, Medicaid programs have suggested such drastic cuts in Medicaid reimbursements to pharmacies that pharmacy operators have elected not to participate in these programs.

For a community pharmacy, such a decision can be substantial. Depending on the patient population of a specific pharmacy, Medicaid may comprise a significant part, perhaps even a majority, of their patient population. And decisions to turn away vulnerable populations such as Medicaid beneficiaries can result in substantial negative publicity: in Massachusetts in the year 2000, pharmacy decisions to limit Medicaid participation were met with substantial backlash from the media and the public.

Similar to Medicare, Medicaid payment policy can affect the purchase and subsequent use of pharmaceuticals. The use of traditional managed care formularies is prohibited in Medicaid, but pharmaceutical manufacturers must rebate back to the states the difference between the price paid to the pharmacy and the manufacturer's best price charged to other purchasers. States may, however, establish prior authorization programs or preferred drug lists to promote the use of some products over others.[30] Medicaid policy impacts pharmacists when they must implement such programs, often navigating various payment requirements without any additional compensation.

Some states have attempted to expand access to the lower drug prices negotiated by Medicaid to non-Medicaid beneficiaries. The Maine program, known as Maine Rx, attempts to negotiate lower drug prices from drug manufacturers for the state, which would then offer the savings to the uninsured. The state estimates it would help more than 300,000 people who do not have prescription drug coverage. In January 2003, the United States Supreme Court heard oral argument about the legality of such a program in Maine. In *Pharmaceutical Research and Manufacturers of America v. Concannon,* 01-188, the issue is whether the Constitution and the federal Medicaid law allow such state governments to use the Medicaid program to leverage discounts for populations beyond the defined Medicaid population. The Pharmaceutical Research and Manufacturers of America contends the state program violates Medicaid law and is an unconstitutional regulation of interstate commerce. Twenty-eight states are supporting the Maine program, and about a dozen are poised to pass similar laws quickly if the Supreme Court sides with the state.

In a few states, Medicaid programs have been expanded to include payment for more advanced services by pharmacists. In Mississippi, specially trained pharmacists are eligible for disease-state management payments for patients with dyslipidemia, asthma, diabetes, and those using anticoagulant therapy.[31] In practice, however, few pharmacists have obtained the necessary disease-state certification to secure payment.

In Wisconsin, pharmacists may secure additional payment for specific services, including, for example, intervening on late prescription renewals to improve patient compliance or recommending lower cost drugs.[32] In Iowa, certain pharmacists and collaborating physicians are eligible for case management services when provided to designated at-risk patients.[33]

The Missouri Medicaid program added payment for pharmacists and physicians for disease management services in early 2003.[34] High-risk patients are asked to enroll in the program, with payment to participating providers at fixed rates for assessments and follow-up interventions. Participating providers must complete specific training about the program and the targeted disease states of asthma, depression, diabetes, and heart failure.

In Washington State, payment for pharmacist-provided services is limited to counseling associated with assessing patient appropriateness for emergency contraceptive therapy.[35] Pharmacists authorized to prescribe such therapy under a collaborative practice agreement with a physician or other prescriber may secure payment for the consultation whether the therapy is prescribed and dispensed or not.

CMS has outlined the parameters for approving Medicaid plans to pay for additional pharmacist services.[36] CMS will reimburse states for what they call "cognitive" or "disease management" services under the "Other Licensed Practitioners" category of the federal regulations, but will not pay for those services as an add-on to the dispensing fee.[37] To secure CMS payment, the state must amend its Medicaid plan and describe, among other things, the practitioners providing the service, the specific services to be provided, relevant state law authorizing the provision of such services, any training or certification requirements, the unit of service (e.g., 15 minutes) and average length of the service envisioned, and procedures for communicating with the patient's primary care provider to ensure coordination of care.[38]

IMPACT OF MEDICARE AND MEDICAID PAYOR POLICY

When state and federal governments choose to pay for pharmaceuticals and pharmacist services under Medicare or Medicaid, pharmacists face another challenge: meeting the payors' requirements. A now common component of healthcare are the standards set for third-party payment, such as mandatory second opinions for nonemergency surgery. In pharmacy, such policies include limitations in covered services or in the frequency of providing such services, and the impact can be substantial. From restricted networks which limit pharmacist participation in patient care to limits on payable services, payor policy shapes pharmacist activity.

Occasionally, the payor policy of Medicare or Medicaid can influence the medication prescribed and dispensed. For example, patients requiring medication for respiratory disorders have a choice: albuterol delivered through a metered-dose inhaler is not covered by Medicare, but the same medication delivered through a nebulizer is payable. To qualify for the nebulizer product, prescribers are required to determine why inhaler-delivered medication is not appropriate. But in a review of claims for one Medicare region in 2001, nearly 300 claims had insufficient documentation in the suppliers' or physicians' records to determine whether the prescriber considered the use of a metered-dose inhaler.[39] Whether the payor rules were followed is unclear, but most would assume that the availability of Medicare payment was a factor in the decision.

If a patient is unable to afford the medication (or convinces the prescriber they would rather not make such payment when an alternative is available), the nebulizer treatment will likely be prescribed—even if the MDI delivery would be therapeutically preferable. If the choice is between a substandard delivery mode or no medication, the choice is easy. Similarly, in Medicaid, implementation of prior authorization programs are intended to guide providers to use lower-cost medications as a first line of treatment before more expensive options. Implementation of such programs often resides substantially with pharmacists, as prescribers rarely track the various requirements of Medicaid and other third-party payors.

Revision of the Medicare system to add coverage for outpatient medications is a popular topic among policymakers and will be essential for improving the delivery of pharmaceutical care to the nation's seniors. A poorly designed program, however, such as the existing limited system, could pose additional problems. Payor policy does guide care delivery, and the impact of such decisions must be considered in the design of new programs.

In considering payment for pharmacists' services, the limited, but expanding, payment from Medicare and Medicaid is often perceived as a barrier to further expansion of these services. Such limitations are problematic for beneficiaries who could benefit from pharmacists' medication therapy management services, and also create barriers for pharmacists. Many private payors use the lack of public payment for such services as a justification for not covering these services within their own programs. Importantly, however, payor policy (even when the payor is a government program such as Medicare or Medicaid) does not prohibit legal pharmacist activity—it merely limits the availability of third-party payment. Payment denial can limit services, when affected patients are unable to pay for the services themselves.

Some payor policies, particularly those of Medicare, prohibit charging for services that are not covered under the program, requiring the provider to forgo providing such services or to provide them at no cost. With enactment of the Benefits Improvement and Protection Act of 2000 (effective February 1, 2001), for example, all drugs and biologicals covered under Medicare Part B must be submitted on an assigned basis regardless of the physician's provider agreement with Medicare.

CONCLUSION

Understanding the Medicare and Medicaid programs is important to navigating pharmacy practice in any environment. Whether affecting the medications prescribed and dispensed or the services provided by pharmacists, payor policy is important.

NOTES

1. The Nation's Health Care Dollar, CY 2000. CMS, Office of the Actuary, National Health Statistics Group, June 2002.

2. 42 USC 1395cc.

3. *Id.*

4. Medicare Enrollment: National Trends 1966-1999, available at http://cms .hhs.gov/statistics/enrollment/natltrends/hi_smi.asp. Accessed November 1, 2002.

5. Program Expenditures/Trends, Table 26, 2002 CMS Statistics, CMS Office of Financial Management, U.S. Department of Health and Human Services.

6. 42 USC 1395d for Part A, 42 USC 1395j for Part B.

7. "Coalition to Secure Pharmacist Provider Status—Patients to Benefit from Pharmacist Services Under Medicare," Press Release of the American College of Clinical Pharmacy, March 6, 2001.

8. National Coverage Analyses, available at http://www.cms.gov/ncdr.

9. Title XVIII, Medicare Part B.

10. Davis M. et al. Prescription Drug Coverage, Utilization, and Spending Among Medicare Beneficiaries. *Health Affairs* 1999;18(1):231-243.

11. Definitions of Services, Institutions, Etc. for the Medicare Program, 42 USCA § 1395x.

12. How to Bill for Influenza and Pneumococcal Vaccinations. Centers for Medicare and Medicaid Services, available at http://www.cms.hhs.gov/quality/3g8.htm.

13. Section 1861(dd) of the Social Security Act.

14. Testimony of the American Pharmaceutical Association to the Senate Health, Education, Labor and Pensions Committee, hearing "Regarding Pain Management and End-of-Life Care," October 13, 1999.

15. Medicare Hospital Inpatient Prospective Payment System, Centers for Medicare and Medicaid Services, available at http://cms.hhs.gov/providers/hipps/default.asp.

16. O'Sullivan J. Medicare: Prescription Drug Coverage for Beneficiaries. Congressional Research Service, April 19, 1999.

17. Mueller C., Shur C., and O'Connell J. Prescription Drug Spending: The Impact of Age and Chronic Disease Status. *American Journal of Public Health* 1997; 87(10): 1626-1629.

18. *Id.*

19. How to Bill for Influenza and Pneumococcal Vaccinations. Centers for Medicare and Medicaid Services, available at http://www.cms.hhs.gov/quality/3g8.htm.

20. "For the purpose of enabling each State...to furnish (1) medical assistance on behalf of families with dependent children and of aged, blind, or disabled individuals, whose income and resources are insufficient to meet the costs of necessary medical services. . . ," 42 U.S.C. 1396 (2001).

21. A Profile of Medicaid. Medicaid Chartbook 2000 from Centers for Medicare and Medicaid Services, p. 12.

22. Medicaid: A Brief Summary, p. 12, available at http://cms.hhs.gov/publications/overview-medicare-medicaid/default4.asp. accessed November 2002.

23. Medicaid: A Brief Summary, available at http://cms.hhs.gov/publications/overview-medicare-medicaid/default4.asp. accessed November 2002.

24. A Profile of Medicaid, Medicaid Chartbook 2000 from Centers for Medicare and Medicaid Services, p. 27.

25. State Medicaid Manual, Part 2—State Organization and General Administration, 2501. Federal Medical Assistance Percentages (FMAP)—State-By-State Tables.

26. National Pharmaceutical Council. *Pharmaceutical Benefits under State Medical Assistance Programs*, Section 4: Medicaid and Pharmacy Program Characteristics, December 1998, pp. 4-17.

27. *Id.* at 4-43.

28. *Id.* at 4-32.

29. A Profile of Medicaid. Medicaid Chartbook 2000 from Centers for Medicare and Medicaid Services, p. 27.

30. 42 U.S.C. 1396r-8(d).

31. Carlson B. Others Await Promise of Mississippi's Experiment With Pharmaceutical Care, *Managed Care* 1999; 8(3), available at www.managedcaremag.com/archives/9903/9903.states.shtml.

32. Hogue M. and Whitmore S., The History of the Wisconsin Medicaid Pharmaceutical Care Project: Part II, *Wisconsin Pharmacist,* March/April 1997.

33. Iowa Medicaid Pharmaceutical Case Management Initiative, available at http://www.iarx.org.

34. Correspondence from George Oestreich and Robert Berringer, DMS Pharmacy Program, November 5, 2002.

35. Medicaid Reimbursement for Emergency Contraceptive Pills and Services, available at http://www.pharmcare.org/resources/5-6-2.asp.

36. Correspondence from Eugene A. Gasser, Division of Medicaid and State Operations with the Centers for Medicare and Medicaid Services, to Bob Sharpe, Deputy Secretary for Florida Medicaid, October 12, 2001.

37. *Id.,* paragraph 3, 4.

38. *Id.,* paragraph 5.

39. *Review of Payments for Inhalation Drugs Made by Region C Durable Medical Equipment Regional Carrier.* Department of Health and Human Services Office of Inspector General, Report A-06-00-00053, October 2001.

Chapter 18

Certification in Pharmacy: Advanced-Level Credentials, Including Specialty Certification

Richard J. Bertin

INTRODUCTION

Pharmacy, like most professions serving a societal need, has evolved a series of credentials for its practitioners. Some of these credentials are regulatory, administered by governmental agencies specifically to protect the public. Others, usually at a higher level than the regulatory baseline, are voluntary in nature and indicate that the holder has demonstrated an advanced level of knowledge and skill.

Pharmacist credentialing has become a topic of important discussions in the profession of pharmacy in recent years. These discussions, inherently complex, have sometimes been further complicated by the lack of a common lexicon. Many different words are used to describe the process by which pharmacists are educated, trained, licensed, and otherwise recognized for their competence and achievements. Many different organizations—public and private—are involved in assessing pharmacists' knowledge and skills, granting credentials, and accrediting programs and institutions. This chapter will focus on certification, after providing an overview of the credentialing context in which it exists.

Compared with many other professions, pharmacy has entered the arena of advanced-level credentialing only recently. The medical profession has been recognizing specialty practice for at least 100 years. Medicine's evolution to its current highly credentialed state provides an interesting study in the professional, economic, and political forces that influence such a transformation.[1] Several other health professions, including nursing, optometry, and dentistry, also have a long history of advanced-level credentialing of qualified members. The most likely explanation for pharmacy's delay in developing such credentials is that pharmacy has been a rather undifferenti-

Pharmacy Law Desk Reference
© 2007 by The Haworth Press, Inc. All rights reserved.
doi:10.1300/5790_18

ated profession for most of its history. The vast majority of pharmacists simply dispensed and/or compounded prescription orders written by a physician and had little clinical or other opportunity to demonstrate abilities beyond those assessed by the written and practical licensure examinations administered by state boards of pharmacy.

This situation began to change in the 1970s, when leaders in the profession began to acknowledge the emergence of specialized practices of its members and the need for consistent standards and the assessment of knowledge and skills of pharmacists in those practices. In 1971, the American Pharmaceutical Association (now American Pharmacists Association) convened a Task Force on Specialties in Pharmacy, which sought extensive input on the subject from within and outside the profession.[2] The ultimate outcome of this discussion was the establishment of the Board of Pharmaceutical Specialties (BPS) in 1976, and the recognition of the first specialty in pharmacy: nuclear pharmacy. Since that significant event, several other specialties have been recognized by BPS and other postlicensure credentials launched. These will be discussed in more detail later in this chapter.

COUNCIL ON CREDENTIALING IN PHARMACY

The Council on Credentialing in Pharmacy (CCP) is a coalition of thirteen national pharmacy organizations founded in 1999 to provide leadership, standards, public information, and coordination for professional voluntary credentialing programs in pharmacy. Members of the CCP include the following organizations:

Academy of Managed Care Pharmacy
Accreditation Council for Pharmacy Education (formerly the American Council on Pharmaceutical Education)
American Association of Colleges of Pharmacy
American College of Apothecaries
American College of Clinical Pharmacy
American Pharmacists Association (formerly the American Pharmaceutical Association)
American Society of Consultant Pharmacists
American Society of Health-System Pharmacists
National Association of Boards of Pharmacy
Board of Pharmaceutical Specialties
Commission for Certification in Geriatric Pharmacy
Pharmacy Technician Certification Board
Pharmacy Technician Educators Council

In an attempt to provide clarity and reference for the profession on topics of credentialing, the CCP developed an important reference paper on the topic: the CCP White Paper on Credentialing in Pharmacy. This document has formed the basis of much of the content of this chapter.[3]

SIX ESSENTIAL DEFINITIONS

Discussions of credentialing are often complicated by a lack of common understanding of key terms and the contexts in which they are used. To clarify these misunderstandings, one must first distinguish between processes (e.g., credentialing) and titles (a credential). Distinctions must also be made between processes that focus on individuals (e.g., credentialing and certification) and those that focus on organizations (accreditation). Finally, it is essential to understand that for practicing pharmacists, some credentials are required (e.g., an academic degree or a state license) while others are earned voluntarily (e.g., certification).

Beyond these distinctions, it is also necessary to understand the definitions of the words that commonly come up in discussions of credentialing and to be able to distinguish the sometimes-subtle differences among them. A comprehensive glossary of such words and their definitions appears in Appendix A of this chapter. The following definitions are provided here because an understanding of these terms is a prerequisite to any meaningful discussion of credentialing in pharmacy.

- A *credential* is documented evidence of a pharmacist's qualifications. Pharmacist credentials include diplomas, licenses, certificates, and certifications. These credentials are reflected in a variety of abbreviations that pharmacists place after their names (e.g., PharmD for "doctor of pharmacy," an earned academic degree; RPh for "registered pharmacist," which indicates state licensure; and acronyms such as BCNSP for "board-certified nutrition support pharmacist," which indicates that an individual has demonstrated advanced knowledge or skill in a specialized area of pharmacy).
- *Credentialing* is the process by which an organization or institution obtains, verifies, and assesses a pharmacist's qualifications to provide patient care services.
- *Accreditation* is the process by which a private association, organization, or government agency, after initial and periodic evaluations, grants recognition to an organization that has met certain established criteria.

- A *certificate* is a document issued to a pharmacist upon successful completion of the predetermined level of performance of a certificate training program or of a pharmacy residency or fellowship.
- A *statement of continuing education credit* is a document issued to a pharmacist upon participation in an accredited continuing education program.
- *Certification* is a voluntary process by which a nongovernmental agency or an association grants recognition to a pharmacist who has met certain predetermined qualifications specified by that organization. This formal recognition is granted to designate to the public that this pharmacist has attained the requisite level of knowledge, skill, or experience in a well-defined, often specialized, area of the total discipline. Certification usually requires initial assessment and periodic reassessments of the individual's qualifications.

IMPORTANCE OF CREDENTIALS IN PHARMACY

"Credential" and "credentialing," like the words "creed" and "credence," derive from the Latin verb *credere,* which means "to trust," "to entrust," or "to believe." A pharmacist's credentials are indicators that he or she holds the qualifications needed to practice the profession of pharmacy and is therefore worthy of the trust of patients, of other healthcare professionals, and of society as a whole.

In the profession of pharmacy, the interest in credentials has been catalyzed in recent years by several factors. First among them is the pace of change and the increasing complexity of healthcare. A second factor is the pharmacist's expanding clinical role. Interest in credentialing has also been stimulated by the growing trend toward specialization in pharmacy practice and by the need to document the pharmacist's ability to provide specialty care. Another contributing factor has been the need to help ensure lifelong competence in a rapidly changing, technologically complex field. The need to provide a means of standardization of practice has also had a role. Such a motivation was key, for example, to the development of the Federal Credentialing Program, which is creating a national database of health professionals that will include pharmacists.[4]

Finally, economic realities enter the picture. Pharmacists who are providing cognitive services or specialized care need to be reimbursed for the services they provide. Payors rightfully demand validation that pharmacists are qualified to provide such services. Credentials, and in many cases, more specifically, certification, can help provide the indication of quality service that Medicare and Medicaid, managed-care organizations, and other third-party payors require of pharmacists today and in the future.

OVERVIEW OF CREDENTIALING IN PHARMACY

Pharmacist credentials may be divided into three fundamental categories.

- *College and university degrees* are awarded to mark the successful completion of a pharmacist's academic training and education.
- *Licensure* is an indication that the pharmacist has met minimum requirements established by the state in which he or she intends to practice.
- *Postgraduate degrees and certificates* are awarded to pharmacy practitioners who have completed programs of various types (e.g., residencies) that are intended to develop and enhance their knowledge and skills, or to those who have successfully documented a specialized level of knowledge and skill through an assessment process.

These three paths to pharmacist credentialing are illustrated in Figure 18.1. Much of the remainder of this chapter will focus on the optional practice credentials available to pharmacists.

The certification of pharmacy technicians is also covered briefly at the end of this chapter. This topic is receiving increased attention from the pharmacy profession, as technicians assume greater responsibility for dispensing functions. A White Paper on Pharmacy Technicians, endorsed by many of the profession's membership organizations, suggests that standardization of technician education and practice regulation will occur in the future.[4]

ADVANCED PRACTICE CREDENTIALS FOR PHARMACISTS

Developing and Enhancing Knowledge and Skills

Pharmacy practitioners who wish to broaden and deepen their knowledge and skills may participate in a variety of postgraduate education and training opportunities. They include the following.

Academic Postgraduate Education and Training

Pharmacists who wish to pursue a certain field of study in depth may enroll in postgraduate master's or doctor of philosophy (PhD) programs. Com-

Education	Entry into Practice	Practice
Pharmacists		
Doctor of pharmacy (PharmD) degree (ACPE)	Licensure (RPh) (State boards of pharmacy)	License renewal (State boards of pharmacy) State-specific criteria may include mandatory continuing education (ACPE)
		Postgraduate education (optional) Advanced degrees MS, PhD (college/schools of pharmacy) Postgraduate training (optional) Residency (ASHP) Traineeship (ASHP) Fellowship (ACCP, ASHP) Certificate programs (ACPE) Continuing education (ACPE)
		Certification (optional) Specialty (BPS) Nonspecialty (CCGP) Disease management (NISPC) Multidisciplinary (various)
Pharmacy technicians		
Education/training (ASHP/state boards of pharmacy)	Registration/ licensure in some states (Boards of pharmacy)	Certification (PTCB) Generally optional

FIGURE 18.1. U.S. pharmacy credentials and oversight bodies. *Source:* Adapted from Council on Credentialing in Pharmacy's Reference Paper on Pharmacy Credentialing, 2003.

mon fields of study for master's candidates include business administration, clinical pharmacy, and public health. Common fields for PhD studies include pharmacology, pharmaceutics, pharmacy practice, and social and administrative sciences.

BS-level pharmacists who have been in the workforce may also return to a college or school of pharmacy to earn the PharmD degree. These programs, which are tailored to the individual's background and experience, may follow "nontraditional" pathways; however, they must produce the same educational outcomes as traditional PharmD degree programs.

Residencies

- Credential earned: Residency certificate
- Credential awarded by: Residency training program
- Program accreditation: The American Society of Health-System Pharmacists (ASHP) (independently or in collaboration with other pharmacy organizations)

A residency is an organized, directed postgraduate program in a defined area of pharmacy practice. Pharmacy practice residencies focus on the development by the resident of professional competence in the delivery of patient care and practice management activities. Specialized pharmacy practice residencies focus on the knowledge, skills, and abilities needed to provide care in a specialized area of pharmacy practice (e.g., critical care, drug information, pharmacotherapy, or oncology). Residencies are usually twelve months in duration, although certain specialized residencies require an additional twelve (or continuous twenty-four) months for completion.

The American Society of Health-System Pharmacists is the recognized accrediting body for pharmacy practice and specialty residency programs in pharmacy. The ASHP Commission on Credentialing (COC), a committee of the ASHP Board of Directors, is responsible for the development of standards for residency programs, administering the accreditation process, and granting accreditation. The COC consists of fourteen appointed pharmacists who have served as residency program directors and who represent a variety of practice settings, as well as two "public" members. ASHP partners with appropriate organizations, including the Academy of Managed Care Pharmacy (AMCP), the American College of Clinical Pharmacy (ACCP), the American Pharmacists Association (APhA), and the American Society of Consultant Pharmacists (ASCP), in developing standards and/or accrediting residency programs of a specialized or practice-setting-specific nature.

The majority of pharmacists who pursue residency training currently do so by completing a pharmacy practice residency. These residencies are usually based in a particular practice setting or practice type, such as a hospital, ambulatory care clinic, community pharmacy, managed-care organization, or home or long term care practice. Specialized residency training often involves additional education and training experiences beyond the pharmacy practice year, usually in specialized areas of practice such as pharmacokinetics, the care of specific types of patients (e.g., pediatrics), or a focus on specific diseases (e.g., oncology).

The Centers for Medicare and Medicaid Services (CMS), an agency of the federal government, recognizes residency accreditation bodies within the health professions, including ASHP in its role as the accrediting body for pharmacy residency training. Consequently, ASHP-accredited residency programs are eligible for inclusion by a Medicare "provider" (i.e., usually a hospital) in the calculation of (and reimbursement for) the entity's costs for providing services to Medicare beneficiaries. The rules and regulations guiding this reimbursement policy are reviewed regularly by CMS and are subject to change.

Fellowships

- Credential earned: Fellowship certificate
- Credential awarded by: Fellowship training program
- Program accreditation: No official accreditation body

A fellowship is an individualized postgraduate program that prepares the participant to become an independent researcher. Fellowship programs, like residencies, usually last one to two years. The programs are developed by colleges of pharmacy, academic health centers, colleges and universities, and pharmaceutical manufacturers.

There is no official accreditation body for fellowship programs; however, the American Association of Colleges of Pharmacy and American College of Clinical Pharmacy have issued guidelines that are followed by many fellowship program directors.

Several pharmacy organizations, including the American College of Clinical Pharmacy, the American Society of Health-System Pharmacists, and the American Pharmacists Association, award the honorary title of "Fellow" to selected members as a means of publicly recognizing their contributions to the profession. A Fellow of ASHP, for example, may write "FASHP," for "Fellow of the American Society of Health-System Pharmacists," after his or her name. The two uses of the word "fellow"—one denoting an individual participating in a postgraduate training program and the other denoting receipt of an honorary title—should be clearly distinguished.

Certificate Training Programs

- Credential earned: Certificate of completion
- Credential awarded by: Educational institutions and companies, pharmacy organizations, and others
- Provider accreditation: Accreditation Council for Pharmacy Education (ACPE) (formerly the American Council on Pharmaceutical Education)

A certificate training program is a structured and systematic postgraduate continuing education experience for pharmacists that is generally smaller in magnitude and shorter in duration than degree programs. Certificate programs are designed to instill, expand, or enhance practice competencies through the systematic acquisition of specified knowledge, skills, attitudes, and behaviors. The focus of certificate programs is relatively narrow; for example, the American Pharmacists Association offers programs in such areas as asthma, diabetes, immunization delivery, and management of dyslipidemias.

Certificate training programs are offered by national and state pharmacy organizations and by schools and colleges of pharmacy and other educational groups. The programs are often held in conjunction with a major educational meeting of an organization. The Accreditation Council for Pharmacy Education approves providers of such programs.

Traineeships

Traineeships, in contrast to certificate training programs, are defined as intensive, individualized, structured postgraduate programs intended to provide the participant with the knowledge and skills needed to provide a high level of care to patients with various chronic diseases and conditions. Traineeships are generally of longer duration (about five days) and involve smaller groups of trainees than certificate training programs do. Some are offered on a competitive basis, with a corporate sponsor or other organization underwriting participants' costs. Pharmacy organizations currently offering traineeships include the American College of Apothecaries, the American Society of Consultant Pharmacists, and the American Society of Health-System Pharmacists' Research and Education Foundation.

Certification

- Credential earned: Certification in area of practice
- Credential awarded by: Board of Pharmaceutical Specialties; Commission on Certification in Geriatric Pharmacy; National Institute for Standards in Pharmacist Credentialing; other multidisciplinary programs
- Provider accreditation: No official accrediting body for pharmacy. General accreditation is available from the National Commission for Certifying Agencies (NCCA) and the American National Standards Institute (ANSI)

Certification is a credential granted to pharmacists and other health professionals who have demonstrated a level of knowledge and skill in a specific and relatively narrow area of practice that exceeds the minimum requirements for licensure. Certification is granted on the basis of successful completion of rigorously developed eligibility criteria that include a written examination and, in some cases, an experiential component. The certification process is customarily undertaken and overseen by a nongovernmental body.

The development of a certification program includes the following steps:

1. *Role delineation.* This step defines the area in which certification is to be offered. This is done through a process called role delineation or "task analysis." An expert panel of individuals in the proposed subject area develops a survey instrument to assess how practitioners working in the area rate the importance, frequency, and criticality of specific activities in that practice. The instrument is then sent to a sample of pharmacists who are practicing in that field who respond concerning their own practices. The responses are compiled into a formal description of the characteristics and parameters of the practice area.

2. *Development of content outline.* On the basis of responses to the role delineation survey, a content outline for the certification program is developed.

3. *Preparation of examination.* The written examination component of the certification program is developed on the basis of the content outline.

4. *Other activities.* Appropriate measures are taken to ensure that security and confidentially of the testing process are maintained, that the examination and eligibility criteria are appropriate, and that the knowledge and skills of those who are certified do, in fact, reflect competence.

A professional testing consultant or firm typically assists in the development of the role delineation and the examination itself to ensure that the examination meets professional standards of psychometric soundness and legal defensibility. National standards have been developed for accrediting certification programs across a wide variety of professions. The Council on Credentialing in Pharmacy has approved Guiding Principles for Pharmacy Credentialing Activities with which the profession's certification programs are expected to comply.[5] These principles appear as Appendix D at the end of this chapter. Pharmacists considering any advanced credentialing opportunities, and particularly certification programs, should determine compliance of the program with these basic quality principles.

Certifying Agencies for Pharmacists Only

Three groups, the Board of Pharmaceutical Specialties, the Commission for Certification in Geriatric Pharmacy, and the National Institute for Standards in Pharmacist Credentialing, offer certification to pharmacists.

Board of Pharmaceutical Specialties

Established in 1976 by the American Pharmacists Association (then the American Pharmaceutical Association), BPS certifies pharmacists in five specialties: nuclear pharmacy, nutrition support pharmacy, oncology pharmacy, pharmacotherapy, and psychiatric pharmacy. Descriptions of each specialty area are provided in Appendix C in this chapter. Pharmacists who wish to retain BPS certification must be recertified every seven years.

The recognition of each specialty is the result of a collaborative process between the board and one or more pharmacy organizations, which develop a petition to support and justify recognition of the specialty. This petition must meet written criteria established by the BPS.

A nine-member board that includes six pharmacists, two health professionals who are not pharmacists, and one public/consumer member, directs the BPS. A specialty council of six specialist members and three pharmacists not in the specialty direct the certification process for each specialty.

BPS examinations are administered with the assistance of an educational testing firm, resulting in a process that is psychometrically sound and legally defensible. Each of the five specialties has its own eligibility criteria, examination specifications, and recertification process. All five examinations are given on a single day once a year in approximately 30 sites in the United States and internationally.

In 1997, BPS introduced a method designed to recognize focused areas within recognized pharmacy specialties. A designation of "Added Qualifications" denotes that an individual has demonstrated an enhanced level of training and experience in one segment of a BPS-recognized specialty. Added qualifications are conferred on the basis of a portfolio review to qualified individuals who already hold BPS certification. Within the specialty of pharmacotherapy, infectious diseases and cardiology are the two areas of added qualifications currently approved by BPS.

Commission for Certification in Geriatric Pharmacy (CCGP)

In 1997, the American Society of Consultant Pharmacists Board of Directors voted to create the CCGP to oversee a certification program in geriatric pharmacy practice. CCGP is a nonprofit corporation that is autonomous from ASCP. It has its own governing board of commissioners. The CCGP Board of Commissioners includes five pharmacist members, one physician member, one payor/employer member, one public/consumer member, and one liaison member from the ASCP Board of Directors.

To become certified, candidates are expected to be knowledgeable about principles of geriatric pharmacotherapy and the provision of pharmaceutical care to the elderly. Pharmacists who meet CCGP's requirements are entitled to use the designation certified geriatric pharmacist, or CGP. Pharmacists who wish to retain their CGP credential must recertify every five years by successfully completing a written examination.

CCGP contracts with a professional testing firm to assist in conducting the role delineation or task analysis, and in developing and administering the examination. The resulting process is psychometrically sound and legally defensible; it also meets nationally recognized standards. The CGP certification exams are administered twice a year at multiple locations in the United States, Canada, and Australia. CCGP publishes a candidate handbook that includes the content outline for the examination, eligibility criteria for taking the examination, and the policies and procedures of the certification program.

National Institute for Standards in Pharmacist Credentialing (NISPC)

The NISPC was founded in 1998 by the American Pharmacists Association (then the American Pharmaceutical Association), the National Association of Boards of Pharmacy (NABP), the National Association of Chain Drug Stores, and the National Community Pharmacists Association. The purpose of NISPC is to "promote the value and encourage the adoption of

National Association of Boards of Pharmacy disease-specific examinations as the consistent and objective means of documenting the ability of pharmacists to provide disease state management services."

NISPC offers certification in the management of diabetes, asthma, dyslipidemia, and anticoagulation therapy. At the time of its founding, the organization's immediate objective was to design a process that would document the competence of pharmacists providing care for patients with these disease states. The NISPC credential was first recognized in the state of Mississippi, where it was used to enable pharmacists to qualify for Medicaid reimbursement as part of a pilot project in that state. NABP developed the competency assessment examinations and oversees their administration. The NISPC tests are administered nationally as computerized examinations and are available throughout the year.

Multidisciplinary Certification Programs

Some certification programs are available to professionals from many health disciplines, including pharmacists. Areas in which such certification is available include diabetes education, anticoagulation therapy, pain management, and asthma education. Some of these programs are still in the early stages of development. Several of these providers are listed in Appendix B in this chapter; however, the information is not intended to be exhaustive.

PHARMACY SUPPORTIVE PERSONNEL (TECHNICIANS)

A pharmacy technician is an individual who assists in pharmacy activities that do not require the professional judgment of a pharmacist. For example, pharmacy technicians may accept orders from patients, prepare labels, enter drug information into the pharmacy's computer system, and retrieve medications from inventory. The term "pharmacy technician" is used in a majority of states; however, other terms are also used to describe pharmacy support personnel carrying out functions similar to those described above. As pharmacists assume an increasing number of clinical roles, pharmacy technicians are taking more and more responsibility for distributive functions in pharmacies in all settings.

The exact functions and responsibilities of pharmacy technicians are defined by state laws and regulations and are also determined by the willingness of pharmacists to delegate the nonjudgment activities of their practice. Pharmacy technicians always work under the supervision of a licensed pharmacist. The education and training, certification, and continuing education of pharmacy technicians are similar in some ways to those of pharmacists. There is, however, more interstate variation in the regulation of and requirements for pharmacy technicians than for pharmacists.

Education and Training

Most pharmacy technicians today have been trained on the job, either formally or informally. As the responsibilities of pharmacy technicians grow, however, more and more individuals are enrolling in formal training programs. These programs are generally affiliated with a community college, a four-year college, a hospital, or another healthcare organization. Graduates of these programs may be awarded an associate's degree or a certificate of completion.

Not all states have education and training requirements for pharmacy technicians, but some states require board of pharmacy approval of the training program. ASHP is the accreditation body for pharmacy technician training programs. Accreditation of training programs is voluntary in the majority of states.

In early 2003, at the request of the Council on Credentialing in Pharmacy, the Accreditation Council for Pharmacy Education initiated a profession-wide dialogue concerning the possible development of national standards and an accreditation process for pharmacy technician education and training.

Regulation

State boards of pharmacy oversee the regulation of practice of pharmacy technicians. Practices differ substantially among the states. Approximately 60 percent of states currently require registration or licensure of pharmacy technicians by the board of pharmacy. Virtually all state boards of pharmacy have amended their pharmacy practice acts and regulations in recent years, allowing an expanded role for pharmacy technicians in the delivery of pharmacy services. It is anticipated that further changes in the regulation of pharmacy technicians will be made.

Certification

The Pharmacy Technician Certification Board (PTCB) was established in 1995 as a national voluntary certification program for pharmacy technicians. Its founders were the American Pharmacists Association (then the American Pharmaceutical Association), the American Society of Health-

System Pharmacists, the Illinois Council of Health-System Pharmacists, and the Michigan Pharmacists Association.

In collaboration with testing experts, the PTCB developed a national examination, the Pharmacy Technician Certification Examination. The examination is designed to assess the candidate's knowledge and skill base for activities that are most commonly performed by a pharmacy technician, as determined by a national task analysis.

The board administers its certification examination three times a year at more than 120 sites across the nation. A technician who passes this examination is designated as a certified pharmacy technician (CPhT). Pharmacy technicians must renew their certification every two years. To qualify for recertification, they must participate in at least twenty hours of pharmacy-related continuing education that includes an hour of pharmacy law.

A growing number of states require pharmacy technicians to be certified, and/or recognize certification in other ways in their regulations.

CERTIFICATION—THE FUTURE

The pharmacy profession is continuing to evolve in response to a changing healthcare system in the United States. This evolution creates opportunities for pharmacists to provide an expanded range of services within their defined scope of practice. It is incumbent on the profession to assure the public, as well as employers, payers, other health professionals, regulatory agencies, and governmental agencies, that pharmacists and pharmacy technicians who provide specific services possess the knowledge, skills, and abilities to safely and competently perform those services. This will be accomplished through an established and widely understood system of credentialing, including licensure to practice and certification to recognize knowledge and skills evolved beyond general practice to specialty practice in defined areas.

APPENDIX A: GLOSSARY

These definitions have been developed by a variety of organizations involved in credentialing and are generally accepted by those in the pharmacist credentialing arena.

accreditation: The process whereby an association or agency grants public recognition to an organization (or a specific program of an organization) that meets certain established qualifications or standards, as determined through initial and periodic evaluations.

certificate program: A structured, systematic postgraduate education and continuing education experience for pharmacists that is generally smaller in magnitude and shorter in duration than a degree program. Certificate programs are designed to instill, expand, or enhance practice competencies through the systematic acquisition of specific knowledge, skills, attitudes, and performance behaviors.

certified: Adjective that is used to describe an individual who holds certification and that is incorporated into the name of the credential awarded that individual. For example, someone who has earned BPS certification in oncology is a "board-certified oncology pharmacist."

certificate: A certificate is a document issued to a pharmacist upon successful completion of the predetermined level of performance of a certificate program or of a pharmacy residency or fellowship. *See also* STATEMENT OF CONTINUING EDUCATION CREDIT.

certification: The voluntary process by which a nongovernmental agency or association formally grants recognition to a pharmacist who has met certain predetermined qualifications specified by that organization. This recognition designates to the public that the holder has attained the requisite level of knowledge, skill, or experience in a well-defined, often specialized, area of the total discipline. Certification entails assessment, including testing, an evaluation of the candidate's education and experience, or both. Periodic recertification is usually required to retain the credential.

clinical privileges: Authorization to provide a specific range of patient care services. *See* PRIVILEGING.

competence: The ability to perform one's duties accurately, make correct judgments, and interact appropriately with patients and with colleagues. Professional competence is characterized by good problem-solving and decision-making abilities, a strong knowledge base, and the ability to apply knowledge and experience to diverse patient-care situations.

competency: A distinct skill, ability, or attitude that is essential to the practice of a profession. Individual competencies for pharmacists include, for example, mastery of aseptic technique and achievement of a thought process that enables one to identify therapeutic duplications. A pharmacist must master a variety of competencies in order to gain competence in his or her profession.

continuing education: Continuing education for the profession of pharmacy is a structured process of education designed or intended to support the continuous development of pharmacists to maintain and enhance their professional competence. Continuing education should promote problem solving and critical thinking and be applicable to the practice of pharmacy.

credential: Documented evidence of professional qualifications. For pharmacists, academic degrees, state licensure, and board certification are all examples of credentials.

credentialing: (1) The process by which an organization or institution obtains, verifies, and assesses a pharmacist's qualifications to provide patient care services. (2) The process of granting a credential (a designation that indicates qualifications in a subject or an area.)

fellowship: A directed, highly individualized postgraduate program designed to prepare a pharmacist to become an independent researcher.

license: A credential issued by a state or federal body that indicates that the holder is in compliance with minimum mandatory governmental requirements necessary to practice in a particular profession or occupation.

licensure: The process of granting a license.

pharmacy technician: An individual who, under the supervision of a licensed pharmacist, assists in pharmacy activities not requiring the professional judgment of the pharmacist.

privileging: The process by which a healthcare organization, having reviewed an individual healthcare provider's credentials and performance and found them satisfactory, authorizes that individual to perform a specific scope of patient care services within that organization.

residency: An organized, directed, postgraduate training program in a defined area of pharmacy practice.

registered: Adjective used to describe a pharmacist who has met state requirements for licensure and whose name has been entered on a state registry of practitioners who are licensed to practice in that jurisdiction.

scope of practice: The boundaries within which a health professional may practice. For pharmacists, the scope of practice is generally established by the board or agency that regulates the profession in a given state or organization.

statement of continuing education credit: A document issued to an individual upon completion of a continuing education program provided by an organization accredited by the Accreditation Council for Pharmacy Education.

traineeship: A short, intensive, clinical and didactic postgraduate educational program intended to provide the pharmacist with knowledge and skills needed to provide a high level of care to patients with specific diseases or conditions.

APPENDIX B: REFERENCED PHARMACY ORGANIZATIONS AND CERTIFICATION BODIES

Pharmacy Organizations

Academy of Managed Care Pharmacy (AMCP)
100 North Pitt Street, Suite 400
Alexandria, VA 22314
(800) 827-2627
www.amcp.org

American Association of Colleges of Pharmacy (AACP)
1426 Prince Street
Alexandria, VA 22314-2841
(703) 836-8982
www.aacp.org

American College of Apothecaries (ACA)
P.O. Box 341266
Memphis, TN 38184
(901) 383-8119
www.acainfo.org

American College of Clinical Pharmacy (ACCP)
3101 Broadway, Suite 650
Kansas City, MO 64111-2446
(816) 531-2177
www.accp.com

Accreditation Council for Pharmacy Education (ACPE—formerly American Council on Pharmaceutical Education)
20 North Clark Street, Suite 2500
Chicago, IL 60602-5109
(312) 664-3575
www.acpe-accredit.org

American Pharmacists Association (APhA—formerly American Pharmaceutical Association)
2215 Constitution Avenue, NW
Washington, DC 20037-2985
(202) 628-4410
www.aphanet.org

American Society of Consultant Pharmacists (ASCP)
1321 Duke Street
Alexandria, VA 22314-3563
(703) 739-1300
www.ascp.com

American Society of Health-System Pharmacists (ASHP)
7272 Wisconsin Avenue
Bethesda, MD 20814
(301) 657-3000
www.ashp.org

National Association of Boards of Pharmacy (NABP)
1600 Feehanville Drive
Mount Prospect, IL 60056
(847) 391-4400
www.napb.net

National Association of Chain Drug Stores (NACDS)
413 N. Lee Street, P.O. Box 1417-D49
Alexandria, VA 22313-1480
(703) 549-3001
www.nacds.org

National Community Pharmacists Association (NCPA)
205 Daingerfield Road
Alexandria, VA 22314
(703) 683-8200
www.ncpanet.org

Pharmacy Technician Educators Council (PTEC)
800 Robin Hill Drive
San Antonio, TX 78230
(800) 798-3247
www.rxptec.org

Certification Bodies for Pharmacists or Pharmacy Technicians (May Be Multidisciplinary)

Anticoagulation Forum
88 East Newton Street, E-113
Boston, MA 02118-2395
(617) 638-7265
www.acforum.org

Board of Pharmaceutical Specialties (BPS)
2215 Constitution Avenue, NW
Washington, DC 20037-2985
(202) 429-7591
www.bpsweb.org

Commission for Certification in Geriatric Pharmacy (CCGP)
1321 Duke Street
Alexandria, VA 22314-3563
(703) 535-3038
www.ccgp.org

National Asthma Educator Certification Board
American Lung Association
1740 Broadway
New York, NY 10019-4374
(212) 315-8865
www.lungusa.org

Nonpharmacy Accreditation Bodies

American National Standards Institute (ANSI)
Personnel Certification Program
1819 L Street, NW, 6th Floor
Washington, DC 20036
(202) 331-3617
Rswift@ansi.org

National Commission for Certifying Agencies
2025 M Street, NW, Suite 800
Washington, DC 20036
(202) 367-1165
info@noca.org

National Certification Board for Diabetes Educators (NCBDE)
330 East Algonquin Road, Suite 4
Arlington Heights, IL 60005
(847) 228-9795
www.ncbde.org

National Institute for Standards in Pharmacist Credentialing (NISPC)
205 Daingerfield Road
Alexandria, VA 22314
(703) 299-8790
www.nispcnet.org

Pharmacy Technician Certification Board (PTCB)
2215 Constitution Avenue, NW
Washington, DC 20037-2985
(202) 429-7576
www.ptcb.org

APPENDIX C: SPECIALTIES RECOGNIZED BY THE BOARD OF PHARMACEUTICAL SPECIALTIES

Nuclear Pharmacy

Nuclear pharmacy seeks to improve and promote the public health through the safe and effective use of radioactive drugs for diagnosis and therapy. A nuclear pharmacist, as a member of the nuclear medicine team, specializes in procurement, compounding, quality assurance, dispensing, distribution, and development of radiopharmaceuticals. In addition, the nuclear pharmacist monitors patient outcomes and provides information and consultation regarding health and safety issues. Specifically, the nuclear pharmacist

- procures radiopharmaceuticals and other drugs, supplies, and materials necessary for his or her practice;
- compounds radiopharmaceuticals necessary to his or her practice;
- assures the quality of radiopharmaceuticals and of instruments, equipment, and devices necessary for his or her practice;
- dispenses radiopharmaceuticals and other drugs necessary to his or her practice;
- distributes radiopharmaceuticals, other drugs, and other materials necessary to his or her practice;

- assures the health and safety of himself or herself, co-workers, patients, and the public as related to his or her practice;
- provides information and consultation related to his or her practice;
- provides pharmaceutical care to patients and assures optimal patient outcomes within the scope of his or her practice;
- conducts research and development as necessary for his or her practice.

Nutrition Support Pharmacy

Nutrition support pharmacy addresses the care of patients who receive specialized nutrition support, including parenteral and enteral nutrition. The nutrition support pharmacist has responsibility for promoting maintenance and/or restoration of optimal nutritional status, designing and modifying treatment according to the needs of the patient. The nutrition support pharmacist has responsibility for direct patient care and often functions as a member of a multidisciplinary nutrition support team. The nutrition support pharmacist specialist is responsible for the following specialized services:

- provides individual nutrition support care to patients through patient assessment activities and the development, monitoring, and management of a therapeutic plan;
- manages nutrition support services;
- advances nutrition support pharmacy practice.

Oncology Pharmacy

Oncology pharmacy addresses the pharmaceutical care of patients with cancer. The oncology pharmacist specialist recommends, designs, implements, monitors, and modifies pharmacotherapeutic plans to optimize outcomes in patients with malignant diseases. In providing his or her specialized scope of services, the oncology pharmacist specialist

- collaborates with other health professionals in pursuing optimal drug therapy for patients with cancer. This requires that the oncology pharmacist collect and interpret pertinent clinical data and recommend, design, implement, monitor, and modify patient-specific therapeutic plans;

- interprets, generates, and disseminates knowledge in oncology as it applies to oncology pharmacy practice;
- collaborates with other professionals, patients, and the public to recommend, design, implement, monitor, and modify systems and policies to optimize the use of drugs in patients with cancer;
- collaborates with other professionals and the public in addressing risk factors, prevention, screening, and issues associated with cancer survivorship as they relate to oncology pharmacy practice.

Pharmacotherapy

Pharmacotherapy is that area of pharmacy responsible for ensuring the safe, appropriate, and economical use of drugs in patient care. The pharmacotherapy specialist has responsibility for direct patient care, often functions as a member of a multidisciplinary treatment team, may conduct clinical research, and is frequently a primary source of drug information for other healthcare professionals. In providing his or her specialized scope of services, the pharmacotherapy specialist

- collects and interprets data to design, recommend, implement, monitor, and modify patient-specific pharmacotherapy in collaboration with other healthcare professionals to optimize drug therapy;
- interprets, generates, and disseminates knowledge in pharmacotherapy;
- designs, recommends, implements, monitors, and modifies system-specific policies and procedures in collaboration with other professionals and administrators to optimize healthcare.

The term "added qualifications" is used by BPS to denote the demonstration of an enhanced level of training and experience and to document further differentiation of practitioners within specialties that BPS has already recognized in which practitioners focus on specific patient populations or diseases. Creation of this process by BPS in 1997 responded to requests from several segments of the profession in view of the growing complexity of the profession and the needs of healthcare systems. As of January 2004, two areas of added qualifications have been approved within the pharmacotherapy specialty: cardiology and infectious diseases.

Psychiatric Pharmacy

Psychiatric pharmacy addresses the pharmaceutical care of patients with psychiatric disorders. As a member of a multidisciplinary treatment team, the psychiatric pharmacist specialist is often responsible for optimizing drug treatment and patient care by conducting patient assessments, recommending appropriate treatment plans, monitoring patient response, and recognizing drug-induced problems. In providing his or her specialized scope of services, the psychiatric pharmacist specialist

- collaborates with other health professionals in pursuing optimal drug therapy for neuropsychiatric patients. This requires that the psychiatric pharmacist collect and interpret pertinent clinical data and recommend, design, implement, monitor, and modify patient-specific therapeutic plans;
- interprets, generates, and disseminates knowledge in neuropsychiatric pharmacy;
- collaborates with other professionals and administrators to recommend, design, implement, monitor, and modify systems and policies to optimize the use of drugs in the treatment of neuropsychiatric patients.

APPENDIX D: COUNCIL ON CREDENTIALING IN PHARMACY— GUIDING PRINCIPLES FOR PHARMACY CREDENTIALING ACTIVITIES

The development and application of credentialing standards for the pharmacy profession are integral components of CCP's vision and mission statements. The CCP Guiding Principles for Pharmacy Credentialing Activities are intended as guidelines for the development and assessment of new and established pharmacy credentialing efforts.

The CCP Guiding Principles for Pharmacy Credentialing Activities are based, in part, on the "Standards for Educational and Psychological Testing" (revised 1999) developed jointly by the American Educational Research Association, the American Psychological Association, and the National Council on Measurement in Education, and "Standards for Accreditation of Certification Programs" (revised 1995) developed by the National Commission for Certifying Agencies.

Discussions of credentialing are often complicated by a lack of common understanding of key terms and the contexts in which they are used. To

Adopted by the Council in November 2001.

clarify these misunderstandings, the following definitions are adapted from the CCP White Paper on Pharmacy Credentialing:

- A *credential* is documented evidence of an individual's or program's qualifications or characteristics. Credentials may include diplomas, licenses, certificates, and certifications.
- *Credentialing* is the process by which an organization or institution obtains, verifies, and assesses an individual's qualifications to provide services.
- *Accreditation* is the process by which a private association, organization or government agency, after initial and periodic evaluations, grants recognition to an organization that has met certain established criteria.
- A *certificate* is a document issued to an individual upon successful completion of the predetermined level of performance of a training program.
- *Certification* is a voluntary process by which a nongovernmental agency or an association grants recognition to an individual who has met certain predetermined qualifications specified by that organization. This formal recognition is granted to designate to the public that this individual has attained the requisite level of knowledge, skill, or experience in a well-defined, often specialized, area of the total discipline. Certification usually requires initial assessment and periodic reassessments of the individual's qualifications.

I. Organizational Principles for a Credentialing Activity

Purpose

- Should have written vision and mission statements in support of excellence in pharmacy.

Structure

- Should be organized in such a way that the credentialing process is free from inappropriate external influence.
- Should have a governing board that is representative of appropriate stakeholders.

Resources

- Should have adequate financial and staffing resources to fulfill its mission.

II. Programmatic Principles for a Credentialing Activity

Testing/Evaluation Mechanism

- Should adhere to rigorous industry standards in its testing and evaluation activities (e.g., those standards developed by the American Educational Research Association, the American Psychological Association, the National Council on Measurement in Education, the National Commission for Certifying Agencies, or other organization recognized as authoritative).

Public Information

- Should publish and make readily available information about organization responsibilities, purpose, policies, and procedures.

Responsibilities to Candidates

- Should have in place mechanisms to ensure fairness and due process for individuals or programs that are candidates for the credential.

Responsibilities to Public and Employers

- Should have in place mechanisms to ensure credibility and understanding of credentials.
- Should publish a listing of credentialed individuals or programs.

Reevaluation

- Should have a program of periodic reevaluation of individuals or programs holding the credential.

III. External Review

- Should meet all above guidelines and/or seek to meet requirements for appraisal/accreditation by a recognized third party, as appropriate.

NOTES

1. Rosemary Stevens, *American Medicine and the Public Interest* (University of California Press, Berkeley, 1998, p. 44).

2. Final Report . . . Task Force on Specialties in Pharmacy. *J Am Pharm Assoc* NS14:618-622

3. Council on Credentialing in Pharmacy, CCP White Paper: Credentialing in Pharmacy, September, 2003. Available at www.pharmacycredentialing.org/ccp/ CCPWhitePaper2003.pdf. Accessed May 10, 2004.

4. White Paper on Pharmacy Technicians: Needed Changes Can No Longer Wait. *J Am Pharm Assoc* 2002; 43:93-107.

5. Council on Credentialing in Pharmacy, "Guiding Principles for Pharmacy Credentialing Activities," November, 2001. Available at www.pharmacy credentialing.org/ccp/guidingprinciples.htm. Accessed May 10, 2004.

Chapter 19

Collaborative Drug Therapy Management

Marla J. Campbell

Collaborative drug therapy management (CDTM) describes an approach to care in which drug therapy management and decision making are coordinated collaboratively by pharmacists, physicians and other healthcare professionals, and the patient. When participating in CDTM, pharmacists share the responsibility for patient outcomes, not just by providing the basic dispensing functions and drug information services but by solving patient and medication-related problems and by making decisions regarding drug prescribing, monitoring, and regimen adjustments.[1] CDTM allows pharmacists to move beyond the identification of drug-related problems to providing solution to those problems. A growing body of literature has provided evidence of cost savings, decreased deaths, and decreased hospitalizations with pharmacists' clinical services, especially in environments where CDTM is practiced.[2]

HISTORY OF PHARMACIST PRESCRIBING
AND COLLABORATIVE DRUG THERAPY MANAGEMENT
IN THE UNITED STATES

Regulation of pharmacist prescribing in the United States can be traced to passage of the Federal Food, Drug, and Cosmetic (FDC) Act of 1938. The act was introduced to address concerns surrounding the availability of antibiotics, led by introduction of the sulfonamides in 1935. Congress

Portions of this chapter are adapted from Carmichael JM, O'Connell MB, Devine B, et al., Collaborative drug therapy management by pharmacists, *Pharmacotherapy* 1997; 17:1050-1061; and Hammond RW, Schwartz AH, Campbell MJ, et al., Collaborative drug therapy management by pharmacists—2003, *Pharmacotherapy* 2003; 23(9): 1210-1225. © American College of Clinical Pharmacy. Used with permission.

passed the act after a disaster in which 107 people died from consuming a toxic base used to compound a sulfanilamide elixir. Regulations were then issued by the Food and Drug Administration (FDA) to enforce this legislation. The 1938 act deemed as "misbranded" any drug that failed to carry adequate directions for use or failed to warn patients about potential lack of safety. Any drug could be exempt from the requirement of adequate directions for use if, because of its potential for toxicity or misuse, it was to be used under the supervision of a physician. Regulations mandated these exempted agents carry the wording "Caution: to be used only by or on the prescription of a physician, dentist, or veterinarian." Another provision was the wording "Warning—may be habit forming," required on certain narcotic and hypnotic drugs. These regulations became the forerunner to our present-day system for designating prescription drugs and controlled substances. Until this time, pharmacists had been able to prescribe medications legally.[1]

The activity of pharmacists renewing, and thereby continuing, a patient's medication without authorization from the patient's physician was a secondary issue in the 1938 FDC debates. The FDA saw the practice of pharmacists providing renewals of medications directly to patients as unfavorable. No definition had differentiated a prescription drug from a nonlegend, over-the-counter (OTC) drug. The two classes of drugs were not legally differentiated until passage of the Durham-Humphrey Amendment in 1951. At that time, it became illegal for pharmacists to renew legend drugs without authorization from the patient's physician.[3,4] Thus, the practice of physician prescribing and pharmacist dispensing became law.

During the same period, many of the products previously manufactured by the individual pharmacist became available from pharmaceutical manufacturing companies.

In the 1960s, pharmacists in the Indian Health Service (IHS) began assuming an active role in drug therapy management. The activity of pharmacist prescribing was first documented in this setting.[5] In 1973, under a grant from the National Center for Health Services Research and Development, IHS developed the Pharmacist Practitioner Program, where some specially trained pharmacists provided drug therapy management services in collaboration with physicians.[6,7,8]

In 1972, individual states began exploring the issue of pharmacist prescribing, heralded by the Health Manpower Experimental Act of 1972, a unique experiment in California. Health Manpower Pilot Projects were created with the purpose of training students of the allied health professions in areas that were then beyond their legal scope of practice. To include prescribing by pharmacists, nurses, and physician assistants in these pilot projects, California Assembly Bill 717 was introduced in 1977, with a provision for sunsetting in 1983. The bill authorized prescriptive authority only to those directly involved with the pilot projects. The project was so successful in saving healthcare dollars that the California Pharmacists Association, with assistance from the California Society of Hospital Pharmacists, introduced legislation in 1981 to enable prescribing by all pharmacists in the state.[6,9] This legislation allowed registered pharmacists functioning in licensed acute and intermediate healthcare facilities to adjust the dosage of a patient's drug regimen pursuant to a prescriber's authorization, order laboratory tests, perform physical assessments, and administer medications. This law has been expanded twice since then and now enables pharmacists to initiate drug therapy (1983) and expands the types of practice sites to include clinics and systems licensed as healthcare service plans (e.g., managed-care organizations; 1994).[10,11,12,13] The specific duties outlined by each protocol are site and practice specific.

In time, the recognition of pharmacists as drug therapy experts has spread to the national level. In 1974, the Department of Health, Education, and Welfare enacted a drug regimen review regulation for nursing homes in an attempt to improve the quality of drug prescribing in that healthcare setting. A 1984 study by Thompson described the activities of clinical pharmacists who prescribed under physician protocol in a skilled nursing facility.[14] In the clinical pharmacist intervention group, cost savings attributed to fewer deaths, more patients discharged to lower levels of care, and fewer drugs per patient than the patients in the traditional care group were estimated to be $70,000 annually for every 100 beds.

Legislation enabling pharmacists to prescribe under protocol was first passed in Washington State in 1979. The protocols were initially used in institutions, but currently most are used in managed-care and community settings.[15,16]

Florida was the third state to provide prescriptive authority to pharmacists. The Florida legislature created a third class of drugs in 1986. In contrast to the California and Washington provisions for prescribing under protocol (i.e., dependent prescribing), Florida pharmacists have independent prescribing from within a limited formulary. The medications on the formulary are for the management of minor illnesses and include oral, urinary, and otic analgesics; hemorrhoid medications; antinausea preparations; antihistamines and decongestants; anthelmintics; topical antifungals and antimicrobials; topical antiinflammatory preparations; otic antifungals and antimicrobials; keratolytics; vitamins with fluoride; lindane shampoos; antidiarrheals; smoking cessation products; and ophthalmics. The formulary is subject to specific conditions spelled out in the state's pharmacy practice act.[17]

In 1995, the Veterans Health Administration (VHA) updated the granting of prescribing authority for practitioners in the Veterans Affairs (VA) system. "General guidelines for establishing medication prescribing authority for clinical nurse specialists, nurse practitioners, clinical pharmacy specialists, and physician assistants," VHA Directive 10-95-019, delineated the prescribing role of these midlevel practitioners within the VA healthcare system. Clinical pharmacy specialists are defined as those with master of science or doctor of pharmacy degrees, pharmacists who have completed an accredited residency, specialty board-certified pharmacists, or pharmacists with equivalent experience. The scope of practice for each type of practitioner is determined by the practice site. The scope of practice statement identifies each individual's prescriptive authority and describes routine and nonroutine professional duties and general areas of responsibility. Prescription orders written by authorized practitioners within their approved scope of practice do not require a physician cosignature. Because states cannot regulate the activities of the federal government or its employees when acting within the scope of their employment, state laws and regulations related to medication orders and prescriptions do not affect scope of practice statements in the VA system.[1]

A later directive, VA Directive 2001-82, revoked the 1995 directive and indicated that by June 30, 2002, the authority of these practitioners would be based on the status of CDTM in the individual practitioner's state of licensure, registration, or certification, rather than the state in which the VA facility was located. Concern that implementation would hamper the ability of the VA system to provide care to veterans led to an extension on the deadline until June 30, 2004. Many VA CPSs sought to become licensed in states that specifically outlined CDTM, regardless of the state they were currently physically practicing in.

Two further directives have been issued since then (VA Directive 2002-083 and VA Directive 2003-004) that clarify scope of practice for midlevel professionals in the VA.

The final distinction was on the prescribing of controlled versus noncontrolled substances. For a midlevel practitioner to prescribe controlled substances, that level of privilege needed to be explicitly stated in the practice act of the state that they are currently licensed in. Although most CDTM legislation does not prohibit dependent prescribing of narcotics, few specifically describe it. Montana and North Carolina are two examples of states where specific DEA recognition has been granted.

For prescribing of noncontrolled substances, the VA specifies the internal scope of practice for the professional. The CPS does not need to hold a license in a state that specifically outlines prescribing privileges (dependent or independent prescribing). The new directive adequately covers medications that would be most likely to be prescribed in the course of chronic disease management (antihypertensives, anticoagulants, etc.).

At the national level, legislation was introduced in 2001 and 2003 in both the U.S. Senate and House of Representatives which proposed to amend the Social Security Act to recognize pharmacists as healthcare providers for Medicare patients. In 2002, the American College of Physicians/American Society of Internal Medicine issued a policy statement that contained qualified support for the concept of collaborative drug therapy management in certain practice settings.[18]

The recognition of other professions of the value of CDTM and the success seen in pioneer states such as Washington has spurred other states to enact or pursue legislation to enable pharmacists to prescribe as part of collaborative drug therapy management agreements. Currently, forty-two states and the federal government have some form of collaborative drug therapy management authority for pharmacists.

DEFINITIONS OF CDTM BY DIFFERENT PHARMACY ORGANIZATIONS

Depending on the reference, there are discrepancies among listings of the number of states with CDTM. This is due to different definitions and interpretations of what CDTM constitutes. A consistent definition has not been universally adopted. The following are different pharmacy organization definitions of CDTM.

American Pharmacists Association (APhA)

"Under mutually agreeable practice protocols and guidelines," CDTM activities may include, but not be limited to, the following activities by pharmacists:

- Initiating, modifying, and monitoring a patient's drug therapy
- Ordering and performing laboratory and related tests
- Assessing patient response to therapy
- Counseling and educating a patient on medications
- Administering medications[19]

American College of Clinical Pharmacy (ACCP)

ACCP defines "collaborative drug therapy management by pharmacists" (CDTM) as follows:

A collaborative practice agreement between one or more physicians and pharmacists wherein qualified pharmacists working within the context of a defined protocol are permitted to assume professional responsibility for performing patient assessments; ordering drug therapy-related laboratory tests; administering drugs; and selecting, initiating, monitoring, continuing, and adjusting medication regimens.

As a working definition, ACCP considers a drug therapy management protocol to be

a written plan that delegates prescriptive authority to pharmacists under designated circumstances. It serves to guide their conduct, direct the course of action, and delineate the functions, procedures, and decision criteria to be followed. It has been mutually agreed upon by the collaborating physicians(s) and pharmacists(s), and has been reviewed by an appropriate body responsible for quality assurance within the practitioners' practice setting.[6]

American Society of Consultant Pharmacists (ASCP)

A collaborative practice agreement is a voluntary, written agreement between a pharmacist and a prescriber that permits expanded authority for the pharmacist, such as the ability to initiate or modify drug therapy and order laboratory tests. Collaborative practice agreements are intended to optimize patient care outcomes, and may include protocols, practice guidelines, care plans, and formulary systems.[20]

Most organizational definitions are derived in least in part from the NABP Model State Pharmacy Act and Model Rules. The National Association of Boards of Pharmacy (NABP) is the independent, international, and impartial association that assists its member boards and jurisdictions in developing, implementing, and enforcing uniform standards for the purpose of protecting the public health.

NABP Model State Pharmacy Act and Model Rules of the National Association of Boards of Pharmacy (Section 105, June 2003)

"Collaborative pharmacy practice" is that practice of pharmacy whereby one or more pharmacists have jointly agreed, on a voluntary basis, to work in conjunction with one or more practitioners under protocol whereby the pharmacist may perform certain patient care functions authorized by the practitioner or practitioners under certain specified conditions and/or limitations.[21]

A "collaborative pharmacy practice agreement" is a written and signed agreement between one or more pharmacists and one or more practitioners that provides for collaborative pharmacy practice for the purpose of drug therapy management of patients.

"Drug therapy management" means the review of drug therapy regimen(s) of patients by one or more pharmacists for the purpose of evaluating and rendering advice to one or more practitioners regarding adjustment of the regimen. Decisions involving drug therapy management shall be made in the best interest of the patient. "Drug therapy management" may include

1. Implementing, modifying, and managing drug therapy according to the terms of the collaborative pharmacy practice agreement;
2. Collecting and reviewing patient histories;
3. Obtaining and checking vital signs, including pulse, temperature, blood pressure, and respiration;
4. Ordering and evaluating the results of laboratory tests directly to drug therapy, when performed in accordance with approved protocols applicable to the practice setting; and
5. Such other patient care services as may be allowed by law.

Table 19.1 lists states that have CDTM formalized in state statute or practice regulations. Table 19.2 lists additional states where interpretation allows for some form of collaborative practice.

The National Association of Boards of Pharmacy conducts an annual survey on pharmacy law. In states where CDTM is not in statute the individual state boards of pharmacy responses detailing interpretation of CDTM authority are listed here:[22,23]

Illinois. CDTM is not addressed in laws or regulations, but pharmacists may do so if acting as an agent of the prescriber.

Iowa. CDTM is not specifically addressed in law or regulation. However, on June 2, 2000, the Iowa Board of Pharmacy Examiners issued a declaratory order specific to whether pharmaceutical case management (as defined in the relative Medicaid waiver) was within Iowa pharmacists' scope of practice. The board ruled that "PCM services that are delivered in the manner described in the petition to fall within the scope of practice of pharmacy in the State of Iowa." However, the Iowa Board of Pharmacy responded to the National Association of Boards of Pharmacy 2001-2002 Survey that there is not collaborative drug therapy authority in the state of Iowa.

South Carolina. The South Carolina's Board of Pharmacy responded to the National Association of Boards of Pharmacy 2001-2002 Survey that there is not collaborative authority in the State of South Carolina. However several definitions in the practice act suggest otherwise:

> practice of pharmacy means . . . drug administration . . . provision of those acts and services necessary to provide pharmacy care and drug therapy management; drug therapy management is that practice of pharmacy which involves the expertise of the pharmacist in a collaborative effort with the practitioner and other health care providers to ensure the highest quality health Care services; and prescription drug orders means a lawful order from a practitioner . . . and including orders derived from collaborative pharmacy practice.

Tennessee. Tennessee Board of Pharmacy responded to the National Association of Boards of Pharmacy 2001-2002 Survey that there is collaborative drug therapy authority in the state of Tennessee. However, it is not specifically cited in law.

> Pharmaceutical Care is defined as including, "developing relationships with licensed practitioners to enable the pharmacist to accomplish comprehensive management of the patient's pharmacy related care and to enhance a patient's wellness, quality of life and optimize outcomes; and communicating to the health care provider any knowledge of unexpected or adverse response to drug therapy, or resolving unexpected or adverse response; and having a pharmacist accessible at all time to patients and healthcare providers to respond to their questions and needs.

If a stringent litmus test of an outpatient anticoagulation clinic where a pharmacist adjusts doses of warfarin under a defined protocol were applied then many of the states in Table 19.2 would not be considered to actually have CDTM. A few states in Table 19.1 would also fail this test due to limitations on the outpatient setting.

Different interpretations can be linked back to the strategies that different states have used to enable collaborative practice authority. APhA's Policy and Advocacy Department has identified the following principal avenues for obtaining CDTM:[24]

1. Direct legislative language: Legislation must be passed to enact CDTM agreements followed by the promulgation of regulatory rules following passage of legislation

2. Empowering language (direct or indirect) in scope of practice acts (either pharmacy or medical) which allows for physician delegation of such authority to pharmacists
3. Silence in statute and/or regulations that neither prohibits nor specifically provides for CDTM authority
4. Regulatory language
5. State attorney general interpretation

So CDTM may (and certainly does) exist in states where it is not recognized in statute or regulations because no law *prohibits* it from existing. (i.e., Alabama) This approach becomes problematic when attempting to bill for CDTM services. In an inpatient setting the pharmacists services are incorporated on overall hospital billing, DRG codes, etc. In an outpatient setting it is more of a challenge. Patients can be billed on a cash basis and in retail settings there has been some success with alternative billing forms but most commonly, incident-to billing is used for secondary providers such as APRNs and PAs. To satisfy the requirements for incident-to billing, the service provided must be within the scope of practice of the secondary provider.

For pharmacists to participate effectively in collaborative drug therapy management, the following conditions should exist: a collaborative practice environment; access to patients; access to medical records; a defined level of education, training, knowledge, skills, and abilities; documentation of clinical activities; and payment for pharmacists' activities.

REQUIREMENTS FOR COLLABORATIVE DRUG THERAPY MANAGEMENT

Collaborative Practice Environment

The pharmacist wanting to participate in CDTM first needs to identify a physician or practitioner group who wishes to collaborate with the pharmacist.* The physician or health system is necessary to identify patient populations, disease states, and drug-related issues that would be candidates for drug therapy management. The pharmacist and the provider define a scope

---

*Adapted with permission from ref. 1 Carmichael JM, O'Connell MB, Devine B, et al. Collaborative Drug Therapy Management by Pharmacists. Pharmacotherapy 1997;17: 1050–61and ref. 6. Hammond RW, Schwartz AH, Campbell MJ, et al. Collaborative Drug Therapy Management by Pharmacists—2003. *Pharmacotherapy* 2003;23(9):1210–1225

of practice that delineates routine and nonroutine professional duties and areas of responsibility.

The environment can be in any practice setting as long as the remaining conditions are met.

Access to Patients and Medical Records

Direct communication with patients is imperative for pharmacists to function successfully as drug therapy managers. In addition to an established agreement with the provider, the pharmacist-patient relationship is a key element of CDTM. In this relationship, the patient grants the pharmacist responsibility to perform services, and the pharmacist promises competency in performance of these services. Physicians and patients should understand that this relationship complements, rather than replaces, the physician-patient relationship.

The pharmacist must have access to medical records that include the patient's history, problem lists, progress notes, laboratory and procedure results, as well as previous drug therapy prior to entering a collaborative drug therapy management agreement. The CDTM agreement should also address patient privacy and confidentiality issues. Pharmacists working in a health-system environment may have easy access to computerized medical records. Other practice settings may have obstacles to access that will need to be overcome.

Education, Training, Knowledge, Skills, and Ability

Pharmacists are uniquely trained for the task of CDTM. Contemporary pharmacy education has provided pharmacists with more extensive and in-depth training in pharmacology and drug therapy management than any other healthcare professional. Training in patient interviewing, counseling, and patient assessment have resulted in competency to collect patient data, enhance patient adherence to a therapeutic plan, and monitor drug therapy for response to therapy and avoidance of adverse effects.

Pharmacists with a PharmD degree have more clinical training compared to those with a bachelor of science degree in pharmacy. However, bachelor of science pharmacists can acquire the skills and experience required for collaborative drug therapy management with additional training (i.e., nontraditional PharmD programs or residency programs) and/or clinical experience.

There are also various types of certificate programs that can help them to achieve the necessary competencies for a specific disease state. Ultimately, of course, the collaborating practitioners at the practice site should determine the credentials or specific education and training requirements for an individual collaborative practice agreement.

Documentation of Activities and Quality Assurance

Timely and appropriate documentation of all activities related to CDTM is required. Policies and procedures should be in place to ensure that the documentation is shared appropriately and available to other providers caring for the patient. To conform with the Health Information Portability and Accountability Act (HIPPA), regulations and guidelines for patient privacy and confidentiality should be incorporated into the plan. Pharmacists engaged in CDTM should meet all relevant standards for quality assurance and adhere to the same measures of quality as other health professionals in the practice setting. Measuring adherence to practice guidelines and comparing patient outcomes to benchmark data or literature reports are essential to quality assurance.

Payment for Services

Pharmacy continues to seek recognition as providers of patient care services by the federal government and other payors. Appropriate payment for pharmacists' CDTM and other direct patient care services will be a logical result of this recognition. Continued demonstration of improved outcomes from CDTM will be integral to gain support for compensation for services.

NOTES

1. Carmichael JM, O'Connell MB, Devine B, et al. Collaborative drug therapy management by pharmacists. *Pharmacotherapy* 1997;17(5):1050-61.

2. Schumock GT, Butler MG, Meek PD, Vermeulen LC, Arondekar BV, Bauman JL, for the 2002 Task Force on Economic Evaluation of Clinical Pharmacy Services of the American College of Clinical Pharmacy. Evidence of the economic benefit of clinical pharmacy services: 1996-2000. *Pharmacotherapy* 2003;23(1): 113–32

3. Marks HM. Revisiting "the origins of compulsory drug prescriptions." *Am J Public Health* 1995;85:109-15.

4. Swann JP. FDA and the practice of pharmacy: prescription drug regulation before the Durham- Humphrey amendment of 1951. *Pharmacy in History* 1994; 36:55-70.

5. Brands AJ. Treating ambulatory patients. *U.S. Pharmacist* 1977;2:70-4.

6. Hammond RW, Schwartz AH, Campbell MJ, et al. Collaborative Drug Therapy Management by Pharmacists—2003. *Pharmacotherapy* 2003;23(9):1210-1225

7. United States Public Health Service. The pharmacist as a provider of primary care—Indian Health Service, Volume 1: National Center for Health Services Research and Development. (contract Number HSM 110-HSRD, USPHS, April 1, 1973, to March 31,1975).

8. Copeland GP, Apgar DA. The pharmacist practitioner training program. *Drug Intell Clin Pharm* 1980;14:114-9.

9. Health Manpower Pilot Projects. Final report to the legislature, state of California and to the Healing Arts Licensing Boards. Prescribing and dispensing pilot projects. Office of Statewide Health Planning and Development, Division of Health Professions Development. November, 1982.

10. An interview with Gordon Duffy, Assemblyman, 32nd District. CSHP *Voice.* 1978;5:11.

11. California Assembly Bill 1868, 1981.

12. California Senate Bill 502, 1983.

13. California Assembly Bill 1759, 1994.

14. Thompson JF, McGhan WF, Ruffalo RL, Cohen DA, Adamcik B, Segal JL. Clinical pharmacists prescribing drug therapy in a geriatric setting: outcome of a trial. *J Am Geriatr Soc* 1984;32:154-9.

15. Christensen D, Fuller T, Williams D. Prescriptive authority protocols. 1993 Washington state survey. Washington State Board of Pharmacy, 1993.

16. Christensen D. Prescriptive authority for pharmacists: current status and future opportunities. Presented at the American Society of Hospital Pharmacists annual meeting, Reno, Nevada, June 5-9, 1994.

17. Flanagan ME. Update on state prescribing authority. *Am Pharm* 1995; NS35:13-8.

18. Pharmacists scope of practice. *Ann Intern Med* 2002;136:79-85.

19. Highlights of the APhA 144th Annual Meeting & Exposition, Los Angeles, March 8-12, 1997. *JAPhA* NS 37(4):459-461.

20. http://www.ascp.com/public/pr/policy/collaborative.shtml accessed November 10, 2003

21. NABP Model State Pharmacy Act and Model Rules of the National Association of Boards of Pharmacy. Section 105. June 2003

22. ASHP List of States by Statutory and Regulatory Authority June 21, 2002 http://www.ashp.com/gad/Issues/CDTM/CDTMStateComparisons.pdf   accessed July 7, 2003

23. National Association of Boards of Pharmacy Survey of Pharmacy Law—2001-2002, National Association of Boards of Pharmacy, Park Ridge, Illinois, 2002, pp. 82–83.

24. Cannistra J. Expanding Collaborative Practice in a Non Collaborative World. *Pharmacy Today* 2002; July:1,20,35

TABLE 19.1. Attributes of state and federal regulations governing collaborative practice.

State	Year	Types of collaborative practice agreements	Level of review of approval required	Medications included	Environments	Educational requirements/demonstrated competencies	Other aspects addressed
Alaska[a]	2002	Written protocols	Physician, BOP	All	All	No additional	Initiate and modify drug therapy
Arizona	2000	Written protocols (drug therapy management agreement)	Physician, BOP, drug therapy management advisory committee	All	Healthcare institutions including hospitals, staff models of a healthcare organization, nursing care instruction, community health center	One of the following: – Pharmacy practice residency accredited by ASHP/APhA – Current board specialty certification for the BPS or current certification as a licensed geriatric pharmacists – Doctor of pharmacy degree and completion of an ACPE-approved certificate program in each of the practice areas of practice covered in the drug therapy management agreement – Bachelor's degree in pharmacy, satisfactory completion of an ACPE-approved certificate program in each area of practice covered in the drug therapy management agreement, an appropriate credentialing issued by the governing body of a qualifying Arizona practice site	Implement, monitor, and modify drug therapy
Arkansas	1997	Protocol for each specific patient	Physician	All	All	Must be credentialed in one of the following areas of disease state management: asthma, anticoagulation therapy, diabetes, dyslipidemia Copy of credential must be kept on file at BOP Those completing diabetes mellitus training eligible for reimbursement from insurance companies	Completion of course approved by BOP enables pharmacist to administer certain medications, including immunizations and vaccinations, to patients aged 18 years or older

State	Year	Types of collaborative practice agreements	Level of review of approval required	Medications included	Environments	Educational requirements/demonstrated competencies	Other aspects addressed
California	1981/ 2002	Policies, procedures, protocols	Facility	All	1981: Licensed healthcare facilities, licensed providers who contract with licensed healthcare service plans. 2002: Expanded to all settings	Clinical residency or clinical experience as specified by facility	Administering injections; patient assessment; laboratory tests; initiating and adjusting drug regimens. January 2002: EC in community pharmacy; protocol with authorized prescriber; training course required
Connecticut	2002/ 2003	Written protocols specific to patient	Physician, available for inspection by Department of Public Health and Consumer Protection	All	Hospital–inpatient. 2003: Nursing homes	Determined by institution, criteria filed with commission of pharmacy	Authority to implement, modify, and discontinue drug therapy; administration; laboratory tests
Delaware[b]	1999	Administration of injectables (medications, biologics, and vaccines) protocol	Pharmacy regulatory council of the board of medical practice. Prescriptions and/or protocols must be available for inspection by BOP	Injectable medications, biologicals, and adult immunizations	All. The scope of the protocol must be limited to that physician's patient population	Curriculum approved by the BOP and a current CPR certificate and a minimum of two hours continuing education every licensure period	Pharmacist may also administer injectables pursuant to a valid prescription. Authority to perform capillary blood tests as a means to screen or monitor disease risk factors.
Florida	1986/ 1997	Formulary only (mostly OTC); legislation to establish protocols introduced in 1997	None	1986: Specified formulary only; no narcotics or injectables. 1997: All	Pharmacies	No additional except: CE course required to order lab tests. Smoking cessation certification required to prescribe nicotine transdermal systems	For OTC formulary: No pregnant or nursing women; only drug supplies for less than 34 days; no refills
Georgia[c]	2000	Protocol	Physician	All	All	Course of study approved by BOP; annual CE on modification of drug therapy	

State	Year	Type	Who	Drugs	Settings	Requirements to administer medications	Activities
Hawaii	1997/2002	Policies, procedures, protocols	Healthcare professionals, facility administrator	All	1997: Hospital 2002: All settings	Appropriate training that includes ACPE programs, curriculum based on programs from an ACPE-accredited college of pharmacy, state or local health department programs, or programs recognized by BOP	Patient assessment, ordering lab tests, administering drugs and injectables, modifying drug therapy; Transmission of a prescription to another pharmacist
Idaho[a]	1998	Written protocols	Physician	All	All	No additional	Initiate and modify drug therapy, patient assessment, ordering lab tests
Indiana	1996	Policies, protocols, and procedures	Hospital and admitting practitioner	All except narcotics	Acute care settings; private mental health institutions	No additional	Changing duration of therapy, drug strengths, dosage forms, frequencies, or routes of administration; stopping and adding drugs
Kentucky[d]	1996	Collaborative care agreements	None	All; narcotics not specified	All	No additional	Physical assessment; ordering clinical tests; initiating, continuing, or stopping drug therapy; drug modification and monitoring; therapeutic interchange
Louisiana[e]	1999	Written protocols	LA State Board of Medical Examiners and LA Board of Pharmacy	All	All	No additional	
Maine[f]	2004	EC protocol	To be determined	EC	Not specified	Approved training program on EC	Standardized fact sheet developed by BOP must be provided to patient
Maryland[g]	2002	Therapy management contract (condition or disease state specific)	Board of physician quality assurance and BOP	All	All (Therapy contracts are not required for institutional settings)	PharmD or equivalent training plus one of the following: specialty certification, accredited residency NABP credentialing, certificate program AND 1000 hrs clinical experience or 320 hrs in structured experience program approved by BOP	Modification, continuation, discontinuation of drug therapy; ordering lab tests; patient care monitoring
Minnesota	1998	Written patient-specific protocol with dentist, optometrist, physician, podiatrist, or veterinarian	None	All	All	No additional for general protocols Vaccines: ACPE-accredited vaccination program or graduated in 2001 or thereafter	Administration for first doses and medical emergencies; modifying drug therapy 2003: Administration of vaccines

State	Year	Types of collaborative practice agreements	Level of review of approval required	Medications included	Environments	Educational requirements/demonstrated competencies	Other aspects addressed
Mississippi	1987	Guidelines, protocols	BOP	All	Institutional settings; in outpatient settings, specific protocols required for each patient	Study course (of at least 20 hours) approved by BOP	Initiating and modifying drug therapy; administration; ordering lab tests
Montana[h]	2001	Written protocol	None	All	All	No additional	Initiating and modifying drug therapy; administration including immunizations for 18 or older; EC
Nebraska	1998	Not addressed	None	All	All	No additional	Administration including immunization
Nevada	1990	Protocols	Available for inspection by BOP	All, except narcotics	Licensed medical facilities: hospitals, hospices, managed-care settings, home health care, skilled nursing facilities	No additional	Initiating, modifying, and monitoring drug therapy
New Jersey[i]	2004	Written protocol or guideline with licensed physician	To be determined by regulations	To be determined by regulations	To be determined by regulations	To be determined by regulations	Modifying, continuing, or discontinuing drug or device therapy; ordering or performing laboratory tests; ordering clinical tests; administration including immunizations
New Mexico	1993/2002	1993: Protocols 2002: Specific vaccination and EC protocols	BOP approves practitioner license	All	All	Pharmacist clinician: 60 hrs of physical assessment with either 9 months of clinical experience or a 150-hr, 300-patient contact MD-supervised preceptorship and successful passing of a BOP-approved examination. Pharmacists certified by Indian Health Service Pharmacist Practitioner Program must provide documentation of 600 patient contacts with the past 2 years and an affidavit from supervising physician	Monitoring drug therapy; ordering laboratory tests; patient assessment; prescribing and modifying drug therapy. Practitioner and pharmacist must meet every 2 weeks to discuss patient management (every 60 days in nursing homes)

State	Year	Authority/Agreement	Regulating body	Patient population	Settings	Requirements	Scope of practice
North Carolina	1999	Written protocol	NC Medical Board and NC Board of Pharmacy	All	All	Certification renewed annually by completing an additional 10 hrs of ACPE credit beyond the 16 required for license. Meets one of the following: BCPS certification, certified geriatric practitioner, ASHP residency, PharmD, 3 years of clinical experience and approved certificate program in area of practice, BS PharmD and 5 years clinical experience and 2 certificate programs. Clinical pharmacy practitioner designation renewed annually	2002: Administering vaccinations and prescriptive authority for EC. Implementing, modifying drug therapy; ordering lab tests. 2004: Official DEA recognition to prescribe controlled substances
North Dakota	1995/ 2001	Collaborative agreement with licensed physician	BOP and board of medical examiners	All, except narcotics	Institutional settings: skilled hospitals; skilled nursing facilities; swing bed facilities; clinics	35 hours of CE. For authority to *initiate* drug therapy: ScD, PhD in clinical pharmacy, MS or PharmD OR certified as Fellow by Board of Pharmaceutical Specialties OR completed an accredited fellowship or residency. No additional to modify drug therapy. 2001: To perform CLIA waived lab tests—board approved course and instrument training plus CLIA certificate. 2001: To administer injectables and immunizations—board approved course and BCLS	Pharmacist must notify physician when initiating or modifying drug therapy. Physician limited to collaborative agreements with no more than 3 pharmacists. 2001: Authority to perform CLIA waived lab tests. 2001: Authority to administer medications and immunizations
Ohio	1999	Depends on setting. Outpatient: Consult agreement signed by pharmacist, physician, and patient	Depends on setting. Outpatient: Physician. Hospital: Approved by facility. Long term care: Policies developed by facility are approved by BOP	All	All	Depends on setting. Outpatient and long term care: No additional. Hospital inpatient: Competencies set by facility. Specific course required for administration of immunizations	Outpatient: Monitoring and modifying drug therapy. Hospital inpatient: Allows pharmacist to act as agent of physician

397

State	Year	Types of collaborative practice agreements	Level of review of approval required	Medications included	Environments	Educational requirements/demonstrated competencies	Other aspects addressed
Oregon[a]	1980	Hospital inpatient and long term care: policies for agreements set by facility / Patient-specific written protocols	None / Protocols on file at BOP	All	All	No additional	
Pennsylvania	2002	Written protocols	Physician protocols on file at BOP and board of medicine	All	Institutional	No additional / State BOP to establish educational guidelines for authority to administer injectables	Administration of injectables, ordering lab tests / Pharmacist must carry liability insurance
Rhode Island	2001	Written protocols	None	All	All	Advanced training: Residency OR board certification OR certification from an accredited professional organization or education institution	
South Carolina	1998*	Not explicitly addressed	Not addressed	Not explicitly addressed	Not explicitly addressed	Not addressed	*2002: The BOP has not taken a stance on interpretation of the statute
South Dakota	1993	Protocols	Practitioner or the legal authority of the licensed health facility	All, except narcotics	All	No additional	Administering, initiating, and modifying drug therapy; research investigators
Texas	1995	Written protocols with specific physicians	Must be available for inspection by BOP	All	All	Specific clinical CE (6 hrs)	Administration, physical assessment, ordering lab tests, implementing and modifying drug therapy / Written protocol defined as a physician's order, standing order, standing delegation order, or other identified protocol

State	Year	Protocol	Authorizing body	Scope	Setting	Certification	Administration of prescription drug therapy
Utah	2001	Written protocols	Outpatient: Division of Occupational and Professional Licensing and Physician's Licensing Board; Inpatient: Facility approva	All		No additional except training and BCLS certification required for administration	
Vermont[a]	1992	Medication or dosing protocols	Medical staff of institution	All	Institutional settings	No additional	Adjustment of doses; VT Breg 4.512: "This section should not be construed as giving prescribing privileges to pharmacists."
Virginia	1999	Written protocol with MD, DO, or podiatrist	BOP and board of medicine	All	Protocols not required in inpatient facilities	No additional	Modification, discontinuation of drug therapy; ordering lab tests; Requires written consent from patient on file; $750 fee to board for each protocol that has to be reviewed
Washington	1979	Protocols	BOP	All		No additional	Initiating and modifying drug therapy; physical assessment; ordering lab tests; Protocols must be renewed every 2 years
Wyoming	1999	Written protocols	Physician	All		No additional	Implement and modify drug therapy; physical assessment; ordering lab tests
Federal government	1995	Protocols within scope of practice	Appropriate facility-based authorizing body or chief of staff	Dependent on state license held by pharmacist**	All	Clinical pharmacy specialist; One of the following: MS, PharmD, accredited residency, specialty board certification, or 2 years clinical experience	No protocol or cosignature required within scope of practice; policies required to assure practice is within identified scope of practice **As of January 8, 2003; For NON-controlled substances the individual VA institution specifies the internal scope of practice for the professional.

State	Year	Types of collaborative practice agreements	Level of review of approval required	Medications included	Environments	Educational requirements/demonstrated competencies	Other aspects addressed
							The CPS does not need to hold a license in a state that specifically outlines prescribing privileges. To prescribe controlled substances the CPS needs to have this authority stated in the practice act of the state licensed in

Source: Adapted from Carmichael JM, O'Connell MB, Devine B, et al. Collaborative Drug Therapy Management by Pharmacists. *Pharmacotherapy* 1997; 17:1050-1061; Hammond RW, Schwartz AH, Campbell MJ, et al. Collaborative Drug Therapy Management by Pharmacists—2003. *Pharmacotherapy* 2003; 23(9):1210-1225.

Note: BOP = board of pharmacy; EC = emergency contraception

[a]Regulations not statute

[b]In state statute

[c]2003: Awaiting regulations

[d]2004: Authority to administer immunizations under physician protocol

[e]2003: Regulations are required to enact CDTM; regulations have not been promulgated.

[f]In state statute; regulations to be determined

[g]$250 fee to board for each pharmacist/physician agreement that has to be reviewed; 2003: Regulations adopted.

[h]2004: Official DEA recognition to prescribe controlled substances

[i]Regulations will be written jointly by NJ BOP and NJ State Board of Medical Examiners.

[j]Current directive #2003-04 expires January 31, 2008.

TABLE 19.2. Additional states where interpretation allows for some form of collaborative practice.

State	Year	Types of collaborative practice agreements	Level of review of approval required	Medications included	Environments	Educational requirements/demonstrated competencies	Other aspects addressed
Illinois[a]	N/A	Pharmacist may practice CDTM if acting as agent of prescriber	N/A	Not specified	All	Not specified	Initiate and modify drug therapy
Iowa[b]	1996	Written protocol	Physician	All	Retail and health-system pharmacies that meet eligibility requirements for the Medicaid Demonstration Project	No additional	Implementing, modifying drug therapy; clinical assessment; ordering lab tests
Kansas	1996	Medical Practice Act interpreted to permit delegation to pharmacist	None	All	All	No additional	Copy of protocol for immunizations kept at primary care provider's office / Information reported to state immunization registry
Michigan	1991, under state public health code	Responsibility delegated by MD or DO	None	All, except C-II drugs and steroids	All; Medical Practice Act interpreted to permit delegation to pharmacist	None specified	Pharmacist must record the name of the delegating MD or DO on the prescription
Tennessee[c]	N/A	Not specified	None	Not specified	Not specified	Not specified	Pharmaceutical care is defined as including "developing relationships with licensed practitioners to enable the pharmacist to accomplish comprehensive management of the patient's pharmacy related care

and to enhance a patient's wellness, quality of life and optimize outcomes; and communicating to the health care provider any knowledge of unexpected or adverse response to drug therapy, or resolving unexpected or adverse response; and having a pharmacist available at all times to patients and health care providers to respond to their questions and needs." (Tennessee BOP)

2004: Pharmacy students who have completed their second year and a 12-hour course on vaccines may administer adult vaccinations under the supervision of a practicing pharmacist.

Wisconsin[d]	2000	Medical Practice Act interpreted to permit delegation to pharmacist	None	All	All	No additional

Source: Adapted from Carmichael JM, O'Connell MB, Devine B, et al. Collaborative Drug Therapy Management by Pharmacists. *Pharmacotherapy* 1997; 17:1050-1061; Hammond RW, Schwartz AH, Campbell MJ, et al. Collaborative Drug Therapy Management by Pharmacists—2003. *Pharmacotherapy* 2003; 23(9):1210-1225.

Note: BOP = board of pharmacy

[a]Not addressed in laws or regulations

[b]Guideline not statute and hence subject to interpretation

[c]Not specifically cited in law

[d]Guideline rather than statute

Chapter 20

Supportive Personnel in Pharmacy Practice

Thomas George

There is a certain inevitable futility in indecision.

Voltaire

The American Society of Health-System Pharmacists (ASHP) defines pharmaceutical care as the direct, responsible provision of medication-related care for the purpose of achieving definite outcomes that improve a patient's quality of life. The Joint Commission on Accreditation of Healthcare Organizations (JCAHO), which has profoundly affected health and pharmaceutical care, has redefined the accreditation process by placing patient outcomes at the center of their standards.

As a result, we continue to develop and expand pharmacy roles to meet the objective of pharmaceutical care. The key to achieving this is the development of a highly trained, well-defined corps of supportive personnel. Pharmaceutical care (as we have defined it) cannot be implemented without concomitantly expanding the roles of support personnel—even beyond the advanced roles that are being accepted today.

Today, supportive personnel can be found pursuing professional careers in clinics, hospitals, community and chain pharmacies, home care pharmacies, long term care facilities, and mail service pharmacies.

HISTORICAL PERSPECTIVE

What is the role of supportive personnel in pharmacy practice? We can trace the formal use of supportive personnel back to World War II, when

Note: The legal concepts, laws, doctrine, and cases used in this chapter have been edited for purposes of educational clarity. For specific legal advice, pharmacists and pharmacy support personnel should seek competent legal counsel.

Pharmacy Law Desk Reference
doi:10.1300/5790_20

workforce shortages led to the use of assistant pharmacists. Originally, all pharmacy supportive personnel received informal, on-the-job training. In the early 1940s formal training programs for pharmacy supportive personnel were introduced by the military. More structured programs were developed during the late 1950s. In 1958, the ASHP published qualifications and responsibilities for a "pharmacy helper-storekeeper." In 1966, a joint committee of the ASHP and American Colleges of Pharmacy (AACP) approved a statement recognizing "hospital pharmacy technician-helpers." This coincided with the Department of Health, Education, and Welfare recommendation to develop "pharmacist aide" curricula in junior colleges and other educational institutions. During the 1970s, in response to requests from hospital pharmacy administrators, formal training programs continued to expand to meet the needs of the profession. The ASHP accredited the first technician training program in 1983. Community and chain pharmacies, however, had little interest in formally trained support staff and continued to train technicians on the job. This dichotomy in education still exists today, with the majority of pharmacy support personnel being trained on the job. This is due, in part, to the proliferation of chain pharmacies, the pharmacist workforce shortage, the limited number of formal educational programs available, and the lack of uniform training standards.

Recently, pharmacy supportive personnel have been recognized as skilled and professional workers. Even the term "pharmacy technician" is a relatively new title. Over the years, supportive personnel have been known by a variety of names, including pharmacy helpers, pharmacy clerks, pharmacy assistants, pharmacy aides, pharmacy support personnel, qualified pharmacy employees, support staff, unlicensed personnel, unlicensed assistants, and even pharmacy technologists. Collectively, state pharmacy practice acts used more than eleven different terms to describe pharmacy supportive personnel. Many of these terms are still in use today because they are embedded in the antiquated pharmacy practice acts of various states. A majority of states, however, have adopted the term "pharmacy technician" to describe the most skilled and professional member of a pharmacy support staff.

For the purposes of this chapter, the following definitions from the Pennsylvania Society of Health System Pharmacists serve well to define the various types of pharmacy supportive personnel that can be found in practice today.

> *Certified pharmacy technician:* A pharmacy technician who has met the minimum requirements of the Pharmacy Technician Certification Board (PTCB) by sitting for and passing the National Pharmacy Technician Certification Examination or who has transferred previously approved state certification to PTCB standing and who maintains her

or his certification according to the continuing education requirements outlined by the PTCB.

Pharmacy technician: A skilled worker who has been trained to assist
the pharmacist in preparing and dispensing medications.

Clerk/aide: A worker employed to assist in the performance of clerical,
billing, administrative, and minor technical tasks in the pharmacy.
Pharmacy aides work closely with pharmacy technicians. They are often
clerks or cashiers who primarily answer telephones, handle money,
stock shelves, and perform other clerical duties. Pharmacy technicians usually perform more complex tasks than do pharmacy aides,
although in some jurisdictions their duties and job titles overlap.

Secretary/assistant: A category of worker employed to assist in the performance of clerical and administrative tasks in the pharmacy.

Some jurisdictions use a general definition for supportive personnel. For
example, Nevada uses the following definition: "Supportive personnel
means persons who perform technical services in a pharmacy that do not require the judgment of a pharmacist but which are related to the preparation
and distribution of drugs under the direct supervision of the pharmacist who
is responsible for all of the work performed in the pharmacy." Supportive
personnel, by regulation, may be further defined to mean technicians and
technicians in training. The U.S. Department of Labor Bureau of Labor Statistics recognizes two types of supportive personnel, the pharmacy technician and the pharmacy aide.

This chapter concentrates on the legal aspects of pharmacy technician
practice, since technician activities can differ significantly from the usual
business activities of clerks, administrative assistants, and secretaries. Although some of the discussions here will apply to all types of pharmacy supportive personnel, the reader should also refer to legal treatises covering
general business and employment law.

SCOPE OF PRACTICE

Until recently, state regulation did not keep up with the continually expanding role of support personnel, especially pharmacy technicians. For
example, in 1988 eight states still did not allow technicians to practice in a
community setting. Now, however, many states have begun to address these
roles and look at training requirements, certification, registration, and even
licensure. The National Association of Boards of Pharmacy (NABP) formed
a specific task force in 1999 to examine the regulation of pharmacy technicians and the role they play in delivering pharmaceutical care.

This task force recommended three levels of supportive personnel: the "pharmacy technician," the "certified pharmacy technician," and a much higher level of supportive personnel, the "pharmacist assistant." The task force specified the scope of practice that would be allowed for each level of support personnel under the supervision of a pharmacist. The pharmacy assistant would have limited dispensing privileges but could not practice independently without a supervising pharmacist. This is similar to how paralegals practice. While the Task Force on Standardization of Technicians' Role and Competencies recommended the pharmacy assistant, the NABP Committee on Law Enforcement/Legislation advocated against this level of support personnel, and as a result, the NABP did not adopt the third level of pharmacist assistant. The ASHP and the American Pharmacists Association (APhA) likewise oppose the creation of this category of supportive personnel. The responsibility of a pharmacy technician may include any or all of the following activities under the supervision of a registered pharmacist. Each of these activities present an area in which the technician, technician supervisor, pharmacist, and employer may be exposed to legal liability due to noncompliance with federal and state laws and regulations or because the individual in question has performed below established standards of practice and other quasi-legal requirements such as institutional policies, professional standards, and JCAHO requirements.

Accepting a Written Prescription Order

Pharmacy technicians and other support personnel may accept a prescription order from the patient when it is brought into the pharmacy. This expedites the dispensing process. The pharmacy technician may check the prescription order for the following information:

Name of patient—Many times this information needs to be written by the pharmacy technician above the prescriber's writing for purposes of clarification.

Address of patient—A street address and city are required for controlled substances under federal and state law. Some jurisdictions and many pharmacies also require an address on all prescription orders. A phone number also may be required.

Age of patient—The age is helpful for third-party billing and also to differentiate between people with the same first and last names, i.e., senior and junior or I, II, III. The age of the patient is important to the pharmacist to check the appropriateness of the drug prescribed and its dosage. Serious harm may come to patients, especially infant, pediatric, or geriatric patients, if they receive an inappropriate dosage.

Billing information—Billing information is required by the pharmacist at the time of dispensing the prescription order for patients who have health insurance policies that will pay for prescription drugs.

Allergy information—The pharmacy technician or aide should ask the patient or customer if he or she has any drug or food allergies. If the patient has no known allergies, a notation should be made on the back or the face of the prescription order. The abbreviation NKA is customarily used to denote "no known allergy." This information, as well as any allergies the patient may have, should also be entered on the patient profile in the pharmacy computer. A prescription order should never be dispensed until a determination is made as to whether the patient has any allergies.

The most recent expansion of permitted technician activities includes the ability to accept verbal renewal authorizations and verbal requests for new prescription orders. Some jurisdictions permit only renewal authorizations, while others permit technicians to take both new prescription orders and renewal authorizations. A third group of jurisdictions permits technicians to take renewals only when there is no change in strength or directions. If there is, the technician must refer the call to the pharmacist.

Preparing and Dispensing the Prescription Order

The pharmacy technician may perform the following tasks that involve the dispensing of a prescription order under the supervision of a registered pharmacist:

Prepare or modify a patient profile: A new patient profile will need to be created when a new patient brings in a prescription order. Existing profiles can be updated with allergy, billing information, or other notes.

Enter the prescription order data on the patient profile: The pharmacy technician may key prescription order data into a computer system. The interpretation of the prescription order requires an extensive training program that includes both written and on-the-job training. Each pharmacy will have a very specific policy and procedure involving the task of preparing a profile.

Manually fill a prescription order: After the information is entered in the patient profile, the next step is to prepare the prescription order for dispensing. The technician will assist in the preparation of the prescription order for dispensing. This task may include obtaining the product, counting the prescribed number of tablets, capsules, etc., pouring the indicated quantity into the appropriate size container, choosing the correct trade formulation and package: e.g., for such products as ophthalmic (eye), otic (ear), topical (cream or ointment), or nasal products, and labeling the product. The container selected for dispensing the prescription medicine must conform to state and federal law. Usually this requires the use of childproof or safety closures for prescription containers. Consent by the patient is required for the use of non–safety closures. Any prescription order requiring extemporaneous compounding or mixing of multiple ingredients is generally left to the pharmacist to prepare. Such compounds may be prepared by the technician following explicit directions and under direct supervision by the pharmacist.

Prepare the label: The computer-generated label from a pharmacy computer profile system will be prepared automatically when all pertinent information is entered. The label usually contains the following information:

> Name of patient
> Date of dispensing
> Directions for use
> Name of medication
> Name of prescribing physician
> Name of drug manufacturer
> Pharmacist's initials
> Prescription order number
> Expiration date
> Auxiliary labels

The label may be affixed to the medication container of the prepared drug or left off until checked by the pharmacist. This is a policy determined by the pharmacy and state regulations. In certain situations or in certain communities with different ethnic groups, it may be necessary to prepare labels in different languages. Failure to do so may result in liability if the patient or customer fails to take the drug correctly because the directions were unclear.

When all of these steps have been completed, the supervising pharmacist will check the work of the technician. The pharmacist, who then completes the task of dispensing the prescription order, does a comprehensive review of the prescription order, the patient profile, the drug selected, the quantity, the label, and the price. At this time, the pharmacist will provide the patient with the required drug information to maximize the use of the prescription medication. This may include the use of auxiliary labels. In some cases, technicians affix auxiliary labels to the medication container, but this will still be verified by the supervising pharmacist.

The pharmacist has a legal, professional, and ethical responsibility to determine or assess the patient's needs regarding counseling and provide the patient with as much drug information as required to ensure the proper use of each prescription medication. The legal requirement arises from individual state laws passed as a result of the Omnibus Budget Reconciliation Act of 1990. In some jurisdictions, technicians and other supportive personnel may make the offer to counsel, but a pharmacist must do the actual patient counseling. The specifics of these counseling requirements may be found in the pharmacy practice acts of each state.

Third-Party Administration Responsibilities

Primarily this involves determining the correct benefit plan information. Today, most patients carry a prescription card that identifies themselves and their insurer. These cards contain the following information:

Name of insured (cardholder)
Group number
Identification number
Dependent information, i.e., who is covered, spouse, children
Expiration date of coverage
Amount paid by patient, i.e., copay
Carrier (name of provider of pharmacy services)

In a computerized pharmacy, the third-party information is stored until it is needed for real-time claim adjudication. Once the third-party administrator or pharmacy benefit management company processes adjudicated claims, a reimbursement check is issued to the pharmacy along with a statement of claims. The statement of claims is used for reconciliation. Failure to follow employer policies with regard to third-party billing may result in substantial revenue loss for the employer and expose the technician or aide to legal liability.

Inventory Control

Technicians are also involved in coordinating inventory control, which may include controlled substances or scheduled drugs. These inventory activities include establishing inventory levels of prescription and OTC drugs, establishing ordering procedures, checking in orders, monitoring price changes, and checking expiration dates. Outdated drugs must be removed from inventory and properly disposed of according to the prevailing state law.

Additional Institutional Responsibilities

In addition to the above activities, institutional practice may include the following responsibilities: packaging and labeling medications based on physician orders, assembling a twenty-four-hour supply of medication for each patient (filling unit doses), filling and refilling automated dispensing cabinets, preparing commercially unavailable medications, preparing sterile intravenous and other parenteral medications, delivering medications, repackaging unit dose medications, maintaining anesthesia and other drug trays, maintaining nursing unit medications, inspecting and maintaining emergency carts, and inspecting and maintaining medication storage areas.

Advanced Roles for Pharmacy Technicians

What are some of these new and advanced activities? They include daily quality assurance activities, nuclear pharmacy activities, oncology practice, coordinating the introduction of new technology, managing new automation and technology, such as computerized dispensing or robotic equipment, first dose and stat dose dispensing, preparing written communications, implementing or revising policies and procedures, and assisting clinical pharmacists with data collection and analysis activities.

Technicians also train other technicians by providing in-service programs, outside training programs, and continuing education. Pharmacy technicians may also have positions as system coordinators, supervisors, and pharmaceutical buyers, further increasing their responsibility and liability.

Technicians are also checking the work of other technicians. This is sometimes known as tech-check-tech. This activity was first utilized by Veterans Administration hospitals where supervisory technicians check the unit dose fills done by other technicians. Several states now permit this activity by regulation.

REGULATION

Based on a recent NABP survey, twenty-four states required registration and five required licensure of pharmacy technicians. This was not always the case, however. Historically, pharmacy has opposed both recognizing technicians or other supportive personnel and expanding their scope of practice. This was based on the prevailing attitudes of pharmacists who took a protectionist position when it came to job assurance. Among all pharmacy supportive personnel, only the pharmacy technician requires registration or licensure.

In terms of regulation, we can expand the definition of the term "pharmacy technician." For purposes of national voluntary certification as described previously, pharmacy technicians are defined as individuals working in a pharmacy who, under the supervision of a licensed pharmacist, assist in pharmacy activities not requiring the professional judgment of the pharmacist. A majority of jurisdictions include in their pharmacy laws and regulations a distinction between activities requiring professional judgment (those permitted to be done only by pharmacists) and nonjudgment activities (those permitted to be done by technicians and other pharmacy supportive personnel).

It is important to apply terms such as certification, licensure, and registration carefully and in ways that are consistent with their use throughout the health field. Several states use the term "license" in their regulations, but in actuality, the licensing process is nothing more than registration. The following definitions are useful in evaluating the type of legal recognition afforded to pharmacy technicians:

Certification is the process by which a nongovernmental agency or association grants recognition to an individual who has met certain predetermined qualifications specified by that agency or association.

Licensure is the process by which an agency of government grants permission to an individual to engage in a given occupation upon finding that the applicant has attained the minimal degree of competency necessary to ensure that the public health, safety, and welfare will be reasonably well protected.

Registration is the process of making a list or being enrolled in an existing list. This author believes that the majority of states will use this approach coupled with certain requirements for registration such as certification, documented and/or approved on-the-job training, and educational requirements such as a high school diploma or a certain number and type of college credits. These added requirements are now appearing in state board regulations that specify criteria for training programs, examinations, and evidence of continued competency. A minority of jurisdictions uses the current PTCB certification to qualify a person for technician registration.

There are several important differences between licensing, registration, and certification. Licensed professionals who fall below an acceptable level of practice can be fined, reprimanded, and have their licenses suspended or revoked. Suspensions and revocations are usually given some type of legal recognition in other jurisdictions, so the practical effect is that the professional can no longer practice. Society is thus protected from a dangerous practitioner. The situation is different for supportive personnel, however. Most jurisdictions do not require licensure. Therefore, the means to remove a dangerous individual from practice does not exist. Even with registration, a technician is free to move to another jurisdiction that does not require registration. The same scenario applies to certification. In some jurisdictions, if a technician loses his or her certification, the technician can still work, albeit in a lesser capacity. The technician can also work in other states.

When an employee is not licensed, the burden of ensuring competency falls on the employer. The employer, however, must do this within the confines of existing employment laws that strongly favor the employee. These laws, while protecting the employee, restrict the ability of employers to oversee employee conduct.

All jurisdictions require supervision of pharmacy technicians. The degree of technician supervision required, however, varies from state to state. The majority of jurisdictions require direct supervision of support personnel, especially those states that have expanded technician activities and formally recognize pharmacy technicians by registration or licensure. Direct supervision is most often defined as requiring that the pharmacist be physically present to observe the technician and provide supervision. The pharmacist supervisor must be on the premises and aware of the activities of the technician or technicians, but does not necessarily have to be in the same physical space or room. Going down the street for lunch or to the bank with a mobile phone for communication, which has been known to occur on occasion, would be stretching the interpretation and clearly be a violation of pharmacy regulations in all jurisdictions. Some jurisdictions require that the technician must be under the direct supervision of a licensed pharmacist who is physically present and capable of observing the actions of the pharmacy technician.

How many technicians can one pharmacist supervise? No, not as many as you can get away with. A majority of states now specify how many technicians a pharmacist can supervise. The ratio of pharmacists to technicians varies in each of these states depending on the practice setting. Many states allow ratios of 1:2 or 1:3 in institutions, but only corresponding ratios of 1:1 or 1:2 in a community setting. Some jurisdictions are silent on this issue or have vague regulations that do not specify specific ratios.

Currently, most jurisdictions permit pharmacist-to-technician ratios of 1:2 or 1:3. This is a trend away from more restrictive ratios in the 1:1 to 1:2 range. Some states will permit expansion of these ratios on request or based on the number of *certified* pharmacy technicians employed.

The reader is cautioned to check current state board of pharmacy regulations for specific state licensure and registration requirements governing pharmacy support personnel and for specific pharmacist-to-technician ratios.

TRAINING

At the present time there are no uniform national training standards for pharmacy technicians or other pharmacy support personnel. This has severely limited the recognition of pharmacy technicians and is primarily responsible for the underutilization of support personnel. The wide disparity in training, education, and levels of responsibility has produced and continues to nourish a pervasive futility among all levels of pharmacy practitioners attempting to define their roles in the healthcare system. Substandard training programs and those that purport to train support personnel result in ill-trained individuals who can be a danger to patients. This disparity also makes it difficult for employers to find and hire well-trained, professionally mature individuals to fill their support personnel needs. The burden of ensuring competency that may fall on the employer also increases.

Technician training programs differ in many ways, the most important being experiential contact hours, program content, didactic components, and overall length. Typical programs are divided into didactic training, laboratory and practical training, and clinical training. Clinical experiential training most frequently takes place in community or chain pharmacies and hospital pharmacies. Programs typically strive to offer both types of clinical experience, but due to high student numbers and a lack of suitable facilities many students do not participate in both rotations. Programs purporting to train people as pharmacy technicians have as few as 56 didactic contact hours with no experiential training. Accredited programs range from 540 to more than 2,100 contact hours. The ASHP requires a minimum of 600 contact hours and with a minimum duration of 15 weeks for accreditation. Depending on the program chosen, students can earn diplomas, certifications, or associate degrees. The Pharmacy Technician Educators Council advocates that all technician training programs evolve into two-year associate degree programs. A typical two-year associate degree program curriculum is illustrated in Table 20.1.

Most institutions require candidates for admission to an associate degree program to meet the following requirements for admission: One course each of algebra, chemistry, and biology at either the senior high school or college level with a minimum grade of "C" within the past five years. They

TABLE 20.1. Sample two-year associate degree curriculum.

Course title	Credits
Semester I	
Chemistry	3
Introduction to Pharmacy Practice	3
Rhetoric I	3
Computer Science elective	3
Psychology	3
Total credits	15
Semester II	
Rhetoric II	3
Pharmacy Calculations	3
Human Biology	4
Pharmacology I	3
Medical Terminology	3
Total Credits	16
Semester III	
Pharmacology II	3
Elective or Microbiology	3 or 4
Introduction to Sociology	3
Pharmacy Techniques	4 (Sterile products, preparation, and dispensing.)
Social Science Elective	3
Total credits	16-17
Semester IV	
Pharmacy Law	3
Clinical Pharmacy	9 (Clinical internship 320 contact hours)
Elective	3
Total credits	15
Total degree credits	62-63

also recommend combined verbal and math SAT scores (nonrecentered score) of 800 or ACT scores of 17, or demonstration of college-level academic performance. College Board scores are usually not required for those applicants who have been out of high school for five or more years.

Continuing education for technicians is required in some jurisdictions, but the majority of states have not addressed this issue. The PTCB requires 20 contact hours of continuing education over a period of two years, at least one of which must be in pharmacy law. Programs relating to patient counseling or functions outside the scope of practice for pharmacy technicians are not acceptable.

LIABILITY ISSUES

Today, pharmacy technicians are performing more activities once exclusively performed by pharmacists. At the same time, pharmacists are assuming responsibility for supervising pharmacy technicians and are moving into clinically oriented services focused on the patient's drug therapy outcome. In order to gain an appreciation for what is occurring and examine the legal implications for pharmacy technicians, we need to examine some of the traditional activities and new, advanced roles for pharmacy technicians discussed above.

If we look at these activities, we see that traditionally they have all been done by pharmacists, who, until recently, were solely liable for any dispensing errors. If you add to these activities the new, advanced roles for pharmacy technicians, you have a situation that results in increased liability exposure for pharmacy technicians and other support personnel.

Although this chapter has attempted to provide a comprehensive list of pharmacy technician activities and corresponding responsibilities, the reader should be aware that not all jurisdictions allow technicians to perform all of these activities.

EXCLUSIONARY ACTIVITIES

Many jurisdictions specify what activities pharmacy technicians and other supportive personnel are not permitted to do (for example, take new prescription orders or chart orders by telephone, take renewal authorizations, distribute medications pursuant to prescriptions or chart orders unless verified by a pharmacist, and perform any action requiring a judgmental decision such as drug utilization review, prescription order clarification or therapy modification, or patient counseling).

A minority of jurisdictions specify activities that do not require a pharmacist, pharmacy intern, pharmacy technician, or technician in training. These activities may be performed by a pharmacy aide and include processing sales, including operating a cash register, stocking shelves, delivering medication to patients or within hospitals, and data entry, including entry of prescription information.

MALPRACTICE AND OTHER LIABILITIES

State and federal regulations control professional behavior through training requirements, assessment of competence, and licensure. Prosecutors can punish those professionals who fail to abide by these regulations with fines, license suspension or revocation, and even incarceration, yet the most powerful method for assuring professional competence is the lawsuit for malpractice.

Malpractice actions serve two basic purposes. First, they provide compensation for the harm one party has caused to another. Second, these actions serve as deterrents against substandard and irresponsible conduct. They are constant reminders that pharmacy technicians and other support personnel are held accountable for their actions.

Who is liable for the negligence of a pharmacy technician? Under the doctrine of *Respondeat Superior,* the pharmacist who supervises the technician would be liable along with the pharmacy technician. This doctrine states that an employer is responsible for the negligent acts of his or her employee. The classic example is that of a corporation with delivery truck drivers. If an accident occurs due to the delivery truck driver's negligence, while that driver is operating one of the company trucks and is on company business, the doctrine of *Respondeat Superior* would apply. This doctrine holds both the employer (the company) and the employee (driver) liable.

Consider this scenario. A technician negligently places the wrong drug in a unit dose cassette. It is administered and the patient has a severe allergic reaction that requires emergency treatment. The doctrine applies to the technician, the supervising pharmacist, and the hospital that employs them.

The scope of practice, as permitted by licensure, registration, or certification, defines what support personnel may do. Acting outside the scope of practice exposes the employer, pharmacist, and support personnel to liability. Some examples include acting without the supervision of a pharmacist, acting as pharmacists, i.e., counseling, performing discretionary acts, violating federal DEA regulations, or failure to meet licensing requirements, i.e., continuing educational requirements. In addition, acting outside the scope of authorized practice may allow an employer to shift blame and place the individual outside their malpractice liability insurance coverage.

Another area of concern is legislated technician and pharmacist liability. A number of states have specific regulations that hold the pharmacist liable for the actions of the pharmacy technician. Examples of typical language used in such regulations include "when direct supervision is required, a licensed pharmacist shall be jointly responsible and liable for the actions of a pharmacy technician" and "the pharmacist on duty shall be directly responsible for the conduct of a pharmacy technician." Pharmacists who violate statutes or regulations concerning the distribution of pharmaceutical products may be liable under the doctrine of *Negligence Per Se*. This conduct is treated as negligence without the need for proof because it is a violation of a statute or regulation designed to protect the public. If the pharmacist has clearly violated the statute or regulation, he or she has breached the duty of care. At this point, the plaintiff need only prove causation and damages. Likewise, pharmacy technicians are also exposed to liability through this doctrine. A likely scenario for a pharmacy technician would be where the technician incorrectly takes a telephoned prescription order from a prescriber, causing the patient to receive the wrong drug which then harms the patient. In a jurisdiction that does not permit the technician to accept verbal prescription orders, the doctrine of *Negligence Per Se* would apply.

MALPRACTICE ACTIONS

If we look at the types of malpractice cases filed, we see that approximately 75 to 80 percent are due to mechanical-type errors, such as the wrong drug being dispensed, the wrong directions being placed on the label, or the wrong strength of the drug being dispensed. The balance of cases (20 to 25 percent) is due to what are termed intellectual errors. These are cases in which the pharmacist has made an error in judgment or has provided incorrect advice. As technicians take over more drug dispensing functions, they are more likely to be involved in mechanical-type errors. In other words, pharmacy technicians are now more actively engaged in the type of activities that, if performed incorrectly, may result in the greatest percentage of malpractice cases.

The seriousness of medication errors is illustrated by the following Massachusetts case. A technician failed to dilute a dose of enalaprilat that the physician had prescribed to control a premature infant's blood pressure. The error resulted in a 750 mcg dose instead of the intended 6 mcg dose. The pharmacist who was responsible for checking the technician's work did not discover the error. The family claimed the infant suffered neurological damage as a result of the error and was awarded $7.1 million in damages at trial. In this case, the plaintiff did not bring suit against the hospital because of a state statute that limits damages to $20,000. Whatever the final outcome of the case is, the pharmacist and technician, but not their employer, will share the liability. The impact of such limited liability statutes on healthcare employees is yet unknown but certainly merits close attention.

As if that liability exposure is not enough, technicians may also be involved in intellectual errors. Typical scenarios include not advising the pharmacist of known drug interactions, providing the wrong information to patients, and providing advice when not permitted by law.

An overview of recent lawsuits affecting pharmacy technicians provides valuable insight and instruction. A review such as this is not meant to be alarming, although it may seem that way. Its purpose is to illustrate that the patient's interests and well-being must be paramount for all pharmacy personnel.

The importance of this concept is emphasized by a Virginia case in which a four-day-old baby died from an accidental overdose of potassium. According to the lawsuit the baby was born premature but with no significant abnormalities. A doctor prescribed potassium chloride to be administered through a feeding tube through the baby's belly button. The baby died of cardiac arrest. An autopsy found that hyperkalemia was the immediate cause of death. Blood potassium levels were nearly four times normal. The technician who improperly prepared and delivered the lethal dosage was fired by the medical center. The settlement was confidential, but a similar case with a fatal overdose of potassium was settled for $750,000.

In a Michigan case involving a pharmacy technician, the court found that the drugstore had voluntarily assumed a legal duty to advise customers properly of potential adverse drug interactions through its computerized information system. The case arose because a physician prescribed the decongestant Tavist-D and an antibiotic for the plaintiff's cold. The prescription orders were dispensed at the drugstore where the plaintiff had been getting Parnate, a prescription antidepressant. The computer showed an interaction between Tavist-D and Parnate, but a pharmacy technician apparently overrode the warning and filled the Tavist-D prescription order. Since the interaction warning was bypassed, the supervising pharmacist was not aware that the patient was taking Parnate. The technician failed to advise the pharmacist of the interaction warning and the Tavist-D was dispensed.

In a New Hampshire case, a pharmacist assistant placed a label on a vial and filled it with the number of tablets of medication called for on the label. Evidence showed that the vial contained the wrong medication, which resulted in the recipient's emergency hospitalization. The pharmacists involved were cited by the New Hampshire Board of Pharmacy for failing to examine the contents of the vial to make certain that it contained the medication actually prescribed. In these cases, even though the pharmacists were held liable, the technicians involved were also liable as co-actors.

Will a technician have to face a lawsuit by a pharmacist who is supervising them? The answer here is yes. Although the pharmacist is a co-actor and shares liability for the negligence, the pharmacist may proceed against the technician to collect a portion of the plaintiff's award or settlement. The doctrine of *Contribution* allows recovery from other joint tortfeasors in these situations. For example, in a Minnesota case, a technician made an error in preparing a parenteral nutrition solution that was not discovered by the pharmacist in charge. The technician faced liability along with the hospital and the pharmacist. Also, consider this Omaha case, where a hospital was sued because of a pharmacist error and paid $950,000 in damages. The hospital then sued the pharmacist to recover the award. The same scenario could occur if a technician made the error instead of the pharmacist. Both the hospital and the supervising pharmacist could sue the technician. In the Massachusetts case described above, the pharmacist defendant could have joined the technician, if the technician had not been included in the plaintiff's claim.

Technicians can also face liability and legal difficulties from other activities. A lawsuit was threatened against a pharmacy technician when the technician named a pharmacy patient and referred to the patient as a drug abuser while presenting a seminar on confidentiality to other technicians. The technician may have violated confidentiality laws and libeled or slandered the patient. Another issue that arises is whether the technician was within his scope of employment when the seminar was given. If the presentation was done at a national conference and not sponsored by the technician's employer, the technician may have been acting outside his scope of employment. If, on the other hand, the seminar was a work-related in-service, the technician would be acting within his scope of employment and his employer may share some liability.

With the passage of the Health Insurance Portability and Accountability Act of 1996 (HIPPA) we have the first ever federally mandated privacy laws. Up until the act went into effect in April 2003 only state laws covered individual privacy rights. The law applies to all healthcare workers and requires that healthcare organizations have written policies on privacy procedures and educate their employees on these procedures. The act authorizes specific federal penalties if a patient's right is violated. Patients are now permitted to see their medical records, which include pharmacy profiles and dispensing records.

In-service training is vital to reduce the risk of a lawsuit. Supportive personnel should familiarize themselves with their employer's policies, HIPPA requirements, and state laws. Training should include how to answer the phone, providing medical information, and what constitutes inappropriate conversation. In a similar vein, support personnel should understand that good patient and customer relations go a long way to reduce the potential for a claim. Perceived or real rudeness, lack of courtesy, and unexplained delays in dispensing prescription orders can foster an atmosphere ripe for litigation.

In an unusual Texas case, a pharmacist was found guilty of deceptive business practices because a prescription order was dispensed substituting the generic drug metronidazole in a bottle labeled as containing the brand name drug Flagyl. The pharmacist tried to blame the pharmacy technician who was on duty for mislabeling the prescription container. In similar scenarios, pharmacy technicians may be asked by their employers to participate in such fraudulent practices under the threat of losing their job. Consider the situation in which a technician knows that his or her employer is intentionally and consistently dispensing outdated drugs. Not only is the technician exposed to civil liability should harm come to the patient, but he or she is exposed to criminal liability for violating state and federal pharmacy regulations by dispensing expired drugs.

CONCLUSION

The threat of liability, both civil and criminal, is very real in pharmacy technician practice and will increase as technicians gain greater responsibilities. Pharmacy technicians as well as other support personnel must be aware of the consequences associated with negligent practice and adopt an attitude that places the welfare of the patient first and foremost. In addition, a thorough understanding of state and federal pharmacy regulations and drug laws is also required to ensure that no criminal liability occurs. Finally, practicing sound risk-management activities can reduce the potential for professional malpractice actions.

BIBLIOGRAPHY

Abood, R. and D. Brushwood. 2001. *Pharmacy Practice and the Law.* Gaithersburg, MD: Aspen Publishers, Inc.

American Society of Health-System Pharmacists. 2001. *Model Curriculum for Pharmacy Technician Training,* Second Edition. Bethesda, MD: ASHP.

Brushwood, D. 1994. Legal justification for licensure of pharmacy technicians. *Journal of Pharmacy Technology* 10 (March/April):61-63.

Bureau of Labor Statistics. 2005. Pharmacy technicians, aides. In *Occupational Outlook Handbook.* Washington, DC: U.S. Department of Labor.

Daniels, B. and M. Jensen. 1997. New roles for pharmacy technicians in the managed care setting. *Drug Benefit Trends* 9(6):12, 14-17.

Keresztes, J., S.M. Lang, and M. Palmer. 2001. National Pharmacy Technician Conference: Looking toward the future. *J Pharm Technol.* 17:S1-26.

National Association of Boards of Pharmacy. 2003. *2003-2004 National Association of Boards of Pharmacy Survey of Phatrmacy Law.* Mount Prospect, IL: NABP.

Young, D. 2002 Pharmacists, technician found liable for millions in medication error. *Am J Health Syst Pharm.* 59(12):1143-1144.

Chapter 21

Quality Improvement Initiatives for Pharmaceutical Care

Garry Carneal

INTRODUCTION

This chapter explores how quality improvement activities based upon various accreditation programs and regulatory avenues impact the health-care system in the United States. The analysis also looks at the challenges confronting pharmaceutical services, particularly in managed care settings, when establishing voluntary quality standards and accreditation programs.

MEASURING QUALITY IMPROVEMENT IS AN ONGOING CHALLENGE

Some believe the term *quality* is overused or misused in such a way that it sometimes undermines the ability of healthcare systems to actually improve patient care. To some extent, the overindulgence of this term can be explained by the complexity and fragmentation of the healthcare system itself, creating the need to use a variety of different approaches and tools to accurately measure quality.

Simply stated, one approach to quality benchmarking does not fit all applications or needs. This is especially true for pharmaceutical services.

As highlighted in Table 21.1, there are several different ways to measure quality. Most traditional health-related accreditation programs rely on process and structure measures. For example, accreditors often assess or audit a healthcare organization's written policies and procedure (P&Ps), and how these P&Ps are implemented. This type of benchmarking is referred to as a "process" measure. For others, the end game is really focused on implementing a performance or outcome measurement system that attempts to

Pharmacy Law Desk Reference
doi:10.1300/5790_21

TABLE 21.1. Types of quality benchmarks.

Types of measures	Descriptions
Structure	Does the organization have the capacity to deliver quality care? (e.g., size of the network, board certification of physicians, compliance with safety codes)
Process	Does the organization operate in a manner that promotes quality care? (e.g., provider credentialing)
Outcome/performance	Does the organization actually provide quality care?
Best practices/evidence-based	What are the models of care that promote quality and patient safety?
Individualized information management	What does each stakeholder value as quality-based care?

directly identify the causal relationship between a quality improvement activity and how patient health is actually improved. An example of this approach is a health plan that implements an immunization program and then measures how the immunizations decrease sickness in the targeted population of covered lives.

Typically, an interdependent relationship exists between the various types of quality measures identified in Table 21.1. For example, measuring health outcomes is useless unless there are well-established structures and processes supporting the targeted healthcare initiatives (e.g., a consistent baseline needs to be established).

Sometimes the linkage or correlation between processes or structures with improved performance is difficult to clearly establish due to a myriad of confounding variables. For example, a health plan may offer a case management or disease management program to reduce the incidence of asthma (such as the distribution of appropriate medications dispensed through an inhaler). However, certain environmental, genetic, and/or behavioral factors that the health plan cannot control for could greatly impact the health condition of an asthmatic even if the patient is dutifully following the instructions of the health plan.

Often, the complexity, fragmentation, flexibility, and ongoing evolution of the healthcare system make it difficult to apply quality measurement systems in a meaningful way over time. As a result, accreditation agencies and others must use different approaches to measure and document quality improvement activities, which in turn must be constantly updated and checked for validity.

THE ACCREDITATION MOVEMENT

Major Players

Over a dozen nonprofit accreditation organizations operating in the United States focus on promoting quality-based healthcare operations. Three of the best known agencies are the Joint Commission for the Accreditation of Healthcare Organizations (JCAHO or Joint Commission), the National Committee for Quality Assurance (NCQA), and URAC (formerly known as the Utilization Review Accreditation Commission and the American Accreditation HealthCare Commission).

JCAHO

JCAHO,[1] based in Oakbrook Terrace, Illinois, is the oldest and largest nonprofit accreditation organization in the United States and evaluates thousands of hospitals and healthcare organizations annually. Since 1951, JCAHO has developed state-of-the-art, professionally based standards and evaluates the compliance of healthcare organizations against these benchmarks. The Joint Commission is best known for auditing facility-based operations such as hospitals and chronic care facilities.

JCAHO is governed by a twenty-eight-member Board of Commissioners that includes nurses, physicians, consumers, medical directors, administrators, providers, employers, labor representatives, health plan leaders, quality experts, ethicists, health insurance administrators, and educators.

JCAHO's evaluation and accreditation services are provided for the following types of organizations:

- Hospitals (e.g., general, psychiatric, children's, and rehabilitation)
- Managed care networks
- Home care organizations (e.g., personal care and support services, home infusion and other pharmacy services, durable medical equipment services, and hospice services)
- Nursing homes and other long term care facilities (e.g., subacute care programs, dementia programs, and long term care pharmacies)
- Assisted-living facilities (e.g., coordinate personal services, twenty-four-hour supervision and assistance)
- Behavioral healthcare organizations (e.g., mental health and addiction services)

- Ambulatory care providers (e.g., outpatient surgery facilities, rehabilitation centers, infusion centers, and group practices)
- Clinical laboratories

JCAHO's standards address an organization's level of performance in key functional areas, such as patient rights, patient treatment, and infection control. In addition, the standards set forth performance expectations for activities that affect the safety and quality of patient care. JCAHO develops its standards in consultation with healthcare experts, providers, measurement experts, purchasers, and consumers.

In 1997, JCAHO launched "ORYX: The Next Evolution in Accreditation" to integrate the use of outcomes and other performance measurement data into the accreditation process. A planned component of the ORYX initiative is the identification and use of standardized, core performance measures that can be applied across accredited healthcare organizations in a particular accreditation program. Future sets of core performance measures for each accreditation program will be identified in a staggered approach. In 2001, JCAHO announced the four initial core measurement areas for hospitals: acute myocardial infarction; heart failure; community-acquired pneumonia; and pregnancy and related conditions.

NCQA

NCQA,[2] based in Washington, DC, was first established in the late 1970s by several industry trade groups. NCQA was later spun off as an independent nonprofit that began accrediting managed care in 1991. NCQA's Board of Directors is made up of fifteen representatives covering employer, provider, legal, and other stakeholder interests.

NCQA is best known for its work in assessing and reporting on the quality of care for health maintenance organizations (HMOs) through NCQA's accreditation and performance measurement programs. NCQA also accredits the following:

- Point-of-service plans
- Managed behavioral healthcare organizations
- Credentialing verification organizations
- Preferred provider organizations
- New health plans (special accreditation program)
- Physician organization certification
- Disease management organizations

NCQA also sponsors the Health Plan Employer Data and Information Set (HEDIS) performance measurement tool that is used by most HMOs in the United States. HEDIS is designed to provide purchasers, consumers, and other stakeholders the information to compare the performance of health plans. To date, over sixty different measures are implemented.

NCQA also publishes annually the *State of Managed Care Quality* report that takes a comprehensive look at the health plan quality performance. In addition, NCQA has created the Quality Compass, a national database of HEDIS and NCQA accreditation information from hundreds of health plans. This database includes national and regional averages and benchmarks, which help to establish targets for improvement and put plans' results into a more meaningful context.

URAC

URAC,[3] based in Washington, DC, is a nonprofit charitable organization founded in 1990 to establish standards for the healthcare industry. URAC began as a single, specialty accreditation agency for health utilization management functions in managed care settings, but the accreditation agency has diversified over the years and now offers over a dozen different accreditation programs covering a wide spectrum of healthcare activities.

URAC's broad-based twenty-four-member board includes representation from all constituencies affected by healthcare—employers, consumers, regulators, healthcare providers, and industry stakeholders. Moreover, hundreds of volunteers serve on URAC's committees and/or otherwise support URAC's activities.

URAC's main accreditation programs cover the following:

- Case management (CM) services
- Claims processing
- Consumer directed healthcare
- Core quality activities
- Credential verification organization (CVO) operations
- Disease management (DM) services
- External and independent reviews
- Health calls center operations
- Health network operations (e.g., preferred provider organizations, specialty networks)
- Health plan operations (e.g., health maintenance organizations, specialty health plans)

- Health plan consumer satisfaction (in conjunction with J.D. Power and Associates)
- HIPAA privacy compliance activities
- HIPAA security compliance activities
- Health provider credentialing programs
- Health utilization management (UM) services
- Health Web site services
- Workers' compensation network operations
- Workers' compensation UM services

URAC uses a modular approach to accreditation. This empowers companies to actually get accredited for only the services that they offer. The URAC modular accreditation system allows a diverse range of healthcare organizations to apply for URAC accreditation with the flexibility to achieve accreditation for a wide spectrum of healthcare services. A central goal of this approach is to adapt quickly to the evolving healthcare system and company types.

Each clinical accreditation applicant must apply for "Core Accreditation."* The Core Standards incorporate the basic elements necessary to promote quality for any type of healthcare organization. In most cases, the accreditation applicant adds the appropriate modules. Each module is a set of standards established for a particular healthcare function.

Set of Standards Addressing a Healthcare Function = Module

Examples of URAC modules include the credentialing of providers in a network, and various medical management functions such as UM, CM, DM, and independent review services. As a result of this methodology, an application is usually submitted that includes the Core Standards and the module(s) covering the functions that the applicant is ready to become accredited for:

Core Standards + Module(s) = Application for Accreditation

The modular accreditation system also allows healthcare companies to apply for accreditation even when no specific URAC module applies to their services. This is referred to as a Core "stand-alone" application. As described in more detail below, many pharmaceutical-related services would qualify for URAC's Core stand-alone accreditation or Vendor Certification.

---

*This requirement does not apply to URAC's Health Web Site Accreditation Program.

Recognizing that many different performance measurement systems are already in use today, URAC has elected to not reinvent the wheel by developing and issuing yet another measurement set. However, URAC's core quality management (QM) standards do require organizations to measure, and then improve, their performance. URAC is intentionally nonprescriptive when it comes to what measures of quality must be used (in part due to the reasons highlighted previously). Each organization has its own unique needs, demands, and challenges, so URAC is flexible. However, the measurement system must be objective, be statistically valid, and identify changes in performance over time. As a general rule, most of the well-known performance measurement systems—such as HEDIS or ORYX—can be used to satisfy the data collection requirement of URAC's QM standards.

Market and Regulatory Drivers

With the healthcare industry evolving so rapidly, fueled in part by technological advances driving change, accreditation has assumed a more central role in safeguarding the quality and safety of patient care. Here are some of the reasons why the healthcare accreditation industry has expanded over the past several decades:

- *Patients.* Accreditation ensures that a healthcare organization has passed a rigorous, comprehensive test that meets national standards for quality health. Moreover, if there are concerns about coverage, consumers will have the right to basic due process protections that could be otherwise lacking in some cases.
- *Purchasers.* Accreditation is important to employers because it helps them select healthcare vendors that meet high quality standards, and thereby promote the delivery of quality healthcare to their staff/employees. As a result, accreditation is often required as part of the request for proposal or request for information (RFP/RFI) bid process when healthcare is purchased.
- *Regulatory recognition.* Accreditation is important to legislators and regulators by promoting or assuring the quality of healthcare operations under their oversight, and protecting consumer rights in the healthcare system. The accreditation process evaluates quality procedures, operations, and accountability for healthcare organizations through nationally recognized, publicly available standards, thus increasing transparency for consumers, providers, and regulators. As a result, state and federal agencies often recognize or otherwise "deem" vari-

ous accreditation programs as part of the regulatory process. Through external accreditation, the regulatory burden on state agencies can be reduced, since accreditation offers a rigorous, transparent, private-sector alternative to direct regulatory oversight.

- *Provider protections.* Accreditation is important to physicians and healthcare providers because it ensures that provider concerns are addressed within health management organizations. Accreditation standards ensure providers' voices are heard throughout the healthcare system. For example, most accrediting bodies require the use of dispute resolution systems to resolve provider grievances. Most also require that providers participate on quality and credentialing committees within the accredited companies.

- *Organizational improvement.* Accreditation is important to healthcare organizations because the standards ensure they have a rigorous process in place to track and monitor quality, making their operations more cost-efficient and cost-effective and more attractive to various stakeholders.

  — Accreditation standards are revised periodically (e.g., every two to three years), helping healthcare organizations to keep current with the latest quality benchmarks and best practices.

  — Accredited organizations can demonstrate their quality and accountability to a spectrum of stakeholders interested in the healthcare system, including consumers, employers, health insurers, providers, purchasers, regulators, workers' compensation industry, etc.

  — The standards make healthcare organizations more marketable by differentiating them from their competitors.

  — Most accredited companies apply for reaccreditation, demonstrating the lasting value that accreditation has for these organizations.

- *Accreditation benchmarking.* Due to the ever-changing healthcare system, a typical accreditation agency offers a more flexible approach to quality benchmarking than other approaches. For example, a regulatory approach is often too static or limited to keep apace with today's healthcare system. Whereas states and the federal government can often update their quality oversight initiatives only through the enactment of a new law or through an administrative rule-making process that can take months or years, accreditation agencies can update their standards more regularly through their committee systems. As a result, accreditation standards are often more relevant to current industry practices than outdated regulations.

Risk Management Strategy

Accreditation also serves as an effective risk management tool. It reduces liability by validating the organization conforms to national standards of practice and provides review and feedback on operations by national experts.

- Accreditation standards are sometimes used by the court system as a way of establishing sound business practices and/or to establish negligence. Therefore, if a company has successfully achieved accreditation, it can use the accreditation as part of its defense strategy. Courts also have been known to look to accreditation standards when regulatory requirements or common law is nonexistent or ambiguous.
- Professional liability carriers and their brokers often will grant premium discounts for Errors and Omissions (E&O) and Officers and Directors' (D&O) insurance policies. Occasionally, insurers will require accreditation as part of their underwriting criteria.
- Accreditation programs can be used by companies as a proxy or method to establish a national compliance strategy in meeting various state and local jurisdictional requirements. Simply put, accreditation can establish a national baseline for benchmarking quality operations.

Overview of Benefits

As highlighted above, many benefits can be derived through the accreditation process:

- Leads to improved patient care and strengthens community confidence.
- Demonstrates the organization's commitment to safety and quality.
- Promotes national standardization of best practices.
- Facilitates the written documentation (e.g., through policies and procedures) of an organization's business operations and strategies.
- Provides a competitive advantage in the marketplace (e.g., enhances the organization's image to the public, purchasers, and payers).
- Recognized by insurers and other third parties.

Challenges

Like most enterprises in life, no business is perfect. Accreditation programs or the agencies that sponsor them have been criticized periodically for all or some of the following issues:

- Accreditation is too costly (both in terms of application fees and incidentals, and the time invested to prepare for an accreditation audit).
- Accreditation standards can miss the mark or become outdated.
- Consumers and employers often do not rely on accreditation information as a meaningful way to direct how they use or contract for healthcare services.
- The results derived from an accreditation audit are confusing or insufficient to be relied on by outside stakeholders.
- The types of accreditation measurement approaches highlighted in Table 21.1 often do not guarantee a successful outcome and/or provide clear information on how to compare healthcare organizations.

As a result of these and other concerns, accreditation agencies must periodically reexamine the efficacy of their programs to ensure the ongoing integrity of their quality benchmarking approaches.

THE ROLE OF REGULATORY OVERSIGHT

Many healthcare operations impacting the delivery of pharmacy services and prescription drugs are regulated directly and/or indirectly by the state and federal governments. For example, most states regulate mail-service pharmacies, license pharmacists, and specify how pharmacies dispense drugs. In addition, the federal government oversees pharmaceutical services through the Controlled Substance Act of 1970, which requires pharmacies to register with the Drug Enforcement Administration (DEA).* Several state and federal agencies also indirectly regulate how pharmaceutical care is delivered as the purchaser of coverage (e.g., through an RFP process or regulations supporting programs such as Medicare and Medicaid).

Exhibit 21.1 provides three examples in which states briefly reference the quality assurance requirements for pharmacies, pharmacists, state phar-

---

*The DEA is responsible for enforcing federal controlled drug laws. Title 21 USC (United States Code) is the controlled drug law. Title 21 CFR (code of federal regulations) consists of the working regulations that are based on the USC.

EXHIBIT 21.1. STATE LAWS REFERENCING PHARMACY QUALITY REQUIREMENTS

California Business and Professional Code

§ 4125. Quality Assurance Program

(a) Every pharmacy shall establish a quality assurance program that shall, at a minimum, document medication errors attributable, in whole or in part, to the pharmacy or its personnel. The purpose of the quality assurance program shall be to assess errors that occur in the pharmacy in dispensing or furnishing prescription medications so that the pharmacy may take appropriate action to prevent a recurrence.

(b) Records generated for and maintained as a component of a pharmacy's ongoing quality assurance program shall be considered peer review documents and not subject to discovery in any arbitration, civil, or other proceeding, except as provided hereafter. That privilege shall not prevent review of a pharmacy's quality assurance program and records maintained as part of that system by the board as necessary to protect the public health and safety or if fraud is alleged by a government agency with jurisdiction over the pharmacy. Nothing in this section shall be construed to prohibit a patient from accessing his or her own prescription records. Nothing in this section shall affect the discoverability of any records not solely generated for and maintained as a component of a pharmacy's ongoing quality assurance program.

(c) This section shall become operative on January 1, 2002.

Minnesota Statutes Annotated: Health, Chapter 151. Pharmacy—Board Of Pharmacy

151.22. Liability for Quality of Drugs

Every pharmacist in charge or proprietor of a pharmacy shall be responsible for the quality of all drugs, medicines, chemicals, and poisons procured for use and sold therein, except proprietary medicines or other articles sold in the original package of the manufacturer.

Vernon's Texas Statutes and Codes Annotated: Occupations Code—Title 3. Health Professions, Subtitle J. Pharmacy and Pharmacists—Chapter 564. Program to Aid Impaired Pharmacists and Pharmacy Students; Pharmacy Peer Review—Subchapter C. Pharmacy Peer Review

§ 564.101. Definitions

In this subchapter:

(continued)

(continued)

(1) "Pharmacy peer review committee" means:

(A) a pharmacy peer review, judicial, or grievance committee of a pharmacy society or association that is authorized to evaluate the quality of pharmacy patient care; or

(B) a pharmacy peer review committee established by a person who owns a pharmacy or employs pharmacists that is authorized to evaluate the quality of pharmacy services or the competence of pharmacists and suggest improvements in pharmacy systems to enhance patient care....

macy boards, or other related activities. Most states have similar passing references embedded in their regulations.

However, no state or federal legislation appears to have adopted a law establishing comprehensive quality improvement standards, which cover organizations that manage the delivery of pharmaceutical services such as pharmacy benefit managers (PBMs).* This is in contrast to the scope of standards set forth in a typical accreditation program offered by JCAHO, NCQA, or URAC.

In the future, state and federal officials may adopt a more comprehensive approach promoting the quality oversight of pharmaceutical services. For example, the NAIC adopted in early 2003 the Health Carrier Prescription Drug Benefit Management Model Act. As described in recent NAIC minutes:

> The purpose of the model is to provide standards for the establishment, maintenance, and management of prescription drug formularies and other pharmaceutical management procedures used by health carriers that provide prescription drug coverage. The model law was drafted to address an issue of increasing concern to consumers—the use by health carriers of formularies and other pharmaceutical benefit management procedures to manage prescription drug utilization. It

---

*The Westlaw search just looked at state and federal statutory codes with the following search query: "pharmacy pharmaceutical /p quality & medical health insurance." Basically this search query picked up all state and federal laws that reference pharmacy services and the term "quality." A total of 138 state statutes and 1 federal statute were identified. There may be administrative rules or regulations that identify more details supporting quality improvement activities. Another search was run to identify the number of state and federal laws addressing "pharmacy benefit managers." Thirty-eight statutory cites were found in about thirty states, and three federal references in the U.S. Code. But the search results only produced one passing reference (in the state of Vermont) regarding the quality-based activities of PBMs.

sets out standards for the establishment, maintenance and management of prescription drug formularies and other benefit management procedures to assure that consumers have appropriate access to medically necessary prescription drugs. The model law also establishes a medical exceptions process that will permit consumers to request a non-formulary prescription drug or to request an exception to a dose restriction or step therapy requirement.[4]

Over the next several years, several states will likely consider adopting this model legislation or similar regulations.

PHARMACEUTICAL-BASED ACCREDITATION/CERTIFICATION PROGRAMS

In addition to the regulatory provisions, numerous voluntary standards have been adopted by the pharmacy industry and accreditation groups that cover distinct pharmaceutical market segments and related services.

The author could not identify any stand-alone accreditation programs implemented nationally that provide a comprehensive approach to quality assessment for pharmaceutical services. However, several other countries appear to offer stand-alone accreditation programs, including the Pharmaceutical Society of New Zealand[5] and Canada's National Association of Pharmacy Regulatory Authorities.[6] This section highlights case examples of pharmacy standards that have been developed and are geared to specific market segments or services.

Pharmaceutical Care Management Association

The Pharmaceutical Care Management Association (PCMA), based in Washington, DC has published two sets of standards dealing with the operations of managed care pharmacies and pharmacy benefit managers.[7] These standards cover a full range of activities, including the following:

- Staffing and training requirements
- Quality assurance programs
- Equipment and facilities
- Prescription processing and dispensing verification
- Formulary management process
- Patient education and counseling
- Drug utilization review

- Guidelines for handling controlled substances, including inventory controls and special handling requirements
- Confidentiality requirements

Regarding quality assurance, the PCMA Pharmacy Practice Standards require the following:

> The managed care pharmacy shall have a Quality Assurance program designed to ensure the accuracy and quality of the prescription medicines dispensed and the services offered. There shall be written procedures and policies that describe the review and verification of key steps in the prescription dispensing process. They are designed to assure the accuracy of the dispensed prescription medicine.[8]

The Quality Standards proceed to outline eight examples of a quality assurance procedure. They are as follows:

- Outline the quality assurance verifications employed during the prescription processing and dispensing procedures.
- Specification of the duties of pharmacy personnel and specification of training requirements and training objectives.
- Facility requirements for support functions, such as housekeeping and security.
- Proper use, maintenance, and ongoing monitoring of equipment used in the processing and dispensing of prescriptions orders.
- Requirements for materials used in the dispensing process.
- Procedures for documentation of Quality Assurance key steps in the prescription processing and dispensing procedures.
- In-process and distribution controls and procedures that protect product identity and stability.
- Appropriate and timely investigation of inquiries regarding dispensed prescription medicines.[9]

However, PCMA has not officially endorsed the adoption of these standards into a formal accreditation program.

Accreditation Council for Pharmacy Education

The Accreditation Council for Pharmacy Education, based in Chicago, Illinois, accredits professional programs in pharmacy for the baccalaureate in pharmacy and the doctor of pharmacy degrees. ACPE highlights the goal of its accreditation programs to include the following:

> A professional program is evaluated on the extent to which it accomplishes its stated goals and is consistent with the concept that pharmacy is a unique, personal service profession in the health science field. In the application of these standards, literal conformity in every detail is not required. Variations are to be expected, and superiority in certain qualities may compensate, at least in part, for deficiencies in others. Many college and school programs exceed Council standards in one or more of the various elements comprising accreditation. In pharmaceutical education, as in American education generally, there is diversity. In this diversity there is potential strength. The accreditation process, therefore, seeks to maximize potential strengths while assuring basic expectations for quality pharmaceutical education.[10]

American Commission for Health Care, Inc.

The American Commission for Health Care, Inc. (ACHC), based in Raleigh, North Carolina, offers a "Specialty Pharmacy Accreditation Program." ACHC, which rolled out the program in 2000, describes the program as follows:

> A Specialty Pharmacy company is one that dispenses medications, usually self-injectable, biotechnology drugs to a client's home, physician's office, or clinics specializing in certain chronic disease states. These medications benefit a targeted patient population with a chronic and sometimes life-threatening disease. Examples of Specialty Pharmacy drug classifications and medications include growth factor such as Genotropin and Humatrope, antihemophilics such as Hemofil and Bioclate, interferons such as Avonex and Rebetron, or HIV/AIDS medications such as Eqiver or Viracept.[11]

National Association of Boards of Pharmacy

The National Association of Boards of Pharmacy (NABP), based in Mount Prospect, Illinois, represents the state boards of pharmacy in all fifty states and the District of Columbia. In addition to developing licensing standards and administering exams for pharmacists, NABP also has developed an accreditation program geared to Internet-based pharmacy practices:

> In response to public concern of the safety of pharmacy practices on the Internet, the association developed the Verified Internet Pharmacy Practice Sites (VIPPS) program in the spring of 1999. A coalition of state and federal regulatory associations, professional associations, and consumer advocacy groups provided their expertise in developing the criteria which VIPPS-certified pharmacies follow.
>
> To be VIPPS certified, a pharmacy must comply with the licensing and inspection requirements of their state and each state to which they dispense pharmaceuticals. In addition, pharmacies displaying the VIPPS seal have demonstrated to NABP compliance with VIPPS criteria including patient rights to privacy, authentication and security of prescription orders, adherence to a recognized quality assurance policy, and provision of meaningful consultation between patients and pharmacists.[12]

JCAHO Long Term Care and Hospital

The JCAHO[13] offers two notable accreditation programs that cover facility-based pharmaceutical services in long term care and hospital settings.

Long Term Care Pharmacy Accreditation

The accreditation of long term care pharmacies resides in the home care accreditation program of the Joint Commission. Any organization that meets the general eligibility requirements for accreditation of the Joint Commission and provides pharmacy dispensing services to patients residing in a nursing home or other long term care facility, such as assisted living and rehabilitation facilities, can be accredited for long term care pharmacy services.

In addition, the Joint Commission accredits long term care consultant pharmacists under a different service. Clinical/consultant pharmacist services are defined as the provision of professional care and services by a qualified pharmacist to optimize outcomes of medication therapy and minimize the adverse effects of medications. This includes assessing the appropriateness of medication orders, the ongoing evaluation and review of the patient's medication regimen and pharmacy care plan, the ongoing monitoring of medication effects in individual patients, the provision of drug information, oversight of the medication use process to improve patient safety, and other related cognitive medication-related services. This is also under the auspices of the home care accreditation program.*

Hospital Pharmacy Accreditation

The JCAHO does not accredit or survey hospital pharmacy services per se. Rather, it surveys and accredits the entire hospital, including the medication use or medication management processes within it.

Surveyors interview hospital leaders early in the survey. The surveyors want to see how the senior leaders work together to plan, design, implement, and improve patient care services. Other interviews examine the specific roles played by hospital administration, by medical staff and nursing leaders, and by departmental directors. These other interviews take place later in the survey so that the surveyors can use knowledge of the hospital's performance to direct their questions. Surveyors will interview the

- CEO/person responsible for strategic planning and resource allocation,
- medical staff leaders,
- nursing leaders, and
- hospital department directors, including the director of pharmacy.

During this activity, the surveyors will evaluate the organization's performance improvement efforts in medication use, how the organization evaluates significant adverse drug reactions and medication errors, and medication-related sentinel events. Surveyors will also examine how the hospital has implemented and improved the planning and design of its processes, including medication use. The surveyors will review medication storage areas and equipment, such as automated dispensing machines and infusion pumps.†

When significant medication issues are found during the survey, a pharmacist surveyor may be sent back to conduct a more thorough analysis of the organization's medication use processes, as part of a focused survey or unannounced-for-cause survey.

---

*All standards for which the long term care pharmacy is evaluated can be found in the *2003 Comprehensive Accreditation Manual for Home Care.*

†The standards used for the survey process can be found in the *Comprehensive Accreditation Manual for Hospitals.* The medication use standards are currently a section in the "Care of the Patient" chapter. However, the medication standards have been significantly revised for 2004 and appear, as a separate chapter titled "Medication Management."

NCQA HEDIS Measures

As referenced above, HEDIS measures have become the industry standard for measuring health plan performance. Embedded within HEDIS are several measures that are associated with accurate and appropriate delivery of the pharmacy benefit. Table 21.2 highlights several examples. As a result, integrating medial and pharmacy claims data is necessary to meet the HEDIS requirements.

TABLE 21.2. Examples of HEDIS measures requiring pharmacy data.

Domain	Measure	Description	Pharmacy data to report
Effectiveness of care	Beta-blocker treatment after a heart attack	Percent members thirty-five years or older who were hospitalized with a diagnosis for AMI and who received a Rx for Beta-blockers on discharge	Members who received an outpatient Rx within thirty days before admission for AMI to seven days after discharge
	Eye examinations for people with diabetes	Percent members thirty-one years or older with type I or II diabetes who had a retinal examination within the year	Identification of population: those members dispensed insulin, oral hypoglycemics, antihyperglycemics
	Antidepressant medication management	Percent members eighteen years or older diagnosed with a new episode of depression, treated with medication: acute and continuation phase follow-up	Members diagnosed with a new episode of major depressive disorder treated with antidepressant meds
Use of services	Outpatient drug utilization	Summary of drug use: average number and cost of Rx's PMPM, total number and cost of Rxs stratified by age and payer	"Prescription" is defined as one thirty-day (or less) supply of pharmaceuticals or one supply requiring a copay

Source: Novarro, Robert P. "Prescription Drug Benefits in Managed Care." In Peter R. Kongstvedt (ed.), *The Managed Health Care Handbook,* Fourth Edition (p. 445). New York: Aspen, 2001; table adapted from Goodwin, Amelia, "Quality Improvement Initiatives in Managed Care." In R. P. Navarro (ed.), *Managed Care Pharmacy* (p. 300). New York: Aspen, 1999.

Note: AMI = acute myocardial infarction; Rx = prescription.

URAC Core and Vendor Certification

Pharmaceutical organizations can get accredited either through URAC's Core "stand-alone" accreditation program (as referenced above) and/or through URAC's Vendor Certification Program.

Regarding the Vendor Certification, URAC will allow a Core-eligible applicant to undergo vendor certification for a limited number of self-selected standards within any URAC module in conjunction with a Core application. After successful completion of its review, URAC would award Core Accreditation to the applicant, along with a certificate of compliance for the additional, specifically named standards. The vendor can then utilize its Core Accreditation plus its Vendor Certification to assist clients and potential clients to achieve or maintain URAC accreditation by using its product or services for the performance of that function. For example, another applicant for URAC UM accreditation would be recognized as in compliance for a standard or standards when it submits evidence of using a "URAC Certified Vendor" product or service. Areas that could be recognized or certified by URAC under certification program include drug UM programs, software systems, elements of a disease management program, drug formulary applications, and so on.

CONCLUSIONS

The expansion of the use of prescription drugs by patients in the United States has been dramatic during the past few decades. This trend should continue as Americans get older and deal with a wide range of chronic conditions. Of course, this creates new cost and quality pressures on the healthcare delivery system.

One public policy question that confronts all the stakeholders who provide, distribute, dispense, finance, or receive medications is whether pharmaceutical companies should be encouraged to pursue a higher level of organizational and system accountability.

For example, one could argue that URAC's Case Management Accreditation Program has benefited medical management companies and health plans in several different ways by

- creating national quality benchmarks.
- standardizing best practices and quickly popularizing new ones.
- identifying national operational standards promoting efficiency.

- serving as a substitute for state and federal legislation (no state has adopted comprehensive enabling legislation for case management organizations).
- supporting an organization's risk management strategy.[14]

Could individual pharmacies, pharmacy chains, PBMs, drug manufactures, mail-service pharmacies, and state Medicaid programs benefit in the same way?

One could argue that a comprehensive accreditation program for pharmaceutical services could enhance business operations, reduce liability exposure, and promote quality. The range of services could be covered in the same way as URAC's modular approach to quality assessment or through a series of different accreditation programs. The mainstream accreditors could also help various stakeholders debate and sort out in a more public forum how pharmaceutical drugs are dispensed and paid for. For example, PBM-related standards would require many of us to really think through how medical necessity and benefit determinations overlap in pharmaceutical coverage decisions, and how denials of care are made and reconsiderations are handled.

The current danger for the pharmaceutical industry is the fact that no universal organizational standards have been adopted. An argument can be made that comprehensive quality-based standards adopted nationally could improve the system on many fronts. Assuming that no industry market segment can develop credible standards on their own and regulatory oversight would likely create a patchwork quilt of inconsistent requirements, teaming up with one or more accreditation agencies may be the best bet.

NOTES

1. See www.jcaho.org.
2. See www.ncqa.org.
3. See www.urac.org.
4. NAIC Meeting minutes, December 8, 2002. See also www.naic.org.
5. See www.psnz.org.nz.
6. See www.napra.org.
7. *PCMA Pharmacy Practice Standards* and *PCMA Pharmacy Benefit Management Standards,* first published in 1990, revised in 2000. See www.pcmanet.org.
8. *PCMA Pharmacy Practice Standards,* pp. 4-6.
9. *Id.*
10. See www.acpe-accredit.org.

11. See www.achc.org. Among other programs, ACHC also offers another accreditation program for home infusion services. The program is described as follows:

> The Infusion therapy continuum of care includes IV drug mixture preparation, IV administration, therapy monitoring, patient counseling, and education. It is the administration of medications using intravenous, subcutaneous and epidural routes. The IV therapies include IV antibiotics, prescribed primarily for diagnosis such as osteomyelitis; sepis, cellulites total parenteral nutrition, pneumonia, sexually transmitted diseases and others. Services for Home Infusion include RN, IV, and pharmacy. ACHC accredits infusion nursing, pharmacy services, clinical respiratory care, home medical equipment, rehab technology supplier, and post mastectomy fitter services.

12. See www.nabp.net/vipps.

13. Personal communication, Margaret VanAmringe and Anita Epstein, Joint Commission on Accreditation of Healthcare Organizations, 601 Thirteenth Street NW, Suite 1150 N, Washington, DC, 20005.

14. URAC, *Case Management Trends: An Overview of Recent Industry and Regulatory Developments,* 2002. (2003, URAC).

Chapter 22

Electronic Prescribing

F. Nicholas Willard

INTRODUCTION

From a regulatory perspective, the use of a computer to assemble the required elements of a prescription order is immaterial. On the other hand, transmitting prescription information electronically raises a number of legal and policy questions. To date, however, the literature on electronic prescribing has focused either on its promised benefits or on the practical, operational, and financial considerations that have impeded prescriber acceptance rather than on the regulatory issues raised by electronically transmitting prescription data between prescribers and pharmacies.

The absence of literature is not surprising given the difficulty of drawing general conclusions about the widely varying nature of states' respective pharmacy laws: inevitably, there are exceptions. Further, electronic prescribing is an evolving technology: while competing systems share common characteristics, software developers have also made discrete technological choices that in turn raise different issues depending upon the jurisdiction in which they are deployed. Most law lags behind technological innovation, and pharmacy law is no different. Finally, pharmacy law is not the only source of legal guidance for pharmacists and regulators on electronic prescribing issues. Dispensing a legend drug upon receipt of a lawful prescription order is not merely a healthcare matter. The process can also be accurately defined as a commercial transaction involving a prescriber, a pharmacist, and a consumer. To the extent a prescription transaction can be conducted electronically, it is governed not only by existing pharmacy law but also by applicable electronic commerce law, namely the Uniform Electronic Transactions Act and the Electronic Signatures in Global and National Commerce Act.

The purpose of this chapter is to provide an overview of the extent to which current pharmacy law accommodates electronic prescribing. For reference, it will provide a brief summary of the major benefits and operational

Pharmacy Law Desk Reference
© 2007 by The Haworth Press, Inc. All rights reserved.
doi:10.1300/5790_22

characteristics of electronic prescribing technology. It will examine applicable electronic commerce law and its intriguing impact on pharmacy laws and regulations. It will also identify compliance issues for which state pharmacy law in large part neither addresses nor provides adequate guidance for practicing pharmacists. Finally, it will analyze the legal and policy issues raised by the U.S. Drug Enforcement Administration's (DEA) pending regulatory strategy for authorizing electronic prescriptions for controlled substances.

Because the intent is to provide an overview of regulatory issues, the chapter will use the following terms and meanings to avoid the confusion that would result from relying on state pharmacy law to provide a consistent set of relevant definitions. *Prescription* means a lawful order for a drug or device issued by an authorized prescriber for a specific patient. *Electronic prescription* means a lawful order that is created and issued electronically without having taken physical form in the prescriber's office. Electronic prescription orders are executed with the prescriber's electronic signature. *Electronic signature* means an electronic sound, symbol, or process attached to or logically associated with a record and executed or adopted by a person with the intent to sign the record. *E-Fax prescription* means the type of electronic prescription order that is transmitted from the prescriber's computer to the pharmacy's facsimile machine using facsimile simulation software. *Facsimile prescription* means an exact image copy of a written prescription order transmitted by a facsimile machine. *Written prescription* means a lawful order printed, typed, or handwritten on paper in the prescriber's office. Written prescription orders are executed with the prescriber's manually affixed, handwritten signature.

ELECTRONIC PRESCRIBING: BENEFITS AND OPERATIONAL CHARACTERISTICS

From its introduction, electronic prescribing software was quickly identified and hyped as a "magic bullet" or "killer application" capable of improving patient safety by taking the illegible, handwritten prescription order out of the clinical equation. The earliest electronic prescribing systems were relatively simple, stand-alone applications capable of storing the required content of a prescription order in system memory and causing the content to be printed on paper in the prescriber's office. The prescriber signed the printed prescription in his or her own hand and either presented it to the patient for delivery to the pharmacy or transmitted it via a facsimile machine to the pharmacy of the patient's choice.

Since the early 1990s software vendors have consistently added to electronic prescribing capabilities, not only to take advantage of advances in connectivity and standards development but also to respond both to physicians' demands for improved ease of use and pharmacists' increasingly complicated practice demands. For example, using facsimile simulation software and bit-mapping technology to save an image of the prescriber's handwritten signature in system memory, electronic prescribing software simplified the prescriber's workflow by transmitting the prescription data in electronic form from the prescriber's computer to a pharmacy's facsimile machine. Similarly, with the 1997 adoption of a national Electronic Data Interchange (EDI)* standard for prescription data and increasingly capable EDI network switches, developers added the ability to transmit prescription information in electronic form from a prescriber's computer to a pharmacy's computer, thus relieving pharmacists of the task of reentering data and the liability of transcription errors.

In the past several years, electronic prescribing has continued to evolve. Recent innovations have produced integrated software packages that enable prescribers—using wireless local area networks, handheld personal digital assistants, and point-and-click menus—to access patient records, check for harmful drug-drug and drug-allergy interactions, and ensure formulary compliance before creating a clinically appropriate prescription at the point of care.[†] As the volume of legible, correctly blended, and formulary-adherent electronic prescriptions grows, pharmacists can expect to make far fewer than the estimated 150 million annual telephone calls they currently make

---

*Electronic Data Interchange is a standard format for exchanging business data. An EDI message contains a string of data elements, each of which represents a singular fact, such as a prescriber's name, prescriber's address, and so forth, separated by a delimiter. The entire string is called a data segment. One or more data segments framed by a header and trailer form a transaction set, which is the EDI unit of transmission (equivalent to a message). A transaction set often consists of what would usually be contained in a typical business document, form, or, for purpose of this chapter, a prescription order.

†Significantly, the recently enacted Medicare prescription drug benefit legislation builds on such capabilities by requiring the secretary of the U.S. Department of Health and Human Services (HHS) to establish standards that would apply to electronic prescribing programs established by Medicare prescription plans. Under the proposed standards, prescribers would not be required to create and transmit prescription orders electronically. However, the legislation specifies the types of information that Medicare prescription drug plans must make available electronically to pharmacies and prescribers under an electronic prescribing program, to include (1) information on eligibility and benefits (including formulary drugs, any tiered formulary structure, and prior authorization requirements); (2) information on the drug being prescribed and other drugs in the patient's medication history (i.e., prospective drug utilization review); and (3) information on the availability of lower-cost, therapeutically appropriate alternative drugs. Pursuant to the legislation, the Secretary of HHS would have to promulgate final standards no later than April 1, 2008. While the implications of new Medicare requirements are beyond the scope of this chapter, see Section 1860D-4(e) of The Medicare Prescription Drug, Improvement, and Modernization Act of 2003 (Public Law No. 108-173) for further information.

to deal with unclear handwritten prescription orders, drug utilization review issues, and formulary questions.

Technically, electronic prescribing means the use of an automated data entry system to create an electronic record containing the required content of a prescription order and issuing a prescription order based on the information in the record. Before creating the electronic record, electronic prescribing systems require a prescriber to log on to the software, using either a single or multifactor authentication procedure that not only logically associates the prescriber with his or her electronic prescribing activities but also provides an audit trail. An example of a single factor authentication procedure would be requiring the prescriber to log on with a user name and personal identification number (PIN) or password. Minimally, multifactor authentication could require the user to log on not only by entering a user name and PIN but also by (1) swiping an encoded card through an electronic reader, (2) "signing in" by using a digitized pen on a tablet or other image digitizing device, (3) entering a number randomly generated by an electronic token, or (4) biometric confirmation of the user's identity. To provide additional security, the vast majority of electronic prescribing systems require the prescriber to perform the authentication procedure again when an input device has been turned off or has been idle for a specified period of time. Most electronic prescribing systems rely on single factor authentication procedures because they provide a reasonable and auditable degree of security and are simpler to use for the prescriber.

Generally speaking, electronic prescribing software issues prescription orders in one of two ways: (1) the electronic record can be printed on paper in the prescriber's office or (2) it can be transmitted electronically from the prescriber's computer over a private or public network to either the pharmacy's computer or its facsimile machine.* The manner in which electronic prescribing systems issue prescription orders is dependent on a combination of factors: patient choice, applicable state law, the electronic prescribing system's capabilities, and the receiving pharmacy's technological capabilities. Today, due to patient request, half of all prescription orders issued by electronic prescribing systems are written prescription orders, either for delivery to the patient or transmission from the prescriber's facsimile machine to the pharmacy's facsimile machine. Less than 1 percent of the electronic prescriptions issued by such systems are transmitted computer-to-computer, with the remainder being transmitted computer-to-facsimile

---

*Because of security concerns raised by the general use of the Internet, electronic prescription orders are not transmitted via electronic mail. Theoretically, electronic mail could be used if a national standard for digital signatures existed. See below for a discussion of digital signature technology.

machine. In other words, 99 percent of all electronic prescription orders are transmitted to facsimile machines because the vast majority of pharmacies are incapable of receiving computer-to-computer transmissions.*

Electronic prescription orders transmitted computer-to-computer are formatted in the only nationally recognized EDI standard for transmitting prescription data between prescribers and pharmacies, the SCRIPT standard developed by the National Council for Prescription Drug Programs (NCPDP).† Because it is infeasible and, in some states, illegal to provide direct, dedicated connectivity between each physician practice site and each pharmacy, computer-to-computer transmissions are routed between the prescriber's and the pharmacy's operating systems by an EDI network switch via a private network. EDI network switches transmit SCRIPT-formatted electronic records to EDI-enabled pharmacies via leased lines or encrypted circuits, using 128-bit encryption.

If the pharmacy the patient has chosen is not EDI-enabled, electronic prescription orders are transmitted to a pharmacy's facsimile machine. Computer-to-facsimile transmissions use facsimile simulation software (resident either at the EDI network switch or at the prescriber's computer, depending on system design) to transmit the prescription information over telephone lines. The use of facsimile simulation software essentially enables the prescriber to use the pharmacy's facsimile machine as a remote printer: i.e., the e-Fax prescription order takes physical form for the first time when it prints on the pharmacy's facsimile machine.‡

---

*The precise number of pharmacies capable of receiving and responding to computer-to-computer EDI prescription transmissions is difficult to determine. However, according to information available from ProxyMed, Inc., a leading provider of EDI network connectivity, the only large retail chain drugstore organizations that are EDI capable are Eckerd, Publix, Rite Aid, and Walgreens.

†On February 27, 2002, the National Committee on Vital and Health Statistics (NCVHS) recommended to the secretary of HHS that the NCPDP SCRIPT standard be adopted as the message format standard for prescription orders pursuant to its Health Insurance Portability and Accountability Act of 1996 (HIPAA) mandate regarding "the adoption of uniform data standards for patient medical record information (PMRI) and the electronic exchange of such information." HHS Secretary Tommy Thompson adopted the NCVHS recommendation for PMRI message format standards on March 21, 2003, as part of the Consolidated Health Informatics (CHI) initiative.

‡In contrast, a facsimile prescription order is a copy of an original paper-based document. When a prescriber transmits a prescription order by a facsimile machine (sometimes called "telecopying"), the facsimile machine optically scans the original paper document, treating the contents (text or images) as a single fixed graphic image and converting it into a bitmap. In this digital form, the information is transmitted as electrical signals through the telephone system to a telephone number associated with a printer or other output device. The receiving facsimile machine (i.e., printer) reconverts the bitmap image and prints a paper copy of the document.

It is important to note that the SCRIPT standard does not support bitmapped images. In other words, any electronic prescription order formatted in SCRIPT (all computer-to-computer transmissions) cannot feature a graphical image of the prescriber's original handwritten signature or handwritten drug product selection instructions. On the other hand, electronic prescribing systems that are not based on the SCRIPT standard, which include most but not all systems that transmit e-Fax prescription orders, routinely employ graphical images replicating a prescriber's handwritten signature and handwritten drug product selection instructions.

ELECTRONIC COMMERCE LAW

Recently enacted state and federal economic commerce laws combine to both clarify and circumscribe how and what policymakers must consider in addressing electronic prescribing issues under the nation's pharmacy laws. In broad terms, where pharmacy law requires a paper prescription order, handwritten signatures, and handwritten instructions, such requirements are no longer enforceable.

The Uniform Electronic Transactions Act

The Uniform Electronic Transactions Act (UETA) is a model act drafted by the National Conference of Commissioners on Uniform State Laws (NCCUSL)* with the goal of providing uniformity among state laws with respect to electronic signatures and electronic records. The "Official UETA" was approved by the NCCUSL and recommended for enactment in all the states at the NCCUSL's annual conference in Denver, Colorado, July 23-30, 1999. As of April 21, 2004, the District of Columbia and forty-four states have enacted the UETA.† The UETA is a law of general application, i.e., unless the enacted UETA exempts another provision of state law from its scope, the UETA applies.

---

*The NCCUSL is an organization of attorneys, judges, and law professors that drafts proposals for uniform legislation and works with state legislatures toward their enactment.

†The following states have enacted the UETA: Alabama, Arizona, Arkansas, California, Colorado, Connecticut, Delaware, Florida, Hawaii, Idaho, Indiana, Iowa, Kansas, Kentucky, Louisiana, Maine, Maryland, Massachusetts, Michigan, Minnesota, Mississippi, Missouri, Montana, Nebraska, Nevada, New Hampshire, New Jersey, New Mexico, North Carolina, North Dakota, Ohio, Oklahoma, Oregon, Pennsylvania, Rhode Island, South Dakota, Tennessee, Texas, Utah, Vermont, Virginia, West Virginia, Wisconsin, and Wyoming. All references are to the "Official UETA" because there are slight variations in the versions adopted by the respective states.

The primary purpose of the UETA is to provide legal recognition to electronic records, electronic signatures, and electronic contracts:

1. A record or signature may not be denied legal effect or enforceability solely because it is in electronic form.
2. A contract may not be denied legal effect or enforceability solely because an electronic record was used in its formation.
3. If a law requires a record to be in writing, an electronic record satisfies the law.
4. If a law requires a signature, an electronic signature satisfies the law.[1]

The UETA defines an "electronic signature" as "an electronic sound, symbol, or process attached to or logically associated with a record and executed or adopted by a person with the intent to sign the record."[2] Further, the UETA defines a "transaction" as "an action or set of actions occurring between two or more persons relating to the conduct of business, commercial, or governmental affairs."[3]

The UETA does not require parties to use or accept electronic signatures, electronic contracts, or electronic records, but rather seeks to facilitate the use of these instruments by upholding their legal effect. As such, the UETA is technology neutral and does not require a specific type or method that businesses and consumers must use or accept in order to conduct transactions electronically. However, the UETA would not prevent a state legislature or state agency from requiring a specific technology for electronic transactions, provided the requirement was adopted in conformance with the federal Electronic Signatures in Global and National Commerce Act.

Electronic Signatures in Global and National Commerce Act

President Clinton signed the Electronic Signatures in Global and National Commerce Act into law on June 30, 2000. The legislation, commonly referred to as the "E-Sign Act,"[4] became effective October 1, 2000. The E-Sign Act was originally based on the UETA and at one point was designed with the intent that any provisions of the E-Sign Act that overlapped state law would "sunset" after adoption of the UETA in all fifty states.[5] However, after much debate and compromise, the E-Sign Act developed into a separate piece of legislation.

The principal purpose of the E-Sign Act is to establish that a signature, contract, or record relating to a transaction involving interstate or foreign commerce may not be denied legal effect or enforceability simply because it is in electronic form:

(a) In general

Notwithstanding any statute, regulation, or other rule of law (other than this subchapter and subchapter II of this chapter), with respect to any transaction in or affecting interstate or foreign commerce—

(1) a signature, contract, or other record relating to such transaction may not be denied legal effect, validity, or enforceability solely because it is in electronic form; and

(2) a contract relating to such transaction may not be denied legal effect, validity, or enforceability solely because an electronic signature or electronic record was used in its formation.[6]

As in the UETA, the E-Sign Act defines an "electronic signature" broadly as "an electronic sound, symbol, or process attached to or logically associated with a record and executed or adopted by a person with the intent to sign the record."[7] A "transaction" is defined to mean "an action or set of actions relating to the conduct of business, consumer, or commercial affairs between two or more persons" and includes such conduct as "the sale, lease, exchange, licensing, or other disposition of (i) personal property, including goods and intangibles, (ii) services, and (iii) any combination thereof."[8]

The E-Sign Act applies to all electronic records, electronic signatures, and electronic contracts relating to a transaction unless specifically exempted from its scope. Like the UETA, the E-Sign Act does not exempt any law governing prescription transactions.[9] Consistent with the UETA, the E-Sign Act does not require parties to use or accept electronic records, electronic signatures, or electronic contracts[10] and is technology neutral, although it achieves such neutrality through its unique "reverse preemption" provisions.

The E-Sign Act authorizes a state statute or regulation to modify, limit, or supersede the E-Sign Act's provisions authorizing the use of electronic records, electronic signatures, and electronic contracts *only* if the state law (1) constitutes an adoption or enactment of the Official UETA (i.e., as approved and recommended by the NCCUSL), or (2) specifies alternative procedures or requirements for the use or acceptance of electronic signatures or records for establishing the legal effect, validity, and enforceability of contracts or records *and* those alternative procedures or requirements are (3) consistent with Titles I and II of the E-Sign Act and (4) do not require, or give greater legal status or effect to, a specific technology for creating, storing, generating, and receiving, communicating, or authenticating electronic signatures or records, and (5) if enacted or adopted after June 30, 2000, makes specific reference to the E-Sign Act.[11]

Despite the preemption provisions, the E-Sign Act authorizes federal or state regulatory agencies to issue regulations specifying performance standards to assure accuracy, record integrity, and accessibility of records that would otherwise violate the prohibition against giving greater legal status or effect to a specific technology. Such a requirement would survive preemption provided it (1) serves an important governmental objective and (2) is substantially related to the achievement of that objective. However, such a requirement would not allow a federal or state agency to require the use of a particular type of software or hardware in order to comply.[12]

With one exception, the E-Sign Act prohibits any federal or state agency from imposing or reimposing any requirement that a record be in a tangible printed or paper form. To do so, the agency must show that there is a compelling interest relating to law enforcement or national security and that requiring a hard-copy record is essential to attaining such interest. It should be noted that the legislation provides no guidance on how "compelling" the interest will need to be in order to void the broad intent of the E-Sign Act.[13]

IMPACT ON PHARMACY LAW: ELECTRONIC PRESCRIPTION ORDERS AND ELECTRONIC SIGNATURES

The combined effect of the E-Sign Act and the UETA is that the vast majority of federal and state laws requiring paper documents and contracts, handwritten signatures, and paper-based record keeping relating to transactions in interstate and intrastate commerce are no longer enforceable. Significantly, the impact of the E-Sign Act and the UETA on state and federal laws governing the manufacture, marketing, and distribution of legend drugs, to include controlled substances, is not widely acknowledged or understood.

Dispensing a drug pursuant to a lawful prescription order can clearly be described as a transaction under both the E-Sign Act and the UETA. In addition, neither Congress nor any of the states that have adopted the UETA exempted prescription transactions from the scope of the respective statutes. Clearly, where the UETA has been enacted, state pharmacy laws requiring written prescription orders and handwritten signatures cannot be enforced. Further, it would appear that current DEA regulations and conforming state provisions requiring written prescription orders and handwritten signatures for controlled substances are also not enforceable.

Although some might argue that prescription transactions constitute intrastate commerce, federal laws governing the manufacture, marketing, and distribution of drugs and controlled substances derive their authority from the Commerce Clause of the U.S. Constitution because such activities involve interstate commerce, i.e., the E-Sign Act applies to the laws and regulations of the U.S. Food and Drug Administration and the DEA because pharmaceuticals, even when distributed locally, are transported in interstate commerce. Just as important, it can also be expected that prescription transactions conducted electronically over telephone lines, the Internet, or private EDI networks will be deemed to affect interstate commerce as well.*

In other words, a "willing" pharmacist would appear to be legally authorized to dispense both controlled and noncontrolled substances upon receipt of an electronic prescription order issued pursuant to the execution of an electronic signature that complies with the definition set forward in the UETA and the E-Sign Act. A pharmacist could decide not to dispense pursuant to an electronic prescription order but could not justify rejecting the prescription order on the ground that it is illegal unless it in some way violates a requirement of pharmacy law that specifically applies to electronic prescription orders. In addition, the E-Sign Act and the UETA (where enacted) would invalidate any handwriting requirements of state pharmacy law or federal Medicaid regulations† for communicating a prescriber's drug product selection instructions.

As a general rule, community pharmacists look to state pharmacy law rather than electronic commerce law to determine whether they are authorized to dispense upon an electronic prescription order. Although the UETA and the E-Sign Act provide broad legal support for electronic prescription orders and electronic signatures, neither was designed to provide the specific operational guidance that pharmacy law theoretically should provide pharmacists. To the credit of the vast majority of states, pharmacists have been granted authority—independent of electronic commerce law—to dispense electronic prescription orders. However, with few exceptions, current state pharmacy law either does not adequately or uniformly address or has failed to respond to a number issues that are central to electronic prescribing technology and electronic commerce law.

As a result, regulatory matters remain relatively unsettled, particularly with respect to requirements for prescription orders for controlled substances. The following section will address various issues that state law eventually will need to address in order to facilitate an expansion of electronic prescribing practices and thus enhance patient safety. The final section will address the DEA's current regulatory situation and the plans it is

---

*Federal courts have indicated that telephones and the Internet are part of interstate commerce regardless of the geographical use of either system. In *United State v. Alvelo-Ramos*, the district court found that cellular phones, even if only used intrastate, are part of interstate commerce because the phones were manufactured in another state and could be used for interstate and international calls. *United States v. Alvelo-Ramos*, 957 F. Supp. 18, 19 (D. Puerto Rico, 1997). In *American Libraries Association v. Pataki*, the court came to the "inescapable conclusion that the Internet represents an instrument of interstate commerce." *American Libraries Association v. Pataki*, 969 F. Supp 160, 173 (S.D.N.Y. 1997).

†42 C.F.R. § 447.331(c). For a pharmacist to receive reimbursement for a brand name, multisource product dispensed to a Medicaid beneficiary, the physician must certify in his or her own handwriting that a specific brand is medically necessary for a particular patient.

considering for addressing electronic prescription orders for controlled substances.

STATE LAW REQUIREMENTS OF PRESCRIPTION ORDERS

Taking into consideration the technical characteristics of electronic prescribing and the implications of electronic commerce law, most state policymakers have and will continue to face complex challenges in establishing a reasonable and operationally feasible regulatory environment for creating, transmitting, and dispensing electronic prescription orders. To accommodate electronic prescribing and to avoid confusion in the community pharmacy setting, state pharmacy laws and regulations generally require adjustment in three areas: manner of issuance, format, and validation (security).

Manner of Issuance Issues

Providing authority for the transmission of electronic prescription orders is a prerequisite for electronic prescription orders. However, the matter is not limited simply to authorizing pharmacists to dispense: state pharmacy law should also support the transmission infrastructure on which electronic prescribing relies to deliver electronic prescription orders to pharmacies. As will be noted below, a significant number of states have adopted conditions that, on face value, ignore technological reality and thus could be interpreted to prohibit the transmission of electronic prescription orders.

Since the early 1990s, policymakers and regulators have worked steadily to provide the necessary authority for electronic prescription orders. With a few exceptions, pharmacists need not look to the UETA or the E-Sign Act to find authority to accept electronic prescriptions. By the spring of 2004, only the District of Columbia* and Nebraska† had not amended or clearly inter-

---

*The District of Columbia has enacted the UETA. Even though applicable district pharmacy law authorizes only written or oral prescriptions, the effect of the UETA is to authorize pharmacists to accept lawful electronic prescriptions.

†When Nebraska enacted the UETA, it had a preexisting Digital Signatures Act that provides legal sanction for only two types of electronic signatures for nongovernmental electronic transactions. See Neb. Rev. Stat. § 86-1701 and Neb. Admin. R. & Regs. Title 437. The Nebraska Pharmacy Practice Act provides only explicit guidance for written or oral prescriptions. However, within the statutory definition of signature, the Nebraska Pharmacy Practice Act includes the term "digital signature" as defined in the Digital Signatures Act. Neb. Rev. Stat. § 71-1, 24(36). The UETA would not invalidate any provision requiring a specific electronic signature technology. However, it would appear that the E-Sign Act might preempt Nebraska's Digital Signatures Act because the latter gives greater legal status and effect to specific electronic technologies. If so, the Pharmacy Practice Act's digital signature requirement may also be invalid.

preted applicable pharmacy law to authorize pharmacists to dispense electronic prescription orders. Forty-one states specifically authorize pharmacists to dispense upon an electronic prescription order.* Three of these forty-one states—Nevada, Ohio, and Washington—require electronic prescribing system vendors to obtain approval from their respective Boards of Pharmacy before deploying the systems. Of the eight states whose pharmacy statutes do not specifically authorize electronic prescription orders, regulators in Arizona, Indiana, North Dakota, and Oklahoma rely on a definition of "prescription" that includes "other means of communication" for authorization, regulators in Idaho, Pennsylvania, and South Dakota rely on their state's enactment of the UETA for authority,[†] and regulators in Alabama sought the necessary guidance from the Alabama attorney general pursuant to the Alabama UETA.[‡]

Authorizing pharmacists to dispense pursuant to electronic prescription orders does not remove every regulatory barrier to transmitting prescription orders electronically. At least seventeen states specifically require that electronic prescriptions be transmitted directly to the pharmacy, with no intervening person having access to the prescription drug order.[§] Historically, the prohibitions were likely adopted to ensure that pharmacy benefit managers did not gain access to electronic prescription orders for purposes of either "steering" prescription orders to mail-service pharmacies or initiating therapeutic substitution activities. While direct transmission requirements would not affect e-Fax prescription orders transmitted directly over the public telephone network, these requirements, applied literally, would prohibit the use of most if not all private EDI networks to route prescriptions from prescribers to pharmacies, either computer-to-computer or computer-to-facsimile machine. Such an interpretation would severely inhibit the expansion of electronic prescribing practices.

---

*Alaska, Arkansas, California, Colorado, Connecticut, Delaware, Florida, Georgia, Hawaii, Illinois, Iowa, Kansas, Kentucky, Louisiana, Maine, Maryland, Massachusetts, Michigan, Minnesota, Mississippi, Missouri, Montana, Nevada, New Hampshire, New Jersey, New Mexico, New York, North Carolina, Ohio, Oregon, Rhode Island, South Carolina, Tennessee, Texas, Utah, Vermont, Virginia, Washington, West Virginia, Wisconsin, and Wyoming.

†Guidance obtained from interviews with Board of Pharmacy personnel. Vendors of electronic prescribing software must receive approval from the executive director of the Board of Pharmacy in Idaho and South Dakota.

‡Opinion Letter of August 21, 2003, from Alabama Attorney General Bill Pryor to Larry D. Dixon, executive director of the Alabama State Board of Medical Examiners. General Pryor opined that the Alabama UETA authorized the electronic transmission of prescriptions and the use of electronic signatures and that the Alabama Board of Pharmacy may adopt rules and regulations "concerning the receipt of [electronic] prescriptions by electronic signatures."

§Arkansas, Delaware, Georgia, Hawaii, Iowa, Kansas, Maine, Maryland, Massachusetts, Michigan, Mississippi, Montana, North Carolina, Virginia, Washington, West Virginia, and Wyoming.

To perform their basic function, EDI networks must have access to an electronically transmitted prescription order. The network must have access to the prescriber's identity to verify that he or she is authorized to transmit via the network. The network must also have access to the identity, electronic "address," or facsimile number of the pharmacy to which the electronic prescription order has been issued to route it correctly.

Many EDI networks also provide a value-added service benefiting both the prescriber and the pharmacy that requires access to the electronic prescription. For electronic prescription orders formatted in the SCRIPT standard, private network switches scan each prescription order to ensure that information required by law has been entered into the appropriate data field specified by the SCRIPT standard. The network does not actually "read" the prescription order; it merely confirms that the required data fields are populated. If data are missing in a required field, the network automatically rejects the prescription order and notifies the prescriber. If all required data are provided, the prescription order is routed to the pharmacy to which it was addressed. This functionality is designed to minimize call backs by ensuring to the extent possible that pharmacies receive complete electronic prescription orders.

To deliver an electronic prescription order that has been encrypted and formatted according to the SCRIPT standard to a pharmacy's facsimile machine, the EDI network must also have access to the prescription order to decrypt* the content and convert it to a format that can be received and printed at the pharmacy's facsimile machine. The content of the electronic prescription order is not altered by such an intervention: the electronic prescription order that reaches the pharmacy contains the exact same information it contained when the prescriber transmitted it.[†]

In general, third-party intervention prohibitions and/or direct transmission requirements should not be interpreted to apply to EDI networks, provided that the content of the prescription order is not changed while en route. In fact, several states have provided explicit legal sanction for EDI networks, which are sometimes referred to as "computer transition systems,"[14] "a commercial intermediary,"[15] or "data communication devices."[16] Further, the security and confidentiality of prescription information transmitted via such networks is governed under the federal privacy rules established pursuant to HIPAA. Without the express written authori-

---

*In general, while pharmacy facsimile machines can convert data in digital form into print, they do not have decryption capability.

[†]In Maryland, EDI networks must demonstrate the integrity, confidentiality, and security of transmissions in a manner approved by the Board of Pharmacy. Md. Regs. Code tit. 34 §20.02.B-C.

zation of the patient, protected health information cannot be used by covered entities (healthcare providers, health plans, and healthcare clearinghouses) or their business associates (to include EDI networks) for any purpose other than treatment, payment, and healthcare operations.

Format Issues: Drug Product Selection Instructions

With few exceptions, state pharmacy law does not provide specific guidance for how prescribers' drug product selection instructions are communicated in electronic prescription orders. Clearly, the existing requirements for written prescription orders cannot be applied to electronic prescription orders. Where handwritten signatures and/or handwritten instructions are required, applicable electronic commerce law makes such requirements unenforceable. Further, even though bit-mapping technology can be used to replicate handwritten signatures and instructions (to include handwritten initials, check marks, and abbreviations), few if any vendors employ technology that meets the implicit requirement that such handwriting be created contemporaneously with the creation of the prescription order (see below for a discussion of bit-mapped, "digitized" electronic signatures). Finally, bit-mapping technology cannot be employed in electronic prescription orders transmitted computer-to-computer because the SCRIPT standard format does not support graphical images.*

In sum, requiring electronic prescriptions to comply with the same requirements for communicating drug product selection instructions in written prescription orders is neither reasonable nor enforceable. To accommodate the requirements of electronic commerce law and the limitations of electronic prescribing technology, state law should be amended to provide guidance to pharmacists on how drug product selection instructions may be separately addressed in electronic prescription orders.

For example, Washington law provides for different mechanisms for communicating drug product selection instructions, depending on whether the prescriber issues a written or an electronic prescription order. For written prescription orders, prescribers must use a form that has two signature lines at opposite ends of the bottom of the form. The signature line on the right side of the form must be labeled "Dispense as Written" while the one on the left is labeled "Substitution Permitted." Pursuant to this requirement, the prescriber communicates his or her instructions by signing the ap-

---

*In prescription orders formatted according to the SCRIPT standard, drug product selection instructions are transmitted as numeric values: "Ø" for substitution permitted and "1" for substitution not allowed by prescriber. See SCRIPT Standard Format Implementation Guide, Version 4, Release 3 (October 2003).

propriately labeled line.[17] For electronic prescription orders, the requirement is both linguistically and technologically neutral: prescribers are required to indicate their "preference" on whether drug product selection is authorized.[18] In short, the Washington requirements for electronic prescription orders accommodate both computer-to-computer and computer-to-facsimile machine transmissions.

Validation and Security Issues: Electronic Signatures

A prescriber's handwritten signature is one of several criteria* on which pharmacists have historically relied to validate or authenticate a written prescription order. For electronic prescription orders, only electronic commerce law provides consistent guidance for what constitutes the legal equivalent of a handwritten signature, i.e., an electronic signature. Where state pharmacy law does address electronic signatures, the guidance is not only inadequate but also frequently in conflict with the controlling electronic commerce laws. As of early 2004, only eight states even provide an electronic signature definition and, of these, only Massachusetts, Washington, and Wyoming have adopted electronic signature definitions that are consistent with the definition set forward in the UETA and the E-Sign Act.

As previously noted, the UETA and the E-Sign Act define an electronic signature broadly as "an electronic sound, symbol, or process attached to or logically associated with a record and executed or adopted by a person with the intent to sign the record." Because electronic prescription transactions are within the scope of both bodies of law, an electronic signature that meets this definition cannot be denied legal effect or enforceability under state pharmacy law. In other words, the test of whether an electronic signature is valid is not that it has the visual appearance of an original handwritten signature but rather whether it meets the requirements of the UETA and E-Sign Act definition. Under the UETA, so long as the electronic signature can be shown to be the act of the prescriber—such as by demonstrating the efficacy of the security procedures used to generate and execute the prescription— the electronic signature is legally attributable to the prescriber.[19]

Thus, because the UETA and the E-Sign Act are technology neutral, the generosity of their common electronic signature definition thus allows soft-

---

*Pharmacists also rely on a critical examination of the prescription's clinical contents as well as on the prescriber's name, address, and DEA number. Although advised to the contrary, most prescribers order preprinted prescription blanks that include their DEA numbers, whether the prescription is for a controlled substance or not. Because each DEA number is unique to the prescriber, pharmacists also rely on it to authenticate written prescriptions.

ware developers to employ a wide range of legally valid electronic signatures for electronic prescribing. It should be noted that the validity of an electronic prescription order depends more on the security features of the electronic prescribing software and transmittal process than any symbol or mark that may be displayed or printed at the pharmacy. What is displayed or printed is the "evidence" that a valid electronic signature has been executed rather than what the prescriber actually did when he or she executed the prescription order: indeed, after a prescriber has logged on to the electronic prescribing application, in most cases he or she clicks on a button displayed on a computer monitor or the display of a PDA to print a prescription locally or to transmit it electronically.

The most widely used and accepted symbol for validating an electronic prescription order is known as a "digitized" or replicated signature. Simply put, a digitized signature is a bit-mapped, exact image copy of the prescriber's original handwritten signature. Obtained either by scanning an original signature handwritten on paper or writing a signature with a digitizing pen on a tablet or other image digitizing device, a digitized signature can be saved to computer memory, displayed on a computer monitor, and printed on paper.* Further, it need not be executed contemporaneously with each prescription: the stored image can be retrieved from memory and "pasted" into each electronic prescription order a prescriber creates.

Because regulators and pharmacists are inclined to accept a digitized signature on its face, most electronic prescribing systems use bit-mapping technology to capture and save both handwritten signatures and handwritten drug product selection instructions to create and transmit e-Fax prescription orders, by far the most frequently transmitted electronic prescription order. When received and printed at the pharmacy's facsimile machine, such prescription orders are generally accepted as valid *facsimile* prescription orders rather than electronic prescription orders because they *appear* to be exact image copies of written prescription orders.

Although regulators and pharmacists may be more comfortable with digitized signatures, it is not likely that this particular technology could be mandated. The UETA would not prohibit a state from requiring that a specific electronic signature technology be used, but the E-Sign Act generally preempts any state or federal requirement that accords greater legal status or effect to a specific technology or technical specification for electronic records and electronic signature. However, as previously noted, the E-Sign

---

*At least five states (Colorado, Missouri, Nevada, Texas, and Wyoming) authorize the issuance of written prescription orders executed with digitized signatures, provided such prescriptions are printed on paper that utilizes security features that will ensure that the prescription order is not subject to any form of copying and/or alteration.

Act does authorize a state or federal agency to adopt requirements that would otherwise violate the prohibition against mandating a specific technology provided such requirements specify performance standards assuring the accuracy, record integrity, and accessibility of records that must be retained.[20] While a digitized signature possesses no special characteristic that would allow it to meet such performance standards, a digital signature does.

A digital signature should not be confused with a "digitized" signature. A digital signature is a mathematical form of signature that is based on the asymmetric encryption capabilities of Public Key Infrastructure (PKI) systems. Using PKI standards, a prescriber can "sign" an electronic prescription order and encrypt it with a "private key" under his or her control that is issued by a certification authority. A recipient pharmacist can decrypt the electronic prescription order only by use of a "public key" that is issued by the same certification authority. The primary benefits of a digital signature is that (1) it confirms or authenticates the identity of the sender; (2) the sender cannot deny that he or she sent the electronic prescription order (sometimes referred to as the quality of "nonrepudiation"); (3) the content of the prescription order is accessible only to those possessing the public key; and, most important, (4) if the content of the prescription order is changed or altered in transmission, the digital signature is automatically invalidated and the transaction is void.

In short, pursuant to the UETA* and the exception to preemption provisions of the E-Sign Act, it would appear that a state or federal agency could adopt a requirement mandating the use of PKI-based digital signatures for electronic transactions simply by specifying that record integrity is a performance standard that not only serves an important governmental objective but also is substantially related to the achievement of that objective.† Not surprisingly, digital signature technology's ability to ensure the integrity of an electronically transmitted record in combination with its other features (authentication of the identity of the sender, nonrepudiation, and a strong encryption standard) are the primary reasons the DEA has actively been considering mandating the technology for electronic prescriptions for controlled substances. If adopted, state pharmacy law would also require amendment to conform to the DEA requirements.

---

*Indeed, the Official UETA states, "To the extent a State has a Digital Signature Law, the UETA is designed to support and compliment [sic] that statute." See UETA, Prefatory Note.

†Wyoming, a state that has adopted the UETA, is the only jurisdiction that specifically requires the use of digital signature technology for electronic prescriptions that are transmitted computer-to-computer. However, it is unclear that the requirement escapes preemption by the E-Sign Act. The Wyoming rules were adopted without the required reference to the E-Sign Act in March 2002, long after the federal statute's effective date.

ELECTRONIC PRESCRIPTION ORDERS
FOR CONTROLLED SUBSTANCES

Requiring the use of PKI-based digital signature technology has been under DEA consideration since 1998-1999.* It is now clear that the DEA recognizes that the E-Sign Act imposes no legal barriers to requiring PKI-based digital signatures for electronic prescription orders; in June 2003, the agency published proposed rules based on the technology for electronic orders for Schedule I and II controlled substances.[21] However, operational complexity and public policy issues appear to have extended the DEA's review of whether to issue similar rules authorizing electronic prescription orders for controlled substances.

PKI-based digital signature technology may well be the "gold standard" for secure electronic transactions and thus the optimum solution to supporting the DEA's goal of preventing the diversion of controlled substances in an electronic environment. However, mandating its use for controlled substance prescription orders should not only support the DEA's mission; it should also be operationally reasonable for all stakeholders and facilitate rather than inhibit prescribers' adoption of electronic prescribing practices. Given that the DEA has repeatedly failed to meet publicly announced deadlines for proposing rules, it would appear that the development of the proposed standard has encountered obstacles.[†]

---

*Technically, the DEA's approach to authorizing electronic prescription orders for controlled substances is consistent with the philosophy set forth in both the UETA and the E-Sign Act. The DEA would not require prescribers to issue electronic prescription orders for controlled substances. The DEA plan, known as the Electronic Prescriptions for Controlled Substances project, would authorize the use of electronic prescription orders and establish the standards by which electronic prescription orders would be issued. For a detailed analysis of the DEA's project, see Office of Diversion Control, U.S. Drug Enforcement Administration, *Public Key Infrastructure Analysis Concept of Operations* (October 26, 2000).

†For example, establishing and administering a nationally accepted infrastructure for PKI systems that is capable of supporting an estimated 450,000 active clinicians and 70,000 pharmacies in real-time constitutes a complex and costly proposition. Moreover, establishing a separate technological standard for electronic prescription orders for controlled substances would impose new development costs for vendors to integrate legacy electronic signature technologies for prescription orders for noncontrolled substances with PKI-based digital signature technology for prescription orders issued for controlled substances. Given the low volume that prescription orders for controlled substances represent, few vendors are likely to incur the costs willingly. Further, because the security of PKI-based digital signature technology is inherently superior to other electronic signature technologies, state regulators may be tempted to extend the standard to apply to all electronic prescription orders. Such an outcome would simplify matters for vendors but would be a costly complication for retail pharmacies, particularly those that lack EDI capability (a facsimile machine is not capable of decrypting an asymmetrically encrypted record). In short, the vast majority of pharmacies would not be able to receive digitally signed electronic prescription orders until their computer systems were upgraded.

Pending publication of a proposed rule on electronic prescription orders, the DEA has erroneously taken the position that the E-Sign Act did not invalidate its current regulations; the DEA insists that a pharmacist may dispense a Schedule II controlled substance only pursuant to a written prescription order signed by the prescriber[22] or, in the case of a controlled substance in Schedules III-V, pursuant to a written prescription order signed by the prescriber, a facsimile prescription, or an oral order that is immediately reduced to writing.[23] In October 2003, the DEA's Office of Chief Counsel stated that "at present, the use of electronic prescriptions for controlled substances is prohibited."[24] Moreover, the April 2004 publication of the eighth edition of the DEA's *Pharmacist's Manual* also included guidance consistent with the existing regulations.[25]

Further complicating the regulatory environment, the DEA has interpreted its current regulations to authorize pharmacists to dispense certain controlled substances upon an electronic prescription order under certain conditions. In December 2000, the DEA issued an informal guidance authorizing pharmacists to dispense a Schedule III-V controlled substance pursuant to an electronic prescription order, provided the pharmacist treated it as oral prescription order: i.e., it would have to be verified, presumably via a telephone call to the prescriber, and immediately be reduced to writing.[26] In April 2001, the DEA issued a similar but formal guidance for prescription orders for controlled substances received over the Internet.[27]

Although it would appear that the DEA's current enforcement approach clearly flouts the E-Sign Act, no interested party has seen any practical advantage to challenging the DEA's authority. Were the DEA challenged, it is unlikely that the agency could prevail. To enforce a prohibition against the use of electronic prescription orders for controlled substances, the DEA would have to initiate a new rule pursuant to the E-Sign Act to "impose or reimpose any requirement that a record be in a tangible printed or paper form"[28] on the ground that there is a "compelling governmental interest relating to law enforcement or national security" and that the "requirement is essential to attaining such interest."[29]

In sum, therefore, it would appear that all interested parties (to include state regulators, pharmacists, and software vendors) are content to accept the DEA's interpretation of the effect of the E-Sign Act. In order words, it would be fair to say that until the DEA actually adopts regulations for electronic prescription orders for controlled substances, there will be no legal challenge and pharmacists will not dispense pursuant to a prescription order for a controlled substance unless the prescription order complies with the current requirements, even though the latter are unenforceable.

CONCLUSION

With the exception of those states that have adopted direct transmission requirements, there are few if any legal barriers in pharmacy law to the electronic transmission of prescription information. Even where state pharmacy law does not provide clear guidance to pharmacists, the effect of electronic commerce law should remove any doubt that pharmacists have legal authority to dispense pursuant to an electronic prescription order. Because of the technology's promised contribution to enhanced patient safety and reduced operational costs, policymakers and practicing pharmacists almost universally endorse electronic prescribing. As a result, software vendors are deploying electronic prescribing products as quickly as they can sell them, despite the fact that the DEA's proposed regulatory environment may require reengineering.

That being said, it is clear that in order to facilitate the expansion of electronic prescribing practices, state policymakers should undertake a careful review of their existing requirements with a view toward providing guidance to pharmacists on the requirements of electronic prescription orders that not only accurately reflects the technology's characteristics, capabilities, limitations, and connectivity infrastructure but also accommodates technological innovation. Finally, recognizing that states will seize upon regulatory schemes that will differ in the details, such schemes must be consistent with and reflect the requirements of prevailing electronic commerce law.

NOTES

1. UETA § 7.
2. *Id.* § 1(8).
3. *Id.* § 1(16).
4. 15 U.S.C. §§ 7001-7006, 7021, and 7031.
5. See 145 Cong. Rec. S3584 (daily ed. April 12, 1999) (remarks of Sen. Abraham); 145 Cong. Rec. S13547 (daily ed. October 29, 1999) (remarks of Sen. Leahy); 145 Cong. Rec. S13549 (daily ed. October 29, 1999) (remarks of Sen. Hyde); 146 Cong. Rec. S5227 (daily ed. June 15, 2000) (remarks of Sen. Hollings).
6. 15 U.S.C. § 7001(a).
7. *Id.* § 7006(5).
8. *Id.* § 7006(13).
9. *Id.* § 7003(a)-(b).
10. *Id.* § 7001(b)(2).
11. *Id.* § 7002(a)(1)-(2).
12. *Id.* § 7004(b)(3)(A).
13. *Id.* § 7004(b)(3)(B).

14. Code Vt. R. 19.3.1.5(A).

15. Md. Regs. Code tit. 34 § 20.02.B.4.

16. Tex. Admin. Code tit. 22 § 291.34(b)(4)(A)(ii).

17. Wash. Rev. Code § 69.41.120.

18. Wash. Admin. Code § 246-870-030(9).

19. UETA § 9.

20. 15 U.S.C. §7004 (b)(3). To escape preemption, the adoption of a regulation requiring a specific technology after June 30, 2000, must make specific reference to the E-Sign Act. 15 U.S.C. § 7002(a)(2)(B).

21. *Federal Register* 68, No. 124 (June 27, 2003): 38557-38581.

22. 21 C.F.R. § 1306.11(a).

23. *Id.* § 1306.21(a).

24. Letter from Charles Trant, Associate Chief Counsel, U.S. Drug Enforcement Administration, to Wendell Morgan, Associate Counsel, Alabama State Board of Medical Examiners, October 24, 2003.

25. See Office of Diversion Control, U.S. Drug Enforcement Administration, *Pharmacist's Manual* (Washington, DC, 2004).

26. Letter from Patricia Good, Liaison and Policy Section, Office of Diversion Control, U.S. Drug Enforcement Administration, to Clifford Berman, General Counsel, Allscripts Healthcare Solutions, Inc., December 27, 2000.

27. *Federal Register* 65, No. 82 (April 27, 2001): 21181-21184.

28. 15 U.S.C. § 7004(c)(1).

29. *Id.* § 7004(b)(3)(B).

Chapter 23

Telepharmacy: Identifying Legal Issues for Pharmacists

Edward D. Rickert
Melissa A. Madigan

INTRODUCTION

Over the past several decades, the practice of pharmacy has undergone tremendous change. The profession is slowly evolving from the traditional, product-oriented profession depicted by characters such as Mr. Gower, the hapless druggist in the Frank Capra classic *It's a Wonderful Life,* to a service-oriented profession in which the cognitive services provided by the pharmacist, both to patients and to other members of the healthcare team, are as important as the drug product he or she dispenses.

As we carry on with our journey into the twenty-first century, the profession will undoubtedly continue to evolve. Much has already been written about how managed care and the increased emphasis on conserving our healthcare dollars has opened the door for pharmacists to demonstrate that pharmaceutical care can decrease healthcare costs and improve the overall quality of care. A current shortage of pharmacists, combined with the need for pharmacists to provide higher-level patient care, decrease medication errors, and improve patient access to care, is causing the industry to rely more and more on modern communications technologies to assist pharmacists in delivering more efficient and effective patient care.

Healthcare delivery using advanced communications technologies has long been under review by state and federal lawmakers. Since 1993, over 400 "telehealth"-related bills had been proposed or are currently being

The authors would like to thank Keri Sullivan, a prelaw student at Villanova University, for her assistance in preparing this chapter.

Pharmacy Law Desk Reference
© 2007 by The Haworth Press, Inc. All rights reserved.
doi:10.1300/5790_23

considered by state legislatures, along with over 100 such bills at the federal level.[1] At the forefront of this trend is the medical profession, where advanced communications technologies were first used to deliver cost-effective medical care to patients in underserved, rural areas, and where such technologies have since demonstrated their benefits within a number of medical specialties, including radiology, cardiology, and critical care medicine.

In an effort to resolve the many issues identified as barriers to the provision of cost-effective, quality pharmaceutical care services, especially for those patients with limited access to pharmacies and pharmacists, successful adaptations to certain telemedicine technologies have been made, particularly the use of communications equipment that provides "face-to-face" interactions with patients. Other innovations utilizing advanced communications technologies include the incorporation of automated dispensing devices in clinic settings, remote dispensing sites staffed by pharmacy technicians while supervised by pharmacists at a distance, order review and entry by pharmacists located at a centralized location prior to dispensing by pharmacy or nonpharmacy personnel at a remote location, pharmacy call centers, and centralized prescription filling systems. Each of these innovations addresses the lack of available pharmacists, the lack of accessible care in some areas, and the need to remove pharmacists from the technical duties associated with the prescription dispensing process so that they may focus on providing cognitive services to patients.

Also necessary to the future improvement of patient care is the use of communications technologies between the pharmacy and medical professions. The electronic transmission of prescription information is probably one of the most vital, yet most difficult to implement, applications of communications technologies. Its widespread use can remedy several issues, including prescription errors due to misread handwriting, noncompliance associated with patients who may not get their initial prescriptions dispensed, the amount of time spent by pharmacists on prescription input functions, and the inaccessibility of vital patient health information, including lab and other test results, to pharmacists.

The National Association of Boards of Pharmacy (NABP)* defines the "practice of telepharmacy" as "the provision of pharmaceutical care through the use of telecommunications and information technologies to pa-

---

*The NABP is the "independent, international, and impartial association that assists its member boards and jurisdictions in developing, implementing, and enforcing uniform standards for the purpose of protecting the public health" and "the only professional association that represents the state boards of pharmacy in all fifty United States, the District of Columbia, Guam, Puerto Rico, the Virgin Islands, New Zealand, eight Canadian Provinces, and three Australian states." (www.nabp.net)

tients at a distance."[2] Although many of the telepharmacy practices now in place were originally designed to provide pharmacy services to rural areas where access to pharmacy services is lacking, the use of telepharmacy has also been helpful in providing service in urban settings, where the pharmacist shortage and increased prescription demands have left many retail and hospital pharmacies severely understaffed. Indeed, the NABP Model Act does not limit the availability of telepharmacy services to rural areas, and national pharmacy groups, including the American Pharmacists Association, have adopted official positions that embrace the use of technology as a means of freeing up an overworked pharmacist's time, thereby allowing these healthcare professionals to spend more time on direct patient care activities.* The focus of these and other pharmacy organizations has been to avoid placing arbitrary limits on the availability of telepharmacy services, and instead to encourage the use of technology to assist pharmacists in providing pharmaceutical care in all practice settings.

It is clear that the use of these technologies in pharmacy practice, or "telepharmacy" practice, is quickly becoming an integral part of modern pharmacy practice. It is equally clear that with the adoption of these practices come legal hurdles, obstacles, and pitfalls that need to be addressed. This chapter is intended to identify and analyze the more significant of these legal and regulatory issues.

LICENSURE

A number of licensure issues exist that may hinder the widespread use of telepharmacy-related technologies across the country. Currently, the regulation of the practice of pharmacy is left to the state legislatures and court systems in each of the fifty states. State boards of pharmacy are authorized

---

*At its annual meeting in March 2004, the APhA House of Delegates adopted as APhA's official policy the following statement concerning the use of Automation and Technology in Pharmacy Practice:

1. APhA supports the use of automation and technology in pharmacy practice, with pharmacists maintaining oversight of these systems.

2. APhA recommends that pharmacists and other pharmacy personnel implement policies and procedures addressing the use of technology and automation to ensure safety, accuracy, security, data integrity and patient confidentiality.

3. APhA supports initial and on-going system-specific education and training of all affected personnel when automation and technology are utilized in the workplace.

4. APhA shall work with all relevant parties to facilitate the appropriate use of automation and technology in pharmacy practice.

This policy statement applies equally to all pharmacy practice settings, whether urban or rural.

to define the "practice of pharmacy" and regulate the activities of pharmacists and pharmacy establishments. Relative to the issue of telepharmacy, the primary questions that must be answered are, Where does telepharmacy practice fit within the legal-regulatory definition of pharmacy practice? In other words, Are telepharmacy practices legal? Should telepharmacy be regulated differently than traditional pharmacy practice? and Where does the practice of pharmacy take place when the pharmacist and patient are located in different states?

The answers to these questions vary significantly from state to state. Only a handful of states even utilize the term *telepharmacy* in their laws or regulations.[3] Most states address the issue through the regulation of "nonresident pharmacies," those located outside the state that is doing the regulating. The vast majority of states require nonresident pharmacies that dispense prescription medications to in-state resident to register with the state board of pharmacy.[4] Occasionally, such a requirement applies only if the nonresident pharmacy dispenses prescriptions into the state for resident patients on a regular and ongoing basis, as opposed to on a limited or incidental basis.[4]

NABP has incorporated the "practice of telepharmacy within and across state lines" into its definition of the "practice of pharmacy."* This recognition of the "practice of telepharmacy" several years ago, coupled with the growing demand for this type of pharmacy service, likely led to the formal recognition of telepharmacy by several state boards of pharmacy in recent years. With that formal recognition has come a variety of different approaches to licensing and regulating the practice.

Some might question whether a separate licensure scheme should be required for telepharmacy, or whether existing laws and regulations that regulate traditional pharmacy are sufficient. Initially, the components of telepharmacy practice—specifically order review, drug utilization review, and dispensing activities—are the "practice of pharmacy" under the laws and regulations of most, if not all, states. As such, there should be no need to create a separate licensure classification specific to the practice of tele-

---

*NABP's Model Act defines "Practice of Pharmacy as "the interpretation, evaluation, and implementation of Medical Orders; the Dispensing of Prescription Drug Order; participation in Drug and Device, selection; Drug Administration; Drug Regimen Reviews; the Practice of Telepharmacy within and across state lines; Drug or Drug-related research; the provision of Patient Counseling and the provision of those acts or services necessary to provide Pharmaceutical Care in all areas of patient care, including Primary and Collaborative Pharmacy Practice; and the responsibility for Compounding and Labeling of Drugs and Devices (except Labeling by a Manufacturer, repackager, or Distributor of Non-Prescription Drugs and commercially packaged Legend Drugs and Devices), proper and safe storage of Drugs and Devices, and maintenance of proper records for them."

pharmacy. Rather, modifications to existing laws to address issues unique to telepharmacy practice can be made to allow the practice of telepharmacy under existing state licensing schemes.

For example, in Texas, the pharmacy act was amended to provide a definition for "telepharmacy services," which permits the practice under Texas's already existing Class A and C pharmacy licenses. The Texas statute states:

TELEPHARMACY SYSTEMS.

(a) In this section, "telepharmacy system" means a system that monitors the dispensing of prescription drugs and provides for related drug use review and patient counseling services by an electronic method, including the use of the following types of technology:
(1) audio and video;
(2) still image capture; and
(3) store and forward.
(b) A Class A or Class C pharmacy located in this state may provide pharmacy services, including the dispensing of drugs, through a telepharmacy system in a facility that is not at the same location as the Class A or Class C pharmacy.[6]

This regulatory scheme simply identifies the type of technology that can be employed to provide traditional pharmacy activities, including dispensing, DUR, and patient counseling, and permits those activities to be provided under a pharmacy's existing Class A or C pharmacy license. No separate "telepharmacy" license is required. This approach makes sense and eliminates the requirement of multiple licensure for pharmacies that practice traditional pharmacy but utilize telepharmacy technology for some purposes.

Similarly, in Illinois, although the legislature has not directly addressed the use of technology to provide telepharmacy services, the pharmacy board and Department of Professional Regulation have granted variances to allow telepharmacy services to be provided to hospitals under the existing Division II pharmacy license classification.* Under the Illinois licensing

---

*In March 2004, the Board of Pharmacy and the Illinois Department of Professional Regulation granted a variance to a pharmacy that provides pharmacy services to hospitals but does not dispense prescription medications to those hospitals. The variance allowed the pharmacy to provide remote order review, order entry, and DUR services for hospitals, and removed any requirement that the pharmacy comply with record keeping and drug inventory control requirements. *See,* IDPR Order Granting Variance, March 12, 2004 (Public Record).

scheme, a Division II license is issued to "pharmacies whose primary pharmacy service is provided to patients or residents of [long term care facilities and hospitals], and which are not located in the facilities they serve."[7] Thus, the existing license classification expressly permitted the provision of pharmacy services from a remote location, and all that was required to allow remote order review and DUR services was board and department approval of a variance which recognized that the facility providing those services was not involved in the dispensing of any medications to the facilities that it served.

One benefit of having a separate licensure classification for telepharmacy is that some of the requirements associated with traditional pharmacy can present significant barriers to the implementation of telepharmacy services. These include physical space requirements which provide that in order to be licensed a "pharmacy" must meet certain minimum square footage requirements. A pharmacy that is simply providing order review and processing for another pharmacy may not need as much space as a traditional pharmacy. Similarly, licensing laws that require the pharmacy to maintain an inventory of drugs, or equipment such as mortars, pestles, prescription balances, and the like, also present challenges for would-be telepharmacy practitioners. Such requirements may make sense under the traditional view of pharmacy as a product-oriented profession, but make little sense when the type of pharmacy services to be provided from a "pharmacy" are purely cognitive, nondispensing services.

As an example of the problems created by some of the traditional pharmacy requirements, consider a pharmacy in a rural area that wants to provide services to a medical office located in an adjacent county or town which had no pharmacy of its own. One way to provide that service would be to place a medication "dispensing machine" at the doctor's office, along with a computer link that would allow the pharmacist located at a remote location to view, via video feed, the medications "dispensed" from the machine, as well as the patient, for purposes of patient counseling. The doctor could transmit an order to the pharmacy, where the pharmacist would review the order, perform DUR activities, and electronically request that the dispensing machine label and release the prescription medication to the patient. The pharmacist could remotely view the labeled medication for accuracy, and also provide counseling via the computer video link to the doctor's office. This type of pharmacy service is currently being provided in many locations across the country.[8] If however, the law of the state required the space where the dispensing machine is located to be licensed as a pharmacy, that could present a disincentive for the doctor to agree to the placement of the unit. Even if the doctor were to agree to place the unit in his or her office, if the state's law required that the "pharmacy" be of a certain physical size,* that too could create an obstacle to the implementation of a service that would promote patient care, by keeping the pharmacist involved in the medication therapy review and dispensing process.

Similarly, some state laws require a pharmacy to maintain an inventory of drugs in order to obtain a license. If the only pharmacy service provided by the pharmacy is order review and DUR services, why would there be any need for that pharmacy to maintain any inventory of drugs? The same is true of laws that require pharmacies to have dispensing and compounding equipment in all pharmacies. Such equipment would be absolutely necessary in a pharmacy that provides compounding and dispensing services but has no place in a pharmacy engaged exclusively in the provision of the cognitive, nondispensing telepharmacy services. Clearly, if telepharmacy services are to flourish, changes must be made to these types of archaic laws. In addition, there may be some requirements that would be unique to telepharmacy practice but are not needed in a traditional pharmacy. In order to meet these conflicting needs, it may be necessary for states to create a new and separate licensure classification by statute. Alternatively, the specific requirements could be left to the rule-making process, so that variances from requirements that may not make sense in a particular setting could be obtained, to accommodate the practice without requiring legislative change.

Additional issues are raised when a pharmacy desires to provide telepharmacy across state lines. The issues raised include the question of where the practice of pharmacy occurs and, with that, which state should have jurisdiction and regulatory authority over the pharmacy, as well as the individual pharmacists engaged in telepharmacy practice. The answer to this question varies significantly from state to state. A handful of states have indirectly answered this question by requiring individual, nonresident pharmacists to be licensed in the state where the patient is located, at least when it comes to dispensing medications into the state.† NABP has taken the position that the practice of pharmacy takes place in the state where the patient is located, and recommends that states require all nonresident pharmacists providing any pharmaceutical care services, as op-

---

*Illinois, for example, requires that pharmacies be at least 300 square feet of contiguous space. 225 ILCS § 85/14.

†For example, Tennessee pharmacy rules require the pharmacist in charge of the nonresident pharmacy to have a Tennessee pharmacist license, and Arkansas rules require at least one pharmacist employed by the nonresident pharmacy to have an Arkansas pharmacist license. NABP, *infra* note 2, at 45.

posed to only those who dispense medications to their patients, be licensed in their states.*

However, requiring full licensure of pharmacists severely limits the ability of pharmacists to provide care on a nationwide basis and could present a significant barrier to the provision of telepharmacy services. Although the process that allows the reciprocation of pharmacist licensure is one that is far quicker, easier, and less expensive than those in place for other professions, obtaining and maintaining licenses in each of the fifty states is one that few pharmacists are willing to contemplate.

Moreover, state laws that attempt to regulate the activities of nonresident pharmacies and pharmacists through licensure requirements may be susceptible to challenge under the Commerce Clause of the United States Constitution. Although, under Article X of the U.S. Constitution, states have the authority to regulate activities that affect the health, safety, and welfare of their citizens, which would include the provision of pharmaceutical care to in-state residents, that power is not absolute. The Commerce Clause of the Constitution limits states' ability to erect barriers against interstate trade.†
The Commerce Clause, Article I, Section 8, Clause 3 of the Constitution grants Congress the power to "regulate Commerce with foreign nations and among the several states." The Commerce Clause has been interpreted by the U.S. Supreme Court to be both an affirmative grant of power to Congress to regulate commerce between the states and an implied prohibition on the states to do the same:

---

*The NABP Model Act "Section 301, Unlawful Practice" states "except as otherwise provided in this Act, it shall be unlawful for any individual, whether located in or outside this State, to engage in the Practice of Pharmacy in this state unless currently licensed to practice under any facet of the provisions of this Act. The provision of Pharmaceutical Care services to an individual in this state, through telephonic, electronic, or other means, regardless of the location of the pharmacist, shall constitute the Practice of Pharmacy and shall be subject to regulation." NABP, *supra* note 6, at 41. The comment accompanying Section 301 reemphasizes the Association's position that full licensure should be required of pharmacists across state lines but, recognizing the difficulty in promulgating such a requirement, recommends that states, in the alternative, mandate a less stringent nonresident pharmacist "registration" requirement in place of full pharmacist licensure. It states that "NABP recognizes that protection of the public health should extend across state borders. Accordingly, the NABP Model Act incorporates the Practice of Telepharmacy across state lines with the scope of the 'Practice of Pharmacy' and requires full licensure for all pharmacists practicing within a particular jurisdiction by any means. Alternatively, states may choose to implement a nonresident pharmacist 'registration' rather than require full licensure for pharmacists providing pharmaceutical care services from outside the state to patients within the state." NABP, *infra* note 4, at 49.

†The practice of healthcare has been held to be interstate trade for the purposes of antitrust laws. See, e.g., *Arizona v. Maricopa County Medical Soc'y.*, 457 U.S. 332 (1982).

Where a statute regulates even-handedly to effectuate a legitimate local public concern, and its effects on interstate commerce are only incidental, it will be upheld unless the burden imposed upon such
commerce is clearly excessive in relation to the putative local benefits. If a legitimate local purpose is found, then the question becomes
one of degree. And the extent of the burden that will be tolerated will
of course depend on the nature of the local interest involved, and on
whether it could be promoted as well with a lesser impact on interstate
activities.

In the case *Pike v. Bruce Church, Inc.,* 397 U.S. 137, 142 90 S.Ct. 844,
847, 25 L.Ed.2d 174 (1970), *Bruce Church* prescribes a balancing test,
under which the local interest must be sufficiently compelling to justify a
burdening interstate commerce. Under *Bruce Church* the Court will also determine whether there might exist less onerous—or more direct—methods
of accomplishing the local purpose. Also see the case *Baldwin v. G.A.F.
Seelig, Inc.,* 294 U.S. 511, 524, 55 S.Ct. 497, 501 (1935) (purported goal of
protecting quality of milk must be met by means "more direct and certain
than the creation of a parity of prices between New York and other states.").

The potential conflict between a state's power to regulate health professionals and the prohibition against restraints on interstate commerce has yet
to be addressed by the courts. To determine whether a state law that requires
licensure for nonresident pharmacies or pharmacists to become licensed
imposes an undue burden on the out-of-state provider, the burden of obtaining licensure would have to be weighed against the benefits of regulation
and the reasons for the regulation. On the one hand, it can be argued that the
need to protect the health and well-being of in-state residents far outweighs
any minimal burden created by requiring an out-of-state pharmacy or pharmacist to obtain a license in the state where the patient resides and where,
therefore, care is being provided. On the other hand, when care is provided
to residents residing in all fifty states, the requirement imposed on the
nonresident pharmacy provider to obtain a license in all fifty states may be
extremely burdensome. The burden is that much greater when, in addition
to requiring licensure, each of the individual states requires compliance
with their pharmacy practice laws. That issue is addressed more fully in the
next section.

CONFLICTS OF LAW

The answers related to where the practice of pharmacy takes place in the
context of telepharmacy and multistate practice is significant to the issues

associated with conflicts of law. Conflicts between the laws of the various states create confusion as to which state's law a pharmacist is required to follow in any given situation involving nonresident patient prescription orders. For example, suppose the pharmacist's home state did not recognize as valid prescriptions independently written by a physician assistant, while the patient's home state recognized physician assistant prescription orders. Would such a prescription be valid? The premise that the practice of pharmacy takes place in the patient's home state would likely cause one to conclude that such a prescription order would be valid and that the pharmacist can, in effect, violate his home state's law and dispense the prescription order. But does it make sense that a nonresident physician assistant, not licensed in the state, would have a broader scope of authority than one located within the state? Would that broader scope of authority exist if the patient were a state resident who traveled to the nonresident physician assistant? If not, does it make sense that prescriptions of nonresident patients might be considered valid but the prescription orders of in-state patients, written by the same practitioner, might not? What if the pharmacist's home state mandated generic substitution, while the patient's state left the decision of generic substitution up to the pharmacist and required the patient's affirmative consent? If the patient desired the brand name product, would the pharmacist be able to dispense the prescription order according to the patient's wishes and the laws of the patient's home state, or would the pharmacist be required to dispense a generic product, as mandated by her home state? Again, would the pharmacist be required to break his or her own state's law to fill the prescription?

Certain states have addressed these very conflicts in their pharmacy practice acts and regulations. For example, although the state of Arkansas mandates that nonresident pharmacies follow its generic substitution laws when dispensing prescriptions orders for its residents, it makes an exception to this requirement when doing so would violate such laws of the state in which the pharmacy is located.[9] The laws in Maryland are similar in that they state outright that laws addressing nonresident pharmacies do not require such pharmacies to violate the laws or regulations of the state in which they are located.[10] Such clauses resolve many conflicts of law issues associated with multistate practice, but only a few states seem to have included such language in their pharmacy practice acts or regulations.* For those pharmacies in states without such clauses, NABP recommends and requires of its VIPPS (Verified Internet Pharmacy Practice Sites) certified pharma-

---

*Montana and New Mexico are two other states that have included conflicts of law clauses in their pharmacy laws or regulations. See, e.g., Mont. Admin. R. 24.174.1009 (2002), or N.M.A.C. 16.19.6.24 (2003).

cies that pharmacies follow the more stringent law or regulation.* Often-times, however, following the more stringent law does not prevent one from violating the less stringent law. In addition, the determination as to which law is more stringent is not always clear-cut. Take, for example, the case of mandatory generic substitution. Is the state law that mandates substitution more stringent than the law that requires patient consent? The answers are not always obvious.

These types of conflicts are a significant concern to pharmacies that are engaged in multistate practice and may be an impediment to the growth of telepharmacy. In addition to the difficulty of knowing and complying with the laws of all states in which the pharmacies provide service is the question of whether a state board of pharmacy will prosecute a pharmacy for violat-ing its law through activities performed in an effort to comply with another state's conflicting laws or regulations. Again, the Commerce Clause im-poses limits on how far a state can go when regulating conduct that occurs outside its borders, even where traditional health and safety concerns are raised. It can be argued that absent deference to the law of the state in which the pharmacy provider is located, state laws regulating telepharmacy prac-tice are unconstitutional under the Commerce Clause.

The Supreme Court has held that state laws or regulations affecting inter-state commerce which, if duplicated by other states, would result in con-fusing or contradictory edicts, would by definition directly impact inter-state commerce. Such laws are therefore per se invalid under the Commerce Clause.[11] The concern expressed by the Court in *Healy,* and countless other commerce clause cases, is that if one state may regulate extraterritorially, so may they all. Such widespread attempts to regulate beyond state boundaries could have sweeping regional or national effect, which the Court has found to be constitutionally suspect:

> If [one state] may enact a contemporaneous affirmation statute, so may each of the border States and, indeed, so may every other State in the Nation. . . . [U]nless a beer supplier declined to sell in one of the States for an entire month, the maximum price in each State would be

---

*VIPPS pharmacies must "[c]omply with all applicable statutes and regulations govern-ing the practice of pharmacy where licensed or registered, and comply with the more stringent law or regulation as determined by conflicts of law rules. VIPPS pharmacies must maintain and enforce policies and procedures that address conflicts of law issues that may arise be-tween individual states or between state and federal laws and regulations. Said policies and procedures must assure compliance with applicable laws including generic substitution laws and regulations, and must prohibit unauthorized therapeutic substitution from occurring with-out necessary patient or prescriber authorization and outside of the conditions for participa-tion in state or federal programs such as Medicaid." NABP, VIPPS Criteria. http://www.nabp.net/vipps/consumer/criteria.asp. Accessed October 15, 2003.

capped by previous prices in the other States. This maximum price would almost surely be the minimum price as well, since any reduction in either State would permanently lower the ceiling in both. Nor would such "price gridlock" be limited to individual regions.

At least one court has reviewed these concerns in the context of a law that attempted to regulate the practice of pharmacy by a nonresident mail-order pharmacy. In *National Pharmacies, Inc. v. Feliciano-De-Melecio,*[12] a New Jersey operator of a mail-order pharmacy brought suit challenging a Puerto Rico statutory scheme which regulated the registration and licensing of pharmacists in Puerto Rico. The pharmacy alleged that the Puerto Rico Pharmacy Act unconstitutionally burdened interstate commerce by requiring the out-of-state entity to comply with Puerto Rico residency and pharmacy practice requirements. The court reviewed the standard for considering dormant Commerce Clause challenges, noting that the Constitution prohibits states from regulating in a manner that would discriminate against or unduly burden interstate commerce and would thereby impede free trade in the national marketplace, and that courts should view with suspicion state regulations which attempted to control commercial activity wholly outside the state's borders. However, rather than declaring the Puerto Rico licensing law unconstitutional, the court interpreted the law narrowly, finding that it applied only to pharmacies physically located in Puerto Rico. Thus, the nonresident pharmacy was permitted to provide pharmacy services in Puerto Rico but was not required to comply with the requirements of the local Puerto Rico laws.

The problems caused by requiring a pharmacy engaged in the nationwide practice of telepharmacy to become licensed in and to comply with the laws of all fifty states could be addressed by the passage of a federal law creating a uniform national licensure. That is the approach favored by the American Telemedicine Association, which advocates such an approach for the practice of telemedicine.[13] However, unless and until such uniform national standards are created and implemented, state regulators should be encouraged to pass laws and regulations, or interpret existing laws and regulations, in a manner that will not unduly interfere with the practice of telepharmacy.*

---

*Deference to the law of the state where the dispensing pharmacy is located was the approach advocated by proponents of mail-service pharmacies when that type of pharmacy practice was first being introduced to state legislatures. See, e.g., Testimony of Delbert D. Konnor, Minutes of Kansas House Committee and Public Health and Welfare, HB 3064, March 3, 1992, Attachment 2, 1-15. ("It is not unfairly burdensome for a reputable pharmacy to comply with the requirements of any single state. The problem occurs when any pharmacy, including a mail service pharmacy, is required to comply with requirements of several states at once.") This approach was viewed as necessary to remove the impediments to mail-order pharmacy practice across state lines, and a similar approach may be needed to allow the interstate practice of telepharmacy.

ELECTRONIC TRANSMISSION
OF PRESCRIPTION INFORMATION

The actual transmission of a prescription order from the prescriber's office to the pharmacy has been a task fraught with technological and regulatory difficulties. Although the electronic transmission of a drug order from one place to another seems like a simple concept, practical and technological issues related to its lack of acceptance by the medical community, incompatible computer systems, and high costs, as well as regulatory issues involving state restrictions on such practices and concerns related to patient information security and confidentiality, have prevented its widespread incorporation into daily medical and pharmacy practice.

On the regulatory side, states are attempting to accommodate the use of electronic prescription orders. As of mid-2002, thirty-seven states allowed the intrastate transmission of prescription orders from prescribers to pharmacies, while thirty-five allowed the interstate transmission of such orders.[14] NABP advocates the use of computers to electronically transmit prescription orders. In fact, in 2001, NABP endorsed federal proposals to allow the electronic transmission of controlled substance prescription orders,* and encouraged states to adopt recommended regulations to make legal electronically transmitted orders and to accommodate the various technologies currently used to transmit such orders.[15]

Conflicts of law issues present a practical hurdle to the implementation of e-prescribing. Pharmacies that practice across state lines may have difficulty complying with the differing requirements set forth in each state. Also, companies that provide the communications hardware and software face difficulties designing products that are marketable and compliant with legal requirements in all fifty states. Recognizing that this is a real and present concern to the widespread adoption of e-prescribing, the Department of Health and Human Services, in a proposed rule that addresses e-prescribing under the Medicare Reform law, is proposing that federal e-prescribing laws preempt all contrary state laws. The proposed rule provides:

> The MMA addresses preemption of State laws at section 1860D-4(e)(5) of the Act as follows:

---

*Although the U.S. Drug Enforcement Administration has not yet published a proposed rule on the electronic transmission of controlled substance prescriptions, efforts have been put forth to establish an electronic framework for controlled substance prescription transmission, which incorporates Public Key Infrastructure/digital signature technology intended to ensure the electronic system provides for message/record integrity, authentication, and nonrepudiation. See www.deadiversion.usdoj.gov/ecomm/e_rx/e_standard.htm. Accessed October 21, 2003.

(5) Relation to State Laws. The standards promulgated under this subsection shall supercede any State law or regulation that—-

(A) is contrary to the standards or restricts the ability to carry out this part; and

(B) pertains to the electronic transmission of medication history and of information on eligibility, benefits, and prescriptions with respect to covered part D drugs under this part.

We propose to interpret this section of the Act as preempting State law provisions that conflict with Federal electronic prescription program drug requirements that are adopted under Part D. We view it as mandating Federal preemption of State laws and regulations that are either contrary to the Federal standards, or that restrict the ability to carry out (that is, stand as an obstacle to) the electronic prescription drug program requirements, and that also pertain to the electronic transmission of prescriptions or certain information regarding covered Part D drugs for Part D enrolled individuals. Consequently, for a State law or regulation to be preempted under this express preemption provision, the State law or regulation would have to meet the requirements of both paragraphs (A) and (B).[16]

A federal law that preempts the applicability of contrary state laws would create the type of uniformity that is needed to remove the legal and practical barriers associated with e-prescribing specifically and telepharmacy generally.

The HHS proposed rule addresses only the e-prescribing part of the equation, however. State laws that provide for electronic prescribing, and even the HHS preemption proposal, do not fully address all of the issues raised by the practice of telepharmacy. For telepharmacy, of perhaps more importance than the transmission of a prescription from the prescriber to the pharmacy is the transmission of the prescription information from one pharmacy to another pharmacy. For example, in order for two pharmacies to share prescription information and allow order review, verification, and DUR services to be provided at one location, while the preparation of the product for dispensing and patient consultation occurs at another, there must be a means for allowing the transmission of the prescription information from one location to the other.

Issues raised in connection with this component of telepharmacy include whether the pharmacy that receives the prescription from the patient (if in paper form) or the prescriber (if in fax, verbal, or electronic form), can in effect transfer that information to another pharmacy for processing. Digital imaging technology now allows a pharmacy to create an exact digital image of a prescription, and electronically store and transmit the image to other locations. However, is the image created a valid "prescription" that can be filled by a pharmacy? In our so-called paperless society, can the image serve as the original prescription for filing purposes, or must the pharmacy maintain the original paper prescription? Assuming the image can be treated as a prescription, in terms of record keeping, where should that image be stored? Can the pharmacy that receives the prescription initially transfer that information to another pharmacy location to allow remote order review, processing, or filling activities, or do applicable prescription transfer rules limit the transfer of prescription information to refill situations? State laws and regulations must adequately address these issues in a manner that does not create arbitrary technical barriers to the provision of telepharmacy services.

Fortunately, many states, as well as the federal government, have addressed the issue of electronic record keeping. First, the federal Electronic Signatures in Global and National Commerce Act,[17] which took effect in October 2000, provides that many existing state and federal laws requiring written and hand-signed documents as well as record-keeping requirements that require original paper records to be maintained are preempted and no longer enforceable. The intent of the law was to eliminate legal barriers to using electronic technology to form and sign contracts, collect and store documents, and send and receive notices and disclosures. The law is not pharmacy specific but has been viewed as invalidating state laws that require a physician's signature on a written prescription or any requirement that paper records, as opposed to electronic forms of those records, be maintained.[18]

Most states have also passed laws that require recognition of electronic signatures and records, and many of those laws are pharmacy specific. For example, Florida pharmacy regulations expressly permit a pharmacy to maintain electronic images of prescriptions, "in lieu of retaining the actual original prescriptions," provided that the computer system is capable of capturing, storing, and reproducing the exact image of the prescription, including the reverse side of the prescription, if necessary.[19] Similarly, Illinois pharmacy laws allow prescription records to be maintained in an alternative data retention system, such as a direct digital imaging system, provided that:

(1) the records maintained in the alternative data retention system contain all of the information required in a manual record;
(2) the data processing system is capable of producing a hard copy of the electronic record on the request of the Board, its representative, or

other authorized local, State, or federal law enforcement or regulatory agency; and

(3) the digital images are recorded and stored only by means of a technology that does not allow subsequent revision or replacement of the images.[20]

Illinois law also permits two or more pharmacies to share a common electronic prescription file to maintain required dispensing information, and allows those pharmacies to utilize that file for purposes of electronically transferring information from one location to another for dispensing purposes.[21] These types of laws, though not originally drafted with telepharmacy practice in mind, support telepharmacy applications, by allowing two or more pharmacies to share the information required to provide tlepharmacy services. Regulators must be cognizant of laws and regulations that may, even unintentionally, interfere with the provision of telepharmacy services.

THE VALIDITY OF THE PRESCRIPTION ORDER AND THE PHYSICIAN-PATIENT RELATIONSHIP

One of the primary issues that has arisen concerning the transmission of prescription orders by electronic means is related to the validity of the prescription order. Within the confines of traditional medical practice, where patients see their physicians and are prescribed necessary drugs, this is not an issue. Whether the prescription order is written or electronically transmitted to a pharmacy, the validity of the order is not in question. It is when the action of prescribing occurs outside of this traditional physician-patient interaction that concerns arise. Primarily, this occurs when patients are able to obtain prescription medications from online pharmacies without ever actually having to see a physician. A prescription order is generated upon the completion of a medical questionnaire by the patient and review of that information by a physician hired by the pharmacy. It is this "electronic prescription order" that has regulators, as well as the medical and pharmacy professions, concerned.

The Federation of State Medical Boards (FSMB) Model Guidelines for the Appropriate Use of the Internet in Medical Practice state that "a documented patient evaluation, including history and physical evaluation adequate to establish diagnoses and identify underlying conditions and/or contra-indications to the treatment recommended/provided, must be obtained prior to providing treatment, including issuing prescriptions, electronically or otherwise." Further, these guidelines state that "it is the expectation of the

[FSMB] that e-mail and other electronic communications and interactions between the physician and patient should supplement and enhance, but not replace, crucial interpersonal interactions that create the very basis of the physician-patient relationship."[22]

Guidelines recently adopted by the American Medical Association (AMA) state that physicians should obtain medical history information and perform a physical examination before prescribing medications online. These guidelines also maintain that some Web sites prescribing medications to patients electronically do not meet the minimum standards of medical care since they do not establish valid patient-physician relationships and instead dispense drugs based solely on online questionnaires and consultations.[23]

NABP also is of the position that prescription orders generated as a result on an online questionnaire or consultation are invalid and cannot be legally dispensed.[24] State legislation has begun to address this issue, and currently eleven states, Alabama, Arizona, California, Missouri, Nevada, New York, Oklahoma [osteopaths only], Ohio, Oregon, Virginia, and West Virginia, have laws explicitly requiring in-person physical examination before prescribing. At least one other state has proposed legislation in this area, and fifteen have "policies" to this effect.[25]

Some have opined that medications dispensed pursuant to a prescription written by a physician based on an online diagnosis are "misbranded" and therefore a pharmacy dispensing a drug based on such a prescription order is violating the Federal Food, Drug, and Cosmetic Act (FDCA). This theory stems from wording found in Sections 502(f) and 503 of the FDCA. Section 502(f) states that a drug shall be deemed "misbranded" unless its labeling bears "adequate directions for use." Section 503 exempts pharmacists from this requirement if the drug is dispensed pursuant to a prescription and is labeled with such data as the name/address of the dispenser, prescription number and date, prescriber name, etc; however, Section 503(b)(2) revokes this exemption if the diagnosis is made by mail. This means that if a diagnosis is made by mail, then the "adequate directions for use" requirement found in Section 502(f) would have to be followed. FDA regulations addressing this area, however, suggest that writing "adequate directions for use" for a prescription-only drug for a layperson is impossible, making it unfeasible for a pharmacy to legally dispense a drug pursuant to a prescription order obtained as a result of a diagnosis by mail. Although it appears that these sections were specifically tailored to the problems being experienced today, they were actually written to remedy a similar problem encountered during the 1930s when it was common for patients in rural areas to write to physicians describing symptoms and for physicians to prescribe medications without ever seeing the patient. Inaccurate diagnoses as a result of such practices were common. A growing body of law seems to indicate that legal principles applicable to ink-on-paper mail also apply to e-mail, making such statutes applicable to the problems being experienced today. In fact, the language is narrow enough to get at the problem pharmacies—those routinely dispensing medications pursuant to prescription orders obtained online—but is not applicable to those legitimate pharmacies doing business on the Internet, which are already adequately regulated.[26] At this time, it is not believed that the FDA has utilized this theory to prosecute dispensers of medications based on prescription orders written based upon online questionnaires.

Of course, situations arise in everyday medical and pharmacy practice in which a physician will prescribe a medication without first examining a patient. For example, doctors routinely prescribe antibiotics, or medications to control the symptoms of a cold or flu, following a telephone consultation with a patient. On-call physicians will often authorize refills for patients not under their direct care. A consultant oncologist at a large teaching hospital might prescribe chemotherapy medications for a patient located remotely, based on telephone or Internet communications with the local physician, the patient, and review of medical records and laboratory reports. If a physician located in a remote location has the ability to make a prescribing decision based on a review of such information without physically examining the patient, shouldn't a pharmacy that receives such a prescription order be permitted to defer to the prescriber's professional judgment and dispense the prescription order without fear of regulatory action? States must take care not to pass laws that have as their purpose the economic protection of local professionals, as opposed to what is best for the patient. Further, regulators concerned about the practices of rogue Internet pharmacies and physicians who are out to make a quick buck must avoid interfering with the professional judgment of legitimate pharmacies and physicians providing patient care.

HEALTH INFORMATION PRIVACY AND SECURITY

The privacy and security regulations stemming from the federal Health Insurance Portability and Accountability Act of 1996 (HIPAA), which address the privacy and security of patient health information, are especially helpful to concerns related to telemedicine and telepharmacy issues. Electronically stored health information once held the capability to be passed anywhere with few or no restrictions. HIPAA privacy regulations now require healthcare providers to protect individually identifiable healthcare records from unauthorized disclosures and to notify patients of the potential uses of information collected.[27] Under these regulations, all pharmacies, including those providing telepharmacy services, must implement safeguards to protect individually identifiable health information.

Prior to the implementation of HIPAA privacy and security requirements, there existed a patchwork of state regulations addressing patient health information. Although such a structure was adequate when pharmacy practice was a paper-based, localized activity, electronic, multistate practice resulted in expanded access to patient information and issues related to conflicts of law. The new federal regulations provide a uniform minimum level of protection for patient health information. State laws or regulations more stringent than the HIPAA rules remain in effect; only those less stringent or in conflict with the federal rules are preempted.

The regulations protect medical records and other individually identifiable health information. Most significantly, the regulations provide for:

- Patient access to see and obtain medical records and request corrections to such records;
- The provision to patients of the healthcare provider's Notice of Privacy Practices indicating how they may use personal medical information and their rights under the new privacy regulation. Patients may ask providers to restrict the use or disclosure of their health information beyond the practices included in the Notice, but the provider does not have to agree to such restrictions.
- Limitations on the use of personal medical information. Generally, health information may not be used for purposes unrelated to healthcare, and healthcare providers may use or share only the minimum amount of protected information needed for a particular purpose. In addition, patients must sign a specific authorization before providers can release their medical information to outside business for purposes not related to their healthcare (e.g., marketing).[28]

OTHER LEGAL ISSUES

Another concern related to telepharmacy practice, as well as any type of pharmacy practice, is the issue of malpractice. To state a claim for malpractice, or professional negligence, a plaintiff must prove that the pharmacist owed a duty of care, that the pharmacist's conduct fell below the standard of care, that an injury occurred, and that the pharmacist's negligent conduct caused the injury.

Historically, a pharmacist could not be held liable for professional negligence except in cases involving dispensing errors. A pharmacist's duty was limited to dispensing medication pursuant to the prescription order as written by the doctor—making sure that the right medication in the right dose was give to the right patient. No other duty existed. A recent study, however, conducted by Pharmacists Mutual Insurance Company, which examined the types of pharmacy liability claims submitted to the company between 1989 through 2001, indicates an increase in the number of claims alleging negligence based on the inadequate performance of some cognitive service, such as drug therapy monitoring or patient counseling.[29] The study also indicates the most common types of errors made by pharmacists are mechanical errors, including dispensing of the wrong drug or wrong dose, oftentimes due to misreading the prescription order.

Electronically transmitted prescription orders can decrease the incidence of many types of errors, including, most significantly, errors caused by the misreading of a physician's often illegible handwriting. There are court cases, however, that suggest advances in technology may expose the pharmacist to new or additional liability risks.

One case, *Baker v. Arbor Drugs,*[30] addressed the scope of the pharmacist's duty to monitor prescription orders for drug interactions, where the pharmacy promoted the ability of its computer system to track and detect drug interactions. The plaintiff's decedent, who had been receiving the antidepressant drug Parnate® for several years, presented a prescription order to the defendant pharmacy for Ceftin® and Tavist-D®. The prescription orders were entered into the pharmacy computer by a technician, who apparently overrode the computer alert that indicated a drug interaction between Parnate®, which had been dispensed in the past, and Tavist-D®. The pharmacist testified in her deposition that she would not have dispensed the Tavist-D® had she known that the decedent was taking Parnate®. The prescription orders were dispensed, however, and the patient experienced a hypertensive attack, suffered a stroke, and later committed suicide, all allegedly because of the pharmacist's error.

At the time of the lawsuit, Michigan law, like the law in nearly every other state, held that a pharmacist could not be held liable for negligence as long as the prescription order was properly dispensed with the correct drug and dose prescribed by the physician, and that a pharmacist has no duty to warn or monitor drug usage. In its opinion, the Court affirmed that this was the law in Michigan, but held in this case that by utilizing a computer system that screened for drug interactions and advertising that feature to the public, the defendant pharmacy assumed a duty to monitor for potentially harmful drug interactions. Thus, by failing to detect the Parnate/Tavist-D interaction in this case, a jury could find that the pharmacy breached the duty and could be held liable for professional negligence. The lesson to be learned from the *Baker* decision is twofold. First, once a pharmacy has access to the information needed to provide pharmaceutical care, it must use that information to see that quality care is provided. It would appear that the more information that is available to the pharmacists, the greater is his or her responsibility to monitor the appropriateness of patient drug therapy, and failure to detect and act on drug interactions, inappropriate drug regimens, or other problems associated with the prescription order could expose the pharmacist to malpractice liability. The second lesson is, of course, that the information contained in the pharmacy's computer system is only as good as the person who accesses, enters, or uses the information. If unskilled, poorly trained, or incompetent pharmacists or technicians ignore the information provided to them, or do not know how to effectively use the information for the patient's benefit, errors can and will occur, regardless of the level of sophistication of the computer system. This risk is multiplied when the pharmacist is providing care from a location remote to the patient, based on a patient profile, prescription order, or other information accessed electronically from a location that is remote from the patient.

Finally, of course, the issue of conflicts of laws can be significant. When a pharmacist reviews an order in one state, authorizes dispensing by a pharmacy or other healthcare provider located in another state, to a patient located in a third state, and pursuant to a prescription order written by a doctor located in a fourth state, which state's malpractice laws would apply if an error occurred somewhere in the chain? This is another issue that will need to be addressed by the courts as the provision of telepharmacy care continues to expand.

Telemedicine also must address other legal matters such as anti-kickback statutes and fraud and abuse issues. Referrals by and between telemedicine partners, and a host's subsidization of a system's capital or operating costs raise significant anti-kickback concerns. 42 U.S.C. § 1320a-7b(b) provides for criminal penalties for any person who knowingly and willfully offers, pays, solicits, or receives any remuneration, including any kickback, bribe, or rebate, in return for referring or inducing the referral of an individual to a person for the furnishing or arranging for the furnishing of any item or service payable in whole or in part a federal healthcare program, or purchasing, leasing, ordering or arranging for the recommending purchasing, leasing, or ordering any good, facility, service, or item payable under a federal healthcare program. This statute is extremely broad in scope.[31] Statutory exceptions and regulatory safe harbors exist, but they are narrow and specific.

CONCLUSION

The way in which medical and pharmacy care is provided in this country is rapidly changing. These changes are providing a wealth of opportunity for the physicians and pharmacists who are prepared to adapt to the changes and become a more integral part of the healthcare team. One can anticipate additional legal action, enforcement measures, and further legislation in the telemedicine and telepharmacy areas. Pharmacists and physicians must be aware that with increased opportunity comes an increased risk. Changes in the way medicine and pharmacy are practiced may create an increased exposure to liability. As long as physicians and pharmacists continue to act reasonably as healthcare professionals, putting the health and safety of patients above all other concerns, the potential benefits of telemedicine and telepharmacy are certain to outweigh the risks.

NOTES

1. Telemedicine Information Exchange (TIE), Legislative, Legal and Policy Issues in Telemedicine & Telehealth, Legislation Search. See tie.telemed.org/legal/search.asp. Accessed October 2, 2003.

2. NABP, Model State Pharmacy Act and Model Rules of the National Association of Boards of Pharmacy (Model Act), 11 (June 2003).

3. See, e.g., Tex. Code Ann. § 562.110 (2002) for the section of the Texas Pharmacy Practice Act that addresses Telepharmacy Systems, and N.D. Admin. Code § 61-02-08 (2003), for North Dakota State Board of Pharmacy rules on Telepharmacy Pilot Projects.

4. National Association of Boards of Pharmacy (NABP). 2002-2003 Survey of Pharmacy Law 45 (2002).

5. See, for example, the Alaska Pharmacy Practice Act, which requires nonresident pharmacy registration only if a pharmacy "regularly ships" prescriptions into the state (Alaska Stat. § 08.80.158), and the Kentucky Pharmacy Practice Act, which requires such registration if the pharmacy ships into the state "other than on an incidental basis" (Ky. Rev. Stat. § 315.0351).

6. Texas Ann. Stat. § 562.110.

7. 225 ILCS § 85/15 (c).

8. See, Telepharmacy takes pharmacists online off-site, Pharmacy Annual Report. Some pharmacies are piloting telepharmacy systems. *Drug Store News,* August 18, 2003. Available on-line at www.findarticles.com/p/articles/mi_m3374/is_10_25/ai_108969719. Accessed November 22, 2004.

9. Ark. Reg. § 04-04-0001 (2003).

10. Md. Ann Code art. 12, § 403 (2003).

11. *Healy v. Beer Institute,* 491 U.S. 324, 336-337, 109 S.Ct. 2491, 2499, 105 L.Ed.2d 275 (1989). See also *Brown-Forman Distillers Corp. v. New York State Liquor Authority,* 476 U.S. 573, 578-579, 106 S.Ct. 2080, 2084, 90 L.Ed.2d 552

(1986) (same); *Edgar v. MITE Corporation,* 457 U.S. 624, 642, 102 S.Ct. 2629, 2640-2641, 73 L.Ed.2d 269 (1982) (state regulations affecting tender offers which prevented offeror from making offer to non-Illinois residents); *Bibb v. Navajo Freight Lines, Inc.,* 359 U.S. 520, 529, 79 S.Ct. 962, 967-968, 3 L.Ed.2d 1003 (1959) (Illinois mudguard regulations "out of line with the requirements of almost all the other States" and in direct conflict with Arkansas' similar regulation); *Southern Pacific Co. v. Arizona,* 325 U.S. 761, 775, 65 S.Ct. 1515, 1523, 89 L.Ed. 1915 (1945) (Arizona's uniquely restrictive train car-length regulation required trains to be broken up at state borders).

12. 221 F.3d 235 (1st Cir. 2000).

13. See Coleman M. The Cyber Waiting Room: A Glimpse at the New Practice of Telemedicine. www.tilj.com/content/healtharticle11159902.htm. Accessed February 28, 2004. See also Nationalizing Pharmacy Practice Standards, Proceedings of the American Society for Pharmacy Law Developments in Pharmacy Law Seminar XV. St. Petersburg, Florida, November 11-14, 2004. (Excerpts to be published at www.aspl.org).

14. NABP, *supra* note 2, at 62.

15. NABP, 2001-2002 Committee and Task Force Reports. Report of the Task Force on Electronic Transmission of Prescriptions 2-3 (2002). See www.nabp .net/ftpfiles/task_force_reports/CommTFBook2002.pdf. Accessed October 15, 2003. As a result of the recommendations of this Task Force, NABP incorporated into its Model Act definitions of "digital signature" and "electronic signature" and rules that recognized the validity of electronic prescription orders.

16. 42 CFR Part 423 (2004).

17. 15 U.S.C § 7001 *et seq.*

18. An excellent discussion of the applicability of the federal E-Sign law to pharmacy practice can be found at Vivian, E-Signatures Pharmacy Practice, *U.S. Pharmacist,* 26:02 (Available on line at www.uspharmacist.com/oldformat.asp? url=newlook/files/Phar/ACF952D.html&pub_id=8&article_id=665.) Accessed November 22, 2004.

19. Florida Administrative Code, Rule 64B16-28.140.

20. 225 ILCS § 85/18.

21. 225 ILCS § 85/19.

22. Federation of State Medical Boards, Policy Documents, Model Guidelines for the Appropriate Use of the Internet in Medical Practice. See www.fsmb.org. Accessed October 17, 2003.

23. American Medical Association. AMA adopts new guidelines to help physicians ensure safe and secure Internet prescribing. See www.ama-assn.org/ama/ pub/article/1616-7802.html. Accessed October 17, 2003. In their guidelines, the AMA stated "physicians who prescribe medication using the Internet should either be licensed in the states where their patients live or meet the regulatory requirements of individual state medical boards" and recommend that such physicians adopt additional safeguards, including the following:

- "having adequate dialogue with patients about treatment options, risks and benefits; following up with the patient as appropriate;

- maintaining an updated medical record that is readily available to the patient and to his or her other healthcare professionals (subject to the patient's consent);
- including the electronic prescription information as part of a patient's medical record;
- clearly disclosing physician-identifying information on the World Wide Web such as name, practice address and financial interests in any products prescribed."

24. NABP, Report of the Task Force on Expanded Use of the Internet in Pharmacy Practice and Regulation 2 (2001). See www.nabp.net/ftpfiles/task_force _reports / Task_Force_on_Expanded_Use_of_the_Internet_in_Pharmacy_Practice _and_Regulation.doc. Accessed October 17, 2003.

25. Arent, Fox, Kintner, Plotkin & Kahn, PLLC, *State Laws Explicitly Requiring Physical Examination Before Prescribing.* See www.arentfox.com/quickGuide/ businessLines/telemed / e-health_telemed / e-health_state/map-statelaws/map-state laws.html. Accessed October 17, 2003.

26. David B. Brushwood, Responsive Regulation of Internet Pharmacy Practice, 10 *Annals Health L.* 75, 82-84 (2001).

27. 21 CFR § 160 *et seq.* (2003), 21 CFR § 164 *et seq.* (2003).

28. U.S. Department of Health and Human Services, Fact Sheet: Protecting the Privacy of Patients' Health Information. See www.hhs.gov/news/facts/privacy.html. Accessed October 21, 2003.

29. The claim study can be found at www.phmic.com. Accessed March 22, 2004.

30. 544 N.E.2d 727 (Mich. App. 1995)

31. See, e.g., *United States v. Greber,* 760 F.2d 68 (3d Cir.), *cert. denied,* 474 U.S. 988 (1985) (payment for actual services rendered may violate statute if "one purpose" of the payment was to induce referrals); *United States v. Bay State Ambulance & Hospital Rental Service, Inc.,* 874 F.2d 20 (1st Cir. 1989) (giving a person an opportunity to earn money may constitute an improper inducement); *Hanlester Network v. Shalala,* 51 F.3d 1390 (9th Cir. 1995), *petition for rehearing pending* (mandatory requirement of referrals in exchange for remuneration is unnecessary to violate the statue).

Chapter 24

Medication Error Reporting

Jennifer Devine

INTRODUCTION

Medication errors have been widely publicized over the past two decades—Betsy Lehman, the *Boston Globe* reporter, died from an overdose during chemotherapy, and Ben Kolb, an eight-year-old, died during minor surgery due to a drug mix-up. Although these medication errors were widely publicized in the news, it was not until the release of the 1999 IOM report, *To Err Is Human: Building a Safer Health System* (hereinafter IOM Report), that policymakers and other stakeholders elevated issues surrounding medication errors and patient safety to the national level.

As these issues were elevated to the national level, healthcare professionals, policymakers, legislators, and other stakeholders began discussing strategies and obstacles to improving patient safety and reducing medication errors. One strategy that was identified to reduce medication errors was the full implementation of reporting programs. It was concluded that medication error reporting programs provide important opportunities for healthcare facilities and practitioners to document, identify, and learn about medication errors. It was also recognized that a significant obstacle to the full implementation of reporting programs is the lack of legal protection against disclosure of the reports in civil and administrative proceedings. Without such legal protection, healthcare facilities and practitioners would be reluctant to track and report medication errors, thereby reducing opportunities to identify and prevent medication errors.

Since the IOM Report, numerous federal and state legislative bills have been introduced to encourage medication error reporting. Although no federal protection has been implemented as of June 2004, Congress continues to work to pass bipartisan federal legislation that will provide protection and encourage medication error reporting. Federal protection for medication error information shared with regional, state, and national medication

Pharmacy Law Desk Reference
doi:10.1300/5790_24

error reporting programs will help reduce medication errors and improve patient safety.

MEDICATION ERROR REPORTING PROGRAMS

Most experts recognize that a number of methods are used to measure medication safety—observation, computer monitoring, practitioner intervention, chart review, and voluntary reporting.[1] This chapter focuses on the latter—voluntary reporting programs and the challenges and obstacles to their full implementation. Full implementation of error reporting programs can provide practitioners, healthcare facilities, and other organizations at local, regional, state, and national levels information for improving healthcare systems and patient safety.

Currently, there are numerous reporting efforts at the local, regional, state, and national levels. They vary in size, purpose, and scope. For example, some reporting programs are localized, while others are national; some are mandatory, while others voluntary; and there are paper-based systems and Internet-accessible systems. These efforts have contributed to improving patient safety, but their full potential has yet to be realized due in part to the lack of legal protection.

At the local level, most individual healthcare facilities have some form of an internal medication error reporting program. These programs often focus on individual practitioner errors and do not reach to capture system failures in the healthcare facility and beyond. Unfortunately, many healthcare facilities are not willing to share their data or reports externally with regional, state, or national reporting efforts.

Although limited in numbers, there are collaborative efforts at the local and regional level that proactively share reports with third parties. The purpose of such collaborative efforts is to share and learn about potential or actual errors and exchange preventive measures from one facility to the other. One example of a regional collaborative effort that reports medication errors is the Pittsburgh Regional Healthcare Initiative (PRHI). PRHI is comprised of approximately forty hospitals in southwestern Pennsylvania that have agreed to share and compare medication errors using the Medmarx system.[2]

States also have instituted reporting programs. The IOM reported that approximately one-third of states have some form of adverse event reporting system.[3] One example of a state reporting program is New York's Patient Occurrence Reporting and Tracking System (NYPORTS). NYPORTS, a mandatory reporting system for all adverse events, including medication errors, occurring in hospitals, is operated by the New York State Department of Health.[4] The purpose of the NYPORTS system is to provide the information to New York State for trend analysis and to provide information to healthcare facilities on their reporting pattern and allow facilities to compare themselves to other facilities in the region and the state. In 1999, a total of 15,127 cases were submitted electronically to NYPORTS.[5] Despite efforts to encourage reporting into NYPORTS, an analysis of 1999 data continues to show significant underreporting of reportable occurrences.[6]

There are also federal programs such as the Food and Drug Administration's MedWatch Program. MedWatch is a voluntary program for healthcare practitioners and consumers to report serious adverse events or product problems.[7] Over 500,000 reports were received by the MedWatch program from November 1997 through December 2000.[8] Through the MedWatch program, the FDA conducts postmarketing surveillance of medical products to identify safety concerns so that the agency can take necessary action.[9]

Furthermore, the Joint Commission on Accreditation of Healthcare Organizations (JCAHO) has operated a sentinel event reporting system for hospitals since 1996. It is designed to help healthcare organizations identify sentinel events and take action to prevent their occurrence.[10] A sentinel event is an "unexpected occurrence involving death or serious physical—including loss of limb or function—or psychological injury, or the risk thereof."[11] Although reporting sentinel events to JCAHO is not legally mandated, neither is it considered totally voluntary. If hospitals fail to report an event and JCAHO learns of it from a third party, the hospital is required to conduct an analysis of the root cause, and if the root cause analysis is not completed, the hospital may risk loss of accreditation.[12]

There also are national programs such as the Medication Errors Reporting (MER) Program and Medmarx. The MER Program is a voluntary program available to all healthcare practitioners and is operated by the United States Pharmacopeia (USP) in cooperation with the Institute for Safe Medication Practices (ISMP).[13] Since 1991, the MER Program has received nearly 8,000 reports of actual and potential medication errors.[14] These reports have identified errors in various healthcare delivery settings, including hospitals, nursing homes, physicians' offices, community pharmacies, emergency response vehicles, and home care.

A complementary database to the MER Program is the Medmarx Program, also operated by USP. Medmarx is an Internet-accessible, deidentified, anonymous medication error reporting database designed for healthcare facilities and health systems.[15] Medmarx started collecting data in 1998, and USP has issued three reports based on data from 1999, 2000, and 2001. At the end of 2002, the total records in the Medmarx database exceeded 325,000.[16]

Like many voluntary programs, Medmarx and the MER Program are based on the premise that patient safety can more effectively be improved in a culture that emphasizes systematic changes in healthcare facilities rather than focusing on individual blame. In order to implement systematic changes in healthcare facilities, reporting programs must collect, analyze, and disseminate information on medication errors to people in a position to effect change.

The collection of medication or medical error reports is not a goal in itself. The purpose of voluntary reporting programs is to analyze the information provided in the reports and to implement effective, sustainable interventions that will prevent errors from recurring.[17] A substantial obstacle in collecting and analyzing medication error reports is the fear of healthcare facilities and practitioners about liability associated with medication errors.

LEGAL LIABILITY FOR MEDICATION ERROR REPORTING

Background

Many healthcare facilities and practitioners are hesitant to report medication errors for fear that such reports may be used in a legal suit. The most likely legal suit for a healthcare facility or practitioner would be medical malpractice. A malpractice suit is based on professional misconduct or unreasonable lack of skill.[18] In order to recover for malpractice, a plaintiff must establish the following elements: (1) the existence of the healthcare practitioner's duty to the plaintiff; (2) the applicable standard of care and its violation; (3) a compensable injury; and (4) a causal connection between the violation of the standard of care and the alleged harm.[19]

In order to help establish these four elements, medication error reports could potentially be requested from facilities, practitioners, or medication error reporting programs through discovery in a malpractice suit. The following reports could be requested: (1) a medication error report that contains facts or analysis involving a specific incident in a current malpractice suit; (2) other medication error reports that involve a specific healthcare facility or practitioner named in a current malpractice suit (e.g., all medication records involving a specific facility); or (3) medication error reports from any healthcare facility or practitioner with common characteristics to facts in a current malpractice suit (e.g., same type of medication but different practitioner or facility). Although a discovery demand (through a subpoena) could be made for such reports, one cannot assume that such reports would legally need to be disclosed. Whether such data are legally discoverable will depend on state law and the specific facts surrounding the case.

Protections for Medication Error Reports

A basic principle in law is that the public "has a right to every man's evidence."[20] This basic legal principle is subject to exceptions that prevent disclosure of evidence, such as the attorney-client privilege, self-critical analysis privilege, and peer review privilege. These exceptions were enacted to strike a balance between the need for open and effective discovery and the desire to encourage specific behavior that may result in a public benefit, such as improving healthcare. Two exceptions—the self-critical analysis privilege and the peer review privilege—provide the basis for potential protection for reports submitted to medication error reporting programs.

Self-Critical Analysis Privilege

The self-critical analysis privilege was recognized over thirty years ago in *Bredice v. Doctors Hospital, Inc.,* a case in the U.S. District Court for the District of Columbia.[21] In *Bredice,* the court found that the minutes and records of medical staff reviews by committees of doctors were essential to the improvement of patient care and that confidentiality was essential to ensuring their effectiveness.[22] Although there was no statutory protection for the records and minutes, the court held that the records were not discoverable by the plaintiffs.[23] This case created an exception to the basic principle that the public has the right to every man's evidence. This exception was later referred to as the "self-critical analysis privilege."

Most courts evaluate the following four criteria to determine if the self-critical analysis privilege can be applied: (1) whether the information resulted from a critical self-analysis undertaken by the party seeking protection; (2) whether the public has a strong interest in preserving the free flow of the type of information sought; (3) whether the information is of a type whose flow would be curtailed if discovery were allowed; and (4) whether the document was prepared with the expectation that it would remain confidential and has in fact been kept confidential thus far.[24] If one can establish these four elements, the courts will then weigh the interest in maintaining confidentiality against a competing interest—the public's need for all available evidence.[25]

Although the self-critical analysis privilege using these elements has been applied in the healthcare field a number of times, it has not been uniformly accepted. Courts that have recognized the privilege have also limited and applied it inconsistently.[26] The lack of consistent application of the privilege leaves many healthcare facilities and practitioners without a guarantee that a court will bar medication error reports from legal discovery.

Furthermore, courts have yet to address the application of the self-critical analysis privilege concerning reports voluntarily submitted to a medication error reporting program. However, some courts have applied the self-critical analysis privilege in cases involving safety reports.

In *Tice v. American Airlines,* the defendants successfully established the applicability of the self-critical analysis privilege to safety reports that were commissioned by American Airlines.[27] The safety reports resulted from American Airlines' top-to-bottom self-analysis of its operations (done in order to maximize safety and prevent personal injuries and other torts.)[28] In *Tice,* American Airlines satisfactorily established the four elements required to obtain the self-critical privilege. The court noted that "the flow of internal airline safety information would be somewhat curtailed if discovery" of these documents were allowed.[29]

A second federal court addressed the issue of voluntary safety reports.[30] Although in this case the court did not accept the self-critical analysis privilege application for safety reports (similar to the reports prepared under the *Tice* case), the court determined that the documents should be entitled to protection under a federal common law privilege.[31] Therefore, two federal court cases have provided protection to safety reports voluntarily submitted to reporting programs.

These two cases may provide some important precedent when practitioners and healthcare facilities attempt to obtain protection for medication error reports voluntarily submitted to national programs.

The self-critical analysis privilege is one possible privilege that could be invoked by practitioners or healthcare facilities that have performed a self-evaluation and documented such analysis on a medication error report. However, most states have provided statutory protections to peer review committees (or similar committees) on the premise of the self-critical analysis privilege. Therefore, most states will rely on specific statutory protections, such as state peer review laws, to prevent medication error reports from being disclosed.

Peer Review Privilege

Most states have implemented quality improvement or peer review statutes based on the self-critical analysis privilege afforded to medical review committees, as in the *Bredice* case. Currently, every state, except one, statutorily protects various records and deliberations of peer review committees from discovery.[32] New Jersey does not have a law protecting peer review documents.[33]

A common characteristic of these state laws is that persons who engage or participate in the collection, reporting, evaluation, or use of such quality improvement information often are granted immunity and are not obligated or permitted to testify in any civil or administrative proceeding.[34] The underlying purpose of such laws is to foster accurate and thorough quality assessment and assurance activities by protecting related information from subpoena or discovery in civil and administrative proceedings.[35] The rationale underlying the need for peer review protection is to ensure the effectiveness of professional self-evaluation in the interest of improving the quality of healthcare.[36]

State quality improvement and peer review statutes vary greatly in the scope of information protected and entities covered. This variation in state law can impact the extent to which medication error reports are provided protection. For example, some states may limit protection to records prepared by peer review committees and not extend protection to records provided to these committees.[37] Other states extend protection more broadly to include "the investigations, proceedings, and records of a committee."[38] Therefore, in the first example, a medication error report may not be protected, whereas in the latter example, if the medication error report was part of an investigation, proceeding, or record of the committee, it may be considered protected.

States also vary in the way they address the issue of waiver—disclosure of peer review protected information to third parties. Historically, there was little need to share information beyond the four walls of the hospital.[39] Therefore, most peer review statutes do not directly address the issue of waiver. In some states, the issue has been addressed through case law; several states have refused to find a waiver of a peer review privilege when presented with the issue.[40] Other states have yet to consider a case specific to waiver of the peer review privilege, thereby leaving the outcome uncertain.

The extent and application of state protections vary, thereby failing to establish clear and consistent legal protection for medication error reports provided to local, state, and national databases. Due to the variety in state legal protection, healthcare facilities and practitioners in some states are discouraged from sharing reports beyond the four walls of their hospitals. In other states, healthcare facilities and practitioners are comfortable sharing reports to local, state, or regional databases.

Because of these inconsistent applications of the law, medication errors are not being reported in a consistent and uniform manner nationally, which reduces the chances of identifying trends and implementing effective corrective measures. The IOM Report specifically addressed the lack of clear and consistent protection for medical error reports, including medication errors, and provided recommendations to improve the current legal environment.

THE INSTITUTE OF MEDICINE

Background

The Institute of Medicine (the Institute) was established in 1970 by the National Academy of Sciences to secure the services of eminent members of appropriate professions in the examination of policy matters pertaining to the health of the public.[41] The Institute acts under the responsibility given to the National Academy of Sciences by its congressional charter to be an adviser to the federal government and, upon its own initiative, to identify issues of medical care, research, and education.[42]

In 1998, the Institute established the Committee on Quality of Health Care in America and charged it with the task of developing strategies and recommendations that would result in a substantial improvement in the quality of healthcare delivered to Americans.[43] The committee released two reports that set forth its strategies and recommendations. The first report, *To Err Is Human: Building a Safer Health System,* was released in 1999 and focused on patient safety.[44] The second report, *Crossing the Quality Chasm: A New Health System for the 21st Century,* was released in 2001 and focused on how the healthcare delivery system can be designed to innovate and improve healthcare.[45] The reports set forth a national agenda for improving healthcare in the United States. This section focuses on the first report and the recommendations and strategies surrounding medication error reporting.

The IOM Report: To Err Is Human

The IOM Report, *To Err Is Human: Building a Safer Health System,* elevated the issue of medical errors, including medication errors, to the national level and laid out a national agenda by setting forth strategies and recommendations for improving patient safety. One of the most critical issues addressed in the IOM report is medical errors, including medication errors.

The IOM reported that medical errors in the United States are a significant public health problem and estimated that between 44,000 (Colorado study) and 98,000 (New York study) preventable deaths, and as many as 500,000 preventable injuries, occur each year in the United States.[46] Even when using the conservative estimate of 44,000, deaths due to medical errors exceed the number attributable to the eighth leading cause of death.[47]

Deaths due to preventable adverse events exceed deaths attributable to vehicle accidents (43,458), breast cancer (42,297), or AIDS (16,516).[48]

In addition, the IOM Report specifically addressed the issue of medication errors. The IOM reported that medication errors are estimated to account for about 7,000 deaths annually.[49] Medication errors account for one out of 131 outpatient deaths and one out of 854 inpatient deaths.[50] One of the studies cited by the IOM Report found that almost 2 percent of admissions experienced a preventable adverse drug event, resulting in an average increased hospital cost of $4,700 per admission or about $2.8 million annually for a 700-bed teaching hospital.[51] Furthermore, the IOM Report recognizes that the current estimates of incidence of medication errors are undoubtedly low because many errors go undocumented and unreported.[52]

The IOM Report recognized that errors could be prevented by designing safer healthcare systems and by avoiding the traditional culture of blame that focuses on individuals. The title of the IOM Report—*To Err Is Human: Building a Safer Health System*—encapsulates the premise of the report. In other words, the healthcare sector needs to build a safer system by breaking down "[t]raditional clinical boundaries and a culture of blame" and systematically designing safety into the process of care to ensure that patients are safe from accidental injury.[53] In order to accomplish this goal, the IOM Report set forth specific recommendations.

IOM Recommendations

The patient safety recommendations contained in the IOM Report lay out a four-tiered approach: (1) establishing a national focus to create leadership and enhance knowledge concerning patient safety; (2) identifying and learning from errors through reporting systems; (3) setting performance standards and expectations for safety; and (4) implementing safety systems in healthcare organizations.[54] In establishing these four approaches, the IOM recognized that reporting systems play an important role in the patient safety national agenda and that a critical component of a comprehensive strategy to improve patient safety is to create an environment that encourages organizations to identify errors, evaluate causes, and take appropriate actions to improve performance in the future.[55]

In order to build a safer health system through identifying and learning from errors, the IOM Report set forth three recommendations: (1) a mandatory reporting system should be established by state governments; (2) the development of voluntary reporting efforts should be encouraged; and (3) Congress should pass legislation to extend peer review protection to data related to patient safety.[56]

The IOM Report envisioned two systems of reporting medical errors that would be operated separately. One system would be a mandatory system for the collection of serious adverse events and would not be protected from public disclosure. The second system would be a voluntary external one for less serious events that have legal protections. Thus, the IOM Report recognized that appropriate legal protection for medical error reports should be provided in order to have a successful voluntary reporting program. The IOM Report established a specific recommendation for protection of information submitted to voluntary reporting programs. Recommendation 6.1. of the IOM Report states:

> Congress should pass legislation to extend peer review protection to data related to patient safety and quality improvement that are collected and analyzed by health care organizations for internal use or shared with others solely for purposes of improving safety and quality.[57]

The implementation of this recommendation would encourage the reporting of medical errors, including medication errors, by healthcare practitioners and facilities by creating a more conducive legal environment. The environment would encourage practitioners and facilities to report medical errors and thereby increase the chances of identifying trends and implementing effective corrective measures that would help improve the quality of care in America. It is believed that the full potential of reporting systems and the ability to identify trends cannot be realized until the fear of reprisal by practitioners and facilities is reduced. This recommendation by the IOM Report has become a critical piece of the national agenda for improving patient safety.

PATIENT SAFETY LEGISLATION

Federal Legislation

Currently, there is no federal protection for healthcare facilities and practitioners against the disclosure of medication error information that is voluntarily shared with local or national reporting programs. Without such protection, facilities and practitioners are less likely to perform a self-critical analysis or report medication errors due to the threat of disclosure in civil litigation or administrative proceeding. The threat of disclosure of medication error reports discourages the identification and reporting of medication errors by facilities and practitioners, which reduces the chances to identify trends and implement corrective measures. Furthermore, the sharing of such reports among facilities may result in national identification of process improvements and risk prevention strategies. Absent clear state or federal legal protection, medication errors are not reported in a consistent and uniform manner, which may decrease the ability to reduce medication errors at the national level.

The Response to the IOM Report

Recommendation 6.1 of the IOM Report was a call to action for Congress to create a more conducive legal environment for voluntary reporting programs. Congress responded to the IOM call to action by holding a hearing within two weeks to discuss the IOM recommendations. Furthermore, during the 108th Congress (January 2003-December 2004), the House of Representatives passed a patient safety bill—HR 663—by a near unanimous vote in March 2003. A similar patient safety bill was unanimously approved (20-0 vote) by the Senate Health, Education, Labor, and Pensions Committee in June 2003. The Senate bill has passed. The bills were an effort to encourage reporting by establishing a federal privilege for information submitted to patient safety reporting programs (referred to in the bill as Patient Safety Organizations).

During the 108th Congress, senators and representatives moved closer to resolution on many outstanding issues on the above bills; however, important distinctions remain regarding the extent of legal protection, patient and practitioner confidentiality, and qualification of patient safety organizations. As the 108th Congress came to a close, these issues remained. The 2nd Session of the 108th Congress, which began in January 2004, focused on patient safety and medical error reporting as important issues. Many believe and hope that a bill encouraging voluntary reporting will be introduced again during the 109th Congress.

General Principles for Patient Safety Reporting Systems in Response to the IOM Report

Also in response to the IOM Report, over 100 healthcare organizations, including the American Medical Association, National Committee for Quality Assurance, American Nursing Association, American Hospital Association, the Joint Commission on Accreditation of Healthcare Organizations, and the United States Pharmacopeia, supported legal protection for patient safety reporting programs as set forth in the General Principles for Patient Safety Reporting Systems.[58] The General Principles contained five principles that

1. encouraged an environment for safety;
2. emphasized the importance of data analysis;
3. established confidentiality protection for patients and healthcare practitioners;
4. recognized the need for reporting programs to facilitate information sharing; and
5. embraced the notion of the necessity of a federal privilege (legal status).[59]

The last principle (legal status) contained four criteria to ensure the establishment of a clear federal legal privilege. The criteria are as follows:

1. the privilege for information submitted to a reporting system should extend to any data, report, memorandum, analysis, statement, or other communication developed for the purposes of the system;
2. the sharing of information to a patient safety reporting program should not waive the established privilege;
3. information received by the reporting program should be exempt from the Freedom of Information Act and other similar state laws; and
4. a federal privilege should not preempt state evidentiary laws that provide greater protection.[60]

The General Principles have been used by legislators and policymakers in determining the appropriate scope of a federal privilege that would protect information submitted to patient safety reporting systems. The five legislative bills introduced during the 107th Congressional Session incorporated many, if not all, of the General Principles for Patient Safety Reporting Systems. If reporting programs are to have a patient safety impact, these General Principles should continue to be used by national and state policymakers, legislators, and stakeholders in seeking to improve patient safety reporting program efforts and results.

State Legislative Activity

The IOM Report was a call to action not only to federal policymakers and legislators but also to states. The states responded to the IOM Report by attempting to address the patient safety issue through legislation. At least eleven medical-error-related bills were introduced during the 1999 legislative session for states; thirty-four during the 2000 session; and sixty-one during the 2001 session.[61] Nine percent of the bills introduced in 1999 were enacted, 29 percent in 2000; and 20 percent in 2001.[62] The bills addressed issues concerning whistleblower protections, studies on patient safety, reporting requirements, and public disclosure of information.[63] Twelve bills dealing with some aspect of error reporting were introduced during the 2001 session.[64] For example, California and Minnesota introduced voluntary reporting legislation, whereas New York State introduced legislation that would require mandatory reporting.[65]

Furthermore, in a recent survey of pharmacy law, nine states responded that the board of pharmacy required pharmacies to maintain some type of continuous quality improvement program to monitor and prevent quality-related events.[66] The nine states are Arizona, California, Connecticut, Florida, Kentucky, New Mexico, North Carolina, Oregon, and West Virginia.[67]

Some of the state legislation has been specific to medication error reporting and other legislation has been much broader. It is clear that states have a strong interest in patient safety, and additional legislation is likely to be introduced and passed as a way to improve patient safety and reduce medical errors, including medication errors.

CONCLUSION

The reduction of medication errors and the improvement of patient safety will continue to be an important issue that states and federal policymakers will be forced to address. Voluntary reporting will play an important role in improving patient safety; however, the obstacles that hinder reporting programs from their full potential must be addressed. Most important, federal legislators must pass legislation that establishes a federal privilege in order to encourage reporting. Although such legislation should not be considered the complete solution to medication errors, it is a vital step toward ensuring that reporting can occur in a consistent, uniform, and open environment. Reporting in such an environment will encourage healthcare practitioners, facilities, and national organizations to report, analyze, and identify solutions and provide recommendations for patient safety improvements.

NOTES

1. Phillip Schneider, *Am. J. of Health-Syst. Pharm.* 29:2313-4, at 2313 (2002).

2. Donna Young, *Am. J. of Health-Syst. Pharm.* 59:1014, 1016, 1026. News (2002).

3. Kohn, Linda T., et al., *To Err Is Human: Building a Safer Health System.* Washington, DC: National Academy Press, at 79 (2002) (hereinafter the IOM Report, *To Err is Human*).

4. See www.health.state.ny.us.nysdoh/healthinfo/pschodhi.htm. NYPORTS is implemented pursuant to New York State Public Health Law Section 2805-1, Incident Reporting.

5. The New York Patient Occurrence and Tracking System Annual Report, at 5 (1999), www.healthstate.ny.us/nysdoh/commish/2001/nyport.htm.

6. *Id.*

7. See www.fda.gov/medwatch/report.hcp.htm.

8. Thomas J. Moore et al., Reported Adverse Drug Events in Infants and Children Under 2 Years of Age, 110 *Pediatrics,* November, at 53 (2002).

9. John Henkel, *FDA's Head Up on Medical Product Safety,* www.fda.gov/fdac/features/1998698_med.html.

10. See www.jcaho.org/accredited+organization/patient+safety/index.htm.

11. *Id.*

12. Lucian Leape, Reporting of Adverse Events, 347 *New Eng. J. Med.,* 20 (2002).

13. See www.usp.org.

14. E-mail received from U.S. Pharmacopeia's Center for the Advancement of Patient Safety, January 21, 2003.

15. See www.usp.org.

16. Medmarx, *Summary of Information Submitted to Medmarx in the Year 2001, A Human Factors Approach to Understanding Medication Errors,* www.usp.org.

17. Roger L. Williams, Testimony Before the Health Subcommittee of the House Energy and Commerce Committee—*Reducing Medical Errors: A Review of Innovative Strategies to Improve Patient Safety,* 107th Congress, May 8, 2002.

18. Black's Law Dictionary 959 (6th ed., 1990).

19. *Kosberg v. Washington Hospital Center, Inc.,* 394 F.2d 947, 949 (1968).

20. *United States v. Nixon,* 418 U.S. 683, 709 (1974) (quoting *United States v. Bryan,* 339 U.S. 323, 331 (1950), *Blackmer v. United States,* 284 U.S. 421, 438 (1932), *Blanzburg v. Hayes,* 408 U.S. 665, 688 (1972).

21. *Bredice v. Doctors Hospital, Inc.,* 50 F.R.D. 249 (D.D.C. 1970), aff'd without opin., 479 F.2d 920 (1973).

22. *Id.* at 253.

23. *Id.* at 255.

24. James M. Healy et. al., Confidentiality of Health Care Provider Quality of Care Information, 40 *Brandeis L.J.* 595 (2002) [quoting *Dowling v. American Hawaii Cruises, Inc.,* 971 F.2d 423, 246 (9th Cir. 1992)].

25. Eric M. Grasha, Discovering Pharmacy Error: Must Reporting, Identifying, and Analyzing Pharmacy Dispensing Errors Create Liability for Pharmacists?, 63 *Ohio St. L.J.* 1419 (2002/2003).

26. See, e.g., *Granger v. Nat'l R.R. Passenger Corp.,* 116 F.R.D. 507, 508 (E.D. Pa. 1987) (portions of Amtrak accident report detailing the cause of the accident and the factors contributing to the accident were not protected by the critical self-analysis privilege, but portions dealing with opinions and recommendations regarding the accident would not be discoverable because the production of these portions would tend to hamper self-evaluation); *Recihold Chemical, Inc.,* 157 F.R.D. 526 (adopting

a qualified self-critical analysis privilege for reports prepared after the fact for the purpose of self-analysis of the cause and effect of past pollution.)

27. *Tice v. American Airlines,* 192 F.R.D. 270 (2002).

28. *Id.* at 273.

29. *Id.*

30. *In re Air Crash, Near Cali, Colum.* On December 20, 1995, 959 F. Supp. 1529 (S.D. Fla. 1997). The court determined that the American Airlines Safety Action Partnership (ASAP) program materials were entitled to a qualified privilege. ASAP is a voluntary pilot self-reporting program designed to encourage pilots to report incidents and violations. *Id.* at 1531.

31. *Id.* at 1531.

32. IOM Report, *To Err Is Human, supra* note 3, at 103.

33. Elise D. Brennan, *Peer Review Statutes,* American Health Lawyers Association. Annual Meeting, at 6 (1998) [hereinafter Brennan, *Peer Review Statutes*].

34. Jason M. Healy, Confidentiality of Health Care Provider Quality of Care Information, 40 *Brandeis L.J.* 595, 638 (2002).

35. *Id.* at 638.

36. Brennan, *Peer Review Statutes, supra* note 33, at 1.

37. *Id.* at 8 (quoting Kan. Stat. Ann § 65-4950 (1993) and *Hill v. Sandu,* 129 F.R.D. 548 (D.Kan. 1990)).

38. Fla. Stat. § 766.101.

39. Brennan, *Peer Review Statutes, supra* note 33, at 15.

40. See e.g., *Hillsborough Country Hospital Authority v. Lopez,* 678 So.2d 408 (Fla. App. 2d Dist. 1996); *Little v. Hicks,* 236 A.D. 2d 794, 653 N.Y.S. 2d 740 (4th Dept. 1997); and W*heeler v. Central Vermont Medical Center,* 155 Vt. 85, 582 A.2d 165 (1989).

41. Institute of Medicine, *Crossing the Quality Chasm: A New Health System for the 21st Century.* Washington, DC: National Academy Press (2001) (hereinafter the IOM Report, *Crossing the Quality Chasm*).

42. *Id.* at v.

43. *Id.* at ix.

44. *Id.*

45. *Id.* at ix.

46. IOM Report, *To Err is Human, supra* note 3.

47. *Id.* at 22.

48. *Id.*

49. *Id.* at 23.

50. *Id.*

51. *Id.* at 23.

52. *Id.* at 29.

53. *Id.* at vii.

54. *Id.* at 5.

55. *Id.* at 7.

56. *Id.* at 7 and 9.

57. *Id.*

58. Sharon King Donohue, Health Care Quality Infroamtion Liability and Privilege, 11 *Ann. Health L.* 147 (2002) (quoting U.S. Pharmacopeia, General Principles for Patient Safety Reporting Systems (2000), at www.usp.org/patientsafety.htm).

59. General Principles for Patient Safety Reporting Systems, at www.usp.org.

60. *Id.*

61. Lynda Flowers, *State Responses to the Problem of Medical Errors: An Analysis of Recent State Legislative Proposal*, National Academy for State Health Policy, at 3 (2002).

62. *Id.* The following states enacted legislation in the 2001 session: California, Connecticut, Georgia, Indiana, Maryland, Massachusetts, Minnesota, Nevada, New Hampshire, Virginia, and West Virginia. *Id.* at 7.

63. *Id.* at 3.

64. *Id.* at 12.

65. *Id.*

66. National Association of Board of Pharmacy, *Survey of Pharmacy Law,* at 87 (2002).

67. *Id.*

Chapter 25

VIPPS™: Creating a New Regulatory Model for the Internet Age

Carmen A. Catizone
Moira Gibbons

HISTORICAL BACKGROUND

The Internet Rocks Pharmacy Practice

The Internet's impact on society and the practice of pharmacy can best be described as revolutionary. Although some people may choose to debate who actually invented the Internet, most would agree that the Internet's fostering of electronic communication and maintenance of complex and enormous amounts of data transformed many traditional activities from a paper-confined, local activity to a paper-free, global opportunity. The Internet altered how people seek and find information and communicate with one another. For pharmacy, centuries of order and meticulous regulation to ensure that every movement produced the desired result transformed into a wireless chaos creating a new environment with few rules and even fewer boundaries. Within the paper prescription order and face-to-face patient world of the pharmacist, the Internet became the precursor of innovation and harbinger of unwanted change.

The Internet's dramatic impact on pharmacy practice is directly related to how the practice has been organized and regulated. The individual states continue to define and regulate pharmacy practice through multiple laws and rules.* These regulations detail the pharmacy practices and procedures that must be adhered to, and the consequences that will occur when the regula-

---

*An example of a searchable database of U.S. states' pharmacy practice laws and rules is NABPLAW.net. For more information, visit www.nabp.net, and click on "Who We Are" and "Publications."

Pharmacy Law Desk Reference
© 2007 by The Haworth Press, Inc. All rights reserved.
doi:10.1300/5790_25

tions are not followed. Historically, the entrance into this regulatory framework was, and primarily still is, the presentation of a piece of paper to the pharmacist. That 4 × 6 piece of paper filled with a scribbled, coded language communicates to the pharmacist what medications should be dispensed to the patient and initiates the process of practicing pharmacy. That piece of paper, the prescription order, has defined pharmacy practice since its beginnings centuries ago,[1] and the regulatory system has worked well when applied to paper-based pharmacy practice. The advent of the Internet, however, resulted in state legislatures and pharmacy boards scrambling to update laws and regulations, eliminated pharmacy's dependence on paper prescription orders, and offered a revolutionary alternative: electronic communications and unseen, virtual patients.

Emergence of Rogue and Illegal Pharmacy Sites

In the early 1990s, the U.S. Food and Drug Administration (FDA) and state boards of pharmacy discovered a collection of offshore operations in the Caribbean offering prescription medications to U.S. patients. Federal and state regulators became aware of these businesses through advertisements in magazines, complaints from patients, and investigative work. These operations offered to mail prescription medications to U.S. patients regardless of whether the patient could furnish a legitimate prescription order. The practice of these offshore ventures was in direct violation of a host of federal and state laws governing the practice of pharmacy, including those prohibiting the introduction of misbranded or unapproved drugs into interstate commerce[2] and the operation of a pharmacy without a license.[3] Further investigation revealed that the businesses solicited patients and delivered medications using a paper-based system and reputable delivery services such as the U.S. Postal System or common carriers.

Patients using these sites mailed paper order forms to post office boxes and provided payment for their purchases with money orders or credit cards. Payment involving credit cards lacked the ease and security of today's electronic systems and crudely involved the writing of the patient's name, card number, and card expiration date on the order form. Once the order form was received, the offshore operation would route the request directly through the credit card processing system. Despite the allure of obtaining prescription medications without a prescription order, these offshore operations did not fare well. Patients were not comfortable submitting their credit card information to unknown, foreign businesses and were leery that the correct medications would be shipped. The limitations and traceability of their paper and postal system–based operations allowed the FDA and state boards of pharmacy to close these offshore distributors before they were able to expand in number and effectively penetrate the U.S. market.*

Had it not been for the advent of computers and the Internet, this aberrant practice might have garnered a mere footnote in the chronicles of illegal, failed practice ventures. As millions of U.S. patients gained access to and familiarity with the Internet, the availability of prescription medications and illegal distribution of prescription medications via this medium seemed to be the next logical step of the integration of the Internet into all aspects of people's lives. Where offshore businesses operated inefficiently and were constrained by the limits of paper and mailings, the Internet enabled the distribution of prescription drugs through anonymous, electronic, and largely unregulated means. In fact, the Internet almost completely disguised the paper and audit trails of the "prescription" and payment, and placed virtual pharmacies and distribution centers in the homes and offices of Americans across the country. In late 1998 and early 1999, unlawful offshore operations were replaced with a vengeance by illegitimate online distributors that could ship medications into the United States from anywhere in the world, including our own backyard.†

The National Association of Boards of Pharmacy (NABP)‡ witnessed this introduction of Internet pharmacies with some amazement and concern. Acknowledging the entry into practice of legitimate Internet pharmacies such as planetRx.com and drugstore.com, NABP realized that a powerful communication medium could be harnessed to provide patients and pharmacists with information and tools that did not formerly exist. How-

---

*NABP directly ordered medications from several sites and documented the process and delivery.

†One of several "pioneering" domestic rogue sites was The Pill Box Pharmacy, based in San Antonio, Texas. In May 2002, the U.S. Department of Justice indicted The Pill Box Pharmacy's parent company, as well as one of its owners, pharmacist Bill Stallknect, based upon, among other things, allegations of improper dispensations for prescription narcotics exceeding $7.7 million. These dispensations allegedly resulted from online or telephonic consultations without the benefit of physical examination. In addition, the Texas State Board of Pharmacy revoked the licenses of both The Pill Box Pharmacy and Stallknect in June 2002. Another pioneer was KwikMed, which offered online consultations and prescription drugs without requiring a customer to have been physically examined. KwikMed was recently indicated for allegations of fraud and introducing misbranded drugs into commerce. For an abbreviated list of alleged rogue online pharmacies, see Appendix A.

‡The NABP is the professional organization whose membership consists of all state boards of pharmacy in the United States, the District of Columbia, Guam, the Virgin Islands, Puerto Rico, eight provinces of Canada, three states in Australia, New Zealand, and South Africa. NABP was established in 1904 to develop uniform standards and procedures for pharmacist licensure and for the transfer of licensure. Since its inception, NABP has been repeatedly called upon to develop programs and services to assist the state boards in the charge to protect the public health, safety, and welfare.

ever, this enthusiasm was tempered by the stark discovery that legitimate Internet pharmacies were not the only operations staking a claim on the unregulated frontier of the Internet. With boldness unforeseen in other areas of pharmacy, rogue and illegal sites were popping up all over the Internet offering prescription medications without any knowledge of or regard for state pharmacy laws and regulations. A typical rogue site would offer to sell popular prescription medications, usually medications used to treat obesity, impotence, allergies, smoking cessation, pain, etc., without requiring the patient to submit a prescription order. To the contrary, these sites would charge patients a fee to complete an online or telephonic questionnaire without ever requiring the patient to be physically examined by a physician. In turn, the cyberdoc would issue a "prescription" or authorize a drug to be dispensed by an affiliated pharmacy.

As the number of Web sites increased, NABP detected a stark division between legitimate pharmacies and rogue or illegal sites. In 1998, NABP identified more than 150 Web sites operating on the Internet and offering prescription medications. The range of prescription drugs offered was no different from the traditional brick-and-mortar pharmacies. The regulatory challenge to state boards of pharmacy and the FDA was significant because cyberspace sites replaced the traditional pharmacist's dispensing area and the well-recognized prescription counter. The traditional regulatory model of focusing on the brick-and-mortar pharmacy or a pharmacist as the regulatory apex was no longer applicable in this new electronic, paperless, Internet world.

THE VIPPS™ PROGRAM

In February 1999, NABP announced its intentions to develop its Verified Internet Pharmacy Practice Sites (VIPPS™) Program. The response to that announcement drew national attention and interest from the pharmacy community and emerging dot-com wonder world. In March of that year, NABP convened a special meeting of interested parties: government agencies, including the U.S. Drug Enforcement Administration (DEA), the FDA, and the Federal Trade Commission (FTC), as well as professional associations and consumer groups, such as the American Pharmacists Association (APhA), the American Medical Association (AMA), the Citizen Advocacy Center (CAC), the Federation of State Medical Boards (FSMB), the National Association of Chain Drug Stores (NACDS), the National Community Pharmacists Association (NCPA), and the Pharmaceutical Research and Manufacturers of America (PhRMA). The meeting provided NABP with feedback on its proposal and draft criteria to be used in determining which pharmacy sites would be eligible for VIPPS™ certification.

The draft criteria were widely circulated and comments solicited. The comments received by NABP were reviewed internally with a series of task forces and focus groups from a varied representation of pharmacy, government, and consumer interests. NABP released the final VIPPS™ in May 1999. The criteria addressed such issues as drug utilization review, conflicts of law, patient consultation, and maintenance of a quality assurance/quality improvement program, among others. As trends and innovations in Internet pharmacy practice evolve, so too do the VIPPS™ criteria. For example, the criteria now require VIPPS™-certified pharmacies to maintain and enforce policies and procedures to ensure that prescription medications are not prescribed and dispensed based upon online consultations in which the patient has not benefited from an in-person physical examination.*

After approving the VIPPS™ criteria, NABP initiated an intense public relations program targeting patients in all walks of life, prospective applicants, regulatory authorities, and healthcare organizations. The hallmark of this program was promotion of the VIPPS Seal™ as the means to identify legitimately operating, licensed online pharmacies that were prepared to meet the challenges of Internet pharmacy practice. NABP actively worked with the FDA to promote tips and guidelines for those seeking to purchase prescription medications online. NABP collaborated with the Medicare program to publish a guide for patients regarding Internet pharmacy safety.[4] In addition to the FDA and Medicare programs, the FTC also recommended the VIPPS™ program to the public. To this day, widespread support for the VIPPS™ program continues to come from a variety of news media and associations, from www.cnn.com and[5] *Time*[6] magazine to *The New York Times*[7] and the *Wall Street Journal*,[8] as well as the AMA and the FSMB.

VIPPS™ CERTIFICATION PROCESS

Beginning in the summer of 1999, NABP began accepting applications for VIPPS™ certification. NABP awarded VIPPS™ certification to its first Internet pharmacies in the fall of 1999 to drugstore.com, planetRx.com, and Merck-Medco (now Medco Health Solutions). By the end of 1999, a fourth online pharmacy, CVS.com, had earned the prestigious VIPPS™ award.

The four-member freshman VIPPS™ class, and many other Internet pharmacies, completed the rigorous review and on-site inspection steps that

---

*See Appendix B for the current VIPPS™ criteria.

form the foundation of the VIPPS™ certification process. The VIPPS™ certification process consists of "paper" and "person" phases. Initially, the pharmacy's application, Web site, and submitted policies and procedures are reviewed and evaluated for compliance with the VIPPS™ criteria. In addition, VIPPS staff members contact the boards of pharmacy and verify the applicant pharmacy's licensure with each applicable board. Observations, licensure verification issues, and recommendations are all documented. In the "person" phase, one or more VIPPS™ inspectors travel to at least one of the pharmacy facilities to perform an on-site inspection whereby operations and systems are reviewed, and key personnel are interviewed, including pharmacy, human resources, information technology, shipping, and administrative staff. VIPPS™ staff members prepare a report documenting findings and recommendations and, if necessary, request a response from the pharmacy. Typically, the applicant may be required to revise policies and procedures or forms to demonstrate compliance with VIPPS™ standards.

If, upon reviewing all materials, including the pharmacy's response, the VIPPS™ Committee believes that the applicant pharmacy appears to meet the intent of the VIPPS™ criteria, the pharmacy is awarded VIPPS™ certification. VIPPS™ staff uploads important "vital statistics" about the newly certified pharmacy to the NABP Web site so that patients can access such details as the name of the parent company, CEO, pharmacy address, toll-free phone number, pharmacist-in-charge, state license numbers, and services provided by the pharmacy. Next, VIPPS™ staff provides the pharmacy with a special code to download the VIPPS Seal™ from NABP's Web site. The pharmacy is required to maintain the VIPPS™ Seal as a hyperlink between its site and the NABP Web site for several reasons. Most important, the "Click to Verify" VIPPS Seal™ is a secure link to NABP's database. Patients can verify that the pharmacy posting the seal is, indeed, VIPPS™ certified and has not posted the VIPPS Seal™ on its site without NABP's authorization. If the Seal is posted on an authentic VIPPS™ certified site, the patient can access the aforementioned vital statistics for the pharmacy. On the other hand, if a Web site improperly posts the VIPPS Seal™, patients who click to verify the site will be greeted with a message informing them that the Web site is not VIPPS™ certified and requesting that they contact NABP to report the occurrence.

Once a pharmacy achieves VIPPS™ certification, NABP staff conducts annual reviews, which include licensure reverification and a Web site survey. VIPPS™ certified pharmacies are randomly inspected at least once every three years as part of the recertification process.

NEW REGULATORY STRATEGY

In developing the VIPPS™ program, NABP learned that the traditional approach to regulation, which focused on a physical site (a pharmacy) or a person (a pharmacist), would not be effective in this new Internet domain. The traditional brick-and-mortar pharmacy, licensed and inspected under the accepted model of regulation, did not necessarily exist in the uncharted realms of the Internet. Similarly, the pharmacist, who typically practiced at a facility located somewhere in the regulatory confines of a state, could now be located anywhere and even outside of the United States. One of the most frightening realizations about pharmaceutical cyberspace was the possibility that the traditional pharmacy and pharmacist did not exist at all, but, instead, had been replaced with a U.S. storefront supplied by unscrupulous and anonymous U.S. pharmacies, or worse, a clandestine garage in a third world country staffed by someone wholly lacking in pharmacy knowledge and qualifications, whose primary goal was to distribute prescription medications or counterfeit versions of such medications at huge profits.

The final challenge to successfully applying traditional pharmacy regulation to Internet pharmacy practice involved the last step in the prescription dispensing process: the delivery of the prescription product. Once again, the Internet rearranged the model. Patients no longer traveled to a traditional, licensed and inspected, brick-and-mortar pharmacy to "pick up" their medications. In the Internet world, patients remained at home or in their office for the delivery of packages containing any desired medication, from the most powerful and dangerous narcotic to the most routine antihistamine, shipped from places unknown and possibly unregulated. State boards of pharmacy and the FDA generally lacked the resources and authority to enter the homes or offices of these patients to determine whether illegal activities were occurring. Usually, however, federal and state regulatory authorities were more interested in the suppliers of these prescription medications, as opposed to the recipients. Nevertheless, identifying the source of illegal cyberspace shipments frustrated regulatory authorities, particularly in instances of international distributors. Although deliveries from these suppliers could be halted at the U.S. border,[9] determining the persons behind these shipments and prosecuting international sources proved to be a daunting task. NABP's VIPPS™ program captured the effective tools of traditional regulation and employed a new approach that focused on patient knowledge and empowerment. NABP believed that knowledgeable and informed patients would be able to apply sound judgment when deciding whether to order medications over the Internet. The strategy of the VIPPS™ program was to highlight the importance of using licensed and legitimate

U.S. online pharmacies in order to avoid receiving improper medications or counterfeit drugs from unknown and unregulated sources.

An unfortunate test of VIPPS™'s nontraditional regulatory model was performed in 2001, following the September 11 terrorist attacks. NABP shared with regulatory authorities data that had been supplied by patients utilizing the VIPPS™ "Report-a-Site" Web form.[10] Patients notified NABP of suspiciously operating online pharmacies that preyed upon patients' fears of bioterrorist threats by offering to sell, without a valid prescription order, ciprofloxacin and other antibiotics to treat anthrax. Law enforcement authorities used this information to identify, track, and prosecute illegally operating Web sites. The "Report-a-Site" feature has become an important regulatory component of the VIPPS™ program. The public continues to use this cyber-venue to notify NABP about scores of suspiciously operating Internet pharmacies. NABP, in turn, reviews these Web sites and, if a location can be determined, reports these sites to applicable state and/or federal pharmacy regulatory authorities for investigation and possible prosecution.

CONCLUSION

Cyberspace has left an indelible mark on the healthcare industry. It has revolutionized the practice of pharmacy, from the manner in which we receive prescription orders to the methods used to communicate with patients. While legislatures and boards slowly amend pharmacy practice laws and regulations to carefully define what constitutes a valid prescription order and to prohibit online consultations that occur without the benefit of a physical examination, NABP's award-winning VIPPS™ program will continue to assist patients in identifying legitimately operating e-pharmacies that have met stringent pharmacy practice criteria, and will steadfastly support pharmacy regulatory authorities in their pursuit of illegally operating pharmacy-related Web sites. The VIPPS™ program epitomizes the new regulatory strategy of today and tomorrow and the dramatic adaptations in the delivery of healthcare. No longer are patients passive recipients of care delivered by a patriarchal system that places all information and control in the hands of a few. Today's patients are active participants in their own care and use every resource available to them to obtain the information needed and select the best care or provider available.

The Internet has allowed and fueled this transformation and requires that healthcare regulation include the patient as an empowered and active participant in the selection and delivery of care.

The success of the VIPPS™ program in the United States has led to the request that NABP expand VIPPS™ internationally. The importation of

Canadian drugs illegally into the United States is prompting law makers, concerned citizens, and regulators to look to innovative programs such as VIPPS to deal with a phenomenon that defies traditional regulation and will not be stopped at the U.S. border. NABP, in conjunction with the National Association of Pharmacy Regulatory Authorities (NAPRA), unveiled the Canadian VIPPS™ program in 2003. Like their U.S. counterparts, Canadian patients will also be able to easily locate legitimate online Canadian pharmacies. The expansion of the VIPPS™ program outside of the United States is only the beginning of the new regulatory strategy that will impact healthcare regulation and forever change some of the practice and regulatory models that once defined the profession of pharmacy in the United States and throughout the world.

APPENDIX A: ABBREVIATED LIST OF ROGUE ONLINE PHARMACIES WITH NOTES

Name of alleged rogue entity	URL/Web address	Prosecuting Entity	Date of Pros.	Notes
Norfolk Men's Clinic and Norfolk Pharmacy	www.norfolk pharmacy.com www.norfolk mensclinic.com	U.S. DOJ and WV AG	2/2002	Owners criminally convicted of conspiracy to commit violations of FDCA, fraud, etc. In September 2000, the WV AG filed charges against Norfolk Men's Clinic and Norfolk Pharmacy for allegations of selling prescription medications without valid prescriptions.
The Pill Box Pharmacy	www.thepillbox.com	TX BOP and U.S. DOJ	3/2002	Indictment based upon, among other charges, allegations of conspiring to illegally dispense controlled substances related to the operation of an Internet pharmacy. In June 2002, TX BOP revoked the pharmacy license and the pharmacist-owner's license.
Kwikmed, Inc and Cymedic Health Group	www.kwikmed.com	Federal government	10/2002	Indictment based upon allegations of conspiracy, mail fraud, introducing misbranded drugs into commerce, and other charges.
Total Remedy & Prescription Center II	www.CyberHealth Services.com	CA BOP	5/2002	The BOP charged a pharmacy and pharmacists for, among other things, illegally filling Internet prescriptions issued without a good faith prior medical exam.
RXNetwork and USA Prescription	www.USA Prescription.com	FL Dept. of Health	6/2002	Board issued an emergency order suspending the license of RxNetwork, which supplies several online pharmacies including USA Prescription, for prescribing activity that poses and immediate and serious danger.

Name of alleged rogue entity	URL/Web address	Prosecuting Entity	Date of Pros.	Notes
Nationpharmacy.com and Mainstreet Pharmacy	www.nation pharmacy.com	U.S. DOJ and OK BOP	3/2001	OK BOP revoked the pharmacy license and the owner's pharmacist license for, among other things, failure to establish effective controls against diversion. In June 2002, a physician was sentenced to prison for his role in a conspiracy to distribute controlled substances via Internet prescriptions. Dr. Ricky Joe Nelson prescribed medications through www.nationpharmacy.com.
Medi Clinic Online and Worldwide Marketing, Inc	www.mediclinic online.com	PA AG	2/2002	Pharmacist and others indicted for illegally selling prescription "lifestyle" medications online.

Note: AG = Attorney General; BOP = Board of Pharmacy; U.S. DOJ = United States Department of Justice

APPENDIX B: VIPPS™ CRITERIA

Licensure and Policy Maintenance

Qualifying VIPPS Pharmacies (see definitions) must:

1. Provide NABP with the information necessary to verify that the VIPPS pharmacy is licensed or registered in good standing to operate a pharmacy and/or engage in the practice of pharmacy with all applicable jurisdictions;
2. Provide NABP with the information necessary to verify that all persons affiliated with the site, including those affiliated through contractual or other responsible arrangements, that are engaging in the practice of pharmacy are appropriately licensed or registered and in good standing in all applicable jurisdictions;
3. Maintain and enforce a comprehensive policy and procedure that documents how the pharmacy's policies and procedures are organized, authorized for implementation, revised, retired and archived; and
4. Comply with all applicable statutes and regulations governing the practice of pharmacy where licensed or registered, and comply with the more stringent law or regulation as determined by conflicts of law rules. VIPPS pharmacies must maintain and enforce policies and procedures that address conflicts of law issues that may arise between individual states or between state and federal laws and regulations. Said policies and procedures must assure compliance with

applicable laws including generic substitution laws and regulations, and must prohibit unauthorized therapeutic substitution from occurring without necessary patient or prescriber authorization and outside of the conditions for participation in state or federal programs such as Medicaid.

Prescriptions

Qualifying VIPPS Pharmacies, in accordance with applicable state and federal laws and regulations, must:

5. Maintain and enforce policies and procedures that assure the integrity, legitimacy, and authenticity of the Prescription Drug Order and seek to prevent Prescription Drug Orders from being submitted, honored, and filled by multiple pharmacies. Maintain and enforce policies and procedures that assure that prescription medications are not prescribed or dispensed based upon telephonic, electronic, or online medical consultations without there being a pre-existing patient-prescriber relationship that has included an in-person physical examination.

Patient Information

Qualifying VIPPS Pharmacies, in accordance with applicable state and federal laws and regulations, must:

6. Maintain and enforce policies and procedures ensuring reasonable verification of the identity of the patient, prescriber, and, if appropriate, caregiver, in accordance with applicable state law;
7. Obtain and maintain in a readily accessible format, patient medication profiles and other related data in a manner that facilitates consultation with the prescriber, when applicable, and counseling of the patient or caregiver;
8. Conduct a prospective drug use review (DUR) prior to the dispensing of a medication or device in accordance with applicable state law; and
9. Maintain and enforce policies and procedures to assure patient confidentiality and the protection of patient identity and patient-specific information from inappropriate or non-essential access, use, or distribution while such information is being transmitted via the Internet and while the pharmacy possesses such information. [The NABP Guidelines for the Confidentiality of Patient Health Care Information as It Relates to Patient Compliance and Patient Intervention

Programs can serve as a useful resource for addressing the confidentiality and security of patient data.]

Communication

Qualifying VIPPS Pharmacies, in accordance with applicable state and federal laws and regulations and VIPPS program criteria must:

10. Maintain and enforce policies and procedures requiring pharmacists to offer interactive, meaningful consultation to the patient or caregiver;
11. Maintain and enforce policies and procedures establishing a mechanism for patients to report, and the VIPPS Pharmacy to take appropriate action regarding, suspected adverse drug reactions and errors;
12. Maintain and enforce policies and procedures that provide a mechanism to contact the patient and, if necessary, the prescriber, if an undue delay is encountered in delivering the prescribed drug or device. Undue delay is defined as an extension of the normal delivery cycle sufficient to jeopardize or alter the patient treatment plan;
13. Maintain and enforce policies and procedures establishing mechanisms to inform patients or caregivers about drug recalls; and
14. Maintain and enforce policies and procedures establishing mechanisms to educate patients and caregivers about the appropriate means to dispose of expired, damaged, and unusable medications.

Storage and Shipment

Qualifying VIPPS Pharmacies, in accordance with applicable state and federal laws and regulations and VIPPS program criteria, must:

15. Ship controlled substances to patients via a secure and traceable means; and
16. Assure that medications and devices are maintained within appropriate temperature, light, and humidity standards, as established by the United States Pharmacopeia (USP), during storage and shipment.

Over-the-Counter Products

Qualifying VIPPS Pharmacies must:

17. Comply with all applicable federal and state laws regarding the sale of Over-the-Counter Products identified as precursors to the manufacture or compounding of illegal drugs.

Quality Improvement Programs

Qualifying VIPPS Pharmacies must:

18. Maintain a Quality Assurance/Quality Improvement Program.

Reporting to NABP

Qualifying VIPPS Pharmacies must:

19. Notify NABP within thirty (30) days of any change of information provided as part of the verification process, including change in pharmacist-in-charge, or involving data displayed on the VIPPS Web site. VIPPS pharmacies shall notify NABP in writing within ten (10) days of ceasing operations. The written notification shall include the date the pharmacy will be closed, and an affirmation that all VIPPS Seals and references to the VIPPS program have been removed from the Web site and wherever else they are displayed.

Last Modified: August 30, 2002

NOTES

1. George A. Bender, *Great Moments in Pharmacy* 60-61, 87 (1967).
2. 21 U.S.C. §§ 331(a), 331(d), 355(a).
3. See, e.g., W. Va. Code § 30-5-6a.
4. See www.medicare.gov/Prescription/Home.asp.
5. CNN staff, Online Drug Sales Save Money, But May Raise Risks, FDA Says, cnn.com, March 21, 2000.
6. Christine Gorman, Look Who's Running Drugs, *Time,* July 29, 2002.
7. Sana Siwolop, Buying Your Pills Online May Save Money, But Who's Selling Them?, *The New York Times,* September 29, 2002.
8. Tara Parker-Pope, Shoppers Should Be Aware When Buying Drugs Online, *Wall Street Journal,* February 16, 2001.
9. See, e.g., 19 U.S.C. § 1581.
10. See www.nabp.net/vipps/consumer/report.asp.

Index

Page numbers followed by "f" indicate figures; those followed by "t" indicate tables; and those by "n" are notes.

Abbreviated New Drug Applications (ANDAs)
  and antitrust laws, 162
  FDA role, 30
  and FOIA, 13
  and patents, 129-134
Abortifacients, 291
Abuse. *See also* Addiction
  and liability, 116n, 122
  in minors, 327
  potential for, 43-45
  and telemedicine, 487
Academy of Managed Care Pharmacy, 359, 370
Accreditation. *See also* Certificate training programs
  benefits, 429-431
  challenges, 432
  comprehensive, 441-442
  defined, 367, 377
  of fellowships, 360
  of hospitals, 439
  for institutional setting, 438-439
  of internet pharmacies, 438
  and managed care, 435
  nonpharmacy, 372
  programs. *See also* Accreditation Council for Pharmacy Education
    ACHC, 437
    JCAHO, 438
    NABP, 437, 438
    NCQA, 426, 440t
    ORYX, 425-426
    PCMA, 435
    URAC system, 427-429, 441

Accreditation *(continued)*
  of residencies, 359
  and risk management, 431
  for technician training, 366, 413
Accreditation Council for Pharmacy Education (ACME)
  certificate training programs, 361
  contact information, 370
  and continuing education, 211
  quality standards, 436
  and technicians, 366
Acetone, 88
ACHC. *See* American Commission for Health Care
Acquisitions. *See* Mergers and acquisitions
Active ingredients, 129, 134. *See also* Adulteration
Adalat, 162
Added qualifications, 375
Adderall®. *See* Amphetamine
Addiction
  and alcohol, 217
  and liability, 116n
  to narcotics, and hospitals, 85
  and warning labels, 382
Address
  change of, 60
  of consumer, 322
Adjudication, 12. *See also* Court cases; Litigation
Administrative agencies
  and accreditation, 429-430
  adjudication, 12
  in California, 186-203